HUANG YONG
Liber Amicorum
Leading and Riding the Tide of China's Competition Law

Forewords by Zhang Qiong, William E. Kovacic, Maureen K. Ohlhausen and Allan Fels AO

Editors

Bai Yong and Wang Ziwen

Concurrences

Paris - New York - London

All rights reserved. No photocopying: copyright licences do not apply. The information provided in this publication is general and may not apply in a specific situation. The publisher accepts no responsibility for any acts or omissions contained herein. Enquiries concerning reproduction should be sent to the Institute of Competition Law, at the address below.

Copyright © 2025 by Institute of Competition Law
106 West 32nd Street, Suite 144 New York, NY, 10001, USA
www.concurrences.com
book@concurrences.com

First Printing, October 2025
978-1-954750-30-2 (Hardcover)
Library of Congress Control Number: 2025918278

Cover Design: Yves Buliard, www.yvesbuliard.fr
Book Design and Layout implementation: Nord Compo

Concurrences Books

Tributes

James F. Rill – A Life in Antitrust, *2024*
Eleanor M. Fox – Antitrust Ambassador to the World, *2021*
Herbert Hovenkamp – The Dean of American Antitrust Law, *2021*
Frédéric Jenny – Standing Up for Convergence and Relevance in Antitrust, (Vol. I & II), *2019 & 2021*
Albert Foer – A Consumer Voice in the Antitrust Arena, *2020*
Richard Whish – Taking Competition Law Outside the Box, *2020*
Douglas H. Ginsburg – An Antitrust Professor on the Bench (Vol. I & II), *2018 & 2020*
Wang Xiaoye – The Pioneer of Competition Law in China, *A. Emch, W. Ng (eds.), 2019*
Ian S. Forrester – A Scot without Borders (Vol. I & II), *A. Komninos (eds.), 2015*
William E. Kovacic – An Antitrust Tribute (Vol. I & II), *2013 & 2014*

Practical Books

Competition Law and the Challenges of Insular Economies – A Focus on French Polynesia and the Pacific Region, *J. Peyre, E. Silvestro, V. Terrien, T. Emen, Y. Lecornu (eds.), 2025*
Competition Inspections under EU Law, 2nd Edition, *N. Jalabert-Doury, 2025*
Navigating the DMA: Application Across National Jurisdictions, *G. Muscolo & A. Massolo (eds.), 2025*
Artificial Intelligence and Competition Policy, *A. Abbott, T. Schrepel (eds.), 2024*
State Aid & National Enforcement, *J. Derenne, D. Jouve, C. Lemaire, F. Martucci (eds.), 2024*
The 2023 U.S. Merger Guidelines: A Review, *Sean Sullivan (ed.), 2024*
Competition Inspections in 25 Jurisdictions 2nd Edition – A Practitioner's Guide, *N. Jalabert-Doury (ed.), 2024*
EU Antitrust Enforcement – Law, Economics, History, *Policy & Practice, Wouter P. J. Wils, 2024*
The EU Foreign Subsidies Regulation, *Andreas Reindl, Isabelle Van Damme, 2024*
Compendium of Antitrust Damages Actions – ICC – 2nd edition, *J.W.H. Denton AO, F. Brunet, S. Williams, C. Inthavisay (eds.), 2023*
Pharmaceutical Antitrust: An Analysis of US and EU Law, *M. Thill-Tayara, G. Gordon (eds.), 2023*
Innovation Paradox in Merger Control, *G. Gurkaynak, 2023*
Antitrust and the Digital Economy, *Y. Katsoulacos (ed.), 2023 (in collaboration with CRESSE)*
Judicial Review of Competition Cases, *D. Ginsburg, T. Eicke (eds.), 2023*
Competition Law Treatment of Joint Ventures, *B. Bleicher, N. Campbell, A. Hamilton, N. Hukkinen, A. Khan, A. Mordarian (eds.), 2022 (in collaboration with the IBA)*
Information Exchange & Related Risks, *Z. Marosi, M. Soares (eds.), 2022 (in collaboration with the IBA)*
Rulemaking Authority of the US Federal Trade Commission, *D. Crane (ed.), 2022*
The International Competition Network at Twenty, *D. Anderson & P. Lugard (eds.), 2022*
Competition Case Law Digest – 5th Edition, *F. Jenny, N. Charbit (eds.), 2022*
Competition Inspections in 21 Jurisdictions – A Practitioner's Guide, *N. Jalabert-Doury (ed.), 2022*
Perspectives on Antitrust Compliance, *A. Riley, A. Stephan, A. Tubbs (eds.), 2022 (in collaboration with the ICC)*
Turkish Competition Law, *G. Gürkaynak, 2021*
Competition Law – Climate Change & Environmental Sustainability, *S. Holmes, D. Middelschulte, M. Snoep (eds.), 2021*
Merger Control in Latin America – A Jurisdictional Guide, *P. Burnier da Silveira, P. Sittenfeld (eds.), 2020*
Competition Inspections under EU Law – A Practitioner's Guide, *N. Jalabert-Doury, 2020*
Gun Jumping in Merger Control – A Jurisdictional Guide, *C. Hatton, Y. Comtois, A. Hamilton (eds.), 2019 (in collaboration with the IBA)*
Choice – A New Standard for Competition Analysis? *P. Nihoul (ed.), 2016*

PhD Theses

Intent in Competition Law, *M.S. Garnier, 2025*
Three Essays in Law and Economics: Digital Markets and Abuse of Dominance, *J. Mouton, 2025*
The Economics of Digital Markets – Essays in Theoretical and Empirical Industrial Organization, *E. Arnaud-Joufray, 2024*
Abuse of Platform Power, *F. Bostoen, 2023*
Reform of Chinese State-Owned Enterprises, *X. Bai, 2023*
Competition & Regulation in Network Industries – Essays in Industrial Organization, *J-M. Zogheib, 2021*
The Role of Media Pluralism in the Enforcement of EU Competition Law, *K. Bania, 2019*
Buyer Power, *I. Herrera Anchustegui, 2017*

General Interest

Why Competition? Voices from the Antitrust Community and Beyond, *D. Crane, D. Gerard, R. Tritell (eds.), 2024*
Competition Law Dictionary, *D. Healey, R. Whish, W. E. Kovacic, P. Trevisán (eds.), 2024*
The 5 Labours of Europe, *P.-E. Partsch, 2024*
Great Antitrust Enforcers, *W. E. Kovacic, 2023*
Competition – How to Speak Like an Expert, *E. Combe, 2023*
Women and Antitrust – Voices from the Field (Vol I & II), *E. Kurgonaite & K. Nordlander, 2020*

e-Book versions available for **Concurrences+** subscribers

Foreword

Riding the Crest of the Tide: My Observations on Professor Huang Yong and China's Competition Policy & Antimonopoly Law

ZHANG QIONG[*]

Vice Minister of the Legislative Affairs Office of the State Council

Midsummer Beijing – torrential rains wrapped in scorching heat – cannot dim the cool clarity that this manuscript brings to my desk. As I open this collection, painstakingly compiled by Professor Huang Yong together with friends from academia and practice at home and abroad and by his own students, every line throbs with the intellectual trajectory of his decades-long devotion to competition policy and Antimonopoly Law. It radiates the patriotic heart of a jurist who grew up with the nation's reform and opening-up, and it serves as a living footnote to China's competition law – from its first fragile shoots to today's vigorous bloom. Having known Yong for twenty years as a former leader, colleague and friend, I am flooded with memories as I set pen to paper.

From the Legislative Frontline to National Brain Trust: A Practitioner of China's Competition Policy and Rule of Law

My acquaintance with Professor Huang began at the very start of China's Antimonopoly Law. In 2005, when the law was formally placed on the national

---

[*] Zhang Qiong, Vice Minister of the Legislative Affairs Office of the State Council, Head of the Expert Advisory Group of the first State Council Anti-Monopoly Committee and the Convenor of the Expert Advisory Group of the second State Council Anti-Monopoly Committee.

legislative agenda, I was Vice-Minister of the State Council Legislative Affairs Office and led the drafting coordination. Professor Huang was already a noted competition-law scholar. I still remember vividly how he expounded the value of antimonopoly in a market economy, decoded foreign legislative history and intent, distilled the jurisprudential meaning of economic principles in foreign precedents, and reflected on China's own legislative needs and priorities.

In the dozen years since the Antimonopoly Law was adopted and implemented, we have worked ever more closely on the platform of the Expert Consultation Committee under the State Council Anti-Monopoly Commission. I served as Chair of the first committee and Huang as Deputy Chair; in the second committee I became Convener and he remained a core member. Whenever we confronted the construction of China's competition-policy legal framework – or thorny new issues such as platform-economy or data monopolies – Huang unfailingly offered recommendations that were both forward-looking and workable, grounded in solid theory and acute practical insight.

In recent years, wave upon wave of platform economy, digital economy and artificial intelligence has tested every antimonopoly jurisdiction's ability to adapt. I personally follow these trends closely, and I often meet Huang at forums and seminars. His sweeping vision, penetrating analysis and witty delivery invariably win thunderous applause.

From Academic Depth to Policy Empowerment: Competition Policy Steps into the National Spotlight

Huang's scholarship beats with a pulse of truth-seeking pragmatism, giving it extraordinary vitality and influence. It is precisely this quality that allowed him to turn the once "cold stove" of competition policy into something hot, ultimately bringing it into the top-level design of national governance.

Thanks to the efforts of Huang and other scholars, the 2007 Antimonopoly Law inserted into its text the duty for the State Council Anti-Monopoly Commission to "research and formulate competition policies." Yet competition policy remained an unfamiliar concept; industrial policy still dominated the policy landscape. Huang keenly realized that although foreign antimonopoly laws emerged from mature market economies, China's Antimonopoly Law was enacted while the country was actively integrating into globalization – a historical uniqueness rarely seen in global antimonopoly history. The Chinese statute therefore shoulders a special mission: to take the enactment and implementation of the Antimonopoly Law as its lever and make competition policy a major undertaking in support of the nation's economic restructuring.

Over the following years Huang led or authored multiple research reports, ceaselessly conveying to the decision-making level the principle of "priority to competition policy." In one report he proposed the phrase "gradually establish the foundational status of competition policy," urging the clarification of coordination mechanisms between competition policy and industrial, fiscal and investment policies. Efforts bore fruit: in 2015 the phrase "strengthen the guiding role of competition policy and industrial policy on innovation" entered the Central Committee's "Opinions on Deepening Structural Reform and Accelerating the Implementation of an Innovation-Driven Development Strategy"; the same document and the "Opinions on Advancing Price Mechanism Reform" explicitly called for "gradually establishing the foundational status of competition policy" and "speeding up the creation of coordination mechanisms between competition policy and industrial, investment and other policies, and implementing a fair-competition review system." In October 2015, the Fifth Plenum of the 18th CPC Central Committee adopted the "Proposal for the 13th Five-Year Plan," which stated that industrial policy should be "oriented and competitive." Although the words "competition policy" did not appear, their placement in the same sentence with industrial policy was unimaginable in earlier documents.

The rest of the story is well known. The "fermentation" of competition policy led to the birth of the fair-competition review system, its inclusion in the new Antimonopoly Law and a dedicated State Council administrative regulation; the "strengthening of the foundational status of competition policy" was written into the 2019 Fourth Plenum document. Competition policy stepped to the forefront and now plays a key role in national governance. Behind these milestone breakthroughs, Huang's behind-the-scenes contributions should not be overlooked.

From Traditional Fields to the Digital Frontier: Leading the Escape from Traditional Antimonopoly Paradigms

Huang's scholarly vision has always resonated with the cutting edge of the times. When the global digital-economy tide swept in, bringing platform monopolies and data barriers that shook traditional antimonopoly frameworks, he refused to rely on "old theories for new problems" or to drift with the current of "copy-and-paste." Instead, he went back to first principles: Where did China's digital economy come from? What developmental laws does it follow? What are its future directions? Only then did he pose the question of how Chinese antimonopoly can advance the digital economy.

I believe several of Huang's insights merit close attention. First, how to rationally assess the applicability of international experience. The digital economies of

China, the United States and Europe differ in scale, developmental stage, core strengths and institutional environments; therefore broad borrowing must be tempered by a stance of "using foreign experience for China's purposes." Second, how to align with China's comparative advantages in digital development. China's digital economy owes its rise to a vast market and abundant venture capital; hence the institutional design and its implementation must fit that development pattern. Third, how to balance rule-setting with market-cultivation. For instance, public-data openness is expanding; if rules are set before the data-factor market is mature, market distortion may ensue.

This summary is far from exhaustive, but it shows Huang's fundamental commitment: research must answer new challenges, and theory must solve real problems. This style keeps him at the research frontier while rooting him firmly in Chinese soil.

From the Classroom Podium to International Bridge: Telling China's Competition-Law Story to the World

Huang likes to call himself a mere schoolteacher; to me he is an "academic diplomat."

In 2018, on the tenth anniversary of China's Antimonopoly Law, he led the Competition Law Center of the University of International Business and Economics in hosting that year's "China Competition Policy Forum," bringing together heads of competition agencies from 14 countries, regions and international organizations across six continents. The event became a vivid testament to his global academic influence.

Years earlier, while researching the Sherman Act in the United States, he witnessed the high drama of landmark cases such as Microsoft and Boeing-McDonnell Douglas. From that experience he gained deep insight into antimonopoly's national-policy dimension and its international coordination. Upon returning home he wrote a brilliant doctoral dissertation on "International Competition Law Studies." Over the years he has delivered lectures on Chinese competition law at the American Bar Association, Stanford, Penn, Chatham House, Oxford and other leading universities and think tanks worldwide, and he has visited antimonopoly agencies in the United States, the EU, the UK, Italy, Portugal, Japan and Korea, spreading China's antimonopoly voice.

Huang's theoretical constructs – such as "Antimonopoly Law under incomplete market conditions" and "competition policy in gradualist reform" – offer the world a window onto Chinese antimonopoly and have earned him international scholarly acclaim.

Zhang Qiong

Closing Reflections

This volume is more than a retrospective of Professor Huang's academic career; it is the epitome of a generation of competition-law jurists. From late-night battles in the legislative chamber to policy advocacy; from meticulous cultivation of traditional fields to pioneering innovation in the digital age; from domestic immersion to international dialogue – Professor Huang has spent four decades proving that true scholarship must move in tandem with social development, and that true scholars must serve their country.

As these essays go to press, I extend to Professor Huang my warmest congratulations. May he continue to ride the crest of the wave on the path of competition policy and Antimonopoly law, and may China's competition-law cause, propelled by researchers and practitioners like him, stride toward an even brighter tomorrow.

Foreword

Huang Yong and the Intellectual Architecture of Chinese Competition Policy

WILLIAM E. KOVACIC[*]
The George Washington University Law School

Successful competition law systems depend upon contributions from institutions that supply knowledge and human resources crucial to the formulation and implementation of policy. Paramount among these institutions are universities and research think tanks. No competition law system flourishes without the architecture of ideas and people that these academic hubs supply.

In the still brief history of China's competition law system, Huang Yong stands out as one of the nation's most important intellectual architects. His scholarship has deeply influenced the substance, process, and structure of China's antimonopoly regime. In the classroom, Professor Huang has provided powerful analytical tools and valuable practical guidance to thousands upon thousands of students. He has become a much-demanded lecturer for audiences around the globe. He has provided astute advice to public bodies and private firms as a consultant. He has given invaluable support and guidance to junior academics. In all of these endeavors, he has displayed true mastery of the technical details and broad policy considerations of competition law at home and abroad. Of course, Professor Huang is not alone in building the intellectual architecture or competition policy in China, yet his influence in developing competition policy a focus of intellectual inquiry, scholarship, and policy discourse is unsurpassed.

A central vehicle for Professor Huang's work has been the development of the Center for Competition Policy (Center) at the University of International

---

[*] Global Competition Professor of Law and Policy, George Washington University Law School, and Visiting Professor, Dickson Poon School of Law, King's College London.

Foreword

Business and Economics (UIBE) in Beijing. Professor Huang created the Center and has made it an important platform for teaching, research, and convening events that shape policy. One notable accomplishment has been to increase understanding of competition policy issues, in China and abroad, by convening conferences, seminars, and workshops. In designing these events, Professor Huang has served the vital function of integrating theory with practice – joining up conceptual insights from the academy and injecting them into current debates about policy and to alter the course of policy itself. In doing so, Professor Huang has demonstrated how academic hubs can assist academics, practitioners, and regulators in forming common understandings about developments in industry and in government and, over time, nurture a consensus about the design and implementation of competition policy. Seen this way, academic hubs are striking examples of what Allan Fels, a leading scholar in the fields of economic regulation and public administration and the former chair of the Australian Competition and Consumer Commission, has called "co-producers" – institutions external to the regulatory agency on which regulators can draw to increase their own capability and achieve better regulatory results. Professor Huang has shown that academic hubs should be viewed as vital – perhaps, indispensable – ingredients of the intellectual infrastructure over which good competition policy travels.

I close by noting that the motivation for this tribute is deeply personal. In all that I have done as an academic and public official since meeting Professor Huang many years ago, not a day has passed when I did not use something I learned from Professor Huang. I have seen firsthand that he is a superb teacher in the fullest sense. For the joy of being part of his extended family of former students and fellow researchers, I am most grateful.

Foreword

MAUREEN K. OHLHAUSEN[*]
Co-chair of Wilson Sonsini's antitrust and competition practice

Early in my tenure as a Federal Trade Commissioner, I was very fortunate to meet Dr. Huang Yong, then Vice Chair of the Expert Advisory Board of the State Council on the Antimonopoly Commission Expert Advisory Board. In my first of many visits to China, I helped mark the fifth anniversary of China's Anti-Monopoly Law at the 2013 China Competition Policy Forum – Competition Policy in Transition in Beijing, organized by Dr. Huang. This event featured leaders of the Chinese antitrust authorities and prominent Chinese scholars in a wide-ranging debate on the future of competition law in China, and it illustrated Dr. Huang's commitment to promoting competition as a societal value and developing a modern competition regime in China.

As I got to know Dr. Huang better, I realized that the conference was also a reflection of his personality. Of course, that should not be a surprise to anyone familiar with the Chinese zodiac as Dr. Huang, like me, was born in the Year of the Tiger. Tigers are supposed to be bold, confident, competitive, and driven to be leaders. They are not afraid to fight for what they believe in. Dr. Huang's storied career has exemplified these Tiger qualities, and he has had an enormous, positive impact on competition in law in China through his long relationships with the officials, scholars, and practitioners that put competition principles into action.

Now, there have been myriad changes in the practice of competition law since 2013, some for the good and some less so, many of them driven by concerns about the global impact of digital platforms and increasingly of AI. This in turn has raised questions about merger control, the regulation of market power in digital markets, and the impact of other regulations in fostering or hampering competition. Fittingly, the articles in this volume tackle all of these topics and more.

In the area of digital platform regulation, **Meng Yanbei** considers how such platforms should be regulated under anti-monopoly laws in China and asserts that the enforcement agencies and industry regulators should work together to

---

[*] The Honorable Maureen K. Ohlhausen is co-chair of Wilson Sonsini's antitrust and competition practice. She served as a Commissioner and Acting Chairman of the Federal Trade Commission from 2012 to 2018.

effectively regulate digital platforms in China. **Zhang Chenying** proposes competition law reforms to construct a new antitrust framework for the Internet and recommends parallel regulation by competition and sectoral regulators. **Jorge Padilla** and **Vanessa Zhang** explore different approaches to digital regulation in major jurisdictions and how digital regulation increasingly functions as a "Behind-the-border Trade Barrier," concluding that such regulation is becoming a critical vector of geopolitical competition and the main arena for trade conflicts.

Turning to AI and data, **Chen Bing** surveys the challenges of effectively regulating digital platforms, urging a more comprehensive regulation around data. **Roger Xin Zhang, Yun Dong** and **Hangchen Guo** examine new issues sparked by AI technology, including self-preferencing, refusals to deal and data-blocking mergers, and they offer proposals on data interoperability and algorithms. **Jia Yuan** explains how China's AML and Anti-Unfair Competition Law should be coordinated to effectively regulate abuse of data advantages and ensure fair accessibility to data.

Merger control is a perennial topic in the field of competition law, and **Yu Yan** examines the growing emphasis on the entrenchment of market power in recent contentious transactions in the EU, the US and China, identifying troubling examples of competition agencies circumventing traditional analytical framework to impose more rigorous measures for the mergers of companies with market power. **Elizabeth Xiaoru Wang, Sophie Na Yang** and **Qian Yujie** cover the changing dynamics of merger review under disrupted supply chains, rising geopolitical tensions, trade conflicts, and shifting tariff policies and how China's merger review regime functions in practice. **Jet Deng** emphasizes that sectoral dynamics and policy considerations now play a decisive role in merger outcomes, and that proactive, well-informed engagement with China's regulatory authorities is vital for transaction success. **Bai Yong and Wang Ziwen** examine the discretionary powers of SAMR to review deals that fall outside the mandatory filing thresholds in China and call for heightened vigilance and a diversified approach reflecting practical concerns. **Deng Feng, Wang Huiqun,** and **Guo Xiaoli** highlight the increased authority and prominence of Chinese antitrust enforcement agencies foresee challenges in developing economic analysis methods in response to economic growth and transformation of Chinese market. **John Yong Ren, Christine Fengyi Zhang, Schiffer Mengmeng Shi** and **Daniel Zu Gui** provide a comprehensive analysis of China's AML from its legislative inception in 2003 to its current enforcement under the SAMR, highlighting the maturity of China's merger control system.

Turning to conduct matters, **Ding Maozhong** notes that the regulations supporting the essential facility doctrine have not been applied in practice in China and proposes to address this by slightly tweaking the current language of the relevant AML provision. **Jiang Shan** observes that while the 2022 Anti-Monopoly Law established a presumption of anti-competitive effects of RPM, the new regulatory structure remains unclear and urges clarifications on how RPM should be analyzed under AML, including adopting the abbreviated rule of reason without any safe harbor. **Cen Zhaoqi** surveys the evolution of regulation concerning loyalty rebates in the EU and evaluates its implications for China through an overview of landmark cases. The article underscores the need for case-specific analysis and robust proof standards to distinguish procompetitive discounts from exclusionary practices. **Huang Wei** analyzes major excessive pricing and refusal to deal cases in China including InterDigital (2013), Qualcomm (2015), and Yangtze River Pharmaceutical (2023), and argues that Chinese regulators have taken enforcement action only when there is a clear demonstration of competitive harm. **Zhan Hao** and **Song Ying** highlight increasing antitrust litigation in China in a review of recent landmark cases, predicting increased parallel proceedings with combinations of administrative and civil processes tackling the same conduct simultaneously.

Institutions and the overall regulatory environment are also major influences on the competitive landscape. **Elenor Fox** examines challenges from balancing necessary state restraints and free competition, proposing tight collaboration between competition authorities and internal market trade authorities, an avoidance of overly restrictive local regulations, and the maintenance competitive neutrality as recommended by the OECD. **Rasul Butt** chronicles the evolution of Hong Kong's competition law since its full implementation in 2015 and contrasts it with China's AML under the "One Country, Two Systems" model of governance.

Looking to Europe, **Frederic Jenny** examines whether environmental sustainability aligns with the competition model, competition's role in achieving sustainability, and how sustainability can be integrated into competition law enforcement. The article conducts a comparative analysis of how the relevant policies have been developing in different jurisdictions, focusing on Chinese Anti-Monopoly Law (AML) in particular. **Clemence Carlier** and **Johannes Lüer** review the recent EU enforcement trend of tighter scrutiny of information exchange between competitors and criticizes the suitability of existing guidance and lack of transparency with a potential for over-deterrence.

Finally, returning to the overall subject of this volume, **Sheng Jiemin** recounts a long friendship with Professor Huang Yong and lauds his accomplishments and scholarly work. **Jin Shanming** surveys Professor Huang Yong's work, legal theory and practice as a legislator, a scholar and a practitioner, and his contribution to the shaping the AML framework in China.

The breadth of this volume is a microcosm of the impact of Dr. Huang's scholarship, leadership, and friendship on the evolution of competition law in China. My congratulations to Dr. Huang and to all the authors on their contributions.

Foreword

Allan Fels AO
Melbourne and Munesh University Australia

It is an honour for me to pay tribute to the outstanding contribution by Professor Huang Yong to the establishment, enactment and implementation of China's antimonopoly law.

Personally I have been an observer of China's competition law since my first competition related visit to China in 1995 until the present time and I have been able to personally observe his multifaceted contributions.

Over the many years and especially in the last 25 years or so Professor Huang Yong has been a leading contributor in every dimension to China's competition law as a researcher, teacher, advisor, practitioner, and educator to the world not to mention his very considerable contribution in establishing the UIBE as a leading global forum for the study of Competition law and as a person who has educated and trained generations of followers whether academics, government officials or legal practitioners.

In all these activities, Professor Huang has been an outstanding performer whether in teaching, writing, lecturing and other ways of explaining and educating about the nature of the law and its implementation and as a major contributor to policy making itself as recognised for example in his appointment to be a member of the expert advisory board of the state council antimonopoly commission

He has been a go to person for foreign experts wanting to understand the intricacies of the Chinese law, intricacies which he has explained in various English language articles and lectures around the world.

I congratulate Professor Huang Yong on his work thus far in his career but we look forward to many continuing contributions.

Contributors

Jin Shanming
Chinese Academy of Social Sciences

Eleanor Fox
New York University

Frédéric Jenny
Economics ESSEC Business School

Rasul Butt
Hong Kong Competition Commission

Jorge Padilla
Compass Lexecon

Vanessa Yanhua Zhang
Compass Lexecon

Clémence Carlier
Clifford Chance

Johannes Lüer
Clifford Chance

Yu Yan
RBB Economics

Cen Zhaoqi
Zhong Lun Law Firm

Sheng Jieming
Peking University

Deng Feng
Peking University

Wang Huiqun
Central University of Finance and Economics

Guo Xiaoli
Shanghai University of Finance and Economics

Jiang Shan
University of International Business and Economics

Bai Yong
Clifford Chance

Wang Ziwen
Clifford Chance

John Yong Ren
T&D Associates

Christine Fengyi Zhang
T&D Associates

Schiffer Mengmeng Shi
T&D Associates

Daniel Zu Gui
T&D Associates

Tony Jiang
Intel China

Elizabeth Xiaoru Wang
Econic Partners

Sophie Na Yang
Econic Partners

Qian Yujie
Compass Lexecon

Jet Deng
Dacheng

Zhan Hao
AnJie Broad

Song Ying
AnJie Broad

Meng Yanbei
Renmin University of China

Zhang Chenying
Tsinghua University

Jia Yuan
Sichuan University

Ding Maozhong
Shanghai University of Political Science and Law

Chen Bing
Nankai University

Roger Xin Zhang
Tencent

Dong Yun
Tencent

Guo Hangchen
Tencent

Huang Wei
Tian Yuan

Editorial Board

Su Runsheng
Zhou Lixia
Tang Jinglun
Xie Jue

Table of Contents

Foreword by Zhang Qiong I

Foreword by William E. Kovacic VII

Foreword by Maureen K. Ohlhausen IX

Foreword by Allan Fels AO XIII

Contributors XV

Editorial Board XVII

Table of Contents XIX

Huang Yong Biography & Publications XXIII

Introduction XXVII

PART I: Frontier Issues and Comparative Studies in Antitrust Law

1. Huang Yong: A Distinguished Trailblazer in China's Antitrust Law Realm 3
   Jin Shanming

2. Attacking State Restraints: Building on the groundwork of Professor Huang Yong 13
   Eleanor Fox

3. Competition and Environmental Sustainability: Lessons from the European Debate 21
   Frédéric Jenny

4. "One Country, Two Systems" of Competition Law 41
   Rasul Butt

5. The Complex Geopolitics of Digital Regulation: The Three Body Problem 49
   Jorge Padilla and Vanessa Yanhua Zhang

6. Unrestricted Enforcement Risk on Information Exchange and Unilateral Disclosure under EU Competition Law? 87
   Clémence Carlier and Johannes Lüer

7. Re-emergence of Entrenchment of Market Power in Merger Controls 101
   Yu Yan

8. Anti-monopoly Regulation on Loyalty Rebates in the European Union and its Implications 109
   Cen Zhaoqi

PART II: Law and Practice of China's Anti-Monopoly Law

1. My Friend Huang Yong 121
   Sheng Jieming

2. The Developments and Evolution of Chinese Merger Control 125
   Deng Feng, Wang Huiqun and Guo Xiaoli

3. On the Pattern Setting of Anti-monopoly Regulatory Framework for Resale Price Maintenance 143
   Jiang Shan

4. Below-Threshold Transactions in China: Roads Less Travelled, but Worth Revisiting 175
   Bai Yong and Wang Ziwen

5. China's Anti-Monopoly Law and its Merger Review: Retrospect and Prospect 193
   John Yong Ren, Christine Fengyi Zhang, Schiffer Mengmeng Shi and Daniel Zu Gui

6. Analyzing China's Draft Guidelines for Non-Horizontal Merger Review (July 2025): Comparative Reflections on US 2020 and 2023 Guidelines 241
   Tony Jiang

7. Key Facts on China's Merger Reviews During the Time of Uncertainties 249
   Elizabeth Xiaoru Wang, Sophie Na Yang and Qian Yujie

8. Understanding China's Merger Control Through Industry Lenses: Market Trends and Review Procedures 263
   Jet Deng

9. China's Antitrust Litigation Practice: Review and Outlook 277
   Zhan Hao and Song Ying

PART III: Focuses on Data and Digital Era

1. Re-examination of the Relationship between Anti-Monopoly Regulation and Industry Regulation of Digital Platforms 297
   Meng Yanbei

2. Anti-monopoly Regulation of Internet Platform from the Perspective of the Public Character 313
   Zhang Chenying

3. Competition Law Regulations on Abuse of Data Advantages 327
   Jia Yuan

4. Problems of Application of the Essential Facilities Doctrine in China and its Solution 345
   Ding Maozhong

5. New Development of Anti-Monopoly Regulation on Data in China 379
   Chen Bing

6. Monopoly Concerns and Regulatory Approaches in the Artificial Intelligence Industry 399
   Roger Xin Zhang, Dong Yun and Guo Hangchen

7. China's Antitrust Practice in SEPs: Excessive Pricing and Refusal to Deal 427
   Huang Wei

Thank You 437

Huang Yong

Biography & Publications

Biography

Basic Information

Huang Yong, born in Beijing in November 1962, holds a Bachelor of Laws from Peking University, as well as a Master of Laws and a Doctor of Laws from the School of Law at the University of International Business and Economics (UIBE). He currently serves as Director of the Competition Law Center at UIBE, Professor at law, doctoral supervisor, Head of the Department of Economic Law of UIBE, and the State Council Special Government Allowance expert.

Major Social and Professional Roles: Member of the Expert Advisory Group of the State Council Anti-Monopoly and Anti-Unfair Competition Commission; Member of the Central Committee of the China Democratic National Construction Association (CDNCA); Vice Chair of its Central Committee on Energy, Resources, and Environment; Deputy Director of the Financial and Economic Affairs Committee of the Standing Committee of the 16th Beijing Municipal People's Congress; Specially Invited Consultant to the Supreme People's Court; Researcher at the Judicial Protection Research Center for Intellectual Property Rights; Hearing Officer for the Supreme People's Procuratorate; Member of the Expert Committee of the State Administration for Market Regulation (SAMR); Member of the Expert Group on Business Environment Optimization under SAMR; Member of the Expert Committee of the China Consumers Association; Vice Chair of the Expert Committee of the National 5G Industry Intellectual Property Operation Center; Vice Chair of the Competition Commission of the China National Committee of the International Chamber of Commerce (ICC China); Executive Council Member of the Economic Law Research Association of the China Law Society; Chair of its Competition Law Committee; Arbitrator at the China International Economic and Trade Arbitration Commission (CIETAC).

Huang Yong has long been engaged in research and teaching in the fields of economic law and international economic law. His main teaching subjects include

Economic Law and Competition Law. As a recognized expert in competition law, he participated throughout the drafting and revision process of China's Anti-Monopoly Law and was one of the key advocates for incorporating the concept of "competition policy" into the statutory text. He has continuously promoted supporting reforms and institutional improvements following the law's enactment. He has organized multiple sessions of the China Competition Policy Forum, hosted by the Anti-Monopoly Commission of the State Council, which have been widely recognized for inviting senior officials from major competition enforcement agencies in China, the United States, and the European Union. In April 2021, he was invited to deliver a keynote lecture to the Standing Committee of the National People's Congress (NPC), titled "Improving the Anti-Monopoly Legal System and Strengthening the Foundational Role of Competition Policy", which was chaired by the then Chairman of the NPC Standing Committee.

Education

From September 1981 to June 1985, Huang Yong studied at the Department of Law, Peking University, earning a Bachelor of Laws degree.

From September 1990 to June 1993, he pursued part-time graduate studies at UIBE, earning a Master of Laws degree.

From September 1999 to June 2002, he continued part-time graduate studies at UIBE and obtained a Doctor of Laws degree.

Since August 1985, he has served at the School of Law, UIBE, successively as Teaching Assistant, Lecturer, Associate Professor, Professor, and Doctoral Supervisor.

Academic Achievements

Books Published: "Studies on International Competition Law", "Analysis of Landmark Cases in Anti-Monopoly Law", "Commentary on Classic Cases of Unfair Competition Law in China and Abroad", "Case Studies on Prohibited Restrictive Agreements", [...] Among these, "Studies on International Competition Law" received the Outstanding Work Award in the 2003 National Foreign Economic and Trade Research Achievement Awards and again won the Outstanding Work Award at the Second National Awards for Legal Textbooks and Research Achievements, hosted by the Ministry of Justice in 2006.

Papers Published: "Essential Facilities Doctrine and Its Application in Intellectual Property Space under China's Anti-Monopoly Law" and "Pursuing The Second Best: The History, Momentum, and Remaining Issues of China's Anti-Monopoly Law" were published in leading international journals in the field of antitrust, such as the Southern California Law Review, Antitrust Law Journal, Competition Policy International, and Antitrust Source.

Domestically, his article "The Anti-Monopoly Law's Response to and Support for China's Economic System Reform" was published in the Theory Edition of People's Daily, and other works have appeared in SSCI, CSSCI, and core Chinese academic journals and major newspapers. His article "China's Anti-Monopoly Law: A Statute Focused on Overall Coordination" was reprinted in full by Xinhua Digest.

Research Projects: Huang Yong has undertaken dozens of research projects commissioned by various institutions, including the Anti-Monopoly Commission of the State Council, the Legislative Affairs Commission of the Standing Committee of the National People's Congress, the former Legislative Affairs Office of the State Council, the National Development and Reform Commission (NDRC), the Ministry of Justice, the Ministry of Commerce, the State-owned Assets Supervision and Administration Commission (SASAC), SAMR, the European Union, the European Environment Agency, the EU-China Trade Project (EUCTP), and the Asian Development Bank (ADB).

Academic Exchanges: He has delivered lectures on Chinese competition law at numerous prestigious institutions, including Chatham House (Royal Institute of International Affairs, UK), the American Bar Association (ABA), Stanford University, University of Pennsylvania, New York University, George Washington University, Georgetown University, American University, George Mason University, University of Oxford, University of Zurich, Nagoya University, Seoul National University, City University of Hong Kong, National Chengchi University, and Fu Jen Catholic University in Taiwan. He has also been invited to visit antitrust enforcement agencies in the United States, European Union, Japan, South Korea, Italy, the United Kingdom, Portugal, etc.

Awards and Honours

In 1988, Yong was recognised as an "Outstanding Educator in Higher Education" by the Beijing Municipal Government. In 1998, Yong was named an "Excellent Young Backbone Teacher" in Beijing. In 2005, he was selected for the New Century Excellent Talents Support Program by the Ministry of Education. In 2007, he was awarded the title of "Education Innovation Model" in Beijing. In 2016, received the Best Asian Antitrust Academic Paper Award in the United States. Also in 2016, Yong was named one of the Most Influential Figures in Chinese Intellectual Property by China Intellectual Property magazine. In 2017, he received the Outstanding Achievement Award from China Law and Practice magazine in Hong Kong.

Introduction

BAI YONG
Partner, Clifford Chance, Beijing

WANG ZIWEN
Associate, Clifford Chance, Beijing

It is with great admiration and warmth that we gather these contributions to celebrate the extraordinary life and career of Professor Huang Yong – a visionary scholar, a beloved mentor, and a dynamic force in the field of competition law in China.

Professor Huang Yong has been a pioneering witness to the birth and evolution of China's competition law, standing at the forefront of its theoretical and practical development from its very inception. A true educator whose students now populate every corner of the legal profession, his profound insights and tireless dedication have shaped generations of legal minds – from government officials crafting national policy to practitioners navigating antitrust enforcement, as well as countless experts and scholars across the field.

Beyond the classroom, Professor Huang's influence extends across cutting-edge issues in competition law including policy formulation, digital markets and AI regulation, intellectual property challenges, and addressing destructive "race to the bottom" competition patterns, to name but a few. Yet his impact reaches far beyond antitrust matters. With a scholar's wisdom, a lawyer's analytical rigor, and a citizen's sense of social responsibility, he actively engages in broader policy discussions and public discourses, offering sage counsel on some of the most critical legal and economic challenges of our time and embodying the ideal of an intellectual serving society.

What truly sets Professor Huang apart is the boundless energy and enthusiasm he brings to every endeavour. Whether mastering the latest legal developments,

Introduction

traversing the globe to share his expertise at conferences, or engaging with friends and colleagues with infectious zeal, he leaves those around him – especially us, his younger admirers – both inspired and struggling to keep pace.

On a more personal note, we must confess we're all devoted followers of his vibrant WeChat Moments updates, where his wisdom, humour and zest for life shine through. These posts perfectly capture his dynamic personality – constantly in motion, constantly motivating. And then, of course, there is Huang Yong the connoisseur – a man who savours the art of living as much as the intricacies of law. His discerning palate and deep appreciation for fine cuisine remind us all that intellectual brilliance and a passion for life's pleasures are not merely compatible, but mutually enriching.

This *liber amicorum* is a testament to the profound impact Professor Huang Yong has had on his field, his students, and his friends. It is a celebration of a life lived with curiosity, generosity, and an unquenchable thirst for knowledge and connection. We offer these reflections with gratitude, respect, and the deepest affection for a teacher, a scholar, and a friend who continues to light the way for so many.

May these pages honour not only his achievements but also the joy, wisdom, and indomitable spirit he shares with us all.

PART I
Frontier Issues and Comparative Studies in Antitrust Law

Huang Yong: A Distinguished Trailblazer in China's Antitrust Law Realm

JIN SHANMING[*]

Professor, Institute of Law, Chinese Academy of Social Sciences

Abstract

Professor Huang Yong emerges as an indispensable academic luminary in the development of China's antitrust regime, contributing as a legislative expert, scholar, and public advocate. His work bridges legal theory and practice, shaping both the Anti-Monopoly Law's framework and the enforcement of competition policy. Through academic research, policy advising, and international engagement, he has advanced the study and implementation of competition law in China and strengthened its dialogue with the global legal community.

---

[*] Jin Shanming, Professor and Doctoral Supervisor at the Institute of Law, Chinese Academy of Social Sciences; Director of the Economic Law Department.

I. Introduction

1. In the sphere of antitrust law in China, Professor Huang Yong from the Law School of the University of International Business and Economics (UIBE) emerges as an indispensable academic luminary. As a key participant throughout the legislative journey of China's Anti-Monopoly Law, a member of the Expert Advisory Board of the State Council Anti-Monopoly Commission, and a "China's voice" in the global competition law community, Professor Huang Yong has dedicated over four decades to the study of economic law and competition law. Guided by a firm belief in "applying knowledge to serve society", he bridges the gap between theory and practice with scholarly integrity. Through his endeavors, he has crafted a multifaceted portrait of a contemporary legal scholar who "studies for the people" and penned a compelling chapter in the broader narrative of the rule of law in service of the public good. His academic career is magnificent, his insights are far-reaching, his social image shines brightly, and he shows his responsibility in participating in politics and deliberating on state affairs, leaving an indelible, impactful mark on the grand narrative of China's antitrust development.

II. Academic Heritage: The Academic Background from Peking University to UIBE

2. Professor Huang Yong began his academic journey at Peking University, by the serene shores of Weiming Lake. In 1981, he gained admission to the Law Department of Peking University, where he underwent a rigorous and systematic legal education. During his undergraduate years, he showed a strong interest in the field of economic law – a discipline that resonated both with the national imperative of cultivating legal expertise in the transformation of China's economic system in the early stage of reform and opening up, and with his personal ideal of advancing governance through law. At that time, China was surging forward on the tide of reform and opening up, and the economic system reform was in full swing. The demand for legal talents was like a parched earth yearning for rain. Professor Huang Yong, much like a tide – riding pioneer seizing the tide of reform, embraced economic law with a deep sense of purpose during his undergraduate years. He was determined to wield the sword of law to hack through the brambles and thorns of social development and pursue his lofty vision of "bringing about good governance in the world". It was then that the seed of his rule-of-law ideal took quiet root in his heart.

3. In 1985, after graduating from Peking University, Huang Yong was recommended to join the Department of International Economic Law of the UIBE as a lecturer. At that time, the Department of International Economic Law of UIBE had just been established for one year. The words and deeds of Professor Feng Datong (an alumnus of Peking University and the first dean of the Department of International Economic Law of UIBE) profoundly shaped his academic outlook. Professor Feng's rigorous style of "putting a stack of small cards on the lectern, walking from one end of the podium to the other, speaking at a steady pace without a single superfluous word" when giving lectures, and the logical training of "drawing a legal relation diagram on the blackboard every time he walked back and forth" became important nourishment for Huang Yong's early academic training.

4. Huang Yong went on to complete his master's and doctoral studies at UIBE (under the supervision of Professor Feng Datong and Professor Shen Daming, respectively), systematically studying international economic law. From 1996 to 1997, he served as a visiting scholar at the University of Connecticut in the United States, where he witnessed the practice of US antitrust law firsthand, laying the foundation for his subsequent shift toward competition law research. From Peking University to UIBE, from domestic to overseas, Huang Yong's academic trajectory gradually came into focus: shaped by a global perspective and grounded in domestic realities, his scholarship took root at the intersection of economic law and competition law.

III. Academic Depth: A "Legislator and Interpreter" in the Field of Competition Law

5. If one were to capture Professor Huang Yong in a phrase, "a living textbook of China's Anti-Monopoly Law" would be the most appropriate. Since 2005, he has been deeply involved in the drafting and revision of China's Anti-Monopoly Law, playing key roles from legislative expert consultant to a member of the Expert Advisory Board of the State Council Anti-Monopoly Commission. His scholarly insight is woven into the very fabric of China's competition law system.

(I) Legislative participation: a witness from "inception" to "refinement"

6. In February 2005, Professor Huang Yong was appointed as a member of State Anti-monopoly Law Legislation Expert Advisory Committee. In July 2006, he was named an expert for the legislation of the Anti-Monopoly Law of the Legislative Affairs Commission of the Standing

Committee of the National People's Congress. During the critical period of drafting the Anti-Monopoly Law, he played an instrumental role in shaping its legal framework and refining key clauses. He put forward significant proposals on several controversial issues such as "the identification of monopolistic agreements", "the review standards for concentration of undertakings", and "the regulation of administrative monopolies". One notable contribution was his advocacy for establishing the foundational status of competition policy in the legal system – a legislative principle aimed at harmonizing antitrust enforcement with industrial policy. This idea was ultimately codified in Article 4 of the general provisions during the 2022 amendment to the Anti-Monopoly Law.

7. Beyond the Anti-Monopoly Law, Professor Huang Yong has also contributed to the expert review of numerous legislative instruments, including the Foreign Trade Law, the Anti-Unfair Competition Law, and the Bankruptcy Law. His scholarship spans a well-integrated framework of competition law, economic law, and foreign-related law.

(II) Academic writings: bridging theory and practice

8. Professor Huang Yong has consistently embraced a pragmatic academic ethos rooted in the belief that "learning from books alone is shallow; true understanding comes through practice". Guided by a problem-oriented approach, he has ventured into the evolving landscape of antitrust law like a fearless explorer, advancing into uncharted territories. He not only keeps abreast of international cutting-edge trends, as if standing on the top of a mountain looking into the distance, observing the development trend of global jurisprudence; but also takes root in the soil of Chinese practice, just like a big tree deeply rooted in the earth, absorbing the nutrients of local experience.

9. His representative work, *International Competition Law* (2003), stands as a bright pearl in the academic community. This book systematically examines the tension and cooperation in the enforcement of international competition law, weaving together a dense and nuanced analytical web that captures complex legal phenomena. It is hailed as the "pioneering work in China's international comparative study of competition law", and justly earned him several major academic awards. Another work, *Anti-trust Law Cases and Commentaries* (2002), takes a different approach, using cases as a guide, it provides a vivid practical reference for the implementation of the Anti-Monopoly Law. Through in-depth examination of landmark U.S. antitrust decisions, the book reads like a collection of gripping stories – translating abstract legal principles into concrete, relatable narratives that immerse the reader and illuminate legal reasoning. It is a textbook example of "explaining the law through cases, with clarity and engagement".

10. In terms of academic writings, Professor Huang Yong has demonstrated outstanding scholarly capacity through both the depth and breadth of his research contributions. He has published in leading international journals such as the *Antitrust Law Journal*, where his work offers the global academic community a window into the evolution of China's antitrust regime. His landmark article, *Pursuing The Second Best: The History, Momentum, and Remaining Issues of China's Anti-Monopoly Law*, unpacks the logic behind China's antitrust choices and the key challenges that remain, enabling the world to better understand China's antitrust regime, the Chinese market economic system, and economic development. At the same time, he has published a wide range of high-quality articles in leading domestic journals and influential media outlets such as *Law Science, China Development Observation*, and *People's Daily*. Through these contributions, he has fostered a discourse that integrates international vision with localized insights, building an intellectual bridge between Chinese and international legal communities and promoting the prosperity of academic research.

(III) Research projects: from national priorities to global governance

11. Professor Huang Yong's research projects have always resonated with national strategies. He has led major national-level projects, including the *Research on Antitrust Rules in the field of Platform Economy* for the State Council Anti-Monopoly Commission, the *Ex-post Evaluation of the Implementation of the Fair Competition Review System* for the State Administration for Market Regulation, and the *Coordination Mechanism between Trade Policy and Competition Policy* for the Ministry of Commerce. At the international level, he has contributed to projects commissioned by international organizations such as the European Union (e.g., *Study on China's Urban Social Security Legal Framework*) and the Asian Development Bank (e.g., *Comparative Research on Competition Law*). These research endeavors have not only provided robust theoretical support for policy-making, but also facilitated international dialogue on China's competition law. His scholarly contributions serve as beacons of insight, illuminating the path of policy formulation, enabling China's competition law to shine brightly on the global stage, and demonstrating a global vision and a sense of global responsibility.

IV. Social Responsibility: The "Multifaceted Roles" from Legal Academia to Law Practice

12. As a scholar, Professor Huang Yong's influence goes far beyond his study. Guided by the philosophy of "applying knowledge to serve society", he plays multiple roles in the fields of teaching and educating people,

participating in the administration and discussion of state affairs, and international exchanges, and fulfilling the mission of "rule of law for the people".

(I) Teaching and educating people: the "gardener" cultivating legal talents

13. On the podium of the UIBE, Professor Huang Yong lectures on courses such as "Competition Law, "Economic Law", and "Law of Macroeconomic Regulation". His classroom is like a magical stage, and the three-dimensional teaching method of "case + theory + practice" attracts the attention of countless students. He often uses trending cases such as "Alibaba Antitrust Case" and "Tencent Music Exclusive Copyright Case" as an introduction, and tells the story like an experienced storyteller, narrating the complex case details, immersing students in the experience as if they were in the fierce court debate scene; he introduces economic analysis tools, such as the SSNIP test for market definition, which is like handing students a magic key to open the door of wisdom, and helping them explore a new realm of thinking; he also invites antitrust officials, legal professionals and executives to enter the classroom to participate in the discussion, just like bridging theory and practice, so that students can get close to the forefront of practice and appreciate the real legal world.

14. He often advises his students, "Competition law scholars should not only understand the law but also understand the industry, technology, and market. Otherwise, they will be like the blind men describing an elephant and unable to respond to the new challenges of the digital economy era." Under his careful guidance, many doctors, like eagles spreading their wings, have entered practical departments such as the Supreme People's Court and State Administration for Market Regulation or served as competition policy consultants in Internet companies, becoming the mainstay of China's competition law construction. At the founding conference of the Institute of Foreign-Related Rule of Law, he said with great pride, "The training of foreign-related rule of law talents at the UIBE must be 'precise, specialized, and accurate', and every key competition policy position must have our graduates." This enthusiasm and responsibility for educating people, like warm sunshine, illuminates the students' path forward and also demonstrates his grand vision of "having students all over the world".

(II) Participating in the administration and discussion of state affairs: the "proposal provider" serving social governance with professionalism

15. As a member of the Central Committee of the China National Democratic Construction Association and a deputy to the Beijing Municipal People's Congress, Professor Huang Yong has transformed his academic expertise

into wisdom for participating in politics and policy-making, just like a painter holding a wonderful brush, sketching out a series of wonderful blueprints on the canvas of social governance. His suggestions, such as "strengthening anti-monopoly law enforcement in the platform economy", "improving the fair competition review system", and "strengthening the capacity building of anti-monopoly law enforcement agencies", are like shining pearls and have been included in the legislative research outline of the Financial and Economic Affairs Committee of the Standing Committee of the Beijing Municipal People's Congress many times, providing important reference for policy formulation.

16. In April 2021, he was invited to deliver the 23rd special lecture of the Standing Committee of the 13th National People's Congress, entitled "Improving the Anti-monopoly Legal System and Strengthening the Basic Position of Competition Policy". At the lecture, Chairman Li Zhanshu personally presided over it, and the audience was attracted by his wonderful explanation. This is not only a high recognition of his academic authority but also highlights his outstanding contribution to serving social governance with professional knowledge, making him a model of "making suggestions for the country and speaking for the people".

(III) International exchanges: the "messenger" telling china's legal stories well

17. In the international academic circle of competition law, Professor Huang Yong is like a loud horn, conveying the "Chinese voice" to the world. He has delivered keynote speeches at world-renowned universities such as the Royal Institute of International Affairs, Stanford University, and the University of Zurich. Like a cultural ambassador, he used vivid language to explain to the world the "overall coordination" characteristics of China's Anti-Monopoly Law, allowing the world to have a deeper understanding of China's market economy, China's economic governance, and China's anti-monopoly law. He was also invited to visit antitrust law enforcement agencies such as those in the US, the EU, and Japan, like a friendly ambassador, actively promoting the dialogue between China and foreign competition policies.

18. Recalling that when the EU's "Digital Markets Act" (DMA) was formulated, participants expressed their opinions and debated fiercely at the China-EU Competition Policy Session. Professor Huang Yong proposed the Chinese position that "data interoperability needs to balance innovation and competition". This view won the approval of the participants, contributed valuable Chinese wisdom to the research and formulation of international rules, and demonstrated the elegance of " Chinese solutions, the world's attention".

V. Honors and Recognition: The "Footnotes" to an Academic Career

19. With over 40 years of dedication to academic and practical work, Professor Huang Yong has won numerous honors. These not only illuminate his remarkable academic journey but also inspire others and contribute to society.

(I) In the field of teaching: the "medal of the hard-working person" on the podium

20. In the field of teaching, he has successively won the titles of Beijing "Advanced Teacher in College Teaching", Beijing "College Outstanding Youth Teacher", and Beijing "Educational Innovation Pace-setter". These honors bear witness to his outstanding teaching achievements and are a high recognition of his hard work in "propagating the doctrine, imparting professional knowledge, and resolving doubts".

(II) In the field of academia: the "witness of achievements" in theoretical exploration

21. In the field of academia, he was selected into the Program for New Century Excellent Talents of the Ministry of Education, won the Best Antitrust Business Article Asian Antitrust Category, was rated as one of "China's most influential people in IP of the Year" by *China Intellectual Property*, and won the "Outstanding Achievement Award" by Hong Kong *China Law & Practice*, among many other awards. These honors are like bright pearls inlaid on his academic crown, demonstrating his profound academic attainments and outstanding academic influence.

(III) In the field of social work: the "manifestation of value" in public service

22. In the field of social work, he was awarded the titles of "National Outstanding Member of the China National Democratic Construction Association" and "Advanced Individual of the Special Committee of the Central Committee of the China National Democratic Construction Association". These honors are a high recognition of his active participation in social affairs and enthusiasm for public welfare undertakings, much like a bouquet of flowers, affirming his outstanding contributions on the social stage.

23. Faced with so many honors, Professor Huang Yong always maintains a humble attitude, like a wise person indifferent to fame and fortune. He often says, "Competition law is the 'economic constitution', and its life lies in implementation. My academic mission is to make this law

truly a real 'weapon' to maintain market fairness and promote innovative development." This pure original intention and lofty ambition are sincerely admirable, and it is also the source of his motivation to keep moving forward.

VI. Conclusion: Legislator, Scholar, and Practitioner Working Together with Competition Law

24. "To ordain conscience for Heaven and Earth, to secure life and fortune for the people, to continue lost teachings for past sages, and to establish peace for all future generations" is a true portrayal of Professor Huang Yong's academic pursuit. From a student at Peking University to a professor at UIBE, from a legislative expert to a political representative, Professor Huang Yong's academic life is like an exciting movement, always in harmony with the development of China's competition law. With a solid academic foundation as the cornerstone, keen sense of problem-solving as the beacon, and an open international perspective as the wings, he perfectly embodies the responsibility and commitment of a contemporary Chinese competition law scholar in the two-way interaction between theoretical construction and legal practice. He once said in an interview, "The value of a scholar lies not only in how many papers and works he produces but also in whether he can use knowledge to respond to the questions of the times and meet the needs of society." This is perhaps the most moving footnote to Professor Huang Yong's academic life, and it has also set the most vivid example for young scholars, inspiring countless legal scholars to continue exploring and advancing on the path of rule of law.

Attacking State Restraints: Building on the groundwork of Professor Huang Yong

ELEANOR FOX*
Professor Emerita, New York University School of Law

Abstract

The task of eliminating unreasonable and unnecessary state restraints is both more necessary and more difficult than ever before. This essay explores these challenges. To capture the space that falls between the silos of competition law and free movement law, it suggests that we need to create a trade-and-competition violation. Short of that aspiration, which will be hard to meet in view of assertions of sovereignty, this essay proposes tight collaboration between competition authorities and internal-market trade authorities. It also urges continued and important attention to overly restrictive local regulations, many of which violate the principle of competitive neutrality.

---

* Eleanor M. Fox, Professor of Law Emerita and Walter J. Derenberg Professor of Trade Regulation Emerita at New York University School of Law, served as a member of President Carter's Antitrust Commission NCRALP (1978-79) and President Clinton's international competition advisory committee ICPAC (1997-2000).

Attacking State Restraints: Building on the groundwork of Professor Huang Yong

Introduction[1]

1. State restraints are some of the most harmful restraints on competition. Professor Huang Yong has been a pioneer in framing the problem for China and doing what he could and can in trying to control state restraints that severely harm the market. He was instrumental in securing Chapter 5 in the Anti-Monopoly Law and in securing Fair Competition Review of regulations.[2]

2. This essay in his honor argues two points. 1) A number of other jurisdictions, backed by the OECD, frame the law reform project as one of assuring competitive neutrality. But competitive neutrality is a corner of the problem; the big problem is unreasonable and unnecessary state restraints. This section examines the OECD recommendation on competitive neutrality. 2) The task of eliminating unreasonable and unnecessary state restraints (hereinafter "state restraints") is both more necessary and more difficult than ever before. This section explores the challenges and proposes a trade-and-competition violation. Short of that aspiration, it urges tight collaboration between competition authorities and internal-market trade authorities.

3. We begin with appreciation of the harms from state restraints. We then proceed to competitive neutrality, and then to the challenges of the big problem.

I. The Immense Harm from State Restraints and the Relevance of Competition Law and Policy

4. In 1995 Fox & Ordover wrote, thinking globally: "It is debatable [...] whether much would be accomplished [...] on harmonization only on a cartel principle without removing tensions at other notable points, for example, [...] anticompetitive government action."[3]

5. In 2005, Professor Tim Muris wrote:[4]

   "Protecting competition by focusing solely on private restraints is like trying to stop the water flow at a fork in a stream by blocking only one channel."...

---

[1] This essay is adapted from Eleanor Fox, The Promotion of Competitive Neutrality by Competition Authorities – Attacking State Restraints and Assuring Competitive Neutrality, OECD Global Forum on Competition, Dec. 8, 2021, https://one.oecd.org/document/DAF/COMP/GF(2021)10/en/pdf.

[2] See Huang Yong, Pursuing the Second Best: The History, Momentum, and Remaining Issues of China's Anti-Monopoly Law, 75 Antitrust L.J. 117 (2008).

[3] Eleanor M. Fox and Janusz A. Ordover, The Harmonization of Competition and Trade Law – The Case for Modest Links of Law and Limits to Parochial State Action, 19 World Competition 5, 11 (1995).

[4] Timothy Muris, Principles for a Successful Competition Agency, 72 U. Chi. L. Rev. 165, 170 (2005).

> "[R]egulatory success in attacking private restraints increases the efforts that firms will devote to seeking public restraints. Indeed rational firms are likely to prefer public restraints. Public restraints can be far more effective at restraining competition."[5]

6. These are immutable observations. Yet the law is hardly robust in eliminating undue state and local privileges and restraints. The difficulty lies not in identifying the restraints as harmful to competition. The difficulty is three-fold. One, it lies in distinguishing restraints unnecessary to a (reasonable) view of the public interest in government action, for government must be given room to operate and bona fide state regulation often has by-product effects that we tolerate. The second difficulty is institutional: designing a competition system that allows judicial/administrative challenge to undue state restraints without (for a number of jurisdictions) threatening powers of the legislature and the executive. The third is political: states and their political leaders resist giving up the power they have, even when it would serve the greater good.

7. Advocacy does not face these problems. Competition authorities can assess state measures, expose their costs, and argue for reforms. Success depends on persuasion. Persuasion is a good but weak tool. Persuasion is not likely to work in the worst cases of vested interests and cronyism where those with power want to keep their privileges. Competition law enforcement (where law allows) is obviously a much stronger tool than advocacy, but legislative prohibitions – if they can be adopted at all – must be judiciously crafted and probably, to be adopted, must be weaker than optimal. A number of jurisdictions have overcome the challenges of defining the scope of state restraints to be prohibited by law, while safeguarding prerogatives of the executive.[6] The most prevalent and accepted enforcement is at local, municipal, and provincial level, and applies to rules and regulations rather than higher law. Yet, disciplines against higher (unreasonable, disproportionate, protectionist) law can be vital to make cross-border markets more competitive and to realize the promise of regional integration.[7]

II. The OECD 2021 Recommendation on Competitive Neutrality

8. The OECD project on competitive neutrality is an important piece of the effort to eliminate law that unreasonably restrains competition. It is framed as "competitive neutrality" – thus, in terms of assuring a level

---

[5] Id. at 170.

[6] Eleanor Fox & Deborah Healey, When the State Harms Competition, 79 Antitrust L.J. 769 (2014).

[7] Eleanor Fox, Integrating Africa by Competition and Market Policy, 60 Rev. of Industrial Organization 305 (2022), available on SSRN, https://papers.ssrn.com/sol3/papers.cfm?abstract_id=3873432.

playing field for private actors who would otherwise face a competitive disadvantage with public actors. Why? The framing suggests that we care centrally about disadvantages to private firms, as opposed to making the market work. To be sure, disadvantage to private firms vis-a-vis state-privileged firms can be a clue to harm to competition, but it is also true that we could achieve competitive neutrality by privileging all firms equally (everyone gets the subsidy) without curing the competitive harm. Laws that are not competitively neutral are only a piece of undue state restraints.

9. The 2021 OECD recommendation[8] actually recognizes that the big project is limiting government restraints that harm competition (rather than only those that harm competitors). Thus, recitals provide:

> "RECOGNISING that competition promotes efficiency, helping to ensure that goods or services offered to consumers more closely match consumer preferences, producing benefits such as lower prices, greater choice, improved quality, increased innovation, and higher productivity;
>
> "RECOGNISING that government actions may distort competition in the market …"

10. The Recommendation then pivots between neutrality (vis-à-vis private rivals) and market harms:

> "CONSIDERING that governments are increasingly developing tools to address distortions related to competitive neutrality …"

11. adherents should ensure competitive neutrality. They should do so by: …

> "1. Ensuring that the legal framework applicable to markets in which Enterprises currently or potentially compete is neutral and competition is not unduly prevented, restricted or distorted. To this effect Adherents should: …
>
> "iii. Carry out competition assessments that identify and revise existing or proposed regulations that unduly restrict competition …".

12. As a thought experiment, we might notionally remove the words "neutral" and "neutrality." The effect would be a recommendation to ensure against government actions and measures that "unduly prevent, restrict or distort competition." Thus, a recommendation against undue government restraints.

13. We might conclude that the project of competitive neutrality is mis-framed.

---

8 See Recommendation of the Council on Competitive Neutrality, OECD, adopted 30/05/2021, https://www.oecd.org/competition/competitive-neutrality.htm.

III. Competition LAWs Against Undue State Restraints

14. The competition laws of a number of jurisdictions reprehend undue state and local restraints. These were compiled and analyzed in Fox & Healey, *When the State Harms Competition.*[9] An appendix by the authors published by UNCTAD highlights sample statutory provisions (as of 2014).[10] The sample provisions span a range, including: 1) competition laws that apply equally to state owned enterprises, 2) application of competition law to enterprises granted exclusive rights and special privileges, 3) control over corrupt public procurement, including provisions that allow the competition agency to challenge public officials complicit in private bid-rig conspiracies, 4) in the case of common markets, provisions to assure free movement of goods and services that reprehend unreasonably restrictive cross-border state/provincial measures, 5) provisions against abuse of competitive neutrality, 6) prohibition of abuse of government administrative power to harm competition (China), and 7) provisions giving standing to the competition authority to challenge state acts as illegal under constitutions or other (than antitrust) statutes.

15. Much of the competition agency activity challenging government restraints involves local/municipal restraints. Among the jurisdictions most active in this area are Russia and Lithuania. Peru is one of the jurisdictions most active in annulling regulations that are "bureaucratic barriers." Peru annuls thousands of such regulations a year. The European Union is the most prominent jurisdiction that has a holistic appreciation of combined state and private restraints – a natural emanation from the common market framework. The EU framework, which supports challenges to hybrid cross-border public-private restraints, has great potential for regional free trade agreements and common markets, as suggested below.

16. National competition laws' control of undue state restraints is a good candidate for a list of best practices. Internationally, it is at least as important as seeking convergence of substantive cartel principles or any other substantive principles.[11]

IV. The Need to Overcome the Silo Problem; Fusing Public and Private Restraints – a Potential New Violation

17. The sharp separation of public and private restraints is a problem. While there are some private restraints that exist without state facilitation, public restraints are often adopted to support private vested interests; often

---

9   Fox & Healey, supra note 6.
10 https://unctad.org/system/files/official-document/ditcclp2015d6_en.pdf.
11 See Fox & Ordover, supra note 3, at 11.

corruptly so, as in the (common) case of procurement officials in league with bid riggers. Often there is an interplay between private interests that have captured the regulator, and unreasonable, excessive laws. For example, Mexico adopted a vested-interest restraint that pushed the price of cross-border telephone calls up to the highest levels in the world.[12] Saskatchewan potash producers played off the dumping laws and the antitrust laws.[13] The US aluminum industry hid behind government's plan to control the flood of imports from Russia.[14] The Italian matches industry succumbed to national producers, who enjoyed the right to parcel out quotas and keep out the Swedes and Germans, meeting their match in EU law, which caught both the public and private restraints.[15] The intertwining of private and public restrains is perhaps most noticeable in developing countries with high levels of corruption, where researchers observe that goods do not flow over the borders that economic logic would predict, and firms stay dominant in their markets.[16]

18. Restraints may be public, they may be private, they may be both. If the competition agency is empowered to challenge both in the same investigation at the same time, they are much more likely to have access to data that will yield evidence that connects the dots to anticompetitive offenses. Procurement bid-rigging is a good example.

19. The problem distinctly surfaces in connection with the promise of regional integration. Regional integration offers many benefits through scale, scope and "vision from the top." The promise is especially great and needed in a region of developing countries where competition agencies are often too small or under-resourced to fend for themselves. In theory, regionalism can overcome these limitations. Yet border restraints of member nations (often hybrid, procured by leading firms) are a serious problem, and unless the border restraints fall, the region – such as the whole African continent, will never be effectively integrated, despite a common market.[17]

20. The European Union institutional framework provides an attractive starting point for a solution. EU law prohibits unreasonable state restraints

---

12 See Eleanor Fox, WTO's First Antitrust Case – Mexican Telecom: A Sleeping Victory for Trade and Competition, 9 JIEL 271 (2006).

13 See Bloomkest Fertilizer v. Potash Saskatchewan, 203 F. 3d 1028 (8th Cir. 2000).

14 See Frederic Jenny, Competition, Trade and Development Before and After Cancun, in Fordham Corp. L. Institute, Chapter 26, 631, 633-35 (B. Hawk ed. 2004).

15 Consorzio Industrie Fiammiferi (Italian Matches), Case C-198/01, EU:C:2003:430.

16 See, e.g., Simon Roberts, Common Law Prescriptions and Competitive.
Outcomes: Insights from Southern and East Africa, Chapter 8 in RECONCILING EFFICIENCY AND EQUITY: A Global.
Challenge for Competition Policy (D. Gerard and I. Lianos, eds. Cambridge 2019).

17 See Integrating Africa, supra note 7. See also Eleanor Fox, Competition Law, Developing Countries, and Regional Agreements: Tearing Down Silos and Building Up Scaffolds, Afronomics Law, August 2, 2021, https://www.afronomicslaw.org/category/analysis/symposium-introduction-markets-competition-and-regional-integration-global-south.

as well as unreasonable private restraints. It spells out, through its case law, what is an unreasonable state restraint. While protecting legitimate states' rights to protect their people, it condemns state acts and measures that unreasonably and disproportionately harm trade and competition in the Union. Importing and building on the model in their own ways, nations and regions can develop a trade-and-competition violation. Short of that aspiration, they can foster a mode of tight collaboration between trade (internal market) authorities and competition authorities, who can and should join forces to understand and prohibit unreasonable hybrid restraints.[18] Likewise, on national and cross-border levels, competition officials and prosecutors can and should tightly collaborate in proving and prohibiting fused competition/corruption offenses. There are models, as in the Brazilian "car wash" scandal.

Conclusion

21. Undue state restraints are a huge problem that can undermine effectiveness of competition law, both nationally and cross-border. Competitive neutrality is a corner of the problem. Most competition laws are not fit for the task of effectively disciplining the most harmful and unreasonable state restraints. Nor do other laws (such as commerce clauses) do the job. As a consequence, unreasonable state restraints boldly "wander around," undisciplined. Empowering competition authorities to challenge unreasonable state restraints, whether or not tethered to competitive neutrality, would significantly improve competition in nations, in regions, and in the world.

---

18 Integrating Africa, supra.

Competition and Environmental Sustainability: Lessons from the European Debate

FRÉDÉRIC JENNY*

Emeritus Professor of Economics ESSEC Business School
Chairman OECD Global Forum on Competition

Abstract

The increasing recognition of climate change as an existential threat, has prompted calls for integrating sustainability into competition policy and competition law enforcement. This article examines whether and when environmental sustainability aligns with the competition model, the role competition plays in achieving sustainability, and how sustainability can be integrated into competition law enforcement. A key difference between countries is the scope of efficiency benefits considered for exemptions, with the EU Commission focusing mostly on "in-market" benefits to consumers affected by restrictions, while the CMA and the ACM in the Netherlands are more open to consider "out-of-market" and broader societal benefits. The article notes that China's Anti-Monopoly Law explicitly includes public interest and sustainable development goals, and its framework allows for exemptions related to sustainability in all areas of competition law, including merger control, a more comprehensive approach than the EU, even if obtaining such exemptions in China in practice remains challenging.

---

* Frederic Jenny, the professor of Economics at ESSEC Business School in Paris. He is Chairman of the OECD Competition Committee (since 1994), Co-Director of the European Center for Law and Economics of ESSEC (since 2010) and Senior Fellow of the GW Competition and Innovation Lab at The George Washington University. He was previously No. Executive Director of the Office of Fair Trading in the United Kingdom (2007-2014), Judge on the French Supreme Court (Cour de cassation, Economic Commercial and Financial Chamber) from 2004 to August 2012, Vice Chair of the French Competition Authority (1993-2004) and President of the WTO Working Group on Trade and Competition (1994-2003).

Competition and Environmental Sustainability: Lessons from the European Debate

1. In a celebrated article entitled "Climate Change Is An Existential Threat: Competition Law Must Be Part Of The Solution And Not Part Of The Problem"[1] published in 2020, Simon Holmes argued that: "It is increasingly accepted that we face a "climate emergency" and that "business as usual" is not an option". He strongly argued for an integration of climate change and sustainability considerations into competition policy. Since then, the relationship between competition and sustainability has become a topic of high interest for competition authorities in Europe.

2. Besides Simon Holmes' wake-up call, several developments have contributed to the emergence of this topic.

3. The Intergovernmental Panel on Climate Change (IPCC) was established in 1988 to provide policymakers with regular scientific assessments on the current state of knowledge about climate change. The reports on climate change, published every two years by the IPCC, have convinced a large number of governments of the urgency of the situation and the need to prioritize resource conservation as a key policy objective.

4. In September 2000, the United Nations established eight Millennium Development Goals (MDGs) to be achieved by 2015. The Millennium Declaration was signed at that September global summit held at the UN headquarters in New York, and the 149 international leaders in attendance committed to combating disease, hunger, poverty, illiteracy, discrimination against women, and environmental degradation. The MDGs were derived from this Declaration, and specific indicators and targets were attached to them. The Millennium Development Goals are fairly wide-ranging, but one of them, the seventh goal, is: "to promote environmental sustainability".

5. In Europe, the European Green Deal, which was approved in 2020, is a set of policy initiatives by the European Commission with the aim of making the European Union (EU) climate-neutral in 2050. The plan is to review each existing law on its climate merits, and also introduce new legislation on the circular economy (CE), building renovation, biodiversity, farming, and innovation.

6. An interesting constitutional feature of the European Treaty is that Article 11 of the TFEU mandates that environmental protection requirements must be integrated into the definition and implementation of all Union policies, including competition law[2]. This means that competition law enforcement must take into account not only traditional competition objectives but also broader EU policy goals, such as environmental sustainability.

---

[1] Simon Holmes, "Climate Change Is An Existential Threat: Competition Law Must Be Part Of The Solution And No. Part Of The Problem" Competition Policy International Antitrust Chronicle, July 2020.

[2] Article 11 TFEU Article 11: "Environmental protection requirements must be integrated into the definition and implementation of the Union's policies and activities, in particular with a view to promoting sustainable development".

7. Europe is not the only place in the world where questions are raised with respect to the integration of sustainability issues into competition law and policy. As we shall see later, China is also a country where sustainability must be integrated in the enforcement of the Anti Monopoly Law (AML).

1) Environmental Sustainability

8. Literally, "sustainability" means the ability to sustain. Sustainability focuses on meeting the needs of the present without compromising the ability of future generations to meet their needs. It thus has a dynamic dimension because it relates to both the present and the future.
9. The concept of sustainability has been developed along three dimensions: an economic dimension, an environmental dimension, and a social dimension. So, although concern about sustainability is frequently associated with the fight against climate change, it is in no way limited to this particular aspect.

2) Complex Relationship Between Competition and Environmental Sustainability

10. Several questions can be raised about the interface between competition and environmental sustainability.
11. The first question is whether environmental sustainability is compatible with the competition model?-A second is when and how, if ever, competition plays a role in achieving environmental sustainability? The third is how to integrate sustainability in competition law enforcement?
12. With respect to the first question (whether environmental sustainability is compatible with the competition model), differing views are possible:
13. At first sight, it seems that the goal of competition is not sustainability, but the allocation of available resources in the most efficient way. Allocating scarcity in a static framework is not, in most cases, directly conducive to conserving resources for the future. On the other hand, to the extent that there is a link between static competition and dynamic innovation and to the extent that technological innovation can possibly lead to the adoption of cleaner technologies, one could argue that competition can be, at least indirectly, a mechanism which could ultimately contribute to saving our environment.
14. Thus, when we think about innovation future resource enter explicitly into the competition discussion only in a limited way. Also the link between competition and innovation is rather complex and subject to some controversy among economists.

15. There may be ways to make competition more beneficial for sustainability and the fight against climate change. Indeed, if the prices of resources today reflected not only the current opportunity cost of these resources but also the social cost of the loss of opportunities tomorrow that their use today entails, we could be more careful about how we use them. If that were the case, there would be a closer link between competition and sustainability.

16. Thus, the absence of a direct link between competition and the progressive use of cleaner technologies could be explained as a regulatory failure to ensure that prices of inputs in the production process reflect their true opportunity cost.

17. For example, the idea of imposing a carbon tax on polluting producers has gained political support in various countries. From an economic standpoint, a carbon tax should be set in such a way that the cost of emitting CO_2 (including the tax) for polluters using "dirty technology" be equal to the social cost of carbon, which is the present value of estimated environmental damages over time caused by an additional ton of carbon dioxide emitted today. This tax rate should also rise over time to reflect the growing damage expected from climate change. An increasing price over time would also provide a signal to emitters that they will need to do more and that their investments in clean technologies will be economically justified.

18. The adoption of such a carbon tax would force firms to internalize the environmental costs of their emissions, and correct the market failures accruing from the fact that currently polluters do not bear the cost of the full societal impact of their actions.

19. In 1990, Finland was the first country to introduce a carbon tax. Since then, about 70 carbon emission schemes have been implemented. With respect to Europe, 23 countries have implemented carbon taxes, ranging from a rate of less than €1 per metric ton of carbon emissions in Ukraine to more than €100 in Sweden, Liechtenstein, and Switzerland. As of June 2024, Switzerland and Liechtenstein levied the highest carbon tax rate at €120.16 ($130.81) per ton of carbon emissions, followed by Sweden (€115.34, $125.56) and Norway (€83.47, $90.86). Currently the lowest carbon tax rates can be found in Poland (€0.09, $0.10) and Ukraine (€0.72, $0.77). The average carbon tax rate among the 23 European countries was €49.23 as of April 1, 2024[3].

20. Carbon taxes are effective tools for incentivizing firms to limit their CO_2 emissions, but the levels and scopes of taxation implemented are usually considered insufficient. Furthermore, to be effective, taxation must be accompanied by enabling policies.

---

[3] Alex Mengden: Carbon Taxes in Europe, Tax Faoundatio Europe, 2024 June 18, 2024.

21. There are a number of political forces which prevent governments from setting the carbon tax at the appropriate level (i.e. at a level which represents the estimated discounted value of the damage associated with the use of the carbon emitting technology).

22. Among the forces pushing back against the adoption of carbon taxes, is the fact that a flat tax on the amount of carbon emission can disproportionately impact lower income groups who spend a higher share of their earnings on energy bills and basic goods carrying embedded carbon costs. There is also the concern that such a tax will reduce the competitiveness of firms using domestic energy sources by raising their cost compared to the costs of foreign firms. Thus there is a perceived risk of firms leaving the country to protect their competitivity.

23. The second question is whether competition plays a role in achieving environmental sustainability?

24. There is a widespread feeling that the profit motive, which fuels firms on competitive markets, has led to many short-term decisions that have depleted our resources.

25. What the recent debate about the importance of sustainability adds is the fact that because the cost of resources today does not reflect the cost of the losses of opportunities to-morrow that their use today entails, there could be a negative externality across time as a result of the competitive market mechanism.

26. Such a negative externality may not materialize if a sufficiently large proportion of consumers attach a high value to clean products and technologies and are willing to pay a sufficiently high premium for climate-compliant products and services. In such cases, it will be in the interest of some (or all) firms to offer "Clean" products at a higher price on the market, and in that case economic competition could be compatible with a climate-compliant economy.

27. However, such a result will not materialize in two cases.

28. First, it will not materialize if consumers do not care about sustainability (if they only care about today), or in other words, if sustainability does not enter their utility function. In this case, there may be a contradiction between the public policy objective and the competitive markets outcomes.

29. Second there may a possibility that a behavioral bias on the part of consumers will lead to a market failure. This would be the case, for example, if consumers proclaim to care about sustainability and to be concerned about the depletion of resources but nevertheless refuse to pay more for cleaner products. From this standpoint, it is interesting to draw a parallel with the issue of privacy. Consumers declare that they care about privacy but when it comes to making choices about which internet site to use, they do not seem to reward the platforms that best protect their privacy.

It cannot be excluded that the same phenomenon is at work with respect to sustainability.

30. This helps to distinguish between four possible scenarios with respect to the relationship between competition and environmental sustainability.

31. First, is the case where competition and a sustainable environment are complementary. This would happen when consumers value sustainable products and production processes and are willing to pay more for climate-compliant products. In such a case, the promotion of competition will directly facilitate the achievement of a sustainable environment since some or all the competing firms will have an incentive, given the consumer behavior, to choose to produce sustainable products.

32. Second, is the case where, due to biases, consumers are not willing to pay more for sustainable goods or services, either because they do not care about sustainability or because they do not behave in a way that is consistent with their professed preferences. In such cases, suppliers who could choose cleaner technologies to produce cleaner products are unlikely to be compensated for the extra cost they would incur if they decided to produce in a more sustainable manner. Each competitor will thus be confronted with a "first mover disadvantage" and will choose dirty technologies over clean technologies (if the former are cheaper than the latter). In this instance, more competition will lead to less environmental sustainability.

33. Third is the case where firms want to collude in order to limit competition on quality. In this case less competition goes together with less sustainability of the products or services sold.

34. Fourth, is the case where competitors use the excuse of sustainability to limit competition on some other dimension (prices, market shares etc.) of their competitive strategies. This refers to the "greenwashing strategies" in which colluding firms attempt to conceal collusion under the guise of sustainability.

35. Overall, the direct relationship between competition and sustainability is complex and requires a detailed analysis of each case.

36. The fact that the relationship between competition and environmental sustainability is complex also applies in the context of merger control.

37. Tristan Lécuyer and Annabelle Leclercq[4] give convincing examples of cases where the traditional competition approach to competition may be in contradiction with an environmental sustainability approach. For example, they suggest that "a merger in the forestry industry that would result in increased output post-merger, and hence lower prices, due to merger-specific synergies. Under the current framework, this merger would

---

[4] Tristan Lécuyer and Annabelle Leclercq: "Is green becoming a grey area? A discussion on sustainability and merger control ", Competition Law & Policy Debate, 2023, Vol. 8, No. 2.

be seen favourably as it increases consumer welfare. However, increased output would be achieved through a greater number of trees being cut, which arguably constitutes a negative externality on the environment".

38. But anticompetitive mergers may also have a positive effect from the sustainability standpoint. Tristan Lécuyer and Annabelle Leclercq also refer, for example, to the case of a merger between two energy producers where part of the merger rationale is to close a particularly polluting power plant and they state: "Under the current framework, this merger would be seen as anticompetitive as it would reduce the quantity of energy supplied, and therefore leads to higher prices for consumers. However, from a broader perspective, this merger would generate a positive externality since the plant closure would reduce CO_2 emissions which benefits society as a whole".

3) Competition Law Enforcement And Environmental Sustainability

39. A lively discussion has developed in Europe over the question of whether competition law enforcement can directly contribute to achieving sustainable development goals.

40. Some authors, such as Cento Veljanovski[5] argue that: "the fact that the Commission has not in the last two decades prosecuted (a case of anticompetitive agreement that otherwise generates substantial environmental benefits) indicates either that such agreements do not exist or, what is more likely, a deliberate strategy of the Commission not to prosecute such cases. The one area where the Commission's enforcement strategy could potentially be too restrictive is its treatment of conservation cartels. However, since it has only prosecuted one such cartel, it is difficult to tell whether antitrust is deterring cooperative solutions to natural resources problems. At the other end of the spectrum, there is little evidence that EU antitrust has deterred industry initiatives that promote sustainability and environment protection which are not greenwashing collusion, or that condoning anticompetitive agreements leads to the more rapid take-up of sustainability and environmental protection".

41. Others, like Schinkel and Spiegel[6] argue that: "The public interest in general, and Sustainable Consumption and Production (SCP) in particular, are elusive concepts, and it is not obvious how to weigh them against the potential anticompetitive effects of various restraints of trade. Moreover it is not even obvious that horizontal agreements necessarily

---

5 Cento Veljanovski: Collusion as Environmental Protection – An Economic Assessment, Journal of Competition Law & Economics, Vol. 17 (2021).

6 Maarten Pieter Schinkel and Yossi Spiegel: "Can collusion promote sustainable consumption and production?" International Journal of Industrial Organization Volume 53, July 2017, Pages 371-398.

boost the incentives of firms to invest in SCP. Hence, it is unclear whether competition policy is the right mechanism to promote SCP, even if the competition authority has the expertise to determine the right level of SCP and how much society is willing to sacrifice in order to achieve it". They also state that "assuming that consumers are willing to pay extra for sustainable products like cleaner energy, sustainable meat, holiday travel, or fair trade clothing, can horizontal agreements among competing firms promote SCP? [...] when consumers value sustainable products and firms choose investments in sustainability before choosing output or prices, coordination of output choices or prices boosts investments in sustainability and may even enhance consumer surplus when products are sufficiently close substitutes and the marginal cost of investment in sustainability is relatively low. By contrast, coordination of investments in sustainability leads to lower investments and harms consumers".

42. In contrast, Maurits Dolmans[7] argues that: "we can no longer afford to turn a blind eye to competition that exploits externalities that hurt the environment and the climate. Nor can we ignore the coordination problems that hamper solutions. Antitrust should be a part of an integrated climate policy, and the social cost of carbon emissions should be taken into account when assessing an agreement or conduct's impact on consumer welfare".

43. Simon Holmes[8] concurs and is of the view that: "The urgency of the climate change threat means we need to reappraise our approach to everything. A 2010 paper by the UK competition authority concluded that 'the advantages and disadvantages of taking into account wider environmental benefits are finely balanced'. In 2010, I would probably have agreed, but whatever the rights and wrongs of that conclusion in 2010, our current appreciation of climate change means that 'balance' has changed significantly: the scales have tilted. We must put more weight on environmental factors and move the dial radically in the direction of permitting arrangements that contribute to combatting climate change, in particular, and to protecting the environment and sustainable production in general. [...] Other areas where competition law may be relevant to sustainability issues include the approach to 'abuse' in Article 102 cases and the analysis of mergers".

44. The controversy about the extent to which competition law should or could accommodate environmental sustainability issues turns around a number of issues:

45. First, what is the goal of EU competition law? Economists have suggested that the goal of competition law in Europe should be the protection of

---

[7] Maurits Dolmans: "Sustainable Competition Policy" Competition Law and Policy Debate CLPD, Vol 5, Issue 4 and Vol 6 issue 1 March 2020.

[8] Simon Holmes: Climate change, sustainability, and competition law, Journal of Antitrust Enforcement, 2020, 8, 354–405, April 2020.

consumer welfare. This goal was endorsed by Mario Monti in 2001 and served as the basis for the 2008 Commission's guidance on its enforcement priorities in the area of exclusionary conduct. The supporters of this approach to the EU goals of competition emphasize the necessity to stick to a relatively narrow economic paradigm and express fear that the introduction of "public interest" goals, such as environmental sustainability, will lead to a watering down of competition law enforcement principles. There is a significant potential conflict between the outcomes viewed as positive under a strict consumer welfare benchmark (e.g. greater output and lower prices) and their effects on sustainability (where sustainability outcomes may instead require lower output and higher prices).

46. Other commentators, more often coming from the legal community, argue that one has to go back to the letter of the European Treaty to find the goals of competition law and that the European Treaty does not mention the protection of consumer welfare but refers to competition law as a means to support the integration of the European market. Simon Holmes reminds us that: "The 'constitutional' provisions of the EU Treaties require sustainability and environmental protection to be taken into account when implementing all of the EU's policies and activities" [...] This would support the (preferable) approach to application of the individual exemption – where the benefits of the collaboration can be for wider society rather than the individual purchasing consumer". Simon Holmes adds: "We need to get away from arcane and narrow concepts (such as a narrow focus on short-term price effects) and get back to what the treaties (and their equivalents in national jurisdictions) actually say".

47. Depending on which goals one believes the EU competition law is trying to achieve, the resulting perspectives on the importance of environmental sustainability in competition law enforcement differ.

48. Second, the controversy about the extent to which competition law should or could accommodate sustainability also depends on one's perception of whether competition law is a potential obstacle to sustainability. As already mentioned, some authors argue that there is no contradiction between the two because cases of first-mover disadvantage are rare when consumers are willing to pay for more sustainable goods. Thus, they conclude, that most if not all of the anticompetitive agreements purporting to enhance sustainability belong in fact to the category of greenwashing, and that firms are not deterred from adopting cleaner technologies by competition laws. But other commentators argue that competition law is, in fact, a deterrent to the adoption of sustainable technologies. For example, at COP27 in November 2022, the International Chamber of Commerce (ICC) published a white paper[9] discussing 12 real-life

---

9   International Chamber of Commerce: When Chilling Contributes to Warming How Competition Policy Acts As a Barrier to Climate Action, November 2022.

examples of competing companies seeking to work together but which eventually abandoned these initiatives for fear of breaking competition laws. According to the ICC, this: "illustrated the pressing need for competition policy and enforcement to be updated to facilitate climate action and pursue sustainability. In particular, it showed that modern competition policy needs to integrate sustainability economics, taking account of market failures and collective action problems".

4) Competition Law Developments On Environmental Sustainability In Europe

49. In Europe, a significant number of competition authorities have published guidelines on sustainability and sustainability agreements over the past four years.

50. The Authority for Consumers and Markets (ACM) in the Netherlands first published draft guidelines on "Sustainability Agreements" in 2020 and also published a second draft in 2021. In January 2021, the ACM and the Hellenic Competition Commission (HCC) published a "Technical Report on Sustainability and Competition". In July 2021, the HCC published a public consultation for a "Sustainable Development Sandbox" which it launched in June 2022. At the end of September 2022, the Austrian Federal Competition Authority published its final sustainability guidelines introducing a new sustainability exemption for ecological sustainability agreements. On 1 June 2023, the European Commission (EC) adopted revised "Horizontal Block Exemption Regulations" and "Horizontal Guidelines" including a new chapter on Sustainability Agreements. On 4 October 2023, the Dutch Competition Authority (ACM) published a Policy Rule on its oversight of sustainability agreements. On 12 October 2023, the Competition and Markets Authority (CMA) in the UK published the Green Agreements Guidance on the application of UK competition law to environmental sustainability (ESG) including climate change agreements.

51. Focus will be, first, on the developments both in the Netherlands and in the EU as they are partly interdependent (the ACM in the Netherlands has been the most active European competition authority on the sustainability front) and, second on the similarities and differences between the developments in the EU and in the United Kingdom.

52. One notable difference of appreciation between the ACM and the European Commission is that the Dutch Competition Authority considers that an environmental damage agreement should not be further analyzed from the competition law standpoint if the initial investigation shows that it is plausible that the agreement is necessary for achieving

the environmental benefits and that such benefits sufficiently outweigh the potential competitive disadvantages (if consumers in the relevant market receive an appreciable and objective part of the advantages and if sufficient residual competition remains).

53. A second important difference of appreciation between the two authorities is related to the question of which efficiencies should be considered in order to assess whether it is possible to exempt a sustainability agreement that limits competition.

54. The ACM considered that all benefits, both "in market" benefits (those that accrue to customers affected by the restrictions of competition due to the agreement) and "out of market" benefits (i.e., those that accrue in markets that are not affected by the agreement), should be considered. This approach was a flexible and permissive approach, allowing parties to rely on a broad set of (potentially global) environmental benefits to justify important sustainability agreements.

55. The ACM did not succeed in its attempt to convince the European Commission on this and the European Commission has taken the position that the benefits which can be taken into account to the credit of an anticompetitive sustainability agreement must accrue to the consumers/users affected by any restriction of competition (the relevant consumers affected by the restriction of competition must make up a substantial part of the beneficiaries of the agreement).

56. Even if the Dutch Competition Authority could not convince the EU Commission to adopt its more extensive approach to the relevant efficiencies, it may have been satisfied that its position was fairly similar to the position taken by the UK competition authority (the Competition and Markets Authority, CMA). Indeed, in its Green Agreements Guidance, the CMA is open to recognizing that to satisfy the condition that consumers receive a fair share of the benefits of the anticompetitive agreements, it will take into consideration the benefits accruing to all UK consumers, not only those in the relevant product market.

57. In 2023, the European Commission revised its 2011 Guidelines on horizontal cooperation agreements (HGL) and added a chapter on sustainability agreements. It should be noted that this addition was justified by the Constitutional reasons invoked by Simon Holmes (see above). Since sustainability and carbon neutrality have become the Commission's top priorities with the adoption of the European Green Deal, a need was felt to streamline those priorities into all policy areas, including competition law.

58. A sustainability agreement, as defined by the EC Revised Guidelines, refers to any horizontal cooperation agreement that pursues a sustainability objective, irrespective of the form of the cooperation. Sustainability objectives include: addressing climate change (e.g., by reducing greenhouse gas emissions), reducing pollution, limiting the use of natural resources,

upholding human rights, ensuring a living income, promoting resilient infrastructure and innovation, reducing food waste, facilitating a shift towards healthy and nutritious food, ensuring animal welfare, etc. As a result, the EU DG Comp definition of a sustainability agreement is quite broad and it is broader than the UK CMA definition.

59. Sustainability agreements not affecting parameters of competition fall outside Article 101 TFEU, and the guidelines give a non-exhaustive list of examples. It includes agreements to create a database containing information about sustainable suppliers or distributors without requiring the parties to necessarily purchase from, or sell to them, agreements relating to the organization of industry-wide awareness campaigns or campaigns raising customers' awareness or agreements that do not concern the economic activity of competitors, but their internal corporate conduct (such as competitors seeking to increase their industry's reputation for environmental responsibility by agreeing to eliminate single-use plastics from their business premises, or by agreeing not to exceed a certain ambient temperature in their buildings, or by limiting the volume of printed internal documents).

60. Sustainability agreements which affect one or more of the parameters of competition must be assessed under Article 101 TFEU to determine whether they raise competition concerns, and, if they do, whether these concerns are outweighed by the positive effects of the agreements on competition.

61. According to the guidelines, if an agreement genuinely pursues sustainability objectives this must be taken into account for the purpose of determining whether the agreement restricts competition by object, as this may cast reasonable doubt on whether the agreement is by its very nature harmful to competition. However, no such doubts can exist where the agreement is merely used to disguise a "by object" restriction of competition, such as price fixing.

62. Where a "by object" restriction can be excluded, the agreement may benefit from a block exemption such as those on standardization agreements or R&D agreements. This approach also allows the agreement to benefit from the safe harbors under the Horizontal Block Exemption Regulations (for both R&D and specialization agreements). In the event of inconsistencies between the Commission's guidance on sustainability agreements and its guidance on other types of cooperation, companies may rely on the more favorable guidance.

63. If no block exemption applies, the actual or potential harmful effects on competition resulting from the sustainability agreement must be assessed.

64. Standardization agreements that set requirements to be met by producers, processors, distributors, retailers or service providers in a supply chain in relation to a wide range of sustainability metrics (such as the

environmental impact of production and lay down rules, guidelines or characteristics for products and processes related to such sustainability metrics) often have positive effects on competition, for example by empowering consumers to make informed purchase decisions or leveling the playing field between producers that are subject to different regulatory requirements.

65. However, sustainability agreements may also restrict competition in three main ways: through price coordination, foreclosure of alternative standards, and the exclusion of, or discrimination against, certain competitors. If they disguise restrictions such as price fixing, market or customer allocation, or limitations of output, quality or innovation, they restrict competition by object. If they do not contain by object restrictions, they can benefit from a so-called 'soft safe harbor' if they meet six criteria: transparency and participation, no obligations on non-members, members are free to go further, no exchange of commercially sensitive information that is not objectively necessary and proportionate for the development, implementation, adoption or modification of the standard, and fair (non-discriminatory) access and either limited negative effects or limited market coverage (less than 20% of the relevant market)

66. A sustainability agreement that restricts competition may nonetheless qualify for an individual exemption if it satisfies four cumulative conditions: 1) it contributes to improving the production or distribution of goods or to promoting technical or economic progress (efficiencies must be substantiated and be objective, concrete and verifiable); 2) the restrictions of competition imposed are indispensable to the attainment of the benefits generated by the agreement; 3) consumers need to receive a fair share of the claimed benefits of the agreement and 4) the agreement must not allow the parties to eliminate competition in respect of a substantial part of the products concerned. This condition may be fulfilled as long as the parties still compete vigorously on at least one parameter of competition. For instance, if competitors decide not to use a certain polluting technology or a certain non-sustainable ingredient in the production of their products, competition is not eliminated as long as they continue to compete on the price and/or quality of the final product.

67. The Commission can also provide informal guidance on novel or unresolved issues relating to individual sustainability agreements whose clarification would be in the public interest. The EC will not issue any fines for agreements that were discussed with the regulators and in respect of which either no concerns were raised, or any concerns raised were addressed by the parties.

68. One notable feature of the European competition law discussion with respect to environmental issues is that there has not been any discussion as to whether merger control needs to be adapted to better take into account such issues. This raises two questions: first, can there be a contradiction

between competition and sustainability when it comes to merger control? And, second, is merger control as it exists sufficient to deal with sustainability considerations?

69. Tristan Lécuyer* and Annabelle Leclercq[10] have looked at these questions in detail and they arrive at the following conclusions: first, "the current framework focuses on direct consumers' preferences and ignores environmental externalities", even though: "mergers may generate economic externalities that can have a broader impact on the environment"; second: "properly considering these externalities in a potential revised framework is likely to raise practical challenges" and third: "regulation may be a better instrument to support sustainability objectives".

70. A number of national competition authorities have taken an approach similar to the EU Commission and have publicly expressed their views on sustainability agreements.

71. For example, in the United Kingdom, the CMA's Green Agreements Guidance is part of a broader program of green action by the CMA as part of its public commitment to promote environmental sustainability and help accelerate the UK's transition to a net zero economy in line with the published priorities in its latest annual plan. The Guidance applies to agreements between competitors which are aimed at preventing, reducing or mitigating the adverse impact that economic activities have on the environment, or to assist with the transition towards environmental sustainability ("environmental sustainability agreements" or "ESAs"), including climate change. Examples of environmental sustainability agreements include agreements between competitors to reduce the use of pesticides, stop the use of microplastic polluting materials, or increase recycling rates. Climate change agreements are a sub-set of environmental sustainability agreements and include agreements reducing the negative externalities of greenhouse gases emitted from the production, distribution or consumption of the relevant products, such as an agreement between manufacturers of a product to phase out a highly emitting production process, or an agreement between delivery companies to switch to using only electric vehicles.

72. Thus the scope of applicability of the of the CMA Guidance on sustainability agreements is narrower than the scope of applicability of the EU Guidelines.

73. The UK Guidance distinguishes environmental sustainability agreements which are unlikely to raise any competition concerns, provided certain conditions are met, and agreements which could infringe the prohibition enacted in Chapter I of the Competition Act 1998 unless they benefit from an exemption.

---

10 See note 6.

74. In the UK Guidance, some of the examples of agreements which are unlikely to raise any competition concerns, provided certain conditions are met, are similar to what one finds in the EU Guideline (for example, agreements which do not affect the main parameters of competition (price, quantity, quality, choice, etc.); but there is also a wider list of examples of agreements not mentioned in the EU Guidelines such as: non-appreciable agreements, where the parties have a very small combined market share of the affected market (below 10%) provided that the agreement does not contain by-object restrictions of competition, such as market sharing or price setting; agreements to pool funds for mitigating, adapting to or compensating for the effects of greenhouse gas emissions generated in production; joint lobbying agreements for policy or legislative changes, provided that these are not used to exclude a competitor by lobbying a standard-setting body in a way that controls the standard-setting process; agreements to do something jointly which none of the parties could do individually due to, for example, the level of risk involved or the level of investment required, provided that the businesses involved could not have proceeded using a form of cooperation that is less restrictive of competition; agreements setting non-binding industry-wide targets or ambitions, such as targets to reduce the whole industry's CO_2 emissions, provided that the participating businesses are free to independently determine their own contributions and the way in which they will meet these targets or ambitions; agreements to phase out or withdraw non-sustainable products or processes, provided that there is no appreciable impact on price, quality or choice, and it does not have the object of eliminating competitors or market sharing; and agreements between shareholders to vote in favor of corporate policies that pursue environmental sustainability or against policies that do not do so.

75. The UK CMA Guidance on sustainability standards is similar to that of the EU Guidelines and the requirements for such agreements to benefit from safe harbor are largely aligned under both regimes. There is, however, a slight difference in emphasis between the EC Guidelines and the UK CMA Guidance. Whereas the EC requires that exchanges of commercially sensitive information be kept to a minimum, and that the standards do not lead to a significant price increase or a significant quality reduction, or alternatively that the combined market share of the participants does not exceed 20% in any relevant market, the CMA primarily focuses on preventing a reduction in product choice and a standard-setting agreement will be considered compliant with UK competition law if the participating businesses can sell alternative competing products that do not meet the standards or, alternatively, if the combined market share of the parties is sufficiently small.

76. Finally, the CMA has an open-door policy thanks to which parties can approach it for informal guidance on any question that parties may

have on the application of the Green Agreements Guidance. This UK open door policy is wider than the EC open door policy which only allows parties to a sustainability agreement to consult the Commission on "novel or unresolved issues" relating to individual sustainability agreements whose clarification would be in the public interest. No such requirements exist under the CMA's Green Agreements Guidance, illustrating the CMA's intention to be more actively involved in guiding interested parties. Additionally, in contrast to the EC's regime, which allows only the parties to an agreement to request informal guidance, NGOs and trade associations can also approach the CMA for guidance.

5) Efficiencies Which Can Be Taken Into Consideration

77. Both the European Commission and the UK Competition and Markets Authority impose, as a condition for exemption of an anticompetitive agreement, that consumers receive a fair share of the efficiency benefits resulting from the agreement. However, they differ in a crucial way on the scope of the efficiency benefits which can be taken into consideration.

78. The EU Commission distinguishes between individual use value benefits (for example: better quality of the products) individual non-use value benefits (resulting from the consumer's appreciation of the impact of its sustainable consumption on others) and collective benefits (such as clean air) which accrue to a wider section of society than just the consumers in the relevant market (for example, less polluting fuel for cars may lead to cleaner air for society as a whole, rather than just for the car driver concerned).

79. An important issue is that in the EU, collective benefits can be taken into account only if the consumers who suffer the harm caused by the anticompetitive agreement (e.g., higher fuel prices) form a substantial part of the total group of people who benefit from the positive effects (e.g., cleaner air). In other words, and contrary to what both the Dutch competition authority was pushing for, "out of market" efficiencies (i.e., efficiencies benefitting others than the consumers affected by the anticompetitive agreement) are not counted as collective benefit that can, if the other conditions are met, be counted as sustainability benefits of the agreement.

80. In contrast, the UK CMA's effects-based assessment of climate change agreements will take into account the full climate change benefits of the agreement to all UK consumers, without the need for the beneficiaries of these benefits to substantially overlap with the consumers in the relevant market. An anticompetitive climate change agreement can be exempted in the UK if three conditions are met: first, the agreement's climate change

benefits are in line with, or exceed, existing legally binding requirements or well-established national or international targets (including climate change goals in international treaties); second, UK consumers in general benefit from the agreement; and, third, these benefits outweigh the harm caused by any restrictions included in the agreement.

81. This difference of position on whether or not "out-of-market" efficiencies can be taken into account in the assessment of climate change agreements is a crucial one from a practical standpoint. Indeed, anticompetitive agreements which have a positive impact on climate change may not be exempted from competition law if only the benefits to the buyers of the product concerned are taken into account, even if such agreements greatly increase the consumer welfare of the non-buyers of the goods considered. Some competition authorities (such as the EU) are unwilling to accept a global welfare perspective because such a perspective would require, at least implicitly, an interpersonal comparison of gains and losses of utility between, on the one hand, the consumers who do not buy the goods considered but benefit from the environmental sustainability brought about by the agreement and the consumers who buy the goods and suffer from a reduction in their due to the decline in competition implied by the agreement. It should be noted, however, that the promotion of competition, which may entail a significant negative externality on consumers of other products though the degradation of the climate, also implies an implicit comparison of interpersonal utilities between the consumers who buy the goods considered and benefit from the increased competition and non-buyers who see their welfare diminished due to the negative externality arising out of the increased output due to competition for the goods concerned.

6) Time Perspective Of Competition Analysis

82. A second crucial issue is the appropriate time frame used to consider competition law issues. Environmental sustainability benefits resulting from an anticompetitive agreement between competitors may materialize in the long term and/or be cumulative over time (for example in the form of reduced pollution) even if the cost of the restriction in competition due to the agreement materializes immediately. Thus, the balance between the costs and the benefits of an anticompetitive sustainability agreement may be different depending on the time perspective of the analysis.

83. An interesting case illustrates this point. On September 6 2019, it was reported that the US Antitrust Division of the Department of Justice had opened an investigation into possible collusion by four car manufacturers which had entered into a framework agreement with the State of California on light vehicle emissions and gas mileage standards. In July 2019, the four

manufacturers – Ford, Volkswagen of America, Honda and BMW – had announced that they had reached an agreement in principle with the California Air Resources Board, a state agency, on emissions and fuel economy standards substantially higher than those sought by the Trump administration, although slightly lower than those previously endorsed by the State of California. This case was subsequently dropped by the US DoJ because no agreement between the car manufacturers was found.

84. What is of interest is that the theory of harm under which the prosecution of this case had been envisaged was that the presumed agreement between the car manufacturers would increase the price of cars for consumers in California since the parties were supposed to have committed to selling cars with a higher quality than what would have been the case without the agreement. Hence, this agreement was presumed to lower consumer welfare. However, one could consider such an alleged agreement in a different way. One could also argue that, over time, such an agreement would decrease the (social) cost of car transportation in California by reducing the amount of CO_2 emissions associated with car transportation. Thus, depending on the time perspective chosen for the competition analysis the same agreement could be seen either as reducing consumer welfare (in the short run) or increasing consumer welfare (in the long run).

85. Competition authorities have tended to take a short-term view of the positive and negative effects of horizontal anticompetitive agreements, arguing that only the short term is predictable and that the longer term is more difficult to predict accurately. But this approach is stacked against sustainability agreements for which the benefits are cumulative over time.

86. Recently European competition authorities have shown that when it comes to innovation, they are willing to take a longer view to assess the risk of horizontal mergers on innovation (see, for example the EU Dow Dupont merger decision[11]). One should then hope that they will adopt the same perspective when assessing anticompetitive sustainability agreements.

Conclusion

87. This quick review of some of the developments and some of the issues related to the interface of sustainability and competition in Western Europe suggests a few comments with respect to the situation in China.

88. First, it is clear that the goal of the Anti Monopoly Law (the AML) includes public interest considerations in general and Sustainable Development goals, in particular.

---

11 Commission Decision of 27 March 2017 (Case M.7932 – Dow/DuPont).

89. In 2016 in China, the government announced the National Plan on Implementation of the 2030 Agenda for Sustainable Development, which addressed each of the seventeen Sustainable Development Goals ("SDGs") set by the United Nations in 2015.

90. The goals of the Chinese Anti-Monopoly Law are diverse and include public interest goals as stated by article 1 of the law. This provides a basis for China's AML to play a role in promoting non-economic SDGs. Furthermore, Article 15 of the AML specifically provides that an anti-competitive agreement may be exempted: "for the purpose of achieving the public interest such as energy conservation, environmental protection, disaster relief and rescue". Additionally, with respect to merger control, Article 28 provides that an anticompetitive merger may be allowed if it is in the public interest. Finally, under article 17 some abuses of dominance may have "justifications".

91. The Opinions on Establishment of a Fair Competition Review System in the Development of the Market System issued by the government in 2016 provide for "exceptions" in the fair competition review regime for those concerning sustainable development: "such as (measures) in order to achieve poverty alleviation and promotion of development, disaster relief and rescue, and other social security purposes" and "(measures) in order to achieve energy and resource conservation, ecological environmental protection and other public interest".

92. Second, the Chinese competition law system provides for exemptions related to sustainability in all areas of competition law and is therefore more comprehensive than the EU system.

93. The Chinese mechanism and the conditions for the exemption of anticompetitive agreements contributing to sustainability are thus fairly similar to those in Western Europe. Monopoly agreements which are prohibited per se can nevertheless be exempted through the application of Article 20 of the PRC AML, inter alia, if they are for realizing public interests such as "energy conservation, environmental protection, disaster relief and aid" subject to the demonstration that they do not substantially restrict competition in the relevant market and that consumers share the benefits arising therefrom, if they are necessary for the achievement of their public interest goal and if they satisfy an efficiency tests.

94. But contrary to the EU, merger control is being adapted in China to deal with the issue of sustainability. The State Administration for Market Regulation ("SAMR") released its "Draft Guidelines for the Review of Horizontal Mergers" to solicit public opinions in June 2024. Article 81 of these Draft Guidelines explains how sustainability factors will impact SAMR's assessment of a horizontal merger. If an undertaking can prove that a horizontal merger has a positive impact on public interests, such as, inter alia, "energy conservation or environmental protection", SAMR may

not prohibit it even if the merger may eliminate or restrict competition provided that the horizontal merger has a substantial positive impact on public interest, that there is a causal link between the merger and the positive impact on public interests and that, absent the merger there could not have been an impact on the public interest.

95. Third, however, it seems that in practice it is extremely difficult in China to obtain a sustainability exemption for an anticompetitive agreement, an abuse of market power or an anticompetitive merger and that there are very few cases in which there is any discussion of these issues. From this standpoint the European systems with the guidelines issued by the European Commission or the national Competition Authorities seem to be more user-friendly. In particular the ability of parties to a sustainability agreement, practice or transaction to receive informal advice from the competition authorities without fearing sanctions in the UK, in the Netherlands, in France, and, to a more limited extent at the EU Commission, seems to be a useful tool given the complexity and the novelty of the issues raised by the interface between competition law and the goal of sustainability.

96. Fourth, if it seems clear that the Chinese competition authorities can take into consideration out of market efficiencies in their analysis of an environmental sustainability agreements or mergers, it remains to be seen whether the time frame of their analysis will be a long term perspective or whether they will favor short-term considerations.

"One Country, Two Systems" of Competition Law

RASUL BUTT*

Chief Executive Officer, Hong Kong Competition Commission

Abstract

The paper examines how Hong Kong's competition law has evolved since its full implementation in 2015, and contrasts it with Chinese Mainland's Anti-Monopoly Law under the "One Country, Two Systems" model of governance. Milestones achieved by the Hong Kong Competition Commission ("HKCC") in its first decade of operation are highlighted, including its first enforcement cases and strategic collaborations with both overseas legal and economic talents and local law enforcement agencies. The paper also underscores how the enforcement capabilities of the HKCC have gradually strengthened through academic engagement and cross-jurisdictional cooperation during its formative years. Finally, the paper offers a brief insight into how Hong Kong's competition law will continue to develop in the days to come.

---

* Mr. Rasul Butt ("*Mr. Butt*") is the Chief Executive Officer of the Hong Kong Competition Commission ("*Commission*") – having been appointed to this role since May 2021. Mr. Butt joined the Commission in April 2015 as its Executive Director (Corporate Services & Public Affairs), and was appointed to the position of Senior Executive Director in July 2016 overseeing the policy advisory, advocacy, and corporate functions of the Commission. Starting his career as a lecturer in law at Universiti Teknologi Mara, Malaysia in the early 1990s, Mr. Butt left academia to take charge of the Compliance Department at the futures and options unit of the Arab-Malaysian Banking Group in Malaysia. He returned to Hong Kong in 1999 and thereafter spent more than 16 years at the Urban Renewal Authority where his last position was General Manager (Corporate Planning). His main focus was formulating urban renewal policies and strategies. Mr. Butt obtained his Bachelor of Laws with Honours from the University of Liverpool, United Kingdom, followed by Master of Laws (Public Law) from the University of Wales, Aberystwyth, United Kingdom. He was called to the Bar of England and Wales (Honourable Society of Lincoln's Inn) and the Hong Kong Bar. He also holds a Postgraduate Diploma in Construction Law and Arbitration from the University of Hong Kong, and a Postgraduate Diploma in Islamic Banking and Insurance from the Institute of Islamic Banking and Insurance, London where he is an Associate Fellow. Mr. Butt has a special interest in the development of competition law regimes in Chinese Mainland and the ASEAN region and regularly engages fellow enforcers and members of the academia in promoting competition law and policy.

Introduction

1. Under the "One Country, Two Systems" model of governance, the Hong Kong Special Administrative Region has flourished as a world class city with a host of unique characteristics that stands it apart from other cities in the People's Republic of China. Chief amongst these is its continuous adoption of the Common Law system after the handover in 1997 that entrenches its position as one of the freest economies in the world.

2. In the field of competition law, Chinese Mainland's Anti-Monopoly Law ("AML") has a longer history than Hong Kong's competition law by nearly a decade. Over the years, the AML's jurisprudence has developed at an amazing pace with major investigations conducted by the Chinese authorities resulting in the resolution of competition concerns that has and continues to draw the world's attention. Meanwhile, Hong Kong's own competition law regime also underwent significant development during the ten years of its full implementation.

3. That two sets of competition law could operate within the same country is an intriguing concept for many people; but for us in Hong Kong, we see that as a distinctive feature of the "One Country, Two Systems" model that has been working very well for close to 30 years.

4. The global competition law enforcement community is a very tight-knit one. Some may say that this is by design in that we have international networks and organisations which provide excellent platforms for the exchange of insights and experiences on competition matters. However, one can also say that it is by necessity due to the fast-evolving commercial landscape that poses significant challenges to competition authorities. The ability to access and make reference to overseas jurisprudence and experience in tackling complex and topical competition issues is invaluable and essential.

5. Due to their long history, the development of competition laws in the European Union and the United States of America have had profound impact in the global context. Indeed, every major judgment and decision handed down by the leading authorities in these jurisdictions have been closely followed and referenced. But more and more, the world is taking notice of the actions and decisions of relevant agencies and courts in Chinese Mainland in implementing the AML. For instance, in addressing competition concerns relating to the digital economy, there is growing acknowledgement that Chinese Mainland is at the cutting edge in terms of its deep understanding of relevant issues and its insights on how they should be addressed.

6. It feels like an understatement to say that Professor Huang Yong, whom I have known for over 10 years, is a leading figure in the development of the AML. A doyen of competition law in Chinese Mainland, he is

one of the most respected and sought-after experts in the field. His intellectual brilliance and extraordinary ability to communicate complex legal and economic principles with clarity and elegance never cease to put me in awe, and I feel very privileged to be able to count him as a friend and mentor.

7. Professor Huang's career is a testament to his versatility and dedication. His academic work, as a professor of law and economics at the law school of the University of International Business and Economics in Beijing, has laid the intellectual foundations for much of Chinese Mainland's competition law and policy. Going beyond his academic career, as a core member of the State Council Anti-Monopoly and Anti-Unfair Competition Committee, his influence extends to the highest echelon of policy-making.

8. It needs to be said that Professor Huang's contributions are not confined to academia or in his advisory role to the Central Government. As a "super-connector," Professor Huang has become a global ambassador for competition law, traveling extensively to engage in dialogues and collaborations between China and the rest of the world. He has helped to build bridges between jurisdictions, fostering a shared understanding of increasingly complex competition issues.

A Tale of Two Competition Regimes

9. When the "One Country, Two Systems" model was first conceived, the late Deng Xiaoping had the foresight that after the handover, Hong Kong would be able to reap the benefits of sharing closer economic ties with Chinese Mainland while, at the same time, preserving its unique cultural, business, and legal traditions.

10. Fast forward to today, foreign businesses wanting to "break" into the China market often treat Hong Kong as their first port of call (encouraged, no doubt, by the prospect of being able to operate under a familiar Common Law regime), while Chinese business giants, in turn, use Hong Kong as a springboard for their overseas ventures.

11. Save for limited areas, such as foreign affairs and national defense, Hong Kong operates as a separate legal system with our own laws and an independent judiciary.

12. So what do all these entail in terms of competition laws in our respective jurisdictions?

13. First, in Hong Kong, its cross-sector competition law is enshrined in the Competition Ordinance ("CO") which was enacted in 2012 and which drew inspiration from the competition laws of other jurisdictions such as:
    - European Union (e.g. by importing concepts such as "object" and "effects" restrictions);

- Australia (e.g. by expressly providing for individual accessorial/inchoate liabilities);
- Canada (e.g. in how "bid-rigging" is to be approached and defined);
- United States of America (e.g. by expressly setting out the basic frameworks of leniency in statute); and
- United Kingdom (e.g. by setting up a specialist Competition Tribunal to hear cases and review decisions of the Hong Kong Competition Commission ("HKCC")).

14. In terms of institutional setup and litigation process, the HKCC is an independent statutory body and its enforcement actions are based on an adversarial, judicial enforcement model. Contrasting this position with Chinese Mainland, the AML is primarily enforced through the State Administration for Market Regulation and its provincial-level counterparts. Like other overseas competition legislations, familiar anti-competitive conducts such as cartels and abuse of market dominance are also outlawed by the AML.

At the Beginning

15. For the longest time, there was much debate about whether Hong Kong needed its own competition law.

16. Proponents of the law pointed to the importance of proper regulation and enforcement to ensure that Hong Kong's capitalist market is capable of providing optimal consumer welfare. By contrast, detractors of the (then) Competition Bill likened any attempt to regulate as being akin to "bringing coal to Newcastle" (both pointless and futile) for a city that had thus far enjoyed the longstanding accolade of being the most competitive business environment in the world.

17. Fortunately, the proponents' view eventually carried the day, and on 14 December 2015, the CO finally came into full effect.

18. Upon the HKCC's establishment, one of its first tasks was to carefully study the provisions of the CO in order to work out the exact boundaries of the new law. At the time, the HKCC was also, by law, required to publish extensive guidelines on how it would go about conducting its investigations, enforcing the substantive competition law, and processing applications for block exemptions and individual decisions for exclusion on efficiency grounds.

19. During this process, the HKCC was very fortunate to have been able to seek the help, advice, and feedback from international organisations and competition networks such as the International Competition Network ("ICN"), the Asia-Pacific Economic Cooperation, the International Bar Association ("IBA"), the American Bar Association ("ABA"), and the Organisation

for Economic Co-operation and Development ("OECD"), all of whom, at various stages, had generously provided their insights and suggestions on how the HKCC could prepare itself for the full enforcement of the law.

20. Legal advice was also sought from a host of London Silks as to how key provisions of the CO should be interpreted, and applied.

21. Finally, the HKCC had also seized upon the generous offers from other international competition agencies such as the Canadian Competition Bureau, the (then) Competition Commission of Singapore, and the Australian Competition and Consumer Commission, to host secondees from the HKCC so that they might gain first-hand experience on how established competition agencies enforced their competition laws.

HKCC's First Cases

22. The HKCC conducted its first dawn raid in August 2016; and in 2017, it brought its first two enforcement actions before the Competition Tribunal. The first case concerned cartel conduct of bid-rigging in the IT industry and the second case involved price-fixing and market allocation in the building decoration/renovation industry.

23. Being the first two competition cases in Hong Kong, both required the HKCC and the specialist Tribunal to grapple with questions that were familiar in the context of competition law but nevertheless novel given Hong Kong's unique legal regime. For example:

    - Can the CO readily condemn a particular agreement as being a "by object" infringement absent *local* experiences on the alleged competitive harm?

    - Can a cartel ever be justified on grounds of economic efficiency?

    - What should the proper standard of proof be for competition enforcement actions where the HKCC is seeking a pecuniary penalty?

24. Fortunately again, the HKCC was able to draw from and collaborate with overseas expertise including leading King's Counsel and internationally renowned testifying experts to argue our cases before the Tribunal.

25. To this end, both cases served to illustrate one of the core strengths of Hong Kong's Common Law system, namely its ability to draw the best legal talents and judicial precedents from around the world to forge its own jurisprudence.

26. On both occasions, the HKCC was also able to benefit substantially from working closely with its overseas experts and gain invaluable insights on how they see competition law should develop in Hong Kong.

Hitting Our Stride – Developing and Refining the Leniency and Cooperation and Settlement Policy

27. Following the successful prosecution of the first two cases[1], the business and legal sector in Hong Kong began requesting for more clarity on how subjects of the HKCC's investigations may "settle" their cases through non-contentious means.

28. This in turn led to the HKCC's amendment of its Leniency Policy (to clarify the circumstances upon which an undertaking/individual may apply for leniency) and the Cooperation and Settlement Policy (to set out the different benefits an undertaking/individual may expect in return for their early cooperation).

29. In drafting and refining both important policy documents, the HKCC again leveraged on the expertise of our Non-Governmental Advisors (who functioned as our helpful "sounding board") and had consulted with international organisations such as the ICN, IBA, and ABA. At every turn, our local and international counterparts generously presented their careful, thorough, and insightful comments to the HKCC and the resultant final product still stands as the HKCC's official policy documents.

30. All of these have, in turn, proven critical in assisting the HKCC's enforcement work, allowing us to secure a number of sizeable penalties from undertakings in Hong Kong. For example, in 2023, the HKCC settled an enforcement action with one undertaking for an agreed penalty of HK$150,000,000 (around US$19,336,000) and in 2025, with two undertakings for a total penalty of around HK$22,000,000 (around US$2,800,000).

The Challenges of Today

31. As Hong Kong enters its tenth year of full implementation of the CO, the HKCC is acutely aware that while it is becoming more experienced and confident in its enforcement work, the same "evolution" may also be said about cartelists and dominant undertakings who may wish to "try their luck" when leveraging their substantial market power. Long gone are the days where the HKCC may expect easy investigations/litigation wins because would-be subjects had underestimated its effectiveness.

32. In order to stay ahead of this proverbial "enforcement game", a recent initiative of the HKCC has been to proactively join forces with other law enforcement agencies in Hong Kong (such as the Police Force

---

[1] In the first case, one party was found to have not contravened the CO on the grounds that the relevant employee involved had acted outside the scope of his normal and specific ambit of employment.

33. and the Independent Commission Against Corruption ("ICAC")) and Government / Public Bodies in our detection and investigative work.

33. For example, by harnessing the intelligence network of the Police Force, the HKCC has been able to detect and commence investigations into organised crime-related cartels which may otherwise go undetected, given the stranglehold they may have on otherwise would-be complainants. Similarly, the HKCC has also been able to uncover a range of corruption-driven bid-rigging activities through collaborating with the ICAC.

34. On the academia front, the HKCC has also been collaborating with local and international academic institutes in hosting a number of symposiums and exchanges with leading competition law experts around the world. For example:

- In 2023, the HKCC hosted our second "Competition Enforcers and Academics Summit" to facilitate full and frank exchanges of cutting edge views and ideas on competition law between university academics and enforcers from the Asia Pacific Region; and

- In 2025, the HKCC hosted our second "Competition Exchange" featuring 30 speakers from 14 jurisdictions with the intention of bridging the "East and West" perspectives on competition law.

35. On both occasions, Professor Huang had generously volunteered his time to moderate/speak on specialist panels, and shared his invaluable insight and expertise.

Concluding Remarks – The Road Ahead

36. As the CO enters its second decade of full implementation, the HKCC will continue its enforcement efforts with both humility and cautious optimism. Humility because there is no doubt that this is nothing short of a Herculean task, but, at the same time, cautious optimism because of the knowledge that it does not need to proceed alone.

37. The one thing the competition world is not short of is the willingness amongst leading scholars (such as Professor Huang), specialist organisations, and other competition agencies to generously share their knowledge, know-how, and experiences with each other.

38. And because of this, the competition world will be much better for it.

The Complex Geopolitics of Digital Regulation: The Three Body Problem

JORGE PADILLA[*]

Senior Managing Director, Compass Lexecon

VANESSA YANHUA ZHANG

Executive Vice President, Compass Lexecon

Abstract

This paper explores the complex geopolitics of digital regulation by analyzing how divergent regulatory models in major jurisdictions – namely the European Union, the United States, China, the United Kingdom, and others – are reshaping global economic governance and digital trade. The paper examines how digital regulation increasingly functions as a Behind-the-border Trade Barrier (BTB), complicating cross-border data flows, market access, and competition. Special attention is given to the EU's Digital Markets Act (DMA) and its extraterritorial reach through the so-called "Brussels Effect," which has generated significant friction with the US and raised questions about digital sovereignty and regulatory hegemony. The analysis is situated within the broader context of the US–China technology rivalry, showing how regulatory asymmetries disproportionately affect firms from these two countries while offering middle powers, like the EU, leverage through norm-setting. Finally, the paper explores the potential escalation of regulatory disputes into trade conflicts, discussing

---

[*] Jorge Padilla (D.Phil. (Oxon)) is Senior Managing Director at the economic consultancy Compass Lexecon and Senior Fellow of the GW Innovation and Competition Lab, George Washington University, and CEMFI in Madrid. Vanessa Yanhua Zhang (Ph.D. (TSE)) is Executive Vice President at Compass Lexecon and Senior Research Fellow at the Market & Regulation Law Center (MRLC) of Renmin University.

the limits of existing trade agreements and the increasing use of retaliatory tariffs. The study concludes that digital regulation is becoming a critical vector of geopolitical competition, with far-reaching implications for international economic law and global digital governance.

I. Introduction

1. All countries – developed or developing – stand to benefit massively from the digitization of their economies. Digital platforms acting as intermediaries between business users (suppliers, advertisers, content providers, etc.) and domestic users (consumers, viewers, etc.) play a key role in pushing economies, both in developed and developing countries, towards digitization. That is especially true for large digital platforms, whether global players – such as Alphabet, Amazon, Apple, Meta, Microsoft, and Bytedance – or regional, sub-regional, and national champions – like Yandex in Russia, Alibaba, Tencent, JD and Meituan in China, or Mercado Libre in South America.

2. Yet, the digitization process may be delayed and its benefits may be limited because the economic characteristics of the markets in which those platforms operate are such that, when taken in combination, may lead to an accumulation of market power among a few platforms, often only one. These features include: (a) the importance of collecting user data as an input to improving product quality and possibly as a barrier to entry; (b) the existence of economies of scale and scope; (c) the availability of zero-price products and services; (d) the existence of network effects creating competition *for* the market rather than *in* the market; (e) the multi-sided nature of these markets; (f) the low marginal costs of many platforms; etc.

3. Due to these features, these markets may exhibit limited contestability: once a platform has achieved a prominent position in a digital market, it may be difficult for new entrants to displace it. Furthermore, platforms may leverage their power to monopolize the markets where their business users operate; or may develop strategies, including acquiring potential or emerging rivals, to entrench their dominance and control the accessibility and contestability of the markets within which they themselves operate. Finally, by their very nature, large platforms enjoy an unequal position *vis-à-vis* their domestic users and business users, whose business operations may be wholly, or in part, dependent on access to the platform provider's services. Platforms' domestic users and business users thus risk being treated unfairly or discriminatorily.

4. Governments, legislatures, and competition authorities in developed and developing nations have become concerned with the power of large digital platforms. Some have developed new regulatory tools to discipline their market power. Australia, the European Union (EU), France, Germany,

5. One of such novel regulatory instruments is the EU's Digital Markets Act (DMA).[1] The DMA is purported to address the limitations of traditional competition law in the digital context and, as such, it represents a significant shift in the European Union's approach to regulating digital platforms, aiming to ensure fair and contestable markets. The DMA represents a bold initiative by the EU to assert regulatory authority over digital markets and address concerns about platform dominance.

China, South Korea, Japan, and the United Kingdom (UK) have implemented novel regimes to regulate digital platforms. Similar initiatives are being considered or implemented in various other countries (such as Brazil, India, Mexico, South Africa, Thailand, and Turkey, to name a few). This has led to many different interventions across many jurisdictions and will produce a vast web of rules and regulations aimed at conditioning the conduct of such large digital platforms in many countries.

6. However, its implications for international trade have sparked significant controversy, particularly with the United States (US). The controversy over the DMA underscores the challenges of regulating the digital economy in a manner that balances domestic policy objectives with international trade commitments. As countries seek to assert greater control over digital markets, the risk of regulatory fragmentation and trade disputes increases. The EU's approach, while aimed at promoting competition and consumer protection, may inadvertently create barriers to trade and provoke retaliatory measures, thereby undermining the principles of open and fair international commerce.

7. Balancing the DMA's objectives with the principles of open and fair trade requires careful navigation, emphasizing the need for dialogue and cooperation among global stakeholders. As digital markets continue to evolve, establishing harmonized and inclusive regulatory frameworks will be essential to ensure that competition and innovation thrive in a globally interconnected economy.

8. Engaging in constructive discussions to address mutual concerns and align regulatory approaches could help prevent further escalation and promote a more harmonized framework for digital market governance. Such collaboration would not only benefit international relations, but also contribute to the development of global standards that support innovation, competition, and consumer welfare in the digital age.

9. The remainder of this paper is structured as follows.

10. In Section II, we offer an overview of existing regulatory approaches across key jurisdictions. It begins with the EU's *ex-ante* framework under

---

[1] Regulation (EU) 2022/1925 of the European Parliament and of the Council of 14 September 2022 on contestable and fair markets in the digital sector and amending Directives (EU) 2019/1937 and (EU) 2020/1828 (Digital Markets Act), published in the Official Journal of the European Union as OJ L 265, 21 September 2022, pages 1–66.

the DMA, then contrasts this with the US's *ex-post* antitrust tradition, followed by an examination of China's integrated and state-driven model, the UK's emerging case-by-case method under the Digital Markets Competition and Consumers (DMCC) Act,[2] and a survey of other national approaches that reflect a broader divide between *ex-ante* and *ex-post* regimes.

11. In Section III, we analyze the intersection between digital regulation and international trade, introducing the concept of Behind-the-border Trade Barriers (BTBs), and exploring how digital rules can function as BTBs that distort market access and competition.

12. In Section IV, we turn to the global regulatory contest, examining how the EU seeks to export its standards through the "Brussels Effect", and how this ambition has fueled transatlantic tensions, particularly regarding the DMA. We then focus on the broader economic implications of the lobal regulatory, situating the debate about competing digital regulations in the context of the US–China technological rivalry, and discussing, in particular, how the asymmetric impact of the DMA may disproportionately affect US and Chinese tech firms.

13. In Section V, we explore how global regulatory disputes may escalate into full-blown trade conflicts, analyzing the limitations of existing trade agreements, the potential use of retaliatory tariffs, and the feedback loop between BTBs and such retaliatory measures, thus closing the argument that digital regulation is increasingly a flashpoint of geopolitical contestation.

14. In Section VI, we evaluate the economy-wide implications of trade wars in the technological domain, emphasizing that while strategic gains are possible, economic and institutional costs typically prevail. We consider the distributional effects of such economic confrontations across firms and nations, the global repercussions of technological decoupling, and the associated risks to sustained growth and institutional balance; particularly the danger of many countries drifting from the narrow corridor of liberty and growth.

15. In Section VII, we present the EU's strategic dilemma amid intensifying geopolitical and technological rivalries between the US and China, where regulatory coexistence becomes unsustainable. While the EU aspires to maintain regulatory autonomy and avoid binary alignment, its technological dependency weakens its influence and risks relegating it to a rule-taker role. As China and the US assert divergent economic governance models and seek global technological leadership, the EU faces mounting pressure to define its strategic position. If forced to align with a dominant

---

[2] Digital Markets, Competition and Consumers Act 2024 (c. 13), enacted by the Parliament of the United Kingdom and received Royal Assent on 24 May 2024.

16. sphere, the EU may have to compromise, threatening its long-standing commitment to multilateralism, democratic legitimacy, and autonomous rule-making in global affairs.
16. In Section VIII, we offer some concluding remarks.

II. An Overview of Existing Regulatory Approaches

17. In her seminal book, Digital Empires: The Global Battle to Regulate Technology,[3] Anu Bradford (2023) offers a profound analysis of the geopolitical contest to shape the global digital order. Bradford dissects how these three "digital empires" advance distinct regulatory models, each reflecting their unique political ideologies and societal values. These empires compete as normative actors, seeking to export their digital governance models.

18. Regulatory interventions are minimal in the US, with a focus on antitrust enforcement rather than proactive regulation. The EU model instead prioritizes individual rights, data protection, contestability, and market fairness. Legislation, such as the General Data Protection Regulation (GDPR)[4] and the DMA exemplify this approach. Finally, China's model is characterized by centralized enforcement, integration with broader policies and dynamic adjustments. Although the technology development of those digital platforms were largely driven by bottom-up innovations of these tech companies, regulatory actions were often driven by top-down interventions of the government. China's digital governance is increasingly influential, particularly among developing countries seeking to emulate its unique model. We discuss these three models and a few others in this section.

II.A. The EU ex-ante approach: the DMA

19. The DMA establishes a set of obligations for designated "gatekeepers", defined as large online platforms serving as intermediaries between businesses and consumers with a significant impact on the internal market. Several companies have been identified as gatekeepers, including Alphabet, Amazon, Apple, Booking, ByteDance, Meta, and Microsoft, based on criteria such as annual turnover and user base within the EU. With the exception of Booking and ByteDance, all other gatekeepers are US companies.

---

3   Bradford, A. 2023. Digital Empires: The Global Battle to Regulate Technology. Oxford University Press.
4   Regulation (EU) 2016/679 of the European Parliament and of the Council of 27 April 2016 on the protection of natural persons with regard to the processing of personal data and on the free movement of such data, and repealing Directive 95/46/EC (General Data Protection Regulation). Official Journal: OJ L 119, 4.5.2016, pp. 1–88.

20. Gatekeepers are required to, among other things, allow third parties to interoperate with their services, provide access to data generated by business users, and ensure transparency in advertising. Gatekeepers are also prohibited from practices, such as self-preferencing, restricting users from uninstalling pre-installed software, and combining personal data from different services without user consent.

21. Implementing the DMA poses several challenges, including defining the scope of obligations, ensuring proportionality, and coordinating with existing legal frameworks. Continuous dialogue between regulators, stakeholders, and scholars is essential to address these challenges effectively. The European Commission is responsible for enforcing the DMA. Non-compliance can result in fines of up to 10% of a company's total worldwide annual turnover, and up to 20% for repeated infringements. In severe cases, structural remedies, including divestitures, may be imposed.

II.B. The US ex-post approach

22. Unlike the EU's *ex-ante* approach to regulating digital platforms, the US approach primarily relies on *ex-post* antitrust enforcement. This strategy emphasizes addressing anti-competitive behaviors after they occur, focusing on maintaining market competition and consumer welfare. Key agencies involved include the Department of Justice (DOJ) and the Federal Trade Commission (FTC), which have initiated significant legal actions against major tech companies.

23. The DOJ has pursued multiple antitrust cases against Google. In 2024, a federal court ruled that Google illegally maintained a monopoly in the search engine market, primarily through exclusive agreements that made its search engine the default on various devices. Also in 2024, the DOJ filed a lawsuit against Apple, alleging that the company maintained an illegal monopoly in the smartphone market. The suit focuses on practices such as restricting third-party app stores and limiting interoperability, which allegedly stifle competition and consumer choice. In 2025, the DOJ secured a victory in a case alleging that Google monopolized digital advertising markets, harming publishers and advertisers. Remedies under consideration include divesting parts of its ad tech business.

24. The FTC on its part has challenged Meta's dominance in the social networking space. The FTC argues that these acquisitions were strategic moves to neutralize competition, consolidating Meta's market power. The agency seeks to unwind these deals to restore competitive balance.

25. While the US continues to navigate the complexities of regulating digital platforms through antitrust enforcement, debates persist about its efficacy in addressing the unique challenges of digital markets. Legislative efforts aiming to bolster enforcement capabilities include the proposed American

Innovation and Choice Online Act (AICOA),[5] and the Advertising Middlemen Endangering Rigorous Internet Competition Accountability (AMERICA) Act.[6]

26. Introduced in 2021, AICOA aims to prevent dominant platforms from favouring their own products over competitors'. Key provisions include prohibiting self-preferencing in search results and app stores; restricting the use of non-public data from business users to advantage the platform's own products; preventing actions that impede interoperability or limit user choice. The bill targets platforms with significant market power, defined by user base and market capitalization thresholds. AICOA was introduced in the U.S. Senate by Senator Amy Klobuchar (D-MN) and Senator Chuck Grassley (R-IA) during the 117th Congress. Despite bipartisan support and advancing through the Senate Judiciary Committee in 2022, the bill did not pass before the end of the congressional session. It was reintroduced in the 118th Congress on June 15, 2023, and referred to the Senate Judiciary Committee, but it has not advanced further as of now.

27. The AMERICA Act in turn seeks to address conflicts of interest in digital advertising. It proposes forcing dominant platforms to divest parts of their advertising businesses; enhancing transparency in ad auctions and pricing; preventing platforms from operating multiple roles in the digital ad supply chain. This legislation responds to concerns about platforms like Google controlling both the buy and sell sides of digital advertising markets. The AMERICA Act was introduced in the Senate by Senator Mike Lee (R-UT) on March 30, 2023, during the 118th Congress. It was referred to the Senate Judiciary Committee but has not progressed further.

28. AICOA, the AMERICA Act, and the DMA all seek to promote fair competition and address the market power of dominant digital platforms. They share concerns about practices like self-preferencing and the use of non-public data to disadvantage competitors. However, while the DMA establishes a comprehensive regulatory framework with predefined obligations for "gatekeepers", applying *ex-ante* rules to prevent anti-competitive behaviors, AICOA and the AMERICA Act are more targeted, focusing on specific anti-competitive practices and applying *ex-post* enforcement mechanisms. Indeed, enforcement of AICOA and the AMERICA Act would fall under the purview of the Federal Trade Commission (FTC) and the Department of Justice (DOJ), relying on existing antitrust enforcement mechanisms.

---

5 The American Innovation and Choice Online Act (AICOA) is a proposed U.S. antitrust bill designed to prevent dominant online platforms from favoring their own products and services over those of competitors. It aims to promote competition and fairness in the digital marketplace.

6 The AMERICA Act is a bipartisan U.S. antitrust proposal introduced in the Senate. It aims to prevent conflicts of interest and promote competition in the digital advertising market by targeting dominant players and ensuring transparency.

II.C. The chinese integrated approach

29. China has implemented a multifaceted regulatory framework to oversee and regulate digital platforms, reflecting its unique political and economic context. This framework encompasses antitrust enforcement, data governance, labour protections, and broader economic policies aimed at ensuring the healthy development of the platform economy.[7]

30. The State Administration for Market Regulation (SAMR) serves as China's primary antitrust authority, overseeing market competition and enforcing regulations against monopolistic practices. In 2021, SAMR imposed a record $2.75 billion fine on Alibaba for abusing its market dominance by forcing merchants into exclusivity agreements, a practice known as "choose one from two".[8] This action marked a significant escalation in China's efforts to regulate its tech giants.

31. Also in 2021 SAMR released guidelines addressing anti-competitive behaviors specific to digital platforms, such as self-preferencing and predatory pricing.[9] Major platforms like Alibaba and Meituan underwent multi-year "rectification" periods to align their operations with regulatory expectations. SAMR continues to monitor and guide platform companies to ensure compliance and fair competition in the digital market.

32. While some China's regulatory measures share the same goal as the DMA in addressing the dominance of digital platforms, China's approach is characterized by (a) centralized enforcement (regulatory actions are often driven by top-down directives from central authorities); (b) integration with broader policies (regulations are closely tied to national strategies, such as "common prosperity" and technological self-reliance); and (c) dynamic adjustments (policies are frequently updated to respond to emerging challenges and align with economic objectives). This approach reflects China's unique political and economic system, where regulatory frameworks both ensure healthy development of the market economy and balance state governance priorities.

II.D. The UK case by case approach: the DMCC

33. Like the DMA, the UK's Digital Markets, Competition and Consumers Act 2024 (DMCC Act) aims to regulate dominant digital platforms to foster fair competition and protect consumers. While they share similar

---

[7] Huang, Y., Yin, N., Zhang, V.Y., Zhao, S.(2023): The Impact of Antitrust Regulations on Firm Market Value-Evidence from Chinese and US Internet Platforms, forthcoming at Review of Industrial Organization.

[8] SAMR, "State Administration of Market Regulation Issues Decision on Administrative Penalty and Administrative Guidance for Alibaba Group Holding Limited Monopolistic Conduct in The Online Retail Platform Services Market in China," April 10, 2021, https://www.samr.gov.cn/zt/qhfldzf/art/2021/art_74b25 93fd32a432baf3dcbd163935167.html.

[9] SAMR, "Anti-Monopoly Guidelines of the Anti-Monopoly Committee of the State Council on the Platform Economy" (State Anti-monopoly Development [2021] No. 1), February 7, 2021, https://www.gov.cn/xinwen/2021-02/07/content_5585758.htm.

objectives, their approaches and implementation mechanisms differ in several key aspects.

34. The DMCC Act empowers the Competition and Markets Authority (CMA), specifically its Digital Markets Unit (DMU), to designate certain firms as having Strategic Market Status (SMS). Firms with SMS are subject to tailored conduct requirements and pro-competitive interventions to address specific competition concerns. A firm may be designated with SMS if it has substantial and entrenched market power in a digital activity linked to the UK and a position of strategic significance. This includes firms with global turnover exceeding £25 billion or UK turnover over £1 billion. The CMA can impose specific obligations on SMS firms to ensure fair dealing, open choices, and trust and transparency. For example, the CMA has the authority to implement structural remedies, such as requiring interoperability or data portability, to promote competition. The Act also strengthens consumer rights by banning practices like fake reviews and "drip pricing", where mandatory fees are added late in the purchasing process.

35. As of January 2025, the CMA has initiated investigations under the DMCC Act to assess whether companies like Google and Apple hold SMS in specific digital activities, such as search and mobile ecosystems. These investigations are expected to conclude within a nine-month statutory timeframe.

36. While both the DMCC Act and the DMA aim to curb the dominance of large digital platforms, their methodologies differ. They share common goals, but their differing approaches reflect distinct regulatory philosophies and legal traditions. The DMA applies a uniform set of obligations to all designated gatekeepers, focusing on *ex-ante* regulation to prevent anti-competitive behavior. Instead, the DMCC Act adopts a more flexible, case-by-case approach, allowing the CMA to tailor obligations based on specific market dynamics. The DMCC Act's flexible, tailored framework may offer advantages in addressing specific market dynamics within the UK, whereas the DMA's uniform obligations provide clarity and consistency across the EU. Ongoing implementation and enforcement will reveal the efficacy and impact of each regime in the evolving digital landscape.

II.E. Other countries: ex-ante v ex-post approaches

37. Countries such as Brazil, Japan, South Korea, and Taiwan, have shown varying degrees of alignment with the EU's regulatory policies concerning digital platforms. While some have adopted measures inspired by the DMA (and Digital Services Act, DSA[10]), others have taken more

---

10 The Digital Services Act (DSA) is a landmark regulation enacted by the European Union to create a safer and more transparent digital environment. Adopted on October 19, 2022, as Regulation (EU) 2022/2065, the DSA updates the EU's legal framework for digital services. Its provisions became fully applicable on February 17, 2024, for most platforms, with earlier compliance required for designated Very Large Online Platforms (VLOPs) and Very Large Online Search Engines (VLOSEs).

cautious or divergent approaches, influenced by domestic considerations and international pressures.

38. Brazil has shown a notable inclination towards adopting regulatory measures inspired by the EU's digital policies. In 2022, Brazil introduced a draft bill establishing a digital markets regulatory regime that mirrors the EU's DMA, targeting specific companies with significant market power. Further, in 2024, Brazil's government proposed reforms to its competition law to better address the dominance of big tech firms, suggesting legislation that would allow antitrust authorities to identify certain digital platforms as systemically relevant and impose new obligations on them. These initiatives reflect Brazil's effort to balance fostering competition with encouraging innovation, drawing inspiration from the EU's regulatory framework, while tailoring it to the Brazilian context.

39. Japan has also actively engaged in developing regulations that align with the EU's digital platform policies. In 2024, Japan enacted the Act on Promotion of Competition for Specified Smartphone Software, also known as the Smartphone Software Competition Promotion Act (SSCPA),[11] which aims to enhance third-party competition in the smartphone market. This legislation, while inspired by the EU's DMA, has been tailored to Japan's specific market conditions. Additionally, Japan has sought to increase transparency and fairness in its digital markets through the Act on Improving Transparency and Fairness of Digital Platforms (TFDPA),[12] targeting online mall operators and app store providers. These efforts demonstrate Japan's commitment to fostering a competitive digital environment, drawing from international best practices while considering domestic needs.

40. South Korea initially considered implementing regulations akin to the EU's DMA, aiming to impose *ex-ante* obligations on dominant digital platforms. However, in 2024, the Korea Fair Trade Commission (KFTC) decided to abandon plans for a comprehensive platform regulation modeled after the EU's approach. This decision was influenced by concerns over potential trade conflicts, particularly with the US, and the desire to avoid disadvantaging domestic tech firms. Instead, South Korea has pursued a self-regulatory framework, establishing a legal basis for digital platforms to engage in self-regulation with government support and oversight.

41. Taiwan has been monitoring the EU's digital regulatory developments, but has yet to implement comprehensive legislation similar to the DMA

---

11 Enacted in June 2024, the SSCPA is Japan's legislation aimed at promoting competition in the smartphone software market. It prohibits practices that prevent alternative app stores, in-app payment systems, and browser engines, ensuring fair competition.

12 The TFDPA, effective from February 2021, is Japan's regulation to improve transparency and fairness among specified digital platform providers. It requires designated platforms to disclose terms and conditions and undergo evaluations to ensure fair practices.

(or DSA). The Taiwanese Fair Trade Commission (TFTC) has expressed intentions to strengthen existing competition rules to address challenges posed by large digital platforms, favouring enhancements to current laws over the adoption of new, broad regulations. Additionally, Taiwan has proposed the Digital Intermediary Services Act (DISA),[13] which emphasizes a participatory approach involving public-private collaboration to oversee platform conduct, unlike the EU's more prescriptive regulatory model.

42. In summary, while countries like Brazil and Japan have taken significant steps to align their digital platform regulations with the EU's policies, adapting them to their national contexts, others like South Korea and Taiwan have opted for more cautious or alternative approaches. These decisions are influenced by a combination of domestic priorities, economic considerations, and international relations, particularly with major global players such as China and the US.

III. Digital Regulation and Trade

43. Digital regulations have extra-territorial implications for, at least, two reasons. First, because they can modify trade flows. Regulations may act as Behind-the-border Trade Barriers (BTBs),[14] protecting domestic firms at the expense of their foreign competitors. Second, regulatory models, like those described above, especially those of the three "digital empires", compete for global dominance, influencing international norms and standards. This competition shapes the global structure of the digital world and can have significant geopolitical implications. We discuss digital regulation as a BTB in this section. We then consider the global aspirations of different regulatory regimes and, in particular, of the EU approach.

III.A. Behind-the-border trade barriers (BTBs)

44. The liberalization of international trade since the mid-20th century has brought unprecedented gains in efficiency, innovation, and economic growth. Yet, even as average tariff rates have declined sharply across both developed and developing economies, global trade has become no less contentious. As

---

13   Proposed in June 2022, the DISA is Taiwan's draft legislation focusing on regulating platform accountability, illegal content, transparency, and the disclosure of business information and service terms to protect users' rights. The draft was released for public consultation by the National Communications Commission.

14   Behind-the-border Trade Barriers refer to domestic regulations, standards, and policies that, while not explicitly discriminatory, can impede trade by increasing the cost or complexity of market entry for foreign firms. These barriers differ from at-the-border barriers, such as tariffs or quotas, because they operate within the internal regulatory framework of a country. See Baldwin, Robert E. Nontariff Distortions of International Trade. Washington, DC: Brookings Institution Press, 1970; and Deardorff, Alan V., and Robert M. Stern. "Measurement of Non-Tariff Barriers." OECD Economics Department Working Papers, no. 179 (1998).

the global economy has evolved, the traditional levers of trade policy – tariffs, quotas, and subsidies – have been progressively supplemented and often overshadowed by BTBs. These measures – ranging from technical standards and customs procedures to domestic regulatory frameworks – are now among the most significant determinants of trade outcomes.

45. BTBs are embedded in domestic regulatory environments, influencing trade flows not through direct cost increases at the border, but through the design, implementation, and enforcement of domestic laws. Unlike traditional tariffs or quotas, BTBs do not operate at the point of entry. Instead, they act indirectly by influencing how goods and services are produced, certified, distributed, and consumed within a country. BTBs are deeply political instruments whose effects are contingent on the institutional frameworks in which they are embedded. An effective trade policy must address not only cross-border barriers, but also domestic regulatory coherence and political constraints.

46. While some BTBs are justified by legitimate policy objectives – such as consumer protection or environmental sustainability – others may serve as disguised protectionism or rent-seeking tools. In some instances, BTBs may prompt retaliation, as when opaque regulatory standards are perceived as de facto discrimination. In others, retaliation may take the form of new BTBs, especially where direct tariff retaliation is constrained by international law or economic feasibility.

47. Several structural transformations in the global economy have contributed to the rise of BTBs. Firstly, the emergence of Global Value Chains (GVCs)[15] and the ensuing fragmentation of production across borders means that a regulation in one country can affect the cost structure of an entire international supply chain. In his influential survey, "Global Value Chains",[16] Paul Antràs (2020) highlights how the increasing fragmentation of production has elevated the importance of domestic institutions and behind-the-border conditions in shaping the geography and structure of international trade. In this view, BTBs are endogenous features of trade patterns, not exogenous constraints. Secondly, the changing composition of trade: as economies become more service-oriented and reliant on digital flows, domestic rules on data privacy, financial regulation, and intellectual property become pivotal to trade. Thirdly, the rising demand for regulation: as societies become wealthier and more environmentally aware, the demand for tighter regulations grows.

---

15   Global Value Chains (GVCs) refer to the full range of activities that firms and workers perform to bring a product from its conception to end use and beyond. These activities, such as design, production, marketing, distribution, and support, are often distributed across different countries. GVCs reflect the increasing fragmentation of production across borders, with different stages of the process located in regions that offer comparative advantages in costs, skills, or technologies. See Baldwin, Richard. 2016. The Great Convergence: Information Technology and the New Globalization. Belknap Press of Harvard University Press, 2016.

16   Antràs, Pol. 2020. "Conceptual Aspects of Global Value Chains," The World Bank Economic Review 34, no. 3: 551–574.

III.B. Digital regulation as a BTB

48. The rise of digital trade is a new arena where BTBs are emerging. Data localization requirements, differential privacy regulations, and cybersecurity laws now represent some of the most salient trade frictions. These new BTBs affect sectors that were previously considered "borderless", demonstrating that domestic regulation continues to shape global commerce even in the digital age.

IV. The Geopolitics of Digital Regulation

49. As explained above, regulatory regimes compete for global dominance to influence international norms and standards. The goal of shaping the global regulatory structure of the digital world is particularly salient in the case of the EU. This is the so-called "Brussels Effect",[17] whereby EU regulations extend beyond its borders due to the bloc's market size and regulatory rigour. In this section we explain this effect and discuss the controversy surrounding the extra-territorial implications of EU digital regulation – in particular the DMA.

IV.A. The Brussels Effect

50. The influence of the DMA on the regulations adopted by other countries exemplifies the Brussels Effect. The Brussels Effect, a term coined by Anu Bradford (2020), describes the EU's capacity to unilaterally shape global regulations through its internal market standards. This phenomenon has allowed the EU to project its regulatory preferences beyond its borders, influencing global norms in areas such as data protection, environmental standards, and consumer safety.

51. The Brussels Effect operates through two primary mechanisms: *de facto* and *de jure*. *De facto* influence occurs when multinational companies adopt EU standards globally to maintain access to the EU market, thereby extending these standards beyond EU borders. *De jure* influence involves other jurisdictions formally adopting EU regulations into their legal frameworks.

52. This legislative influence corresponds to what Gal and Padilla (2010)[18] denote as the "follower phenomenon", according to which jurisdictions adopt regulations from other countries, often without tailoring them to local economic and institutional contexts. This emulation is

---

17 Bradford, Anu. 2020. The Brussels Effect: How the European Union Rules the World. Oxford University Press.

18 Gal, Michal S., and A. Jorge Padilla. 2010: "The Follower Phenomenon: Implications for the Design of Monopolization Rules in a Global Economy." Antitrust Law Journal 76, no. 3: 899–928.

often driven by factors such as (a) international pressure (countries may face pressure from international organizations or trade partners to align their antitrust laws with global standards); (b) the desire for legal harmonization (adopting established rules can facilitate cross-border trade and investment by reducing legal uncertainty); and (c) the perceived legitimacy of established rules (rules from jurisdictions like the EU or the US are often seen as tried and tested, lending them an aura of legitimacy).

53. This practice can lead to suboptimal enforcement and unintended consequences in the global economy. First, differences in market structures, firm sizes, and levels of economic development can render imported rules ineffective or even harmful. Second, variations in legal traditions, enforcement capabilities, and judicial independence can impede the effective implementation of foreign rules. Third, societal attitudes towards competition and regulation can influence the reception and effectiveness of antitrust laws.

54. To mitigate the risks associated with the follower phenomenon, Gal and Padilla recommend that jurisdictions assess their unique economic, institutional, and cultural contexts before adopting foreign rules; invest in local expertise and institutions to enhance the effectiveness of antitrust enforcement; implement foreign rules gradually, with necessary modifications, to allow for better integration into the local legal framework; and engage in dialogue with other jurisdictions and international bodies to facilitate the sharing of best practices and experiences.

55. The practical relevance of the Brussels Effect appears to be declining. The limited adoption of the DMA approach internationally is consistent with this observation. This is for at least three reasons. First, EU regulations, including the DMA, face competition from alternative regulatory frameworks, particularly from the United States and China. The US adopts a more *laissez-faire* approach, emphasizing innovation and market freedom, while China employs a state-centric model to regulate and promote healthy development of digital platforms. These divergent models offer competing paradigms that are diminishing the EU's unilateral regulatory influence. Second, the rapid pace of technological innovation, especially in areas like artificial intelligence (AI) and digital services, poses difficulties for the EU's *ex-ante* regulatory apparatus, which appears unlikely to be able to swiftly address emerging technologies, potentially reducing its regulatory relevance in fast-evolving sectors. Finally, the EU's relative economic stagnation and internal political challenges, including differing Member state priorities and regulatory fatigue, may impact its capacity to maintain the Brussels Effect. A declining share of global GDP and the complexities of achieving consensus among diverse member states is bound to weaken the EU's position as a global regulatory leader.

IV.B. The transatlantic controversy on the EU DMA

56. Against a background of diminished regulatory influence, the DMA, by setting stringent standards for digital platforms, effectively compels global companies to adapt their practices to comply with the EU rules, influencing regulatory approaches worldwide. This extra-territorial impact has prompted discussions about the balance between national sovereignty in regulation and the need for harmonized international standards in the digital economy. In addition, to the extent other countries adopt measures inspired by the DMA, though not necessarily identical, the result may be a patchwork of digital regulations complicating compliance for multinational companies. Such proliferation of, possibly diverse, regulatory regimes would pose challenges for international trade, potentially hindering the seamless flow of digital services, and creating barriers for smaller firms lacking resources to navigate diverse regulatory landscapes.

57. Not surprisingly, the DMA has been met with criticism from the US, where policymakers and industry stakeholders perceive it as disproportionately targeting American tech giants. The perception of discrimination has been exacerbated by recent enforcement actions, including the substantial fines imposed on Apple and Meta for non-compliance with the DMA provisions. The affected companies have voiced strong objections to the DMA's enforcement. Apple criticized the fines as unjustified and detrimental to user privacy and innovation, arguing that the DMA's requirements undermine its business model. Meta similarly contended that the imposed changes to its operations resemble a tariff and harm both its services and European businesses. Both companies have indicated plans to appeal the fines and challenge the DMA's provisions through legal avenues, potentially leading to protracted litigation and further straining EU-US relations.

58. The US administration has expressed concerns that the DMA could act as a trade barrier, potentially violating World Trade Organization (WTO) commitments by discriminating against foreign companies. This raises concerns about the potential for retaliatory trade measures. Indeed, President Donald Trump has threatened to impose tariffs on countries that penalize American companies, and the current administration's strong rhetoric suggests a willingness to consider such retaliatory actions. Such measures could lead to a broader trade conflict, affecting not only the digital sector but also other areas of transatlantic commerce.

59. The US administration has characterized the fines recently imposed on Apple and Meta as economic extortion, arguing that they unfairly penalize American firms and could set a precedent for protectionist digital regulations. At the 2025 International Competition Network (ICN) Annual

Conference in Edinburgh,[19] FTC Chair Andrew Ferguson delivered a keynote address, where he described the DMA as a "sledgehammer" approach, lacking nuance and potentially stifling innovation in the digital economy. He expressed concern that the EU's regulatory impulses, particularly regarding AI, could lead to knee-jerk reactions that hinder technological advancement. In particular, Ferguson objected to the DMA's enforcement mechanisms, suggesting that the substantial fines imposed under the Act resemble a form of taxation on American companies. He argued that such measures would disproportionately affect US tech firms and advantage their Chinese counterparts.

60. In response, the EU has maintained that the DMA applies equally to all companies operating within its market, regardless of origin. At the same ICN Annual Conference,[20] European Commission Executive Vice-President Teresa Ribera addressed Ferguson's criticisms of the DMA emphasizing that the DMA is not designed to target specific countries or companies. Instead, she asserted that the legislation aims to protect users and ensure that digital markets remain open to innovation and new entrants, preventing monopolistic dominance by incumbent tech giants. In her remarks, Ribera maintained that the DMA is a forward-looking framework intended to foster a competitive and fair digital economy, rather than a punitive measure against foreign technology firms. She reiterated the EU's commitment to working collaboratively with global partners to address the challenges posed by rapidly evolving digital markets. Ribera also highlighted the European Commission's willingness to engage in dialogue with the US authorities to clarify any misunderstandings about the DMA. She underscored the importance of international cooperation in regulating digital markets, especially in the face of potential trade tensions and the imposition of tariffs.

61. The EU response misses the point. From a US perspective whether the DMA is targeted to large companies rather than to American companies is utterly irrelevant; because most of the large companies under scrutiny are American. For the US, the DMA is a BTB that risks undermining the competitive position of American companies in the global arena. Whether the ultimate goal is to disadvantage US companies against their European rivals or to protect European consumers is also irrelevant from a US viewpoint. Indeed, it is quite unlikely that the DMA and other EU digital regulations facilitate the emergence of European champions. From the viewpoint of the current US administration, the "real race" is between the US companies and those of China, and the outcome of that technological contest is existential.

---

19   Competition in the 21st Century: Heeding The Rallying Cry for Deregulation. Prepared Remarks of Chairman Andrew N. Ferguson. U.S. Federal Trade Commission. International Competition Network Annual Conference 2025, Edinburgh, United Kingdom, May 7, 2025.

20   Transatlantic antitrust ties fray as US and EU regulators squabble, Financial Times, 10 May 2025.

IV.C. The US-China technology race

62. The geopolitical confrontation between China and the US has evolved into a systemic rivalry with global implications, encompassing ideological, economic, military, and technological dimensions. The technological dimension of this rivalry is arguably its most significant and enduring aspect. Both countries view technological leadership as central to national security, economic power, and global influence.

63. Technological leadership is a fundamental pillar of modern state power. It underpins military capabilities, economic productivity, and the ability to set global standards. For the US, maintaining dominance in critical technologies has long been essential to its geopolitical strategy. For China, technological modernization is central to its ambitions for national rejuvenation and to escape the so-called "middle-income trap."[21]

64. The US perceives China's rapid technological advancement, fueled by state-led industrial policy and strategic acquisitions, as a direct challenge to its global supremacy. Conversely, China sees American efforts to restrict its technological development as a form of containment aimed at thwarting its rise. This mutual suspicion intensifies the zero-sum nature of the rivalry and motivates both countries to pursue increasingly aggressive policies to secure strategic advantage.

65. Telecommunications, particularly the global rollout of 5G networks, has become one of the most contentious arenas of US–China technological rivalry. Huawei, China's flagship telecommunications company, embodies this struggle. The US has accused Huawei of espionage, intellectual property theft, and links to the Chinese military, and it has imposed strict export controls and lobbied allies to exclude Huawei from their 5G networks.[22] From Washington's perspective, allowing Chinese firms to build critical infrastructure poses unacceptable national security risks. For Beijing, however, the targeting of Huawei is perceived as an effort to stifle the growth of China's tech champions. The 5G dispute reflects broader concerns about the security of supply chains, data sovereignty, and the balance of power in the global digital economy.

---

21 The middle-income trap refers to the economic stagnation that countries often experience after reaching a certain income level, typically between $1,000 and $12,000 per capita (in constant 2011 US dollars, PPP), but before achieving high-income status. Initially, low-income countries can grow rapidly by mobilizing cheap labor and adopting existing technologies. However, as wages rise and demographic dividends diminish, these advantages erode. To sustain growth, countries must transition toward innovation-driven economies, characterized by higher productivity, advanced human capital, and robust institutions. Many middle-income countries fail to make this transition due to structural constraints. These include weak governance, underinvestment in education and research, inefficient financial systems, and inadequate infrastructure. Furthermore, political economy factors – such as vested interests resisting reform or inequality stifling broad-based human capital development – can impede the shift toward more complex and high-value-added production.

22 Congressional Research Service, "U.S. Restrictions on Huawei Technologies: National Security, Foreign Policy, and Economic Interests", January 5, 2022, https://www.congress.gov/crs-product/R47012.

66. Semiconductors – microchips that power everything from smartphones to missiles – are at the heart of the technological confrontation. The US has imposed a series of export controls to cut off Chinese access to advanced chips, chipmaking equipment, and design software. In response, China has accelerated its efforts to achieve semiconductor self-sufficiency through massive state investment and policy initiatives like "Made in China 2025"[23] and the "Dual Circulation Strategy".[24] However, China remains dependent on foreign technology in advanced node manufacturing, especially from companies such as ASML (Netherlands), and Nvidia (US), etc..

67. AI is another frontier in the US–China technological rivalry. Both countries view AI as a transformative general-purpose technology with enormous commercial and military implications. In the US, AI development is driven primarily by the private sector, with firms like Google, OpenAI, and Microsoft leading innovation. In China, the state plays a significant role, directing capital and setting national strategies to promote AI through initiatives like the "Next Generation AI Development Plan" (2017).[25] Private sector also plays an important role. DeepSeek is a successful example of China's AI innovation efforts and becomes an effective rival of its US peers.[26]

68. Quantum technologies represent another emerging domain of strategic competition. Quantum computing promises exponential gains in processing power, with potential applications in cryptography, logistics, and materials science. Both the US and China have recognized its geopolitical significance, with each investing billions in research and development. China's National Laboratory for Quantum Information Science and its launch of the world's first quantum satellite (Micius) have demonstrated notable progress. In the US, efforts are spearheaded by both the federal government (through the National Quantum Initiative Act[27]) and private

---

23 Made in China (MIC) 2025 is an industrial policy aimed at upgrading China's manufacturing sector from low-cost, labor-intensive production to high-value, innovation-driven industries. MIC 2025 focuses on ten strategic industries: 1. New-generation information technology 2. High-end numerical control machinery and robotics 3. Aerospace and aviation equipment 4. Maritime engineering equipment and high-tech ships 5. Advanced rail transportation equipment 6. Energy-saving and new energy vehicles 7. Electrical equipment 8. Agricultural machinery and equipment 9. New materials 10. Biopharmaceuticals and high-performance medical devices.

24 Introduced in 2020, the Dual Circulation Strategy aims to create a more resilient and self-sustaining economy by balancing domestic and international economic activities. One of its key goals is to promote indigenous innovation to achieve self-sufficiency in critical technologies. The strategy has led to increased efforts in localizing supply chains and promoting domestic innovation.

25 Translation available at https://digichina.stanford.edu/work/full-translation-chinas-new-generation-artificial-intelligence-development-plan-2017/.

26 Eduardo Baptista: "What is DeepSeek and why is it disrupting the AI sector?", Reuters, January 29, 2025, https://www.reuters.com/technology/artificial-intelligence/what-is-deepseek-why-is-it-disrupting-ai-sector-2025-01-27/.

27 The U.S. National Quantum Initiative Act (NQIA), enacted on December 21, 2018, under Public Law 115-368, establishes a comprehensive federal strategy to advance quantum information science (QIS) and technology in the United States. In May 2025, U.S. lawmakers introduced the bipartisan Quantum Sandbox for Near-Term Applications Act (S.1344), aiming to amend the NQIA. This proposed legislation seeks to establish public-private partnerships to accelerate the development of near-term quantum applications by creating testbeds – referred to as "quantum sandboxes" – for innovators to test quantum technologies in real-world environments.

firms such as IBM and Google. The fear of a "quantum leap" in strategic capabilities has led to growing secrecy and export control regimes, with implications for international scientific collaboration.

69. The intensification of technological competition has led both countries to adopt a range of "techno-nationalist" tools. The US has expanded the use of export controls under the Export Control Reform Act (ECRA[28]) and the Foreign Investment Risk Review Modernization Act (FIRRMA[29]), targeting not only Chinese firms but also foreign entities doing business with them. Investment screening by the Committee on Foreign Investment in the United States (CFIUS) has also become more stringent, especially for transactions involving sensitive technologies. China, for its part, has responded with its own export control law and a new Unreliable Entity List aimed at retaliating against foreign companies that comply with US sanctions.[30] This increasingly interventionist approach by both sides risks fragmenting global technology markets and undermining multilateral trade and investment frameworks.

70. The long-term implications of this technological rivalry are profound. On one hand, it may accelerate innovation through competition, incentivize strategic investment, and reshape global supply chains. On the other hand, it threatens to fragment the global economy, weaken international cooperation, and impose efficiency losses through duplication and reduced knowledge diffusion. For third countries, including developing countries (like Brazil) and developed countries (like the EU, Japan and the UK), the bifurcation of global technology presents a dilemma: whether to align with the US-led ecosystem or the Chinese model of development. The future will likely be characterized by selective decoupling, intensified geoeconomic maneuvering, and attempts to form techno-blocs among like-minded nations.

IV.D. Implications of the DMA for the US-China technology race

71. Focusing on the effects of the DMA, the fear in the US is that it may disadvantage US digital firms in their global competition with Chinese technology companies, including ByteDance, Tencent, Huawei, and Alibaba.

---

28 The Export Control Reform Act of 2018 (ECRA) is a pivotal U.S. federal law that modernizes and strengthens the country's export control system, particularly concerning dual-use technologies – items with both civilian and military applications. ECRA has significant international ramifications, particularly in the context of U.S.-China relations. The Act has been instrumental in imposing export controls on Chinese technology firms, such as Huawei, to prevent the transfer of sensitive technologies that could enhance China's military capabilities or surveillance apparatus. The Act is codified in Title 50, Chapter 58 of the U.S. Code.

29 The Foreign Investment Risk Review Modernization Act (FIRRMA) of 2018 significantly expanded the authority of the Committee on Foreign Investment in the United States (CFIUS) to review foreign investments for national security concerns. FIRRMA broadened the scope of transactions subject to CFIUS review, including certain non-controlling investments and real estate transactions near sensitive sites.

30 Ministry of Commerce of PRC, Provisions on List of Unreliable Entities (Ministry of Commerce Order No. 4 of 2020), September 19, 2020, https://m.mofcom.gov.cn/article/b/fwzl/202009/20200903002593.shtml.

The concern is the DMA may, intentionally or inadvertently, weaken US tech firms in global markets by imposing asymmetric compliance costs, undermining business models, limiting innovation incentives, while ignoring the competitive nature of many Chinese competitors.

72. Such a concern is grounded on the following observations. Firstly, while US tech firms operate globally and generate significant revenue in the EU, making them easy regulatory targets, Chinese firms often have limited exposure in the EU due to data sovereignty concerns, cultural barriers, or geopolitical frictions. As noted by Bradford (2023), the divergence among the three models presents challenges for global digital governance. The lack of a unified approach leads to regulatory fragmentation, complicating compliance for multinational companies, and potentially hindering innovation.

73. Secondly, the DMA may undermine the integrated business models of US tech firms, since it targets a number of practices that have been central to their success: (a) self-preferencing; (b) data aggregation across services; and (c) tight control over app distribution to ensure security, brand consistency, and revenue capture. By restricting these strategies, the DMA may reduce the economic viability of vertically integrated platforms, whose global strength is built on scalability, user data integration, and cross-subsidization between services. In contrast, Tencent and Alibaba, while integrated, operate primarily within domestic markets or regions with less regulatory friction. As such, they are less vulnerable to the compliance constraints imposed by the DMA.

74. The DMA also introduces positive externalities that could benefit US firms in the long run. By imposing constraints on dominant firms, it may lower entry barriers for smaller US competitors, fostering more dynamic innovation ecosystems. Moreover, firms that successfully adapt to the DMA may gain a first-mover advantage in complying with stringent data and platform standards, enhancing their global legitimacy. Still, these benefits are speculative and, in any event, the DMA does not operate in a geopolitical vacuum. While it reflects the EU's aspiration to be a norm-setting power in digital governance, this ambition may create strategic vulnerabilities for its allies. The resulting regulatory asymmetry thus carries significant strategic implications, as we discuss next.

V. From Regulatory Disputes to Trade Wars

75. Countries often use regulations strategically to protect their domestic industries through regulation – a phenomenon known as regulatory protectionism.[31] Governments may implement ostensibly legitimate regulations

---

31 Baldwin, Richard E. 2000: "Regulatory Protectionism, Developing Nations and a Two-Tier World Trade System." Brookings Trade Forum 2000 (1): 237–293. See also Fajgelbaum, Pablo D., Pinelopi K. Goldberg, Patrick J. Kennedy, and Amit K. Khandelwal. 2020: "The Return to Protectionism." Quarterly Journal of Economics 135 (1): 1–55.

that disproportionately burden foreign firms, thus acting as BTBs. As we have seen, these measures often escape scrutiny under traditional trade agreements. Furthermore, dispute settlement systems, including the World Trade Organization (WTO), do struggle to adjudicate complex regulatory issues where scientific evidence, risk perception, and societal preferences diverge. When formal dispute mechanisms fail to resolve these tensions satisfactorily, due to ambiguity in rules, slow processes, or non-compliance with rulings, countries may resort to unilateral retaliation. This is evident in cases like the US-EU beef hormone dispute,[32] where conflicting regulatory philosophies (precautionary principle vs. scientific risk assessment) led to persistent sanctions and counter-sanctions despite WTO rulings.

76. From a domestic politics perspective, trade wars rooted in regulatory disputes are often shaped by interest group pressures and political incentives. In democracies, political leaders may be particularly responsive to protectionist demands when regulations are perceived to harm employment or strategically important industries. The US-EU dispute over digital services taxes or the US-China technological war illustrate how domestic political narratives, such as national security, digital sovereignty, or "unfair" treatment, mobilize support for trade retaliation against regulatory measures.[33]

77. Trade wars stemming from regulatory disputes are not irrational or *ad hoc* phenomena; rather, they emerge from a complex interplay of strategic, institutional, and domestic political factors. Regulatory measures, though often rooted in legitimate public policy goals, can provoke international tensions when perceived as protectionist or politically motivated. As trade becomes increasingly entangled with regulatory, technological, and geopolitical concerns, the risk of conflict and retaliation grows, particularly in the absence of strong multilateral governance mechanisms.

V.A. The limits of trade agreements

78. Addressing BTBs through trade agreements is inherently complex due to their embeddedness in domestic regulatory autonomy, the difficulty in distinguishing protectionism from legitimate regulation, and the institutional limitations of trade negotiation frameworks.

---

32 The US–EU beef hormone dispute is a long-running trade conflict that began in the 1980s when the EU banned imports of beef treated with growth hormones, citing health concerns. The US challenged the ban at the WTO, arguing it was not based on scientific evidence and violated trade rules. The WTO ruled in favor of the US, but the EU maintained its ban, leading to authorized US retaliatory tariffs and a prolonged standoff that highlights tensions between trade liberalization and public health regulation. As of 2025, the dispute remains a partially unresolved trade conflict. Although a 2009 Memorandum of Understanding allowed for limited imports of hormone-free US beef into the EU, the fundamental disagreement over hormone-treated beef persists, reflecting ongoing tensions between differing regulatory approaches to food safety and trade.

33 Krugman, Paul R. 1986: Strategic Trade Policy and the New International Economics. MIT Press. See also Putnam, Robert D. 1988. "Diplomacy and Domestic Politics: The Logic of Two-Level Games." International Organization 42 (3): 427–460.

79. Firstly, dealing with BTBs through negotiation is complicated because of the "incompleteness" of trade agreements – that is, because their inability to specify in advance how all future contingencies will be handled. This incompleteness is rational, given the uncertainty about future preferences or political shocks. But as Giovanni Maggi shows in "Trade Agreements as Endogenously Incomplete Contracts" (2015),[34] with Henrik Horn and Robert W. Staiger, the fact that trade agreements often leave domestic regulatory measures under-specified, allows countries discretion in implementing BTBs, and creates space for post-agreement lobbying and regulatory drift.

80. Secondly, BTB barriers are intrinsically linked to a country's regulatory sovereignty. Governments implement domestic regulations to achieve a variety of public policy objectives, such as consumer protection, environmental conservation, and public health. As such, these measures are often rooted in social preferences and legal traditions, making them politically sensitive. Efforts to liberalize or harmonize such regulations through trade agreements are often met with resistance, particularly when they are perceived as infringing upon national sovereignty. This creates a tension between the objectives of market access and the preservation of domestic policy space. In turn, it complicates the process of rule-making in trade agreements, as governments are hesitant to commit to disciplines that could constrain their ability to regulate in the public interest.

81. Thirdly, identifying and addressing BTB barriers requires distinguishing between legitimate regulatory objectives and disguised protectionism. This is a fundamentally subjective task. Measures that appear trade-restrictive from one perspective may be essential for achieving legitimate non-trade goals from another. For example, food safety regulations that impose stringent testing requirements might be seen by foreign exporters as excessive and discriminatory, while domestic regulators may view them as necessary to protect public health. This ambiguity allows room for opportunistic behaviour by governments seeking to protect domestic industries while maintaining the appearance of regulatory legitimacy. The difficulty of establishing clear benchmarks for assessing the trade-restrictiveness of such measures limits the effectiveness of trade agreements in addressing them.

82. Finally, the negotiation and enforcement of disciplines on BTBs are institutionally constrained within trade agreements. Multilateral trade negotiations, such as those under the WTO, have historically focused on reducing border measures and have struggled to reach consensus on deeper regulatory issues. The WTO's Agreements on Technical Barriers to Trade (TBT)

---

34   Horn, Henrik, Giovanni Maggi, and Robert W. Staiger. 2010: "Trade Agreements as Endogenously Incomplete Contracts." American Economic Review 100 (1): 394–419. See also Bagwell, Kyle, and Robert W. Staiger. 2005. "Enforcing Trade Agreements in the Presence of Renegotiation." Review of Economic Studies 72 (4): 1007–1038.

and Sanitary and Phytosanitary Measures (SPS)[35] offer some guidance, but they rely on principles, such as non-discrimination and scientific justification, which are open to interpretation and difficult to enforce consistently. Moreover, enforcement mechanisms in trade agreements often lack the institutional capacity to scrutinize complex regulatory regimes and assess their compliance with international obligations, especially when such assessments require specialized technical or sector-specific knowledge.

83. As the WTO has struggled to adapt to regulatory and digital economy issues, and with its Appellate Body paralyzed, states increasingly bypass multilateral rules and act unilaterally. This vacuum enables tit-for-tat retaliation when regulatory disputes arise, especially in areas where global standards are lacking or contested (e.g., digital taxation, data governance, environmental labeling).

V.B. Retaliatory tariffs

84. In the absence of trade agreements, or to encourage others to negotiate more complete agreements, countries may, and sometimes do, rely on "retaliatory tariffs" – namely, a distinct class of trade measures imposed in response to, and to condition, the actions of trading partners. Unlike conventional tariffs intended to protect domestic industries or raise fiscal revenue, retaliatory tariffs serve a strategic function: they are meant to punish or deter unfavourable trade practices by other countries. They are often justified by invoking the principle of reciprocity or fairness. However, their use is embedded in the logic of strategic trade policy, which acknowledges the interdependence and asymmetry of global trade relationships. Countries with large trade deficits, structural surpluses, or unbalanced regulatory capacities may have differing incentives to engage in retaliation.[36]

85. Retaliatory tariffs are usually temporary, although they can have long-lasting economic and political consequences. They tend to target politically sensitive sectors – such as agriculture or manufacturing in "swing regions" – in order to maximize domestic pressure on foreign governments. Their effectiveness depends on institutional factors; e.g. whether (i) the domestic political system tolerates short-term economic pain, and (ii) the country has sufficient economic size or geopolitical leverage.

86. Countries may retaliate in unrelated unregulated sectors to exert pressure over regulatory disputes. This reflects a strategic logic where countries

---

35 The WTO Agreement on Technical Barriers to Trade (TBT) ensures that technical regulations, standards, and conformity assessment procedures do not create unnecessary obstacles to international trade. The WTO Agreement on Sanitary and Phytosanitary Measures (SPS) governs the use of food safety and animal/plant health regulations. It allows countries to set their own standards but requires that these measures be based on scientific evidence, not arbitrarily discriminatory, and not more trade-restrictive than necessary.

36 Miran, Stephen. 2024. "A User's Guide to Restructuring the Global Trading System." Hudson Bay Capital. Available at https://www.hudsonbaycapital.com/documents/FG/hudsonbay/research/638199_A_Users_Guide_to_Restructuring_the_Global_Trading_System.pdf.

exploit their bargaining leverage across sectors. For instance, if a country cannot retaliate directly against a regulatory measure due to legal or reputational constraints, it may impose tariffs on politically sensitive exports from the offending country to induce policy change. This dynamic increases the likelihood of trade wars escalating across sectors not initially implicated in the dispute, making regulatory conflicts a broader threat to stable trading relations. In contexts of great power competition, particularly the US–China rivalry, regulatory disputes are increasingly framed in geoeconomic terms. Countries weaponize interdependence by leveraging control over standards, data, and technology. Regulatory conflicts become proxies for strategic competition, and trade wars emerge as tools to defend national autonomy or reshape global value chains.[37]

V.C. The interplay between BTBs and retaliatory tariffs

87. Though distinct in form and function, BTBs and retaliatory tariffs are related. BTBs may prompt retaliation. In others, retaliation may take the form of new BTBs, especially where direct tariff retaliation is constrained by international law or economic feasibility. Conversely, retaliatory tariffs may provoke responses in the form of tighter domestic regulation or non-cooperation in regulatory harmonization efforts. The duality between overt, strategic retaliation and covert, institutional protectionism is at the heart of modern trade politics.

88. Pau Pujolas and Jack Rossbach (2024), in their paper "Trade Wars with Trade Deficits",[38] show that, under certain conditions, a country with a large trade deficit – such as the United States – may derive relative advantage in a trade war. This is the case if the deficit country can leverage its large domestic market to extract better terms from its trading partners. They also show that retaliatory tariffs are more effective when wielded by large economies against smaller, open ones, and less so in symmetric relationships.

89. While this model provides theoretical conditions under which trade wars may yield net gains for certain countries, the authors are careful to warn against simplistic policy applications of these results. Their model assumes optimal tariff design and retaliation, which is rarely achieved in practice; long-run political, diplomatic, and supply-chain costs of trade wars are not captured; and the strategic use of tariffs may be misused for domestic political purposes, leading to overreach or economic backlash.

90. These contributions also point to important interactions between BTBs and retaliatory tariffs. When tariffs are politically constrained, governments

---

37 Farrell, Henry, and Abraham L. Newman. 2019: "Weaponized Interdependence: How Global Economic Networks Shape State Coercion." International Security 44 (1): 42–79.

38 Pujolas, Pau and Rossbach, Jack. 2024: "Trade Wars with Trade Deficits." SSRN: https://ssrn.com/abstract=5008591.

may resort to BTBs to achieve the same protective goals. BTBs may provoke retaliatory tariffs if perceived as unfair or discriminatory. Conversely, tariff wars may prompt the deployment of new BTBs. Interest groups that benefit from BTBs or retaliatory tariffs may support political actors who favor economic nationalism, reinforcing these policies.

91. Indeed, as explained by Giovanni Maggi in recent work, these measures are often the product of political bargaining, influenced by interest groups, rent-seeking behavior, and institutional design. In the paper "Are Trade Agreements Good for You?" (2020),[39] co-authored with Ralph Ossa, Maggi shows that when producer interests are aligned across countries, lobbying can push for mutual deregulation, which benefits firms, but may harm overall social welfare. Instead, when producer interests conflict internationally, trade agreements may instead discipline lobbying pressures, resulting in more balanced regulations that improve consumer welfare.

92. In "Choked by Red Tape? The Political Economy of Wasteful Trade Barriers" (2022),[40] co-authored with Monika Mrázová and J. Peter Neary, Maggi focuses on non-tariff barriers that are intentionally inefficient, such as excessive documentation requirements, inspection delays, or duplicative testing. Termed Red-Tape Barriers (RTBs), these barriers are not designed to raise revenue or confer rents but to impose deadweight costs on foreign firms. RTBs emerge when traditional tariffs are constrained (e.g., by WTO rules or trade agreements). Politicians use RTBs as "second-best" instruments of protection, especially under conditions of political uncertainty or when seeking to appease domestic interest groups.

93. Therefore, modern trade frictions are endogenous, path-dependent, and institutionally embedded. They cannot be addressed purely through economic liberalization; they require deeper engagement with regulatory reform, governance, and political incentives.

VI. The Effect of Trade Wars in Technology Races

94. Trade wars emerge when governments perceive that unilateral or reciprocal protectionism can serve national objectives better than continued liberalization. Yet, the empirical evidence overwhelmingly shows that trade wars impose significant economic costs, particularly on consumers, exporters, and supply chain-intensive firms.

---

39 Maggi, Giovanni and Ossa, Ralph. 2020: "Are Trade Agreements Good for You?". NBER Working Paper No. w27252, SSRN: https://ssrn.com/abstract=3615488.

40 Maggi, Giovanni, Mrázová, Monika, Neary, and J. Peter. 2022: "Choked by Red Tape? The Political Economy of Wasteful Trade Barriers". International Economic Review 63(1): 161-188.

VI.A. Economic effects of trade wars

95. By raising tariffs, governments shield domestic firms from foreign competition. This can boost output, preserve employment, and create temporary pricing power. Tariffs can also serve as negotiation tools to secure intellectual property protection, reduce subsidies, or open foreign markets. For example, the US applied tariffs on China to elicit changes in forced technology transfers and state owned enterprise (SOE) practices. Moreover, trade wars can catalyze the diversification of supply chains, especially when national security or strategic resilience becomes a concern. For example, US efforts to reduce dependence on Chinese suppliers in critical sectors – such as semiconductors and rare earths – encouraged reshoring and nearshoring. These shifts are viewed by some policymakers as investments in long-term sovereignty and risk reduction.

96. However, tariffs raise the cost of imported goods, and those costs are largely passed on to consumers. Amiti, Redding, and Weinstein (2019)[41] estimate that the 2018 US tariffs cost the average American household roughly $414 annually through increased prices. Furthermore, when countries retaliate with counter-tariffs, key export sectors suffer. US soybean exports to China fell dramatically after Beijing imposed tariffs, triggering a wave of farm bankruptcies and $28 billion in federal aid. Since global production networks depend on the seamless movement of intermediate goods, tariffs create bottlenecks and force firms to adjust suppliers, often at higher costs. Finally, trade conflicts introduce uncertainty, discouraging capital expenditure. Financial markets responded to trade war escalations with spikes in volatility, and firm-level investment fell in sectors exposed to tariffs or retaliation.

97. In short, trade wars typically lead to prisoners' dilemma-type outcomes, where mutual retaliation reduces welfare for all involved. The more economically interconnected the world becomes, the higher the costs of such conflict.

VI.B. Winners and losers

98. Despite their overall cost, trade wars occur because they are rarely zero-sum propositions: consumers and many firms lose, but some firms and industries, located in some countries, may benefit.[42] How firms are affected depends less on the tariffs imposed and more on their structural capacity

---

41 Amiti, Mary, Stephen J. Redding, and David E. Weinstein. 2019: "The Impact of the 2018 Trade War on U.S. Prices and Welfare." Journal of Economic Perspectives 33 (4): 187–210.

42 Cen, Youjin, Aaron Flaaen, Justin Pierce, and Peter K. Schott. 2023. "Who Benefits from Trade Wars? Evidence from the US-China Trade Dispute." NBER Working Paper No. 31693. See also Chen, Ling, Wenhao Cui, and Zhi Wang. 2023. "The Impact of the 2018–2019 Trade War on Chinese Firms." NBER Working Paper No. 31508.

to absorb trade shocks. For example, during the 2018 trade US-China war, smaller, less capitalized firms, and those reliant on a single export market, experienced larger drops in profitability. In contrast, diversified firms with multiple export destinations and broad product lines were more resilient. More generally, firms with significant market power managed to pass on tariff-induced cost increases to consumers, maintaining or even growing profit margins during the trade war. In contrast, firms in competitive industries lacked this flexibility and suffered greater profit losses. Firms with alternative sourcing options or diversified customer bases fared better.

99. In addition, trade wars can yield tactical benefits, especially for governments seeking strategic or political leverage. Politicians often deploy trade wars to appeal to specific voter blocs or influential interest groups. Such decisions may make short-term electoral sense even if they generate long-term economic inefficiencies.[43] Finally, as we discussed in the previous sections, trade wars are as much about geopolitical signaling as they are about economic protection. Governments may use trade restrictions to protect technological sovereignty and national defense.

VI.C. Worldwide implications of US-China decoupling

100. The technological and economic rivalry between the US and China has escalated into a process of strategic decoupling, affecting trade, investment, supply chains, and digital infrastructure.[44] While the focus of this decoupling is bilateral, its repercussions are global. Liberal democratic states, particularly those in the EU, are under growing pressure to reconfigure their economic strategies, industrial policies, and regulatory frameworks in response to external polarization. These adjustments, if not carefully managed, may destabilize the internal equilibrium necessary for liberal democracy to function effectively.

101. Technological decoupling refers to the deliberate dismantling or reconfiguration of interdependent technological and digital ecosystems. This includes the restriction of cross-border investment, export controls on key technologies (e.g., semiconductors, AI, quantum computing), the imposition of divergent standards, and limits on academic and industrial collaboration.

102. There is no question that the US and China are engaged in technological decoupling. The US has led this effort through measures, such as the Entity List[45] (targeting Huawei, SMIC, and others), the CHIPS

---

43 Grossman, Gene M., and Elhanan Helpman. 1994: "Protection for Sale." *American Economic Review* 84 (4): 833–850.

44 Bown, Chad P. 2019: The 2018 US-China Trade Conflict After Forty Years of Special Protection. Peterson Institute for International Economics.

45 The Entity List is maintained by the U.S. Department of Commerce's Bureau of Industry and Security (BIS). It includes foreign individuals, organizations, and companies that are deemed to pose a significant risk to U.S. national security or foreign policy interests. Entities on this list are subject to specific license requirements for the export, re-export, and transfer (in-country) of certain items.

and Science Act,[46] and expanded export controls on advanced chip technologies. China, in turn, has accelerated its push for technological self-sufficiency under its "dual circulation" strategy and retaliatory export control laws. This trend is rooted not only in economic competition but also in a deepening geostrategic rivalry, as both states seek to limit technological dependence on the other while shaping global norms and standards in their favour.

103. For the EU and the rest of the world, this dynamic presents challenges and choices that impact economic structure, strategic alliances, and regulatory sovereignty. The first and most immediate implication is the disruption of global supply chains. Sectors such as semiconductors, automotive, telecommunications, and pharmaceuticals rely on inputs, markets, and capital from both countries. As US and Chinese firms reconfigure supply chains to avoid geopolitical risks – relocating manufacturing, sourcing alternative suppliers, or localizing R&D – third-country companies face cost increases, supply instability, and the need to realign strategic partnerships. For instance, the Netherlands-based ASML, a world leader in photolithography machines critical to advanced chip production, has been pressured by the US to restrict exports to Chinese customers. Similarly, German automakers – heavily invested in the Chinese market – must navigate increasingly sensitive dual-use technology regulations and geopolitical scrutiny. The UK's decision to exclude Huawei from its 5G network, influenced by US security concerns, has already disrupted telecom infrastructure planning and incurred transition costs. Investment flows are also affected. Chinese foreign direct investment (FDI) into e.g. the EU and UK has declined sharply, particularly in high-tech sectors, due to increased scrutiny under foreign investment regimes. The EU's FDI Screening Regulation (2019)[47] and the UK's National Security and Investment Act (2021)[48] reflect a growing concern about foreign acquisition of critical technology assets. While such controls aim to protect national security, they may also deter benign investment and innovation partnerships.

104. The second implication arises from the bifurcation of digital and technological standards. Both the US and China are promoting their own regulatory models globally – the former grounded in liberal-democratic norms of openness and privacy, and the latter based on state-led governance

---

[46] The CHIPS and Science Act, signed into law on August 9, 2022, is a significant U.S. federal statute aimed at bolstering the nation's semiconductor industry and advancing scientific research. The act authorizes approximately $280 billion in funding to enhance domestic semiconductor manufacturing, research, and development.

[47] The EU FDI Screening Regulation aims to enhance the Union's ability to identify and mitigate potential risks to security or public order arising from foreign direct investments into the EU. It establishes a framework for cooperation between Member States and the European Commission.

[48] The NSIA provides the UK government with powers to scrutinize and intervene in acquisitions that may pose risks to national security. It applies to both foreign and domestic investors.

and data sovereignty. As we have seen, the EU has attempted to chart a third course, asserting its regulatory autonomy through initiatives such as GDPR and the DMA. However, the US-China decoupling dynamic places pressure on this strategy. In a fragmented global landscape, where firms increasingly align with either the US or Chinese regulatory orbit, the EU, the UK and others, risk diminished leverage. US firms can and do resist EU regulatory impositions if they conflict with American standards or export control regimes, while Chinese firms may retreat from European markets entirely.

105. Technological decoupling also affects the flow of knowledge and innovation, particularly in university-industry collaboration and international research networks. The securitization of technology has led to greater scrutiny of academic partnerships, particularly with Chinese institutions. Governments have issued guidelines and funding restrictions aimed at preventing technology leakage and espionage in critical fields such as AI, quantum computing, and biotech. This poses challenges for open science and international academic cooperation. The increasing "weaponization" of research partnerships may limit scientific progress and reduce opportunities for cross-border collaboration, particularly with researchers from China and affiliated countries.

106. Not surprisingly, US and Chinese trading partners, including the EU, are debating the need for *strategic autonomy* and *technological self-sufficiency*. The EU has embraced this concept through its "Open Strategic Autonomy" framework,[49] which seeks to reduce dependence on external actors in key sectors – such as semiconductors, cloud computing, green technology, and pharmaceuticals. Flagship initiatives include the European Chips Act, which allocates over €40 billion to bolster semiconductor production, and the Gaia-X project, which aims to develop a sovereign European cloud infrastructure. The UK faces similar questions about its technological direction and global competitiveness. Post-Brexit industrial strategy emphasizes national resilience, research excellence, and alignment with likeminded partners (especially the U.S., Japan, and Australia) in emerging technologies. However, both the EU and UK struggle with scale, fragmentation, and funding constraints, which limit their ability to compete with the massive industrial policies of the U.S. (e.g., Inflation Reduction Act[50]) and China (e.g., Made in China 2025). However, strategic autonomy efforts

---

49 The European Union's Open Strategic Autonomy (OSA) framework is a comprehensive approach aimed at enhancing the EU's capacity to act independently in critical areas while maintaining openness to international cooperation. This strategy seeks to balance economic openness with the need to reduce strategic dependencies, particularly in sectors vital to the EU's security and economic resilience.

50 The Inflation Reduction Act of 2022 (IRA) is a landmark U.S. federal law enacted on August 16, 2022, aimed at addressing climate change, healthcare affordability, and tax reform. It represents the most significant climate investment in U.S. history and introduces measures to reduce the federal deficit.

raise difficult trade-offs. For example, measures seeking to localize production or subsidize national champions can generate inefficiencies, provoke trade tensions, and conflict with internal market rules or WTO obligations. For example, the European Commission has had to navigate tensions between state aid control and the need for industrial support in sensitive sectors.

107. The geopolitical dimension of technological decoupling forces third-parties, such as the EU and UK, to reassess their strategic alignment, particularly with the United States. The Biden administration has pursued closer coordination with allies on export controls, investment screening, and technology standards, culminating in initiatives such as the US–EU Trade and Technology Council (TTC)[51] and the AUKUS agreement.[52] Following President Trump's "Liberation Day", however, the EU and other traditional US allies have taken a more cautious and autonomous approach. This raises the risk of intra-Western fragmentation. Divergences over digital regulation, data transfers, and industrial subsidies reflect different normative and policy priorities.

108. For traditional US allies, the key challenge is to navigate this new landscape without becoming peripheral actors or passive rule-takers in a bifurcated world. This will require balancing openness with resilience, autonomy with alliance, and innovation with regulation. In doing so, both will need to invest not only in technological capabilities but also in the political and institutional capacity to shape the rules of the emerging digital order.

VI.D. Risks for the narrow corridor of growth

109. In a seminal book, The Narrow Corridor: States, Societies, and the Fate of Liberty,[53] Noble Prize Laureates Daron Acemoglu and James Robinson distinguish between two critical forces in any political order: the "Leviathan", representing the state's capacity to project authority, enforce laws, and provide public goods; and "Civil Society", understood as the collective capacity of non-state actors to organize, resist, and demand

---

[51] The US–EU Trade and Technology Council (TTC), launched in 2021, is a bilateral forum aimed at deepening transatlantic cooperation on trade, technology, and supply chains. It focuses on aligning regulatory approaches in areas such as artificial intelligence, semiconductors, digital governance, and sustainability, while addressing shared concerns like non-market practices and economic coercion. The TTC serves as a platform to promote democratic values in tech governance and strengthen economic ties amid growing global geopolitical competition.

[52] AUKUS is a trilateral security pact between Australia, the United Kingdom, and the United States, announced in 2021. Its primary goal is to enhance defense and technological cooperation in the Indo-Pacific, notably through support for Australia acquiring nuclear-powered submarines. Beyond defense, AUKUS also covers collaboration in cybersecurity, artificial intelligence, quantum technologies, and undersea capabilities, and is widely seen as a strategic counterbalance to China's growing influence in the region.

[53] Acemoglu, Daron, and James A. Robinson. 2019: The Narrow Corridor: States, Societies, and the Fate of Liberty. Penguin Press.

accountability. Too weak a state, and society collapses into anarchy or local despotism; too strong a state relative to society, and the result is authoritarianism. Liberty and sustainable development are only feasible in the "Narrow Corridor", a delicate equilibrium zone in which the state is strong enough to govern effectively but constrained enough not to become despotic.

110. The authors distinguish between four different types of Leviathan. The "Absent Leviathan", where the state is weak or non-existent. The result is a form of statelessness that leaves populations vulnerable to violence, predation, or warlordism. The "Paper Leviathan", where the state that appears strong on paper – possessing constitutions, ministries, and formal institutions – but lacks the practical capacity to implement its authority The state is unable to provide security, enforce contracts, or regulate the economy. Civil Society may be active, but without a functional state partner, liberty remains unattainable. The "Despotic Leviathan", when the state becomes over-powerful relative to society. In this configuration, the state dominates civil society, suppresses dissent, and centralizes control. Such regimes may be effective in extracting taxes or organizing public works, but they do so without meaningful constraints or public accountability. And, lastly, the "Shackled Leviathan", when both the state and society are strong and mutually constrain. This is the only configuration conducive to liberty and sustainable development. Historical examples include the United Kingdom post-Glorious Revolution, the United States post-Constitution, and contemporary liberal democracies with robust checks and balances.

111. Liberal democracies, like the EU, face three principal risks as a result of the current geopolitical tension between the US and China: (a) the rise of technocratic overreach, (b) democratic fragmentation, and (c) the erosion of societal trust. Each of these dynamics threatens to displace the EU from Acemoglu and Robinson's Narrow Corridor.

112. Firstly, in response to geopolitical pressure, states may centralize authority in executive or technocratic bodies to accelerate strategic reorientation. While this may enhance policy agility, it also risks bypassing democratic oversight, civil society engagement, and procedural legitimacy. The result is a drift toward a "Despotic Leviathan".

113. Secondly, and conversely, internal fragmentation – whether due to national sovereignty concerns, populist resistance, or lack of consensus – can lead to political stalemate. This impairs the state's ability to formulate coherent responses, producing regulatory deadlock and policy inaction. In the narrow corridor model, this is the risk of the "Absent Leviathan", where state weakness leads to democratic dysfunction.

114. Thirdly, technocratic policymaking, especially in domains like digital regulation, defense, and industrial policy, can erode public trust if citizens are

excluded from decision-making processes. This demobilization of society weakens the institutional feedback loop essential to balancing state power with societal contestation, thereby undermining the Narrow Corridor's stability.

115. One way or the other the US-China confrontation can drive other countries, especially liberal democracies, out of the Narrow Corridor, which entails the risk of descending into anarchy or drifting toward authoritarianism. Both dynamics carry significant political, economic, and social costs. When a state becomes either too weak or too strong relative to society, political freedoms, civil liberties, and democratic accountability deteriorate. The collapse of the Narrow Corridor undermines the impartial enforcement of laws, leading to arbitrary governance, politicized judiciary systems, and erosion of property rights. Exiting the Narrow Corridor also results in either state predation or market fragmentation, deterring investment, suppressing innovation, and causing economic inefficiencies. The breakdown of the corridor also increases social polarization and entrenches inequality, as state failure or repression disproportionately affects marginalized groups.

116. Falling out of the narrow corridor represents a systemic failure of the balance between coercion and consent, order and accountability. Whether through excessive centralization or structural weakness, societies that exit this corridor face a cascade of consequences: repression, corruption, stagnation, inequality, and conflict. The corridor is not a destination but a process; one that must be continually defended through civic participation, institutional reform, and the containment of both state overreach and societal decay.

117. In particular, we believe the risk of the EU falling out of the Narrow Corridor as a result of the current geopolitical tensions is significant enough to be concerned. What distinguishes the EU's Narrow Corridor is its "hybrid legitimacy": EU institutions possess enough autonomy to act decisively, particularly in market regulation and competition law, but are constrained by democratically elected national governments and an increasingly assertive European Parliament. Civil society, through NGOs, interest groups, and cross-border movements, helped to shape directives and challenge regulatory overreach. However, this equilibrium has always been precarious. The EU lacks a unified demos, and its political authority is frequently challenged by Eurosceptic movements, national vetoes, and institutional complexity. The question today is whether the pressures of geopolitical rivalry and internal fragmentation will tip the balance toward authoritarian centralization or disintegration.

118. The intensification of the US–China geopolitical rivalry places the European Union in a structurally ambiguous position. As a bloc of liberal democracies, the EU remains institutionally and ideologically aligned with the US. Yet it also seeks to preserve its strategic autonomy in the face

of shifting global power dynamics. This dual imperative has given rise to a series of tensions that challenge the EU's position within the Narrow Corridor. First, the EU's reliance on American digital infrastructure and security guarantees threatens its ability to act as a sovereign political entity. The dominance of US firms in cloud computing, digital advertising, and mobile operating systems has produced a form of technological dependency that constrains policy space. Attempts to regulate platform power reflect an effort to reassert control. Yet these measures often rely on enforcement through national authorities with uneven capacity, limiting their effectiveness. Second, economic exposure to China introduces a different form of vulnerability. European manufacturers, particularly in Germany, depend on Chinese markets, while Chinese investments in strategic infrastructure (e.g., ports, telecommunications) have triggered debates about national security and democratic values. The EU's delayed and fragmented response to the Belt and Road Initiative and 5G rollout revealed deep divisions among member states. Third, Russia's increasingly bellicose foreign policy – manifested through its 2022 invasion of Ukraine, hybrid warfare, cyberattacks, and energy coercion – poses a significant external shock that may destabilize this equilibrium.

119. These external dependencies risk pushing the EU toward a path outside the corridor. Under pressure from security and economic imperatives, the Union may centralize authority in Brussels without sufficient democratic mandate, or fracture along national lines as member states pursue divergent alignments. The EU risks becoming a "Despotic Leviathan" led by a few Member States, or an "Absent Leviathan", if resistance from member states produces institutional paralysis, pushing the EU toward the condition marked by ineffective governance and fragmentation. Either outcome would weaken the balance between state capacity and societal oversight that defines the corridor. The challenge is to build strategic autonomy without sacrificing contestability or pluralism. To remain within the narrow corridor under the mounting pressures of global competition and internal political fragmentation, the EU must engage in a dual strategy: strengthening state capacity to act decisively in key policy domains, while simultaneously reinforcing democratic legitimacy, civic participation, and institutional contestability.

120. The EU must find ways to manage its internal diversity without defaulting to lowest-common-denominator politics or rigid uniformity. Asymmetrical integration, allowing coalitions of willing member states to advance common policies, can enable progress without coercing reluctant members. For instance, deeper integration in defense procurement or cloud infrastructure could proceed through enhanced cooperation, while maintaining opt-out clauses for non-participants. Such flexibility reduces friction, preserves unity, and respects national democratic mandates. Rather than viewing geopolitical pressures as justification for technocratic acceleration

or national retrenchment, the EU should treat them as opportunities to deepen its democratic foundations and institutional adaptability. Only by pursuing liberty through legitimacy can the EU remain within the narrow corridor in a multi-polar world.

VII. The Three Body Problem

121. Companies around the world orbit around three competing regulatory powers – China, the EU, and the US. In the current geopolitical context, this is likely to be unsustainable. They face a "three body problem", like Cixin Liu's fictional planet Trisolaris.[54] The planet's orbits around three Suns and, therefore, its path is unpredictable. Civilization collapse is almost unavoidable. There is no solution to the problem; there is one Sun too many.

122. With this in mind, and given that China and the US are unlikely to change their respective courses, or coordinate their orbits, the question is whether the EU will have to abandon its regulatory autonomy and insert itself in one or another sphere of influence. Otherwise, its companies may crash under the weight of three Suns, while their Chinese and US counterparts choose to abandon its orbit anyways.

123. The EU does not seem to have many cards to play. Its ambition to regulate and lead in digital norms is constrained by its technological dependency. Europe lacks indigenous firms of comparable scale to the US or Chinese cloud computing, social media, and AI champions. This limits EU's leverage in enforcing compliance from foreign firms and exposes it to retaliatory pressures. Without technological and industrial weight, the EU is likely to become a "rule-taker", rather than a "rule-maker".

124. The EU has long sought to avoid binary alignment in global geopolitical rivalries, preferring a multi-lateral approach, rooted in the defense of international law, market openness, and regulatory standards. But this is untenable unless the EU manages to grow a high tech ecosystem of its own and achieve digital autonomy. While initiatives, such as the European Chips Act[55] and Gaia-X,[56] the Strategic Compass,[57] the Competitiveness

---

54 Liu, Cixin. 2014: The Three-Body Problem. Translated by Ken Liu. New York: Tor Books.

55 The European Chips Act aims to bolster Europe's competitiveness and resilience in semiconductor technologies and applications. It seeks to strengthen Europe's technological leadership in the field. The regulation entered into force on 21 September 2023.

56 Gaia-X is a European initiative that aims to develop a federated and secure data infrastructure, promoting data sovereignty and interoperability across Europe. It empowers businesses, individuals, and governments with secure, transparent, and sovereign control over data through a decentralized cloud infrastructure.

57 Adopted in March 2022, the Strategic Compass is the EU's comprehensive action plan to bolster its security and defense policy by 2030. It outlines a shared strategic vision among member states. The Compass aims to make the EU a more capable and autonomous security provider, complementing NATO and reinforcing the global rules-based order.

Compass,[58] and proposals for a EuroStack architecture,[59] represent early steps toward reducing external dependencies, the EU's capacity to compete in high-tech sectors remains uncertain and will require sustained investment, innovation, and public-private coordination. Even that may prove insufficient. Sustainable technological leadership depends on more than R&D spending or industrial policy; it requires cohesive, legitimate, and accountable governance structures. Technological competition is not merely a race of innovation, but a test of political resilience.

125. As both Washington and Beijing push for technological self-sufficiency and influence over global standards, the EU is under increasing pressure to define its own strategic posture.[60] The choice of sphere is not trivial. Whatever its choice it will involve significant political and economic cost. Hitherto, the ideological, military, and economic alignment of the EU and the US was undisputed. But populism is giving rise to tensions both within the EU and between the EU and the US. Meanwhile, the degree of economic interdependency between China and the EU has increased constantly over time.

126. Choosing between the US and Chinese spheres of influence is not a choice between different "civilizations",[61] rooted in deep-seated cultural and ideological differences. The clash is between economic governance models, differing not only in institutional design but also in the normative roles assigned to the market and the state. As Tooze (2020) argues,[62] the post-Bretton Woods order was not designed to accommodate a state-capitalist superpower within its liberal framework. The US-China technology war is a proxy for larger struggles over the rules of globalization. The friction arises not from irreconcilable cultural identities, but from deep disagreements about the role of the state in the economy, the legitimacy of industrial policy, and the architecture of global trade governance. In none of these regards the EU is perfectly aligned with either the US or China.

---

58   Announced in 2025, it provides a strategic framework to boost the EU's global competitiveness, focusing on innovation, decarbonization, and economic security. The Competitiveness Compass aims to make Europe a leader in future technologies, services, and clean products, while ensuring economic resilience and reducing dependencies on external markets.

59   EuroStack is a strategic initiative focused on achieving European digital sovereignty by developing a comprehensive, EU-led technology stack. It encompasses efforts to build and integrate European capabilities in areas such as cloud computing, semiconductors, artificial intelligence, and cybersecurity. The initiative seeks to reduce dependency on non-EU technologies and enhance the EU's competitiveness in the global digital economy.

60   For instance, companies like Siemens, Bosch, and Ericsson face increasing pressure to align with Western restrictions on Chinese technologies, even when such alignment threatens market access in China. Similarly, European universities and research institutions are being drawn into security-based screening of technological partnerships, especially in sensitive dual-use areas.

61   Huntington, S. P. (1996). The Clash of Civilizations and the Remaking of World Order. Simon & Schuster.

62   Tooze, A. 2020. Shutdown: How COVID Shook the World's Economy. Viking.

127. Dealing with the three body problem may require addressing the so-called Rodrik's "trilemma of the world economy" (Rodrik's trilemma).[63] This trilemma posits that economic globalization, national sovereignty, and democratic politics are mutually incompatible. A country can at most fully achieve two out of these three objectives, but not all three simultaneously. Attempts to push globalization beyond traditional trade into areas like regulation clash with national democratic choices. When countries try to achieve all three goals at once, tensions inevitably emerge. The implications of the trilemma are depressing: if a country maintains national democracy and national sovereignty, it must limit globalization to protect domestic preferences; if it pursues globalization and democracy, it must cede sovereignty to supranational institutions, leading toward global governance; if it seeks sovereignty and globalization, it must suppress democratic responsiveness, favouring technocratic or authoritarian decision-making. Europe wants to achieve the three goals. This may be impossible if it needs to choose a sphere of influence.

VIII. Concluding Remarks

128. The international trading order has entered a new phase. On the one hand, this new phase is one in which traditional border measures are no longer seen as the principal determinants of trade flows, but where domestic regulations and strategic responses shape the political economy of globalization. BTBs and retaliatory tariffs are no longer side-issues; they are the main arenas in which trade conflicts are fought and resolved. On the other hand, the new international trading (dis)order is characterized by the technological, economic, and military, rivalry between the US and China, that has evolved into a process of strategic decoupling, with far-reaching consequences for trade, investment flows, global supply chains, and digital infrastructure. These geopolitical changes places the EU, and many other middle-powers, especially in the West, difficult position: institutionally and ideologically aligned with the US, but economically dependent on Chinese imports and exports. In this new geopolitical context, asymmetries in digital regulation are interpreted as BTBs and trigger retaliation. As we discussed above, clear example is provided by the EU DMA. To mitigate these tensions the EU could consider dialing down DMA enforcement while reinvigorating *ex-post* enforcement, aligning its digital regulatory framework with the US. This pragmatic response would reflect the fact that there is no chance that the EU regulatory model becomes globally predominant, influencing international norms and practices. Yet, we doubt

---

63 Rodrik, D. 2011: The Globalization Paradox: Democracy and the Future of the World Economy. W. W. Norton & Company. See also Rodrik, Dani. 2018. Straight Talk on Trade: Ideas for a Sane World Economy. Princeton University Press.

such a change would make any difference. The Trump administration is also likely to object to the *ex-post* enforcement of EU competition law if that is seen to affect US firms disproportionately. As former Chinese Premier Deng Xiaoping famously said, "it does not matter if a cat is black or white so long as it catches mice".[64] The Trump administration will likely oppose the black cat of *ex-post* antitrust enforcement, as it does with the white cat of *ex-ante* regulation for as long as it targets (mainly) US mice.

129. **Conflicts of Interest Declaration.** This paper has not been commissioned or funded by any party, and no party had the right to review the paper prior to its circulation. Jorge Padilla and Vanessa Zhang are solely compensated by Compass Lexecon, an economic consultancy. As consultants, they have represented many companies over the years, on both the complainant and defendant side. They hold no paid or unpaid position as officer, director, or board member of non-profit organizations or profit-making entities whose policy positions, goals, or financial interests relate to the article. The list of their clients can be found at www.compasslexecon.com/professionals. This paper does not necessarily represent the views of Compass Lexecon or its clients.

---

[64] In 1962, amidst China's recovery from the Great Leap Forward, Deng Xiaoping invoked a Sichuan proverb: "It doesn't matter if a cat is black or white; if it catches mice, it's a good cat." He used this analogy to advocate for practical solutions over rigid adherence to ideological doctrines, emphasizing that policies should be judged by their outcomes rather than their alignment with a particular ideology.

Unrestricted Enforcement Risk on Information Exchange and Unilateral Disclosure under EU Competition Law?

CLÉMENCE CARLIER[*]
Counsel, Clifford Chance, Paris

JOHANNES LÜER
Senior Associate, Clifford Chance, Düsseldorf

Abstract

EU Competition Law is tightening the screws on information disclosure. The Portuguese Banks judgment confirms that even a single exchange of "strategic information" may constitute a restriction by object, creating a potentially distinct framework from the Horizontal Guidelines' category of "competitively sensitive information". The resulting situation blurs the object/effects divide and escalates enforcement risks for routine communications. After tracing the doctrinal shift, this chapter analyses the narrow residual scope of Article 101(3) TFEU and shows why efficiency justifications rarely survive when unilateral disclosures concern future pricing. Three examples, product advertising, job-market transparency and capital-market reporting, illustrate the insuitability of the relevant guidance and the ensuing compliance dilemma with a potential for over-deterrence. It finally proposes reliable guidance and safe-harbours to urgently restore legal certainty.

---

[*] Clémence Carlier is a counsel in Clifford Chance's antitrust team in Paris/France, Johannes Lüer is a Senior Associate in that team in Düsseldorf/Germany. The views expressed in this article are those of the authors and do not necessarily reflect the views of their respective firms, clients, or any affiliated entities. This article is intended for informational purposes only and does not constitute legal advice.

Unrestricted Enforcement Risk on Information Exchange and Unilateral Disclosure under EU Competition Law

I. Introduction

1. A spectre is haunting the halls of Europe's legal departments: The end of public communications in business is near and undertakings can no longer publicly inform their customers, candidates, and capital markets. Disclosure of information considered long innocuous may potentially qualify as an infringement of EU Competition Law "by object", facing the ire of the European Commission ("Commission") or other arbiters of the level playing field. The practical implications of the recent judgment of the European Court of Justice ("ECJ", together with the General Court ("GC") the "European Courts") in the case *Portuguese Banks*[1] are potentially far reaching and – compounded with other developments in EU Competition Law, e.g. stronger focus on labour markets[2] or scrutiny of unilateral disclosure[3] – create significant uncertainty for businesses: What can businesses safely communicate to customers, candidates and capital markets?

2. This contribution wants to take stock of the current status of the application of EU Competition Law on information exchange and outline key concerns regarding legal certainty considering the recent developments. While the substantive case law focuses on multilateral or reciprocal information exchange, this analysis aims to identify shortfalls in the guidance on the unilateral disclosure of information aimed at the broader public.

3. After revisiting the legal framework based on Article 101(1) of the Treaty on the Functioning of the European Union ("TFEU") and the European Courts' respective case law (II.), the criteria established by the ECJ in *Portuguese Banks* are examined (III.), the Commission's current enforcement mentioned (IV.) before it is shown that the current legal approach fails to provide for legal certainty in practice (V.), leading to a conclusion with concrete asks to the Commission.

II. Legal Framework

A. Basics of Article 101(1) TFEU

4. At the core of EU Competition Law lies Article 101(1) TFEU, which prohibits agreements between undertakings, decisions by associations of undertakings, and concerted practices which may affect trade between

---

[1] ECJ, judgment of 29 July 2024, case C-298/22, *Banco BPN/BIC Português SA et al.*, ECLI:EU:C:2024:638, herein after *Portuguese Banks*.

[2] Commission, press release of 2 June 2025, IP/25/1356.

[3] GC, judgment of 9 July 2025, case T-188/24, *Michelin v. Commission*, ECLI:EU:T:2025:686, herein after *Michelin*.

Member States, and which have as their object or effect the prevention, restriction, or distortion of competition within the internal market.

5. As part of transnational treaties, changes to this provision are very rare[4] and EU Competition Law, thus, develops through its application and interpretation by the Commission and the European Courts. This leads to a legal framework that is defined by a few case-specific decisions of the European Courts as markers and the Commission's soft law instead of coherent and contemporary legislative activity attempting to provide comprehensive guidance.[5] While this *modus operandi* clearly enables the application of the general principles of Article 101 TFEU in light of changing market conditions and technological developments, and often times the Commission has been pioneering enforcement, the most striking development is the approach to information sharing under EU Competition Law.

6. A practice infringes Article 101 TFEU only if two cumulative conditions are met: (i) the conduct constitutes an agreement or a concerted practice, and (ii) it has either an anti-competitive object or effect. Traditionally, these two conditions must be examined separately and in sequence.

7. An agreement or concerted practice in principle would require some form of meeting of minds or forming of a common understanding. The application of Article 101 TFEU by the European Courts resolves the need for such bilateral aspects by relying on the axiom that it can be expected that a reasonable entrepreneur makes use of all available information and, consequently, would act on sensitive information available to him, and deeming information exchange a form of concerted practice, rendering any bilateral requirements *prima facie* obsolete.[6]

8. In the context of information exchange, the assessment under Article 101(1) TFEU thus uses partially distinct criteria in theory:

9. First, it requires demonstrating the confidential and strategic nature of the exchanged information, i.e., that the information is inherently capable, when exchanged, of reducing strategic uncertainty in the market;

10. Second, it involves showing that the information exchange is likely, considering the context in which it was exchanged, to have facilitated

---

[4] In fact, any changes to the predecessor clauses since the initial Art. 85(1) of the EEC Treaty in 1957 were updating the terminology from "common market" to "internal market".

[5] While competition law generally can derive a lot from lean wording and statues in many jurisdictions are based on a few, often ancient provisions, it must be noted that the textual stability of Art. 101(1) TFEU combined with the harmonization of the competition laws of the EU Member States to EU Competition Law has led to no material legislative activity in this field in the EU and its Member States.

[6] Judgments of the GC of 10 November 2017, *ICAP and Others* v *Commission*, T-180/15, EU:T:2017:795, paragraph 57; judgment of the ECJ of 4 June 2009, *T-Mobile Netherlands and Others*, C-8/08, EU:C:2009:343, paragraph 51; judgment of 19 March 2015, *Dole Food and Dole Fresh Fruit Europe* v *Commission*, C-286/13 P, EU:C:2015:184, paragraph 127, and judgment of 8 July 1999, *Hüls v Commission*, C-199/92 P, EU:C:1999:358, paragraphs 161-163.

11. coordination among competitors in practice. This includes the alignment of commercial strategies, which in turn requires the establishment of a sufficiently credible counterfactual scenario against which to assess the effects.

11. If a restriction is blatant, the competition authorities may – but in relation to information exchange never had until recently – considered that the conduct is "by object" likely to negatively impede competition.

B. The specific nature of information exchange

12. Traditionally, information exchanges may arise in various contexts:
    - As part of broader horizontal cooperation agreements (e.g., joint production), where the exchange of cost or pricing data is incidental;
    - As mechanisms that support or enforce a separate anti-competitive agreement.
    - As autonomous arrangements where the exchange of information is the primary economic function;

13. In the first case, the exchange of information will be assessed together with the underlying cooperation agreement.[7] If this agreement is found licit from a competition point of view, so will the ancillary information exchange, if it remains proportionate and necessary.[8]

14. In the second case, the exchange is treated as an accessory to the underlying infringement and is assessed accordingly. The Commission states that such exchanges will normally be considered as agreements and sanctioned as such. Indeed, that information exchanges which facilitate an anti-competitive agreement – regardless of the nature of the information – constitute an accessory to the infringement under Article 101(1) TFEU.

15. Standalone information exchange (third case) forms a distinct category and requires specific applicable framework.

16. That is because, unlike standard clear-cut anticompetitive agreements (such as price-fixing agreements), which inherently restrict competition, information exchanges exhibit considerable diversity in both form (unilateral, bilateral, multilateral) and effect (they may produce both anti-competitive and pro-competitive effects). This duality necessitates a case-by-case assessment of whether a given exchange amounts to concerted practices likely to restrict competition.

17. This is noted by the European Commission in its guidelines to assess this type of conduct, in which it recognizes, as a starting point of this assessment,

---

[7] *Commission*, Guidelines on the applicability of Article 101 of the Treaty on the Functioning of the European Union to horizontal co-operation agreements (2023/C 259/1) ("**Horizontal Guidelines**"), paragraph 369 *et seq.*

[8] *Ibid.*

that information exchanges are a common feature of competitive markets and can generate various types of efficiency gains.[9] These include:
- Resolving information asymmetries, thereby improving market efficiency;
- Enhancing internal efficiency through the comparison of best practices;
- Reducing inventory costs and enabling faster delivery of perishable goods;
- Responding more effectively to fluctuating demand;
- Reducing consumer search costs and improving product choice.[10]

18. Given the ambivalent nature of information exchanges, their treatment European and national competition authorities must naturally reflect this complexity.

19. For a market to function efficiently, a certain degree of transparency regarding current market conditions is necessary. At the same time, however, it is essential that market participants remain uncertain about the future conduct of their competitors. This balance between transparency and uncertainty is fundamental to preserving the competitive process. And the line can potentially be very thin.

20. As a result, an information exchange is never condemned per se, in the sense of U.S. antitrust law. Enforcers are required to conduct an *in concreto* assessment, taking into account the specific characteristics of each practice, including the nature of the information exchanged and the context in which the exchange occurred. This approach aims at ensures that enforcement remains proportionate and grounded in economic and legal reality.

21. As a direct consequence of this casuistic approach, the assessment of information exchanges remains a sensitive and difficult question, and sometimes difficult to predict. However, enforcers are increasingly scrutinizing information exchanges not only as ancillary to other anticompetitive practices but also as standalone infringements. The enforcement of these conducts is not getting any more lenient over time, as illustrated by the two recent instances discussed further below.

C. Overview of the notion of restriction of competition by object under EU law

22. Under EU Competition Law, the notion of a restriction of competition "by object" is designed to facilitate the identification and prosecution of

---

9   Horizontal Guidelines, paragraph 373.
10 *Ibid.*

practices that are so likely to harm competition that it is unnecessary to demonstrate their actual effects. Thus, in such cases, the burden of proof on enforcers is reduced: restrictions "by object" are presumed to harm the functioning of the market whereas other restrictions require proof of actual or potential effects. This presumption is grounded in both the gravity of the restriction and the accumulated knowledge of its likely consequences. When a high degree of inherent harmfulness is established, the authority may dispense with proving effects, provided that the practice falls within a category of conduct consistently found to be anti-competitive. This category includes classic cartel behaviour such as price fixing, market sharing, and output limitation.

23. However, unlike the per se rule in U.S. antitrust law, the EU concept of "by object" does not allow for automatic condemnation. It is not a mechanical classification but one that must be grounded in legal and economic reasoning.

24. This concept must be interpreted strictly and applies only to conduct whose harmfulness is manifest, particularly in light of established experience.[11] Certain forms of coordination between undertakings may, by their very nature, be regarded as harmful to the proper functioning of normal competition.[12] Thus, it is established that certain collusive behaviours, such as horizontal price-fixing cartels, are so likely to have negative effects that it is unnecessary to demonstrate actual effects on the market.[13]

25. In practice, the classification of a restriction "by object" rests on three key criteria:[14]

- The content of the agreement or practice;

- The objectives pursued by the parties, with intent playing a potentially important though not decisive role; and

- The legal and economic context in which the conduct occurs, including the nature of the goods or services affected, and the real conditions of the functioning and structure of the market or markets in question[15].

---

[11] Judgment of the ECJ of 30 January 2020, *Generics (UK) Ltd and Others*, C-307/18, EU:C:2020:52, paragraph 67, of 26 November 2015, *Maxima Latvija*, C-345/14, EU:C:2015:784, paragraph 20, and of 23 January 2018, *F. Hoffmann-La Roche and Others*, C-179/16, EU:C:2018:25, paragraphs 78 and 79.

[12] Judgment of the ECJ of 11 September 2014, *Cartes Bancaires v Commission*, C-67/13 P, EU:C:2014:2204, paragraph 50.

[13] Judgment of the ECJ of 11 September 2014, *Cartes Bancaires v Commission*, C-67/13 P, EU:C:2014:2204, paragraph 51.

[14] Horizontal Guidelines, paragraph 26.

[15] Judgment of the ECJ of 11 September 2014, *CB v Commission*, C-67/13 P, EU:C:2014:2204, paragraph 53; of 19 March 2015, *Dole Food and Dole Fresh Fruit Europe v Commission*, C-286/13 P, EU:C:2015:184, paragraph 117, and of 2 April 2020, *Budapest Bank and Others*, C-228/18, EU:C:2020:265, paragraph 51.

D. Scope for Efficiencies under Article 101(3) TFEU

26. Even when an information exchange is prima facie caught by Article 101(1) TFEU, undertakings may, in theory (and irrespective of whether found to by a "by object" infringement or not), seek exemption under Article 101(3) TFEU. The provision requires a cumulative four-step test: (i) demonstrable efficiency gains; (ii) a fair share of those gains for consumers; (iii) indispensability of the restriction; and (iv) no elimination of competition in a substantial part of the market.

27. Such justification faces an uphill battle. Positive consumer welfare effects (e.g. lower search costs, improved capital-market transparency) are hard to quantify and to weigh against the alleged anti-competitive effect. The Commission's decisional practice confirms that future-pricing revelations are often unlikely to pass the indispensability test, as similar transparency could potentially be achieved through less competition-sensitive channels.

28. In sum, the scope of Article 101(3) TFEU is narrow but non-negligible: it offers no blanket safe harbour for information exchanges, yet it remains a residual defence for transparency that demonstrably enhances market performance. In practice, relying on Article 101(3) TFEU, however, faces high hurdles, as the burden of proof shifts to the undertaking and the economic outcome may be difficult to sufficiently show.

III. Portuguese Banks: Key Takeaways and Analytical Reflections on "by Object" Restrictions Applied to Information Exchange

29. The ECJ's ruling in *Portuguese Banks* marks a significant development in the jurisprudence on information exchanges under Article 101(1) TFEU.

A. Facts

30. The case arose from a decision by the Portuguese Competition Authority, which sanctioned fourteen banks for exchanging information over a ten-year period concerning credit spreads, risk variables, and individual production data.

31. The Portuguese competition authority treated these exchanges as inherently anticompetitive, even in the absence of explicit collusion. The referring court sought clarification on whether a standalone exchange of strategic and confidential information between competitors may, in itself, constitute a restriction of competition "by object" – without the need to prove any accompanying agreement on prices or market conduct. This was necessary, as there was no evidence of an accompanying anti-competitive agreement or anti-competitive effects.

B. Judgment

32. The ECJ's methodology focuses on the three aforementioned cumulative criteria: the content of the exchange, the legal and economic context, and the objectives pursued. Notably, the ECJ states (and thus closes an ongoing debate) that the absence of precedent does not preclude a finding of a restriction by object.[16]

33. The ECJ provided further guidance on what constitutes "strategic" information. Future pricing intentions, such as anticipated changes in credit spreads, are inherently strategic. However, even current or past data may be deemed strategic if it enables participants to infer competitors' future conduct with sufficient precision.[17] Confidentiality is also essential: information not already known to all market participants is more likely to be considered problematic.

34. The ECJ found that the exchange of future credit spread intentions and risk variables met these criteria.[18] While the exchange of disaggregated production data was more ambiguous, the ECJ held that its combination with other strategic data could still contribute to a restriction by object.[19]

35. The ECJ clarified that the frequency of exchanges is not determinative: even infrequent or one-off exchanges may suffice to establish a restriction by object if they reduce uncertainty and align market behaviour.[20] Moreover, the ECJ emphasized that even a single exchange of strategic information may suffice, provided it is capable of reducing strategic uncertainty and aligning competitors' conduct in the market.[21]

36. Overall, the ECJ's reasoning reflects a stricter interpretation of Article 101(1) TFEU, where the nature and context of the information exchanged rather than its frequency or explicit linkage to pricing agreements can suffice to establish liability.

C. Analysis

37. The ECJ upheld its approach, emphasizing that such "autonomous" or standalone exchanges can distort the competitive process by reducing uncertainty and facilitating tacit coordination among competitors.

38. In recent years, the scope of what may constitute a "by object" restriction has expanded, particularly in the context of information exchanges and the Horizontal Guidelines already pre-shadowed that unilateral

---

16 *Portuguese Banks*, paragraph 41.
17 *Portuguese Banks*, paragraph 62 *et seqq.*
18 *Portuguese Banks*, paragraph 71.
19 *Portuguese Banks*, paragraph 73 *et seqq.*
20 *Portuguese Banks*, paragraph 85.
21 *Ibid.*

39. standalone information exchange could be seen as a by-object restriction by the Commission. Indeed, the ECJ confirmed in *Portuguese Banks* that a standalone exchange of information – i.e., one not ancillary to a broader anti-competitive agreement – may constitute a restriction of competition by object. This represents a notable extension of the "by object" category, traditionally reserved for manifestly harmful practices such as price-fixing or market sharing.

40. The judgment underscores the importance of market structure in assessing the anti-competitive potential of information exchanges. In oligopolistic markets with high entry barriers, even limited exchanges may facilitate tacit coordination. The ECJ rejected arguments that the exchanges were justified by regulatory transparency obligations, noting that the conduct went beyond what was legally required.

41. While the judgment provides a structured framework for assessing information exchanges, it also introduces a degree of legal uncertainty. Indeed, the ECJ's emphasis on case-by-case analysis and its reluctance to define clear thresholds for strategic information may complicate compliance efforts. Nevertheless, the judgment affirms that information exchanges – particularly those involving future pricing intentions – must be approached with caution, especially in concentrated markets. This is reinforced by the fact that the judgment lowers the threshold for enforcement, as there is no need to prove actual effects and no safe harbour for isolated or infrequent exchanges.

42. It must be noted that the ECJ in *Portuguese Banks* focused on "strategic information" – i.e. forward-looking, individual data capable of aligning rivals' future conduct, the Horizontal Guidelines and EU Competition Law generally relies on the broader notion of "competitively sensitive information". The latter covers any non-public parameter that is liable to influence a competitor's strategy, even if historical or aggregated. Thus, every "strategic" datum is competitively sensitive, but not vice-versa. Arguably, this limits the scope of the judgment and does not confirm the approach taken in the Horizontal Guidelines *per se*, but this differentiation will in practice not provide the necessary comfort, as in the relevant areas it will not be practicably possible to reliably discern "strategic" from "non-strategic" competitively sensitive information and exclude the "strategic" part.

IV. A New Frontier: Unilateral Disclosure In The Ongoing Michelin investigation

43. The Commission's ongoing investigation into Michelin's public disclosures during earnings calls raises important questions about the boundaries of lawful transparency and unlawful coordination. While the investigation

remains ongoing and the analysis is still preliminary, the Commission's submissions to the GC provides insights into the Commission's approach which included the analysis of hundreds of thousands of earnings calls for certain "bigrams" followed by a qualitative analysis of the sectors with outstanding results in the "bigram" analysis.[22]

44. Unlike the facts in *Portuguese Banks*, the Commission's theory of harm in *Michelin* does not hinge on a covert exchange of data but on the possibility that highly granular, forward-looking statements broadcast during public earnings calls functioned as price signals in an oligopolistic tyre market. The disclosures were formally addressed to investors and largely driven by securities-law transparency duties; nevertheless, the Commission takes the view that they simultaneously enabled rivals to recalibrate their near-term pricing policies with markedly reduced uncertainty. In other words, Michelin exemplifies a public-signalling scenario in which no explicit meeting of minds is required: concerted practice may arise if each firm can confidently anticipate that competitors will pick up and act upon the signal. The case therefore occupies the same grey zone identified in *Portuguese Banks* – blurring the line between legitimate transparency and unlawful coordination – even though the communication channel (earnings call versus bilateral exchange) is fundamentally different.

45. At the heart of the case is the concept of price signalling where competitors do not communicate directly or through a hub-and-spoke arrangement but nonetheless manage to align their strategies through indirect or public channels. Signalling has been a buzzword for antitrust compliance, but actual cases are rare, and the difficulty is providing a concerted practice that at the same time is not already infringing EU Competition Law based on an agreement or joint understanding.

46. In this context, the Commission is exploring whether Michelin's investor communications, ostensibly made in compliance with French financial disclosure obligations, may have gone beyond what was strictly necessary, and instead served to signal future pricing intentions to competitors.

47. The case illustrates the more nebulous notion of a concerted practice, where mutual awareness of each other's conduct – without direct contact – may suffice to establish coordination.

48. The *Michelin* judgment solely addressed whether the Commission's analysis of earnings calls provided sufficient initial reasonable suspicion to warrant an unannounced inspection. The key question will be whether there must be some form of established joint understanding or even agreement in the background to form the basis for effective

---

22 *Michelin*, paragraphs 95 *et seqq*.

signalling via earnings calls. There are indications that investigated parties may be cooperating with the Commission,[23] but that does not necessarily mean that there needs to be an implicit or explicit joint understanding or even agreement on the meaning of the statements made on the earnings calls.

49. As the facts of the investigation emerged, a long shadow was cast over any form of public disclosure: While the investigation remains ongoing, more clarity may still be years out, but the message is that unilateral public disclosure is in the Commission's focus.

V. Practical Implications

50. While the factual background in *Portuguese Banks* was specific and the ECJ's reasoning carefully grounded, the broader implications of the judgment are not easily confined. In practice, businesses face a heightened risk of legal uncertainty when engaging in any form of unilateral disclosure even if directed at consumers, job seekers, or capital markets. The *Michelin* investigation only adds to this uncertainty, without (yet) offering legal clarity.

51. In the following, three practical areas of business communication are considered to illustrate how the current framework fails to offer adequate guidance and may even create chilling effects that go beyond what is justified in competition terms.

A. Product advertising: a necessary practice at the edge of compliance

52. Advertising, especially in B2C markets, is inherently price-driven. It is hard to imagine effective competition without some public price communication to consumers. And yet, when applying the criteria from the 2023 Horizontal Guidelines for assessing information exchange, the boundaries of lawful advertising remain vague.

53. The Horizontal Guidelines emphasize factors such as market characteristics (e.g., concentration, transparency) and whether the exchange qualifies as a "by object" restriction. However, even basic promotional messages might formally tick the boxes:
    - Prices are disclosed, often including the beginning and the end of a special offer;
    - Information is public but not universally known in real-time – and a few days (if not hours) may suffice for matching the pricing strategy;

---

23 *Hirst/Crofts*: "Goodyear said to be among leniency applicants in EU tire cartel probe", 8 July 2025, https://content.mlex.com/#/content/1666759/goodyear-said-to-be-among-leniency-applicants-in-eu-tire-cartel-probe.

- Market structures in consumer goods often show oligopolistic features.

54. Despite this, advertising has never been considered problematic *per se*, nor should it be.

55. The fundamental flaw lies in the mismatch between theoretical criteria and market reality: public advertising does not entail a genuine meeting of minds, but does it reduce strategic uncertainty among competitors in a way that facilitates tacit coordination?

56. Indeed, firms may react to competitor advertising, but potentially the lack of mutual assurance or feedback mechanism excludes a concerted practice. On the other hand, even if the consequential application of the framework would lead to the conclusion that price advertising is fostering coordination, the alternative of customers having to find out non-public prices individually would be even more concerning (and invite abuse). The Commission's criteria are, in this context, ill-suited to draw a reliable line, creating compliance challenges where none should exist.

B. Job advertising and labour market signalling: between compliance and contradiction

57. Labour markets are increasingly under competition law scrutiny. At the same time, public job postings often include salary ranges or non-monetary benefits, sometimes due to statutory obligations (e.g., equal pay laws) or to compete for talent.

58. Transposing the *Portuguese Banks* logic or the Commission's framework to this domain raises further concerns:
    - Can the disclosure of salaries be seen as "strategic" information?
    - Is there an obligation to withhold information that is otherwise required by law or market practice?

59. The Horizontal Guidelines remain silent on the interaction between competition law and mandatory transparency obligations, merely stating that such requirements must not be used to infringe Article 101(1) TFEU and disclosure should not go beyond what is necessary.[24] But this caveat is unhelpful for companies navigating overlapping regulatory demands.

60. The result is a regulatory vacuum where firms are left guessing whether lawful and sometimes mandatory disclosures might retroactively be seen as "facilitating coordination."

61. Especially in tight labour markets, withholding such information would harm applicants and contradict public policy goals – highlighting once more the need for clarity and safe harbours.

---

24 Horizontal Guidelines, paragraph 372.

C. Capital market disclosures: transparency in tension with enforcement

62. Financial markets impose their own set of disclosure requirements, particularly under frameworks like IFRS or national securities law. These disclosures often include detailed forward-looking statements, cost structures, and investment intentions, all of which could, under the logic of *Portuguese Banks*, be deemed "strategic information."

63. Yet capital markets function on deep transparency. Market participants, investors, and regulators rely on timely and comprehensive information flows.

64. To suggest that such disclosures risk breaching Article 101 TFEU is to pit competition law against the very conditions of efficient capital markets.

65. So far, the Commission has not addressed this tension. The current enforcement posture in *Michelin*, however, suggests that even lawful disclosures may become problematic if they coincide with competitors' reactions – a standard that is not only vague but also economically questionable.

66. Such ambiguity is particularly problematic in concentrated sectors where firms are already cautious. Overdeterrence might lead to underreporting or reduced granularity, harming market integrity and investor confidence.

D. The need for regulatory coordination and clear safe harbours

67. In each of the areas discussed above, the criteria developed in case law and guidelines fail to provide a workable yardstick. The concept of strategic information is too elastic, and the absence of clear exemptions for disclosures required or encouraged under other legal regimes is a regulatory blind spot.

68. As shown particularly under V.A. above, the formal criteria may lead to unwanted results and – particularly concerning in light of the Commission's efforts to ease bureaucratic burden – the the Horizontal Guidelines and the recent case-law may require detailed legal and economic analysis, which will not be available to small- and medium-sized enterprises, not only in terms of costs but also of feasibility of such sophisticated analysis. In this context it must be stressed that putting essential business activities under general suspicion and referring entities to the narrow route to justification appears highly detrimental to the pro-competitive effects of these activities, as the shifted burden of proof under Article 101(3) TFEU gives undertakings a late start.

69. Therefore, the Commission should:
    - Clarify the limits of unilateral disclosure liability under Article 101(1) TFEU;

- Provide safe harbours for standard business activities such as advertising, HR-related transparency, and financial market disclosures, at least where these are (i) required by law, (ii) consistent with legitimate market expectations, or (iii) clearly non-collusive in context;
- Explicitly recognize the importance of regulatory comity, ensuring that competition enforcement does not undermine other public policy goals.

VI. Conclusion

70. The *Portuguese Banks* judgment and the ongoing *Michelin* investigation mark consequent developments in the enforcement of EU Competition Law. Businesses must adapt to a stricter, more nuanced regime where even isolated disclosures may trigger liability under EU Competition Law. The balance between transparency and competition remains delicate and increasingly tilted toward caution.

71. The guidance provided by the Commission, carefully drafted to avoid any self-restriction, combined with the actual enforcement initiative in practice leads to a tangible risk of over-deterrence which may chill legitimate business communication, including to the detriment of consumers. Given the disparate current guidance and the risks associated with arguing a justification under Article 101(3) TFEU, the Commission is called upon to clarify how it intends to apply these new developments and provide for business-compatible safe harbours ensuring, enabling and encouraging pro-competitive transparency.

72. For practitioners, these developments unfortunately do not provide for concrete guidance besides the confirmation that information disclosure can be a grave competition law infringement. In terms of risk management, this unfortunately provides only for further grey areas that cannot be addressed with clear checklists, so the compliance toolbox for the time being must rely on training of public-facing teams, individual guidance on publications and documentation of justification considerations.

Re-Emergence of Entrenchment of Market Power in Merger Controls

YU YAN[*]
Partner, RBB Economics

Abstract

The author had the privilege collaborating with Professor Huang over the years. It is a profound honour to contribute to this distinguished edition of the Concurrences Book Series, commemorating Professor Huang Yong's exceptional contributions to the advancement of China's Anti-Monopoly Law (AML). Professor Huang's legacy is extensive, encompassing the formulation of the initial AML legislation, shaping its enforcement, and guiding recent reforms. This paper examines the growing emphasis on the entrenchment of market power within merger assessments, a trend that has gained prominence in recent years amid increased intervention in merger controls across various jurisdictions. This scrutiny is particularly pronounced in the domains of digital platforms and innovative industries. The paper reflects the application of the market power entrenchment concept in several recent contentious transactions: the acquisition of eTraveli by Booking.com (EU), the acquisition of GRAIL by Illumina (EU and US), and the merger between HUYA and DouYu (China). These cases illustrate a tendency among competition authorities to circumvent traditional analytical frameworks, reduce the evidentiary burden for prohibiting mergers, or even disregard established legal standards when evaluating transactions involving leading technological enterprises.

---

[*] Yu Yan is an Asia based Partner with more than 18 years' experience in providing economic advices on competition matters.

An Increasing Concern On Mergers Leading To An Entrenchment Of Market Power

1. In recent years, competition agencies across jurisdictions, including the European Union, United Kingdom, United States, China, and others such as Australia have intensified their oversight of merger controls. This heightened intervention manifests through various forms, such as the introduction of novel or speculative theories of harm, the adoption of "dynamic" counterfactuals lacking robust factual support, and the review of mergers and acquisitions that fall below filing thresholds. Many of these interventions target digital platforms that are already subject to stringent regulatory scrutiny,[1] as well as leading firms in technological and innovative sectors.

2. In particular, competition agencies become more interested whether a merger may entrench or extend an existing dominant position. Theoretically, a merger entrenching market power may be problematic if it creates monopoly power, or defence existing dominance to the extent of causing a substantial lessening of competition (SLC), a principle well-established in US case law and the 2023 US Merger Guidelines.[2]

3. In practice, however, vaguely articulated theories of harm in the context of an entrenchment of market power can be speculative and capture benign and efficiency driven mergers, and competition authorities tend to broaden the definition of the entrenchment of market power overtime.

4. For instance, despite the implementation of the DMA, the European Commission remains vigilant in scrutinising digital mergers, often proposing counterintuitive or speculative theories of harm. This approach was particularly evident in its review of the Booking/eTraveli transaction, where the parties' business activities did not overlap. The Commission advanced a distinctive conglomerate theory of harm, termed the "ecosystem theory of harm," and applied a reduced intervention threshold under the pretext of preventing market power entrenchment.

5. Although less intrusive, the concerns related to the removal of potential competition also caught significant attention in the US. In addition to the emphasis of killer acquisition concerns in the 2023 horizontal merger guidelines, FTC raised a vertical killer acquisition concern in its review of the Illumina/GRAIL transaction, which is even more speculative in nature.

6. In China, the flexibility in enforcement tools available to the authorities in China, however, has not led to a more complacent approach on

---

[1] See Regulation (EU) 2022/1925 (Digital Markets Act), available at: https://eur-lex.europa.eu/eli/reg/2022/1925/oj; and Digital Markets, Competition and Consumers Bill, available at: https://bills.parliament.uk/bills/3453.

[2] U.S. Department of Justice and Federal Trade Commission, *Horizontal Merger Guidelines* (2023), section 2.6, available at: https://www.justice.gov/d9/2023-12/2023%20Merger%20Guidelines.pdf.

digital mergers, particularly when the transaction involves a large digital platform, and with a similar intent to mitigate a merger entrenching an existing market power. In 2021, SAMR already blocked the Huya/Douyu merger in the name of the merger would enhance Tencent's dominance in the gaming sector.

Booking/Etraveli: Ecosystem Theory of Harm

7. Booking and eTraveli both operate online travel agents (OTAs) services and Booking.com proposed to acquire eTraveli in October 2022.[3] The parties don't compete directly but serve some overlapping customers. Booking is a pre-eminent accommodation OTA in Europe, operating an online platform that connects hotels/accommodation sites looking to find consumers with consumers arranging accommodations. Booking competes with dozens of rival accommodation OTAs in Europe; and eTraveli, on the other hand, is a flight OTA, providing similar services but connecting airlines and flight passengers. It is worth noting that in Europe, a significant proportion of flight tickets are sold directly by the airlines.[4]

8. As some (but not all) consumers tend to book hotels and flights for a given trip, the proposed transaction intended to bring together the booking of flights and accommodation under one single OTA as a "Connected Trip", thus, to provide more convenient services to such customers.

9. This cross-selling generates efficiencies since the parties' services are complementary, and there is no elimination of direct competition between the parties; and the complementarity of flights and accommodation could offer a more seamless product experience for travellers, and potentially even generate a pro-competitive incentive to reduce prices. However, this "Connected Trip" concept provided the basis for prohibition based on "ecosystems" and "network effects".

10. Under the Non-Horizontal Merger Guidelines (NHMG),[5] a typical conglomerate theory of harm suggests that the merged entity could seek to leverage Booking's leading position in the core market (accommodation OTA) into the neighbouring market (i.e. flight OTA), to the extent of significantly undermining the effective competition in the neighbouring market. It is effectively an expansion of the remit of dominance. For example, it could offer accommodation customers a discount if they also book a flight.

---

3   European Commission, Case M.10615 – Booking Holdings/eTraveli Group, 25 September 2023, paras 1, available at: https://ec.europa.eu/competition/mergers/cases1/202451/M_10615_10430872_121034_7.pdf.

4   European Commission, Case M.10615 – Booking Holdings/eTraveli Group, 25 September 2023, paras 269, available at: https://ec.europa.eu/competition/mergers/cases1/202451/M_10615_10430872_121034_7.pdf.

5   EUR-Lex NHMG, available at https://eur-lex.europa.eu/legal-content/en/txt/?uri=celex%3a52008xc1018%2803%29.

11. Whilst theoretically plausible, this concern was not the focus of the Commission's investigation, as market study revealed that consumers typically book a flight weeks before the accommodation purchase, and by the time most consumers seek to book a hotel, the flights would have been secured,[6] practically rendering it impractical for the merged entity to influence flight purchase decisions through its accommodation market strength, the empirical evidence do not a typical conglomerated effects theory of harm.

12. Instead of clearing the transaction, the Commission explored an inverse theory, questioning whether the merger would allow the merged entity to use its relatively modest position in flight OTA to strengthen its leading position in accommodation OTA. That is, whether the merger would allow Booking to leverage its brand strength and customer inertia to attract customers *earlier* in the travel purchase journey, which would increase barriers to entry and expansion for rival OTAs, and "hamper rival hotel OTAs' ability to compete on the merits".

13. Whilst such a concern aligns with Article 2 of the Merger Regulation,[7] which prohibits transactions that strengthen a dominant position, the Commission further justified this by suggesting that flights and accommodation constitute an "ecosystem".

14. Theoretically, if a merger enables a firm to offer a multi-product package that rivals cannot replicate, single-product competitors may struggle to compete, potentially lessening competition. Concerns also arise over consumers making sub-optimal choices, such as paying more for a "Connected Trip" compared to selecting providers independently.

15. However, this argument aligns with the foreclosure assessment in the NHMG, and it is not a novel concept, and the "ecosystem" tag does not justify the Commission abandoning the framework set out in the NHMG for assessing foreclosure.

16. More importantly, market evidence suggests minimal impact from cross-selling accommodation to eTraveli's flight customers. Limited customer base overlap, consumer preferences for mixing providers, and the existence of rivals offering combined services (e.g., Expedia) indicate no significant competitive advantage.[8] Modelling by the parties also estimated an

---

[6] Various statements in the EU decision confirm that consumers generally book flights well in advance of arranging hotel accommodations. For instance, paragraphs 588 and 753 explicitly note that consumers typically secure flights first, primarily due to perceived limitations in flight availability and the necessity of coordinating flight schedules with hotel check-in and check-out dates, which also affects accommodation pricing (European Commission, Case M.10615 – Booking Holdings/eTraveli Group, 25 September 2023, paras 588, 753, available at: https://ec.europa.eu/competition/mergers/cases1/202451/M_10615_10430872_121034_7.pdf).

[7] EUR-Lex Merger Regulation, available at https://eur-lex.europa.eu/legal-content/en/txt/?uri=celex%3a32004r0139.

[8] RBB Brief on Booking/eTraveli, available at https://www.datocms-assets.com/79198/1725913641-brief-68-bookingetraveli-september-2024-final.pdf.

incremental accommodation market share increase of tenths of a percentage point, while the Commission's adjusted model projected a less than 5% increase,[9] begging the question as to whether it meets threshold for a significant impediment to effective competition (SIEC).[10]

17. It is particularly concerning that the Commission took the stance that any non-zero sales increment constitutes an SIEC without robust justifications, raising concerns about whether exploiting economies of scale or scope could be misconstrued as an efficiency offence.

HUYA/DouYu (China): Enhancement of Dominance

18. In China, the digital sector is governed by a complex, evolving legislative framework, notably since 2021. There isn't one single comprehensive law; instead, various laws and regulations address different aspects of the digital economy.[11]

    - Anti-Monopoly Guidelines for the Platform Economy (2021): These guidelines provide specific rules for the platform economy, addressing anti-competitive agreements, abuse of dominance, merger control, and administrative monopolies. They also provide a legal definition of digital platforms.[12]

    - Horizontal Guidance published by SAMR in 2024:[13] no novel concepts, consistent with past approaches in general.

19. Despite flexible enforcement tools, Chinese authorities have not adopted a lenient stance on digital mergers, particularly those involving major platforms, aiming to prevent market power entrenchment. In 2021, SAMR blocked the merger between HUYA Inc and DouYu International Holdings Limited. This signified a major regulatory action in the digital space. Both HUYA and DouYu mainly operate

---

9 European Commission, Case M.10615 – Booking Holdings/eTraveli Group, 25 September 2023, paras 310, available at: https://ec.europa.eu/competition/mergers/cases1/202451/M_10615_10430872_121034_7.pdf.

10 RBB Brief on Booking/eTraveli, available at https://www.datocms-assets.com/79198/1725913641-brief-68-bookingetraveli-september-2024-final.pdf.

11 Other related legislations include Anti-Unfair Competition Law, which prohibits various unfair competition practices, including those in the online space; Data Security Law (DSL) (2021), which focuses on the security of a broad range of data (not just personal information) and imposes obligations on organizations processing data to ensure data security. It also has extraterritorial reach, potentially applying to data processing activities outside of China that harm national security or public interests, or the rights and interests of Chinese citizens or entities; Internet Information Service Algorithm Recommendation Management Regulations (2022), which aim to govern the use of algorithms for personalized recommendations on internet platforms, aiming to provide users with more control over their data and the content they see, as well as promoting transparency in algorithm operations; and various regulations related to consumer rights, intellectual property rights, advertising, and specific industries also impact digital markets in China.

12 Available at https://www.gov.cn/xinwen/2021-02/07/content_5585758.htm.

13 ibid.

interactive video entertainment businesses in particular online game live streaming in China. Prior to the merger, HUYA is already solely controlled by Tencent, and Tencent also jointly control DouYu with its initial founding team.[14] The proposed merger essentially allows Tencent to acquire the remaining shares of DouYu and gain sole control of the entity.

20. Following its investigation, Tencent concluded that HUYA and DouYu are direct competitors in supplying game live streaming, entertainment live-streaming, e-commerce live streaming and short video markets. Tencent, on the other hand is active in the game live streaming upstream market via operating online gaming services.

21. The main concern raised in the final decision is that the proposed merger will enhance Tencent's dominance position in the Chinese game live-streaming market via removing the limited competition from DouYu of which Tencent did not have a full control prior to the transaction, thus lead to an adverse effect on competition. In addition, Tencent would gain a strong control in both upstream and downstream markets post-merger, which would allow it to engage in foreclosure strategies in both directions to the extent that potential competition will be undermined.

22. SAMR conducted a market shares analysis and claims that the combined share of HUYA and DouYu in the respective market will be in the range of 40% to 80%, depending on the metrics in use.[15] However, the decision failed to explain the degree of change in DouYu's incentive to compete independently following the completion of the transaction. After all, Tencent already jointly own DouYu prior to this transaction according to SAMR. The decision does indicate high barriers to entry into such the game live streaming market in China mainly due to the challenges in obtaining game copyrights, investment capital and live streaming broadcasters.

23. In contrast, SAMR's retrospective review of the Meituan/Dazongdianpin merger adhered to conventional frameworks, assessing ecosystem enhancements through barriers to entry rather than novel theories.[16]

24. Generally speaking, SAMR has shown a willingness to adhere to existing analytical frameworks in assessing challenging digital mergers.

---

14 Available at https://scjg.hubei.gov.cn/bmdt/zjyw/202107/P020210713339045725099.pdf.

15 As stated in the published decision, in the domestic game live streaming market in China, in terms of turnover, Huya and Douyu contribute more than 40% and 30% respectively, and more than 70% in total; in terms of the number of active users, the market contributions of both parties exceed 45% and 35% respectively, and more than 80% in total; in terms of anchor resources, the market contributions of both parties exceed 30%, and more than 60% in total, available at https://www.gov.cn/xinwen/2021-02/07/content_5585758.htm.

16 The merger between Meituan and Dazongdianpin combined two leading Chinese online-to-offline (O2O) service platforms, and it was announced on October 8, 2015. In 2021, SAMR conducted a retrospective review of the merger, and the author of this paper advised SAMR as their external economist and assessed the likely effects on competition of the completed transaction.

The recent Horizontal Merger Guidance published by SAMR echoes this general position.[17]

25. This, however, could simply reflect a lower level of transparency in SAMR's merger review process in comparison, thus a bigger leeway in their decision makings process. In other words, a merger entrenching existing market power or dominance may be just easily challenged by SAMR nowadays compared with in other jurisdictions such as the EU.

Illumina/GRAIL (US and EU): Vertical Killer Acquisition Concern

26. Entrenchment of market power could also arise from a removal of potential competition – this is widely understood and recognised in the 2023 US Horizontal Merger Guidelines.

27. Generally speaking, the concerns related to the removal of potential competition could take various forms, for example it could arise when an established company acquires a startup developing a rival product (often known as the killer acquisition concern). It could also refer to the loss of future competition, where the startup might have entered or expanded in the market, and/or the loss of dynamic competition, where the mere possibility of entry by the startup could have constrained the incumbent, even if the startup's success was uncertain.

28. In its recent investigation on the acquisition of GRAIL by Illumina, FTC extended the conventional killer acquisition concern to a vertical context.

29. Illumina, a global genomics company, develops next-generation sequencing (NGS) systems, while GRAIL develops blood-based cancer tests using genomic sequencing. In 2021, GRAIL began limited commercialisation in the US, prompting investigations by the FTC and the EU Commission, the latter via member state referrals, later overturned by the EU General Court.

30. Both FTC and EU Commission raised concerns of the loss of future competition through vertical foreclosure.

31. In particular, the EU Commission found that Illumina would have had the ability and the incentive to engage in foreclosure strategies against GRAIL's rivals. It could for instance refuse to supply its NGS systems to GRAIL's rivals, increase the prices, or degrade quality and delay supplies. The Commission considered that those strategies would have resulted in a significant detrimental effect on competition in *developing and marketing NGS-based cancer detection tests* in the European Economic Area (EEA).

---

17   2024 Chinese Horizontal Merger Guidance, available at https://www.gov.cn/zhengce/zhengceku/202412/content_6993767.htm.

32. Similarly, FTC defined a relevant product market for the "research, development, and commercialization" of MCED tests, which was later upheld by the Fifth Circuit.[18] In essence, the FTC uncharacteristically argued for a broader product market, so as to include potential competitors that could be harmed.

33. Despite ongoing legal challenges in both continents, the parties decided to complete the transaction in 2021. Ultimately, Illumina decided to divest GRAIL following the decision of the Fifth Circuit Court, which rules in FTC's favour.

34. From an economic perspective, this transaction is worth noting as the theory of harm articulated by agencies extended the conventional killer acquisitions in a horizontal setting to one in a vertical setting. By doing so, additional uncertainties are inevitable since the agencies would need to establish robust evidence in forecasting likely market dynamics in both the upstream and downstream markets. Moreover, the theory of harm is ultimately about the possible reduction in competition on innovation in the market for the future development and supply of MCED tests (downstream), however, the agencies do not appear to allow much consideration of any pro-competitive efficiencies in this regard.

Implications Of Future Merger Controls

35. Competition authorities are increasingly focused on market power entrenchment in digital and innovative sector mergers, possibly driven by challenges in ex-post enforcement, particularly in the EU and UK. Competition agencies across jurisdictions demonstrated an increasing interest in a long-term impact of a merger, raised concerns on future competition and innovation, particularly when a merger involve players in digital or other innovative sectors.

36. This trend is likely to be influenced by rapidly evolving industries, the importance of innovation for productivity, industrial policy shifts, and non-competition considerations like sustainability and national security. However, the inclination to circumvent established frameworks, lower evidentiary burdens, or bypass legal standards is concerning. Authorities need to exercise their powers within their mandates to ensure legal certainty and procedural integrity.

---

18 The Fifth Circuit rejected Illumina's argument that the relevant product market should be limited to the "*existing* commercial market for MCED tests." Instead, the court held that there was sufficient evidence that the relevant product market included MCED test companies that are not presently in the consumer market but are in the research and development stage. Refer to the Fifth Circuit's opinion in *Illumina, Inc. v. FTC*, Case No. 23-60167, dated December 15, 2023.

Anti-monopoly Regulation on Loyalty Rebates in the European Union and its Implications

CEN ZHAOQI[*]

Partner, Zhong Lun Law Firm

Abstract

This essay examines the evolution of antitrust regulation concerning loyalty rebates in the EU and its implications for China. Initially, in the EU, cases like Hoffmann-La Roche (1979) adopted a form-based approach, deeming loyalty rebates by dominant undertakings inherently abusive without requiring in-depth analysis of actual or likely effects. This shifted with the Intel case (2009), which introduced a more effects-based approach, mandating analysis of whether rebates could foreclose a competitor as efficient as the dominant undertaking (AEC test). This balanced assessment considers both anti-competitive effects and potential efficiencies. China's first major loyalty rebate ruling-the Tetra Pak case (2016)-penalized loyalty rebates under "other conducts of abuse of dominant market position confirmed as such by the authority for enforcement of Anti-monopoly Law under the State Council" provisions. However, critics argued this approach lacked rigorous economic analysis. The subsequent Eastman case (2019) further demonstrated China's strict stance, punishing loyalty rebates that effectively restricted trading counterparties' choice.

In summary, referring to the EU's law enforcement, judicial cases and experience in the identification of loyalty rebates, and based on China's anti-monopoly

---

[*] Cen Zhaoqi is a partner at Zhong Lun Law Firm.

Anti-monopoly Regulation on Loyalty Rebates
in the European Union and its Implications

legislation and enforcement practices, this essay underscores the need for case-specific analysis and robust proof standards to distinguish procompetitive discounts from exclusionary practices.

Introduction

1. "Loyalty Rebate (Fidelity Rebate)" is "a discount given by an undertaking to a transaction counterparty based on cumulative transaction volume, transaction amount, transaction share, or other performance of loyalty within a certain period of time."[1]

2. Discounts are common business practices. If discounts are solely based on the purchase volume of the buyer, they can usually reflect the requirements of economies of scale, promote market competition, and benefit consumers. Moreover, usually an increase in sales volume helps undertakings further amortize their fixed costs, thereby reducing the average total cost of goods. It is permitted under the *Anti-Monopoly Law* (hereinafter "*AML*") for suppliers to offer discounts based on the contribution of the buyer's purchase volume to the reduction of their own average total costs. However, when a supplier is in a dominant market position, since most of the goods in the relevant market are provided by the dominant supplier and other competitors cannot provide sufficient output, most buyers cannot completely break away from the supplier. A dominant supplier, by granting loyalty rebates, can influence the buyer's purchase decision on the "non-competitive part of demand" by restricting the buyer's "competitive part of demand". The anti-competitive effect of the loyalty rebates is manifested in preventing the buyer from purchasing products from other competitive suppliers, or limiting the quantity the buyer can purchase from other competing suppliers, thereby excluding competitive suppliers, and should be regulated by the *AML*.

3. This article starts from the law enforcement cases involving loyalty rebates in the European Union (hereinafter "EU") and combines the practices of anti-monopoly law enforcement in China, in order to analyze the key points for determining the anti-monopoly regulation of loyalty rebates.

I. Overview of the EU's Anti-monopoly Regulation of "Loyalty Rebates"

4. Competition law limits the types of discounts that undertakings with market dominance can implement. A legitimate discount scheme may be considered a normal business activity if implemented by an undertaking

---

1 *See* Gong Shang Jing Zheng An Zi [2016] No. 1, Page 34.

without a dominant position, but may constitute abusive conduct if implemented by a dominant undertaking. Since the *Hoffmann-La Roche* case in 1979, the EU has established a generally applicable principle that undertakings with market dominance can offer efficiency-related discounts, but can only offer rebates for achieved efficiency, not for loyalty. It was not until the *Intel* case that the court changed its criteria and evidence requirements for determining the loyalty rebates. This article explains and summarizes typical enforcement cases regarding loyalty rebates in the EU.

1. The *Hoffmann-La Roche* case (1979)

5. Hoffmann-La Roche (hereinafter "*Roche*") had a market share ranging from 47% to 96% in the various vitamin markets involved in the case. Roche was found by the European Commission to have violated EU competition law by reaching "fidelity agreements" with downstream customers. The Court of Justice held that "an undertaking which is in a dominant position on a market and ties purchasers – even if it does so at their request – by an obligation or promise on their part to obtain all or most of their requirements exclusively from the said undertaking abuses its dominant position within the meaning of Article 86 of the Treaty, whether the obligation in question is stipulated without further qualification or whether it is undertaken in consideration of the grant of a rebate. The same applies if the said undertaking, without tying the purchasers by a formal obligation, applies, either under the terms of agreements concluded with these purchasers or unilaterally, a system of fidelity rebates, that is to say discounts conditional on the customer's obtaining all or most of its requirements – whether the quantity of its purchases be large or small – from the undertaking in a dominant position."[2]

6. The Court of Justice believed that the effect of loyalty rebates is to apply dissimilar transaction conditions to equivalent transaction with other trading parties in that two purchasers pay a different price for the same quantity of the same product depending on whether they obtain their supplies exclusively from the undertaking in a dominant position or have several sources of supply. According to the Court of Justice, although the loyalty rebates in dispute also involves the purchase quantity, its nature is different from the general quantity discount, because the general quantity discount is only associated with the current purchase volume of the relevant purchaser. But the quantity of purchase involved in the loyalty rebates discussed in *Hoffmann-La Roche* is not an objectively determined quantity standard for all purchasers, but rather a purchase quantity and discount plan derived from the analysis and estimation of the objective and potential demand of each customer. In other words, the goal that

---

2 *See* Case 85/76, Hoffmann-La Roche & Co. AG v Commission, EU:C:1979:36, para. 89.

the dominant undertaking seeks to achieve is not the maximum quantity but the maximum demand of the purchasers.

7. In the *Hoffmann-La Roche* case, the Court of Justice adopted a "form-based approach" to determine whether loyalty rebates constitute an abuse of market dominance. The judgement implies that no extensive investigation of effects is required to conclude that loyalty rebates constitute abuse of dominance. That is, in deciding whether the conduct is abusive, not more indications of harmful effects are required.

8. Cases after *Hoffmann-La Roche* also followed the same form-based approach, that is, a dominant undertaking can be deemed to have violated competition law by offering loyalty rebates, and in-depth analysis of actual or likely effects is not required. In the *Michelin II* case, the court held that for the purposes of establishing an infringement of Article 102 TFEU, "it is sufficient to show that the abusive conduct of the undertaking in a dominant position tends to restrict competition or, in other words, that the conduct is capable of having that effect".[3]

2. The *Intel* case (2009)

9. In 2009, the European Commission complained that Intel had abused its dominant position on the market for x86 microprocessors by granting loyalty rebates to its customers for purchasing all or almost all of their supply needs from Intel. The European Commission held that certain rebates may bring lower prices to consumers. However, when an undertaking has a dominant market position, if the rebates are given on the condition that the counterparty reduces or completely stops purchasing from competitors, then according to the case-law of the European Court of Justice, such rebates will constitute an abuse of market dominance. At the same time, the European Commission clarified that they were not against the rebates themselves, but only against the specific conditions attached to the rebates. The European Commission determined that Intel has infringed the EC Treaty and imposed a fine of €1.06 billion on Intel for the infringement.

10. In 2014, the General Court upheld the decision of the European Commission, but at the same time it rejected the necessity of adopting the As Efficient Competitor (hereinafter "AEC") test, saying that there was no need to consider the impact of rebates on the market. According to the *Hoffman-La Roche* case, the General Court held that loyalty rebates were inherently anti-competitive and upheld the decision of the European Commission. On the appeal brought by Intel, the Court of Justice set aside the judgment made by the General Court and held that "the European

---

3   *See* Case T-203/01, Manufacture frangaise des pneumatiques Michelin v Commission, EU:T:2003:250, para 239.

Commission is required to engage with evidence such as the AEC test when invoked by the investigated party. This duty applies with respect to: a) assess the possible existence of a strategy aiming to exclude competitors that are at least as efficient as the dominant undertaking from the market; and b) analysis of the capacity to foreclose is also relevant in assessing whether a system of rebates may be objectively justified."[4]

11. The *Intel* case reflects a preference for a relatively strict norm in the EU, which shifted from a form-based approach to a more effects-based approach. Although the Court of Justice did not formally overturn the *Hoffman-La Roche* case, it made the following clarification on the scope of application of the *Intel* case. The Court of Justice clarified that the following factors that are mandatory in the European Commission's analysis: "the Commission is required to analyze not only factors such as the extent of the dominant position of the undertaking in question, the share of market covered by the contested rebates and the conditions and arrangements for granting the rebates in question, their duration and their amount, but also the possible existence of a strategy aiming to exclude competitors that are at least as efficient as the dominant undertaking from the market".[5]

12. After the *Intel* case, loyalty rebates used by a dominant undertaking are no longer considered to be abusive *per se*. The European Commission used an AEC test to check whether Intel's behavior could be expected to lead to harm to consumers. Essentially, the idea that loyalty rebates are anticompetitive may be characterized as a rebuttable presumption. At the same time, the Court of Justice has set stricter standards for administrative enforcement procedures and the burden of proof, namely the special responsibilities and obligations of the European Commission to apply the AEC test in investigating loyalty rebates cases. In particular, with regard to the AEC test, the Court of Justice believes that "the capability of such loyalty rebates to foreclose a competitor as efficient as the dominant undertaking, which competitor is supposed to meet the same costs as those borne by that undertaking, must be assessed, as a general rule, using the AEC test. Even though that test is merely one of the ways of assessing whether an undertaking in a dominant position has used means other than those that come within the scope of 'normal' competition, it seeks specifically to assess whether such an as-efficient competitor, considered in abstract to, is capable of reproducing the conduct of the undertaking in a dominant position and, consequently, whether that conduct must be considered to come within the scope of normal competition, that is to say, competition on the merits."[6]

---

[4] See Case C-413/14 P, *Intel Corp. v European Commission [2017]* EU:C:2017:632, para 139 & 140.

[5] *See* Case C-240/22 P, *Intel Corporation v Commission* [2024] EU:C:2024:915, para 180.

[6] *See* Case C-240/22 P, *Intel Corporation v Commission* [2024] EU:C:2024:915, para 181.

13. After the *Intel* case, the regulatory model of adopting effects-based approach for loyalty rebates cases got further affirmation. For example, in the *Unilever* case, the court held that "although, by reason of their nature, exclusivity clauses give rise to legitimate concerns of competition, their ability to exclude competitors is not automatic."[7] In the *Qualcomm* case, the General Court confirm that "the alleged exclusivity clauses can only be anticompetitive if, in fact, they are capable of foreclosing rivals and that the Commission must take proper account of 'all the relevant factual circumstances surrounding the conduct concerned' rather than resort to presumptions [...] this is a matter of both substance and due process."[8]

14. The European Commission also addresses the issue of adopting the effects-based approach and AEC test standards in the *Guidance on the Commission's Enforcement Priorities in Applying Article 82 EC Treaty to Abusive Exclusionary Conduct by Dominant Undertakings* (hereinafter "Guidance"). For example, paragraph 23 of the Guidance provides that "with a view to preventing anti-competitive foreclosure, the Commission will normally only intervene where the conduct concerned has already been or is capable of hampering competition from competitors which are considered to be as efficient as the dominant undertaking". And paragraph 36 states that "the capacity for exclusive purchasing obligations to result in anti-competitive foreclosure arises in particular where, without the obligations, an important competitive constraint is exercised by competitors......If competitors can compete on equal terms for each individual customer's entire demand, exclusive purchasing obligations are generally unlikely to hamper effective competition unless the switching of supplier by customers is rendered difficult due to the duration of the exclusive purchasing obligation." It can be seen that the European Commission believes that competition law does not favor uncompetitive undertakings and is designed to encourage effective competition and pursue maximum efficiency. For example, in cases involving loyalty rebates, "the Commission intends to investigate, to the extent that the data are available and reliable, whether the rebate system is capable of hindering expansion or entry even by competitors that are equally efficient by making it more difficult for them to supply part of the requirements of individual customers."[9]

15. In summary, from the *Hoffman-La Roche* case to the *Intel* case, the EU competition law enforcement agency's attitude towards loyalty rebates has

---

[7] *See* Case C-680/20, *Unilever Italia Mkt. Operations Srl v Autorità Garante della Concorrenza e del Mercato* [2023] EU:C:2023:33, para. 51.

[8] *See* Case T-235/18, *Qualcomm, Inc. v Commission*, [2022] EU:T:2022:358, para. 411.

[9] *See Guidance on the Commission's Enforcement Priorities in Applying Article 82 EC Treaty to Abusive Exclusionary Conduct by Dominant Undertakings,* para 41.

changed from strict to prudent. This tendency towards relatively strict regulations is the result of the shift from a form-based approach to a more effects-based approach. With strict standards and burden of proof, competition law enforcement agencies will also face greater challenges.

II. Overview of China's Anti-Monopoly Enforcement of "Loyalty Rebates"

16. From the perspective of China's anti-monopoly enforcement practices, cases involving loyalty rebates in China are the *Tetra Pak* case and the *Eastman* case. The basis for the penalty in the *Tetra Pak* case is Article 17 (7) of the *AML*, which states that "other conducts of abuse of dominant market position confirmed as such by the authority for enforcement of Anti-monopoly Law under the State Council".

17. In 2016, the AML enforcement agency concluded after investigation that in the liquid-food paper-based aseptic packaging materials, packaging equipment and technical services markets of Chinese Mainland, Tetra Pak and its related subsidiaries abused Tetra Pak's dominant position to implement monopoly conducts such as tying, restricted transactions, and loyalty rebates without justifiable reasons. In the *Tetra Pak* case, AML enforcement agency classified the two types of loyalty rebates Tetra Pak offered to the customers into: (1) retrospective cumulative rebate; (2) customized target rebate.

18. In *Tetra Pak* case, AML enforcement agency's analysis of anti-competitive effects of the involved loyalty rebates mainly focused on the following two aspects:
    (1) The inducement effect of loyalty rebates. Different from the general incremental rebate model, the retrospective cumulative rebate implemented by Tetra Pak has a special case, that is, when the buyer's purchase volume reaches the threshold of the specified rebate, the total payment drops sharply. Therefore, when the buyer's purchase volume is close to the threshold, in order to obtain more products at a lower total price, even if they are not forced to trade, they will often "voluntarily" choose to increase the purchase volume to obtain rebate. Customized target rebate refers to the rebate granted if certain customers' purchase volume meets or exceeds target percentage (as opposed to a customer's total demand) or target quantity. Therefore, given that the total rebate amount under the loyalty rebates model comes from the price reduction of all purchased goods, the buyer will purchase more of supplier's goods to reach the threshold to obtain rebate, which constrains the buyer's purchasing decision and thereby excludes competing supplier.

(2) The exclusion effect of loyalty rebates. The loyalty rebates implemented by Tetra Pak transmits the market power of the "non-competitive market demand" to the "competitive market demand", that is, Tetra Pak's loyalty rebates forced competing firms to increase discount/rebate to match Tetra Pak's price and compete with it. To compete for a part of the purchase volume, competitors must not only offer a rebate no lower than Tetra Pak for the competitive part, but also must compensate customers for the rebate on the non-competitive part that they lose due to reducing purchases from Tetra Pak, which results in competitors offering a price lower than Tetra Pak's discounted price for the competitive part. When the demand for the competitive part is limited, the price that competitors need to match will be very low, which increases the difficulty for competitors to participate in the competition and may even lead to their withdrawal from the competition. This will also induce customers to further choose Tetra Pak, block competitors, and exclude and restrict market competition.

19. *Tetra Pak* case is China's first anti-monopoly case regarding loyalty rebates, which made a precedent for anti-monopoly enforcement case involving loyalty rebates. However, on the issue of law enforcement standards and burden of proof, some scholars believe that "the qualitative conclusion of the Tetra Pak rebate in this case may be completely correct in terms of 'factual and legal significance', but in terms of 'theoretical significance', the logic presented in the Decision still has two major questions: first, the competitive effect of retrospective cumulative rebate is only understood in a purely derogatory manner, without considering the possible positive significance; second, the determination of the illegality of loyalty rebates adopts a form-based approach rather than an effect-based approach, and the conclusion lacks strong data or evidence support."[10]

20. After the *Tetra Pak* case, the *Eastman* case also involved loyalty rebates. In 2019, the AML enforcement agency issued a penalty decision against Eastman for abuse of market dominance by restricting transaction in Ester Alcohol-12 market in Chinese Mainland, violating the provision of "restricting its trading counterparties to trade exclusively with the undertaking or trade exclusively with the designated undertakings without justifiable reasons" (Article 17 (4) of *AML* (2008)). Apart from the *Tetra Pak* case and *Eastman* case, there are no other typical cases of loyalty rebates.

21. In enforcement practices, with the development and changes of the identification standard of loyalty rebates, AML enforcement agency needs to

---

10 *See* LI Junfeng, Determination of the Monopoly Illegality of "Loyalty Rebate" – – Based on the Administrative Penalty Case of Tetra Pak, Contemporary Law Review, 2019, Issue 2.

adapt more economic analysis method to analyze competition damages. In the meanwhile, the AML enforcement agency also bear more burden of proof, which puts higher requirements and challenges on the law enforcement capabilities and levels of AML enforcement agency.

III. Key Points and Implications for the Determination of Loyalty Rebates

22. Although there is no explicit legal provision for regulating loyalty rebates in China's the *AML*, according to the Article 22 (4) of *AML*, "any undertaking with a dominant market position shall be prohibited from engaging in any of the following conducts of abusing dominant market position: [...] (4) restricting its trading counterparties to trade exclusively with the undertaking or trade exclusively with the designated undertakings without justifiable reasons". According to Article 17 of the *Provisions on the Prohibition of the Abuse of Dominant Market Position*, "any undertaking with a dominant market position shall be prohibited from engaging in any of the following restricted trade practices without justified reasons: (1) restricting the counterparty to only conduct transactions with it [...] The above restrictive trade practices may be implemented directly or indirectly through punitive or incentive measures, or otherwise." Therefore, the behavior of granting loyalty rebates is usually regarded as indirect transaction restriction through punitive or incentive measures and is regulated by the *AML*.

23. In summary, referring to the EU's law enforcement, judicial cases and experience in the identification of loyalty rebates, and based on China's anti-monopoly legislation and enforcement practices, as mentioned above, the main issues to be considered in the identification of loyalty rebates include:

1. The factual proof standard of loyalty rebates

24. The effect-based approach should be adopted, rather than applying the "illegal per se" rule to directly determine or presume that loyalty rebates model is illegal. When conducting anti-monopoly assessments on loyalty rebates, the following factors should be comprehensively examined: (1) the status of relevant market; (2) the market position of dominant undertaking and its competitors; (3) the market share blocked by the loyalty rebates; (4) the conditions, duration and extent of the rebate, mainly including whether it is a purchase ratio standard or a quantity standard, whether it is a standardized or customized threshold, whether it is a total volume rebate or an incremental rebate, etc.; (5) whether there are justified reasons, or whether there are other less exclusive alternative conducts.

2. The burden of proof regarding anti-competitive effects of loyalty rebates

25. AML enforcement agency should bear the burden of proof, especially the burden of proving the anti-competitive effect of loyalty rebates. AML enforcement agency need to evaluate the degree of market blockade, the status of competition between upstream and downstream, and the degree of impact on customer welfare, etc. At the same time, it is necessary to evaluate the procompetitive effects arising out of exclusive dealing, such as enhancing efficiency, reducing transaction costs, ensuring quality or reliability, or preventing free-riding, and that such effects may justify or counterbalance the exclusionary effects of the conduct under certain conditions.

3. The justified reasons of loyalty rebates

26. In general, if the grating of loyalty rebates is necessary to protect intellectual property rights, product safety or data security, it may be a justified reason under the *AML*. In addition, situations where customers prefer to source their demand from a single provider, there are multiple scaled competitors capable of competing ex-ante for the contract, and there might be benefits (e.g. in terms of relationship-specific investments) from such forms of contracting.

PART II
Law and Practice of China's Anti-Monopoly Law

My Friend Huang Yong

SHENG JIEMIN*
Professor, Peking University Law School

1. Huang Yong and I are bosom friends from different generations. We have known each other for years. My wife says we share deep and lasting friendship. Our friendship originated at Peking University. Huang Yong's mother is a professor in Faculty of Western Languages and Literature; I taught at the Law School for 40 years. I met Huang Yong's mother first, then him. Huang Yong is a true man of Peking University. He was born in the university community, began his education at the university kindergarten, then affiliated primary school and affiliated middle school, and eventually he was admitted to the Law School (then still known as the Faculty of Law), where he graduated with honours. Huang Yong embodies the unique character nurtured by Peking University – rigorous in academics, yet free-spirited in life.

2. In my exchanges with Huang Yong, aside from academics, we talk about food the most. I have attended his home-cooked banquets on multiple occasions. At these gatherings, Huang Yong would design the menu then cook personally. His dishes highlight natural flavors of the ingredients, combine innovative culinary arts, blending culinary traditions with elegance and harmony while presenting beautifully on plate. There is a saying in Laozi's *Tao Te Ching*: "Governing a great nation is like cooking a small fish" – subtle, precise, requiring just the right touch. In my view, doing scholarly work is much the same as creating fine cuisine. Huang Yong not only excels at crafting exquisite dishes, but also at writing profound essays and pursuing deep intellectual inquiry.

---

* Professor, School of Law, Peking University.

3. Huang Yong possesses a keen sensitivity to emerging trends and new challenges at the frontier of competition law. I often hear him say that the first thing he does after waking up each morning is to browse domestic and international news on politics and economics, as well as newly released laws, regulations, and government policies. This habit keeps him closely attuned to real-world market dynamics and potential competitive trends. Because he consistently updates his knowledge base, the research topics he chooses, the papers he writes, and even the themes he presents at forums are always fresh and original. He has insightful, innovative, and in-depth perspectives on cutting-edge legal issues in China – such as the rule of law in digital economy, and the promotion and development of private enterprises, which are currently emphasized by national policy. Moreover, his insights are deeply rooted in reality and capable of addressing practical problems. Just like his dishes – sourced from fresh ingredients and served with authenticity – his academic work carries the same qualities: freshness, clarity, and integrity.

4. China boasts a rich culinary tradition with its Eight Great Cuisines. A true gourmet, Huang Yong often integrates flavors from both northern and southern Chinese cuisines as well as Western influences in his home-cooked banquets, creating novel and intriguing taste experience. Likewise, in his academic pursuits, Huang Yong places great emphasis on integrating knowledge across disciplines. His legal expertise is solid and profound, and he skillfully applies economic analysis methods to his research on competition law. In his antitrust studies on preventing the abuse of intellectual property rights, Huang Yong delves deeply into theories of intellectual property protection; his research on the interplay between intellectual property law and competition law – including their conflicts, synergies, and complementarities – is outstanding. His research capabilities and findings have earned recognition and accolades within the intellectual property community. In my view, there are few scholars in China's academic circles who truly understand the intersection of antitrust law and intellectual property law, and Huang Yong is one of them.

5. Huang Yong's academic achievements are widely recognized. Many admire his sharp intellect (all his hair was sacrificed for intelligence). But from my observation, beyond being left with more wisdom than hair, Huang Yong is remarkably diligent, conscientious, and hardworking. When writing a paper, he would revise it multiple times, refining from structure, arguments, to logic with meticulous attention to detail and careful consideration of originality, contemporaneousness and real-world effect. Every word is weighed and polished until he feels fully satisfied. The same level of dedication is seen in his application to academic lectures. I recall several events where we conducted Q&A-style dialogue – I as the moderator and he as the speaker. His presentations were brilliant, articulate, and full of insightful examples drawn effortlessly. Audience

consistently rated them as classic and inspiring. Yet, what many didn't know was the tremendous effort he put in behind the scenes. Even though he had already mastered the subject thoroughly, he would stay up late – often until the early hours of the morning – preparing for the lecture the day before. His notebook was filled with detailed outlines, notes, and annotations, showing an extraordinary level of preparation. On competition law forums, the two of us have collaborated the most closely, and seamless. Still, before each session, he would often pull me aside beforehand to walk through his planned content and structure in detail. This helped me understand how best to support him – when to introduce, transition, or summarize – ensuring the most polished and effective delivery possible. Huang Yong's scholarly style – rigorous, grounded, diligent, and dedicated – deeply impresses me.

6. As time goes by, Huang Yong has now been teaching for 40 years. As his senior from alma mater and close friend, seeing him today with students all over the world and a distinguished body of scholarly work, I feel genuinely delighted for him. On this occasion, I sincerely wish him to continue making greater contributions to the development of China's competition law and antirust system and to international legal exchanges. May he continue to nurture and inspire more talents in China's antitrust academic community. May he keep pursuing scholarship with rigor, and at the same time, savor life with grace. And may he always remain a free-spirited, erudite, wise, and worldly scholar – one who truly understands both knowledge and life.

28 May 2025, at the Plum Retreat

The Developments and Evolution of Chinese Merger Control

DENG FENG[*]
Professor, Peking University Law School

WANG HUIQUN
Assistant Professor, Central University of Finance and Economics

GUO XIAOLI
Assistant Professor, Shanghai University of Finance and Economics

Abstract

Over the past 30 years, China's merger control legal institution has evolved from non-existence to a fully developed framework. With the vast scope of the Chinese market, the expanding scale of Chinese enterprises, and the continuous growth of foreign investments in China amidst globalization, the enforcing system has accumulated over 6,000 cases of adjudicatory actions and related knowledge. It has rapidly become one of the most important judicial jurisdictions globally, while gradually exhibiting distinct localization features. This process can generally be divided into three stages of institutional change. At the same time, the latest rule updates reflect a growing trend towards systematization and standardization. Throughout this process, antitrust enforcement agencies have seen an increase

---

[*] Deng Feng, Ph.D. in Law, Professor at the Law School, Peking University. Email: fengdeng@pku.edu.cn. Wang Huiqun, Ph.D. in Law, Assistant Professor at the Law School, Central University of Finance and Economics. Email: huiqun_wang@cufe.edu.cn. Guo Xiaoli, Ph.D. in Political Science, Assistant Professor at the Shanghai Institute of International Organization and Global Governance, Shanghai University of Finance and Economics. Email: guoxiaoli@mail.shufe.edu.cn. The authors would like to thank He, Ziyi, a doctoral student at the Law School of Peking University, for her help in data collection and organization during the writing of this paper. The authors are responsible for the content of the paper.

in their authority within the broader economic regulatory framework, with an ongoing expansion of their authority, power and growing prominence in adjudicatory action capabilities. This paper presents the major rule changes in recent years and the latest judicial review cases, and briefly analyzes the main characteristics and key challenges faced by China's merger control legal institution from the perspective of institutional dynamics.

1. Unlike the concept of "Merger Control" in antitrust theory, the term "concentration of undertakings" in China reflects the influence of the European Union's (EU) terminology, as seen in the "Anti-Monopoly Law of the People's Republic of China" (hereinafter referred to as the "Anti-Monopoly Law") enacted in 2007.[1] In terms of institutional capacity and knowledge accumulation, the concentration of undertakings essentially inherited mechanisms from the 1994 "Foreign Trade Law," which was gradually implemented. The the Ministry of Commerce (MOC), responsible for international trade regulation, gradually gained formal enforcement jurisdiction over the merger control legal institution (through the Anti-Monopoly Bureau of the MOC) and accumulated corresponding enforcement experience. Subsequently, in the 2018 government restructuring,[2] three departments – the National Development and Reform Commission (NDRC), responsible for monopoly agreements (i.e., cartels, originating from the 1993 "Price Law"); the MOC, responsible for concentration of undertakings; and the State Administration for Industry and Commerce (SAIC), responsible for abuse of market dominance – were merged into the State Administration for Market Regulation (SAMR).[3] At the end of 2021, the merged enforcement agency was officially established as the State Anti-Monopoly Bureau (SAB), under the SAMR.[4] The evolution of these enforcement powers and jurisdictional changes is embedded within the broader transformation of China's legal system, forming a path dependence within institutional change. The forces that overcome path dependence or drive institutional change stem from external pushes related to China's participation in globalization since 2001 and the legal supply-demand generated by the development of the Chinese market economy.

---

[1] Anu Bradford, Adam Chilton, Katerina Linos and Alexander Weaver: The Global Dominance of European Competition Law Over American Antitrust Law, Journal of Empirical Legal Studies,16, No. 4, 2019, pp. 731–766.

[2] Deng Feng: "The Three-in-One Antitrust Agencies: Avoiding Tunnel Vision," *Caijing* Magazine, July 9, 2018, Issue No. 533, pp. 122-125.

[3] The Central Committee of the Communist Party of China issued the "Plan for Deepening the Reform of Party and State Institutions," The Central People's Government of the People's Republic of China, https://www.gov.cn/zhengce/2018-03/21/content_5276191.htm#2, last accessed on July 18, 2025.

[4] Xinhua News Agency: "National Antimonopoly Bureau Officially Established," https://www.news.cn/2021-11/18/c_1128075788.htm, last accessed on July 18, 2025.

2. In the evolution of law as a knowledge system, institutional demands continually generate claims on legal rules and practices. At the same time, through the interplay of rules, theories, interpretations, and the interactions between companies and legal professionals in practice, the characteristics and style of the Chinese model have emerged between path dependence and evolutionary dynamics. Although it cannot be said that the underlying knowledge or justification for enforcement decisions is unique to China, similar practices and way of thinking have existed in different judicial jurisdictions at various historical stages. However, within the current global spectrum of judicial characteristics or styles, Chinese features have indeed started to emerge – despite the fact that comparative law methods are currently the mainstream in Chinese legal scholarship as a latecomer in legal development.

3. The Chinese characteristics of the merger control legal institution, or what may be called the "Chinese path dependence," including the institutional achievements already realized and the areas that still need improvement, all stem from the aforementioned logic of institutional change. Therefore, understanding the evolution of China's merger control legal institution should be approached from the perspective of overall institutional or constitutional arrangements, market upgrades, expansion, and iteration, as well as the institutional capacity of the legislative and enforcement departments themselves and the issues, environments, and challenges they face. The functioning of the legal system is not only embodied in the abstract provisions of the law but also manifested in the dynamic practice of the system in reality.

4. So, under the current institutional framework in China, what are the institutional characteristics of merger control legislation? Are there design logics that differ from those in foreign jurisdictions? What typical enforcement models and regulatory paths have emerged during its operation? Furthermore, do the features currently presented have long-term stability, or are they merely institutional arrangements at a specific stage of development that may be adjusted in the future with the evolution of regulatory concepts, the updating of technological tools, or even changes in market structures? These questions are not only related to the rationality and effectiveness of the merger control legal institution itself, but also concern the institutional logic and power distribution structure of the overall antitrust law. Therefore, this paper will analyze the legislative model, enforcement paths, and possible evolutionary trends of China's merger control legal institution, attempting to address this series of questions and provide a more systematic theoretical observation and empirical foundation for understanding the institutional construction in this field.

I. Three Stages of Institutional Change

5. The merger control legal institution involves corporate mergers and acquisition, conglomeration, reorganization (hereinafter referred to as merger), competitive behaviors, especially product pricing, and corresponding market analysis knowledge. Its origin and development in China began with the anti-dumping and anti-subsidy practices established in the 1994 "Foreign Trade Law," where the MOC, as the enforcement agency, gradually began engaging in market analysis, marking the beginning of its economic analytical capabilities. Although the law did not address monopolies, it outlined practices that were difficult to implement, such as "unfair competitive practices to eliminate competitors," and placed them under the broader concept of "foreign trade order."

6. With China's formal accession to the WTO in 2001, the amended 2004 "Foreign Trade Law" clearly granted the MOC the authority to eliminate actions that "implement monopolistic behavior in foreign trade activities, harming fair market competition" and "endangering foreign trade order."[5] Based on this authorization by black lettters of law, the MOC formally initiated the merger control review system, which was later defined in the 2008 "Anti-Monopoly Law" as the concentration of undertakings. This system, rooted in China's foreign investment laws, combined the merger review with the foreign investment review system, particularly centered around the "Foreign Trade Law." The 2004 "Administrative Licensing Law" further institutionalized nearly all government actions under "administrative licenses," [6] laying the foundation for the merger control antitrust review system, influenced by the civil law tradition, particularly the French and Japanese models. From 1994 to 2008, this fusion of foreign investment market entry control system and full administrative regulation can be considered as the first stage.

7. In 2007, the "Anti-Monopoly Law" formally established the merger control review system and largely adopted an EU-style framework. Subsequently, on August 3, 2008, the State Council issued the "Regulations on Merger Notification Standards," which established a reporting threshold requirements centered on turnover to identify concentration transactions that might have a significant impact on the market. With China's accession to the WTO and the global consensus on institutional practices, China's merger control legal institution rapidly developed alongside the market expansion.

---

5 Article 32 of the "Foreign Trade Law of the People's Republic of China" stipulates: "In foreign trade operations, monopoly behaviors that violate relevant anti-monopoly laws and administrative regulations are prohibited. If monopoly behaviors are carried out in foreign trade operations and harm fair market competition, they shall be dealt with in accordance with relevant anti-monopoly laws and administrative regulations. If such violations also harm foreign trade order, the competent department of the State Council for foreign trade may take necessary measures to eliminate the harm."

6 Deng Feng: "The Costs and Limitations of the Administrative Licensing Law," Beijing: *Hongfan Review*, Vol. 2, Issue 2, edited by Wu Jinglian and Jiang Ping, China University of Political Science and Law Press, 2005, pp. 44–92.

8. In terms of specific administrative legislation, on July 15, 2009, the MOC, in collaboration with the People's Bank of China and other departments, issued the "Methods for Calculating Turnover for Financial Sector Merger Notifications," providing guidelines for turnover calculations for mergers in the financial sector. On November 21 of the same year, the MOC published the "Measures for Merger Notification" and "Merger Review Procedures," providing specific standards and processes from both the corporate and enforcement agency perspectives.

9. On May 10, 2011, the MOC issued the "Interim Measures for Investigation and Handling of Failure to File Merger Notifications," in response to frequent instances of Chinese companies deliberately or negligently failing to fulfill their notification duty in merger control filings. This was largely due to the adoption of the EU's framework of substantive damage evaluation *ex ante* and merger contractual performance should be after administrative licensing, followed by an "administrative license" approval model. The Measures defined situations where mergers had not been legally reported and set out investigation and handling procedures, standardizing investigative actions and expanding enforcement powers to penalize concealment or evasion of notification duty.

10. Although the 2007 "Anti-Monopoly Law" did not specify antitrust behavioral remedies, the hotspot and controversial Coca-Cola–Huiyuan Juice merger case led to increased debate.[7] In this case, enforcement agencies were confronted with a binary choice of either approving or prohibiting a merger under an administrative licensing model. This triggered the need for more refined and commercially practical legal remedies that were better aligned with market, corporate, and business behaviors. On December 4, 2014, the MOC issued the "Regulations on the Imposition of Additional Restrictive Conditions on Merger Notifications (Trial)," marking the formal introduction of behavioral remedies for actions suspected of harming competition. This can be seen as the beginning of a shift from the fully administrative licensing model, established in 2004, to a more integrated approach that combines economic analysis, market research methods, and the characteristics of business and market practices (classified under economic law in the civil law tradition).

11. Meanwhile, the 2008 merger notification standards, which set the core threshold at a turnover of 400 million yuan, became increasingly insufficient as China's market expanded and corporate sizes grew rapidly under globalization. The low notification threshold, coupled with an administrative licensing model (where mergers are prohibited without approval), led

---

7 Deng Feng, "Transmission, Leverage, and the Positioning of China's Antitrust Law: A Case Study of the Coca-Cola-Huiyuan Antitrust Review," *China Legal Science*, 2011, Issue 1, pp. 179-190; Sun Jin & Yu Zhe, "Uncertainty and Countermeasures in China's Antitrust Regulation of Foreign Mergers and Acquisitions – A Discussion Based on the Prohibited Coca-Cola-Huiyuan Merger Case," *East China Legal Review*, 2010, Issue 3; Pan Zhicheng, "Analysis of the MOC's Reasons for Prohibiting Coca-Cola's Acquisition of Huiyuan," *Legal Science*, 2009, Issue 7.

to an overwhelming caseload for enforcement agencies. Over 90% of merger cases were approved as "harmless," meaning that the majority of merger filings did not result in exclusionary or anti-competitive effects on relevant markets. These mergers typically shared common characteristics, such as low market share in the relevant market or the post-merger entity not conducting economic activities within China. To improve the efficiency of merger reviews and reduce the burden on applicants, antitrust enforcement agencies identified common characteristics of mergers that were unlikely to have anti-competitive effects. On February 11, 2014, the MOC issued the "Interim Provisions on the Application Standards for Simplified Merger Cases," establishing a simplified merger notification system and formalizing a process for these cases, effectively implementing a "segregation of simple and complex cases" approach for straightforward cases.

12. By this point, the basic legal framework for China's merger control legal institution had been largely completed, marking the second phase of its development.

13. With the development of China's market economy and globalization, debates and discussions about economic development strategies began to emerge. This shift in anti-monopoly policy started with the "Several Opinions of the Central Committee of the Communist Party of China and the State Council on Promoting Price Mechanism Reform," issued on October 12, 2015, which clearly stated the goal to "gradually establish the foundational position (in market economy) of competition policy." At the same time, during this period, the Chinese government's hallmark institutional reform policy was the "delegating powers, streamlining administration, and optimizing services" approach. On June 1, 2016, the State Council issued the "Opinions on Establishing a Fair Competition Review System in Market System Construction," which expanded antitrust law reviews to include scrutiny of local administrative legislation. After the 19th National Congress of the Communist Party of China in 2017, "competition policy" was explicitly outlined as the foundational aspect of China's market economy model, further increasing the importance and attention given to anti-monopoly law within the overall legal system.

14. However, during this stage, regulatory policies in economic sectors such as internet platforms, finance, and capital markets gradually began to show a "strong regulation" trend.[8] The position of antitrust departments within the government rose, and many significant enforcement cases sparked widespread attention across society and globally. This period can be seen as the third phase of China's antitrust law, but with regard to the concentration of undertakings, it was mainly marked by enhanced enforcement rather than structural changes.

---

[8] Li Jian, "The Implementation of Antitrust Law in the Platform Economy: Starting from the Goal of Economic Efficiency," *Chinese and Foreign Legal Studies*, 2022, Issue 1.

15. After the 20th National Congress of the Communist Party of China in 2022, competition enforcement was further strengthened as part of the "combining delegation of powers with strengthened regulating enforcement" policy.[9] Antitrust law was comprehensively reinforced within this institutional framework, and relevant administrative regulations and rules underwent extensive updates. The "Merger Notification Measures," "Merger Review Measures," and the "Interim Measures for Investigation and Handling of Failure to File Merger Notifications" were substantially integrated into the "Interim Provisions on Merger Review," which took effect on December 1, 2020. In 2023, following the updates to the "Anti-Monopoly Law" in 2022, the new "Merger Review Provisions" replaced the previous regulations, becoming an important set of rules for merger notifications, reviews, conditional mergers, penalties, and other areas in the concentration of undertakings domain. This update aligns with the overall reform of the anti-monopoly law system.

Table 1: Summary of China's Anti-Monopoly Law and Regulations

Legal Effect	Name of Laws and Regulations	Effective Date	Issuing Authority	Amendments
Law	"Anti-Monopoly Law of the People's Republic of China"	2008.8.1	National People's Congress	1. Revised version passed on 2022.6.24, effective on 2022.8.1.
Administrative Regulation	"Regulations on Merger Notification Standards"	2008.8.3	State Council	1. New revised version issued on 2018.9.18, effective the same day. 2. New revised version issued on 2024.1.26, effective the same day.
Departmental Regulations	"Methods for Calculating Turnover for Financial Sector Merger Notifications"	2009.8.15	Ministry of Commerce	None, currently effective.
	"Merger Notification Measures"	2010.1.1	Ministry of Commerce	1. Repealed on 2021.5.10.
	"Merger Review Measures"	2010.1.1	Ministry of Commerce	1. Repealed on 2021.5.10.
	"Interim Provisions on Merger Review"	2020.12.1	State Administration for Market Regulation	1. Revised version passed on 2022.3.24, effective on 2022.5.1; 2. "Merger Review Provisions" issued on 2023.3.10, effective on 2023.4.15.

---

9 The report delivered at the 20th National Congress of the Communist Party of China states: "Strengthen antitrust and anti-unfair competition measures, eliminate local protectionism and administrative monopolies, and regulate and guide the healthy development of capital in accordance with the law," https://www.gov.cn/xinwen/2022-10/25/content_5721685.htm,, last accessed on July 18, 2025.

Legal Effect	Name of Laws and Regulations	Effective Date	Issuing Authority	Amendments
Normative Documents	"Interim Provisions on Asset or Business Divestiture in Merger Control"	2010.7.5	Ministry of Commerce	Repealed by "Provisions on Imposing Additional Restrictive Conditions on Mergers (Trial)," which took effect on 2015.1.5; Repealed on 2021.5.10.
	"Interim Provisions on Evaluating the Competitive Impact of Mergers"	2011.9.5	Ministry of Commerce	1. Repealed on 2021.9.1.
	"Interim Measures for Investigation and Handling of Failure to File Merger Notifications"	2012.2.1	Ministry of Commerce	1. Repealed on 2021.5.10.
	"Merger Control Antitrust Review Guidelines"	2018.9.29	State Administration for Market Regulation	None, currently effective.
	"Merger Control Compliance Guidelines"	2023.9.5	State Administration for Market Regulation	None, currently effective.
	"Discretionary Guidelines for Administrative Penalties in Merger Control (Trial)"	2025.2.19	State Administration for Market Regulation	None, currently effective.
	"Horizontal Merger Control Review Guidelines"	2024.12.10	State Administration for Market Regulation	None, currently effective.

16. In the third phase, from the perspective of legal rule changes, the amendments to the "Anti-Monopoly Law" in 2022 did not bring substantial changes to the merger control legal institution, mainly adding the clock suspension rule, proactive investigations, and increasing penalty standards. However, looking at the overall rule system for the concentration of undertakings, the main changes focus on the following aspects: First, the merger notification thresholds have been significantly raised,[10] with the core turnover threshold for merger notification in China increasing from 400 million yuan to 800 million yuan. Second, the compliance

---

10 Deng Feng: "New Regulations on Merger Notification Standards: Mature, Scientific, and Cutting-Edge Exploration in China," *China Market Supervision Newspaper*, February 6, 2024, p. 3.

obligations for enterprises have been strengthened, with various regulatory authorities issuing numerous compliance guidelines, and the merger control review field is no exception. Third, the discretionary power of enforcement agencies has begun to be standardized and institutionalized, including the development of documents such as the "Merger Control Compliance Guidelines," "Discretionary Guidelines for Administrative Penalties in Merger Control (Trial)," and the "Horizontal Merger Control Review Guidelines." At the same time, enforcement agencies have also elevated the "Merger Notification Standards," which cover the entire merger notification process and standards, to the level of national standards.

II. Recent Rule Updates

17. The "Merger Review Provisions" officially issued on March 10, 2023, not only elaborated on the revisions to the law but also drew on past practices, incorporating a comprehensive and detailed update of the specific rules based on the positioning and description of the market and regulatory environment in the new era. First, at the general principles level, four new principles were introduced, including the constraint on the effect of centralized review authority delegation, the principle of equal treatment for private and public undertakings, the responsive principle of post-assessment to promote improvements, and the construction of an information system. Second, key procedural rules such as the "first-to-file" rule, "turnover," "negotiation application," "filing documents," "commercial secret information labeling," and "supplementary information" were further detailed. The clock suspension rule in the higher-level law was specified, and comprehensive additions were made regarding remedies for restrictive conditions. Third, clear obligations were imposed on agents, and relevant rules for supervising enforcement personnel were thoroughly improved. Fourth, the provisions concerning whistleblowing, the rights of the investigated parties, and corresponding legal responsibilities were refined.[11]

18. Regarding notification standards, the State Council issued Order No. 773 on January 22, 2024, making significant revisions to the notification thresholds. The new standards, while maintaining the original structure, have substantially raised the turnover thresholds: the global total turnover standard was increased from 10 billion RMB to 12 billion RMB; the total turnover in China was raised from 2 billion RMB to 4 billion RMB; the individual undertaking's turnover in China was increased from

---

11 Deng Feng: "Progress and Prospects of the Merger Control System," State Administration for Market Regulation Official Website, https://www.samr.gov.cn/zt/ndzt/2023n/2023jzz/zjgd/art/2023/art_11d88240cb4e443a952077207d652231.html, last accessed July 17, 2025.

400 million RMB to 800 million RMB. Notably, under the framework of China's Anti-Monopoly Law, the "Draft Revised Provisions on Merger Notification Standards" introduced a clause concerning "killer acquisitions" aimed at strengthening the regulation of large platforms acquiring high-valuation, low-revenue startups.[12] However, this section was removed in the final published version.

19. In addition, in September 2023, the SAMR issued the "Antitrust Compliance Guidelines for Merger Control," the first compliance guidance document in the field of merger control regulation. It outlines aspects such as compliance risks, compliance management, and compliance assurance. It encourages undertakings with merger control needs to establish antitrust compliance management systems, particularly for companies with annual revenues above a certain threshold. The document also defines the responsibilities of compliance management departments, including the development and implementation of compliance management systems, identifying and assessing compliance risks, and providing compliance advice and training.

20. On December 10, 2024, the SAMR issued the "Guidelines for Horizontal Merger Control Review," marking the first specialized guidance document for horizontal merger control review in China. The guidelines, comprising twelve chapters and eighty-seven articles, systematically summarize the practices and experiences of China's antitrust enforcement agencies in horizontal merger control review, particularly providing clear analytical paths for complex transactions that may have or could have exclusionary or anti-competitive effects. This further enhances the transparency and predictability of the review process.

21. To standardize administrative penalties in the field of merger control, SAMR issued the "Discretionary Penalty Guidelines for Illegal Merger Control Practices (Trial)" (hereinafter referred to as the "Penalty Guidelines") on February 19, 2025. The guidelines clarify the penalty standards for illegal merger control activities, distinguishing between illegal practices with or potentially having exclusionary or anti-competitive effects and those without such effects. It sets different initial fines and conditions for aggravated or mitigated penalties. The "Penalty Guidelines" represent a step toward the normalization and standardization of China's merger control penalty system.

---

12 See Article 4 of the "State Council's 'Draft for Comments' on the Revised Regulations on Merger Notification Standards": If a merger does not meet the notification threshold stipulated in Article 3 of this regulation but simultaneously meets the following conditions, the parties involved must submit a pre-merger notification to the State Council's antitrust enforcement agency. Failure to notify prohibits the implementation of the merger: 1. One of the merging parties has a turnover exceeding RMB 100 billion in the previous accounting year in China; 2. The market value (or valuation) of the other merging party or parties, as specified in Articles 2(1), 2(2), and 2(3), is not less than RMB 800 million, and the turnover in China in the previous accounting year accounts for more than one-third of its global turnover.

III. Changes in Enforcement Agencies

22. A new round of government reforms began in 2018, which integrated the antitrust enforcement responsibilities of the SAIC (Antitrust and Unfair Competition Enforcement Bureau), the NDRC (Price Supervision and Antitrust Enforcement Bureau), the MOC (MOFCOM) (Antitrust Bureau), and the State Council Antitrust Committee Office into the SAMR. The State Council Antitrust Committee was retained, with its specific duties being handled by SAMR. This integration of enforcement agencies has been long advocated by antitrust scholars. However, the merger of agencies, the improvement of institutional capabilities, and the reorganization of work processes have not occurred simultaneously. Therefore, while the agencies are unified, full integration and fusion are still under development.[13]

23. Since the unification of enforcement agencies, the period from 2015 to 2017 has seen a beginning of strengthening of supervision, with competition policy gradually gaining a more prominent position compared to industrial, fiscal, and financial policies. Multiple factors have led to the Antitrust Bureau receiving formal recognition within the Chinese government structure, corresponding to the expansion of both personnel and institutions. This expansion of institutions and staff is particularly important given the growing number of cases.

24. At the same time, the relationship between central and local authorities in merger control review has also evolved. Prior to 2023, merger control review was under the central government's authority, with SAMR handling the enforcement work. Unlike the "Provisional Regulations on Prohibiting Monopoly Agreements" and the "Provisional Regulations on Prohibiting the Abuse of Market Dominance", which authorized local market regulation departments to enforce antitrust rules, local agencies were not authorized to carry out merger control reviews. In recent years, as the number of merger control cases has steadily increased, the shortage of personnel and resources at the central level has become increasingly prominent. Starting in 2023, the "Merger Control Review Provisions" allowed SAMR's Antitrust Bureau to delegate merger control reviews to local enforcement agencies at the provincial, autonomous region, and municipal levels, based on work requirements. This is a crucial improvement for merger control legal institution.[14] On one hand, this "delegated authorization" can enhance the investigative capabilities of enforcement

---

13 Deng Feng: "The Integration of Antitrust Agencies: Avoiding Tunnel Vision," *Caijing Magazine*, July 9, 2018, Issue No. 533, pp. 122-125.

14 Article 2, Paragraph 2 of the "Regulations on the Review of Operator Concentrations" stipulates: "The State Administration for Market Regulation may, based on work needs, delegate provincial, autonomous region, and municipality-level market regulatory departments (hereinafter referred to as provincial market regulation departments) to carry out the review of operator concentrations."

agencies based on regional market divisions; on the other hand, it helps accumulate knowledge and experience at the local level, indirectly addressing the issue of insufficient personnel. Currently, enforcement agencies have begun pilot programs in five provinces (municipalities), such as Beijing, to delegate review tasks to lower-level agencies, establishing a two-tier review system.[15]

IV. Institutional Performance

25. The number of merger control cases in China has continued to grow, reflecting increased market activity and frequent mergers and acquisitions. As of 2024, since the establishment of the merger control legal institution, enforcement agencies have concluded over 6,400 cases, of which more than 6,000 were unconditionally approved, 64 were conditionally approved, and 3 were prohibited.[16] These cases span multiple industries, particularly in the internet, real estate, finance, electricity, and metal products sectors. Notably, in recent years, the penalties for illegal merger practices have been significantly strengthened. For example, in 2022, 32 cases of illegal mergers were penalized, with 27 cases (84.4% of the total) involving the internet industry, highlighting the intense focus on this sector.[17]

26. In 2024, SAMR concluded 643 merger control cases, of which 623 were unconditionally approved, 19 were withdrawn by the filing parties after acceptance, and one case was approved with restrictive conditions (the acquisition of shares in Takeda Electric Wire Co., Ltd. by JX Metal Co., Ltd.).[18] In 2023, SAMR concluded 797 merger control cases, with 782 being unconditionally approved, accounting for over 98%.[19] In 2022, SAMR received 867 merger control notifications and concluded 794 cases, representing year-on-year increases of 5.2% and 9.8%, respectively. Among them, 5 were approved with restrictive conditions, and 2 transactions were abandoned due to an inability to resolve competition concerns.[20] In 2021,

---

15 State Administration for Market Regulation Official Website: Optimizing the Antitrust Review Rules for Operator Concentrations to Protect Fair Competition and Stimulate Market Vitality – Interpretation of the "Regulations on the Review of Operator Concentrations."

16 The above data is calculated based on the cases disclosed by the MOC and the State Administration for Market Regulation.

17 King & Wood Mallesons: "Gathering Strength, Advancing with the Times – Review of China's Antitrust Law in 2022 (Concentration Review)," https://www.kwm.com/cn/zh/insights/latest-thinking/review-of-anti-monopoly-law-of-china-in-2022-concentration-review.html, last accessed July 18, 2025.

18 State Administration for Market Regulation, Official Website: "In 2024, the State Administration for Market Regulation approved 623 concentration cases unconditionally," published January 27, 2025.

19 "Annual Report on China's Antitrust Enforcement (2023)," compiled by the National Antitrust Bureau, p. 8. State Administration for Market Regulation, Official Website: "In 2023, the State Administration for Market Regulation concluded 797 concentration cases," published January 26, 2024.

20 "Annual Report on China's Antitrust Enforcement (2022)," compiled by the National Antitrust Bureau, p. 15.

SAMR concluded 727 merger control cases, a 53% increase compared to the previous year, including 1 prohibition and 4 conditional approvals.[21] The table below summarizes the number of cases concluded in recent years.

Table 2: Summary of Cases Concluded from 2019 to 2024

Year	Total Cases Closed	Notes
2024	643 cases	623 cases unconditionally approved 19 cases withdrawn after acceptance 1 case approved with conditions
2023	797 cases	782 cases unconditionally approved 11 cases withdrawn after acceptance 4 cases approved with conditions
2022	794 cases	787 cases unconditionally approved 5 cases approved with conditions 2 cases abandoned by the parties
2021	727 cases	720 cases unconditionally approved 1 case prohibited 4 cases approved with conditions 2 cases abandoned by the parties
2020	472 cases	468 cases unconditionally approved 4 cases approved with conditions
2019	465 cases	465 cases unconditionally approved 5 cases approved with conditions

V. Judicial Review

27. Due to the adoption of the civil law litigation system, merger control reviews in China must comply with administrative law both in terms of procedure and decision-making. Substantive reviews have gradually shifted to align more with the antitrust law model since 2014. Given that merger control operates in the form of administrative approval, it is a form of preemptive administrative review. If a company disagrees with the decision made by the administrative enforcement agency, it can appeal to the court, invoking the administrative litigation process to have the court review the enforcement agency's decision.[22]

28. According to the case database from "Peking University Law Database" (Beida Fabao), which searches judicial precedents and experiences since the enactment of the "Anti-Monopoly Law" in 2007, there were no cases involving lawsuits filed against unlawful merger control decisions

---

21 "Annual Report on China's Antitrust Enforcement (2021)," compiled by the National Antitrust Bureau, p. 2.

22 Hou Liyang: "The Dilemmas and Responses of Antitrust Administrative Litigation in China: An Empirical Analysis Based on 165 Court Judgments," *Legal Studies*, 2022, Issue 1.

before 2025. However, in 2025, the first administrative lawsuit targeting enforcement agencies as defendants was filed.

29. In March 2025, the Beijing Intellectual Property Court published an administrative judgment regarding the case of Beijing Topix Pharmaceutical Co., Ltd. ("Topix") suing the SAMR.[23] This was the first case involving merger control review since the implementation of the "Anti-Monopoly Law" in 2008. After reviewing the case, the court dismissed all of Topix's claims. As Topix did not appeal within the statutory period, the judgment has now become final. The core of this case was SAMR's decision No. 42 of 2023 concerning the acquisition of partial shares of Topix by Senhong Pharmaceutical Co., Ltd. ("Senhong") in September 2023. After a comprehensive review, SAMR determined that the transaction could potentially have exclusionary or restrictive effects on competition in the Baclofen injection market within China and required Senhong and the post-concentration entity to lift exclusive agreements, divest in-progress businesses, and reduce drug prices, among other obligations.[24] Dissatisfied with this decision, Topix applied for administrative reconsideration within the statutory time limit. In February 2024, SAMR issued Administrative Reconsideration Decision No. 127, maintaining the original decision. Topix then filed an administrative lawsuit in March 2024. The Beijing Intellectual Property Court organized evidence exchange and cross-examination, and determined that SAMR's decision was factually clear, legally applicable, and procedurally correct, ultimately dismissing Topix's lawsuit.

VI. Path Dependence and Institutional Embeddedness

30. The broad legislative authorization granted to administrative agencies is not only one of China's characteristics as a transitioning country but also aligns with the gradual reform strategy, coined by Deng Xiaoping in 1979, of "crossing the river by feeling the stones" (trails and errors). The development of China's merger control review system profoundly reflects this characteristic, where enforcement agencies continuously accumulate experience in response to real-world problems, rather than designing and implementing systems according to predefined models and ideas. Starting with the "Foreign Trade Law," enforcement agencies, based on antidumping, anti-subsidy, and foreign investment regulations, began exploring market conditions and corporate strategies, and taking regulatory actions based on competitive facts related to pricing strategies, all while

---

23 Beijing Tuobixi Pharmaceutical Co., Ltd. v. State Administration for Market Regulation, Beijing Intellectual Property Court (2024) Jing 73 Xing Chu 5180 Administrative Judgment.

24 State Administration for Market Regulation Official Website: Announcement on the Antitrust Review Decision Regarding the Acquisition of Shares of Beijing Tuobixi Pharmaceutical Co., Ltd. by Xiansheng Pharmaceutical Co., Ltd. with Additional Restrictive Conditions, released on September 22, 2023.

31. Once the "Anti-Monopoly Law" provided clearer rules, the legal provisions for merger control remained relatively general, with specific rules primarily relying on administrative agencies' normative documents and case handling developed in practice.[25] After more than 30 years of accumulating knowledge through thousands of cases, by 2025, China elevated the processes of merger control to national standards.[26] This progression can be seen as an example of organizational learning and institutional change on a global legal history scale.

32. Even when making horizontal comparisons within China's economic regulatory system – such as food safety regulation, product quality regulation, or labor regulation – merger control stands out significantly due to the professional, complex, and numerous challenges it faces. Coupled with the rapid development of China's market and the growing importance of mergers as a means for industrial growth, the achievements in this area remain impressive. Even when compared to other departments in antitrust law enforcement, such as those dealing with monopoly agreements, abuse of market dominance, and China's unique anti-administrative monopoly and fair competition reviews, the merger control legal institution's increasing level of standardization, process regularization, and its incorporation of international rules and new economic analysis methods show a high degree of normativity and institutional construction.

33. A more appropriate theoretical perspective for explaining this phenomenon is institutional dynamics, which comprehensively considers multiple factors, including organizational structure, institutional environment, enforcement personnel, management, leadership, and changes within the institutions.[27]

34. Similarly, the path dependence in China's merger control review is also apparent. This includes sensitive path dependencies at the starting point and the high cost of changing the outcome.[28] Clearly, the system's origins reflect institutional considerations regarding foreign trade order, and it is rooted in the administrative approval mechanism, which had distinctive Chinese characteristics, used during its early formation. The system's comprehensive review of foreign-invested enterprises, its high sensitivity to pricing behavior, and its design logic aimed at protecting national interests collectively constitute the early features of the system. Likewise,

---

25 Deng Feng: "The Chinese Characteristics of Antitrust Merger Review," *Caijing* Magazine, April 16, 2021.

26 State Administration for Market Regulation released the "Regulations on Operator Concentration Review" in October 2023, which are important detailed rules in the field of operator concentration.

27 See James Q Wilson, Bureaucracy: What Government Agencies Do and Why They Do It, New York: Basic Books, 1989. See also Avner Greif, Institutions and the Path to the Modern Economy: Lessons from Medieval Trade, Cambridge University Press, 2006.

28 See S. J. Liebowiz and Stephen E. Margolis, Path Dependence, Lock – in, and History, *Journal of Law, Economics, & Organization*, Vol. 11, No. 1, 1995, Pp205-226.

the understanding and cognition of the "Anti-Monopoly Law" when it was enacted in 2008 formed the second level of path dependence. By 2014, the basic framework of the merger control legal institution was established, and this framework became a source of institutional resistance during the 2022 revision of the "Anti-Monopoly Law."

35. The institutional resistance to reforms from the merger control legal institution itself mainly manifests on two levels: First, although the declaration thresholds have been increased, easing the procedural obligations for most enterprises, China, as the world's second-largest economy and a country continually advancing its globalization strategy, still adopts substantial standards and an administrative licensing model similar to the EU,[29] rather than adopting the filing and proactive review mechanism represented by the U.S., or exploring more optimized alternative paths.[30] Second, due to the constraints of the 2004 "Administrative Licensing Law" and the subsequent "Administrative Penalties Law," merger control review was formally categorized as an administrative licensing process (a similar issue also arises in the context of monopoly agreements and abuse of market dominance, but it is particularly prominent in the merger control field). At the same time, judicial review of merger control cases is uniformly incorporated into the administrative litigation process, leading to a series of institutional constraints and inefficiencies in both enforcement and judicial phases. The current administrative model in China is influenced by the French tradition, with some elements borrowed from Japan. Under this model, a merger application between two large companies is treated legally the same as an application for a driver's license, which creates significant controversy in practice due to the formalistic classification logic and exposes the institutional tension in the system's ability to handle complex market behaviors.

36. Another institutional obstacle faced by merger control, as part of the broader antitrust law and economic regulation system, stems from its marginal position within the overall legal framework, leading to issues of "institutional embeddedness." [31] Specifically, the next set of challenges for the merger control review system, based on institutional embeddedness, includes:

    1. Despite institutional reforms in 2018 and the establishment of a unified enforcement agency in 2021, the merging of previously separate enforcement departments under different regulatory agencies only completed the institutional integration, without a fundamental

---

29 Ye Jun: "A Study on the Legal Definition Model of Operator Concentration," *China Law Review*, 2015, Issue 5.

30 Li Jian: "Effectiveness and Transformation of the Mandatory Declaration System for Operator Concentration," *Journal of Law, Jiaotong University*, 2021, Issue 4.

31 See Karl Polanyi: The Great Transformation: The Political and Economic Origins of Our Time, Beacon Press, 1944.

change in the legal rules, enforcement mindset, and practices.[32] This is reflected in the 2022 revision of the "Anti-Monopoly Law" and its subsequent implementation process: although the law was updated, the supporting departmental regulations were not structurally reformed but instead continued the original division of labor with only formal adjustments. Specifically, regarding merger control, the review of joint ventures did not coordinate the relationship with monopoly agreements under the new unified enforcement agency; nor was there a connection between the assessment of potential competition harm and enforcement of market dominance abuse. Furthermore, in some mergers where control changes are driven by regulatory requirements rather than market forces, there has yet to be an effective response to the need for fair competition review or anti-administrative monopoly regulation.

2. The competition assessment in corporate mergers is actually constrained by the company's own governance and the fulfillment mechanisms in the merger contracts. China's corporate governance is also modeled after the French tradition,[33] and the implementation characteristics of business contracts are constrained by China's contract law, which blends elements of the "United Nations Convention on Contracts for the International Sale of Goods (CISG)" with the civil law tradition's classical contract theory (the will theory model). The division or even conflict between different legal departments creates many challenges for determining the merger control judgment. For example, in a tender offer, how to balance the efficiency required and the prevention of competitive harm, and whether the delay in fulfilling the merger contract due to China's way of contractual business performance constitutes a restriction on competition, or how to determine whether contract amendments or updates are part of a joint transaction or multiple separate transactions, are typical examples of such challenges.

3. Although there are differences in the strength of competition policies and their adjustment paths across various jurisdictions worldwide, China's unique institutional characteristics exacerbate the uncertainty in merger control reviews. These characteristics include: the lack of a precedent-based case law system, the extent and practice of information publicity, the central-local govermental relationship, the substantive treatment differences between state-owned and private enterprises, and the choice between regulation or anti-monopoly

---

32 Deng Feng: "The Merger of Antitrust Agencies: Avoiding Tunnel Vision," *Caijing Magazine*, July 9, 2018, Issue 533, pp. 122-125.

33 See Deng Feng: Path Dependence of Corporate Governance in China, *Peking University Law Journal*, Vol. 20, Issue 1, 2008, pp. 58-65.

measures.³⁴ These institutional factors, closely intertwined with corporate governance structures and government-business relations, collectively influence the judgment and discretion in assessing the competitive impact of corporate mergers.

VII. Conclusion

37. With the expansion of China's market and the evolution of business models, platform enterprises have become a key force driving the country's economic development. At the same time, current policies, influenced by the need for administrative control and the nationalism in the market economy triggered by geopolitical conflicts, pose challenges to China's merger control legal institution. In the future, challenges will emerge in areas such as economic analysis methods driven by platforms,³⁵ the issue of personal privacy protection, and the coordination and division of labor between national security reviews and corporate merger control.

38. As part of China's anti-monopoly law, the true challenge for merger control lies in the growth of knowledge and the updating of legal theories.³⁶ This means that companies, enforcement agencies, and practicing lawyers should deepen their understanding of the market, particularly China's transitional market, as well as Chinese corporate governance and business practices. Based on the updating of knowledge and theories, China's merger control legal framework will be better equipped to respond to economic growth and transformation with more effective regulatory measures.³⁷

---

34 Deng Feng, Wang Huiqun: "Regulation or Antitrust? Conflicts and Dilemmas in Platform Legal Adjustments," in *40 Questions on Platform Economy*, edited by Huang Yiping, Peking University Press, 2022. Deng Feng, Guo Xiaoli, Wang Huiqun, Li Shuhao, Wang Fengquan, "Antitrust Challenges of Platforms," in Huang Yiping et al., *Platform Economy: Innovation, Governance, and Prosperity*, CITIC Publishing House, July 2022, Chapter 12.

35 Li Jian: "Antitrust Law and Market Definition in Bilateral Markets: Law and Economics in the 'Baidu Case,'" *Law and Business Review*, 2010, Issue 5; Wang Xiaoye, "The Theory and Practice of Antitrust Regulation in China's Digital Economy," 2022, Issue 5; Sun Jin, "Antitrust Regulation of Digital Platforms," *Chinese Social Sciences*, 2022, Issue 5, and other studies.

36 See Roscoe Pound: Comparative Law and History as Bases for Chinese Law, Harvard Law Review, Vol. 61, 1948, pp. 749–762.

37 Deng Feng: "Towards Responsive Regulation: A Review and Analysis of the Revision of the 'Operator Concentration Review Regulations,'" *China Market Supervision Journal*, March 30, 2023, A8.

On the Pattern Setting of Anti-monopoly Regulatory Framework for Resale Price Maintenance

JIANG SHAN[*]

Professor, University of International Business and Economics

Abstract

For the anti-monopoly regulation of resale price maintenance (RPM), no solid consensus on the regulatory framework has been reached worldwide. In China, the ambiguity of the RPM regulation scheme under the 2007 Anti-Monopoly Law has led to practical divergence between illegal per se and rule of reason in public enforcement and private litigation. The 2022 Anti-Monopoly Law partially resolves these differences by establishing a presumption of anti-competitive effects of RPM, but the new regulatory structure remains unclear. To construct the anti-monopoly regulatory framework of RPM at this new starting point, important clarifications should be made as follows: the analytical mode should be categorized as the abbreviated rule of reason, safe harbor should not be applied, the connotation and legal consequences of the presumption of anti-competitive effects should be clarified, the framework of defenses including direct and indirect evidence should be defined, the pro-competitive effects and the parties' burden of proof should be delineated, and the tradeoff mechanism between pro-competitive and anti-competitive effects should be improved. Only in this way, can we set a coherent pattern of the anti-monopoly regulatory framework for RPM, and shape the stable expectation of market competition order.

---

[*] Jiang Shan, Professor, University of International Business and Economics. The author wants to thank Ziqiang Liang, Yi Hong, Jia Yin and Kemian Wang for translating the paper.

On the Pattern Setting of Anti-monopoly Regulatory Framework for Resale Price Maintenance

Introduction

1. For a long time, RPM has been an important area of antitrust law attracting significant attention but remains fraught with disagreement.[1] The reason for this attention lies in the fact that while RPM manifests in a simplicity in form, its impact on competition is highly complex and involves a collision between market competition order and business models. This complexity has led to divergent views on the regulation of RPM under antitrust law, which remain unresolved to this day. The main manifestations of this division include, on one hand, the differing approaches in major legal jurisdictions regarding the analytical mode of RPM regulation, choosing between illegal per se or the rule of reason; and on the other hand, even within a specific jurisdiction such as China, there are cognitive differences and practical divergences between law enforcement agencies and judicial bodies regarding the regulation of RPM. The structural updates of the provisions in the 2022 Anti-Monopoly Law provide a broader interpretative space to address these disputes,[2] but they also bring about a series of new issues: Does the presumption of anti-competitive effects mean the end of the rule of reason analysis? Is there still room for a successful defense against the presumption of anti-competitive effects? How can the balance between pro-competitive effects and anti-competitive effects be weighed? Answers to these questions are key points that cannot be avoided in the legal interpretation of RPM. Clarifying them will help to set the pattern of the regulatory framework of RPM under Chinese law, thereby providing more stable expectations for the formation and operation of business models and the shaping of market competition order.

---

[1] Regarding the maximum price limit, there is a general consensus in the field of economics that it can eliminate double marginalization… However, the welfare effects of minimum price limits and fixed resale prices are unclear, as they vary depending on market structure and product characteristics. Generally speaking, minimum price limits and fixed resale prices can be discussed under the category of RPM. See Haixiao Gu: *The Economic Logic and Legal Regulation of RPM–With Comments on Article 14 of Chinese Anti-monopoly Law*, Journal of Henan Administrative Institute of Politics and Law, No. 4, 2008. In this paper, the term "maximum resale price maintenance" is used to refer to the maximum price limit, with RPM used as a collective term for the other two types of resale price limits.

[2] The revised Paragraph 1 of Article 18 of the Anti-Monopoly Law remains unchanged: "Undertakings are prohibited from concluding the following monopoly agreements with their trading counterparts: (1) on fixing the prices of commodities resold to a third party; (2) on restricting the lowest prices for commodities resold to a third party; and (3) other monopoly agreements confirmed as such by the authority for enforcement of the Anti-monopoly Law under the State Council." Paragraph 2 adds: "The agreements as specified in subparagraphs (1) and (2) shall not be prohibited if the undertakings can prove the agreements do not have the effect of eliminating or restricting competition." Paragraph 3 adds: "Where undertakings can prove that their market share in the relevant market is lower than the standard set by the authority for enforcement of the Anti-monopoly Law under the State Council and that other conditions stipulated by the authority for enforcement of the Anti-monopoly Law under the State Council are met, the agreement shall not be prohibited."

Jiang Shan

I. A New Starting Point for the RPM Anti-Monopoly Regulation under Chinese Law

2. In China, after more than a decade of development, a partial consensus has been reached in the administrative enforcement and judicial application of RPM regulation under anti-monopoly law, but significant disagreements remain. Today, the legislative progress of Article 18 of the Anti-Monopoly Law marks a new starting point for the legal interpretation. In this regard, reviewing the evolution of the RPM anti-monopoly regulation in China and understanding the underlying logic behind the reshaping of the legal normative structure are essential to opening a new chapter in its legal interpretation.

(1) The evolution of RPM anti-monopoly regulation in China

3. To examine the evolution of RPM anti-monopoly regulation under Chinese law, it is necessary to compare and analyze the practices of public enforcement and private litigation. In this context, "there is a significant divergence in the regulatory approach to RPM: enforcement agencies believe that the presumption of illegality rule should be applied and that this practice should generally be prohibited unless the investigated parties provide strong grounds for exemption; court judgments, on the other hand, tend to adopt the rule of reason, giving full consideration to the balance between pro-competitive and anti-competitive effects of the practice concerned."[3] These two regulatory tracks initially developed in parallel, occasionally intersecting in legal applications, and recently have been left unresolved in the anti-monopoly administrative litigation, highlighting the bottleneck of RPM anti-monopoly regulation under the 2007 Anti-Monopoly Law. Some commentators have even pointed out that "the judicial bodies' approach, although reasonable, is not legal; while the administrative enforcement agencies' approach, although legal, is not reasonable."[4] The key question is whether this divergence stems from improper application of legal interpretation techniques, or from legislation leaving excessive room for ambiguity. This issue warrants further examination.

4. In the public enforcement track, from the Moutai case, the Wuliangye case, and the Milk Powder Manufacturers case, to the Eyeglass Lens Manufacturers case, the Hankook Tire case, the Mercedes-Benz case, the Medtronic case, the Yangtze River Pharmaceutical Group case, and the Bull Group case, the attitude of enforcement agencies toward vertical PRM

---

3   Jiang Shan: *On the Knowledge Transformation and Methodological Reconstruction of Anti-Monopoly Law Interpretation*, Modern Law Science, No. 6, 2018.

4   Liyang Hou: *Localized Enforcement against Retail Price Maintenance: Conflictive Theories, Enforcement Diversity and Possible Solutions*, The Jurist, No. 6, 2016.

has gradually shifted from the rule of reason analytical mode to a mode closer to the illegal per se. The characteristic of this shift is that, in the early stages of administrative enforcement, a detailed layered analysis was conducted between "intra-brand competition" and "inter-brand competition". This was initially introduced in the Moutai case and Wuliangye case, where the RPM of the two brands was clearly discussed: "First, it excluded competition among the distributors of the same brand… Second, it restricted competition among different brands in the Baijiu industry… Third, it harmed consumer interests."[5] However, administrative enforcement cases did not consistently follow this path, sometimes analyzing the competitive effects,[6] and sometimes directly presuming the illegality based on legal provisions,[7] displaying fluctuations and increasingly leaning toward the presumption of illegality rule. This presumption of illegality is also classified as the "Prohibition plus Exemption" regulatory approach, meaning that once RPM agreements are proved to exist, they are presumed to have anti-competitive effects, and the parties involved must prove that the agreements meet the exemption conditions in order to mount a successful defense.

5. In the judicial application track, from the Johnson case to the Gree case, the Hankook case, and the Hainan Yutai case, the judicial system's attitude toward RPM has shifted from predominantly using the rule of reason analytical mode to more recently proposing that in certain cases,[8] public enforcement and private litigation should follow different analytical modes.[9] In the Hainan Yutai case, the Supreme People's Court elaborated on this legal application distinction: "In anti-monopoly civil

---

5   See Administrative Penalty Decision of the Guizhou Provincial Administration for Commodity Prices (Qian Jia Chu [2013] No. 1); and Administrative Penalty Decision of the Sichuan Provincial Development and Reform Commission (Chuan Fa Gai Jia Jian Chu [2013] No. 1).

6   For the Milk Powder Manufacturers case, see "Milk Powder Manufacturers such as Biostime and Others Fined a Total of 668.73 Million Yuan for Violating the Anti-Monopoly Law by Restricting Competition", the National Development and Reform Commission, August 7, 2013, https://www.ndrc.gov.cn/xwdt/xwfb/201308/t20130807_956179.html?; for Medtronic case, Administrative Penalty Decision of the National Development and Reform Commission (Fa Gai Jia Jian [2016] No. 8); and for Yangtze River Pharmaceutical Group case, Administrative Penalty Decision of the State Administration for Market Regulation (Guo Shi Jian Chu [2021] No. 29).

7   For the Eyeglass Lens Manufacturers case, see "Some Eyeglass Lens Manufacturers' Resale Price Maintenance Practices Lawfully Investigated," National Development and Reform Commission, May 29, 2014, https://www.ndrc.gov.cn/xwdt/xwfb/201405/t20140529_956353.html; for the Hankook Tire case, see "Shanghai Hankook Tire Fined 2.1752 Million for Price Monopoly," China News, April 13, 2016, https://www.chinanews.com/auto/2016/04-13/7832464.shtml; for the Mercedes-Benz case, Administrative Penalty Decision of the Jiangsu Provincial Administration for Commodity Prices (Su Jia Fan Long Duan [2014] No. 2); for the Chrysler case, the Administrative Penalty Decision of the Shanghai Municipal Administration for Commodity Prices (No. 2520140077 [2014]); "FAW-Volkswagen Sales Company Implemented Price Monopoly and Fined 240 Million Yuan," China Central People's Government Portal, September 11, 2014, https://www.gov.cn/xinwen/2014-09/11/content_2749003.htm; and for the Bull Group case, Administrative Penalty Decision of the Zhejiang Provincial Administration for Market Regulation (Zhe Shi Jian An [2021] No. 4).

8   For the Johnson case, see the Civil Judgment of the First Intermediate People's Court of Shanghai Municipality (Hu 01 Min Zhong No. 1035 [2018]). For the Gree case, see the Civil Judgment of the High People's Court of Guangdong Province (Yue Min Zhong No. 1771 [2016]). For the Hankook case, see the Civil Judgment of the High People's Court of Shanghai Municipality (Hu Min Zhong No. 475 [2018]).

9   See the Administrative Judgment of the Supreme People's Court of the People's Republic of China (Zui Gao Fa Xing Shen No. 4675 [2018]).

litigation, the court examines whether the monopolistic agreement has the effect of excluding or restricting competition, and on this basis determines whether to support the plaintiff's claim... In administrative litigation, the standard for determining the legality of vertical monopolistic agreements by anti-monopoly enforcement agencies differs significantly from the standard in civil litigation."[10] The problem is, the analysis stops there, and the term "differs significantly" is not further explained in the court's analysis. A closer look reveals that the natural difference between the two is evident: in civil litigation, the plaintiff must prove that the specific competitive harm has occurred to him/her, while in administrative enforcement, the enforcement agency only needs to prove that competitive harm to the competition order exists. Nevertheless, apart from this, there should not, and cannot, be other substantial differences in the analytical mode, methods of proving, and burden of proof.

6. It can be argued that until the Hainan Yutai case, Chinese law still left considerable uncertainty regarding RPM anti-monopoly regulation. On one hand, in public enforcement, the anti-competitive effects of RPM have already been placed under the framework of the presumption of illegality rule, but how to rebut the presumed effects has not been clarified. On the other hand, in private litigation, the anti-competitive effects of RPM remain to be proved, but the methods of proving and the room for defense are still uncertain. Such an amount of uncertainty mainly stems from the long-standing ambiguity in the analytical mode of RPM anti-monopoly regulation under Chinese law, and it is essential to trace the source of these issues.

(2) Reshaping the framework of RPM anti-monopoly Regulation

7. Prior to the legislative amendment, the prevailing view in both China's legal practice and academia overwhelmingly favored that RPM should be subject to the presumption of illegality rule.[11] Some commentators have pointed out that the application of the rule of reason is generally unfavorable to Chinese consumers, as the courts lack sufficient economic analysis capacity to apply the rule of reason. Furthermore, applying the rule of reason to RPM conflicts with the current law of China, which is why the Anti-Monopoly Law adopts the "Prohibition plus Exemption" approach.[12] Others have stated that, for any of the listed typical monopolistic agreements, they are generally presumed to be anti-competitive and thus declared illegal. The participants in the monopolistic

---

10 The Administrative Judgment of the Supreme People's Court of the People's Republic of China (Zui Gao Fa Xing Shen No. 4675 [2018]).

11 See Lei Lan: *The Critique of the Presumption of Illegality of Resale Price Maintenance*, Tsinghua University Law Journal, No. 2, 2016.

12 See Xiaoye Wang: *Criticism of the Application of Rule of Reason in Anti-Monopoly Regulation of Resale Price Maintenance*, Studies in Law and Business, No. 1, 2021.

agreement (the undertakings) can only rebut the presumption of illegality by providing evidence to prove that the exemption conditions are met.[13] Of course, these commentators did not explicitly argue that RPM should be governed by the illegal per se.

8. At the same time, some commentators explicitly supported the application of the rule of reason. Some noted that applying the rule of reason to RPM is consistent with economic research findings, legislative goals, and international enforcement as well as judicial practices, and aligns with China's economic development stage and the development stage of the Anti-Monopoly Law.[14] Other commentators have argued that, in the absence of sufficient empirical evidence showing that most of minimum resale price restrictions harms competition, it would not be wise for China, as an emerging market economy, to adopt either the illegal per se or the "Prohibition plus Exemption" approach to regulate minimum resale price maintenance; the rule of reason is more in line with the actual needs of the market.[15] Still, others have pointed out that, considering the diversity and complexity of the impact of RPM on social welfare when companies make multiple decisions, the antitrust enforcement standards for RPM should shift from the illegal per se rule to the presumption rule based on reasonableness, emphasizing the interrelation between business strategies and the market.[16] In comparison, the views focusing on the welfare impacts of RPM itself is more convincing than the argument based on the economic development stage.

9. There are also some commentators who hold a middle-ground position, arguing that both the illegal per se rule and the rule of reason should be applied with caution. Some have pointed out that adopting a per se illegality approach toward the prevalent vertical price-fixing agreements in China would inevitably raise concerns about selective enforcement, while applying the rule of reason may involve significant legal basis deficiencies.[17] Others have proposed that the rule of reason analysis should be adopted, but certain conditions should be set to prevent such agreements from being treated as de facto legal per se.[18] There are also commentators who support applying the rule of reason but argue that while theoretical analyses of the potential reasonableness of RPM are increasing, empirical

---

13 See Jian Wang: *A Study on the Relationship Between the Identification of Monopolistic agreements and the Exclusion or Restriction of Competition*, Law Science, No. 3, 2014.

14 See Lei Lan: *The Critique of the Presumption of Illegality of Resale Price Maintenance*, Tsinghua University Law Journal, No. 2, 2016.

15 See Wenlian Ding: *Judicial Evaluation of Practices Restricting Minimum Resale Prices*, Journal of Law Application, No. 7, 2014.

16 See Guangliang Ye and Shiqiang Wang: *Resale Price Maintenance and Wholesale Pricing – A Spatial Price Discrimination Model*, China Economic Quarterly, No. 1, 2021.

17 See Maozhong Ding: *The Dilemma and Solutions of Determining the Illegality of Resale Price Maintenance under the Current Framework of the Anti-Monopoly Law*, No. 5, 2015.

18 See Huang Yong and Yannan Liu: *A Sudy of Application of China's Anti-Monopoly Law on the Issue of PPM, Journal of Social Sciences*, Journal of Social Sciences, No. 10, 2013.

10. studies are also increasingly finding an existing causation between high product prices and RPM.[19] Evidently, before the legislative amendment, whether supporting the illegal per se or the rule of reason, both positions necessarily required qualifying "caveats", which naturally directed to one middle-ground choice between the two.

10. With the legislative amendment now in place, Paragraph 2 of Article 18 of the Anti-Monopoly Law clearly states that "The agreements as specified in subparagraphs (1) and (2) shall not be prohibited if the undertakings can prove the agreements do not have the effect of eliminating or restricting competition." This marks the legalization of the presumption of anti-competitive effects for RPM. This shift carries significant structural implications. Some commentators have pointed out the difference between the old law, which "identified" RPM as a monopolistic agreement, and the new law, which "presumes" it as a monopolistic agreement: "The identification is a final conclusion, and the burden of proof is borne by the plaintiff, while the presumption allows for a defense, essentially reversing the burden of proof."[20] Interpretation of the Supreme People's Court on Several Issues Concerning the Application of Law in the Trial of Civil Dispute Cases Arising from Monopolistic Conduct (Judicial Interpretation of Anti-Monopoly Law), effective July 1, 2024, clarifies the burden of proof under Paragraph 2 of Article 18 of the Anti-Monopoly Law.[21] Furthermore, the structural impact of the presumptions of illegality rule on the anti-monopoly regulation of RPM, particularly regarding the analytical mode that this presumption entails and the underlying logic of the associated burden of proof allocation, should be clarified as early as possible.

11. First, it should be determined that under the current normative structure, the anti-monopoly analytical mode for RPM should not be classified as illegal per se. The application of the illegal per se rule has a defined scope, i.e., there are certain agreements or practices which because of their pernicious effect on competition and lack of any redeeming virtue are conclusively presumed to be unreasonable and therefore illegal without elaborate inquiry as to the precise harm they have caused or the business excuse for their use.[22] By contrast, the legal provision allowing for the rebuttable presumption of anti-competitive effects clearly adopts an open stance for defense. Furthermore, according to the past practices in Chinese law, such

---

19 See Jian Li and Fei Tang: *The Illegality of Resale Price Maintenance and Legal Regulation*, Contemporary Law Review, No. 6, 2010.

20 Guangyao Xu: *Identification of Monopoly Behavior in Resale Price Maintenance Cases*, Law Review, No. 3, 2023.

21 Article 21 of Interpretation of the Supreme People's Court on Several Issues Concerning the Application of Law in the Trial of Civil Dispute Cases Arising from Monopolistic Conduct (Fa Shi No. 6 [2024]): "If the alleged monopolistic conduct falls under the monopolistic agreements specified in Subparagraphs (1) and (2) of Paragraph 1 of Article 18 of the Anti-Monopoly Law, the defendant shall bear the burden of proof that the agreement does not have the effect of excluding or restricting competition."

22 Northern Pacific Railway v. United States, 356 U.S. 1, 5 (1958).

anti-competitive presumptions are not irrebuttable, and there is room for the subsequent efficiency defense. Currently, even a de facto presumption of anti-competitive effects has been applied in administrative enforcement, the analytical mode is not strictly aligned with the illegal per se rule. Some commentators have pointed out that the State Administration for Market Regulation often conducts a certain amount of economic analysis based on the economic realities of specific cases and makes a cautious decision after weighing the overall impact [...] Local anti-monopoly enforcement agencies commonly tend to apply the simple illegal per se rule in follow-on enforcement actions.[23] The above assessment is empirically grounded, as the enforcement documents fail to adequately demonstrate the underlying analytical process. Before administrative penalty has been determined, enforcement agencies in practice typically conduct an analysis that extends beyond the scope of the illegal per se rule.

12. Second, it should be clarified that under the current normative structure, the anti-monopoly analytical mode for RPM should not fall under a comprehensive rule of reason. It is generally believed that the illegal per se rule and the rule of reason are part of a continuum: (1) the illegal per se rule, where anti-competitive restrictions are presumed unreasonable (thus illegal) and cannot be rebutted; (2) a presumption of illegality after proving certain elements (e.g., market power), which also does not allow for potential justifications; (3) a rebuttable presumption of illegality, where the plaintiff must first prove certain elements and if the defendant cannot provide a recognizable pro-competitive justification, the presumption of illegality applies; (4) a comprehensive rule of reason, where the plaintiff must first prove anti-competitive effects (actual harm or harm inferred from market power), and if the defendant offers a recognizable pro-competitive effect, the determination of illegality depends on whether the plaintiff can prove that the anti-competitive effects outweigh the pro-competitive effects.[24] Under this classification, the current provision lies in the middle of this continuum between the illegal per se rule and the comprehensive rule of reason. Since there is a presumption of anti-competitive effects, it cannot be classified under the comprehensive rule of reason.

13. Third, in comparison, under the current normative structure, the anti-monopoly analytical mode for RPM should be classified as an abbreviated rule of reason or "quick look". In some respects, the abbreviated rule of reason functions as a screening mechanism to determine whether conduct that would typically be subject to the illegal per se rule should instead be analyzed under the rule of reason because the defendant has offered

---

23 See Yaojia Tang: *The Anti-monopoly Principles of Resale Price Maintenance under Platform Economy*, Journal of Shanghai University of Finance and Economics, No. 4, 2021.

24 See Spencer Waller: *Justice Stevens and Rule of Reason*, SMU Law Review, Vol. 62, p.700-701 (2009).

a plausible pro-competitive justification.²⁵ Based on this, the Chinese law has adopted a hybrid model that combines the above (2) and (3) modes, where the enforcement agency or plaintiff only needs to prove the existence of the RPM practice (without needing to prove market power) to presume anti-competitive effects, but this presumption can be rebutted based on market power and the effects of the behavior. It must be repeatedly emphasized that the illegal per se rule, the abbreviated rule of reason, and the comprehensive rule of reason do not operate as isolated analytical silos.²⁶ Based on this understanding, it is not hard to understand that under Chinese law, the RPM analytical mode is precisely positioned in the middle of the continuum between the illegal per se rule and the comprehensive rule of reason. Moreover, theoretically, the abbreviated rule of reason lacks precisely defined boundaries, and classifying the middle ground between the illegal per se and the rule of reason as the abbreviated rule of reason aligns with categorical logic. On this basis, the role of this analytical mode as a screening mechanism is to invoke the application of either the illegal per se rule or the comprehensive rule of reason based on the rebuttal of the presumption of anti-competitive effects.

14. In other terms, under the new normative structure, summarizing over a decade of accumulated experience on the implementation of the Anti-monopoly Law, it should be clear that RPM regulation should adopt the abbreviated rule of reason. Under this analytical mode, the focus of the examination is identifying whether the RPM provisions in a specific case will invoke a more comprehensive rule of reason analysis or return to the illegal per se path. Based on this, along with the newly introduced safe harbor institution in Paragraph 3 of Article 18, the regulatory framework can be restructured at three levels: Firstly, as a preliminary question, does RPM qualify for the safe harbor? Secondly, how to frame the presumption of anti-competitive effects of RPM and the available defenses? Thirdly, how to substantiate the pro-competitive effects of RPM and establish its balancing mechanism against anti-competitive effects?

II. The Preliminary Question: Does RPM Qualify for the Safe Harbor for Monopolistic Agreements?

15. The concept of a safe harbor in antitrust law is a screening mechanism based on market share, where the market power of an undertaking is assessed to infer whether it could potentially have an exclusionary or anti-competitive effect. In jurisdictions with safe harbor provisions, some

---

25   See Lei Lan: *The Logic of Configuring Modes of Analysis for Monopolistic Conducts*, Business and Economic Law Review, No. 2, 2021.

26   See Herbert Hovenkamp: *The Rule of Reason*, Florida Law Review, Vol. 70, p.128 (2018).

exclude practices like RPM from the safe harbor, while others do not place behavioral restrictions on whether vertical restraints can apply within a safe harbor. Starting from the restructuring introduced by the revision of Article 18 of the Anti-Monopoly Law, the preliminary issue in the anti-monopoly regulation of RPM should be determining whether it is subject to the safe harbor specified in Paragraph 3 of Article 18. That is, whether RPM can be excluded from the regulation of vertical monopolistic agreements due to its low market power?

(1) The inherent logic of the establishment of the safe harbor under monopolistic agreements

16. Paragraph 3 of Article 18 of the Anti-Monopoly Law stipulates that "Where undertakings can prove that their market share in the relevant market is lower than the standard set by the authority for enforcement of the Anti-monopoly Law under the State Council and that other conditions stipulated by the authority for enforcement of the Anti-monopoly Law under the State Council are met, the agreement shall not be prohibited." As a screening mechanism, the safe harbor focuses on exempting vertical restraints that are unlikely to have anti-competitive effects. The key to its effective establishment lies in clarifying to what extent market share can represent market power and how market power and competitive behaviors link together.

17. Undoubtedly, the application of the safe harbor requires an appropriate market share threshold. Compared with other indicators like the Lerner index, market share is widely recognized as the best quantitative proxy of market power. Some commentators suggest setting the threshold at 30%, noting that this aligns with the safe harbor standards for vertical monopolistic agreements in the EU and the U.S. They also point out that if contrary evidence shows that the agreement has the effect of eliminating or restricting competition, the safe harbor shall not apply.[27] This suggestion has a solid consensus basis. However, determining the market share threshold does not constitute the entirety of legal interpretation. Since these thresholds are difficult to define precisely, defining the exact threshold is largely a matter of policy. In fact, the focal point of legal interpretation should be analyzing "other conditions stipulated by the authority for enforcement of the Anti-monopoly Law under the State Council are met," clarifying the meaning of "other conditions," and defining their relationship with market share.

18. Critically, while market share is the core indicator for the safe harbor, it is not the only indicator. This is because while market share may indicate the degree of market power, it constitutes only an imperfect proxy.

---

27 See Xianlin Wang: *On the Implementation and Improvement of Monopoly Agreement Regulation System in China – Based on the Revision of the Anti-monopoly Law of PRC*, Journal of Anhui University (Philosophy and Social Sciences Edition), No. 1, 2020.

This quantitative proxy should be considered alongside other quantitative and qualitative considerations to more comprehensively and objectively reflect the actual market power of an undertaking. Thus, here, "other conditions stipulated by the authority for enforcement of the Anti-monopoly Law under the State Council are met" act as an important interface for defining these additional conditions. The key is whether these additional conditions should contain both quantitative (including market concentration, downstream buyer power, etc.) and qualitative (including market entry and expansion barriers, etc.) considerations. From a theoretical perspective, it is necessary to include both quantitative proxies and qualitative factors. However, according to Paragraph 3 of Article 18 of the Anti-Monopoly Law, the "other conditions" and the "set standard (market share)" must be met simultaneously. In this case, adding "other conditions" based on quantitative proxies should be a key focus of setting up the safe harbor, otherwise, the system will lose its value of simplicity.

19. Specifically, "other conditions" should more broadly include quantitative proxies such as market concentration and downstream buyer power, so as to more precisely characterize market power, and corroborate or rebut the conformity of specific market shares with conditions of safe harbor. This is because market share only reflects the static position of the undertaking in the relevant market, while adding market concentration can better highlight the undertaking's dynamic position, illustrating the competitive constraints imposed by other market participants. Furthermore, in the event that an undertaking exercises its market power in a vertical relationship, the final effect of it not only depends on the competitive situation in the relevant market, but also on the competitive situation in the downstream market. Additionally, downstream buyer power can also be assessed via market share and market concentration. The challenge lies in selecting a proxy that combines market share and market concentration, and formulating market power criteria to determine when countervailing power constitutes sufficient constraints to upstream.

20. In essence, the value of the safe harbor institution lies primarily in protecting agreements among undertakings from antitrust challenges and the uncertainties that such challenges may bring. In this regard, some commentators argue that from the perspective of the purpose of establishing the safe harbor, it mainly exempts certain monopolistic behaviors that have little or no harm to competition from scrutiny, aiming to improve enforcement and judicial efficiency in antitrust, increase undertakings' stable expectations, and reduce compliance costs. Therefore, behaviors that significantly harm competition should be excluded from the application of the antitrust safe harbor.[28] It can be argued that maintaining

---

28 See Guohai Li and Yining Wang: *The Construction of Safe Harbor Rules in China's Anti-monopoly Law*, Journal of Jishou University (Social Sciences), No. 2, 2022.

and enhancing stable expectations is one of the core values of the safe harbor. On this basis, it is crucial to avoid the potential generalization of the safe harbor institution, which could lead to false negative/under-enforcement. Combined with the analytical mode perspective, practices that will be applied with the illegal per se rule, the quasi-illegal per se rule, or the abbreviated rule of reason, if included within the scope of the safe harbor, may lead to false negative/under-enforcement.

(2) RPm is not suitable for safe harbor

21. Pursuant to Paragraph 3 of Article 18 of the Anti-Monopoly Law, the legislator has not expressly specified which types of vertical restraints may qualify for the safe harbor. Judicial Interpretation of Anti-Monopoly Law in 2024 maintains judicial restraint on this matter, expressly reserving regulatory competence to the authority for enforcement of the Anti-Monopoly Law under the State Council.[29] Theoretically, the explanatory framework for this issue should be established on the basis of clarifying the relationships between market power and competitive behaviors with their impacts. If the relationship between market power and competitive behaviors with their impacts is understood as unilateral determinism, there would be no need to examine whether specific behaviors should be excluded from the scope of the safe harbor. In other words, irrespective of the type of vertical restraint employed, falling below the market power threshold would inherently qualify for safe harbor. However, some commentators have insightfully argued that "market power cannot be considered in a vacuum but rather must be combined with at least some information about allegedly anti-competitive practices and possible explanations for their use."[30] If the relationship between the two is understood as bilaterally determined, it is necessary not only to examine market power of the undertakings but also to carefully scrutinize their challenged conduct. Accordingly, what needs to be clarified is: Should vertical price restraints be categorically excluded from the safe harbor? Can vertical non-price restraints categorically qualify for the safe harbor?

22. First, should vertical price restraints be categorically excluded from the safe harbor? Paragraph 1 of Article 18 of the Anti-Monopoly Law enumerates the normative types of vertical restraints regulated, namely "fixing the price for resale" and "restricting the lowest price for resale," also providing a catch-all provision. From the perspective of price-related

---

29　Article 23 of Interpretation of the Supreme People's Court on Several Issues Concerning the Application of Law in the Trial of Civil Dispute Cases Arising from Monopolistic Conduct (Fa Shi No. 6 [2024]): "Where the alleged monopolistic agreement falls under any of the following circumstances, the People's Court shall not support the plaintiff's claim that the defendant shall bear legal liability under Paragraph of Article 18 of the Anti-Monopoly Law: (2) The defendant's market share in the relevant market is below the threshold prescribed by the authority for enforcement of the Anti-monopoly Law under the State Council and meets other conditions specified by such authority."

30　Louis Kaplow: *On the Relevance of Market Power*, Harvard Law Review, Vol. 130, p.1362 (2017).

restrictions, these may include resale price fixation, minimum resale price maintenance (collectively referred to as RPM), and maximum resale price maintenance. From the analytical mode perspective, both maximum resale price maintenance and RPM are currently analyzed under the rule of reason in the U.S, while in the EU, RPM continues to be treated as a core restriction and is consequently excluded from the safe harbor. Under Chinese law, from the structural perspective of the provisions, some commentators have pointed out that "the safe harbor rule applies not only to vertical agreements covered by the 'catch-all provision,' but also extends to expressly prohibited practices of resale price fixation and minimum resale price maintenance. As a result, RPM agreements under China's Anti-Monopoly Law are effectively caught in a tension between two conflicting regulatory forces: on one hand, they are subject to a 'rebuttable presumption of illegality' rule due to their severely anti-competitive nature; and on the other hand, they may simultaneously qualify for the safe harbor rule specifically designed for scenarios without obvious anti-competitive effects."[31] The argument that RPM can qualify for the safe harbor remains contentious, but it also highlights potential structural issues that may arise if such an exemption is applied. In other words, extending the safe harbor to RPM would lead to systemic inconsistencies in the anti-monopoly regulation of vertical restraints.

23. Furthermore, an analysis of the economic effects of vertical price restraints versus vertical non-price restraints also provides a justification for excluding RPM from the safe harbor. As some commentators have pointed out, RPM can enhance the transparency of retail prices and thus facilitate collusion when imperfect observability of rivals' prices is the primary obstacle to the detection of deviations. There is, moreover, a clear distinction between the impact of price and non-price vertical restraints in that respect, which provides a rationale for a tougher antitrust treatment of price restrictions and particularly of RPM.[32] From the perspective of information collection costs, U.S antitrust law generally applies the rule of reason to vertical agreements, further developing the abbreviated rule of reason to reduce information collection costs. This approach can effectively balance error costs and information collection costs, eliminating the need for the safe harbor. In contrast, the EU predominantly adopts effects-based assessment for vertical agreements, which incurs excessively high information collection costs, thus necessitating the inclusion of the safe harbor to exclude certain cases from scrutiny, mitigating these costs.[33]

---

31 Jianzhong Shi: *The Practical Significance and Interpretation of the New Anti-Monopoly Law*, China Law Review, No. 4, 2022.

32 See Jullien, Bruno, and Patrick Rey: *Resale Price Maintenance and Collusion*, The RAND Journal of Economics, Vol. 38, p.997 (2007).

33 See Huiqun Wang: *Chinese Legislative Logic for Safe Harbor Rule for Vertical and Horizontal Agreements under Antitrust law:The Information Cost Approach*, No. 1, The Jurist, 2023.

Under Chinese law, the statutory presumption of anti-competitive effects implies the application of the abbreviated rule of reason, there is no rigid necessity of establishing a safe harbor for RPM to reduce the burden of information collection. Therefore, after comprehensive consideration, to mitigate the risk of false negative/under-enforcement, RPM should be excluded from the scope of the safe harbor based on its nature as a core restriction.

24. In contrast, maximum resale price maintenance (price ceiling), although rarer in practice, holds the potential for efficiency enhancement, for example, through enhanced output or achieving a more desirable equilibrium between price and quality when implemented in competitive markets.[34] Commentators have even argued that maximum price fixing is almost always beneficial to consumers.[35] Just because of this view, in State Oil Co. v. Khan, the Supreme Court of the U.S held that maximum resale price maintenance was lawful and established the rule of reason as the analytical mode.[36] In this case, the Court noted that "the potential anti-competitive harm identified in Albrecht[37] was not as serious as the Court had previously assumed."[38] The Court here applied a structural rule of reason, instead of the abbreviated rule of reason. Moreover, after being subjected to the rule of reason analysis, such behavior has not triggered widespread backlash in practice like RPM (facing explicit legislative bans in multiple states). Furthermore, a systematic interpretation of the legal framework suggests that: on one hand, Paragraph 3 of Article 18 of the Anti-Monopoly Law does not expressly exclude the application of the safe harbor to such behavior; and on the other hand, continuing from the previous description, the regulation of such behavior should not automatically invoke the presumption of anti-competitive effects under Paragraph 2 of Article 18. It can therefore be concluded that including maximum resale price maintenance within the safe harbor would not create conflicts under systematic interpretation, nor would it significantly likely lead to false negative/under-enforcement.

25. Second, can vertical non-price restraints be categorically applied to the safe harbor? To date, while "other agreements identified by the authority for enforcement of the Anti-monopoly Law under the State Council" under Chinese law have not been explicitly specified, major jurisdictions typically include vertical non-price restraints such as exclusive distribution, selective distribution, and franchising arrangements within this category. However,

---

34   See Mathewson: Frank, Ralph Winter, *The Law and Economics of Resale Price Maintenance*, Review of Industrial Organization, Vol. 13, p.82 (1998).

35   See Frank H. Easterbrook: *Maximum Price Fixing*, University of Chicago Law Review, Vol. 48, p.887 (1981).

36   See State Oil Co. v. Khan, 522 U.S. 3 (1997).

37   In this case, the Supreme Court of the US applied the illegal per se to maximum resale price maintenance. See Albrecht v. Herald Co., 390 U.S. 145 (1968).

38   State Oil Co. v. Khan, 118 S. Ct. 275, 283 (1997).

applying the safe harbor to all such conduct may lead to false negative/ under-enforcement. This is because exclusive distribution, selective distribution, and franchising arrangements are not normative categories under China's Anti-Monopoly Law, but rather empirical categories derived from anti-monopoly enforcement practice. Specifically, some arrangements involve purely vertical non-price restraints such as exclusive distribution, while others may encompass both non-price vertical restraints, including territorial restrictions as well as customer restrictions, and vertical price restraints, including RPM, as typically seen in franchising agreements. Given the inherent complexity involved, these empirical categories should still be analyzed on a case-by-case basis, with the applicability of the safe harbor determined according to the specific category of restraints involved. To illustrate, under the EU law, there are five distinct scenarios where restraints are classified as core restrictions and thus excluded from the safe harbor, demonstrating considerable sophistication.[39] Under Chinese law, the establishment of a safe harbor for vertical non-price agreements should integrate both market share and behavioral elements, while explicitly excluding any categories or subcategories that constitute core restrictions.[40] Although the EU regulatory structure offers valuable references, its application must be carefully calibrated to China's specific context, requiring "a thorough understanding of distinctive industry characteristics, unique marketing practices, and distribution channel patterns across different sectors in China's market economy."[41]

26. Overall, the application scope of the safe harbor remains relatively limited in the anti-monopoly regulation of vertical restraints. Specifically, vertical non-price restraints cannot be categorically subjected to the safe harbor, vertical price restraints should not be categorically excluded from safe harbor either; while there exists a clear consensus that RPM shall be excluded from the application of the safe harbor.

III. The Presumption of Anti-Competitive Effects for RPM and Its Defenses

27. On the premise that RPM should be excluded from the safe harbor, the anti-monopoly regulation should further focus on interpreting the presumption of anti-competitive effects. Following the legislative amendment,

---

39 See Commission Regulation (EU) 2022/720 of 10 May 2022 on the application of Article 101(3) of the Treaty on the Functioning of the European Union to categories of vertical agreements and concerted practices, Article 4.

40 See Jiang Shan: *On the Anti-monopoly Regulation of Non-price Vertical Restraints*, Science of Law (Journal of Northwest University of Political Science and Law), No. 1, 2020.

41 Huang Yong and Yannan Liu: A *Study on the Legal Application of Resale Price Maintenance Agreements Under China's Anti-Monopoly Law*, Journal of Social Sciences, No. 10, 2013.

Paragraph 2 of Article 18 of the Anti-Monopoly Law stipulates: "The agreements as specified in subparagraphs (1) and (2) shall not be prohibited if the undertakings can prove the agreements do not have the effect of eliminating or restricting competition." The presumption of anti-competitive effects for RPM under antitrust law is articulated in a concise manner within the revised statutory framework. Article 21 of Judicial Interpretation of Anti-Monopoly Law in 2024 neither provides any elaboration, merely confirming the defendant's burden of rebutting the presumption of anti-competitive effects.[42] The key interpretive issues requiring clarification are: What constitutes the primary content of RPM's anti-competitive effects? What are the legal effects of successfully rebutting anti-competitive effects? And through what procedural framework should such rebuttal be developed?

(1) The connotation of the presumption of anti-competitive effects in RPM

28. Existing consensus holds that Paragraph 2 of Article 18 of the Anti-Monopoly Law establishes a clear presumption of anti-competitive effects for RPM, and this presumption is not extended to vertical non-price restraints. However, the provision leaves several critical issues unresolved: Whether the presumption of anti-competitive effects applies to all types of vertical price restraints? Whether the anti-competitive effects target intra-brand competition or inter-brand competition, or a combination of both? What are the legal consequences corresponding to the success or failure of such defenses, and specifically, under what circumstances would the conduct qualify for the statutory exclusion ("shall not be prohibited")?

29. First, the types of conduct covered by the presumption of anti-competitive effects must be defined by legislation. On one hand, through systematic interpretation, it should be established that: The presumption of anti-competitive effects applies not only to pure RPM agreements, but also extends to RPM clauses embedded within certain vertical non-price restraints. In this regard, the analysis mirrors that in the safe harbor, which will not be reiterated here. On the other hand, in light of prevailing legal theories and enforcement practices across major jurisdictions, the presumption of anti-competitive effects should not extend to behaviors involving maximum resale price maintenance within the context of vertical price restraints, as such measures are generally regarded has price-lowering effect, and thus pro-competitive. Informed by a broad body of enforcement experience, the exclusion of maximum resale price maintenance from the scope of the presumption under Paragraph 2 of Article 18 should become a consensus.

---

[42] Interpretation of the Supreme People's Court on Several Issues Concerning the Application of Law in the Trial of Civil Dispute Cases Arising from Monopolistic Conduct (Fa Shi No. 6 [2024]).

30. Second, whether the anti-competitive effects target intra-brand competition or inter-brand competition, or a combination of both? Some commentators have pointed out that, for conduct subject to either an irrebuttable presumption (illegal per se) or a rebuttable presumption of illegality ("quick look" rule of reason), only abstract anti-competitive effects are required, there being no need to prove a concrete effect of eliminating or restricting competition in individual cases. Once an agreement meeting the relevant formal requirements is reached, such effects may be presumed.[43] From a teleological interpretation perspective, effects that merely restrict intra-brand competition do not inherently raise serious anti-competitive effects. The anti-competitive effects referred to in this provision, even in their "abstract sense," must ultimately refer to inter-brand competition. Consequently, when only intra-brand competition is restricted while inter-brand competition remains sufficient, such circumstances would constitute valid defenses under this framework. Then, in theory, the defense against anti-competitive effects can be presented at two levels: intra-brand competition is unrestricted and inter-brand competition is unrestricted.

31. Furthermore, differing opinions remain as to whether intra-brand restrictions can be rebutted. Some commentators argue that **RPM** inherently restricts "intra-brand competition," and this cannot be rebutted. Therefore, the "competition" mentioned in Paragraph 2 can only refer to the competitiveness of the market, that being the competitive market structure.[44] This judgment contains certain logical flaws. This is because, while **RPM** inherently restricts intra-brand competition, the extent of such restriction is case-specific. In other words, while **RPM** may be presumed anti-competitive in the abstract sense, it should also be allowed to be rebutted in the concrete sense. Otherwise, if no rebuttal is permitted, the presumption of anti-competitive effects at the abstract level may lead to false positive/over-enforcement when the actual degree or intensity of intra-brand competition restriction in a given case is not sufficient. However, such rebuttals do not carry conclusive weight in challenging the "presumption of anti-competitive effects," but rather serve only a supporting function. This is because the presumption ultimately rests on inter-brand competition, and even if restrictions on intra-brand competition are successfully rebutted, this does not constitute a decisive rebuttal against restrictions on inter-brand competition.

32. Third, the legal consequences corresponding to RPM's anti-competitive effects defense must also be examined. Specifically, there are three possible scenarios: (1) If the presumption of substantial weakening of inter-brand

---

43 See Lei Lan: *Assessing the Goodness of Argument for the Per Se Illegal Approach to RPM: Comments on the Antitrust Case between Hainan Price Bureau and Hainan Yutai Technology Feed Co., Ltd.*, Competition Policy Research, No. 4, 2018.

44 See Guangyao Xu: *Identification of Monopoly Behavior in Resale Price Maintenance Cases*, Law Review, No. 3, 2023.

competition is directly overturned, it constitutes a circumstance that "shall not be prohibited", rendering subsequent competitive analysis unnecessary; (2) If the aforementioned presumption cannot be overturned, the legal consequence would be a direct prohibition; (3) The most complex scenario arises when the presumption cannot be directly overturned, but the evidence presented casts sufficient doubt on the validity of this presumption in the specific case. This leads to two possible outcomes: A prohibition if the party subsequently fails to provide efficiency justifications under Article 20 of the Anti-Monopoly Law, or if such justifications are insufficient to offset the aforementioned anti-competitive effects, or if the efficiencies are not passed on to consumers; and conversely, if the efficiency defenses are successfully established, the conduct shall be exempted.

33. The key issue is: how to determine whether a defense against anti-competitive effects is valid? It should be recognized that, first and foremost, such a defense shall be deemed valid if either direct evidence demonstrating the existence of competitive pricing and output, or structural evidence sufficient to rebut the presumption is presented. Second, if the available structural evidence to rebut the presumption is not fully conclusive but "plausible" pro-competitive justifications has been demonstrated, the anti-competitive effects shall be rendered legally indeterminate. In such cases, it suffices to demonstrate either the potential absence of anti-competitive effects or the abstract possibility of pro-competitive outcomes, with the concrete analysis to be further developed during subsequent efficiency defense proceedings. Finally, where neither of the two aforementioned conditions is satisfied, the presumption of anti-competitive effects shall be deemed as unrebutted. This screening mechanism embodies the essence of the abbreviated rule of reason.

(2) The defense framework against the anti-competitive effects of RPM

34. A further issue to be addressed is: How can we concretely determine whether inter-brand competition remains sufficiently robust to overturn the presumption of anti-competitive effects in RPM? In this regard, the explanation must be sought from the incentives behind RPM. Currently, there are three widely recognized rationales for RPM: (1) RPM serves to support a cartel of manufacturers; (2) the practice is a manifestation of retailers' monopoly power, supporting a cartel at the retail level; (3) the practice is implemented unilaterally by manufacturers as part of an efficient distribution system, necessary to elicit adequate service from retailers.[45] Accordingly, the potential defenses may include: the absence of pricing and output patterns consistent with cartel behavior, insufficient market power among retailers or manufacturers, or possible efficiency enhancements.

---

45 See Mathewson, Frank, Ralph Winter: *The Law and Economics of Resale Price Maintenance*, Review of Industrial Organization, Vol. 13, p.65 (1998).

Among them, the efficiency defense is specifically articulated and applied during the presenting of pro-competitive effects and the balancing of pro-competitive and anti-competitive effects. The discussion here is limited to examining the potential for efficiency gains in specific cases.[46]

35. First, a defense may be raised based on the existence of competitive market prices and output. When analyzing RPM's anti-competitive effects, price increases are indeed the most direct indicator of harm to consumer welfare. Conventional wisdom holds that RPM facilitates price collusion among manufacturers or retailers, directly leading to higher product prices and ultimately impairing consumer welfare. However, this analysis requires further refinement for precision. Some commentators argue that, in the ongoing debate concerning RPM, the assertion that RPM inherently leads to higher prices has often been treated as axiomatic. However, any argument advocating stringent intervention against RPM based solely on alleged price increases as proof of competitive harm lacks robust scientific support.[47] It should be noted that higher prices may reflect profit margins reserved for better services, meaning the ultimate criterion for assessment is not price itself, but whether output has been increased.[48] If increased prices genuinely facilitate the effective provision of services, the result of inter-brand competition should be an overall increase in market output. In this regard, some commentators have further argued that, changes in output should serve as the fundamental criterion for assessment: if a practice is found to increase output in a specific case, it should not be prohibited in principle; conversely, if its effect is to reduce output, this may generally give rise to a presumption of illegality.[49] However, some economists have pointed out that examining output and price levels in isolation is insufficient to fully reveal RPM's impact on consumer surplus: By facilitating demand-enhancing services, RPM may simultaneously affect both consumer demand and market competition dynamics, consequently leading to scenarios where price and output could move either in tandem or inversely. Under such circumstances, neither price nor output alone can serve as an accurate indicator of overall social welfare or consumer welfare.[50] A more comprehensive analytical approach should

---

46　It is generally recognized that for conduct other than hardcore cartels, the defendant may challenge both the plaintiff's factual allegations and the underlying economic theories they rely upon. See Gregory J. Werden: *Antitrust's Rule of Reason: Only Competition Matters*, Antitrust Law Journal, Vol. 79, p.753 (2014).

47　See Lei Lan: *Myths about Price Increase as a Competitive Harm and their Debunking: From the Perspective of RPM*, SJTU Law Review, No. 4, 2021.

48　See Richard Posner: *The Rule of Reason and the Economic Approach: Reflections on the Sylvania Decision*, University of Chicago Law Review, Vol. 45, p.19 (1977).

49　See Guangyao Xu: *Antimonopoly Analysis on Maintenance of Resale Price*, Journal of Political Science and Law, No. 4, 2011.

50　As a means of demand-facilitating services, RPM may affect output in two distinct ways: either by causing movement along the demand curve or by shifting the demand curve itself. The former reflects the impact of competitive conditions on output, while the latter demonstrates how demand facilitation affects output. When output increases, total social welfare invariably rises, though the change in consumer surplus remains

therefore be adopted: A price increase coupled with output reduction may be treated as proof of anti-competitive effects, whereas output expansion without significant price increases could serve as valid grounds to rebut the presumption of RPM's anti-competitive effects.

36. Second, establish structural elements that can overturn the presumption of RPM's anti-competitive effects. In this regard, some commentators have pointed out that: "If the relevant market lacks the requisite conditions for anti-competitive effects, the practice may be presumed to aim at output expansion rather than restricting competition. In such cases, no further output analysis is required. Consequently, in RPM cases, a structural analysis of the relevant market must precede any prohibition, thereby excluding RPM that fails to satisfy the requisite conditions for anti-competitive effects."[51] This analysis holds significant practical value, because the aforementioned rebuttal claims based on output levels require robust economic analysis and solid empirical data, and not all defendants or investigated parties possess those required resources and expertise. Furthermore, some commentators have proposed that "the market structure may serve as a 'screening mechanism,' only when specific structural thresholds are met should RPM be subject to stringent prohibition."[52] Here, it must be clarified that market power serves as a reverse screening tool to identify RPM unlikely to have anti-competitive effects, and not vice versa. Otherwise, the regulatory framework for vertical monopolistic agreements would be concurrence with that governing the abuse of dominance. At the same time, it should be noted that while there is no safe harbor for RPM regulation, this does not mean that structural factors alone can never fully rebut the presumption of anti-competitive effects. The concept of a safe harbor is abstract and industry-agnostic, whereas here the rebuttal based on the market structure is concrete and tailored to the specificity of each case. When more direct evidence is unavailable, challenging the sufficiency of the market structure that supports RPM's anti-competitive effects undoubtedly constitutes a critical line of defense. Enforcement agencies or courts inherently possess the discretion to determine, based on case-specific evidence, whether a given RPM produces anti-competitive effects. Such a rebuttal has two possible legal effects: firstly, it may directly rebut the presumption; or secondly, it may cast reasonable doubt on the validity of the presumption (in cases involving ambiguous evidence), thereby necessitating further analysis incorporating behavioral elements.

---

indeterminate. Conversely, when output decreases, consumer surplus always declines, yet the impact on total social welfare remains uncertain. See MacKay, Alexander, and David A. Smith: *Challenges for Empirical Research on RPM*, Review of Industrial Organization, Vol.50, p.214-216 (2017).

51 Guangyao Xu: *Antimonopoly Analysis on Maintenance of Resale Price*, Journal of Political Science and Law, No. 4, 2011.

52 Jian Li and Fei Tang: *The Illegality of Resale Price Maintenance and Legal Regulation*, Contemporary Law Review, No. 6, 2010.

37. Specifically, rebuttals grounded in structural elements should primarily target the major anti-competitive effects that RPM may produce.[53] The structural analysis of RPM currently develops along two dimensions: First, in cases of unilateral RPM implementation, the assessment must focus on whether the undertaking possesses sufficient market power, thus being able to substantially restrict inter-brand competition independently. This evaluation typically employs market share as the major metric, supplemented by the examination of additional elements, including market entry and expansion, as well as downstream countervailing power. Second, in cases of multilateral RPM implementation, the assessment must focus on whether the aggregate market power of the undertakings is sufficiently substantial to create cumulative effects that may significantly restrict inter-brand competition. This evaluation typically employs market share as the major metric, supplemented by the examination of additional elements, including market concentration, entry barriers, downstream countervailing power, and market transparency. Furthermore, with regard to cartels successfully initiated and maintained by distributors,[54] negating market power should simultaneously focus on demonstrating that neither manufacturers nor distributors possess substantial market power. With regarding to cartels successfully initiated and maintained by manufacturers,[55] negating market power should center on proving low market concentration, low entry barriers, and the limited aggregate market share of participating manufacturers. Additionally, the countervailing forces of market power from upstream and downstream players must not be overlooked as a critical factor.[56]

38. Third, establish "plausible" pro-competitive justifications that are able to rebut the presumption of RPM's anti-competitive effects. It must be recognized that while the legal presumption of RPM's anti-competitive effects is abstract in nature, "plausible" pro-competitive justifications are concrete and must be derived from theoretical reasoning tailored to

---

[53] Some commentators distinguish this approach from the affirmative defense of efficiency justification, characterizing it as a negative defense. See Junqi Hao: *Reflection and Balance: Research on the Analysis Mode of Resale Price Maintenance in China*, Competition Policy Research, No. 4, 2017.

[54] For distributor-initiated RPM to succeed, "it requires participation from most or all manufacturers, or the individual manufacturer implementing RPM must possess significant market power [...] Distributors must also wield considerable market power; otherwise, they cannot compel manufacturers to adopt RPM and thereby raise retail prices." Haixiao Gu, *The Economic Logic and Legal Regulation of RPM – With Comments on Article 14 of Chinese Anti-monopoly Law*, Journal of Henan Administrative Institute of Politics and Law, No. 4, 2008.

[55] While RPM can stabilize cartels among manufacturers, "this can only occur when the market structure in which manufacturers operate is conducive to cartel formation." Haixiao Gu: *The Economic Logic and Legal Regulation of RPM – With Comments on Article 14 of Chinese Anti-monopoly Law*, Journal of Henan Administrative Institute of Politics and Law, No. 4, 2008.

[56] "When upstream firms possess absolute market power compared to downstream firms, RPM weakens market competition, leading to product prices reaching double marginalization levels. Conversely, when downstream firms have strong buyer power, RPM may eliminate the double marginalization problem." Yiming Meng and Kai Li, *Analysis of the Competitive Effect of Resale Price Maintenance in the Context of Consumer Preference*, Industrial Economic Review, No. 5, 2022.

scenarios of specific cases. Whether in empirical or theoretical sense, the anti-competitive effects of RPM should not be considered an irrefutable axiom. Rather, legislators have determined that the high probability of its existence has reached a threshold sufficient to warrant the establishment of a presumption rule. The aforementioned defense based on structural factors, such as market power, is primarily developed from experience. However, a defense based solely on structural elements of the market may not be sufficient, and behavioral analysis serves as a crucial supplement. Based on rationale of the abbreviated rule of reason, once a theoretical rebuttal can be raised in scenarios of specific cases, even if it cannot entirely rebut the presumption, it will cast doubt on the validity of such presumption in that specific case. In California Dental Association v. FTC, the Supreme Court of the US outlined the applicability criteria for the abbreviated rule of reason: "Where an observer with even a rudimentary understanding of economics could conclude that the arrangements in question would have an anti-competitive effect on customers and markets."[57] This paves the way for "plausible" pro-competitive justifications. Generally, firstly, one can point out a significant "free-riding" issue and explain how the relevant vertical restraints address this issue; and secondly, one can demonstrate how the relevant vertical restraints encourage distributors or retailers to exert greater efforts and sell more products.[58] Here, the "plausible" pro-competitive justifications refer to efficiency motivations expressed through behaviors in a case-specific context. While it will not directly rebut the presumption of anti-competitive effects, it is sufficient to cast doubt on the validity of such a presumption, thereby invoking a comprehensive rule of reason analysis. Ultimately, whether such efficiency claims can be substantiated depends on the production of concrete proof at the efficiency defense stage.

39. The strength of the aforementioned efficiency claims varies depending on the specific circumstances of each case. The key considerations should focus on the context, details, and logic of the restraint in question, to determine whether market experience is so clear or its implications so inevitable that a quick look analysis, rather than a more protracted examination, would suffice to confidently conclude the restraint's predominant tendency.[59] Certainly, for specific RPM practices that may raise more serious competitive concerns, a correspondingly stronger defense is required. For instance, some commentators have analyzed the practice of dual RPM, where RPM is applied to both primary and complementary products, and pointed out that "rather than eliminating the double marginalization

---

57 California Dental Association v. FTC, 526 U.S. 756, 770 (1999).

58 See Gregory J. Werden: *Antitrust's Rule of Reason: Only Competition Matters*, Antitrust Law Journal, Vol. 79,, p.754 (2014).

59 See California Dental Association v. FTC, 526 U.S. 756, 780-781 (1999).

observed in classic single RPM cases, dual RPM may instead create a new form of 'double marginalization,' potentially leading to even worse welfare outcomes, thus harming consumer welfare."[60] Moreover, RPM can interact with other practices to produce more complex anti-competitive effects. As commentators have noted: "RPM enables manufacturers to discriminate the consumers, thereby facilitating intertemporal price discrimination. This allows manufacturers to extract higher profits through such discrimination and effectively achieve collusive outcomes. Ultimately, RPM results in diminished consumer surplus and reduced social welfare."[61] In such cases, the strength of the rebuttal regarding anti-competitive effects should also be appropriately enhanced accordingly.

IV. Evaluating the Pro-competitive Effects of RPM and the Tradeoff Mechanism

40. In antitrust, the balancing of the pro-competitive and anti-competitive effects of RPM is not a new topic. However, until recently, cases referring to exemption clauses accounted for 20% of the total RPM cases in China, but the actual exemption rate was 0%.[62] The overall situation of defenses is not optimistic, which is related to the lack of clarity in institutional details. Some commentators even argue that whether the list of defenses can achieve legitimate interest protection entirely depends on the regulatory conscience and reflective rationality of the competition authorities.[63] Judicial Interpretation of Anti-Monopoly Law in 2024 elaborates on this issue by enumerating factors relevant to the assessment of competitive effects.[64] The listing of these factors undoubtedly provides a structured framework for balancing pro-competitive and anti-competitive effects.

---

60 Yikai Zhen: *Anticompetitive Effects of Dual Resale Price Maintenance – Based on the Analysis of China's Auto Industry*, China Industrial Economics, No. 5, 2016.

61 Chuanhai Jiang, Zhiwei Wang and Shuai Leng: *Intertemporal Price Discrimination and Resale Price Maintenance*, Journal of Management Sciences in China, No. 7, 2016.

62 See Jun Zhang: *Anti-monopoly Law Implementation Concerning Resale Price Maintenance: Conflict Dilemma and Its Solution*, Contemporary Law Review, No. 4, 2022.

63 Jianzhong Shi and Junqi Hao: *The Legislative Correctness of Principle Prohibition of Resale Price Maintenance and the Improvement of Its Implementation*, Political Science and Law, No. 11, 2017.

64 Article 22 of Interpretation of the Supreme People's Court on Several Issues Concerning the Application of Law in the Trial of Civil Dispute Cases Arising from Monopolistic Conduct (Fa Shi No. 6 [2024]): "When a people's court examines and determines whether an alleged monopolistic agreement has the effect of eliminating or restricting competition in accordance with the provisions of Paragraphs 1 and 2 of Article 18 of the Anti-Monopoly Law, it may comprehensively consider the following factors: (1) The market power of the defendant in the relevant market and the cumulative effect of the agreement in producing similar adverse competitive effects in the relevant market; (2) Whether the agreement has adverse competitive effects, such as raising barriers to market entry, hindering more efficient operators or business models, or restricting competition between or within brands; (3) Whether the agreement has pro-competitive effects, such as preventing free-riding, promoting inter-brand competition, maintaining brand image, improving pre-sale or after-sales service levels, or fostering innovation, and whether such effects are necessary to achieve the intended purpose; (4) Other factors that may be considered."

However, further clarification is urgently needed regarding how the main exemption factors under Article 20 of the Anti-Monopoly Law should be better applied and how the corresponding analytical process ought to be established. In particular, it remains to be clarified how pro-competitive effects such as addressing issue of "free-riding" and "hold-up" should be weighed against the aforementioned presumptive anti-competitive effects.

(1) Proving the pro-competitive effects of RPM

41. To define the pro-competitive effects of RPM, a categorical analysis should be conducted, taking into account Article 20 of the Anti-Monopoly Law and the development of economic theory. According to this article, an undertaking can demonstrate that its behavior promotes competition through three types of efficiencies: "(1) improving technologies, or engaging in research and development of new products; (2) improving product quality, reducing cost, and enhancing efficiency, unifying specifications and standards of products, or implementing specialized division of production; (3) increasing the efficiency and competitiveness of small and medium-sized undertakings."[65] Specifically, subparagraphs (1) to (3) of this paragraph respectively concern the claims of dynamic efficiency, static efficiency, and the efficiency of small and medium-sized undertakings. Given that RPM primarily involves the production and distribution process, the claim of static efficiency should be the most significant. Prior to the legislative amendment, some commentators pointed out that the Anti-Monopoly Law overlooked the efficiency of RPM in the marketing process.[66] This issue remains unresolved in the current legislation and needs to be addressed through future legislative amendments or regulatory instruments.

42. More importantly, there is significant divergence within Chinese antitrust academia regarding the legal nature of exemptions for monopolistic agreements, with various theories proposed, including the competition defense theory, the efficiency defense theory, the public policy defense theory, the composite defense theory, and the denying anti-competitive effects theory, among others.[67] However, from a comparative law perspective, while the efficiency defense may not be the only option, it should undoubtedly be regarded as the core of the defense. In this context, examining economic theory, the efficiencies primarily include: addressing the "free-riding" issue of distributors,[68] obtaining quality or style certifications from reputable

---

65 Additionally, "other conditions" listed in Paragraph 1 of Article 20 of the Anti-Monopoly Law serve as exemption reasons for specific scenarios, and there remains insufficient consensus regarding their application.

66 See Jing Zeng: *On the Predicament and Optimization of the Anti-monopoly Regulations of Maintenance of Resale Price in China*, The Theory and Practice of Finance and Economics, No. 4, 2021.

67 See Lei Lan: *On the Dual-Level Balancing Model for Regulating Monopolistic Agreements in China*, Tsinghua Law Review, No. 5, 2017.

68 See Lester G. Telser: *Why Should Manufacturers Want Fair Trade?*, Journal of Law & Economics, Vol. 3, p.89-96 (1960).

distributors,[69] eliminating double marginalization,[70] promoting market entry,[71] addressing cost and quality issues or moral hazard problems triggered by non-price externalities in contractual mechanisms,[72] avoiding the "cream-skimming effect" among retailers to ensure product diversity,[73] maintaining the price positioning of reputation-based products,[74] overcoming retailers' optimal inventory problems in the face of demand uncertainty,[75] and resolving incentive discrepancies between manufacturers and retailers.[76] Among these, the issue of addressing "free-riding" issue appears more frequently in the efficiency defense and can be analyzed as a typical example.

43. First, it is necessary to demonstrate whether the "free-riding" has actually occurred or is likely to occur. In brief, "free-riding" occurs when consumers obtain pre-sale services from one distributor but purchase the product from another distributor at a lower price. Commentators have pointed out that "whether **RPM** is effective is closely related to the costs borne by manufacturers and retailers for pre-sale services; when retailers bear too much cost, they are bound to free-ride on the pre-sale services and reduce retail prices."[77] Furthermore, some commentators have summarized that the occurrence of "free-riding" typically depends on the establishment of certain assumptions: "(1) the services provided by distributors have a positive effect on final demand; (2) these services are specifically targeted at particular products; (3) the cost of providing the services is relatively high; (4) the provision of services and the purchase of products can be separated."[78] It can be argued that, to prove **RPM** can address the

---

[69] See Howard P. Marvel and Stephen McCafferty: *Resale Price Maintenance and Quality Certification*, RAND Journal of Economics, Vol. 15, p. 358 (1984).

[70] See Joseph J. Spengler: *Vertical Integration and Antitrust Policy*, Journal of Political Economy, Vol. 58, p. 352 (1950).

[71] See Warren S. Grimes: *Spiff, Polish, and Consumer Demand Quality: Vertical Price Restraints Revisited*, California Law Review, Vol. 80, p. 832-833 (1992).

[72] See Benjamin Klein and Kevin M. Murphy: *Vertical Restraints as Contract Enforcement Mechanisms*, Journal of Law & Economics, Vol. 31, p.295 (1988); Richard E. Romano: *Double Moral Hazard and Resale Price Maintenance*, RAND Journal of Economics, Vol. 25, p. 464 (1994).

[73] See Victor P. Goldberg: *The Free Rider Problem Imperfect Pricing and the Economics of Retailing Services*, Northwestern University Law Review, Vol. 79, p. 754-756 (1984).

[74] See George R. Ackert: *Argument for Exempting Prestige Goods from the Per Se Ban on Resale Price Maintenance*, Texas Law Review, Vol. 73, p. 1208 (1995).

[75] See Raymond Deneckere et al.: *Demand Uncertainty and Price Maintenance: Markdowns as Destructive Competition*, American Economic Review, Vol. 87, p. 634 (1997); Howard P. Marvel: *The Resale Price Maintenance Controversy: Beyond the Conventional Wisdom*, Antitrust Law Journal, Vol. 63, p. 60 (1994).

[76] Manufacturers and retailers have differing levels of incentive for the sale of each unit of a product. Since manufacturers benefit more from each unit sold, this disparity leads to insufficient motivation for retailers to undertake promotional efforts for the product. RPM can resolve this imbalance. See Benjamin Klein, *Competitive Resale Price Maintenance in the Absence of Free Riding*, Antitrust Law Journal, Vol. 76, p. 448-449 (2009).

[77] Pinliang Luo and Lianquan Chen: *Retailers' Incentives to Free-ride on Presale Services and RPM Contract*, Industrial Economics Research, No. 1, 2008.

[78] Haixiao Gu: *The Economic Logic and Legal Regulation of RPM – With Comments on Article 14 of Chinese Anti-monopoly Law*, Journal of Henan Administrative Institute of Politics and Law, No. 4, 2008.

"free-riding" issue, it is necessary to demonstrate that the market conditions and business operations meet these assumptions.

44. Of course, these assumptions should not be interpreted o absolutize the reasonableness of RPM. Because, "First, RPM cannot explain maintaining resale price for products with low service demand; second, in various forms of vertical restraints, inducing distributors to provide services does not necessarily have to be achieved through RPM"[79] Therefore, in specific analyses, on the one hand, it is important to distinguish the service demands of different products and focus on whether the product itself constitutes a "complex product" (a product where understanding pre-sale information is crucial).[80] On the other hand, it is necessary to compare the specific scenarios in which services are induced to be provided and confirm the corresponding efficiency value. For instance, in cases where the same brand is distributed by multiple retailers, "the repeat consumption characteristics of the product may cause inter-temporal externalities in retail services, leading to insufficient supply of retail services [...] RPM can internalize the inter-temporal externality in retail services by increasing the compensation for retailers during the consuming trial phase, thereby incentivizing retailers to provide an optimal level of service, and its incentive outcome is superior to other vertical restraints such as minimum sales quantity requirements and exclusive sales territorial allocations."[81]

45. Second, it is important to distinguish whether RPM is initiated by the manufacturer or the distributor, so as to demonstrate the efficiency gains from the agreement. Typically, RPM has a greater likelihood of promoting competition when initiated by the manufacturer. Conversely, "if it is entirely the distributor imposing its will on the manufacturer, the anti-competitive effects are indisputable."[82] Bork also pointed out that "Retailers who agree to a horizontal restraint that the manufacturer does not desire are almost certainly attempting to restrict output for the sake of monopoly gains. If such a restraint would increase efficiency, the manufacturer would not only favor it but would impose it himself."[83] Other commentators argue that, "a single manufacturer producing a differentiated product over which such a manufacturer possesses some degree of monopoly power may find it advantageous to establish minimum retail prices to induce its retailers to offer special services jointly with it,

---

79 Jian Li and Fei Tang: *The Dealer Service Theory in Resale Price Maintenance: Explanatory Power and Limitations*, Oriental Law, No. 6, 2008.

80 See Haixiao Gu: *The Economic Logic and Legal Regulation of RPM – With Comments on Article 14 of Chinese Anti-monopoly Law*, Journal of Henan Administrative Institute of Politics and Law, No. 4, 2008.

81 Zili Wang, Xiaogang He and Weihua Pan: *Intertemporal Externalities, Retail Services, and Resale Price Maintenance*, Contemporary Finance & Economics, No. 2, 2019.

82 Haixiao Gu: *The Economic Logic and Legal Regulation of RPM – With Comments on Article 14 of Chinese Anti-monopoly Law*, Journal of Henan Administrative Institute of Politics and Law, No. 4, 2008.

83 Robert Bork: *The Antitrust Paradox: A Policy at War with Itself*, Basic Books, 1978, p. 289.

thereby increasing total sales."[84] Of course, if RPM is initiated by multiple manufacturers, it is necessary to examine whether it constitutes a cartel.

46. From this perspective, identifying the initiator of the agreement implicitly involves examining the motivations behind the formation of the agreement, as well as the accompanying efficiency considerations. Furthermore, evaluating the market power of the initiator in vertical agreements is directly related to how this power is transmitted through this vertical distribution chain and its impact on competition in the target market of specific distribution levels. Under intra-brand restrictions, vertical undertakings and their trading counterparts in the transaction form a cooperative relationship in the distribution chain. A successful initiation by the supplier implies that it holds a certain level of market power within the vertical chain, and might primarily focus on maximizing their own interests. In contrast, when RPM is successfully initiated by a distributor, the incentive for converting intra-brand restrictions into a means of promoting inter-brand competition is lacking, meaning the supplier has no intention of planning such restrictions, but is rather induced or coerced by the distributor to do so. Moreover, the presence of buyer power in the supply-distribute chain implies a lower likelihood of passing on efficiency to consumers. Accordingly, it may be worth exploring the allocation of varying degrees of burden of proof based on the identity of the initiating party. If the initiator is the manufacturer, the possibility that pro-competitive effects may arise from their actions is higher, correspondingly, a higher market power can be tolerated in the efficiency defense. If the initiator is the dealer, the possibility that pro-competitive effects may arise from their actions is lower, correspondingly, a lower market power can be tolerated in the efficiency defense.

(2) Key points in balancing the pro-competitive and anti-competitive effects of RPM

47. With regard to the framework for balancing the anti-competitive and pro-competitive effects of RPM, there are several questions that require further clarification. The key issue is: how undertakings can demonstrate that "the agreements reached will not substantially restrict competition in the relevant market, and that they can enable the consumers to share the benefits derived therefrom." Here, the proof of pro-competitive effects moves beyond the abstract, plausible stage, and requires concrete, substantiated evidence.

48. First, to prove that "the agreements reached will not substantially restrict competition in the relevant market." Under the EU law, when the relevant competition authorities assess exemptions pursuant to Article 101(3) of

---

84 Lester G. Telser: *Why Should Manufacturers Want Fair Trade?*, Journal of .Law & Economics, Vol. 3, p.104 (1960).

Guidelines on the application of Article 81(3) of the Treaty, "the protection of rivalry and the competitive process is given priority over potentially pro-competitive efficiency gains which could result from restrictive agreements."[85] According to the EU Guidelines on Vertical Restraints, the focus of this demonstration should be on analyzing "the remaining competitive pressures in the market and the effect of the agreement on those remaining sources of competition."[86] This analysis is logically sound, but its applicability under Chinese law is limited. In China's Anti-monopoly law, since the anti-competitive effects have been presumed and rebutted, further inquiry into market structure may no longer serve a meaningful purpose. In contrast, under the U.S law, the focus shifts to examining the balance between pro-competitive and anti-competitive effects. This is a more direct approach to the analysis of competitive impacts and therefore warrants greater emphasis.

49. In the Leegin case, the U.S Supreme Court stated, "Though each side of the debate can find sources to support its position, it suffices to say here that economics literature is replete with procompetitive justifications for a manufacturer's use of resale price maintenance."[87] Moreover, "Notwithstanding the risks of unlawful conduct, it cannot be stated with any degree of confidence that RPM 'always or almost always tend [s] to restrict competition and decrease output."[88] It is important to note that, the emphasis on output is critical. Unlike horizontal monopolistic agreements, RPM, by setting prices above competitive levels, does not necessarily imply that output is always or almost always reduced below competitive levels. This is because, in vertical relationships, limiting price competition may foster non-price competition, which can, in turn, increase output.[89] As highlighted in Leegin's open letter to dealers, the aim was for "our retailer, creating great looking stores selling our products in a quality manner."[90] The central issue, then, is how to ensure that restrictions on vertical price competition can effectively lead to non-price competition. A deeper analysis of the interaction between these two elements is necessary.

50. Where price competition is restricted, promoting competition and achieving greater output depends on the effectiveness of non-price competition. It must be demonstrated that: (1) non-price competition indeed occurs effectively, such as genuine competition among intra-brand distributors in service

---

85 Guidelines on the application of Article 81(3) of the Treaty, para.105 (2004/C 101/08).

86 Commission Notice, Guidelines on vertical restraints (2022/C 248/01), para.296.

87 Leegin Creative Leather Prods., Inc. v. PSKS, Inc., 551 U.S. 877, 889-890 (2007).

88 Leegin Creative Leather Prods., Inc. v. PSKS, Inc., 551 U.S. 877, 894 (2007).

89 As previously analyzed, RPM may intensify retailer competition in demand-enhancing services, thereby expanding market demand and ultimately increasing output. See MacKay, Alexander, and David A. Smith, *Challenges for Empirical Research on RPM*, Review of Industrial Organization, Vol. 50, p.214-216 (2017).

90 Leegin Creative Leather Prods., Inc. v. PSKS, Inc., 551 U.S. 877, 883 (2007).

provision;[91] and (2) the effectiveness of non-price competition is causally linked to the restriction of price competition, meaning that without the price competition restriction, such service-based competition would be ineffective due to problems such as "free-riding".[92] Hence, a valid defense requires not only proving that retailers are providing incremental services, but also demonstrating that high-quality services will not be offered without sufficient profit margins. Furthermore, the balancing of competitive effects should include an evaluation of market externalities and information symmetry. This is because, for a given level of demand, the effect of **RPM** on effort levels and consumer surplus depends on the severity of horizontal externalities and the extent of information asymmetry. When horizontal externalities are significant, RPM leads to higher effort levels and greater consumer welfare; conversely, when information asymmetry is severe, the opposite outcome will occur--The tradeoff between horizontal externalities and information asymmetry directly influences the welfare outcomes of **RPM**.[93]

51. Second, to prove that "they can enable the consumers to share the benefits derived therefrom." Some commentators argue that "any determination of monopolistic behaviors must return to an examination of the competitive harm itself, and cannot rely on the inaccurate concept of 'consumer choice being harmed' as a substitute indicator."[94] As commonly recognized, competitive harms include both disruption to the competition order/mechanism and detriment to consumer welfare.[95] Therefore, whether an efficiency defense is successful depends on how efficiency influences consumer welfare. In light of this, further clarification is needed as to what specific dimensions are encompassed within the benefits conveyed by undertakings and shared by consumers. How can it be demonstrated that consumers have, in fact, shared in the benefits generated? And to what extent must such consumer benefits be proven?

52. In general, the benefits that consumers can share include cost efficiencies and qualitative efficiencies, such as new products and improved products.[96]

---

91   See Lester G. Telser: *Why Should Manufacturers Want Fair Trade?*, Journal of .Law & Economics, Vol. 3, p.94-96 (1960); Robert Pitofsky: *Why Dr. Miles Was Right*, Regulation, Vol.8, p.29 (1984); In U.S. antitrust private litigation and public enforcement cases between 1975 and 1982, approximately 65% and 68% of cases respectively exhibited characteristics of non-price competition when categorized according to the necessity of pre-sale services. Pauline M. Ippolito: *Resale price maintenance: Empirical evidence from litigation*, Journal of Law & Economics, Vol. 34, p.283-284 (1991).

92   See Benjamin Klein and Kevin M. Murphy: *Vertical Restraints as Contract Enforcement Mechanisms*, Journal of Law & Economics, Vol. 31, p.266 (1988); Kevin J. Arquit: *Resale Price Maintenance Consumers' Friend or Foe*, Antitrust Law Journal, Vol.60, p.454 (1991).

93   See Zhichen Liu: *Resale Price Maintenance Asymmetric Information and Antitrust Enforcement*, Economic Research Journal, Supp. 2, 2012.

94   Lei Lan: *Debunking the Theory of Consumer Choice Injury as Competitive Harm: A Theoretical Reflection on the RPM Regime Inspired by Article 17(2) of the Amendment Bill of China's Antimonopoly Law*, Nanjing University Law Journal, No. 2, 2022.

95   See Eleanor M. Fox: *What is Harm to Competition – Exclusionary Practices and Anticompetitive Effect*, Antitrust Law Journal, Vol.70, p.372 (2002).

96   See Guidelines on the application of Article 81(3) of the Treaty, para.93 (2004/C 101/08).

For RPM, its pro-competitive effects are not derived from cost savings, but rather from qualitative efficiencies. Here, service provision should also be regarded as an important aspect of qualitative efficiency. The starting point for this consideration is the genuine demand consumers have for services.[97] This is because, "The welfare changes of consumers depend on their preference for pre-sale services. When additional pre-sale services are inconsistent with consumer preferences, the price increase caused by setting a minimum price may lead to a loss for consumers that outweighs the gain derived from the service."[98] Thus, the direction for demonstrating the availability of competitive benefits is: firstly, direct evidence that the benefits have been shared by consumers, and secondly, indirect evidence based on market structure proving that consumers might share the benefits. Direct evidence generally manifests in output quantities, supply quality, service provision, or diversified choices at or above the competitive level. Here, the assessment of consumer benefits should focus on consumers as a whole, as direct evidence that certain individuals benefit from RPM does not necessarily demonstrate that the benefits generated have been shared by consumers as a whole.[99] More specifically, "output tests should be accompanied by credible evidence or market surveys to demonstrate that consumers, to a greater or lesser extent, value the additional promotional services or price increases in the same way."[100] Indirect evidence, by contrast, is primarily demonstrated through the existence of sufficient intra-brand competition among distributors, with the absence of other intermediary levels, which serve as a structural guarantee that consumers will ultimately get the benefit. It is generally believed that if undertakings compete mainly on price and are not subject to significant capacity constraints, pass-on may occur relatively quickly. If undertakings compete mainly on capacity and capacity adaptations occur with a certain time lag, pass-on will be slower.[101]

53. On this basis, it should be clarified that, on the one hand, the benefits that consumers receive should be compared with the efficiencies claimed by the undertakings. It is generally accepted that "consumers must receive a fair share of the resulting benefit,"[102] which means that "consumers of the

---

97 "In cases where the likely effect of the agreement is to increase prices for consumers within the relevant market it must be carefully assessed whether the claimed efficiencies create real value for consumers in that market so as to compensate for the adverse effects of the restriction of competition." See Guidelines on the application of Article 81(3) of the Treaty, para.104 (2004/C 101/08).

98 Haixiao Gu: *The Economic Logic and Legal Regulation of RPM – With Comments on Article 14 of Chinese Anti-monopoly Law*, Journal of Henan Administrative Institute of Politics and Law, No. 4, 2008.

99 See Case T-131/99, Shaw, para.163 [2002] ECR II-2023.

100 Jun Zhang: *Ideal Regulation Path for Resale Price Maintenance in Anti-Monopoly Law from Perspective of Law and Economics: Concurrently Discussing Some Revisions of China's Anti-Monopoly Law*, Law Review, No. 4, 2020.

101 See Guidelines on the application of Article 81(3) of the Treaty, para.97 (2004/C 101/08).

102 Commission Notice, Guidelines on vertical restraints (2022/C 248/01), para.291.

goods or services purchased and/or (re)sold under the vertical agreement must at least be compensated for the negative effects of the agreement. In other words, the efficiency gains must fully offset the likely negative impact on prices, output, and other relevant factors caused by the vertical agreement."[103] This requirement can exclude situations where the potential benefits are insufficient. For instance, the EU Guidelines on Vertical Restraints states, "Rivalry between undertakings is an essential driver of economic efficiency, including dynamic efficiencies in the form of innovation. In its absence, the dominant undertaking will lack adequate incentives to continue to create and pass on efficiency gains. A restrictive agreement which maintains, creates or strengthens a market position approaching that of a monopoly can normally not be justified on the grounds that it also creates efficiency gains."[104] Thus, from the perspective of the undertaking's market power, a limit is set for the efficiency defense. On the other hand, the benefits that consumers receive should be assessed in relation to the manner in which the undertaking achieves efficiency gains. Generally, it can be assessed whether there exist less restrictive alternatives that could yield comparable consumer benefits. To evaluate whether a restriction is indispensable for achieving the claimed efficiency, "it must be made within the actual context in which the agreement operates and must in particular take account of the structure of the market, the economic risks related to the agreement, and the incentives facing the parties."[105] Additionally, the duration of the restriction should be considered. The analysis of less restrictive alternatives, although not codified under Chinese law yet, has been recognized in major jurisdictions as a crucial safeguard against excessive discretionary balancing in the assessment of competitive effects, and should be thoroughly developed through legal interpretation.[106]

Conclusion: Toward a Patternized Anti-monopoly Regulatory Framework for Resale Price Maintenance (RPM)

54. Under Chinese Anti-Monopoly Law, the regulation of RPM has undergone a long-term evolution, characterized by differences in understanding and divergent paths between law enforcement and judicial judgment, as well as opposing stances in academia. This phase of exploration in the early

---

103 Commission Notice, Guidelines on vertical restraints (2022/C 248/01), para.294.

104 Commission Notice, Guidelines on vertical restraints (2022/C 248/01), para.296.

105 Guidelines on the application of Article 81(3) of the Treaty, para.80 (2004/C 101/08).

106 The provision "and such effects are necessary to achieve the intended purpose" in Paragraph 1 of Article 22 of Judicial Interpretation of Anti-Monopoly Law represents a constructive attempt to advance this analysis

On the Pattern Setting of Anti-monopoly Regulatory Framework for Resale Price Maintenance

application of the law is understandable and acceptable. However, if this status quo persists, it may undermine the stability of market competition and the reasonable expectations for the development of business models. Now, lawmakers have provided a new statutory framework through the amendment of the Anti-Monopoly Law, which offers greater potential for reconciling the long-standing differences between various analytical modes and regulatory paths. However, without further clarification, it is unlikely to achieve a definitive and authoritative resolution. The primary concern lies in whether the presumption of anti-competitive effects signals the end of the rule of reason analysis. After detailed legal interpretation, the answer is negative. This is not only because the theoretical foundations is logically inconsistent, but also due to the inescapable reality that while the presumption of anti-competitive effects largely addresses the issue of under-enforcement, it significantly increases the risk of over-enforcement. Under the new RPM anti-monopoly regulatory framework, prevention of the risks of false positive/over-enforcement should be the central focus. To this end, academics, enforcement agencies, and the judicial bodies must form a new consensus, focusing on advancing legal interpretation, defining the legal application process, and clarifying the burden of proof for the parties involved. This would help establish a more consistent and robust analytical framework for the competitive effects of RPM. The paramount task lies in the interpretation and application of the new Anti-Monopoly Law: to unlock the analytical flexibility of the abbreviated rule of reason by preserving ample space for rebuttal in each stage of analysis, under the rigid shell of the presumption of anti-competitive effects.

Below-Threshold Transactions in China: Roads Less Travelled, but Worth Revisiting

BAI YONG[*]

Partner, Clifford Chance, Beijing

WANG ZIWEN[**]

Associate, Clifford Chance, Beijing

Abstract

This paper explores the discretionary powers of the State Administration for Market Regulation (SAMR) to review deals that fall outside the mandatory filing thresholds in China. Through a detailed analysis of cases and practices, this paper aims to identify key patterns in SAMR's enforcement approach regarding below-threshold transactions, highlighting the interplay between competition concerns and broader policy considerations during call-in reviews, and discussing the potentially diversified toolkit SAMR may employ in its enforcement of below-threshold transactions. It further examines the legal and procedural implications of China's first judicial review of a below-threshold merger case and proposes clarifications toward a more nuanced regulatory framework, advancing more balanced views with respect to appealability and the relevance of pre-existing competition issues in merger review. The paper also calls for vigilance regarding transactions that fall below control thresholds.

[*,**] Bai Yong is partner in Clifford Chance's antitrust practice and head of antitrust, Greater China. Wang Ziwen is associate in Clifford Chance's antitrust practice, based in Beijing, China. The views expressed in this article are those of the authors and do not necessarily reflect the views of their respective firms, clients, or any affiliated entities. This article is intended for informational purposes only and does not constitute legal advice.

Below-Threshold Transactions in China:
Roads Less Travelled, but Worth Revisiting

I. Introduction

1. In recent years, the enforcement of *the Anti-Monopoly Law of China* ("AML")[1] has gained significant momentum, with the State Administration for Market Regulation ("SAMR") actively engaging in a variety of cases. The scope of antitrust enforcement has expanded beyond mandatory filing reviews to include a growing focus on transactions that fall below statutory merger filing thresholds. While the AML and its implementing regulations provide the fundamental criteria for mandatory filings, SAMR retains broad discretionary powers to review transactions that may raise competition concerns, even if they do not meet the prescribed turnover thresholds.[2]

2. While still limited in numbers, these so-called "below-threshold" or "call-in" cases have garnered increasing attention, particularly in sectors characterised by rapid innovation, high market concentration, or strategic importance.[3] The regulation of such transactions presents challenges faced globally, and it is an area where China continues to explore and clarify its approach.

3. This paper aims to unpack the legal framework, enforcement practices, and policy rationale underlying SAMR's approach to below-threshold transactions. Chapter One serves as an introduction. In Chapter Two, the paper briefly outlines the legal framework governing below-threshold reviews in China, setting the stage for subsequent discussions. Chapters Three and Four analyse a series of representative case studies to identify emerging trends and enforcement priorities, highlighting the growing relevance of non-competition factors in call-in reviews. It follows that the paper seeks to provide clarity and guidance based on SAMR's decisional practices regarding these reviews. Chapter Five explores the implications of China's first judicial review of a below-threshold merger decision, examining and clarifying key issues related to the evolving relationship between administrative enforcement and judicial oversight. Chapter Six further proposes that beyond below "value" threshold cases, SAMR should also keep an eye out for transactions below "control" thresholds. Chapter Seven concludes.

II. Legal Framework Of Below-Threshold Mergers In China

4. The AML and its implementing regulations establish a twin test for mandatory merger filings in China; namely, a transaction must be notified to SAMR if both of the following conditions are met: (a) the transaction

---

[1] Anti-Monopoly Law of the People's Republic of China (promulgated by the Standing Comm. Nat'l People's Cong., Aug. 30, 2007, amended June 24, 2022, effective Aug. 1, 2008), http://en.npc.gov.cn.cdurl.cn/2022-06/24/c_1058449.htm.

[2] Guohai Li & Xiao Wang: *On the Regulation of Below-Threshold Concentrations under the Anti-Monopoly Law*, 29 J. Cent. S. Univ. (Soc. Sci.) 63, 63-64 (2023), https://doi.org/10.11817/j.issn.1672-3104.2023.04.007.

[3] See generally, Magali Eben & David Reader: *Taking Aim at Innovation-Crushing Mergers: A Killer Instinct Unleashed?*, 42 Y.B. Eur. L. 286 (2023), https://doi.org/10.1093/yel/yead013.

constitutes a "concentration of undertakings"; and (b) the parties meet the prescribed turnover thresholds.[4]

5. Even if a concentration does not meet the prescribed turnover thresholds, SAMR may still require a filing if there is evidence that the transaction has or may have the effect of eliminating or restricting competition. The basis legal framework for such review is provided under Article 26 of the Anti-Monopoly Law and Article 4 of the *Regulations of the State Council on Filing thresholds for Concentrations of Undertakings* (the "Regulations").[5] Such power is also widely referred to as the call-in power.[6]

6. The application of call-in reviews is subject to SAMR's wide discretionary assessment. In particular, the use of the term "may" in the legal provisions also indicates that SAMR has broad latitude in determining whether and how it will call in a deal for review. As will be discussed in detail below, SAMR has so far wielded such call-in powers in a few instances, and in all these cases, exhibited a great level of discretion in this process.

7. Aside from the general rules above, it should be noted that two sector-specific guidelines also provide useful references for gauging whether a below-threshold transaction may trigger regulatory interest.

8. In the platform economy sector, Article 19 of *the Anti-Monopoly Guidelines for the Platform Economy*[7] highlights that transactions involving start-ups, emerging platforms, or low/zero-price business models may raise concerns despite low turnover, particularly in markets with high concentration or limited competition.

9. Additionally, in the pharmaceutical sector, Article 30 of *the Anti-Monopoly Guidelines for the Pharmaceutical Sector*[8] notes that transactions involving

---

[4] Under the *Regulations of the State Council on Notification Thresholds for Concentrations of Undertakings*, a transaction must be notified to SAMR if it constitutes a "concentration" and if it is "notifiable". Specifically:
  - A "concentration" includes:
    ○ a merger;
    ○ acquisition of control through equity or asset transactions; and
    ○ acquisition of control or the ability to exert decisive influence through contracts or other means (Article 2 of the Regulations).
  - The turnover thresholds are met if:
    ○ the parties' combined global turnover in the previous fiscal year exceeds RMB 12 billion, with at least two parties each having over RMB 800 million in turnover within China; or
    ○ the parties' combined turnover within China exceeds RMB 4 billion, with at least two parties each exceeding RMB 800 million in turnover within China (Article 3 of the Regulations).

[5] Regulations of the State Council on Notification Thresholds for Concentrations of Undertakings (promulgated by the State Council, Jan. 22, 2024, effective upon promulgation), Decree No. 773, https://www.gov.cn/zhengce/content/202401/content_6928387.htm.

[6] Anna Tzanaki, *Towards a Merger Control Framework for Addressing Likely Harmful Below-Threshold Mergers*, Autorité de la concurrence (Jan. 2025), https://www.autoritedelaconcurrence.fr/sites/default/files/24.%20Anna%20Tzanaki%20-%20adlc.pdf.

[7] Anti-Monopoly Commission of the State Council of the PRC, *Anti-Monopoly Guidelines for the Platform Economy* (Feb. 7, 2021), available at https://www.gov.cn/xinwen/2021-02/07/content_5585758.htm.

[8] Anti-Monopoly and Anti-Unfair Competition Commission of the State Council of the PRC, *Anti-Monopoly Guidelines for the Pharmaceutical Sector* (Jan. 23, 2025), available at https://www.samr.gov.cn/zw/zfxxgk/fdzdgknr/fldzfys/art/2025/art_4f615267290d443f9b4e571774ed3d2a.html.

small-scale or early-stage pharmaceutical companies may warrant review, even if they fall below the thresholds, where there is evidence of potential anti-competitive effects.

III. Practice Of Below-Threshold Reviews In China

10. The call-in review of below-threshold transactions in China is not frequently seen – in particular, there is even more limited information regarding the use of such call-in powers. This article provides below a brief overview of the key practices of SAMR concerning below-threshold transactions, based on a review of public information that is available to us.

Didi/Uber China

11. In August 2016, Didi Chuxing acquired Uber's China operations, resulting in a combined market share exceeding 90% in the ride-hailing sector. Despite this, Didi did not notify the transaction to the Ministry of Commerce ("MOFCOM"), arguing that Uber China's revenue did not meet the RMB 400 million domestic turnover threshold required for merger notification under Chinese law back then.[9] MOFCOM responded by invoking relevant laws and regulations, which allow the authority to investigate transactions that may eliminate or restrict competition, even if they fall below the filing thresholds.[10] MOFCOM officials subsequently indicated that it conducted an informal review and held multiple interviews with Didi representatives. There is little further public information in this respect.

Er-kang Pharmaceutical/Jiushi Pharmaceutical

12. In late September 2018, Hunan Er-Kang Pharmaceutical ("Er-Kang"), a Chinese pharmaceutical company specialising in pharmaceutical excipients, announced its plan to acquire Henan Jiushi Pharmaceutical ("Jiushi"), a producer of active pharmaceutical ingredients ("APIs") for cold medicines. The two companies had a long-standing exclusive distribution relationship, with Er-Kang serving as Jiushi's sole distributor.[11] The proposed acquisition aimed to vertically integrate their operations.

---

9   Zhang Xi: *Antitrust Analysis of Didi's Acquisition of Uber China*, Peking Univ. Fin. L. Res. Ctr. (Oct. 25, 2018), https://www.finlaw.pku.edu.cn/flyxjr/xk_hljryfl_20181025180039673681/305388.htm.

10 Xinhua News Agency, *MOFCOM Investigates Didi-Uber Merger Case*, XINHUANET (Sept. 2, 2016), https://www.xinhuanet.com/politics/2016-09/02/c_1119503825.htm.

11 SAMR, *SAMR Fines Pharmaceutical Companies RMB 12.43 Million for Monopoly Conduct in Chlorpheniramine API Market*, SAMR (Jan. 2, 2019), https://www.samr.gov.cn/xw/xwfbt/art/2023/art_72cb5638e08842c3b3ab19fe3b2e9c19.html.

13. Although the transaction fell below China's merger filing thresholds, SAMR proactively intervened. According to SAMR's 2019 annual report, the regulator initiated several rounds of discussions with the parties and ultimately persuaded them to abandon the deal in June 2019 – approximately 8.5 months after the announcement. SAMR stated that, despite the deal's size, it would likely harm market competition if completed.[12]

14. The competition concerns were closely tied to the then ongoing antitrust investigations into both companies at the time. SAMR was simultaneously probing Er-Kang and Jiushi for abuse of dominance in the market for chlorpheniramine maleate APIs.[13] In January 2019, SAMR imposed a combined fine of RMB 10.04 million on the two companies for engaging in collective abuse of dominance. The conduct included excessive pricing, refusal to supply, and tying practices that restricted downstream competition.[14] Consequently, SAMR was concerned that the transaction would reinforce previously identified anti-competitive dynamics and complicate future enforcement efforts.

Synopsys/Ansys case

15. On 16 January 2024, Synopsys, a leading U.S.-based provider of electronic design automation ("EDA") software, announced its plan to acquire Ansys, a major simulation and analysis software company, in a cash-and-stock transaction valued at approximately USD 35 billion. The deal aims to combine Synopsys' semiconductor design capabilities with Ansys' physics-based simulation tools, creating a comprehensive design platform to address growing complexity in AI, mobility, and software-defined systems.[15] The deal does not meet the mandatory merger filing thresholds in China, as according to public disclosure, Ansys' China revenue falls below the filing threshold of RMB 800 million.

16. On 14 May 2024, Synopsys received a formal notice from SAMR, requiring it to notify the transaction, despite the deal falling below China's merger filing thresholds.[16] In response, Synopsys submitted its filing on

---

12 SAMR, *Annual Report on China's Anti-Monopoly Law Enforcement (2019)*, SAMR (Dec. 25, 2020), https://www.gov.cn/xinwen/2020-12/25/5573435/files/195171fdee024615933c10d57f141171.pdf.

13 PaRR Global, *Asia Desk: China Wrestling with How to Examine 'Killer Acquisitions' or 'Qia Jian Bing Gou'*, PaRR Global, https://app.parr-global.com/intelligence/view/2182891.

14 PaRR Global, *SAMR Issues CNY 12m Penalty Decision Against Er-Kang, Jiushi Pharma*, PaRR Global, https://app.parr-global.com/intelligence/view/1780535.

15 Synopsys Newsroom, *Synopsys to Acquire Ansys, Creating a Leader in Silicon to Systems Design Solutions*, SYNOPSYS (Jan. 16, 2024), https://news.synopsys.com/2024-01-16-Synopsys-to-Acquire-Ansys,-Creating-a-Leader-in-Silicon-to-Systems-Design-Solutions.

16 MLex, *Synopsys, Ansys Required by China's SAMR to File Below-Threshold Merger*, MLex (accessed June 5, 2025), https://content.mlex.com/#/content/1563658/synopsys-ansys-required-by-china-s-samr-to-file-below-threshold-merger.

10 July 2024,[17] and it is reported that SAMR formally accepted the case in December 2024, approximately five months later.[18]

17. SAMR's decision to intervene was driven by a combination of competition, technological, and geopolitical concerns. From a competition standpoint, Chinese customers and industry associations raised concerns that the merger could lead to bundling and interoperability issues between Synopsys and Ansys software products – both of which are widely used throughout the electronic design and simulation process. These concerns are particularly acute given Synopsys' estimated 30% share of China's EDA software market and Ansys' 17% share in the simulation software segment. The domestic industry remains nascent, with high barriers to entry, further amplifying the perceived risks.[19] SAMR reportedly met with Chinese competitors, downstream customers, and industry groups, who urged the regulator to intervene, citing horizontal overlaps and the risk of reduced competition in the EDA space.

18. Technological sensitivities further complicated the review. Synopsys has been subject to U.S. export controls that restrict the export of certain advanced EDA software to China, which has heightened concerns about the continuity of after-sales support and software upgrades for Chinese customers following the merger.[20] Chinese stakeholders also argued that the deal could adversely impact the security of supply of critical technological inputs due to U.S. export restrictions. Geopolitically, the transaction is unfolding amid a broader high-tech rivalry between the two countries, with both Synopsys and Ansys offering products that are subject to U.S. export restrictions.[21]

19. Finally, on 14 July 2025, SAMR conditionally approved the transaction, subject to a series of structural and behavioural remedies, including divestment, commitments to ensuring supply, no bundling, and ensuring interoperability, among others.[22]

17　MLex, *Synopsys, Ansys Awaiting China Clock to Start Over Review of $35 Billion Deal*, MLex (accessed June 5, 2025), https://content.mlex.com/#/content/1582117/synopsys-ansys-awaiting-china-clock-to-start-over-review-of-35-billion-deal.

18　MLex, *Synopsys-Ansys Deal Faces Uphill Battle in Six-Month Push for China Greenlight*, MLex (accessed June 5, 2025), https://content.mlex.com/#/content/1624253/synopsys-ansys-deal-faces-uphill-battle-in-six-month-push-for-china-greenlight.

19　MLex, *Synopsys, Ansys Required by China's SAMR to File Below-Threshold Merger*, MLex (accessed June 5, 2025), https://content.mlex.com/#/content/1563658/synopsys-ansys-required-by-china-s-samr-to-file-below-threshold-merger.

20　MLex, *Synopsys-Ansys Deal Faces Uphill Battle in Six-Month Push for China Greenlight*, MLex (accessed June 5, 2025), https://content.mlex.com/#/content/1624253/synopsys-ansys-deal-faces-uphill-battle-in-six-month-push-for-china-greenlight.

21　MLex, *Synopsys, Ansys Deal Sparks Concerns in China Over Bundling, Trade Controls*, MLex, https://content.mlex.com/#/content/1559423/synopsys-ansys-deal-sparks-concerns-in-china-over-bundling-trade-controls.

22　SAMR, *Announcement on the Conditional Approval of Synopsys Inc.'s Acquisition of Ansys Inc.* (July 14, 2025), https://www.samr.gov.cn/zt/qhfldzf/art/2025/art_5a07a899349b4855aa914010b3971b63.html.

Simcere/Tobishi case

20. Another noteworthy case centres around Simcere Pharmaceutical Co., Ltd. ("Simcere")'s acquisition of Beijing Tobishi Pharmaceutical Co., Ltd. ("Tobishi"). This case is not where SAMR actively called in the transaction, but where the parties voluntarily filed the case to SAMR, who then confirmed that a filing was needed, and after review, conditionally approved the case.

21. The case needs to be viewed against the broader backdrop of the protracted commercial disputes between the parties. By way of background, Simcere is the exclusive distributor of the Batroxobin API in China as a result of an exclusive supply agreement with the sole global manufacturer of the Batroxobin API, DSM, entered into in 2019. Tobishi, on the other hand, is China's only producer of the Batroxobin injection, the major downstream product of the Batroxobin API that primarily treats sudden hearing loss. Simcere's acquisition of Tobishi was first announced in June 2017, but has remained unresolved for several years due to commercial disputes, including arbitrations in relation to the share purchase agreement. This hostile nature sets the stage for why Tobishi has been averse to the deal. Despite not reaching the filing thresholds, both Tobishi (presumably as a strategy to oppose the deal's progress) and Simcere voluntarily submitted the transaction to SAMR in June and July 2022, respectively.

22. In September 2023, SAMR conditionally approved the acquisition, concluding that the deal could eliminate or restrict competition, as Simcere was the sole supplier of the upstream Batroxobin API and Tobishi was the only supplier of the downstream Batroxobin injection.[23] SAMR imposed both behavioural and structural remedies, which included requiring Simcere to terminate exclusive agreements with DSM, divest its research pipeline, and reduce drug prices. In November 2023, Tobishi challenged this decision with SAMR by way of administrative review, asserting that the remedies were insufficient and that SAMR should have blocked the transaction. This administrative challenge was unsuccessful. Subsequently, Tobishi initiated legal proceedings, arguing that SAMR's decision lacked factual bases, violated procedural requirements, and that the transaction should have been blocked and the proposed remedies are inadequate as they may allow the company to engage in monopolistic practices, such as price manipulation and supply constraints.

23. On 19 March 2025, the Beijing Intellectual Property Court (the "BIPC") published its ruling on an administrative lawsuit initiated by Tobishi against SAMR with respect to SAMR's conditional approval of Simcere's acquisition of Tobishi, the first and only conditionally approved case for

---

23 SAMR, *Decision on Conditional Approval of Simcere Pharmaceutical Co., Ltd.'s Acquisition of Equity in Beijing Tobishi Pharmaceutical Co., Ltd.*, SAMR (Sept. 22, 2023), available at https://www.samr.gov.cn/fldes/tzgg/ftj/art/2023/art_90a71deadd224689b026920807c0389c.html.

a below-threshold transaction.[24] The case marks China's first administrative lawsuit or judicial review concerning merger control review since the implementation of the AML in 2008. In its ruling rendered on and dated 30 December 2024, the BIPC upheld SAMR's conditional approval decision and confirmed the legality of SAMR's review procedures. The court emphasised that SAMR's review was "competition issue-oriented," with no procedural violations or factual errors. It clarified that the review standards applicable to voluntary filings are the same as those applicable to mandatory filings. It also affirmed that blocking a merger is not established as a preferred or prioritised remedy under the AML and that the imposed remedies in this particular case could effectively mitigate adverse competitive effects. The BIPC highlighted that the purpose of the merger control review is to address competition problems that "arise from" a concentration, as opposed to tackling issues that existed "pre-concentration", such as disputes regarding the validity of the share purchase agreement.[25] This landmark lawsuit clarifies several key principles in merger review enforcement and illustrates the panorama of the merger control review process in China, including the various stages of SAMR's decision-making and the remedies available to challenge such a decision.

CK Hutchison case

24. In early March 2025, CK Hutchison Holdings ("CK Hutchison"), a Hong Kong-based conglomerate founded by Li Ka-shing, announced a major divestment of its global port assets. Under a preliminary agreement, CK Hutchison plans to sell its entire stakes in Hutchison Port Holdings and Hutchison Ports Group Holdings – which together represent 80% of its port business – to a consortium led by BlackRock and Terminal Investment Limited, the port investment arm of Mediterranean Shipping Company. The deal also includes the sale of a 90% stake in Panama Ports Company, which operates the Balboa and Cristóbal ports on both ends of the Panama Canal. The total enterprise value of the transaction is estimated at USD 22.8 billion, with CK Hutchison expected to receive over USD 19 billion in cash proceeds.[26]

25. On 28 March 2025, SAMR publicly acknowledged the transaction for the first time. In response to media inquiries, an official from SAMR's Anti-Monopoly Bureau II stated that it had "taken note of the deal" and would conduct a review in accordance with the law to safeguard fair

---

[24] Beijing Intellectual Property Court, *Administrative Judgment in Beijing Tobishi Pharmaceutical Co., Ltd. v. State Administration for Market Regulation*, China Judgments Online.

[25] WeChat Official Account, *First Administrative Judgment on Merger Review in China Comes into Effect*, wechat (June 2025), https://mp.weixin.qq.com/s?__biz=mzi3ota3mjq3mw==&mid=2650328477&idx=1&sn=5fb8 0f67a967865a813b0a75edf3a35e.

[26] Securities Times, *CK Hutchison Plans to Sell Global Port Assets, Expected to Generate USD 19 Billion in Proceeds*, stcn.com (June 5, 2025), https://stcn.com/article/detail/1565759.html.

competition and public interest. This initial response signalled SAMR's intent to assert jurisdiction, even though the transaction primarily involves overseas assets and may fall below the mandatory filing thresholds.[27]

26. On 27 April 2025, SAMR issued a second statement. In response to reports that the transaction might be split into two separate deals to avoid regulatory scrutiny, SAMR warned that "all parties must not circumvent antitrust review in any form" and that no part of the transaction may be implemented without prior approval. SAMR emphasised that any attempt to proceed without clearance would result in legal consequences.[28]

27. SAMR's scrutiny appears to be driven by a combination of competition and geopolitical concerns. While the transaction does not directly involve Chinese port assets, regulators are reportedly assessing whether the deal could indirectly affect China's strategic interests in global port infrastructure. Of particular note is the role of U.S.-based BlackRock as a lead acquirer. In the current climate of heightened tensions between the U.S. and China, especially over control of critical infrastructure and supply chains, SAMR's cautious posture reflects broader geopolitical sensitivities.[29]

IV. Navigating Uncertainties: Towards More Clarity And Guidance

1. Refining standards for call-ins

28. Based on the case studies above, it is evident that while the AML only includes a high level catch-all clause and SAMR has not yet established or pronounced clear standards and guidance for the specific circumstances under which call-in reviews should take place, consistent patterns and focuses can be discerned through a review and assessment of past cases, which can help provide some clarity and guidance.

29. The past decisional practices represent pretty clearly two strings of cases: (i) call-in due to significant competition concerns; and (ii) call-in due to competition concerns plus non-competition concerns.

30. For Didi/Uber China, and Er-kang Pharmaceutical/Jiushi Pharmaceutical cases, the concerns are predominantly competition concerns. In Didi/Uber China case, the combined market share would be extremely high (90%) in

---

27 SAMR, *SAMR Responds to CK Hutchison's Planned Sale of Panama Ports: Review Will Be Conducted in Accordance with Law to Safeguard Fair Competition*, SAMR (Apr. 27, 2025), https://www.samr.gov.cn/xw/mtjj/art/2025/art_d6eda66f9646413586de65756625be43.html.

28 SAMR, *SAMR: Parties to CK Hutchison Port Transaction Must No. Circumvent Antitrust Review*, SAMR (May 27, 2025), https://www.samr.gov.cn/xw/zj/art/2025/art_67506eda5edf4f39b704340c0dd4ad35.html.

29 Cheng Leng & Andy Lin: *China Delays Approval of Hutchison Ports' Sale of Overseas Terminals*, FIN. TIMES (June 5, 2025), https://www.ft.com/content/2f5571ff-90b0-4ba2-8f09-257903e5326a.

the ride-hailing sector, and thus MOFCOM opted to intervene. In Er-kang Pharmaceutical/Jiushi Pharmaceutical case, the concern is more of a vertical integration and abuse concern, given the sole distributorship and the existing antitrust investigations back then.

31. When it comes to the Synopsys/Ansys case and CK Hutchison case, competition concerns still form the basis of SAMR's intervention. This is also consistent with SAMR's role and function as a competition law enforcement authority. However, the situations are more complex and usually compounded by non-competition policy factors, such as geopolitical tensions, supply chain stability concerns, and wider national strategic interest considerations. Nonetheless, instead of depicting this as weaponising or politicising antitrust enforcement,[30] this article proposes that so long as the law is applied in a reasonable and proportional manner, the relevance of non-competition policies per se is part of the balancing of interest test and does not in itself discriminate against the legitimacy of antitrust enforcement. Actually, the potential consideration of non-competition factors is clearly provided under the AML, which is also in line with the practices across the globe,[31] where an increased linkage between merger review and national security review is observed, and many jurisdictions also allow for and indeed consider non-competition factors during review.

32. In light of the above, it is fair to conclude that the typical scenarios where SAMR tends to intervene, or in other words, where there are higher call-in risks, can be either those with significant competition concerns, or those with competition concerns coupled with non-competition concerns. This is also in line with Article 4 of the *Interim Measures for Collecting Evidence on Anti-Competitive Concentrations Not Meeting Notification Standards (Draft for Comments)* published by MOFCOM back in 2009.[32] When conducting a preliminary analysis, MOFCOM may consider several factors, including the market share of the participating undertakings, the geographical scope involved in the concentration, competitors in the same industry, upstream and downstream enterprises, and consumer and public opinion reactions. While the document has been shelved and no further updates are available, it still provides insight into the authorities' views on this matter.

---

30 Daren Bakst & Gabriella Beaumont-Smith: *Five Conservative Principles to Apply Against Weaponized Antitrust*, heritage found. (Aug. 5, 2021), https://www.heritage.org/government-regulation/report/five-conservative-principles-apply-against-weaponized-antitrust.

31 Cullen O'Keefe: *How Will National Security Considerations Affect Antitrust Decisions in AI?* (Future of Humanity Inst., Univ. of Oxford, Technical Report, 2020), available at https://www.fhi.ox.ac.uk/wp-content/uploads/How-Will-National-Security-Considerations-Affect-Antitrust-Decisions-in-AI-Cullen-OKeefe.pdf.

32 Ministry of Commerce (MOFCOM), *Interim Measures for Collecting Evidence on Anti-Competitive Concentrations No. Meeting Notification Standards (Draft for Comments)* (Jan. 19, 2009), available at http://fldj.mofcom.gov.cn/aarticle/zcfb/200901/20090106010097.html.

2. Capitalising on the potentially diversified toolkit for below-threshold deals

33. In the previous section, we examined the types of factors and scenarios in which SAMR should consider intervening in below-threshold cases. We now turn to the question of what tools and measures SAMR can and should adopt to address such transactions effectively. This paper considers that SAMR may effectively make full use of its diversified enforcement toolbox to address below-threshold transactions that warrant attention. This includes employing both hard and soft measures, both ex-ante and ex-post approaches, both based on merger control rules and conduct rules.

34. The most immediate and legally clear option is for SAMR to initiate a formal investigation or issue a notice requiring the parties to submit a filing. This is a well-trodden and enforceable route.[33] In addition, this paper also proposes that there be a range of softer and more flexible tools that SAMR can deploy, both pre- and post-transaction, to manage potential risks.

35. One such mechanism is the "three letters and one notice" system.[34] Under this framework, SAMR can initiate regulatory dialogue with the parties involved, issue inquiries, or provide early warnings about potential competition concerns. This approach was effectively used in the Er-kang Pharmaceutical/Jiushi Pharmaceutical case (although back then, there was no such thing formally called "three letters and one notice"), where SAMR engaged with the parties and issued warnings. Given SAMR's authority and influence in the competition law space, such soft measures often carry significant weight and can prompt parties to reconsider or restructure their transactions voluntarily.[35]

36. In addition to pre-transaction engagement, SAMR may also consider post-transaction monitoring and intervention.

37. First of all, even after a transaction has closed, SAMR retains the authority to call in the deal for review under merger control rules. Alternatively, SAMR may investigate the transaction under the conduct rules of the AML – such as those governing monopoly agreements or abuse of dominance – if the transaction results in anti-competitive effects.

38. This dual-track approach – merger control and conduct enforcement – provides SAMR with the flexibility to tailor its response to the specific nature of the competitive harm. It also aligns with international practice.

---

[33] For instance, SAMR issued the notice requiring notification in the Synopsys/Ansys case. See Form 8-K, ANSYS, Inc. (May 14, 2024), https://www.sec.gov/Archives/edgar/data/1013462/000114036124026369/ef20029334_8k.htm.

[34] Notice on Establishing the "Three Letters and One Notice" System for Antitrust Enforcement, State Administration for Market Regulation & Office of the Anti-Monopoly and Anti-Unfair Competition Committee of the State Council (Nov. 29, 2023), https://www.samr.gov.cn/zw/zfxxgk/fdzdgknr/jzzcxds/art/2023/art_515052484fd94fb1a2d8a648615b4c1c.html.

[35] Jin Liu, *Research on the Soft Law Enforcement Mechanism of Antitrust* (Zhejiang Univ. Press 2023).

For example, recent EU case law confirms that national competition authorities (NCAs) and courts may challenge mergers that fall below filing thresholds, even after the transaction has closed, under the prohibition on abuse of dominance in Article 102 of the Treaty on the Functioning of the European Union ("TFEU"). A case in point is the Towercast judgment (2023).[36] In October 2016, Télédiffusion de France (TDF) acquired Itas, a competitor in the Digital Terrestrial Television (DTT) broadcasting market in France. The transaction did not meet the filing thresholds under either the EU Merger Regulation (EUMR) or French merger control law, and was not referred to the European Commission under Article 22 EUMR. At the time, the French DTT market was highly concentrated, with only three active players: TDF, Itas, and Towercast, with TDF holding a dominant position due to its extensive infrastructure and largest market share. In November 2017, Towercast filed a complaint with the French Competition Authority (FCA), alleging that the acquisition constituted an abuse of dominance under Article 102 TFEU, arguing that the transaction strengthened TDF's dominance and substantially impeded competition in both upstream and downstream wholesale DTT broadcasting markets.[37]

39. The European Court of Justice (ECJ) held that the introduction of ex ante merger control under Regulation 139/2004 does not preclude ex post control of mergers that fall below filing thresholds. National competition authorities and courts may therefore review such acquisitions under Article 102 TFEU, if they involve dominant entities and raise concerns of abusive conduct. Notably, the FCA has extended the Towercast reasoning to Article 101 TFEU, which prohibits anti-competitive agreements. In its May 2024 decision, the FCA investigated a series of asset swaps in the French meat-cutting industry, treating the sale and reciprocal divestiture agreements as potential anti-competitive arrangements under Article 101, despite the fact that none of the transactions met filing thresholds.[38]

40. Similarly, in January 2025, the Belgian Competition Authority (BCA) launched an investigation into a below-threshold acquisition in the artisan bakery sector, relying on Article 101 TFEU rather than abuse of dominance rules. The BCA argued that the transaction between Dossche Mills and Ceres – two major flour suppliers – could distort competition through collusive effects, even though neither party was dominant.[39]

---

36 Case C-449/21, *Towercast SASU v. Autorité de la concurrence*, ECLI:EU:C:2023:207, Judgment of Mar. 16, 2023.

37 Ibid.

38 Autorité de la concurrence, Décision n° 24-D-05 du 2 mai 2024 relative à des pratiques mises en œuvre dans le secteur de l'équarrissage, https://www.autoritedelaconcurrence.fr/sites/default/files/integral_texts/2024-05/24d05.pdf (last visited July 4, 2025).

39 The Belgian Competition Authority Opens Ex Ante Proceedings Into the Possible Abuse of Dominance by Proximus in the Fiber Sector, *Concurrences* (Jan. 2025), https://www.concurrences.com/en/bulletin/news-issues/january-2025/the-belgian-competition-authority-opens-ex-ante-proceedings-into-the-possible.

Ultimately, the parties decided to abandon the deal.[40] These developments suggest that all mergers, regardless of size or dominance, may now be susceptible to ex post scrutiny under EU competition law, particularly where the transaction structure resembles an agreement between undertakings.

41. In sum, while formal investigations remain a critical tool, SAMR's enforcement strategy for below-threshold transactions should also include a broader set of regulatory instruments. These include early engagement, soft warnings, post-merger monitoring, and conduct-based enforcement – all of which can help ensure that transactions falling outside the mandatory notification regime do not escape scrutiny where competition risks are present.

V. Rethinking The Implications Of The First Merger Juridical Review In China

1. Non-appealability of unconditional clearance?

42. As introduced above, the Simcere/Tobishi case for the first time touches upon the appealability or justiciability concerning antitrust administrative actions (i.e., merger review decisions) in China. Specifically, it indicates that the nature of the administrative actions taken by antitrust enforcement authorities (i.e., SAMR's approval) in the context of merger control has been defined as an administrative licence, and based on this clarification, the court holds that:[41]

- If the decision made regarding the merger notification is one of unconditional clearance, the specific administrative action does not alter or increase the rights and obligations of the notifying parties based on the merger agreement. Therefore, the notifying parties do not have the legal interest to initiate administrative litigation as their legitimate rights and interests are not affected.

- If the decision is one of prohibition or conditional approval, the specific administrative action negates the rights and obligations of the notifying parties based on the merger agreement or imposes statutory obligations on the post-merger entity. Consequently, the notifying parties can initiate administrative litigation as their legitimate rights and interests are affected.

---

40 Eubelius, Parties Abandon Non-Reportable Transaction After Belgian Competition Authority Launches Investigation, *Eubelius News* (Mar. 21, 2025), https://www.eubelius.com/en/news/parties-abandon-non-reportable-transaction-after-belgian-competition-authority-launches.

41 Beijing Intellectual Property Court, *Administrative Judgment in Beijing Tobishi Pharmaceutical Co., Ltd. v. State Administration for Market Regulation*, China Judgments Online.

43. While the above propositions sound well argued, and indeed, it is generally accepted that unconditional merger approval decisions do not affect the legitimate rights and interests of notifying parties – and thus do not give rise to standing for administrative litigation – this principle may warrant further assessment and refinement.

44. Take the present case as an example: Tobishi expressed objections to the conditional approval decision and sought a prohibition of the transaction. The court ultimately recognised Tobishi's standing to bring an administrative lawsuit, affirming that the conditional approval decision affected its legitimate rights and interests.

45. By analogy, if SAMR had instead issued an unconditional approval decision for this transaction in the first place, Tobishi would arguably have had an even greater incentive and reason to challenge the outcome in order to seek a prohibition. However, under the current framework as explained in the judgment, Tobishi would lack standing to challenge an unconditional approval (due to lack of impact on its interest) in case of, for example, an unconditional clearance, despite the fact that its interests, in effect, can be more significantly affected. This outcome appears logically inconsistent and paradoxical.

46. Therefore, while it is reasonable to presume that unconditional approvals typically do not infringe upon the rights of notifying parties, it may be worth considering whether the legal framework should allow for exceptions. In certain circumstances, parties or one of the parties may have a legitimate interest in challenging an unconditional approval, particularly in the case of hostile takeovers. Leaving institutional space for such challenges could enhance procedural fairness and accountability in merger control enforcement.

47. Another aspect worthy of attention is that while it is important to ensure that parties whose legitimate interests are affected by merger control decisions have access to judicial remedies, it is equally critical to guard against the abuse of process. In particular, notifying parties should not be permitted to challenge decisions by SAMR without reasonable substantive grounds, merely as a tactic to delay transaction timelines or gain commercial leverage.

48. To address this concern, this paper proposes that a form of procedural estoppel should be considered.[42] Parties seeking to challenge a merger decision should be required to maintain a consistent position throughout the regulatory process, from the initial submission to the litigation stage. For example, if a party such as Tobishi consistently argued that a

---

42 See generally, Andrew S. Y. Li & Hester Wai-San Leung: *The Doctrine of Substantive Legitimate Expectation: The Significance of Ng Siu Tung and Others v Director of Immigration*, HKU Scholars Hub, https://hub.hku.hk/bitstream/10722/133101/2/content.pdf; Lucy Jackson: *Towards an Administrative Estoppel*, (2015) AIAdminLawF 18, https://classic.austlii.edu.au/au/journals/AIAdminLawF/2015/18.pdf.

transaction raised competition concerns and should be blocked, it would be reasonable to allow that party to challenge either a conditional or unconditional approval decision, as such a challenge would be aligned with its original position and aimed at protecting its interests. Conversely, if a party initially submitted the transaction as non-problematic and supported clearance without remedies, it should not be permitted to later reverse its stance and challenge a conditional approval. Such a reversal would constitute a clear abuse of process, particularly if motivated by a change in commercial strategy rather than genuine competition concerns. In other words, where the parties have submitted the filing and presented the transaction as unproblematic, they should not be allowed to later invoke litigation to escape the deal or renegotiate terms under the guise of a regulatory challenge.

49. In sum, while judicial review is a vital safeguard, it must be balanced with procedural integrity. Ensuring consistency of position and good faith participation in the regulatory process will help preserve the legitimacy and efficiency of merger control enforcement, especially in the context of below-threshold transactions.

2. Pre-merger competition issues: leaving it as is?

50. Another widely discussed takeaway from the recent Tobishi judicial decision is the clarification that the purpose of merger control is to address competition concerns arising from the merger, rather than to resolve pre-existing competition issues. While this distinction is conceptually clear and appealing, it may oversimplify the practical realities of merger review and draw an overly artificial line between pre-existing and merger-induced competition concerns.

51. Cases such as Simcere/Tobishi and Er-Kang Pharmaceutical/Jiushi Pharmaceutical illustrate this complexity. In both instances, the transactions involved parties with high market shares and abuse of dominance prior to the merger. These pre-existing dynamics were not merely background context; they were central to the competitive assessment conducted during the merger review. In fact, they often set the stage for the very concerns that the review process seeks to address.

52. Although it is correct to say that merger control is not designed to remedy past anti-competitive conduct, such conduct is often inextricably linked to the potential effects of the merger. For example, in the Er-Kang Pharmaceutical/Jiushi Pharmaceutical case, SAMR initiated a review on its own initiative, driven by concerns over market foreclosure stemming from exclusive distribution arrangements and dominant market positions. These concerns, while rooted in pre-merger conditions, were directly relevant to the assessment of whether the merger would substantially restrict competition. This suggests that in practice – especially in

below-threshold transactions – the competition assessment needs to be comprehensive, contextualised, and holistic. It necessarily includes an evaluation of the existing market structure, the parties' conduct, and the broader competitive landscape. While admittedly pre-existing issues may not be the formal target of merger control review, they frequently inform the analysis of whether a transaction will exacerbate or entrench anti-competitive conditions.

53. Therefore, it is proposed that the merger review should not artificially exclude or insulate pre-existing competition concerns from its scope. Instead, these factors should be recognised as legitimate and often essential components of a comprehensive competitive assessment, particularly in call-in cases where the merger may amplify existing market problems.

VI. Beyond Below "Value" Thresholds – Stay Vigilant on Transactions Below "Control" Thresholds

54. Under the AML, below-threshold transactions and their regulation pertain to "concentration" that does not meet the value-based filing thresholds.[43] While much of the current enforcement focus has been on transactions that fall below the value-based filing thresholds, this paper proposes that comparable vigilance should be applied to transactions that fall below the control thresholds.

55. Such transactions, even if crossing the value thresholds, are not subject to mandatory notification because they do not meet the legal definition of a "concentration". Yet, they may still give rise to anti-competitive effects – particularly in the form of coordinated behaviour, information exchange, etc. These risks are especially pronounced in cases involving cross-shareholdings in competing firms.

56. For instance, the European Commission's recent action in the Delivery Hero/Glovo case underscores this point. There, a minority investment raised serious concerns about potential collusion and information sharing between competitors.[44] Specifically, in July 2018, Delivery Hero acquired a 15–16% non-controlling minority stake in Glovo, a Spanish-based food delivery company. This investment did not confer control and was

---

[43] Regulations of the State Council on Notification Thresholds for Concentrations of Undertakings (promulgated by the State Council, Jan. 22, 2024, effective upon promulgation), Decree No. 773, Article 4 https://www.gov.cn/zhengce/content/202401/content_6928387.htm, which provides that "Where " *a concentration of undertakings*" [emphasis added] does not meet the notification thresholds specified in Article 3 of these Regulations, but there is evidence that the concentration has or may have the effect of eliminating or restricting competition, the anti-monopoly enforcement agency of the State Council may require the undertakings to file a notification.".

[44] European Commission, Commission Fines Delivery Hero and Glovo €329 Million for Participation in Online Food Delivery Cartel, IP/25/1356; See also David Cendon Garcia, *Glovo and Delivery Hero Fined €329 Million for Market Manipulation Across Europe*, EU-Startups (June 3, 2025), https://www.eu-startups.com/2025/06/glovo-and-delivery-hero-fined-e329-million-for-market-manipulation-across-europe/.

therefore not subject to merger notification at the time. Despite lacking control, Delivery Hero gained board representation at Glovo, voting rights in Glovo's general assembly and board, as well as access to Glovo's confidential business plans and strategic documents. The European Commission found that this minority stake facilitated a cartel between the two companies, which lasted until Delivery Hero acquired full control of Glovo in July 2022. The Commission emphasised that owning a stake in a competitor is not inherently illegal, but in this case, the minority shareholding facilitated horizontal coordination and collusion, violating Article 101 of the TFEU. The case signals a growing recognition that minority shareholdings, even absent formal control, may distort competition and should be subject to scrutiny.

57. To address these concerns, a robust framework and toolkit is called for. In the Chinese context, this calls for a more nuanced approach to merger control – one that goes beyond formalistic thresholds and considers the substantive competitive impact of all structural links between undertakings. Particularly in below-threshold cases, SAMR should be empowered to assess not only the size of the transaction, but also the form and its potential to undermine market competition.

VII. Conclusions

58. The evolving landscape of below-threshold merger reviews, albeit still less frequently seen, in China has reflected a nuanced and increasingly sophisticated enforcement regime. This paper demonstrates, through a string of case studies, that SAMR's interventions are often triggered by a combination of market structure, competitive dynamics, and contextual factors. The diversification of enforcement approaches – from formal investigations to soft regulatory tools, from ex-ante intervention to ex-post measures, from merger control enforcement to conduct rules enforcement – can provide a comprehensive toolbox for SAMR to employ. The landmark Tobishi case further highlights the importance of procedural fairness and judicial oversight in merger control. Nonetheless, this paper also critically reflects on the judicial decision and calls for a re-assessment of the appealability of some of the unconditional approvals, seeking to allow for the parties to appeal unconditional approvals under certain circumstances, and the paper also calls for reconsideration of the role of pre-existing competition issues in merger review, which are hard to be artificially insulated from the merger review at issue. These considerations are critical to maintaining the efficacy of the enforcement and appeal process. Finally, this paper advocates for heightened vigilance not only toward transactions falling below value-based thresholds but also those below control thresholds. Structural links such as minority shareholdings

and cross-ownership arrangements can pose significant competition risks and should not escape scrutiny. Overall, a more context-sensitive, holistic, and diversified approach to below-threshold merger control will be of practical meaning to ensuring that China's antitrust enforcement remains robust, fair, and effective.

China's Anti-Monopoly Law and its Merger Review: Retrospect and Prospect

JOHN YONG REN*
Managing Partner, T&D Associates

CHRISTINE FENGYI ZHANG
Partner, T&D Associates

SCHIFFER MENGMENG SHI
Senior Associate, T&D Associates

DANIEL ZU GUI
Senior Associate, T&D Associates

Abstract

This article provides a comprehensive analysis of China's Anti-Monopoly Law (AML) from its legislative inception in 2003 to its current enforcement under the State Administration for Market Regulation (SAMR). The paper traces the AML's evolution through three distinct phases: the drafting period (2003-2008), MOFCOM's enforcement era (2008-2018), and SAMR's unified regime (2018-2025). It examines key developments including the consolidation of three enforcement agencies into SAMR, procedural innovations such as simplified review procedures and "stop-clock" mechanisms, and substantive advancements in merger control practices. The analysis highlights China's unique approach

---

* Dr. John Yong Ren is the Managing Partner of T&D Associates, Christine Fengyi Zhang is the Partner and Dr. Schiffer Mengmeng Shi and Daniel Zu Gui are the senior associates of T&D Associates.

to behavioral remedies, the increasing application of FRAND principles, and the regime's adaptation to digital economy challenges. The paper demonstrates how China's merger control system has matured from a nascent framework to a sophisticated regulatory regime that balances domestic economic priorities with international antitrust standards.

1. 2025 marks the 40th anniversary of Prof. HUANG Yong's widely esteemed, thriving and fruitful academic career at the University of International Business and Economics (*"UIBE"*). Every time I reminisce about our undergraduate days at Peking University four decades ago (from 1981 to 1985), vivid memories of shared classrooms, heated debates, and youthful aspirations come flooding back. Back then, neither could've anticipated how much our paths would cross over the years – while he embarked on a track of academic excellence, dedicating his life to shaping young minds, I ventured into the legal profession, eventually specializing in anti-monopoly law.

2. Remarkably, my professional journey has paralleled the growth and evolution of China's anti-monopoly regime. Since discussions on the Anti-Monopoly Law of the People's Republic of China (*"AML"*) began in the end of 20th century, I have participated and witnessed firsthand its transformation from a concept on the drawing board to an increasingly refined legal framework. The final enactment of the law in 2008 heralded not only a significant legislative achievement but also the start of a new chapter in China's economic governance.

3. At the moment when Prof. Huang extended the invitation for me to contribute to this book, I know exactly what to explore. This article aims to provide a comprehensive overview of the progress and prospects of China's antitrust system, with a particular focus on the merger review.

I. 2003–2008: China's AML Drafting and Preparatory Work – Inheriting the Past and Ushering in The Future

A. Origins and imperatives of China's AML

4. Back in early 2000s, the formulation of China's AML was neither a foregone conclusion nor an effortless endeavor. Although the anti-monopoly rules had far-reaching effects on competition, there was still much dispute as to, *inter alia*, whether such rules were really need and if so, how should relevant mechanism be designed. While the practices in other jurisdictions, such as the US and the EU, offer valuable insights, it remains difficult to predict the effects of implementing anti-monopoly laws in China, given differences in economic conditions and national circumstances

5. Notably, during the drafting process of the AML, some government officials, academic experts and foreign economists argued that monopoly is the natural result of competition. The AML might instead cause more governmental restrictions on competition and lead to low efficiency. However, the concerns of domestic enterprise circles were that, most Chinese enterprises were small-scale with less competitiveness at the moment of China entering the WTO in 2003. The most urgent priority was to strengthen these enterprises rather than to eliminate monopoly. The AML might hinder the implementation of this prioritized strategy.

6. At that time, in the transition from a planned economy to a market-oriented one, it was sensible for China to establish and maintain an orderly market by subjecting the market competition to anti-monopoly rules. Given such a situation, from my perspective, China's AML would largely bear certain unique characteristics, which would reflect the transitional period.

7. Despite domestic and international disputes, skepticism, and widespread concerns, Ms. MA Xiuhong, then Vice Minister of Ministry of Foreign Trade and Economic Cooperation ("MOFTEC", the predecessor of Ministry of Commerce ("MOFCOM")), demonstrated foresight by directing Mr. SHANG Ming (then head of the Fair-Trade Bureau) to prioritize preparations for the imminent enactment of the AML. It was also during the same period when Prof. Huang kindly reminded me to pay close heed to the future antimonopoly laws and regulations, a mini constitution in the economic domain.

1. A very early start in 1980s and the promulgation of Anti-Unfair Competition Law

8. Competition laws entails both anti-monopoly law and anti-unfair competition law. Therefore, the legislators in China at that juncture firstly decided to combine both anti-monopoly rules and anti-unfair competition rules into a single legislation. As early as August 1987, the Legislation Bureau under the State Council formed a board in charge of the draft of anti-monopoly law and proposed in 1988 a draft of the *Provisional Regulations Governing Anti-Monopoly and Anti-Unfair-Competition*[1]. Given, among others, China's market-oriented economy was far from being mature by that time, the Anti-Unfair Competition Law ("AUCL") was promogulated on September 2nd 1993, and it was decided that the anti-monopoly law should be issued separately at a later stage. Inevitably, the framework of the AUCL had a coverage of rules governing anti-monopoly issues. Such a legislative framework was divergent from that of foreign countries who published single rules respectively governing anti-monopoly and anti-unfair competition.

---

1 《反对垄断和不正当竞争暂行条例草案》.

9. Communications with both legislators and Prof. Huang brought to my attention that, the AML to be implemented in China was not totally a new legislation covering a blank area – it would both inherit the past and usher in the future. In the forthcoming AML in 2008, China would not only include the effective anti-monopoly measures in the law by summarizing the practice and experience from the past years, but also work out rules to deal with anti-monopoly contingencies in the future.

2. A significant move after entering 21ˢᵗ century

10. Having considered the aforementioned factors, following the promulgation of the AUCL, the Standing Committee of both the 8th and 9th People's Congress put the AML on the legislation agenda and entrusted the former MOFTEC's State Economy & Trade Commission and the State Administration of Industry and Commerce ("SAIC") to draft the law. A board was therefore established for this purpose.

11. The 10th Five Year Plan urged to "develop and improve the regulations to maintain the market order, prohibit monopolies and unfair competition, and guarantee the effective operation of the market competition mechanism". In addition, after entering 21ˢᵗ century, with the development of a legal culture in China, every year there were more motions and proposals for the National People's Congress ("NPC") and the Chinese People's Political Consultancy Congress ("CPPCC"), urging for the promulgation of an anti-monopoly law.

12. On March 7, 2003, the former MFT, together with the National Taxation Bureau, SAIC, the National Foreign Exchange Bureau, jointly promulgated the *Provisional Regulation Regarding Merger and Acquisition of Domestic Enterprises by Foreign Investors* ("2003 Regulation")[2], effective April 12, 2003. Notably, the 2003 Regulation contained anti-monopoly rules governing both inbound and outbound mergers and acquisitions of domestic enterprises by foreign investors. As China's first major anti-monopoly framework post-WTO accession, the 2003 Regulation signaled the government's commitment to fulfilling its WTO obligations by expediting antitrust legislation and aligning with global competition standards.

B. 2003 – 2008: Drafting and preparatory work of China's AML

1. Key substantive and procedural issues addressed during the drafting process observed by T&D

13. Given the bridging role of China's AML between past and future, I, along with Prof. Huang and my colleagues in T&D Associates ("T&D"), observed during this process that legislative departments and enforcement agencies

---

2 《外国投资者并购境内企业暂行规定》, please see: https://www.gov.cn/gongbao/content/2003/content_62062.htm.

collaborated with legal experts, practitioners in the legal profession, and even solicited input from international and domestic corporations. This drafting process entailed a systematic progression from multi-year legislative research, iterative revisions of preliminary drafts, to the ultimate promulgation of the finalized legislation.

14. Through this collective endeavor, T&D was deeply involved and holistically assisted legislative authorities with Prof. Huang in considering the following critical factors:

    From the perspective of coordination and continuity with existing legal frameworks, although no specialized anti-monopoly law in China in 2003, as mentioned above, indeed there had been antitrust legislation in place made up of laws, administrative regulations, local government rules etc. These include: five articles in the AUCL promulgated in September 1993 covering antitrust areas; the Price Law enacted in December 1997 requiring operators not to conspire with each other and manipulate the market price; Articles 32 and 33 of the Bidding Law issued in August 1999 addressing collusive actions and predatory pricing; the Government Procurement Law promulgated in June, 2002 covering administrative monopoly, especially local boycotting, among others.

    From the perspective of competent authorities and implementation agencies for the AML, in 2003 no special authority or implementation agency in China was in existence solely in charge of the anti-monopoly issues. Multiple governmental organs had the authority, within their specific jurisdictions, to issue and implement rules regarding anti-monopoly problems.

15. At that time, and according to the explicit authorization of the State Council, SAIC assumed the drafting, and implemented rules and measures to counter illegal monopoly and unfair competition, to investigate monopoly in market transactions (specifically, the Anti-Monopoly Division under the Fair Trade Bureau of SAIC was responsible for the drafting and implementation of relevant rules); the MOFCOM addressed the issues of monopolies in foreign investment introduction (mainly in merger and acquisition); the National Development and Reform Commission ("NDRC") oversaw monopoly issues related to price.

16. In addition, the competent industry-specific authority had the right to investigate monopoly in the industry. For example, on January 31st, 1997, the Ministry of Judiciary issued Penalty Rules Regarding Lawyers' Illegal Act, Article 6 of which provides that, "[w]here a lawyer commit any of the following misfeasance, the judicial department at provincial level or local level shall give a disciplinary warning; If the circumstances are serious, the judicial department shall suspend its business from three to twelve months, confiscate the illegal gains if any; [...] (5) monopolize legal service business by taking advantage of judicial authority, administrative organs or other social management organization etc."

Table 1 | Power Division of Three Authorities Prior-AML

	Monopoly Agreement	Abuse of Market Domination Status	Merger & Acquisition	Administrative Monopoly
SAIC (according to AUCL, etc.)	Authorized	Authorized		Authorized
NDRC (according to price law, etc.)	Authority over agreement related to price	Authority over acts related to price (e.g. predatory pricing price discrimination)		Authority over acts related to price
MOFCOM (according to Provisional Regulation Regarding Merger and Acquisition of Domestic Enterprises by Foreign Investors)			Authority over mergers and acquisitions by foreign investors	
Competent industry-specific authority (according to industry rules)	Authorized	Authorized		Authorized

17. To realize the entire purpose of an anti-monopoly law, many scholars proposed to set up a special anti-monopoly executive department as monopoly additionally concerned the government's restriction on competition. This department should not only have the power of law enforcement but also enjoy relevant legislative rights. This would permit this department to retain independence and unity. The enforcement of AML included examination of economic monopoly, restraint on enterprise consolidation, and disposal on the governmental and departmental administrative monopoly. It needed economy analysis as well as legal judgment. Therefore, a unified, independent and authoritative special institute should undertake the enforcement.

18. However, since the newly established department might damage the vested interest of some departments/ministries under the existing systems, some raised voices against establishing special an anti-monopoly executive department, but insisted on maintaining the existing system.

Other Key Issues and Perspectives in the AML

19. Beyond these aspects, regarding the application scope and regulated issues of AML, debates revolved around "strictly [limiting] the application of the exclusion clause" (*i.e.*, exempting those natural monopoly and public

interest sectors), applying it to all monopolies, and "applying exceptions similar to the anti-monopoly laws of various countries in the world" (*i.e.*, exempting industries or fields such as natural monopolies and public interests). There were serious, detailed, and realistic discussions on the extraterritorial effect of the AML, whether administrative monopolies need to be regulated, whether to adopt "behaviorism" or "structuralism" for abuse of market dominance, whether the government shall control the enterprise consolidation, and the "dividing line" between anti-monopoly and intellectual property rights, which have now reached many consensuses.

20. Due to space constraints, the following Section II and III will retrospectively analyze the legislative debates surrounding "the concentration of undertakings review mechanism", thereby reconstructing the intricate and monumental lawmaking journey of China's AML.

2. T&D's role in the drafting process of the AML

21. From 2003 until the formal enactment of the AML in 2008, recognizing the profound significance and foundational nature of the issues addressed by the law, T&D collaborated with Prof. Huang to organize seminars involving authority officials, experts, legal practitioners, and corporate stakeholders. This initiative was aimed to support the legislative process and contribute to the formulation of the AML.

22. Through those efforts, we deepened the understanding of AML's legislative framework and content, actively building a bridge for the legislators to gather feedbacks from market participants and scholars. By sharing research achievements in AML legislation, the market participants and scholars, including Prof. Huang, advanced and facilitated the legislative process, ultimately aiding Chinese lawmakers in revising and finalizing the law.

23. Under the leadership of Legal Affairs Office of the State Council ("**SLO**"), three groups were established based on AML legislation by the end of 2004:

    (1) a leading group comprising several vice ministry level officials from the Government, such as MOFCOM, SAIC and NDRC;

    (2) a working group comprising some bureau and division level's officials from the same ministries; and

    (3) an expert group comprising more than twelve Chinese legal scholars from various legal research institutions and law schools.

24. Starting from February 2005, consultative seminars and meetings have been held by the three groups from time to time to discuss the imminent AML. On February 4th, 2005, the leading group held its first meeting. Mr. Cao Kangtai, the head of the group, presided this meeting. Officials from State

Council, Supreme People's Court and NPC also attended. Attendants were consent to the importance of AML in Chinese legal system and the necessity of enacting AML.

- In 2004, SLO held a closed consultative meeting with three prominent Chinese legal scholars from the expert group[3] at the end of February. This meeting was initiated after SLO had the chance to collect and review the modification comments (Modification Comments) received from various senior governmental bodies, political organizations, and selected members of the academic community regarding the first draft of AML submitted by MOFCOM in March 2004.

25. Prof. HUANG Yong, Prof. WANG Xiaoye, and Prof. WANG Xianlin were among the selected members of the expert group to participate in this meeting and evaluate the comprehensive modification comments. The compiled modification comments include both linguistic points as well as views about the actual drafts, and there was a deluge of varying views from different parties on each issue. Despite these differing perspectives, there was a consensus that promoting fair competition is imminent and the importance and urgency of AML legislation in China is undisputed.

- The June 2004 seminar covered extensive topics including the latest developments in AML formulation, amendments to the AUCL, and China's WTO trade policy compliance. Corporate participants shared legal challenges in cross-border operations – spanning marketing practices, agency systems, pricing policies, and transitional mechanisms – as well as fair competition issues in transnational investments (mergers, acquisitions, joint ventures). Legal scholars and judicial authorities also presented relevant landmark cases.

26. The legislative participants of the seminar included the NPC Finance and Economics Committee, the NPC Legal Affairs Committee, SLO, legislative group members and relevant experts; the SAIC, NDRC and MOFCOM and some corporate representatives. As key market participants, enterprises and their legal counsel deemed it imperative to engage in AML legislative consultations, facilitating interactions with enforcement agencies and courts while strengthening ties with competition law scholars.

- Additionally, on July 1, 2004, the "International Symposium on Anti-Monopoly Law and Economic Development" was convened.

27. In addition to domestic participants, the event invited Mr. Thomas B. Leary, Commissioner of the U.S. Federal Trade Commission ("**FTC**"), and Mr. Re. Hewitt Pate, Assistant Attorney General for Antitrust at the

---

3   The expert group is composed of more than 12 professors from Chinese Academy of Social Sciences (CASS), Renmin University, University of International Business and Economics (UIBE) and others.

U.S. Department of Justice ("DOJ"). The two U.S. officials delineated the evolutionary trajectory of U.S. anti-monopoly laws, emphasizing their interpretive adaptability to economic shifts and operational interdependence with macroeconomic conditions. Particular focus was placed on balancing intellectual property protections with anti-unfair competition regulations.

- On July 30, 2005, T&D assisted in convening the Anti-Monopoly Theories and Practices Symposium. Prof. Huang Yong delivered a keynote speech titled *Characteristics of China's Competition Policy and Its Macro-Level Impact on Business Environments*. Additionally, Prof. Sheng Jiemin lectured on *Legal Issues of Fair Trade in Corporate Market Operations*. Prof. Wang Xiaoye addressed *Competition Law Considerations in Concentration of Enterprises*.

28. The symposium convened participants from the Industry and Transportation Department of the SLO, the MOFCOM Treaty and Law Department, the NPC Legislative Affairs Commission & Financial and Economic Committee, NDRC Legal Affairs Office, SAIC Regulations Department, and the State Council Development Research Center; scholars from universities such as UIBE, Peking University ("PKU"), CASS, and SUFE; and representatives from companies such as CNPC, Air China, China Mobile, Microsoft, Intel, GE, and Cisco.

- In 2005, T&D also supported the Present and Future of Petroleum System Reform on August 26, the Symposium on the Application of Anti-monopoly law in US Health Insurance Sector on October 17 and Forum on Competition Law and Industrial Policy on April 6, 2006.
- On April 15, 2006, T&D supported the Symposium on International Enforcement of AML with participants of officials from NPC, the State Council, MOFCOM, NDRC, SAIC and Professor Eleanor M. Fox at New York University.
- From May 19th to May 20th, 2006, MOFCOM, Asia Development Bank ("ADB") and Organization for Economic-Cooperation and Development ("OECD") co-hosted an international anti-monopoly law seminar in Hangzhou. The main participants of the seminar included Mr. Arthur M. Mitchell, Chief Legal Counsel of the ADB, Mr. Hans-Jurgen Ruppelt, Head of the Retail & Transport Division, German Federal Cartel Office, Mr. William Blumenthal, Chief Legal Counsel of the U.S. FTC, Mr. Gerald F. Masoudi, Chief of the Antitrust Division, U.S. DOJ, Ms. Blanca Rodriguez Galindo, Head of International Relations Unit, DG Competition, European Commission, Mr. Bernard J. Phillips, Chair of the OECD Competition Committee, Mr. Edward Whitehorn, Head of the OECD Competition Division, Mr. Shang Ming, Director of

the MOFCOM Treaty and Law Department, Mr. Wang Changbin, Deputy Director of the MOFCOM Treaty and Law Department.

- On December 19, 2006, Prof. Huang, together with the officials from the Legislative Working Commission of NPC, MOFCOM and SAIC visited Japan's Fair Trade Commission ("JFTC") around Dec 10. Law researchers including the three scholars (Huang, Sheng and Wang) mentioned above all attended a seminar on antitrust held in Hong Kong in the middle of December.

29. After that conference, T&D supported the Anti-monopoly law and Intellectual Property Rights Symposium on November 25, 2006.

Prof. Huang Yong (the first from the left) and experts during Anti-Monopoly law and IPR Symposium (photo provided by T&D)

30. 2006 was an unusual year for China's AML. After a long-time debate, the Standing Committee of the 10th NPC reviewed the draft submitted by the State Council in June, 2006 for the first time and then officially initiated the legislative procedure.

31. The AML draft went under its second review in the 28th meeting of Standing Committee of the 10th NPC from June 24 to the 29, 2007, and the third review is scheduled to take place in August. Since the bills on the Standing Committee agenda are usually examined three times before being voted on, T&D at that time predicted that the AML is expected to be enacted in August or later in 2007.

John Yong Ren, Christine Fengyi Zhang
Schiffer Mengmeng Shi and Daniel Zu Gui

- Before and after the enactment of China's AML on August 30, 2007, intensive seminars addressing AML implementation details were conducted, including:
    - June 2, 2007, the Competition Law Center of the UIBE and the China Price Association held the Symposium on Price Agreement and AML Theories and Practices, co-organized by T&D.
    - July 21, 2007, the Competition Law Center of UIBE and the Fair Trade Bureau of the SAIC jointly held the Symposium on Abuse of Market Dominance and AML Theories and Practices.
    - September 5, 2007, T&D supported the Anti-Monopoly Enforcement of the European Commission with participants of Neelie Kroes, the European Commissioner for Competition, and Emil Paulis, Director of Directorate General for Competition of the European Commission.
    - September 22, 2007, the Competition Law Center of the UIBE held the Symposium on AML Application in the Knowledge Economy Era, co-organized by T&D.

Prof. Huang Yong (the first from the left) and experts during the symposiums (photo provided by T&D)

Prof. Huang Yong (the first from the right), Mr. Shang Ming (third from the right) and foreign experts during the symposium (photo provided by T&D)

- From December 13 to 14, 2007, SAIC hosted the AML *Enforcement International Research Symposium* at Diaoyutai State Guests House of Beijing. The Symposium focused on AML Enforcement issues, and invited influential officials of AML Enforcement Authorities from other jurisdictions, e.g. the U.S. FTC, the U.S. DOJ, the Korea KFTC, DG Competition of European Commission, Japan JFTC, Cartel Bureau of Germany, Australia Competition and Consumer Commission, Russia Antitrust Bureau and delegates from UN, etc.

32. For the domestic side, the other two possible AML Enforcement Authorities, MOFCOM and NDRC also sent officials to this symposium, at the meantime, officials from Legislative Affairs Commission under the Standing Committee of the NPC, Financial & Economical Commission under the Standing Committee of the NPC, Legislative Affairs Office under the State Council, and experts from prestigious AML research institutes, such as Competition Law Center at UIBE, PKU, Renming University, and CASS also participated in this symposium and expressed their opinions regarding the AML Enforcement.

  - On December 20, 2007, MOFCOM, Japan International Cooperation Agency ("JICA") and Japan External Trade Organization ("JETRO") hosted the *China Anti-monopoly Law Symposium* at China World Hotel of Beijing. MOFCOM, NPC and the State Council officials, experts from JICA and JETRO, and professors from Chinese academia respectively delivered speeches at this Symposium. Attorneys from foreign and local law firms including T&D Associates also participated in this Symposium.

33. The Symposium focused on the influence of the newly adopted AML on the enterprise activities, and mainly discussed the outline of the law. Mr. Shang Ming, Director of Department of Treaty & Law under MOFCOM, gave a speech of the new AML and the M&A in China. JICA and JETRO experts primarily talked about Japan's experience in AML legislation and enforcement. Ms. Yuan Jie, Deputy Director of Economic Law Division of Legislative Affairs Commission under the Standing Committee of the NPC, introduced the background of China's AML Legislation. Professor Sakai Kyouhei from Japan Tokyo Metropolitan University, Professor Sheng Jiemin from Peking University and Professor Shi Jianzhong from China Politic and Law University respectively expressed their opinions from the perspective of academic research

- On January 12, 2008, the Symposium on Enforcement of Anti-Monopoly Law & Judicial Proceedings was held by the Competition Law Center of the UIBE and T&D Associates in Beijing. The attendees including:
    o experts in law from PKU, RMU, CASS and UIBE;
    o senior government officials from NPC, SLO, MOFCOM, NDRC and SAIC;
    o judges from the Supreme Court, Beijing High Court, Beijing Intermediate Courts, and Shanghai High Court;
    o EU WTO Senior Experts;
    o in-house counsels and senior officials from multi-national companies and local companies; and
    o lawyers from distinguished local and foreign firms.

From the left to the right: Ms. Mei Lipeng/ Prof. Huang Yong/Prof. Wang Xiaoye/Ren Yong (photo provided by T&D)

34. The main issues discussed on this symposium focused on the judicial review of agencies' decision, and private enforcement in China after the AML takes effect on August 2008. This symposium was a great success. For the first time Judges joined in the discussion; heated debates among the participants made the atmosphere unprecedented active. Nearly all the attendees agreed on a cautious policy to antitrust civil litigations, so as to avoid abuse of court proceedings. Most of the scholars and officials supported administrative primacy.

- On April 19, 2008, Innovation & Competition: Forum on IPR Related Antitrust Rules was held by T&D with participants of officials from NPC, the State Council, MOFCOM, NDRC, SAIC, judges from the Supreme Court and Beijing/Shanghai Courts, DOJ, and Academia.

- On September 21, 2008, Symposium on Enforcement of Anti-Monopoly Law & Economic Analysis was held by T&D with Participants including Carl Shapiro, Transamerica Professor of Business Strategy at the Hass School of Business at the University of California at Berkeley.

Prof. Huang Yong (the third from the left) and experts during Symposium on Enforcement of Anti-Monopoly Law & Economic Analysis (photo provided by T&D)

C. China's AML: Reference to other jurisdictions and re-contextualization

1. T&D's sustained consolidation and analysis of the AML draft amendments and subsequent revisions

35. During the drafting process of the AML, the legislative content had undergone over a decade and a number of refinements and revisions. Throughout these amendments, the draft consistently structured the code

based on the categorization of monopolistic conducts: beyond general provisions, it established four prohibited monopolistic behaviors as separate chapters, supplemented by legal liabilities and supplementary provisions. Notably, the prohibition of monopoly agreements gained increasing prominence during legislative deliberations, leading to its elevation from the original Chapter 3 to Chapter 2, thereby exchanging positions with the prohibition of abuse of dominant market position. The draft persistently defined its primary regulatory targets as "business operators", inheriting the conceptual definition from the AUCL.

36. Although the times are progressing and society is developing, the guiding ideology and internal considerations have been consistently followed by China's antitrust enforcement community: persisting in formulating the AML according to the market economy system, striving to reflect national conditions and adapt to China's economic development level, endeavoring to absorb and draw upon internationally accepted rules, reflecting the policy of opening up, and adapting to the situation of economic globalization.

2. The predecessor and concerns of relevant regulations on review of concentration

37. As this paper focuses on the merger filing process under the China's AML mechanism, we select certain important issues involving the review on the concentration of undertakings during the AML formulation process.

38. Particularly in the aspect of the review of undertaking concentration, the European Union revised the former EC Merger Control Regulation (Original Regulation 4064/89, amended by 1310/97) in 1997. The U.S. DOJ and FTC issued the *Horizontal Merger Guidelines in* 1992, which adopted the Herfindahl-Hirschman Index ("HHI") to calculate market concentration levels.

39. During the 2003 legislative deliberations, heated debates emerged regarding whether to regulate enterprise concentrations. The first camp of objections propositioned that anti-monopoly regulation should be implemented at a more mature stage of market economy development. Given China's then-prevalent small scale of enterprises (particularly compared to global industry leaders), the priority should be fostering enterprise consolidations and corporate group formations. Premature anti-monopoly controls were deemed detrimental to domestic enterprise growth.[4] The second camp pointed that mandatory merger regulations were unnecessary under globalized competition trends.

---

[4] China's majority of industries exhibit significantly low concentration levels by international standards. Based on preliminary estimates from the 1995 Industrial Census, among 521 four-digit industrial sectors classified, only 6% of industries had an HHI Index above 1,800 or CR4 exceeding 5%, accounting for 5-6% of total sales. When factoring in import competition, concentration metrics would be even lower. While recent mergers

40. However, the more prevailing view maintained that the AML and enterprise scale were not inherently contradictory – the regulatory focus should target market competition structures rather than enterprise size *per se*. The newly promulgated 2003 Regulation evidenced[5] that merger control would constitute a core component of future AML. Accordingly, the draft law dedicated a whole chapter to regulating enterprise concentrations.

41. For the fact that the Interim Provisions specifically governed foreign investors' M&A activities in China, foreign stakeholders contended these rules would erect barriers against foreign capital influx while stimulating domestic consolidation waves. As reported by the Financial Times, the Interim Provisions triggered "panic" among international investors, who perceived them as a legislative "prelude" and "prototype"[6] for the impending AML. Such apprehensions persisted throughout China's *AML* legislative process.

42. *For instance, regarding the notification thresholds for concentration of undertakings,* the Interim Provisions adopted the criteria largely aligned with the EU Merger Regulation,[7] diverging significantly from U.S. methodologies. Given China's underdeveloped market mechanisms at the time, the legislators deliberately bypassed the conventional analytical market share based approach, *i.e.*, first defining "relevant markets" and then assessing market shares. Instead, it followed the administratively simpler "turnover threshold" system – mandating merger notifications in case of combined domestic sales over prescribed levels.

43. This approach was conclusively validated at the 2006 Hangzhou Symposium, where participants formally adopted the turnover-based standard while eliminating market share considerations from notification requirements.

---

and acquisitions have slightly increased industrial concentration, the low market concentration across most sectors remains unchanged. For instance, in the home electronics and appliances sector, the CR4 of leading enterprises is approximately 60% (calculated by sales value; this figure would decline when considering imports), still below the U.S. threshold for high-concentration markets.

Quoted from Chen Xiaohong, *"China's Anti-Monopoly Law Requires Merger Control Provisions," China Economic Times,* 12 December 2002.

5   Article 26: Foreign investors shall report to Chinese competent authorities under any of the following circumstances in cross-border M&A transactions:

(1) The annual turnover of any party in the Chinese market exceeds RMB 1.5 billion;
(2) Acquisition of more than 10 domestic enterprises in related industries within one year;
(3) Any party holds a market share reaching 20% in China;
(4) The transaction results in a party's market share reaching 25% in China.

Even if the above thresholds are not met, where competing domestic enterprises, relevant government departments, or industry associations request a review, the national competent authorities may require reporting if the M&A involves substantial market share or other factors significantly affecting market competition, national economic security, or public welfare.

6   Quoted from *Financial Times,* 12 April 2003.

7   See Article 1 of the Council Regulation (EC) No. 139/2004 of 20 January 2004 on the control of concentrations between undertakings (the EC Merger Regulation).

John Yong Ren, Christine Fengyi Zhang
Schiffer Mengmeng Shi and Daniel Zu Gui

II. 2008–2018: Merger Filing Under The AML: From A Tottering Child to An Adolescent Teenager

44. After all the disputes, challenges, discussions, the first AML was ultimately enacted on August 1, 2008. Between 2008 and 2018, China's antitrust enforcement landscape was characterized by the concurrent operations of three competition enforcement authorities: MOFCOM, NDRC and SAIC. Mr. SHANG Ming, after acting as the Director of Law and Treaty Department during the legislation process, became the Director of the new antitrust bureau in MOFCOM since 2008.

45. Among them, MOFCOM, entrusted with the crucial task of merger review, embarked on a transformative journey, evolving from a fledgling entity to a more mature and proficient regulator. This decade witnessed its remarkable growth, manifested through significant advancements across multiple fronts.

46. In the legislative domain, MOFCOM systematically strengthened the foundational pillars of merger review regulations, meticulously crafting a more robust and comprehensive legal framework. The introduction of the simplified merger review procedures in 2014, among others, represented a pivotal breakthrough in institutional refinement, optimizing the review process and enhancing overall efficiency. When examining its enforcement practices, particularly through the lens of conditional approval cases, MOFCOM adopted more economically astute strategies and implemented innovative remedies. Notably, the use of hold separate remedies as behavioral remedies and the prevalence of behavioral remedies over divestiture underscored its growing regulatory acumen. The section is therefore structured to explore each of the mentioned aspects, i.e., legislation, procedures, and enforcement (from the lens of conditional approvals).

A. Legislation: continuous improvement of the fundamental system

47. Between 2008 and 2018, China embarked on a crucial journey of constructing the foundational framework for its merger control regime. During this formative decade, the regime underwent a process of steady development, gradually taking shape as a multi-tiered regulatory structure. At the core of this emerging framework was the AML, which served as the cornerstone upon which subsequent regulations were built. In general, from the Administration Law perspective, there are fourfold layers of antitrust legal sources, i.e., laws, (administrative) regulations, (administrative) rules, as well as guidelines and guidance. This top-down, hierarchical and pyramidal organization laid the groundwork for a more systematic approach to managing undertaking concentrations, allowing higher-tier laws to set broad principles while lower-tier rules and guidelines to offer operational flexibility.

1. Law (Top Tier): the AML

48. Due to the AML's position as a law enacted by the NPC and/or its Standing Committee – supreme legislative authority in China, the goal of AML is to outline the most foundational principles, but intentionally avoid granular details. Generalized languages and provisions in connection with objectives, generic monopolistic behaviors, legal liabilities and penalty afford it the long-term stability. This is not uncommon where the AML delegates rulemaking authority to subordinate bodies to develop implementing regulations and rules.

2. Administrative regulations (Second Tier)

49. Issued by the State Council under the AML's delegation, administrative regulations at the second tier primarily address certain matters in exceptional occasions, with more details than the AML, but refrain themselves from overly technical specifics than rules and guidelines. There's so far only one regulation in the merger control segment in China's antitrust history, i.e., the *Provisions of the State Council on Thresholds for the Notification of Concentrations of Undertakings*.

3. Administrative rules (Third Tier)

50. Third-tier administrative rules formulated by the antitrust competent agency SAMR, properly operationalize the AML's broad principles into actionable manuals and standards. These rules provide an abundant extent of technical, procedural, and industry-neutral mechanics. More frequent occurrences of revisions are hence required so as to adapt and conform to evolving economic dynamics and emerging anticompetitive conducts.

51. SAMR's departmental rules mainly zoom in on three classic monopolistic behaviors regulated under the AML, *namely*, monopoly agreements, abuse of dominance and merger controls.

4. Guidelines & guidance (Fourth Tier)

52. The release of guidelines and guidance documents normally rests within the mandate of two organs, Anti-Monopoly Commission of the State Council and SAMR. This type of legal sources is at the bottom of the pyramid, but occupies the vastest number among all. While not legally binding undertakings in the strict sense, they are most followed and implemented by undertakings for their "soft law" nature.

53. Table 2 below summarizes the main legislation on merger control in China during 2008 to 2018.

John Yong Ren, Christine Fengyi Zhang
Schiffer Mengmeng Shi and Daniel Zu Gui

Table 2 | Main Legislation on Merger Control and Merger Remedy in China (2008 – May 2018)

Date of Enactment	Instrument	Highlights
Laws		
• Promulgated on August 30, 2007 • Effective from August 1, 2008 • Revised from June 24, 24	Anti-Monopoly Law of the People's Republic of China 《中华人民共和国反垄断法》	Defined the concept of concentration of undertakings and its review procedures, while stipulating that concentrations must not be implemented without prior notification and specifies the corresponding legal liabilities.
Administrative regulations		
• Issued on and effective from August 3, 2008 • Revised on September 18, 2018 • Further revised and effective from January 22, 2024	Provisions of the State Council on the Notification Thresholds for Concentration of Undertaking 《国务院关于经营者集中申报标准的规定》	The 2008 version established the initial notification thresholds. The 2018 revision adjusted the name of the enforcement authority (from MOFCOM to SAMR) but did not modify the notification thresholds.
• Issued on July 15, 2009 • Effective from August 15, 2009	Measures for Calculating Turnover for Notification of Concentrations in the Financial Sector 《金融业经营者集中申报营业额计算办法》	Clarified the rules for calculating turnover for special industries such as banking, insurance, and securities.
Departmental rules		
• Issued on November 21, 2009 • Effective from January 1, 2010 • Repealed on May 10, 2021[8]	Measures for the Notification of Concentrations of Undertakings 《经营者集中申报办法》	Standardized the notification process for concentrations and the acceptance of notifications by anti-monopoly enforcement agency.
• Issued on November 24, 2009 • Effective from January 1, 2010 • Repealed on May 10, 2021[9]	Measures for the Review of Concentrations of Undertakings 《经营者集中审查办法》	Refined the review procedures, timelines, and practice for imposing restrictive conditions.
• Issued on and effective from July 5, 2010 • Repealed on January 5, 2015[10]	Interim Provisions on the Implementation of Divestiture of Assets or Business in Concentrations of Undertakings 《关于实施经营者集中资产或业务剥离的暂行规定》	Regulated the implementation of the decisions imposing divestiture of assets or business as restrictive conditions to ensure the smooth completion of such divestitures.

---

8   See: MOFCOM Notice [2021] No.2. It was replaced by the *Interim Provisions on the Examination of Concentrations of Undertakings* (《经营者集中审查暂行规定》) and later by the *Provisions on the Examination of Concentrations of Undertakings* (《经营者集中审查规定》).

9   See: footnote 6.

10 It was repealed with the enactment of the *Regulations on Imposing Restrictive Conditions on Concentrations of Business Operators (for Trial Implementation)* (《关于经营者集中附加限制性条件的规定（试行）》). Moreover, MOFCOM Notice [2021] No. 2 repealed the *Regulations on Imposing Restrictive Conditions on*

Date of Enactment	Instrument	Highlights
• Issued on December 7, 2911 • Effective from February 1, 2012 • Repealed in September 2021[11]	*Interim Provisions on the Assessment of Competitive Effects of Concentrations of Undertakings* 《关于评估经营者集中竞争影响的暂行规定》	Standardized the assessment of competitive effects in concentrations.
• Issued on August 29, 2011 • Effective from September 5, 2011 • Repealed on May 10, 2021[12]	*Interim Measures for the Investigation and Handling of Concentrations of Undertakings Not Notified in Accordance with the Law* 《未依法申报经营者集中调查处理暂行办法》	
• Issued on February 11, 2014 • Effective from February 12, 2014 • Repealed[13]	*Interim Provisions on the Applicable Standards for Simplified Cases of Concentrations of Undertakings* 《关于经营者集中简易案件适用标准的暂行规定》	Clarified the notification standards for simplified cases.
Guidelines		
• Issued on and effective from May 24, 2009	*Guidelines of the Anti-Monopoly Commission of the State Council on the Definition of Relevant Market* 国务院反垄断委员会《关于相关市场界定的指南》	Clarified the methodologies for defining relevant product markets, geographic markets, and technology markets.
• Issued on and effective from January 5, 2009 • Revised on September 29, 2018 by SAMR	*Guidelines on the Documentation for Notification of Concentrations of Undertakings* 《关于经营者集中申报文件资料的指导意见》	Specifies the format and content of notification documents.
• Revised on September 29, 2018	*Case Handle Guidance for Anti-Monopoly Review of Concentrations of Undertakings* 《经营者集中反垄断审查办事指南》	Provided guidance on the review process.

Concentrations of Business Operators (for Trial Implementation) and now it was replaced by the *Provisions on the Examination of Concentrations of Undertakings* (《经营者集中审查规定》).

11 See: MOFCOM Notice [2021] No. 24. It was replaced by the *Interim Provisions on the Examination of Concentrations of Undertakings* (《经营者集中审查暂行规定》) and later by the *Provisions on the Examination of Concentrations of Undertakings* (《经营者集中审查规定》).

12 See: footnote 6.

13 See: MOFCOM Official Websites.
https://m.mofcom.gov.cn/article/b/c/201402/20140200487038.shtml?utm_source=chatgpt.com. It was replaced by the *Interim Provisions on the Examination of Concentrations of Undertakings* (《经营者集中审查暂行规定》) and later by the *Provisions on the Examination of Concentrations of Undertakings* (《经营者集中审查规定》).

Date of Enactment	Instrument	Highlights
• Issued on and effective from January 5, 2009 • Revised in 2014 • Revised on September 29, 2018, by SAMR's *Guidelines on the Notification of Concentrations of Undertakings*（《关于经营者集中申报的指导意见》）	*Guidelines on the Notification of Concentrations of Undertakings* 《关于经营者集中申报的指导意见》	Standardized the requirements and procedures for submitting notification materials.
• Issued on and effective from February 2015 • Revised on September 29, 2018, by SAMR's *Guidelines on Standardizing the Naming of Concentration Cases*（《关于规范经营者集中案件申报名称的指导意见》）	*Guidelines on Standardizing the Naming of Concentration Cases* 《关于规范经营者集中案件申报名称的指导意见》	Unified the naming rules for concentration cases.
• Issued on and effective from 2014 • Revised on September 29, 2018, by SAMR's *Provisions on Imposing Restrictive Conditions on Concentrations of Undertakings*（《关于经营者集中简易案件申报的指导意见》）	*Provisions on Imposing Restrictive Conditions on Concentrations of Undertakings (Trial)* 《关于经营者集中简易案件申报的指导意见（试行）》	Regulated the enforcement of imposing restrictive conditions on concentrations.

54. It can be observed that during this decade, a suite of essential regulations was introduced to flesh out the merger control regime. Following the discussion and debates during the legislation process before 2008, these regulations addressed key areas such as notification thresholds, establishing clear criteria for when undertakings were obligated to notify the authorities of their planned concentrations. Regulations on market definition were also formulated, helping to precisely demarcate the boundaries of relevant markets, and enabling a more accurate evaluation of potential anti-competitive effects. Moreover, detailed procedural rules for merger filings were established, creating a standardized and orderly process for reviewing proposed transactions.

55. The institutional reform in April 2018 represented a significant juncture in the evolution of China's merger control landscape. By centralizing the enforcement authority under the State Administration for Market Regulation ("SAMR"), this reform rationalized the regulatory architecture, eliminating potential fragmentation and inefficiencies in the enforcement process. It was a pivotal step that solidified the foundational work done between 2008 and 2018, and further transformed China's merger control regime into a more robust and comprehensive regulatory framework *(please see Section III infra for details)*.

B. Procedure: the introduction of simplified merger review procedures in 2014

56. In 2014, with an increase in the number of filings, MOFCOM streamlined its law-enforcement mechanisms by, among other things, introducing the simplified merger review procedures. The simplified procedures were designed to streamline the review process for transactions that are less likely to raise significant competition concerns.[14] By separating relatively straightforward cases from more complex ones, MOFCOM was expected to allocate their resources more effectively.

57. This also allows for a quicker assessment of the notified transactions, reducing the time and cost burden on the notifying parties. Figure 1 below summarizes the MOFCOM/SAMR's decided transactions between 2008 to 2018.

Figure 1 | MOFCOM/SAMR's Decided Transaction (2008.8 – 2018.12)[15]

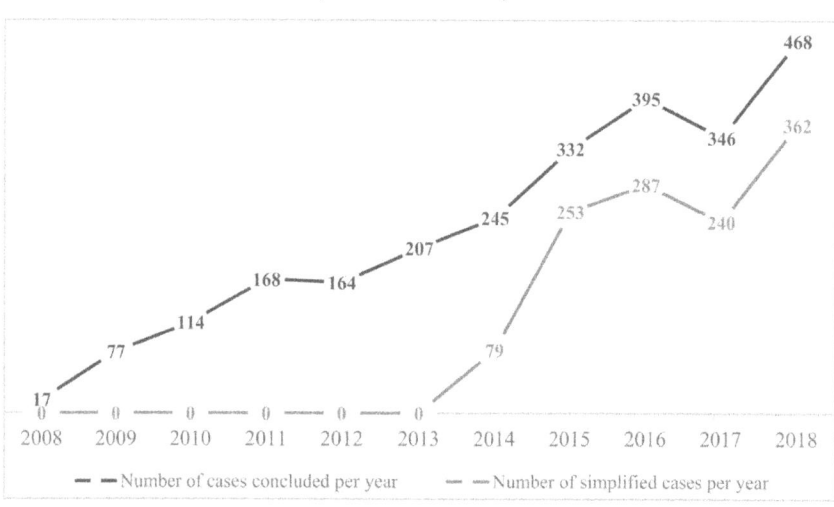

Notes:

1. Source of data includes: China's Annual Report on Anti-Monopoly Enforcement (2020) by SAMR, Yearly Overview for the Commence Work of MOFCOM and other public sources.

2. The number of simplified cases in 2014 is the cases publicized; the number of simplified cases in 2015 and 2016 are the cases notified; the numbers of simplified cases in 2017 and 2018 are

---

14 The relevant thresholds of combined market shares are 15% for transactions involving horizontal relations and 25% for others.

15 The simplified merger review procedures were effective from February 12, 2014, in other words, all filings before that date were made under the normal case procedures. Further, MOFCM/SAMR did not publish detailed case numbers for simplified procedures cases. Rather, the first time that SAMR published its Annual Report on China's Anti-Monopoly Law Enforcement was in 2019. SAMR started to publish unconditional approval cases on a quarterly basis from January 2019 onwards. Prior to this, MOFCOM had reported annual enforcement data sporadically in its Regular Press Conference and Yearly Overview for the Commence Work, but it has not formed dedicated annual report.

the cases concluded. Further, the numbers of simplified cases in 2016 and 2017 are calculated based on percentage published by MOFCOM.

3. Although the statistical parameters are not the same, the discrepancy between the yearly publication/ notification data and the yearly conclusion data will not be very significant, since the review period for simplified cases is relatively short.

58. From 2008 to 2018, the overall number of cases of concentrations of undertakings showed a fluctuating upward trend. In 2008, the total number of cases was only 16. Subsequently, it gradually increased from 2009 to 2013, reaching 207 cases in 2013. From 2014 to 2016, the number continued to grow, reaching 395 cases in 2016. Although the number of cases decreased to 344 in 2017, it rebounded to 445 cases in 2018. Overall, over time, the number of cases of concentrations of undertakings has increased significantly, reflecting the increasingly frequent concentration activities among undertakings in the market.

59. Regarding the number of simplified cases, in 2014, there were 79 publicized simple cases. For some subsequent years, due to the lack of accurate data from public official sources, only approximate numbers could be obtained through speculation. For example, the concluded number in 2017 was approximately 240, and 362 cases were concluded in 2018. Overall, it shows an increasing trend.

60. In terms of the proportion of simplified cases, in 2016, it was estimated that the proportion of simplified case filings accounted for 76% of all filings. In 2017, based on the concluded cases, the proportion of simplified cases was estimated to be 70%. In 2018, simplified cases accounted for approximately 77.4% of all cases. It can be seen that the proportion of simplified cases in all cases of concentrations of undertakings may show an upward trend.

61. This reflects the increasing importance of this procedure in enabling more qualitied cases to be processed quickly through the simplified procedure. As reported, during 2014[16], 2015[17] and 2016[18], almost all simple cases were concluded within 30-days preliminary review period. In 2017, the time required for simple cases was 24 days, which was further shortened to 16 days in 2018.[19]

---

16   Central government official websites, *Commerce Landscape (商务形势)*, February 9, 2025, https://www.gov.cn/guoqing/2015-02/09/content_2816663_19.htm (accessed: May 7, 2025).

17   The State Council Information Office of the People's Republic of China, *Yearly Overview IX for Commerce Work in 2015* (2015年商务工作年终综述之九), February 22, 2016, http://www.scio.gov.cn/xwfb/gwyxwbg-sxwfbh/wqfbh_2284/2016n_8740/2016n02y23r/xgbd_8820/202207/t20220715_191616.html (accessed: May 10, 2025).

18   Chinanews.com, *MOFCOM: Antimonopoly cases filed and closed in 2016 both hit record highs (商务部：2016年反垄断立案审结案件均创新高)*, January 5, 2017, https://www.chinanews.com/cj/2017/01-05/8115031.shtml.

19   https://www.sohu.com/a/288942055_221481 (accessed: May 10, 2025).

C. Enforcement: from the lens of conditional approvals

1. A more economic approach[20]

62. The decade between 2008 to 2018 witnesses a more economic approach taken by MOFCOM to help obtain evidence and to increase the scientific credibility of the merger review[21]

a. Pfizer/Wyeth (2009)

63. In the Pfizer/Wyeth case, MOFCOM, for the first time, used the HHI to gauge market concentration[22]. Defining Chinese Mainland as the relevant geographic market and human medicines (including JIC and N6A) along with animal health products as the relevant product markets, MOFCOM assessed competitive impacts through three key aspects.

64. *First*, it noted that post-merger, the combined market share of the parties would surge to 49.4%, far exceeding that of competitors. *Second*, the HHI analysis revealed a post-merger HHI of 2182, an increase of 336, categorizing the merger as a "dangerous transaction." This established an implicit practical threshold for MOFCOM, as in contrast to the US and the EU, China's regulatory framework lacks explicit written guidelines for such determinations. *Third*, MOFCOM highlighted the high entry costs (average $2.5 – 10 million) and long development cycles (3 – 5 years) in pharmaceutical innovation, arguing that the merged entity could entrench barriers and impede competitors' growth in the domestic market.

b. Thermo Fisher/Life Tech (2013)

65. When Thermo Fisher Scientific Inc. proposed to acquire Life Technologies Corp. in 2013, MOFCOM's review showcased an increasingly economic approach. With 59 horizontal overlaps, an independent third-party consultancy was engaged by MOFCOM for quantitative analysis.[23]

66. MOFCOM's assessment spanned multiple levels. Similar to *Pfizer/Wyeth*, an HHI test identified 13 products for further scrutiny based on post-merger HHI values above 1500 with increases over 100. This reinforced

---

20 For this section, please also refer to one of this article's contributors, Mengmeng Shi's dissertation, *The Divestiture Remedies under Merger Control in the US, the EU and China: A Comparative Law and Economics Perspective*. [Doctoral Thesis, Maastricht University]. Datawyse/Universitaire Pers Maastricht, https://doi.org/10.26481/dis.20171003ms.

21 Fei Deng and Yizhe Zhang: *Interview with Ming Shang, former Director General of the Anti-Monopoly Bureau under the Ministry of Commerce of the People's Republic of China* (Beijing, March 7, 2014). For the text of the interview, *see:* https://www.edgewortheconomics.com/media/publication/65_Fei_Deng_Antitrust_Source_Interview_with_DG_Shang.pdf (accessed: May 9, 2025).

22 For a full text of this decision, please refer to: *MOFCOM Public Notice 2009/77: Conditional Approval for the Notified Merger – Pfizer/Wyeth* (MOFCOM Decision) [September 29, 2009], http://fldj.mofcom.gov.cn/article/ztxx/200909/20090906541443.shtml (accessed: May 8, 2025).

23 For a full text of this decision, *see: MOFCOM Public Notice 2014/03: Conditional Approval for the Notified Merger – Thermo Fisher/Life Tech* (MOFCOM Decision) [January 15, 2014], http://fldj.mofcom.gov.cn/article/ztxx/201401/20140100461603.shtml (accessed May 8, 2025).

the practical thresholds hinted at in prior cases. Additionally, Profit–HHI regression and price rise tests was conducted, projecting that 12 products would see price hikes exceeding 5%.

67. A comprehensive competition assessment, involving on-site inspections, stakeholder surveys, expert consultations, and international consultations with counterparts, further demonstrated MOFCOM's data-driven and economic-oriented review methodology.

68. These cases, alongside others like *Merck/AZ (2014)*[24], underscore MOFCOM's growing reliance on economic analysis to refine its merger review toolkit.

2. Creative remedies imposed

a. Prevalence of behavioral remedies rather than divestitures and possible reasons

69. Between 2008 and end of 2018, a total of 39 cases received conditional approvals. Among these 39 conditional approval cases, pure divestiture remedies were employed in 11 instances, while pure behavioral remedies were utilized in 17 cases. The remaining 11 cases involved hybrid remedies, which combined both divestitures and behavioral measures. For a detailed breakdown, kindly refer to Table 3 below.[25]

Table 3 | Types of Remedies from 2008 to 2018

Types of remedies	Number	Percentage
Pure structural remedies	11	28.2%
Pure behavioral remedies	17	43.6%
Hybrid remedies	11	28.2%
Behavioral remedies included	28	71.8%
Total	39	100%

Source: MOFCOM (August 2008 – April 2018)/SAMR (since April 2018)

70. The data in Table 3 above proves the long-lasting impression that MOFCOM (SAMR) prefers behavioral remedies over pure structural remedies to address competition concerns, which is different from its counterparts in the US and the EU. The following reasons may explain.[26]

---

24 For a full text of this decision, *see: MOFCOM Public Notice 2014/30: Conditional Approval for the Notified Merger – Merck/AZ* (MOFCOM Decision) [April 30, 2014], http://fldj.mofcom.gov.cn/article/ztxx/201404/20140400569060.shtml (accessed May 8, 2025).

25 Also refer to John Ren, Wesley Wang, Mengmeng Shi: *High Profile Concentrations in China: An Analysis on Conditional Approvals in 2018,* CPI Antitrust Chronicle [March 2019].

26 See footnote No. 7.

71. *First,* the merging parties often shy away from divestitures due to high transaction costs, complex asset transfers, and the risk of strengthening competitors. Divestitures involve intricate processes, including handling intangible assets and re-organizing personnel, and the irreversible nature can pose significant risks. In contrast, behavioral commitments, such as maintaining the business *status quo*, are less burdensome and costly, making them a more attractive option for the parties seeking swift transaction approval.

72. MOFCOM's approach also contributes to this trend. Unlike competition authorities in the US and the EU, MOFCOM lacks a clear preference for divestitures. Its compromise-seeking attitude during remedy negotiations allows for greater flexibility. MOFCOM is reluctant to force commitments, and both parties aim to reach an agreement to avoid transaction prohibitions. This dynamic makes behavioral remedies acceptable as long as they address anti-competitive concerns, influenced in part by China's cultural emphasis on harmony and mutual satisfaction.

73. *Second,* China's corporate surveillance traditions further support the use of behavioral remedies. Stemming from the planned economy era, the country has a strong tradition of corporate monitoring. Monitoring costs for behavioral remedies are dispersed among various stakeholders, including industry associations, competitors, and consumers. With numerous market participants, the enforceability of these remedies is enhanced, reducing the overall burden on the competition authority.

74. *Third,* the existence of three independent competition agencies (NDRC, SAIC, and MOFCOM) in China plays a role during 2008 and 2018. In a single-agency scenario, merger review data could seamlessly flow to other internal units. Yet in China, before reform in 2018, with three separate competition agencies – NDRC, SAIC, and MOFCOM – operational realities differ. Their inter – agency dynamics are intricate. A merged entity exhibiting anti-competitive behavior might exploit MOFCOM's approval as a shield against NDRC or SAIC probes, arguing that its actions comply with competition law as it stemmed from the approved merger.

75. *Fourth,* while competition authorities in the EU and the US typically focus on horizontal overlaps – often requiring structural remedies such as divestitures – vertical and adjacent market effects are generally less central and seldom lead to intervention. In contrast, China's merger review adopts a broader approach, with SAMR placing significant emphasis not only on horizontal overlaps but also on vertical relationships and adjacent markets. This broader focus means concerns may arise even in the absence of direct competition, such as the potential for market foreclosure, data access issues, or the leveraging of market power. In such cases, behavioral remedies are often more appropriate, as they can be tailored to address specific conduct concerns – such as ensuring non-discriminatory access,

maintaining information firewalls, or preserving third-party access – without requiring divestitures.

76. *Additionally*, Chinese merger control reviews may also encompass non-competition considerations, such as alignment with industrial policy goals. While these concerns may not justify structural remedies, they nonetheless require a meaningful response from the notifying parties to reassure relevant stakeholders and facilitate regulatory clearance.

77. In this context, behavioral remedies offer a flexible and pragmatic tool. They can be tailored to address both competition and non-competition issues – such as commitments to continue certain business operations, invest in local markets, or comply with relevant trade and industrial policy objectives. As such, behavioral remedies have become the preferred solution in cases in China where structural remedies are either disproportionate or infeasible.

b. Hold separate remedies as a behavioral remedy and possible reasons[27]

78. In the merger control frameworks of the US and the EU, hold separate provisions typically serve as an interim measure within the divestiture process, according to which, the merging parties have to manage the to-be-divested business independently to ensure, to the extent possible, its viability, marketability and competitiveness during the transitional period and until the divestiture is completed.

79. Conversely, in China, MOFCOM deploys hold separate provisions as a distinct form of behavioral remedy. Unlike the use in the US and the EU, this provision requires the merged entity to maintain the separate operation of specific business segments for certain time period after the merger has been consummated. During 2008 to 2018, such remedies were included in five cases, i.e., *ASE/SPIL (2017)*[28], *MediaTek/Mstar* (2013)[29], *Marubeni/Gavilon* (2013)[30], *Western Digital/Hitachi Vivit* (2012)[31] and *Seagate/Samsung HDD* (2011)[32], all of which entailed horizontal overlaps between the parties.

---

27 See footnote No. 7.

28 *MOFCOM Public Notice 2013/61: Conditional Approval for the Notified Merger – ASE/SPIL* (MOFCOM Decision) [November 24, 2017], https://m.mofcom.gov.cn/article/ae/ai/201711/20171102675620.shtml (accessed May 8, 2025).

29 *MOFCOM Public Notice 2013/61: Conditional Approval for the Notified Merger – Mediatek Inc./Mstar* (MOFCOM Decision) [August 27, 2013], http://fldj.mofcom.gov.cn/article/ztxx/201308/20130800269821.shtml (accessed May 8, 2025).

30 *MOFCOM Public Notice 2013/22: Conditional Approval for the Notified Merger – Marubeni/Gavilon* (MOFCOM Decision) [April 24, 2013], http://fldj.mofcom.gov.cn/article/ztxx/201304/20130400100376.shtml (accessed May 8, 2025).

31 *MOFCOM Public Notice 2012/09: Conditional Approval for the Notified Merger – Western Digital/Hitachi Vivit* (MOFCOM Decision) [March 2, 2012], http://fldj.mofcom.gov.cn/article/ztxx/201203/20120307993758.shtml, (accessed May 8, 2025).

32 *MOFCOM Public Notice 2011/90: Conditional Approval for the Notified Merger – Seagate/Samsung HDD* (MOFCOM Decision) [December 12, 2011], http://fldj.mofcom.gov.cn/article/ztxx/201112/20111207874274.shtml (accessed May 9, 2025).

80. Take the first hold separate case – *Seagate/Samsung HDD* – as an example. According to MOFCOM's conditional approval, post-transaction, Seagate was required to operate Samsung HDD as an independent market competitor, which entailed mainly the following specific obligations:
    - Pricing and sales independence. Seagate should establish an independent subsidiary to handle Samsung HDD's pricing and marketing.
    - Information firewall. No exchange of competition information between pricing and sales teams respectively from Seagate and Samsung. Competition information refers to any information that may lead to the coordination of business behaviors, especially information related to prices, production volumes, customers, bidding, and other aspects.
    - Manufactory independence. The production line for Samsung HDD should utilize Samsung's equipment, processes, and production systems.
    - R&D independence. Seagate should establish an independent R&D center for Samsung HDD.

81. The adoption of hold separate behavioral remedies may stem from practical considerations. *Firstly*, these remedies offer flexibility. After several years of implementation, MOFCOM can modify or remove the hold separate requirements upon the merged firm's request, provided that such changes do not pose new competition risks. For instance, in the Seagate/Samsung case, MOFCOM lifted the hold separate requirements in 2015[33], demonstrating that such provisions can be reversed. This reversibility makes them more palatable to merging parties, who may anticipate future relief from these obligations. *Secondly*, unlike divestitures, which often struggle due to challenges in identifying suitable buyers, hold separate remedies sidestep this hurdle entirely, making them a more practical option for addressing competition concerns.

D. Remarks

82. 2008 to 2018 witnessed MOFCOM's transformation from a novice to a more mature regulator. Its remarkable growth was shown in multiple areas. In legislation, MOFCOM strengthened the basis of merger review regulations and created a more comprehensive legal system. The simplified merger review procedures introduced in 2014 were a significant institutional breakthrough that improved the review process and efficiency. In

---

33 *See*: *MOFCOM Public Notice 2015/43: Modifications of the Conditional Approval in Seagate/Samsung HDD* (MOFCOM Decision) [October 22, 2015], http://fldj.mofcom.gov.cn/article/ztxx/201510/20151001144105.shtml, (accessed May 9, 2017).

enforcement, especially in conditional approval cases, MOFCOM adopted more economically intelligent strategies and innovative remedies. The use of hold separate remedies as behavioral ones and the greater prevalence of behavioral remedies compared to divestiture demonstrated its ability of re-contextualization of merger regime from other jurisdictions, such as the EU.

83. In April 2018, China established SAMR, marking a significant milestone in the country's regulatory landscape. By consolidating the functions of the three previous agencies into one unified body, SAMR could provide a more coherent and comprehensive approach to market regulation.

III. 2018 – 2025: SAMR's Era and Flourishing Merger Filing Regime to a Chinese Characterized Phase

84. Ever since the milestone consolidation of tripartite overseeing pillars into one single unified competition authority in 2018, China has been picking up the pace in reshaping its antitrust regime in a fashion aligning itself with its global enforcement counterparts, while increasingly highlighting the Chinese characteristics. This trend and trace are particularly marked by a spectrum of moves and actions that were launched by relevant authorities from then.

85. In particular, retrospectively, this unification not only gives rise to the institutional efficiency within the domestic regulatory landscape, but also brings about fresh colors and flavors for antitrust legislation and enforcement practice in China compared to other jurisdictions.

A. Institutional level: establishment of SAMR

86. As explained in Section II, while MOFCOM was specifically assigned with the task of merger control, SAIC and NDRC respectively oversaw monopolistic agreements and abuse of dominance. Their tasks were, however, separate but closely related. Therefore, with the enforcement of AML since 2008, long existence of criticisms for the shared antitrust responsibilities and functions in China had remained revolving around overlapping mandates, bureaucratic inefficiencies, and divergent enforcement outcomes ever since 2003. These criticisms and concerns then gradually faded away or somewhat were reformed with the staging of SAMR assembling the antitrust enforcement functions in 2018.

87. First of all, antitrust jurisdictional conflicts were substantially reconciled. Due to the intersecting powers arising from previous separated functional setting, one single conduct potentially involves various types of monopolistic circumstances in nature. In such cases, jurisdictions were eligibly exerted by more than one body simultaneously and contradictorily,

or otherwise lax regulation arose.[34] There therefore sometimes came with a too-much-or-too-little paradox. SAMR, on the other hand, becoming the merged successor, currently administers antitrust matters on an all-round basis, effectively optimizing enforcement resources and neutralizing conflicting jurisdictional risks.

88. Second, the centralization of antitrust enforcement into SAMR, to some extent, conduces to elevated enforcement efficiency by firming internal exchange and streamlining decision-making processes. Exemplified by the merger control review, comparatively, prior and post the 2018 consolidation, the average duration from filing to initiation dropped to 24 days in 2019, with a fall-off of 8% from 2018 and 21% from 2017; while clearance followed in an average of 28.3 days, 13% faster than 2018 and 2017.[35] This trend continued in 2020, with an average timeframe further declining to 17.8 days for case initiation and 24.2 days for clearance.[36] This acceleration is not merely a function of internal workflow optimization, but also an achievement of more focused resource allocation and clearer review criteria.

89. Last but not the least, the tripartite convergence further unified regulatory calibers and facilitated strategic coordination to China's antitrust regime. Prior to 2018, the separation of responsibilities among the three antitrust enforcement agencies led to inconsistent enforcement standards, poor information sharing, and regulatory blind spots.[37] A telling example of this disjunction occurred in respect of confiscation of illegal gains – whether or not to use this penalty tool in different cases largely diverged across three agencies. It thus stands reason that the position of SAMR may help facilitate the predictability and uniformity of antitrust enforcement, and foster a fairer, more transparent, and more business-friendly competitive environment.[38]

90. Following on November 18, 2021, the State Anti-Monopoly Bureau was officially listed, restructured from a bureau directly under the SAMR to a newly formed vice-minister-level national bureau by the State Council. As part of this institutional upgrade, three new departments

---

[34] People.cn, *China Establishes SAMR, Embodying "Unified Regulation"* [December 17, 2018], http://legal.people.com.cn/n1/2018/1217/c42510-30471162.html (accessed: May 23, 2025).

[35] SAMR, *China Anti-Monopoly Annual Enforcement Report (2019)* [September 24, 2021], https://www.gov.cn/xinwen/2020-12/25/5573435/files/195171fdee024615933c10d57f141171.pdf (accessed: May 10, 2025).

[36] SAMR, *China Anti-Monopoly Annual Enforcement Report (2020)* [December 25, 2020], https://www.gov.cn/xinwen/2021-09/24/5639102/files/77006c5bccc04555aa05f30c9a296267.pdf (accessed: May 10, 2025).

[37] Meng Yanbei: *The Historical Evolution and Future Prospects of China's Anti-Monopoly Enforcement Regime* [August 1, 2023] https://www.samr.gov.cn/zt/ndzt/2023n/2023jzz/zjgd/art/2023/art_59ed517acd47423fbd48b8b2f44e11c5.html. (Accessed: June 4, 2025).

[38] The State Council Information Office of the People's Republic of China ("SCIO"), *SCIO Holds Press Conference Marking the 10th Anniversary of the Implementation of the Anti-Monopoly Law* [November 16, 20118], http://www.scio.gov.cn/xwfb/gwyxwbgsxwfbh/wqfbh_2284/2018n_7138/2018n11y16r/ (accessed: May 23, 2025).

were created – the Competition Policy Coordination Department, the First Anti-Monopoly Enforcement Department and the Second Anti-Monopoly Enforcement Department. This significant move substantially expands staffing capacity, strengthens China's antitrust regulatory power, and further enhances the uniformity and professionalism of antitrust enforcement.[39]

91. Nevertheless, it still requires a long-run observation and analysis before one can reach any definite conclusion in this regard, in particular against the background of recent introduction of a handful of new antitrust tools such as call-in and stop-clock procedures.

B. Legislative level: continuously refined merger control system

92. A noticeable phenomenon seems to emerge where the SAMR-era greatly opens a completer and more mature chapter for the antitrust legislative system for merger controls in China compared to the past. On one hand, without doubt, years of enforcement practice particularly in merger controls, immensely contributes to China's accumulating experiences and joining the global big league of antitrust regulators. On the other hand, these practical experiences in turn prompted the continuous roll-out of legislative activities in recent year, which prominently facilitated the construction of a relatively comprehensive antitrust framework. This so-called multi-tiered legal structure suggests a number of shifted features, with today being more developed, complete while targeted, enforceable while flexible.

1. A More complete and mature tiered hierarchy of merger controls

93. After officially striding into the SAMR's phase, the antitrust legal system for merger controls in China has been further refined and progressed. Particularly, further to the introduction of the fourfold legislation in Section II, since 2018 and onwards, each layer of antitrust legal sources has undergone revisions and refinements.

---

39 Chinanews, *State Anti-Monopoly Bureau was officially listed, Marking New Milestone in China's Antitrust Regime* [November 18, 2021], https://m.chinanews.com/wap/detail/chs/zwsp/9611949.shtml (accessed: June 9, 2025).

Figure 2 | The Multi-Tiered Pyramidal Hierarchy of China's Antitrust Regime

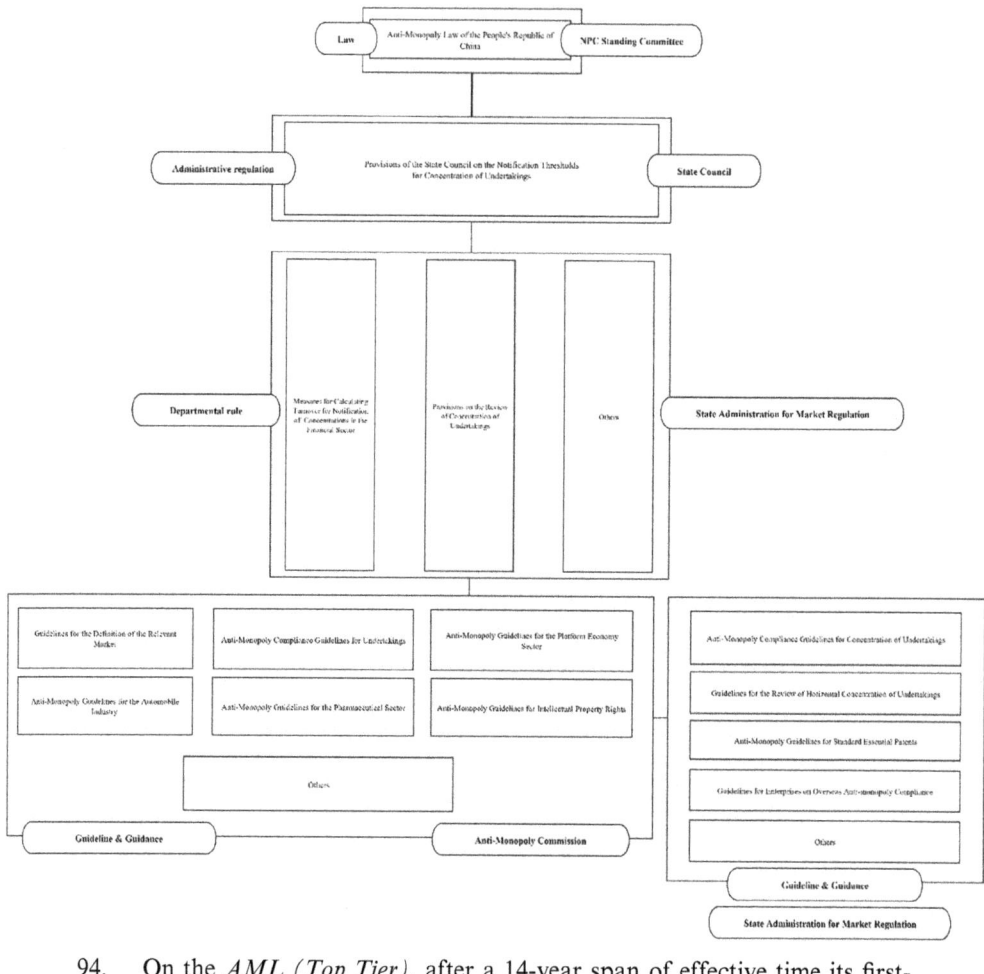

94. On the *AML (Top Tier)*, after a 14-year span of effective time its first-time landmark amendment debuted in 2022 that came into force as from August 1, 2022. This major revision reflects China's evolving priorities in regulating digital giants and aligning antitrust with broader economic strategies, including digital-economy focus, stricter penalties for gun-jumping, procedural enhancements such as call-in and so on.

95. On the *administrative regulations (Second Tier)*, as mentioned above, there's only one regulation in this area, i.e., the *Provisions of the State Council on Thresholds for the Notification of Concentrations of Undertakings*, and it went through a systemic change in 2023 nearly doubling the filing thresholds, a timely reflection and adaption of the latest economic development in China.

96. On the *administrative rules (Third Tier)*, during this period, most of departmental rules were upgraded from "provisional" to formal provisions

following the AML revision. For the merger filings, the *Provisions on Review of Concentration of Undertakings* issued by SAMR on March 10, 2023, is direct at supporting the implementation of the amended AML and further standardizing the merger review procedures. It refines and details, particularly, *among others,* the "stop-clock" mechanism, the handling of below-threshold concentrations, and the classified and tiered review system, etc.[40]

97. On the *guidelines & guidance (Fourth Tier)*, post 2018, an outbreak of the introduction of guidelines and guidance documents is manifestly identifiable. Among the 15 guidelines and guidance documents released to date, SAMR focuses on addressing particular types of monopolistic conduct or specialized areas, including horizontal mergers, non-horizontal mergers, merger control compliance, etc. While the Anti-Monopoly Commission primarily formulates industry-specific guidelines, these guidelines also contain relevant sections in allusion to the merger filings.

2. More communications between SAMR and stakeholders

98. In order to improve the legal system, SAMR expands its engagement with stakeholders such as scholars, lawyers, economists and experts through seminars, workshops, and public consultations to refine enforcement and policy-making. T&D has participated in almost each of these seminars that SAMR hosted and shared our inputs and experiences with the authorities. For example,
    - In September 2023, SAMR convened a symposium in Qingdao Shandong, with a focus on further strengthening the legal framework for merger control. The discussion zeroed in on the *Guidelines for the Antitrust Review of Horizontal Concentration of Undertakings (Draft for Comments)*, aimed to develop the antitrust legal system, refine the merger review rules, standardize the review process for horizontal mergers, and enhance the transparency of antitrust enforcement in merger control. Participants – including representatives from enterprises, law firms and regulatory authorities – engaged in in-depth discussions on key aspects of the draft.
    - Building on this foundation, in August 2024, SAMR held another legislative symposium in Chongqing to further discuss the *Guidelines for the Antitrust Review of Horizontal Concentration of Undertakings (Draft for Comments)* and *Guidelines for the Antitrust Review of Non-Horizontal Concentration of Undertakings (Draft for Comments)*. This event reflected SAMR's careful consideration of

---

40 SAMR, *Refining Antitrust Review Rules for Merger Control to Safeguard Fair Competition and Stimulate Market Vitality – Interpretation of the Provisions on the Review of Concentrations of Undertakings* [March 24, 2023], https://www.samr.gov.cn/zw/zfxxgk/fdzdgknr/xwxcs/art/2023/art_977d8220221d4b00b3f2dbdfc71 216ee.html (accessed: May 23, 2025).

earlier feedback and demonstrated its commitment to an inclusive and consultative rulemaking process. Participants offered additional input on both linguistic consistency and substantive matters, including presumptive standards, market definition, and unique considerations related to the platform economy. SAMR provided timely and constructive responses during the discussions.

- In April 2025, SAMR hosted a follow-up symposium in Wuhu Anhui, with a dedicated focus on the *Guidelines for the Antitrust Review of Non-Horizontal Concentration of Undertakings*. The event featured both plenary and breakout sessions to examine key issues and consider proposed revisions. Discussions centered on ensuring the consistency, practical applicability, and alignment with enforcement practice. Participants engaged deeply on critical topics such as market definition, burden of proof, and emerging concepts, contributing valuable insights to further refine the draft guidelines.

3. Proliferation of guidelines and guidance as "soft law" tools

99. In recent years, antitrust guidelines and guidance measures are increasingly prevailingly deployed as a "soft law" tool in China. Though non-binding legally as they are, these documents and measures are positioned to offer legislative flexibility and swiftness for the enforcer to interpret laws, regulations and rules. Especially in a rapid-changing technological era, this "soft law" tool enables SAMR to deal with the rise of novel concepts and issues on a timely basis, without requiring higher-tier law and regulation reforms.

100. One of the examples is the *Anti-Monopoly Guideline for the Platform Economy Sector* enacted by Anti-Monopoly Commission of the State Council, echoing the nation's wide-spread attention and concern to the digital economy. Such notion was also affirmed by the start of a surge of gun-jumping investigations and probes against Chinese national digital champions in the same year.

101. Another type in this category – guidance or guiding measures developed by SAMR – normally sets forth practical compliance advice, particularly on procedural matters. They are equipped with practical clarity for businesses to understand enforcement priorities and expectations. Undertakings therefore tend to *de facto* abide by them for the sake of avoiding exposure to any non-compliance risks.

102. Notably, on December 20, 2024, SAMR issued the *Guidelines for the Review of Horizontal Concentrations*. Drawing on practical experience accumulated since the implementation of the AML, the guidelines consolidates effective practices and aims to enhance the consistency, standardization, and transparency of China's merger control review regime by

reference to, *e.g.*, guiding cases.⁴¹ On February 19, 2025, SAMR issued the *Discretionary Benchmark for Administrative Penalties for Unlawful Implementation of Concentrations (Trial)*, clarifying the basis and standards for imposing penalties on undertakings that unlawfully implement concentrations.

103. This legislative methodology serves the purpose of balancing legal certainty and practical agility, by bridging formal laws and market realities and responding dynamically to market changes. In point of fact, this approach was in existence early and came into play effectively in the EU's competition system, such as the *Guidelines On The Assessment Of Horizontal Mergers*. However, other voices also arise in relation to the legislative link-up and possible regulatory fragmentation across different sectors, lack of transparency in drafting processes compared to laws, and potential expansion of SAMR's authority beyond the AML's original intent.

4. Industry-tailored rules for targeted regulation

104. China's strategic use of industry-tailored antitrust rules is aimed at addressing sector-specific risks while aligning with broader national priorities. By focusing on unique market dynamics in sectors like the platform economy, automotive, and pharmaceuticals, these rules enable the regulator to accommodate general antitrust principles to evolving challenges.

105. For instance, the *Anti-Monopoly Guideline for the Platform Economy Sector* refines relevant market definition analysis through inclusion of particular metrics and yardsticks like network effects, lock-in effects, and multi-sided roles. In the context of merger control, the enforcement authority has explicitly emphasized their close scrutiny of "killer acquisitions" involving start-ups or nascent platforms. In addition to traditional market share calculations, it further introduces digital-specific indicators such as number of active users, click-through rates, usage duration, etc. This also applies to assessing the competitive effects by considering factors including control over data, user stickiness and multi-homing behaviors, and user's switching costs related to pricing, data migration, negotiation, learning, and search.⁴²

106. Similarly, the *Anti-Monopoly Guidelines for the Automobile Industry*, hinging on both domestic realities and international experience, is designed to prevent and prohibit monopolistic conduct in the automotive industry.

---

41 See, https://www.samr.gov.cn/zw/zfxxgk/fdzdgknr/xwxcs/art/2024/art_4aa779a99c754d86845d7283453a7431.html.

42 SAMR, *Promoting the Regulated, Orderly, Innovative, and Healthy Development of the Platform Economy – Interpretation of the Anti-Monopoly Guidelines for the Platform Economy Sector* [February 7, 2021], https://www.samr.gov.cn/zw/zfxxgk/fdzdgknr/xwxcs/art/2023/art_5815f10f29114683976461e14554f954.html (accessed: May 25, 2025).

Notably, it, *among others*, refines a tailored framework for defining relevant markets, outlining specific considerations in drawing a distinction between wholesale and retail markets, distribution and aftersales service markets.[43]

107. This approach balances regulatory flexibility with targeted oversight, ensuring antitrust merger filing enforcement remains responsive to fast-paced industries without requiring frequent statutory amendments.

5. More attention to ex-ante compliance

108. By weaving together detailed implementing rules and guiding measures comprehensively, China's antitrust system has been maturely developed and achieved end-to-end regulatory coverage that span from *ex-ante* prevention, ongoing procedural governance, to *ex-post* enforcement. It's, however, more noteworthy that currently increasing focus and emphasis of the authorities are attached to the *ex-ante* preventative compliance, comparatively.

109. Such regulatory trends and motives are reflected not only in the *ex-ante* merger control regime itself, but also in the preventive roles that are played by various antitrust compliance guidelines and guidance documents in recent years, such as *Anti-Monopoly Compliance Guidelines on Concentrations of Undertakings*, *Anti-Monopoly Compliance Guide for Undertakings* and *Overseas Anti-Monopoly Compliance Guidelines for Enterprises*. These instruments are mostly self-explained, intended to "guide and support undertakings in establishing and improving their antitrust compliance management systems".

110. In the merger control segment, these *ex-ante* measures enable businesses to proactively and effectively mitigate compliance risks, enhance risk management capabilities, and promote sustainable and sound development. Industry-specific guidelines also provide targeted rhetorics for risk identification and prevention in sectors and practices more prone and vulnerable to monopoly concerns.

C. Enforcement level: evolution and characteristics of SAMR's merger filing review in practice

1. Overview of the total merger filing case reviewed

111. Based on data and information published by China's antitrust regulators, MOFCOM reviewed approximately 2,165 merger filing cases from 2008 to 2018, while SAMR set a new record of a total of 4,267 merger filing cases from 2018 to 2024.

---

43 SAMR, Interpretation of the *Anti-Monopoly Guidelines for the Automobile Industry* [October 30, 2020], https://www.samr.gov.cn/zw/zfxxgk/fdzdgknr/xwxcs/art/2023/art_447fe07e625e447aac004265e6fe4322.html (accessed May 25, 2025).

112. As illustrated in the chart below, the number of cases reviewed annually increased to over 450 following the establishment of SAMR, and surged to more than 600 per year since 2021.

Figure 3 | 2008-2024 Concluded Merger Review Cases[44]

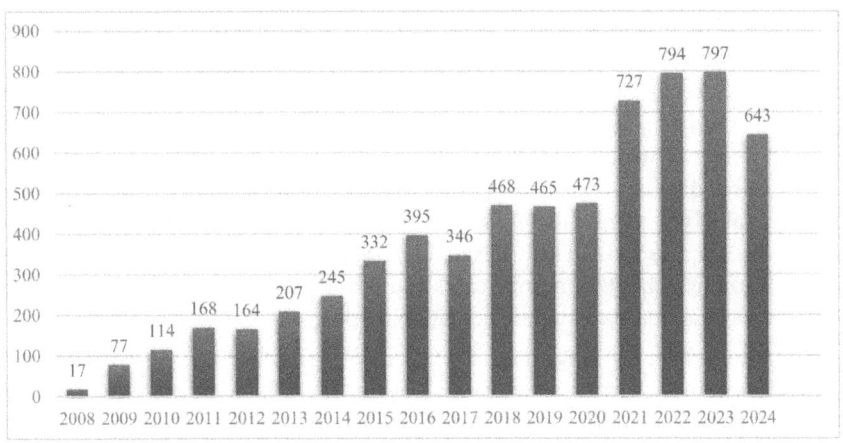

113. In terms of conditionally-approved cases, compared with MOFCOM's period, the number during SAMR's period has remained relatively stable at approximately 4 to 5 per year. An exception occurred in 2024, when only one was conditionally cleared by SAMR.

Figure 4 | 2008-2024 Conditionally-Approved Cases[45]

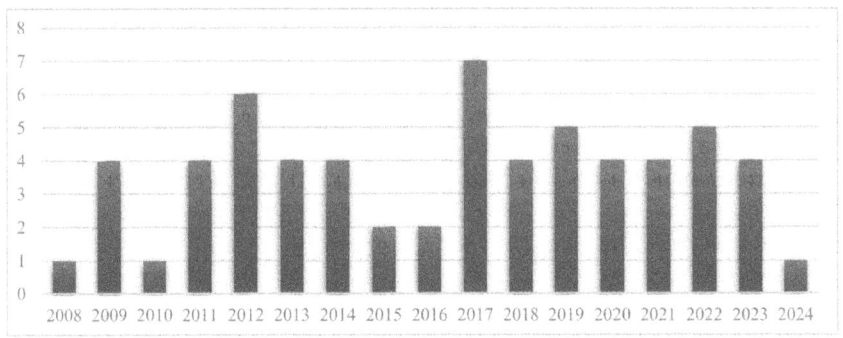

---

44 For data on concluded numbers between 2008-2020, see China Antitrust Annual Enforcement Report (2020) (SAMR); for data between 2021-2023, see China Antitrust Annual Enforcement Report (2021), China Antitrust Annual Enforcement Report (2022) and China Antitrust Annual Enforcement Report (2023) (SAMR); for 2024 data, see SAMR's press release, https://www.samr.gov.cn/xw/zj/art/2025/art_21f523302be74c22922ad59b925bdfa3.html.

45 The number of conditionally approved cases prior to April 10, 2018, is calculated from the official website of MOFCOM (http://fldj.mofcom.gov.cn/article/ztxx/?4); the number of conditionally approved cases after April 10, 2018, is sourced from the official website of SAMR (https://www.samr.gov.cn/fldys/tzgg/ftj/index.html).

2. Procedural evolution of merger review

a. Delegated Pilot Program & E-Filing System

114. To further enhance the efficiency of merger review, SAMR has implemented various measures to reduce the review period, including a pilot program, the internal "Double 20 Days" mechanism, the case review e-filing system, etc.

115. For example, SAMR launched a pilot program on August 1, 2022, delegating part of its antitrust review responsibility for merger filings to local branches in five provinces and municipalities: Beijing, Shanghai, Guangdong, Chongqing, and Shaanxi.[46] Over these years, five branches have accepted a total of 854 merger filings, accounting for 57.74% of all simple cases during the same period.[47] This measure eases SAMR's review workload, enabling it to focus more on normal cases and those involving potential competitive concerns that may require conditional approval.

116. Meanwhile, on August 1, 2022, SAMR rolled out a case management e-system for merger review, which comprises a "filing portal" for notifying parties, a "review portal" for SAMR, and a "delegation portal" for SAMR's local branches. The "review portal" establishes a clear internal requirement for handling simple cases under the "Double 20 Days" mechanism: in principle, the first "below 20 days" should elapse from the submission of a filing to its formal acceptance, and the second from acceptance to approval. Missing the window prompts the system to issue a reminder, to which the case handler must provide an explanation.

117. These measures in place are conducive to shortening the review timeline during the SAMR period, particularly for simple cases. Based on data and information published by SAMR, the average review time from case notification to acceptance was approximately 30 days in 2017, reduced to 26 days in 2018, 24 days in 2019, and further to 22.1 days by 2023. Similarly, the average time from acceptance to approval (including conditionally approved cases) was around 32.5 days in both 2017 and 2018, decreasing to 25.7 days in 2023. In 2024, the review process achieved a new breakthrough, with the average time from filing to acceptance sharply jumping from 22.1 to 18.2 days, and the time from acceptance to approval from 25.7 to 24.7 days.[48]

---

46 SAMR, *Announcement of SAMR on the Pilot Entrustment of Antitrust Reviews for Certain Concentration of Undertakings Cases* [July 8, 2022], https://www.samr.gov.cn/zt/ndzt/2022n/scjgzjlswjjylzzcjchjxzc/zcwj/art/2023/art_df86c1995e92454da0b40f7dc3ffe187.html (accessed: May 25, 2025).

47 See, https://www.gov.cn/lianbo/bumen/202410/content_6982521.htm.

48 See, https://news.cnr.cn/native/gd/kx/20250227/t20250227_527083059.shtml.

Figure 5 | Review Timeline During the SAMR Period[49]

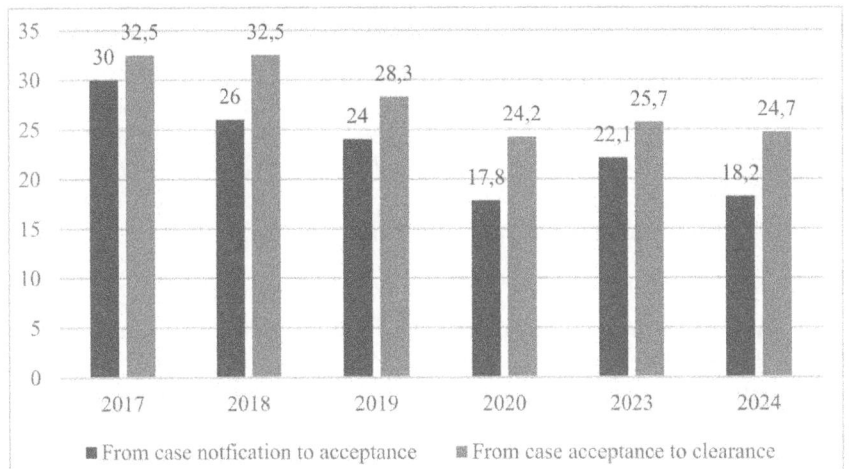

b. Introduction of "stop-clock" mechanism

118. Article 32 of the amended AML formally introduced the "stop-clock" mechanism into China's merger review regime. This development brings an end to the previous "withdraw-and-refile" practice which lacks a legal basis, and grants SAMR the statutory authority and greater flexibility to suspend the review timeline in cases where completing the review within Phase III becomes impossible.

119. However, it does not necessarily mean that SAMR will expedite the process or relax its criteria. As evidenced in *Broadcom/VMware (2023)*, SAMR spent seven to eight months on pre-review.[50] Furthermore, this mechanism does not set forth an explicit legal limit of time on the suspension and therefore may instead add to uncertainty on the review. For example, the *JX Metal/ Tatsuta (2024)* left a record of 11-month (332-day) clock stoppage, extending the total review timeframe from filing to approval to 16.9 months.[51] In practice, there have been more instances where the clock-stop lasts for over a year.[52]

120. The suspension of clock does not imply a halt in SAMR's review process. As a matter of fact, the review often continues to progress, while the clock

---

49 For data between 2017-2019, see China Antitrust Enforcement Report (2019); for data in 2020, see China Antitrust Enforcement Report (2020); for data between 2023-2024, see China news, https://news.cnr.cn/native/gd/kx/20250227/t20250227_527083059.shtml.
Please note that SAMR did not release figures for 2021-2022, so these data points have been omitted from the table.

50 See, https://www.samr.gov.cn/fldes/tzgg/ftj/art/2023/art_cae805a5e37d489ea929af8a4a369f6b.html.

51 See, https://www.samr.gov.cn/fldes/tzgg/ftj/art/2024/art_ee026cc074884d50ade381f916ab943a.html.

52 John Ren, Karen Yang, Martha Wen, *concentrations in china in 2023 and 2024*, CPI Antitrust Chronicle [March, 2025].

stoppage primarily serves as a formality procedure to pause the statutory countdown. In practice, SAMR typically resumes the clock at a later stage – remedy negotiations are concluded or near-completed with a final draft remedy proposal ready. For example, in *Simcere Pharma/Tobishi (2024)* and *JX Metal/Tatsuta (2024)*, the final remedy proposals accepted by SAMR were submitted during the stop-clock period. In *MaxLinear/ Silicon Motion (2023)* and *Broadcom/VMware (2023)*, the submission of the final draft occurred shortly after the clock resumption, followed by SAMR's conditional approval the very next day.[53]

c. Launch of call-in procedure for below-threshold cases

121. Another significant enhancement is also brought into China's merger control regime with the amended AML, that is, establishment of a call-in procedure. Under this mechanism, SAMR is empowered to require a merger notification in cases that do not meet the prescribed turnover thresholds but may give rise to potential competition concerns. Specifically, this procedure is invokable only when there is evidence suggesting that such a below-threshold transaction may have the effect of restricting or eliminating competition. This addresses a regulatory gap, ensuring that transactions involving smaller-scale and highly-innovative undertakings are not excluded from antitrust scrutiny solely based on financial thresholds, particularly in sectors where even modest mergers and acquisitions may substantially affect market competition.

122. Since this new tool becomes available, SAMR seems to have already exercised it in several cases, based on public information, including *Qualcomm/ Autotalks*, *Synopsys/Ansys*, *Keysight/Spirent*, and *CK Hutchison's port sales*. The installment of this procedure reinforces SAMR's commitment to safeguarding market competition.

d. Adoption of "three letters, one notice" system

123. On November 29, 2023, the Anti-Monopoly and Anti-Unfair Competition Committee of the State Council and SAMR jointly issued a notice designing a "Three Letters, One Notice" mechanism, aimed at strengthening antitrust oversight, and promptly preventing and curbing monopolistic conducts.[54] The "Three Letters, One Notice" comprises the Reminder and Urging Letter, the Regulatory Talk Letter, the Case Investigation Letter, and the Administrative Penalty Decision Notice (for undertakings) / Administrative Recommendation Notice (for administrative agencies).

---

53   Ibid.

54   SAMR, *Notice of the Anti-Monopoly and Anti-Unfair Competition Committee of the State Council and SAMR on Establishing the "Three Letters and One Notice" Mechanism* [December 6, 2023], https://www.samr.gov. cn/zw/zfxxgk/fdzdgknr/jzzcxds/art/2023/art_515052484fd94fb1a2d8a648615b4c1c.html (accessed: May 25, 2025).

124. From a merger review perspective, any risk of the unlawful implementation of a concentration, such as failure to file in accordance with the law or violation of a review decision, may trigger the application of the "Three Letters, One Notice" mechanism, which has proven effective in deterring AML violations and enhancing regulatory compliance.

e. Other measures

125. In addition, other notable improvements in SAMR's merger review practices also emerge. For example, releasing the list of approved merger cases is now on a weekly basis under SAMR, shifted from a quarterly basis before during the MOFCOM's period, improving the timeliness and accessibility of information. Another development relates to the publication of the Annual Antitrust Enforcement Reports, which SAMR has been issuing each year since 2019. These reports provide a comprehensive summary of the agency's antitrust work, including detailed statistics and analysis related to merger review activities.

3. Major substantive evolution of merger review

126. In parallel with the procedural improvements outlined above, the substantive aspects of China's merger review regime have also seen advancements since the establishment of SAMR in 2018.

a. General trends in substantive merger review

127. Overall, SAMR's enforcement approach and methodology towards merger review have become more mature, professional, refined, and transparent, forming a tailored review mechanism that aligns with the characteristics of the Chinese market. For instance, review practices have evolved to reflect market developments – such as raising notification thresholds, conducting merger review and investigation based on the specific development status of different industries. The following paragraphs outlines the key characteristics of merger review development under SAMR.

Raised notification turnover thresholds

128. On January 26, 2024, the State Council officially brought into effect the adjustment of the notification turnover thresholds, by revising the Provisions on the Notification Thresholds for Concentrations of Undertakings ("Provisions"). The key highlight is doubling the original RMB 400 million China turnover threshold to RMB 800 million. This change is intended to reduce the number of small-scale cases subject to mandatory filings, thereby lowering institutional transaction costs for concentrations, improving the efficiency and resource allocation of antitrust enforcement, and facilitating investment and merger activities.

Enhanced alignment of antitrust enforcement with evolving industry economy

129. SAMR has increasingly aligned its enforcement goals with the development of China's holistic market economy. In 2021, it started an intensive enforcement campaign targeting the platform economy industry, to strengthen antitrust oversight and prevent the disorderly expansion of capital. Over the course of that year, SAMR penalized major platform companies for failure to notify in the internet sector on four occasions – March, April, July, and November – covering a total of 84 cases.[55] These cases primarily involved Tencent, Meituan, Baidu, JD, 58.Com, etc. all of which received the maximum fines. This wave of enforcement came to an end with the final round of penalties in another 26 internet-related cases on January 5, 2022.

VIE Transactions subjected to merger review

130. At the MOFCOM's times, transactions involving a Variable Interest Entity ("VIE") structure remained a legal gray area. MOFCOM was generally reluctant to accept merger filings involving VIEs, primarily out of the concern that granting antitrust approvals might be interpreted as an official nod to the VIE structure – a stance that conflicted with MOFCOM's foreign investment regulatory framework. For example, in 2012, while conditionally approving Walmart's acquisition of Yihaodian, to avoid the perception of officially recognizing the legality of the VIE structure, MOFCOM imposed conditions refraining Walmart from engaging in businesses restricted to foreign investment.[56]

131. This ambiguity was resolved during the SAMR's period. On April 20, 2020, SAMR publicly announced its review of the establishment of a joint venture between Shanghai Mingchazhegang and Huansheng. Notably, it made overt mention of Mingchazhegang's operation under a VIE structure, marking the first time SAMR clearly acknowledged and reviewed a VIE-related transaction. Further clearer confirmation came with the issuance of the *Anti-Monopoly Guidelines for the Platform Economy Sector* on February 7, 2021, which explicitly provides that concentrations involving contractual control arrangements (*i.e.*, VIE structures) fall within the scope of merger review.[57]

Streamlined Information Requirements for Simplified Cases

132. On September 14, 2024, SAMR issued a notice releasing the revised Notification Form for the Merger Review of Simplified Cases ("Notification Form") and the Public Announcement Form for Simplified Cases ("Announcement Form").

---

55 See, https://www.yicai.com/news/101237163.html.
56 See, http://fldj.mofcom.gov.cn/article/ztxx/201303/20130300058730.shtml.
57 See, Article 18 of the *Anti-Monopoly Guidelines for the Platform Economy Sector*.

133. Under these two updated forms, the number of documents required for a filing has been reduced from three to two. In principle, only a confidential version of the Notification Form and the Announcement Form are now required. Additionally, the number of information items in the Notification Form has been streamlined from 44 to 38.

134. One of the most notable improvements concerns cases where the undertakings involved – i.e., the joint venture to be established or the target company to be acquired – do not, and will not, engage in economic activities in China. In such cases, the notifying parties are no longer required to submit market share data or competitive analysis. Furthermore, for transactions that qualify as simplified cases due to limited market share or a reduction in shareholders in a joint venture, competition analysis is also not required.

b. *Substantive evolution of review in cases with competition concerns*

Increasing use of FRAND

135. Compared with MOFCOM, SAMR has placed significantly greater emphasis on the application of the Fair, Reasonable, and Non-Discriminatory ("FRAND") principle in its conditional merger approvals. Among the 26 conditional cases published by SAMR to date, at least 17 incorporate FRAND-related commitments, accounting for approximately 65% of the total. In contrast, during the MOFCOM's period, only 5 out of 36 conditional approval cases included FRAND obligations.

136. This growing reliance on FRAND commitments reflects SAMR's increasing focus not only on addressing competition concerns but also on promoting equitable access to relevant products and technologies. This is particularly important in sectors such as semiconductors, telecommunications, and other industries where access to critical technologies or essential facilities can directly affect market competition and innovation.

Growing weight given to industry opinions

137. Industry opinions always play a role in merger control review. However, a comparison between pre and post SAMR's period reveals a shift in emphasis. While competition considerations tended to outweigh industry perspectives at the MOFCOM-era, SAMR has placed greater weight on industry opinion in its merger review process.

138. A clear example of this shift is SAMR's conditional approval of the *MaxLinear/Silicon Motion (2023)*[58]. This case stands out as the only one

---

58 Public announcement concerning SAMR's decision approving the acquisition of Silicon Motion Technology Corporation ("Silicon Motion") by MaxLinear, Inc. ("MaxLiner") (issued on July 26, 2023), https://www.samr.gov.cn/fldes/tzgg/ftj/art/2023/art_a685ac0dd85647b3898dff75f68fa2c4.html.

since the implementation of the AML in 2008 that involved no horizontal, vertical, or neighboring relationships between the parties involved in the transaction. Despite this, SAMR imposed remedies to address concerns about the future stable supply of Silicon Motion's main products post-transaction. The competitive analysis in the decision recognized Silicon Motion's strong market position in the relevant product market and emphasized that downstream customers in China "expressed concerns that the transaction might affect the stability of product supply, given their good cooperative relationship with Silicon Motion." Therefore, the issue appeared to stem not from the traditional antitrust concern that the concentration would have anticompetitive effects in the relevant market by altering the parties' economic incentives to supply, but rather from other factors.[59] This decision underscores SAMR's growing responsiveness to industry concerns, even in the absence of traditional competitive overlaps.

139. Further evidence of this trend includes SAMR's growing practice of soliciting industry feedback even before a formal filing is submitted or accepted in high-profile cases. This engagement reflects SAMR's increased sensitivity to industry voices.

Shift from focusing on chinese customers to chinese market

140. Prior to November 2021, the remedies imposed by SAMR primarily focused on addressing the concerns of Chinese customers, with only some targeting the broader Chinese market. For instance, in the *ZF/Wabco* case[60] approved by SAMR in May 2020, the remedy required the merged entity to continue supplying AMT controllers to Chinese customers on FRAND terms. Similarly, in the *Cisco/Acacia* case[61] approved in January 2021, the remedies required the combined entity to maintain the supply of Coherent DSPs to Chinese customers under FRAND principles. In these cases, "Chinese customers" referred specifically to customers headquartered in China.

141. However, this approach shifted beginning with the *SK Hynix/Intel NAND business* case[62] in December 2021. Since then, all conditional approvals have been designed to address the potential impact on the Chinese market

---

59 John Ren, Karen Yang, Martha Wen, *concentrations in china in 2023 and 2024*, CPI Antitrust Chronicle [March, 2025].

60 Public announcement concerning SAMR's decision approving the acquisition of shares of WABCO Holdings Ltd. ("WABCO") by ZF Friedrichshafen AG ("ZF") (issued on May 15, 2020), https://www.samr.gov.cn/jzxts/tzgg/ftjpz/art/2020/art_4426aefc052e4b0bba793d33d7c829e0.html.

61 Public announcement concerning SAMR's decision approving the acquisition of shares of Acacia Communications, Inc. ("Acacia ") by Cisco Systems, Inc. ("Cisco") (issued on January 14, 2021), https://www.samr.gov.cn/jzxts/tzgg/ftjpz/art/2021/art_781c3da9f9cd4d428587b4bb91b12175.html

62 Public announcement concerning SAMR's decision approving the acquisition by SK hynix Inc. ("SK Hynix") of the NAND and SSD Businesses of Intel Corporation (issued on December 22, 2021), https://www.samr.gov.cn/jzxts/tzgg/ftjpz/art/2021/art_fb02fe2b2c194567874cb4999adab0c3.html.

as a whole, signaling a more market-oriented and systemic perspective in SAMR's antitrust enforcement.

142. Although in SAMR's most recent conditional approval – the *JX Metals/Tatsuta* case[63] in 2024, the remedy language still referred to "Chinese customers," the definition was expanded to include not only entities headquartered in China but also the Chinese subsidiaries of multinational companies. In effect, this broader interpretation reflects SAMR's continued emphasis on protecting the overall Chinese market rather than narrowly focusing on the nationality of customers.

More detailed provisions required in remedy proposal

143. Under SAMR's merger review regime, remedies have become increasingly detailed and precise. Notably, certain implementation methods that were traditionally outlined only in the detailed implementation plan ("DIP") – typically prepared after the issuance of a conditional approval – are now prescribed directly within the remedy proposal attached to the approval decision itself.

144. For example, in the most recent conditionally approved case, *JX Metals/Tatsuta*[64], the remedies required that the combined entity must not refuse, restrict, or delay the supply of blackened rolled copper foil and isotropic conductive adhesive film to Chinese customers, unless there is a legitimate justification. Significantly, SAMR also required the parties to explicitly list such justifications in the remedy proposal itself. Previously, such detailed explanations were usually included only in the DIP, rather than the remedy proposal.

145. Another example is *Wanhua Chemical/Yantai Juli* case approved by SAMR on April 7, 2023. Before 2023, the Chinese antitrust authority had imposed price-specific remedies in at least 10 conditionally approved cases. These remedies typically required that the post-merger price of the relevant products (or the patent royalty rate) not exceed a benchmark price (or a benchmark rate). In most of these cases, the decision and/or the remedy proposal explicitly stipulated that the benchmark price should be the *average* selling price of the parties in China for a period prior to the effective date of the decision. However, neither the decision nor the remedy proposal explicitly clarified whether the post-merger price (to be compared with the benchmark price) should be an average price or the price of each individual transaction, order or contract. In practice, the exact meaning of post-merger price is typically defined in the DIP and varies case by case. In some instances, it is defined as the average

---

63 Public announcement concerning SAMR's decision approving the acquisition of TATSUTA Electric Wire and Cable Co., Ltd. ("Tatsuta") by JX Metals Corporation ("JX Metals") (issued on June 11, 2024), https://www.samr.gov.cn/jzxts/tzgg/ftjpz/art/2024/art_cb9e85a768444eb68f5be95d96d490fa.html.

64 Ibid.

price for a certain reporting period or the price stipulated in contracts with customers, while in others, it refers to the price of each individual transaction, purchase order or contract. In *Wanhua Chemical/Yantai Juli* case[65], it is the first time that the decision and the remedy proposal explicitly stipulate that the post-merger price is the annual average price of TDI supplied to customers in the Chinese market after the completion of the transaction.[66][67]

146. This shift reflects SAMR's intent to enhance the enforceability and clarity of conditions from the outset, reducing potential ambiguity and minimizing the risk of disputes during the implementation phase.

IV. Reflections on Two Decades of the AML: From Legislation to Global Influence

147. Since its enactment in 2003, China's AML has undergone a major revision, witnessed the consolidation of its enforcement agencies from three into one, and seen the introduction of a hierarchical system of regulations and guidelines, alongside landmark cases that have shaped its trajectory. As a law firm deeply engaged in AML enforcement since its inception, T&D have been privileged to represent clients in numerous antitrust investigations and merger filings, participating intimately in this transformative journey.

148. When looking back, the drafting process of the AML was marked by fervent debates, forward-looking deliberations, and unparalleled collaboration among legislators, scholars, and practitioners. Their shared commitment to crafting a law that balanced market freedom with regulatory oversight remains vivid in memory.

149. In the realm of merger control, many challenges addressed in recent AML revisions and practices had already been anticipated during legislative discussions.

150. *Micro-level foresight*: In 2007, Professor Huang Yong's seminal article, The Fundamental Relationship Between Intellectual Property Rights and Antimonopoly law, argued that IP protection and antitrust goals ultimately converge in promoting market competition and consumer welfare – a principle later tested in cases like Microsoft/Nokia, Qualcomm/NXP, etc.

---

65 Public announcement concerning SAMR's decision approving the acquisition of Yantai Juli Fine Chemical Co., Ltd. ("Yantai Juli") by Wanhua Chemical Group Co., Ltd. ("Wanhua Chemical") (issued on April 7, 2023), https://www.sac.gov.cn/cms_files/filemanager/samr/www/samrnew/fldes/tzgg/ftj/202304/t20230407_354460.html.

66 The first remedy in the SAMR decision requires that "Where the transaction terms are equivalent, the annual average price of TDI supplied to customers in the Chinese market after the completion of the transaction shall not exceed the average price of the twenty-four months preceding the Commitment Date." See, https://www.samr.gov.cn/fldes/tzgg/ftj/art/2023/art_c2b34c8db90d4415a4025b84a4cf837f.html.

67 John Ren, Karen Yang, Martha Wen, *concentrations in china in 2023 and 2024*, CPI Antitrust Chronicle [March, 2025].

involving the balance of AML and the protection of SEPs and non-SEPs. As early as 2006, during preliminary AML drafting, we advocated for adopting a U.S.-style "deemed approval after Phase I" mechanism for merger reviews to ensure procedural certainty, rather than the EU's more open-ended approach. This concern has since been validated by the introduction of SAMR's "stop-the-clock mechanism."

151. *Macro-level vision*: In 2008, Professor Huang traced China's antitrust philosophy back to *State Council Provisional Regulations on Promoting and Protecting Socialist Competition in* 1980, predicting that transplanting Western "Economic Constitution" into China's context would face unique hurdles. He foresaw tensions between industrial policy and merger control (a recurring issue in semiconductor industry reviews) and debated whether trade remedies might undermine antitrust principles – a prescient analysis now echoed in today's era of deglobalization and trade fragmentation.

152. In any case, over two decades, China's AML has proven resilient against evolving challenges, standing as a testament to the foresight of its architects and China's commitment to a rules-based market economy. It is both an anchor of stability and a dynamic instrument adapting to technological and economic shifts.

153. Looking at the present, some respected legislators and scholars who accompanied the gestation and birth of the AML have gradually stepped down after completing their missions. However, they established numerous institutional frameworks and details during the enforcement of the AML, accompanied the continuous improvement of the AML in practice, overcame various challenges and issues from domestic and international, substantive, and procedural levels, enabling China to gradually become one of the "pivotal" three major antitrust enforcement jurisdictions.

154. Some colleagues who fought alongside me through the storms of these over twenty years remain active on the front lines of anti-monopoly law enforcement and legal practice, continuing to contribute light and heat to China's antitrust institutional development. Among them is Prof. Huang Yong. A group of young enforcers involved in the AML's legislative process have gradually matured, ascended to leadership positions, and become the backbone of current China's AML enforcement.

155. There are also young, professional forces and successors who continuously emerge and devote themselves to antitrust endeavors during this process, bringing fresh blood and innovative ideas to the development and future of China's AML. The drafting and release of new guidelines, including the Platform Economy Guidelines, demonstrate that beyond its foundational role as an "Economic Constitution", the AML possesses vigorous vitality and momentum for growth. It is a law closely aligned with social progress, economic development, and industrial advancement – a cause worthy of our dedication.

Analyzing China's Draft Guidelines for Non-Horizontal Merger Review (July 2025): Comparative Reflections on US 2020 and 2023 Guidelines

Tony Jiang[*]

Vice President for Government Affairs, Intel China

Abstract

On 1 July 2025, China's State Administration for Market Regulation (SAMR) released a draft of the Non-Horizontal Merger Review Guidelines for public consultation[1]. The draft sets out a structured framework for assessing vertical and conglomerate mergers, marking a significant milestone in the evolution of China's antitrust regime. This article provides a comparative commentary on the Chinese draft, juxtaposing its legal and economic foundations with the U.S. Department of Justice (DOJ) and Federal Trade Commission (FTC)'s Vertical Merger Guidelines (2020) and the integrated treatment in the 2023 Merger Guidelines. the article examines the strengths, limitations, and policy choices underpinning China's evolving enforcement framework.

---

[*] Tony Jiang, PhD in Law from University of Business and Economics, Beijing China, under the supervision of Professor Huang Yong. Now serves as Vice President of Global Government Affairs (China) and Assistant General Counsel in Intel Corp, oversees the company's government relations, competition policy, trade/export controls, technical policy, and standards. He also has the extensive working experience in the agency and international cooperation on competition policy.

1   State Administration for Market Regulation (SAMR), Draft Guidelines for Non-Horizontal Merger Review (July 2025), Beijing.

Analyzing China's Draft Guidelines for Non-Horizontal Merger Review (July 2025): Comparative Reflections on US 2020 and 2023 Guidelines

1. Introduction: Toward a Structured Non-Horizontal Review Framework in China

1. Non-horizontal mergers – comprising both vertical and conglomerate integrations – pose distinct challenges to competition authorities. While they do not typically eliminate direct competitors, such transactions may raise foreclosure, coordination, and leveraging concerns. The 2025 SAMR draft introduces a coherent legal-economic approach to such mergers, reflecting both international convergence and adaptation to China's market structure, particularly its platform economy and industrial ecosystems.

2. In contrast to earlier practice, the draft outlines analytical criteria, evidentiary standards, and rebuttable presumptions of harm, with a degree of specificity uncommon in prior Chinese merger guidance. Notably, the draft seeks to bridge the gap between rule-based enforcement and case-by-case analysis, a balance long debated in jurisdictions such as the EU and U.S[2].

2. Key Features of the Draft: Presumptions, Definitions, and Economic Rationale

2.1 Market share thresholds and presumptions of harm

3. One of the draft's key innovations is its tiered approach to market share analysis. SAMR articulates rebuttable presumptions tied to market shares in vertically related or closely linked markets:
   - ≥50%: Presumed anti-competitive unless the parties provide compelling evidence to the contrary;
   - 35%–50%: Enforcement agency "inclined to presume" harm, with intensified scrutiny;
   - 25%–35%: Low likelihood of competitive harm, subject to further review;
   - <25%: Presumption of no harm, barring exceptional circumstances (e.g. rapid entrant expansion, cross-ownership, data integration).

4. This structure provides legal predictability, especially for simplified procedure cases or fast track cases. This also reflects the Chinese agency's long-time inclined methodology towards market share in competition analysis in the enforcement. However, the reliance on static thresholds stands in contrast to the U.S. approach, which eschews bright-line tests in favor of dynamic economic modelling.

---

[2] European Commission (2008), Guidelines on the Assessment of Non-Horizontal Mergers.

2.2 Vertical foreclosure and access concerns

5. The draft provides detailed treatment of vertical concerns, focusing on input and customer foreclosure, information spillovers, and discriminatory access to essential resources. These concepts align with traditional foreclosure theories[3] but are adapted to the realities of Chinese markets – including state-influenced supply chains, vertically integrated industrial champions, and digital platforms.

2.3 Conglomerate mergers and portfolio effects

6. The draft guidelines provide a structured framework for assessing conglomerate mergers, particularly those involving firms in non-overlapping markets that nonetheless exhibit adjacent or complementary relationships. Adjacent markets are defined as those with overlapping customer bases, similar end-uses, or ecosystem dependencies, while complementary markets involve products or services that are technically or functionally interdependent, often used together or requiring interoperability. The guidelines emphasize that such relationships can still lead to anticompetitive effects, including unilateral foreclosure through bundling, tying, refusal to deal, or reducing interoperability, and coordinated effects such as facilitating collusion. A three-step analytical framework is proposed – evaluating the ability, incentive, and effect of potential foreclosure. The guidelines are enriched with illustrative cases that demonstrate how dominance in one market can be leveraged into another, especially when technical bottlenecks, customer lock-in, or high entry barriers exist. They also address ecosystem effects, where control in one part of a digital or platform-based system can amplify market power across related markets. Compared to international standards, the Chinese draft aligns closely with the EU and US approaches, particularly in its economic logic and concern for data concentration and network effects. However, it stands out for its granular distinction between adjacent and complementary markets and its extensive use of case-based reasoning, offering a forward-looking and nuanced enforcement tool for complex multi-market scenarios.

3. Comparative Evaluation: China (2025) vs. United States (2020 & 2023) Guidelines

7. The China 2025 Draft Guidelines and the US 2023 Merger Guidelines both address non-horizontal mergers, but with distinct emphases and frameworks. China's draft explicitly distinguishes between adjacent and complementary market relationships, offering a structured lens to assess how companies

---

3   Huang, Yong: Non-Horizontal Mergers Control: the Analysis on European Commission (2008), Guidelines on the Assessment of Non-Horizontal Mergers, Tsinghua Law Review (2009), 147–159.

may exert influence across related markets. In contrast, the US guidelines focus more broadly on competitive dynamics and economic incentives, without categorizing market relationships in the same way. Both jurisdictions apply similar economic logic in evaluating foreclosure risks, though China formalizes this through a three-step test – assessing the ability, incentive, and effect of potential foreclosure. Ecosystem and platform effects are central to both frameworks, with China providing detailed case examples and the US emphasizing concerns in digital market contexts. Regarding sensitive information, China's draft offers a more detailed treatment of data access and interoperability risks, while the US guidelines recognize such risks as a source of competitive harm. Analytically, China leans on case-based reasoning with illustrative examples, whereas the US approach is grounded in real-world evidence and strategic behavior, reflecting a more flexible, effects-based methodology. Here are some details as below.

1. Evolution of US Approach to Non-Horizontal Mergers

8. The U.S. antitrust agencies have evolved significantly in their treatment of non-horizontal mergers. The 2020 DOJ/FTC Vertical Merger Guidelines provided a structured, economics-based framework with illustrative tools such as the upward pricing pressure (UPP) and vertical gross upward pricing pressure index (vGUPPI)[4]. These tools were supported by a 20% market share screen, although no safe harbor was formally recognized.

9. However, the vertical-horizontal dichotomy was abandoned in the 2023 Merger Guidelines altogether, instead a unified, effects-based framework that assesses vertical and cross-market mergers fusing the same principles as horizontal mergers, was adopted. The 2023 Guidelines emphasize risks of entrenchment, raising rivals' costs, and cumulative competitive harms, particularly in platform and gatekeeper contexts.

2. Market Structure and Thresholds

10. The 2025 SAMR Draft Guidelines codify a tiered system of presumptions based on market share levels:

    ≥50%: Presumed anti-competitive

    35–50%: Likely harmful, requiring scrutiny

    25–35%: May raise concern, further evidence required

    <25%: Presumed not harmful barring aggravating factors

---

[4] DOJ & FTC, Vertical Merger Guidelines, United States, 2020.

11. This stands in contrast to the US 2023 Guidelines, which contain no structural thresholds, and differs from the US 2020 Guidelines, which referenced a 20% threshold as a screen for closer examination but did not establish formal presumptions.

3. Analytical Methodology

12. China's draft emphasizes structured review using both qualitative indicators (e.g., platform behavior, ecosystem lock-in) and limited quantitative evidence. It references use of econometric models but does not require them.
13. The 2020 US Guidelines encouraged tools like UPP and vGUPPI to assess pricing incentives in vertical mergers[5]. The 2023 Guidelines drop these references, instead favoring holistic evaluation grounded in documentary evidence and strategic behavior, regardless of vertical or horizontal labels.

4. Platform Conduct and Digital Ecosystems

14. China's draft provides explicit focus on digital markets, including control of APIs(Application Programming Interface), data aggregation, bundling, and self-preferencing. It introduces specific language on platform gatekeeping and interoperability barriers.
15. The 2023 US Guidelines address platform entrenchment more broadly than the 2020 version, highlighting the risk that vertical or cross-market mergers might fortify digital monopolies. The 2020 Guidelines did not focus specifically on digital platforms.

5. Remedies and Enforcement Preferences

16. Remedy design is largely omitted in China's draft. It does not articulate a policy preference between structural and behavioral remedies
17. The US 2020 Guidelines acknowledged the possibility of behavioral remedies in vertical cases. However, by 2023, the US agencies had adopted a stricter approach, expressing skepticism toward behavioral remedies and favoring structural solutions to prevent entrenchment and exclusionary effects.

---

5 FTC, Hart-Scott-Rodino Antitrust Improvements Act Annual Report, 2020.

6. Summary Comparison Table

Feature	China (SAMR, 2025 Draft)	U.S. 2020 Vertical Merger Guidelines	U.S. 2023 Merger Guidelines
Market Share Thresholds	Yes (≥50%, 35–50%, 25–35%, <25%)	20% as screen (not safe harbor)	No thresholds
Vertical/Non-Horizontal Focus	Explicitly categorized and defined	Specific vertical guidance issued	No separate category
Quantitative Tools	Encouraged, not detailed	UPP, vGUPPI, HHI-based logic	Abandoned, favors qualitative evidence
Platform & Data Issues	Explicit focus (APIs, bundling, self-preference)	Not addressed	Central concern (platform dominance)
Remedy Orientation	Unclear	Behavioral remedies considered	Structural remedies favored
Procedural Predictability	High (structured presumptions)	Moderate	Low (case-by-case, evidence focused)

7. Strengths of the Draft: Legal Certainty and Forward-Looking Analysis

18. The draft introduces several commendable features:
    – Clear analytical framework applicable to both vertical and conglomerate scenarios;
    – Structured thresholds that reduce regulatory ambiguity;
    – Digital-market orientation, responding to challenges in data, platforms, and interoperability, as well as the realities in China's economy;
    – Case-based illustrations, which enhance clarity and practical understanding.

8. Challenges and Areas for Refinement

19. Despite notable progress, the draft presents areas requiring refinement:
    – Over-reliance on market share presumptions may risk formalism and underweight economic effects in complex cases;
    – Lack of economic quantification tools, such as upward pricing pressure indices or vGUPPI, may hinder precision;
    – Unclear approach to remedies could create implementation challenges, especially where behavioral conditions are needed.

9. Conclusion

20. SAMR's 2025 draft marks a significant evolution in China's merger control regime, particularly in its approach to non-horizontal combinations. While it prioritizes procedural predictability and reflects increasing regulatory sophistication, the absence of detailed economic modelling and remedy guidance may limit its effectiveness in complex or fast-moving sectors.

21. Nevertheless, the draft represents a serious and structured effort to modernize China's antitrust tools in line with global practice. In the final version, hopefully the refinements could be reflected on enhancing economic rigor, clarifying threshold application, and improving guidance on remedies.

Key Facts on China's Merger Reviews During the Time of Uncertainties

ELIZABETH XIAORU WANG[*]
Economist, Econic Partners

SOPHIE NA YANG
Economist, Econic Partners

QIAN YUJIE
Economist, Compass Lexecon

Abstract

This article presents an empirical analysis of the People's Republic of China's merger control regime, administered by the State Administration for Market Regulation (SAMR), during a period of significant global uncertainty from 2017 to 2024. Countering prevailing narratives that characterize the Chinese merger review process as protracted, unpredictable, and unduly influenced by industrial policy, this study examines enforcement data to assess its practical application. The analysis demonstrates that despite a substantial and increasing caseload, the vast majority of transactions are cleared expeditiously under a simplified procedure. For complex cases requiring remedies, the review timelines are shown to be comparable to those in the European Union and the United States. Furthermore, the data reveals a remarkably low intervention rate – less than one percent – which is notably lower

---

[*] Elizabeth Xiaoru Wang and Sophie Na Yang are economists at Econic Partners, and Qian Yujie is an economist at Compass Lexecon. We are grateful for excellent research support from Gale Chen. The views and opinions set forth herein are the personal views or opinions of the authors; they do not necessarily reflect the views or opinions of the organizations with which they are affiliated or those organizations' management, affiliates, employees, or clients.

than that of its Western counterparts. The study finds that SAMR exhibits a strong preference for behavioral remedies over structural remedies or prohibitions, thereby facilitating transaction approvals while addressing specific competition concerns.

While acknowledging that transactions within the technology and semiconductor sectors are subject to heightened scrutiny, the article concludes that this does not constitute an insurmountable barrier to clearance. The findings indicate that China's merger review process has remained consistent, predictable, and procedurally robust, even amidst heightened geopolitical and economic tensions. This research provides critical insights for legal practitioners, academics, and multinational corporations navigating the complexities of global M&A transactions involving Chinese jurisdiction.

I. Introduction

1. The past few years have been characterized by unprecedented global uncertainties, reshaping the economic and regulatory landscape for businesses worldwide. In particular, the COVID-19 pandemic disrupted supply chains and altered market dynamics, while rising geopolitical tensions, trade conflicts, and shifting tariff policies introduced additional complexities for mergers and acquisitions. Amid these challenges, changes in key administrations – particularly in major economies like the US and EU – have further contributed to an environment of regulatory unpredictability.

2. China plays a critical role in global mergers and acquisitions, given its massive consumer market, expansive regulatory reach, and influence over multi-jurisdictional dealmaking. There have been concerns about China's merger review process, particularly regarding two key aspects: prolonged and uncertain timelines, and excessive regulatory intervention driven by industrial policy considerations. Some even worry that Chinese merger review would be prohibitive in times of high geopolitical tensions.

3. In this article, we review empirical evidence and key facts to assess how China's merger review regime functions in practice. Data shows that merger cases reviewed in China has growing annually, and a large majority of all transactions are approved quickly. While complex cases may take longer, the review timelines are similar to those in the US and the EU. In terms of merger intervention, China's overall intervention rate has been low. Chinese merger review agency tends to use behavioral remedies to address competition concerns rather than prohibit transactions. Finally, technology mergers face closer scrutiny than those in other industries, but they do not encounter uniquely insurmountable barriers to approval. In summary, amid recent global uncertainties, China's merger review process has been remarkably predictable and consistent.

II. Key Facts about Deal Timing in China

4. Some commentators expressed concerns that merger review timelines in China are excessively long. For example, a Wall Street Journal article in 2023 stated that "Beijing is holding back its required green light for mergers that involve American companies as a technology war with Washington intensifies."[1] A report issued by the U.S. Chamber of Commerce in 2022 also suggested that delays in China's merger review process may create regulatory risks and raise costs of doing business for affected American companies.[2] However, as we will explain in detail in this section, data shows that a large majority of cases have been cleared quickly in the last several years, and while cases cleared with remedies take longer, their review timelines remain comparable to those in the US or EU.

A. SAMR reviews a high volume of cases each year and most are cleared quickly via a fast-track procedure

5. China is an important jurisdiction for global mergers, its merger review agency, the State Administration for Market Regulation ("SAMR") handles a large and steadily increasing number of cases annually. In this article, we focus on patterns and trends of China's merger review since the start of the first Trump Administration in 2017, when geopolitical tensions intensified concerns about the feasibility of obtaining merger approvals in China.

6. As shown in Figure 1, SAMR reviewed 332 cases in 2017, and steadily increased to 473 in 2020. The cases reviewed sharply increased to 727 in 2021 when the agency closed a filing loophole and imposed fines on over 100 transactions for failure to notify. In 2022 and 2023, SAMR reviewed nearly 800 cases. In 2024, the cases reviewed in China declined to 643, when China doubled the filing thresholds.[3] During the period of 2017 to 2024, on average China reviewed 585 cases each year. In contrast, the EU reviewed an average of 375 transactions per year over the same period.

---

[1] Lingling Wei and Asa Fitch: "China's New Tech Weapon: Dragging Its Feet on Global Merger Approvals," Wall Street Journal, April 4, 2023, https://www.wsj.com/articles/chinas-new-tech-weapon-dragging-its-feet-on-global-merger-approvals-d653ca4a.

[2] U.S. Chamber of Commerce. "U.S. Antitrust Legislative Proposals: A Global Perspective," February 2022. https://www.uschamber.com/assets/documents/u.s.-antitrust-legislative-proposals-a-global-perspective-final-locked-2.16.22.pdf.

[3] Nineteen out of the 643 cases were withdrawn by the parties. Among the reviewed cases, 57% were transactions between Chinese firms, 29% between overseas firms (mainly from the US, Japan and France), and 14% involved Chinese and overseas firms. See: 2024 nian shichang jianguan zongju wutianjian pizhun jingying zhe jizhong anjian shencha qingkuang 2024年市场监管总局无条件批准经营者集中案件审查情况 [State Administration for Market Regulation's Review of Unconditionally Approved Concentration of Operators Cases in 2024], last modified January 27, 2025, https://mp.weixin.qq.com/s/mo02CJXkIm9YcT25stMCIA.

Key Facts on China's Merger Reviews During the Time of Uncertainties

Figure 1 | Total Number of Cases Reviewed and Percentage of Simple Cases, 2017-2024

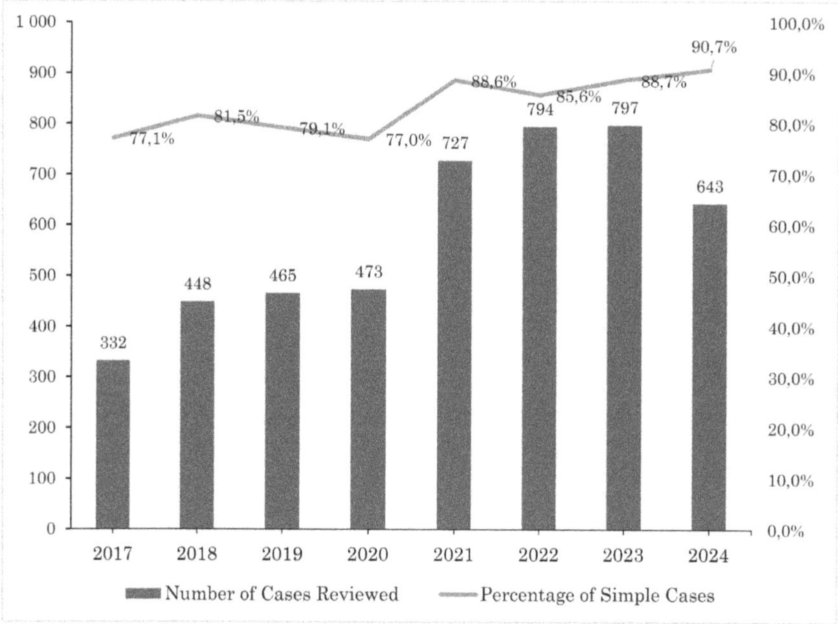

Year	Number of Cases Reviewed	Percentage of Simple Cases
2017	332	77.1%
2018	448	81.5%
2019	465	79.1%
2020	473	77.0%
2021	727	88.6%
2022	794	85.6%
2023	797	88.7%
2024	643	90.7%

Source: SAMR decisions, summarized by the authors.

7. The vast majority of cases in China were reviewed through the "simple cases" fast-track procedure, which applies to transactions unlikely to cause harm to competition. Figure 1 illustrates the share of simple cases in China relative to all cases from 2017 to 2024. In 2024, the proportion of cases reviewed under this fast-track procedure reached a record high of 91%, up from over 80% in previous years.

8. The fast-track procedure has significantly accelerated deal approvals, with most eligible deals cleared within 40 days of filing. As a result, in 2023 and 2024, SAMR's average review time of all cases – measured from formal acceptance to decision – was only 25.7 and 24.7 calendar days, respectively.[4] In the first nine months of 2024, the review time was reduced to 17.3 days after formal acceptance, while the pre-review stage averaged 16.4 days.[5]

---

4 Shichang jianguan zongju 2024 nian jingyingzhe jizhong fanlongduan jianguan gongzuo chengguo saomiao 市场监管总局2024年经营者集中反垄断监管工作成果扫描 [State Administration for Market Regulation 2024 Concentration of Operators Antimonopoly Regulation Progress Update], last modified February 27, 2025, https://www.samr.gov.cn/xw/zj/art/2025/art_21f523302be74c22922ad59b925bdfa3.html.

5 *See*, footnote 4.

9. It is worth noting that despite handling a heavier caseload than the EU, SAMR operates with a much smaller team – only around 20 staff members dedicated to merger reviews, compared to the European Commission's (EC) 117 staff.[6,7] Yet, China remains a critical jurisdiction for global mergers, having reviewed 6,324 cases from 2017 to 2024 (compared to the EC's 3,002).[8,9]

B. For remedy cases, the duration of review in China has increased over time but comparable with the EU and US

10. The average review time for cases cleared with remedies in China has increased in recent years. Remedy cases are often complex, involving competition concerns across multiple product markets and various theories of harm, which naturally extends their review periods. Moreover, SAMR has a mandate to consider China's national economic interests and consult major stakeholders before approving transactions. This consultation process can take many months before a consensus is reached on the terms of the approval.

11. Figure 2 tracks the average duration of a review from initial filing (including pre-review) to approval and the average duration of the formal review (from case opening) for remedy cases from 2017 to 2024. The average formal review period increased moderately over time, from 265 days in 2017 to 474 days in 2024, while the total review period (including pre-review period) increased from 311 days to 511 days.

---

6   On 15 July 2022, SAMR launched a three-year pilot program delegating the review of certain simple cases to the municipal authorities in Beijing, Shanghai and Chongqing and provincial authorities in Guangdong and Shaanxi. In 2023, these local authorities reviewed approximately half of the simple cases. (*See* 2023 nian shichang jianguan zongju jingying zhe jizhong anjian shencha qingkuang jiedu 2023年市场监管总局经营者集中案件审查情况解读 [Interpretation of the State Administration for Market Regulation's Review of Concentration of Operators Cases in 2023], last modified January 24, 2024. https://scjg.tj.gov.cn/tjsscjdglwyh_52651/xwdt/qgxx/gjscjdglzj/202401/t20240124_6518781.html. (accessed November 5, 2024)). All standard cases (including remedy cases) are reviewed by SAMR, *i.e.*, by the 20 officials within SAMR.

7   *See*, European Court of Auditors, Special Report – The Commission's EU merger control and antitrust proceedings: a need to scale up market oversight, November 24, 2020, https://www.eca.europa.eu/Lists/ECADocuments/SR20_24/SR_Competition_policy_EN.pdf.

8   Under the new thresholds, a transaction is notifiable if, in the previous year (1) (a) the combined global turnover of the merging parties exceeded RMB12 billion (approximately USD1.7 billion), or (b) the combined turnover in China of the merging parties exceeded RMB4 billion (approximately USD567.6 million); and (2) the turnover in China of each of at least two of the merging parties exceeded RMB800 million (approximately USD113.5 million). The previous thresholds are RMB ten billion (approximately USD 1.5 billion), RMB two billion (approximately USD 309 million), and RMB 400 million (approximately USD 57 million) respectively. See "China Increases Merger Control Filing Thresholds," O'Melveny & Myers, January 31, 2024, https://www.omm.com/insights/alerts-publications/china-increases-merger-control-filing-thresholds.

9   《shenhua gaige chuangzao gengjia gongping, geng you huoli de binggou jianguan tixi》xinwen fabu hui shilu《深化改革 创造更加公平、更有活力的并购监管体系》新闻发布会实录 [Deepening Reform to Create a Fairer and More Dynamic Mergers and Acquisitions Regulatory System], last modified October 11, 2024, https://m.cqn.com.cn/zj/content/2024-10/11/content_9071637.htm.

Figure 2 | Average Days of Review for Remedy Cases in China, 2017 to 2024

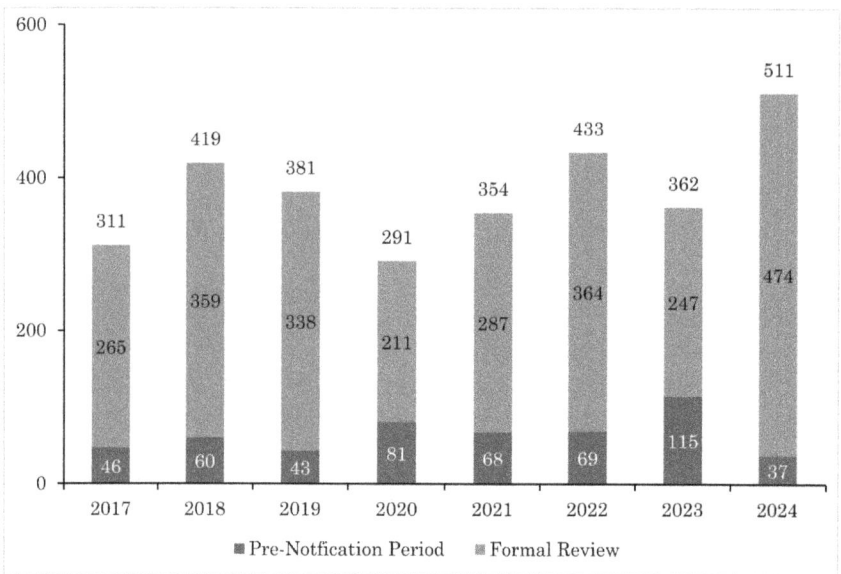

Source: SAMR and MOFCOM decisions

12. The remedy case with the longest review time during this period is *Korean Air/Asiana Airlines* which received clearance in China in 2022.[10] It took 710 days for total review and 643 days of formal review. This transaction involved particularly complex global remedies, and China cleared this transaction ahead of other major antitrust jurisdictions including the EU, Japan, the UK, and the US.[11] Excluding this outlier, the average duration of a remedy case (filing to approval) has remained stable, at about 356 days, during the periods from 2017-2024.

13. Comparison with US and EU data demonstrates SAMR's typical remedy case review duration is largely on par with the US for complex cases and slightly faster than the EU's. Figure 3 compares the length of reviews for complex cases across these three jurisdictions.

---

10 Guanyu Fujia Xianzhixing Tiaojian Pizhun Dahan Hangkong Gongsi Hanya Hangkong Zhushi Huishe Guquan An Fanlongduan Shencha Jueding De Gonggao (关于附加限制性条件批准大韩航空公司收购韩亚航空株式会社股权案反垄断审查决定的公告) [Public Announcement Concerning the Antimonopoly Review Decision Approving the Acquisition of Asiana Airlines, Inc. by Korean Air Lines Co., Ltd. with Restrictive Conditions] (issued by the State Administration for Market Regulation, Dec. 26, 2022), https://www.samr.gov.cn/fldys/tzgg/ftj/art/2023/art_bcb24582268d47c8acd5c29bb76e759b.html (in Chinese).

11 For example, the UK CMA required Virgin Atlantic to start a London-Seoul service, while Japan demanded changes to relevant Korea-bound routes. This multilateral coordination slowed down the overall progress of the transaction. "Korean Air Completes Asiana Acquisition: Everything You Need to Know," Skift Research, December 2024, https://skift.com/2024/12/12/korean-air-completes-asiana-acquisition/. (accessed May 16, 2025).

Figure 3 | Average Duration of Significant Merger Investigations and Remedy Cases in China, the US and by the EC,[12] 2017-2024

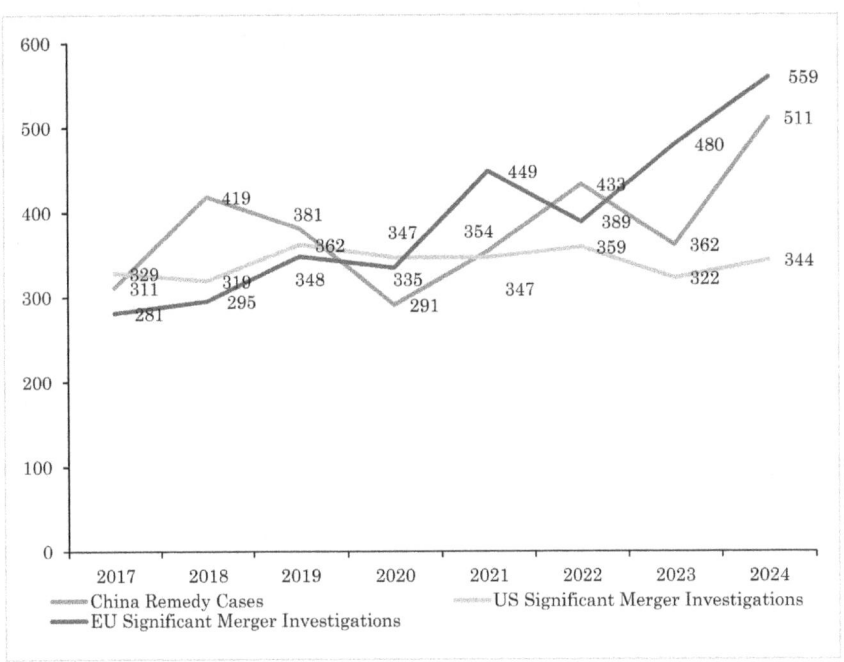

Source: SAMR and MOFCOM decisions. EU and US data from Dechert Antitrust Merger Investigation Timing Tracker[13]

III. Key Facts about Merger Intervention in China

14. Some commentators also raised concerns that SAMR's regulatory actions may be overly intrusive and driven by industrial policies. For example, a study in 2015 found that merger remedies were influenced by industrial policy goals designed to support Chinese companies and industrial development.[14] However, detailed analysis of enforcement statistics shows a different picture.

---

12 Due to data limitations, the duration of investigations in the US only covers the formal review period after HSR filings, while it also includes the pre-filing discussion period in the EU and the pre-case-initiation period in China.

13 "DAMITT 2024 Annual Report: Merger Enforcement at Low Tide on Both Sides of the Atlantic, but 2025 may Bring a Sea Change," Dechert LLP, January 30, 2025, https://www.dechert.com/knowledge/publication/2025/1/damitt-2024-annual-report.html. (accessed May 4, 2025).

14 Healey, Deborah: "Mergers with Conditions in China Caution, Control, or Industrial Policy?." China in the International Economic Order: New Directions and Changing Paradigms, (Cambridge University Press, 2015).

Key Facts on China's Merger Reviews
During the Time of Uncertainties

A. China's intervention rate is low

15. Given China's active government role in the economy, one might assume SAMR would adopt a more interventionist stance than other major antitrust agencies. However, a review of the enforcement statistics tells a different story.

16. The merger intervention rate – including approvals with remedies and outright prohibitions – has been approximately 1% in China since the enactment of AML in 2007. Among the 6,324 cases reviewed by Chinese authorities from 2008 through the end of 2024, only 62 cases (or 0.98%) were cleared with remedies and just three transactions (or 0.05%) were blocked. From 2017 to 2024, the intervention rate decreased to 0.84% with only one prohibition.[15]

17. These statistics do not include rare situations where the parties may abandon a deal in the face of regulatory opposition during the review. The number of such cases is difficult to determine as there is no comprehensive reporting. However, *Intel/Tower Semiconductor* (2023),[16] *Applied Materials/Kokusai* Electric (2021)[17] and *Qualcomm/NXP (2018)*[18] were reportedly abandoned due to potential concerns from Chinese authorities. SAMR also explained that two transactions were withdrawn by the parties due to a failure to resolve SAMR's concerns in 2021 and 2022, although the parties were not named.[19] Also, *Erkang Pharmaceutical/Jiu Shi Pharmaceutical* (2019) fell through reportedly under pressure from SAMR.[20] Regardless, if we assume that there were approximately two

---

15 We have not included transactions abandoned by the parties in the face of regulatory difficulties due to data limitations. We would, however, note that both in the EU and the US, the intervention rate information we discuss includes a significant portion of cases abandoned before or after a complaint or litigation. Still, as explained, publicly available information suggests that few cases are abandoned in China due to competition concerns. Based on the limited information available, two cases a year abandoned due to an inability to resolve competition concerns seems to be a reasonable estimate, *see*, for example, National Anti-Monopoly Bureau 国家反垄断局, Zhongguo fan longduan zhifa niandu baogao (2022) 中国反垄断执法年度报告（2022）[China's Antitrust Enforcement Annual Report (2022)].

16 Anirban Sen, "Intel scraps $5.4 bln Tower deal after China review delay," Reuters, August 13, 2023, https://www.reuters.com/technology/intel-walk-away-54-bln-acquisition-tower-semiconductor-sources-2023-08-16/.

17 "China: Market regulation authority withholds approval for US firm Applied Materials' acquisition of Kokusai Electric," Global Trade Alert, March 21, 2021, https://www.globaltradealert.org/intervention/86463/fdi-entry-and-ownership-rule/china-market-regulation-authority-witholds-approval-for-us-firm-applied-materials-acquisition-of-kokusai-electric.

18 Michael Martina and Stephen Nellis, "Qualcomm ends $44 billion NXP bid after failing to win China approval," Reuters, July 26, 2018, https://www.reuters.com/article/technology/qualcomm-ends-44-billion-nxp-bid-after-failing-to-win-china-approval-idUSKBN1KF18X/.

19 *See*, National Anti-Monopoly Bureau国家反垄断局, Zhongguo fan longduan zhifa niandu baogao (2021) 中国反垄断执法年度报告(2021) [China's Antitrust Enforcement Annual Report (2021)] and National Anti-Monopoly Bureau国家反垄断局, Zhongguo fan longduan zhifa niandu baogao (2022) 中国反垄断执法年度报告（2022）[China's Antitrust Enforcement Annual Report (2022)]. Among the cases reportedly reviewed by SAMR during this period but where SAMR did not complete the review were *NVIDIA/Arm* (2022), and *DuPont/Rogers* (2022). It is possible that the two cases SAMR had in mind were these but there can be differing views as to whether parties withdrew a case because they anticipated insurmountable opposition from the regulator, because the commercial rationale for the deal had fallen away or because there was opposition from other regulators or a number of regulators in other jurisdictions.

20 SAMR disclosed in its 2019 annual enforcement report that it persuaded the parties in Erkang Pharmaceutical/Jiu Shi Pharmaceutical to abandon their merger plans. For Qualcomm/NXP, *see* footnote 19.

transactions a year abandoned by the parties during the regulatory review in China following some indication of competition concerns by the regulator, this would represent a potential increase of 0.3% in China's intervention rate, between 2017 to 2024.

18. Comparatively, the merger intervention rate in China is lower than that in the EU and the US. In the EU, the intervention rate (including Phase I remedies, Phase II remedies, Phase II prohibitions and Phase II withdrawals) was 4.7% from 2017 to 2024.[21] In the US, according to the Hart-Scott-Rodino Annual Report issued by the FTC and the US DOJ, the intervention rate was 1.6% from 2017 to 2023.[22] Figure 4 summarizes China merger enforcement statistics over this period and compares intervention rates with the EU and US.

Figure 4 | Intervention Rate in China, the EU (i.e., intervention by the EC), and the US 2017–2024

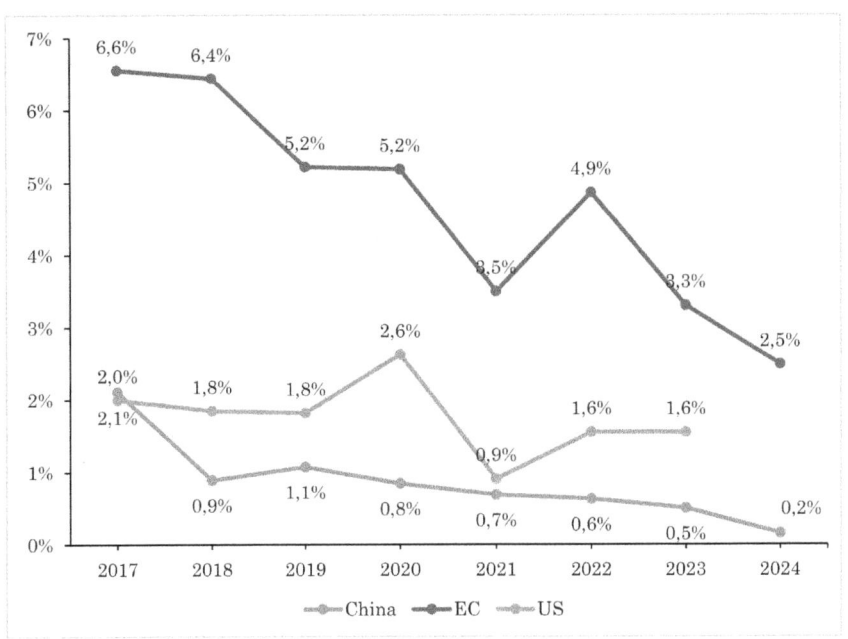

Source: SAMR and MOFCOM decisions, EC Merger Cases Statistics, Hart-Scott-Rodino Annual Reports

---

21 "Statistics on Mergers cases," European Commission, April 30, 2025, https://competition-policy.ec.europa.eu/mergers/statistics_en.

22 Federal Trade Commission, "Annual Competition Reports," accessed November 15, 2024, https://www.ftc.gov/policy/reports/annual-competition-reports. Possibly, when deals abandoned due to unsolved competition concerns (in 2023, a total of 11 cases were withdrawn including those for reasons unrelated to merger review) are factored in, the China intervention rate and the US intervention rate would be comparable.

19. Consistent with its less interventionist track record overall, SAMR is markedly less willing to block mergers. From 2017 to 2024, SAMR issued only one blocking decisions – as noted above. In contrast, the EC prohibited eight transactions during the period.[23] From 2017 to 2023, the US antitrust agencies initiated litigation in respect of 48 cases to prevent or undo mergers.[24] The UK prohibited 10 transactions from April 2017 to April 2024.[25] If propensity to block is the yardstick, SAMR clearly adopts a more cautious approach.

B. SAMR tends to use behavioral remedy to address competition concerns

20. SAMR has traditionally been more willing than its US and EU counterparts to accept behavioral remedies. This reflects SAMR's flexibility in approving pro-competitive transactions while encouraging the parties to propose creative and flexible solutions.

21. During the period 2017 to 2024, SAMR cleared 34 cases with remedies. As summarized in Table 1, only two cases have pure structural remedies – *Danfoss/Eaton* and *Dow Chemical/DuPont*, while the remaining 32 involved some elements of behavioral remedies. Specifically, SAMR imposed purely behavioral remedies in 21 cases and hybrid remedies (including both structural and behavioral remedies) in 11 instances.

Table 1 | SAMR Merger Remedy Classification, 2017-2024

Year	Cases	Type of remedy imposed by SAMR		
		Purely behavioral	Purely structural	Hybrid
2017	7	2	1	4
2018	4	1	0	3
2019	5	4	0	1
2020	4	3	0	1
2021	4	3	1	0
2022	5	4	0	1
2023	4	3	0	1
2024	1	1	0	0
Total	34	21	2	11

---

23 See, footnote 22.

24 See, footnote 23.

25 Competition and Markets Authority, "Transparency data – Merger inquiry outcome statistics," last modified April 10, 2025, https://www.gov.uk/government/publications/phase-1-merger-enquiry-outcomes.

22. SAMR's remedy approach exhibits predictable patterns in addressing standard competition concerns outlined in its decisions. For example, SAMR typically addresses horizontal concerns with structural remedies (often supplemented with behavioral remedies), while vertical and conglomerate issues are typically remedied with behavioral ones. In exceptional cases, SAMR has addressed horizontal concerns with only behavioral remedies (e.g., in II-VI/Finisar and SK Hynix/Intel's NAND and SSD business) but it has not used structural remedies to resolve a vertical or neighboring problem.

23. Also, SAMR consistently applies specific solutions for particular competition issues. Specifically,

- For input foreclosure (*e.g.*, *KLA-Tencor/Orbotech, II-VI/Coherent, ZF/WABCO, Cisco/Acacia*), SAMR requires continued supply of relevant inputs.

- For customer foreclosure, SAMR mandated continued multi-sourcing arrangements (*e.g.*, *II-VI/Coherent*).

- In conglomerate cases, SAMR typically prohibits bundling or tying and ensures product interoperability (*e.g.*, *KLA-Tencor/Orbotech, AMD/Xilinx, Broadcom/VMware*).

24. Behavioral remedies can be understood in the context of SAMR's responsiveness to stakeholder interests, addressing both customer concerns (e.g., supply continuity and interoperability) and industrial policy considerations presented by industry associations. In strategically important sectors like semiconductors and agriculture that receive heightened scrutiny, these behavioral remedies can directly alleviate these concerns by delivering concrete benefits to affected parties. For example, 23 of the 34 remedy cases included a FRAND supply commitment remedy, ensuring the continued supply of relevant products on *fair, reasonable, and non-discriminatory* terms.

C. Transactions in semiconductor and tech sector are under special scrutiny in China

25. In recent years, tech sector deals, especially in semiconductor, have been under close scrutiny by SAMR, accounting for nearly half of intervention cases. SAMR's intervention rate for semiconductor and tech transactions is significantly higher than the all-sector average. From 2019 to 2024, for which sector data are systematically reported, SAMR reviewed 283 tech sector cases,[26] with 4.2% subject to remedies, compared to the 0.8% overall intervention rate. Notably, the China intervention rate for technology cases (4.2%) nearly matches the EC average across all sections (4.1%) during 2019-2024.

---

26 SAMR started publishing systematic industry merger review statistics in China's Antitrust Enforcement Annual Report in 2019.

26. While semiconductor and tech transactions receive significant regulatory attention, over 95% of the cases in these sectors ultimately gain SAMR approval, with a substantial portion cleared through the simplified review process. Moreover, remedy cases in tech sector require roughly the same review time as non-tech cases, indicating no special delays for technology transactions. As shown in Figure 5, the average review time for tech case between 2017 to 2024 is 360 days for remedy cases in tech sector, and 371 days for those in non-tech sectors.

Figure 5 | Average Durations from Filing to Approval for Intervention Cases, 2017-2024

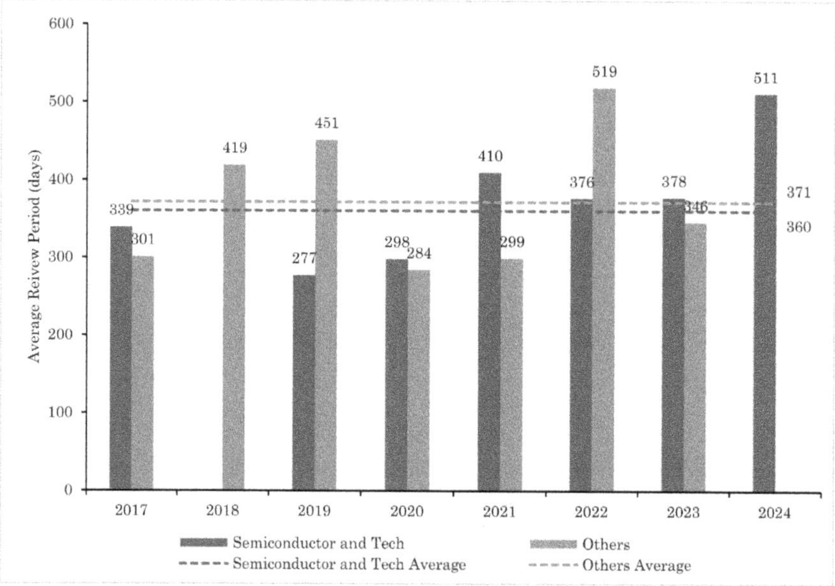

Source: SAMR decisions and statistics, summarized by the authors

27. While SAMR's heightened scrutiny of semiconductor transactions may reflect geopolitical influences, it can also be explained by traditional competition-based considerations such as industry concentration levels or barriers to entry. It is important to note that many of the semiconductor companies are based in the US, while having substantial customer bases in China. Figure 6 shows the industry distribution of intervention cases from 2017 to 2024, revealing that 82% of the semiconductor sector cases involved at least one US merging party.[27]

---

[27] We adopt a broad industry definition because one of the main data sources, China's Antitrust Enforcement Annual Report, updated its industry classification after its first publication. In 2019, the relevant industry is Information and Communication ("信息通信行业"). In 2020-2022, the relevant industries are Internet ("互联网行业") and Semiconductors ("半导体行业").

In other words, China's focus on semiconductor transactions involving US companies is simply because there are more US companies in this space.

Figure 6 | Percentage of remedy cases involving at least one US party,[28] 2017-2024

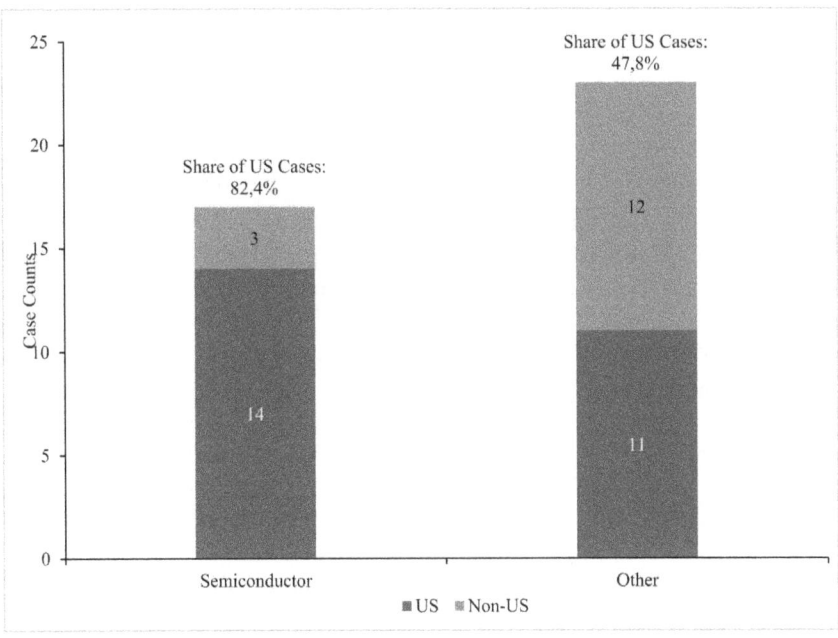

Source: SAMR decisions and statistics, summarized by the authors

28. For tech-related remedy cases, China's key concerns about competition risks include merging parties gaining access to rivals' confidential information in vertical or conglomerate mergers, reduced interoperability with competitors' products in tech deals, or diminished R&D incentives. Under the AML, SAMR must evaluate how mergers impact China's economic development. Semiconductors play a vital role in China's economy, being integral to electronics, automobiles, and countless everyday goods. While China represents more than half of global chip sales, it remains heavily dependent on imports. It is not surprising that amid threats of decoupling and tech rivalry the Chinese authorities pay close attention to these deals.

---

28 In addition to 34 conditional approvals and one blocked transaction, the statistics in this figure also include five cases confirmed withdrawn due to competition concerns based on public information.

IV. Conclusion

29. In an era of unprecedented global uncertainties marked by rising geopolitical tensions and trade conflicts, China's role for global mergers and acquisitions continues to be important. Contrary to common misconceptions about prolonged timelines and excessive regulatory intervention driven by industrial policy, our analysis of enforcement statistics reveals a timely and predictable merger review process in China.

30. During the 2017-2024 period, the large majority of cases in China are reviewed through a fast-track mechanism, which typically grants approval within 40 days. Even for those highly complex transactions where remedies were required, China's review time is comparable to the EU and the US.

31. China's merger intervention rate remains below 1%, lower than the EU and the US. SAMR rarely blocks mergers, preferring behavioral remedies to address its concerns. Although transactions in semiconductor and tech space have been under scrutiny in China, 95% of the cases have been cleared without any remedies and none was blocked.

32. In summary, during the period of significant uncertainties, global mergers, even in semiconductor and tech space involving US companies, remain eminently doable in China. Merger reviews are typically conducted in a timely and predictable manner. SAMR's tendency to favor behavioral remedies offering parties multiple pathways to approval.

Understanding China's Merger Control Through Industry Lenses: Market Trends and Review Procedures

JET DENG[*]

Senior Partner, Dacheng Law Offices, Beijing

Abstract

Since the promulgation of the Anti-Monopoly Law (AML) in 2008, China's merger control regime has matured into one of the most significant and influential systems globally, being a critical consideration for international business strategies. This chapter examines China's merger control framework through an industry-specific lens, focusing on the real estate, finance, natural gas, and manufacturing sectors. Each industry exhibits distinct market structures, competitive dynamics, regulatory priorities, and procedural pathways. This chapter emphasizes that sectoral dynamics and policy considerations now play a decisive role in merger outcomes, and that proactive, well-informed engagement with China's regulatory authorities is vital for transaction success.

---

[*] Dr Zhisong Jet Deng is the Senior Partner of Dacheng Beijing Office and the chair of Competition and Antitrust Practice, Dacheng China Region and has been recognized by Chambers & Partners as one of the "Leading Lawyers for Antitrust Practice in Asia-Pacific" (2014-2025). The author deeply honored to have been invited to contribute to this volume commemorating Dr. Huang Yong's forty-year teaching and scholarly career in China's antitrust law. Dr. Huang – one of the foremost pioneers in the theoretical construction of China's Anti-Monopoly Law, from its initial proposal and legislative drafting through the publication of implementation rules and the establishment of competition authorities – has, over the past decades, provided visionary leadership and transformative insights that have shaped both theory and practice in this field. His mentorship during my Juris Doctor studies and legal practice was invaluable, and this chapter stands as a modest testament to his profound guidance and enduring legacy.

Understanding China's Merger Control Through Industry Lenses:
Market Trends and Review Procedures

I. Introduction

1. Over 150 jurisdictions worldwide have established formal merger control regimes, reflecting the widespread adoption of pre-merger notification and review processes to safeguard competition. Among these, China's merger control system, established by the *Anti-Monopoly Law of the People's Republic of China* (*AML*) which came into effect on August 1, 2008, has rapidly evolved into one of the most influential systems globally. To date, China's antitrust authority[1] has reviewed over 5,000 merger filings – both domestic and cross-border – across a broad spectrum of industries over the past sixteen years.

2. Under China's mandatary pre-merger notification system, transactions – including mergers, equity or asset acquisitions and the establishment of joint ventures – that meet defined turnover thresholds[2] must be notified to the State Administration for Market Regulation (SAMR) and cannot be completed until SAMR grants approval. In practice, these thresholds capture a broad array of deals, including many foreign-to-foreign transactions where the parties maintain significant operations in China. The 2022 amendment to the *AML* significantly boosted penalties for closing a transaction without approval, the maximum fine from RMB 500,000 to as much as 10 percent of the undertaking's prior-year revenue. Given these steep sanctions, multinationals – even those pursuing M&A entirely outside China – gradually exercise heightened diligence to ensure compliance.

3. With the solid legal foundation, comprehensive enforcement tools[3], and decades of practical experience and the accumulated experience, China's merger review practice has evolved into a highly sophisticated regime. It now may employ detailed economic analyses that account for market dynamics, potential foreclosure, coordinated effects, and innovation impacts, with structural and behavioral remedies increasingly imposed in strategically important sectors. Moreover, the regime blends pure competition objectives with broader policy goals: industrial policy, national economic strategies such as "Made in China 2025", and even geopolitical

---

1 Initially, the Ministry of Commerce (MOFCOM) was responsible for merger review, but since the 2018 institutional reform, this authority has been consolidated under the State Administration for Market Regulation (SAMR). This shift streamlined the review process and centralized competition enforcement under one agency.

2 The State Council of China revised the thresholds triggering notification obligation in 2024: (1) the total global turnover of all the undertakings participating in the concentration in the last accounting year exceeds RMB 12 billion, and at least two of these undertakings each have a turnover of more than RMB 800 million within China in the last accounting year; or

(2) the total turnover within China of all the undertakings participating in the concentration in the last accounting year exceeds RMB 4 billion, and at least two of these undertakings each have a turnover of more than RMB 800 million within China in the last accounting year.

3 On December 20, 2024, SAMR formally released China's first special guideline document for the review of concentrations between undertakings, *the Guidelines for the Review of Horizontal Concentrations between Undertakings*, which comprehensively summarizes the practical experience of China's antitrust authority in the review of horizontal concentrations.

concerns now shape the depth and outcomes of reviews – especially in sensitive technology and infrastructure transactions.

4. Adopting a practitioner's perspective, this chapter aims to dissect China's merger control practices through an industry-specific lens, demonstrating how sector-specific dynamics shape both procedural pathways and substantive analysis adopted by SAMR. The chapter is divided into four main sections. It begins with an in-depth, sector-by-sector review – covering real estate, finance, natural gas, and manufacturing – to outline each industry's market structure, transaction trends, and regulatory scrutiny (Part II). It then identifies emerging regulatory trends, such as the increasing complexity of cross-border transactions, the growing policy sensitivity in merger assessments, and the evolution of SAMR's enforcement strategies (Part III). This chapter concludes by summarizing key findings, discussing future directions of China's merger control policy, and offering practical recommendations for businesses navigating this multifaceted landscape (Part IV).

II. Industry-Specific Analysis of Merger Control Procedures

5. This section focuses on four key industries: real estate, finance, natural gas, and manufacturing. Through detailed industry analysis of merger cases from 2021 to July 2024[4], the section seeks to provide both a conceptual understanding and practical insights for practitioners dealing with China's merger notification and review system.

A. Real estate sector

6. The real estate sector in China stands as one of the most vital pillars of the national economy, contributing significantly to GDP growth, employment, and urbanization. It is a highly complex and multifaceted industry, encompassing land acquisition, project development, sales, leasing, property management, and ancillary services such as maintenance and renovation.

7. Statistically, from 2021 to July 2024, the real estate sector accounted for approximately 8% of all merger notifications to the SAMR, totaling 189 cases.

1. Market structure and characteristics

8. The notable volume of merger cases reflects the sector's historically high transactional activity. Nevertheless, it should be recognized that the sector

---

[4] This chapter utilizes cases publicly disclosed by the SAMR between 2021 and July 2024. SAMR, Merger Cases Public Notice, 9 May 2025 (https://www.samr.gov.cn/fldes/ajgs/index.html).

has undergone substantial transformation in recent years, largely due to governmental tightening measures introduced to curb financial risks and prevent housing market bubbles.

9. Real estate markets in China are highly localized. Due to variations in economic development, population density, land use regulations, and consumer preferences, the competitive conditions in metropolis such as Beijing are vastly different from those in smaller inland cities. Regionalism deeply influences market definition in merger reviews, often resulting in city-level or even district-level market delineations.

10. Moreover, the sector features a long and intricate value chain, where different firms specialize in upstream land acquisition and development, midstream construction and marketing, and downstream property operation and management. This segmentation has historically resulted in a fragmented market structure, with relatively low concentration ratios in most submarkets, especially downstream services.

11. That fragmentation is changing. Since around 2022, the real estate sector has entered a phase of consolidation driven by financial distress among private developers, state-led intervention initiatives, and an influx of foreign investors seeking stable assets in premium locations. Although concentration levels remain uneven across regions and segments, the sector is clearly shifting toward a more concentrated market structure.

2. Key features of SAMR's scrutiny

12. The review of real estate sector transactions by the SAMR displays several consistent procedural and substantive features.

13. First, due to the localized nature of real estate markets mentioned above, transactions are typically assessed within narrowly defined geographic scopes. This approach recognizes that housing and commercial property markets operate within confined demand-supply dynamics, largely immune to competitive pressure from distant locations. Therefore, when a merger involves developers or property managers operating in non-overlapping cities, the transaction often raises no substantive competition concerns.

14. Second, the majority of real estate transactions are processed through the simplified procedure, given the generally low market shares of individual parties within defined markets. Even when competitive overlaps exist, regulators typically find limited concerns due to the high degree of market fragmentation and the presence of numerous alternative players. According to public data, nearly 80% of real estate sector notifications between 2021 and 2024 were cleared under the simplified framework.

15. Third, transactions involving purely foreign-to-foreign mergers rarely pose issues unless the acquired assets include substantial commercial holdings in

major Chinese cities. Even in those cases, market shares are usually small relative to the total volume of real estate activities in metropolitan markets.

16. Fourth, market definition and review standards are highly mature and predictable. Real estate is a traditional industry in China that has undergone rapid development and extensive regulatory oversight. Both the definition of relevant markets and the focus areas of regulatory scrutiny have become standardized and well-established. As a result, the level of technical uncertainty in the review process is low, and the outcomes of merger reviews are generally predictable, easing the compliance burden on notifying parties.

3. Industry consolidation trends and regulatory implications

17. The competitive landscape of China's real estate sector is undergoing profound changes, which have significant implications for merger control review.

18. Following the introduction of the "Three Red Lines" policy in 2020 – a set of debt limits imposed on real estate developers – financial pressures mounted on private developers. The policy triggered a wave of defaults and liquidity crises, leading to a surge in distressed asset sales and consolidation activities.

19. State-owned enterprises (SOEs) and government-affiliated funds have played a prominent role in acquiring distressed projects, both to stabilize markets and to ensure social and financial stability. In parallel, foreign investors have demonstrated sustained interest in acquiring real estate assets such as premium office buildings in China.

20. Looking ahead, it is expected that the trend toward industry consolidation will continue, although subject to fluctuations depending on macroeconomic conditions, regulatory interventions, and the evolution of urbanization patterns. Regulatory reviews are likely to remain relatively favorable for non-overlapping or limited-overlap transactions but may become more stringent for deals involving leading players in saturated submarkets.

B. Finance sector

21. China's financial sector has evolved into a diversified, highly competitive industry encompassing banking, securities, insurance, asset management, and various non-bank financial services. Today, the sector includes both large state-owned financial conglomerates and a multitude of smaller, privately owned or regionally focused institutions.

22. From 2021 to July 2024, there were around 135 merger notifications in the financial sector.

Understanding China's Merger Control Through Industry Lenses:
Market Trends and Review Procedures

1. Market structure and characteristics

23. As China's financial industry has matured, the market landscape has become increasingly stratified and fiercely competitive. The banking sector exhibits a clear hierarchy, with the five major state-owned commercial banks at the top – each a global and domestic systemically important bank – followed by nationwide joint-stock banks and a host of regional institutions such as city commercial banks and rural financial organizations occupying complementary positions. Among them, state-owned banks dominate due to their significant scale and capital strength.

24. The securities industry also faces intense competition. Leading brokerage firms maintain their market edge through strong comprehensive capabilities, although overall industry concentration remains relatively low.

25. Across the financial sector, smaller and medium-sized institutions – particularly regional banks and boutique brokerages – face mounting operational pressures. Many have chosen either to exit the market or to merge with larger peers to achieve the scale and resources needed for survival and growth.

2. Key features of SAMR's scrutiny

26. Merger control reviews in the financial sector in China are shaped by several unique factors linked to the sector's regulatory environment, policy priorities, and competitive dynamics.

27. First, despite the significant market shares commanded by top-tier institutions, most merger filings are processed through the simplified procedure. This outcome arises because financial products and services are often segmented by type (e.g., retail banking vs. corporate banking, life insurance vs. health insurance), geographical coverage, and client base. Thus, even when major institutions merge, overlaps may be limited or confined to non-problematic levels in specific market segments.

28. Second, horizontal mergers prevail: larger, financially sound institutions frequently acquire smaller, distressed counterparts to expand geographically, diversify their customer portfolios, or integrate advanced technologies. These transactions typically enhance market stability and service quality, aligning with both competition and financial-stability objectives. Such mergers rarely raise substantial competition concerns because they often strengthen stability and enhance service quality, aligning with policy objectives.

29. Third, cross-sector regulation adds complexity. In addition to the SAMR's antitrust review, financial regulators such as the China Banking and Insurance Regulatory Commission (CBIRC) and the China Securities Regulatory Commission (CSRC) exercise licensing and prudential

oversight. Transactions involving systemically important institutions or complex cross-ownership structures often undergo closer scrutiny to safeguard financial stability.

30. Fourth, pure foreign-to-foreign transactions occasionally require merger notification in China if the involved parties generate sufficient revenue domestically. Although such transactions often receive fast-track clearance due to limited competitive overlaps, they may attract attention if the merger involves institutions critical to China's financial infrastructure, such as global custodians or major institutional asset managers.

3. Industry consolidation trends and regulatory implications

31. Consolidation in China's financial sector has been both cyclical and policy-driven. Four distinct waves of consolidation can be observed[5]:
    - **First Wave (1995–2002):** Triggered by the separation of banking and securities businesses, as part of efforts to impose a clearer regulatory framework and professionalize financial institutions.
    - **Second Wave (2005–2008):** Catalyzed by the fallout from systemic risks and scandals, leading to regulatory interventions that encouraged mergers among troubled institutions.
    - **Third Wave (2008–2015):** Following the global financial crisis, consolidation focused on strengthening the competitiveness of major players and fostering the emergence of national champions capable of international expansion.
    - **Fourth Wave (2016–Present):** Characterized by market-driven consolidation aimed at achieving economies of scale, technological innovation, and risk mitigation under tighter regulatory supervision.

32. More recently, policy initiatives such as the 2020 "New Asset Management Rules" have placed additional pressures on financial institutions to improve capital adequacy, manage non-performing assets more effectively, and optimize balance sheets, further driving merger activity.

33. From a regulatory perspective, China's authorities have adopted a generally supportive attitude towards mergers that enhance systemic stability, expand access to financial services in underserved regions, or promote financial innovation. However, they have simultaneously emphasized the need to avoid excessive market concentration, especially in critical areas such as payment systems, wealth management, or interbank markets.

34. Looking ahead, China's ongoing financial liberalization, including the removal of foreign ownership caps in securities, insurance, and asset

---

5   Fudan Development Institute, Frontiers of Financial Research | The Wave of Mergers and Restructuring Among Financial Institutions, 9 May 2025 (https://fddi.fudan.edu.cn/b4/ff/c21253a701695/page.htm).

management sectors, will likely increase both the frequency and complexity of cross-border merger cases. Foreign institutions seeking to acquire or consolidate operations in China must be prepared for careful regulatory navigation, balancing antitrust, national security, and prudential regulatory concerns.

C. Natural gas sector

35. The natural gas sector in China is a critical component of the national energy strategy. The industry spans an extensive and vertically integrated value chain, encompassing upstream exploration and production, midstream transportation and storage, and downstream distribution and sales.
36. From 2021 to July 2024, there were around 77 merger notifications in the natural gas sector.

1. Market structure and characteristics

37. Upstream activities of the natural gas sector are dominated by a few large state-owned enterprises (SOEs), particularly China National Petroleum Corporation (CNPC), Sinopec, and China National Offshore Oil Corporation (CNOOC). These players control the majority of natural gas production, both conventional and unconventional, including coalbed methane and shale gas.
38. The midstream segment, particularly long-distance pipeline transportation, historically operated under a natural monopoly model. The creation of PipeChina (China Oil & Gas Piping Network Corporation) in 2019 marked a significant step toward reform, aimed at providing open and non-discriminatory access to pipeline infrastructure.
39. Downstream distribution, involving city gas companies delivering natural gas to industrial, commercial, and residential consumers, is relatively fragmented but exhibits localized monopolies. Typically, a single company dominates distribution within a given city or urban district, often operating under exclusive concession agreements granted by municipal authorities.
40. Barriers to entry in the natural gas sector are considerable. High capital requirements, complex regulatory licensing, technological demands for safe extraction and transport, and long project gestation periods all deter new entrants, particularly in upstream and midstream segments.
41. These structural features create a market with high concentration at the production and transport levels, and moderate to high local concentration at the distribution level – a configuration that could lead to competition concerns during merger reviews.

2. Key features of SAMR's scrutiny

42. Merger transactions in the natural gas sector typically present more complex regulatory challenges compared to sectors like real estate or general manufacturing. Several procedural and substantive characteristics of SAMR's review stand out.

43. First, vertical integration prevail: mergers often involve upstream producers cooperating with downstream distributors to secure stable sales channels or downstream companies investing in upstream assets to ensure reliable supply. Vertical transactions trigger regulatory concerns about foreclosure effects, where an integrated entity might restrict or condition access to essential inputs or customers to disadvantage competitors.

44. Second, transactions involving upstream production or midstream transport assets generally undergo normal review procedures rather than simplified ones. Given the high market shares and the concern of market power abuse, SAMR often requires detailed economic analyses, including the evaluation of input foreclosure and customer foreclosure risks.

45. Third, the downstream city gas distribution markets are typically defined on a highly localized basis. Even though the sector appears fragmented at a national level, individual city markets are often dominated by a single supplier, raising potential unilateral effects concerns in cases of horizontal mergers between distributors in neighboring areas.

46. Fourth, merger reviews in this sector often take longer than average due to the need to coordinate with other governmental bodies, such as the National Energy Administration (NEA) and National Development and Reform Commissions (NDRCs), especially when the transactions involve state assets, strategic infrastructure, or large-scale energy supply agreements.

3. Industry consolidation trends and regulatory implications

47. The Chinese natural gas sector is a highly regulated industry where the government exercises significant control over key areas such as pricing mechanisms, market access, and the utilization of infrastructure. As a result, the number of new market entrants remains limited, and the competitive landscape is relatively stable.[6] This is particularly evident in the upstream (exploration and production) and midstream (pipeline transportation and storage) segments, where barriers to entry are notably high.

48. At present, market consolidation is primarily driven by vertical cooperation. Typical examples include long-term, stable supply relationships between upstream producers and downstream players such as city gas distributors or

---

6   In recent years, China has introduced a series of policies and regulations to promote the opening up of the oil and gas market to competition, in order to achieve the goal of "regulating the middle and liberalizing the two ends", but the results have been mediocre.

end-users. In contrast, horizontal mergers and acquisitions are relatively rare in the domestic market, with pure horizontal transactions mostly occurring among foreign enterprises, even if they are linked to the Chinese market.

49. Given the current regulatory environment and industry dynamics, the competitive landscape is expected to remain largely unchanged in the near term. Vertical collaboration will likely continue to be the preferred strategy for companies seeking to optimize their positions across the value chain and enhance market resilience, while large-scale horizontal consolidation or major restructuring appears unlikely in the short run.

D. Manufacturing sector

50. Manufacturing remains the backbone of China's economy, accounting for nearly 30% of the national GDP and employing hundreds of millions of workers. The sector spans an extraordinary range of industries, from traditional heavy industries such as steel and petrochemicals to advanced sectors like electronics, automotive, biotechnology, and renewable energy.

1. Market structure and characteristics

51. The manufacturing landscape in China is highly diversified and characterized by varying degrees of market concentration depending on the sub-sector. Traditional sectors such as textiles, machinery, and basic chemicals are generally fragmented, with numerous small- and medium-sized enterprises (SMEs) competing across national and regional markets.

52. In contrast, high-tech manufacturing sectors, including semiconductors, electric vehicles, and specialized chemicals, have seen the emergence of dominant players, often supported by state-led industrial policies aimed at building globally competitive national champions.

53. China's deep integration into global supply chains further shapes competitiveness: many firms serve as original equipment manufacturers (OEMs) for multinationals or are expanding their own brands abroad.

54. The past decade has witnessed a gradual consolidation trend, driven by the need to achieve economies of scale, enhance innovation capacities, and meet increasingly stringent environmental, quality, and labor standards.

2. Key features of SAMR's scrutiny

55. In the context of merger control, manufacturing transactions exhibit several recurring patterns.

56. First, most mergers are reviewed under the simplified procedure. The general fragmentation of manufacturing markets results in low combined market shares, minimizing substantive competition concerns in most

cases. Simplified procedure cases often clear within 30 to 45 days from acceptance.

57. Second, defining the relevant market can present complex technical challenges. The breadth of products, technological differentiation, and vertical integration across production stages require careful analysis. Authorities often segment markets based on product types, production processes, or end-use applications. For instance, the lithium-ion battery market is subdivided by chemical composition (e.g., NMC, LFP batteries) rather than treated as a single homogenous market.

58. Third, although the manufacturing sector is extensive and diverse, most sub-markets remain highly fragmented with relatively low concentration levels. Numerous players and distributed market shares mean that many transactions do not significantly reduce competition. As a result, unless the transaction involves highly concentrated sub-sectors or market-leading companies, most deals proceed through the review process without triggering major competitive concerns.

59. Forth, for industries deemed strategically important – most notably semiconductors – SAMR routinely assesses not only competitive effects but also material concerns around supply-chain security, technology transfer and national economic interests. As a result, a disproportionate share of conditional clearances in manufacturing M&A involve high-tech deals, where remedies often address access to key inputs, safeguard downstream chip production, or ring-fence critical R&D assets.

3. Industry consolidation trends and regulatory implications

60. The current trend of market concentration in China's manufacturing sector is primarily characterized by horizontal integration in traditional industries as well as vertical cooperation along the value chain. On the horizontal front, companies seek to expand scale and increase market share through mergers, acquisitions, and restructurings, thereby enhancing cost control capabilities and market presence. Vertical cooperation, meanwhile, is increasingly reflected in strategic partnerships and joint ventures between upstream raw material suppliers and downstream manufacturers, as well as between brand owners and distributors. These arrangements aim to build more efficient and integrated supply chain ecosystems while sharing risks and improving resilience.

61. At the same time, driven by the global trend towards manufacturing transformation and upgrading, Chinese enterprises are accelerating their shift towards technological advancement and digitalization. Smart manufacturing has gained momentum, with an increasing adoption of cutting-edge technologies such as the Industrial Internet of Things (IIoT), big data, artificial intelligence (AI), and advanced analytics. These innovations

are reshaping products, enhancing production efficiency, and optimizing service models across the industry.

62. Furthermore, as the domestic market approaches saturation – particularly in mature sectors where capacity utilization has reached high levels – many enterprises are gradually embracing an international expansion strategy. Through initiatives such as overseas investments, acquisitions of foreign companies, and the development of global sales networks, Chinese manufacturers are actively pursuing globalization to tap into new growth opportunities and strengthen their competitive edge on the world stage.

III. Emerging Trends and Practical Considerations

63. China's merger control review process exhibits distinct, industry-specific characteristics, with regulatory focus and priorities varying significantly across sectors.

64. First, as China's merger control regime continues to mature, regulatory priorities and enforcement practices have become increasingly tailored to the unique dynamics and risks of individual industries. For example, transactions in the natural gas industry typically draw scrutiny regarding the transmission of market power through vertical deals and potential foreclosure risks downstream. By contrast, manufacturing sector transactions primarily focus on the precise definition of relevant markets, particularly regarding segmented product markets.

65. In addition, China's competition authorities shift their sectoral priorities over time: public utilities, pharmaceuticals, building materials, internet, new energy vehicles (NEVs), and raw materials have long been key areas of enforcement attention. Since 2024, regulators have further intensified their focus on natural monopoly industries – such as gas, water, electricity, and heating – imposing stricter oversight and more detailed review procedures on both antitrust investigations and merger filings in these sectors.[7]

66. Second, in an era of shifting geopolitical and economic landscapes, cross-border transactions have grown markedly more complex, introducing new layers of regulatory scrutiny and strategic considerations for merger control. These transactions now form an important part of merger control filings in China. On one hand, beyond antitrust review, deals may now trigger foreign subsidies regulation (FSR), foreign direct investment (FDI) screening, and national security review. On the other hand, the difficulty of merger reviews has risen, with political factors, international relations,

---

[7] Xinhuanet, Breaking Monopolies to Stimulate Development and Strengthening Enforcement to Improve People's Wellbeing – Solid and Effective Advancement of Antitrust Enforcement by Market Regulation Authorities in the First Half of 2024, 9 May 2025 (http://www.xinhuanet.com/enterprise/20240806/e2e81c8 a58f843778ccf3d2e8a85dfc8/c.html).

and industrial policy considerations playing a more prominent role in regulatory assessments.

67. According to Chinese merger control rules, even purely offshore transactions without a direct nexus to the Chinese market must be notified if the parties' turnover in China meets the relevant thresholds, and such transactions cannot be implemented prior to clearance. As China remains the world's second-largest economy and many foreign enterprises operate significant local businesses, it is critical for parties to cross-border deals to carefully assess notification obligations and integrate China's review process into the overall transaction timetable. Furthermore, cross-border deals often require multiple merger filings in different jurisdictions. Coordinating these parallel filings to ensure smooth and timely clearances is an important challenge that dealmakers must proactively address.

68. Third, given the increasingly sophisticated and nuanced nature of China's merger control regime, international practitioners must adopt a strategic and well-informed approach to ensure smooth navigation of the notification and review processes. Even for purely offshore transactions, the review process can take substantial time. Deals qualifying for simplified procedure may be cleared in approximately 40 days after submission, while cases under normal procedure without serious competition concerns typically require 3 to 6 months. Therefore, transaction parties should incorporate ample time in their deal planning to accommodate merger clearance and avoid delays in closing.

69. Moreover, different industries face different regulatory focuses during review. It is essential for filing parties to tailor their submissions to address sector-specific issues and proactively prepare for potential competitive concerns. Maintaining effective and transparent communication with the authority is also critical. In appropriate cases, pre-filing consultations can help clarify key issues such as market definition and competitive assessment, thus facilitating a smoother review process and increasing the likelihood of timely approval.

IV. Conclusion

70. China's merger control is deeply shaped by sector-specific dynamics. In sectors like real estate and manufacturing, where markets are often fragmented and competition remains vibrant, merger reviews tend to be relatively straightforward and predictable. By contrast, in finance and natural gas, where systemic risks, public welfare considerations, and infrastructure bottlenecks are prevalent, merger reviews are more complex, requiring deeper substantive assessments.

71. The future of China's merger control landscape will be shaped by several ongoing and emerging trends. These include the rising prominence of non-traditional competition concerns (such as data concentration and innovation impact), the heightened scrutiny of transactions in critical sectors, the growing technical sophistication of regulatory reviews, and the increasing procedural and substantive complexity of cross-border merger cases.

72. Companies engaging in mergers with a China nexus must prepare for a dynamic regulatory environment, where traditional antitrust theories coexist with industrial policy imperatives and geopolitical realities. Anticipating regulatory concerns, engaging early and constructively with authorities, and maintaining flexibility in transaction structuring and remedy negotiation will be essential to navigating this evolving landscape successfully.

73. Over the past sixteen years, China's merger control regime has made remarkable strides toward maturity and global significance. The SAMR has developed into a competent and increasingly transparent regulator, capable of handling complex domestic and international transactions. For businesses and practitioners, mastering China's sector-specific merger control landscape is not merely a matter of legal compliance, but a strategic imperative. Those who understand the intersection of competition, policy, and practice will be best positioned to seize opportunities and navigate challenges in the world's second-largest economy.

China's Antitrust Litigation Practice: Review and Outlook

ZHAN HAO[*]

Managing Partner, AnJie Broad Law Firm

SONG YING

Partner, AnJie Broad Law Firm

Abstract

This note highlights the growing momentum of antitrust litigation in China. In 2024, there was a marked increase in both the volume of antitrust civil cases and the number of rulings in favor of plaintiffs, particularly in cases where monopolistic conduct was identified. In parallel, administrative litigation has played an increasingly important role in reviewing antitrust enforcement, helping to clarify substantive standards such as the identification of monopoly agreements and fine calculations, while also strengthening procedural safeguards in areas such as hearing rights, service, and the completeness of administrative records. Together, these trends contribute to a more rigorous and transparent enforcement environment. Notably, the landmark T Pharma case marked China's first judicial review of a merger control decision and set important precedents for the scope of SAMR's powers and the normative framework for merger assessment. The court affirmed that conditional approvals are permissible even in voluntary filings, that prohibition is not the preferred remedy, and that the focus of merger review lies in addressing competition concerns directly arising from the transaction.

---

[*] Zhan Hao is Managing Partner at AnJie Broad Law Firm and serves as Vice Chairman and China Ambassador of the ICC China Competition Commission. Song Ying is Partner at AnJie Broad Law Firm and a part-time Master of Laws tutor at North China University of Technology.

I. Overview and Trends in China's Antitrust Civil Litigation

A. Case volume and types

1. In recent years – especially in 2024 – the number of antitrust civil cases heard and decided by Chinese courts has risen sharply. According to data released by the Supreme People's Court ("SPC"), from 2013 to 2024, Chinese courts nationwide accepted 1,145 first-instance civil cases alleging monopoly and concluded 1,071 cases.

2. Since its establishment on January 1, 2019, the Intellectual Property Court of Supreme People's Court ("SPC IP Court") has played an increasingly important role in this area. Between 2019 and 2024, it accepted 282 antitrust civil and administrative appeals and concluded 243; in 2024 alone it accepted 137 antitrust appeals[1] and concluded 97[2], meaning nearly half of all such appeals filed since the court's founding were received in a single year. The 2024 conclusion rate approached 40%.

3. The number of newly received monopoly cases by the SPC IP Court has been on the rise year by year. In 2024, it newly received 79 monopoly cases, among which there were 42 monopoly civil disputes and 20 monopoly administrative disputes in the newly received civil second-instance substantive cases.[3]

4. A significant increase has also been observed in the number of cases where monopolistic conduct was actually found. In 2024, courts nationwide identified monopolistic behavior in 31 cases, more than double the number in 2023. The SPC IP Court alone found monopolistic behavior in 17 cases – a 4.6-fold increase from the previous year.[4]

5. Common issues include whether a contract constitutes a horizontal monopoly agreement and must therefore be invalidated, whether monopoly-related profits should be disgorged, and whether and in what amount compensation should be awarded. Vertical monopoly agreement disputes often arise from distribution arrangements between manufacturers and dealers, with many brought as private damages suits following public enforcement actions.

6. Another noteworthy development in 2024 was China's first-ever administrative lawsuit challenging a merger control decision by the State Administration for Market Regulation ("SAMR"). Although the court

---

[1] See https://ipc.court.gov.cn/zh-cn/news/view-3486.html.

[2] Calculated based on the SPC's two announcements, see https://www.court.gov.cn/zixun/xiangqing/462891.html and https://ipc.court.gov.cn/zh-cn/news/view-3486.html.

[3] See https://enipc.court.gov.cn/zh-cn/news/view-4233.html.

[4] See https://www.court.gov.cn/zixun/xiangqing/462891.html.

7. These statistics and cases demonstrate that antitrust litigation in China is becoming increasingly active. Chinese courts – especially the SPC IP Court – are playing a more active and authoritative role in adjudicating antitrust disputes, with rising case volumes and more frequent findings of monopolistic conduct, particularly a rising proportion of rulings in favor of plaintiffs. Businesses are increasingly leveraging antitrust lawsuits as a proactive strategy, not only as a means of defense but also to shape competitive dynamics, challenge unfair practices, and seek damages. Together, these trends reflect a maturing legal environment where both courts and market participants are more engaged in the enforcement of antitrust laws.

upheld SAMR's decision, the case marks a growing willingness among companies to engage in strategic litigation over merger reviews.

B. Publication of new judicial interpretation and typical cases

8. In the past few years, the SPC has actively released guidance and typical cases to provide clarity and consistency in the application of law, thereby enhancing both civil adjudication and administrative antitrust litigation.

9. On June 24, 2024, the SPC promulgated the Interpretation on Several Issues concerning the Application of Law in the Trial of Monopoly-related Civil Dispute Cases (the "2024 Antitrust Judicial Interpretation"), which took effect from July 1, 2024, marking its first comprehensive overhaul of the 2012 rules on antitrust civil disputes. The 2024 Antitrust Judicial Interpretation systematizes both procedural mechanisms and substantive legal standards, providing a more unified and coherent framework for adjudicating monopoly-related disputes.

10. In parallel, the SPC has continued to expand its publication of guiding cases and typical cases, which serve to supplement and refine China's antitrust rules. These cases not only guide civil adjudication but also offer reference value in administrative antitrust litigation. Since the establishment of the SPC IP Court, the SPC has released three guiding cases and six batches totaling 37 typical antitrust cases. Notably, in 2024 alone, two batches comprising nine typical antitrust cases were published (see *Table 1, Items 1-9*). These releases have played a vital role in promoting consistency, improving efficiency in adjudication, and reinforcing fair competition in the market.

11. The published and observed cases span a wide range of industries, particularly those concerning public welfare and emerging sectors. These include pharmaceuticals and healthcare, early childhood education, driver training, taxi operations, auto sales, construction materials, real estate services, agricultural markets, food, residential gas supply, and cable television. There has also been a notable increase in cases involving digital platforms

and new technologies, such as wireless communications and internet-based services. High-frequency dispute areas include:

- **"Choose-one-from-two" practices** and **algorithmic price discrimination** in the internet sector;
- **Patent settlement agreements** and **vertical monopoly agreements** in the pharmaceutical industry;
- **Market dominance abuse** by API manufacturers against formulation producers;
- **Tying and excessive pricing** by public utilities in sectors like water, electricity, and gas;
- **Refusal to license** and **excessive royalties** leading to antitrust-IP intersection disputes.

12. Another significant trend is the rising success rate of plaintiffs. In 2024, among the SPC's published Typical Cases Involving Antitrust and Unfair Competition, four monopoly cases resulted in appellate victories for the plaintiffs. All four concerned sectors with strong public interest implications, such as telecommunications, broadcasting, and retail dining, signaling a more assertive judicial stance in substantively examining monopolistic conduct and rebalancing civil rights and obligations. Additionally, the clarification under 2024 Antitrust Judicial Interpretation of follow-on litigation procedures and evidentiary standards has significantly improved plaintiffs' chances of prevailing in court.

Table 1 | Antitrust Civil and Administrative Cases Published by the SPC in 2024[5]

No.	Case Name	Case No.	Industry	Case Type
1.	"Rice Noodle Producer" Horizontal Monopoly Agreement Case	(2023) Zui Gao Fa Zhi Min Zhong No. 653	Catering	Horizontal Monopoly Agreement
2.	"Public Enterprise of Scrambled Cable Digital Television Signal Service" Abuse of Dominance Case	(2023) Zui Gao Fa Zhi Min Zhong No. 383	Digital TV	Abuse of Dominance
3.	"Natural Gas Company" Tying Case	(2023) Zui Gao Fa Zhi Min Zhong No. 1547	Residential Natural Gas	Abuse of Dominance
4.	"Vegetable Wholesale Market" Abuse of Dominance Case	(2024) Zui Gao Fa Zhi Min Zhong No. 748	Vegetable Wholesale	Abuse of Dominance

---

5   Includes 10 influential cases and 100 typical cases on the fifth anniversary of the establishment of the SPC IP Court and 2024 typical cases concerning monopoly and unfair competition conduct.

No.	Case Name	Case No.	Industry	Case Type
5.	"Automobile Sales" Vertical Monopoly Agreement Follow-On Case	(2020) Zui Gao Fa Zhi Min Zhong No. 1137	Auto Sales	Vertical Monopoly Agreement
6.	"Chlorpheniramine Maleate" API Abuse of Dominance Case	(2020) Zui Gao Fa Zhi Min Zhong No. 1140	Pharmaceuticals	Abuse of Dominance
7.	"Industrial Lubricant" Hub-And-Spoke Agreement Case	(2021) Zui Gao Fa Zhi Min Zhong No. 1315	Industrial Lubricants	hub-and-spoke monopoly agreements
8.	"Rare-Earth Permanent Magnet Materials" Abuse of Dominance Case	(2021) Zui Gao Fa Zhi Min Zhong No. 1482	Rare-Earth Materials	Abuse of Dominance
9.	"Traffic Signal Controller" Horizontal Monopoly Agreement Case	(2024) Zui Gao Fa Zhi Min Zhong No. 455	Traffic Signal Equipment	Horizontal Monopoly Agreement
10.	"Driving School Alliance" Horizontal Monopoly Agreement Case	(2021) Zui Gao Fa Zhi Min Zhong No. 1722	Driver Training	Horizontal Monopoly Agreement
11.	"De-Energized Tap-Changer" Horizontal Monopoly Agreement Case	(2021) Zui Gao Fa Zhi Min Zhong No. 1298	Power Equipment Manufacturing	Horizontal Monopoly Agreement
12.	"Kindergarten" Horizontal Monopoly Agreement Case	(2021) Zui Gao Fa Zhi Min Zhong No. 2253	Education	Horizontal Monopoly Agreement
13.	"Saxagliptin" Patent Infringement Case	(2021) Zui Gao Fa Zhi Min Zhong No. 388	Pharmaceuticals	Horizontal Monopoly Agreement
14.	"Concrete Enterprises" Horizontal Monopoly Agreement Administrative Penalty Case	(2022) Zui Gao Fa Zhi Xing Zhong No. 29	Construction Materials	Horizontal Monopoly Agreement
15.	"Fire Inspection Services" Horizontal Monopoly Agreement Administrative Penalty Case	(2021) Zui Gao Fa Zhi Xing Zhong No. 880	Fire Safety Inspection	Horizontal Monopoly Agreement
16.	"Water Supply & Drainage Services" Public Utility Abuse of Dominance Case	(2022) Zui Gao Fa Zhi Min Zhong No. 395	Public Utilities	Abuse of Dominance
17.	"Funeral Services" Public Utility Abuse of Dominance Case	(2021) Zui Gao Fa Zhi Min Zhong No. 242	Funeral Services	Abuse of Dominance
18.	"Brick & Tile Association" Horizontal Monopoly Agreement Case	(2020) Zui Gao Fa Zhi Min Zhong No. 1382	Building Materials	Horizontal Monopoly Agreement

II. Judicial Review of Antitrust Administrative Penalties in China

13. Antitrust administrative litigation serves as an effective complement to the administrative penalty regime and civil litigation. Judicial review by the courts not only enhances the legitimacy of enforcement actions but also helps refine key standards for identifying monopolistic conduct, thus fostering greater synergy between antitrust enforcement and judicial adjudication. Below, we outline the SPC's adjudicative rules for administrative challenges to horizontal and vertical monopoly agreements.

A. Horizontal monopoly agreements

1. Substance over form: agreements evaluated based on competitive effects

14. Chinese courts, when assessing the existence of horizontal monopoly agreements, focus on the actual impact on market competition rather than the form of the agreement. In Qiandongnanzhou Guilong Driving School. v. Guizhou AMR [(2019) Qian Xing Zhong No. 534], the court emphasized that practices among competitors such as fixing or altering prices, output, market division, or jointly boycotting could constitute horizontal monopoly agreements due to their anti-competitive effects.

15. In that case, several driving schools in Qiandongnan Prefecture – engaged in homogeneous competition – agreed on a minimum cost-based pricing standard under the coordination of local industry associations. Although framed as a measure to avoid "vicious competition" and standardize industry practices, the agreement in effect fixed training prices by limiting price competition. The court held that this conduct restricted market competition and constituted a horizontal price-fixing agreement.

2. Price fixing does not require identical price changes

16. The SPC has adopted a more substantive and effects-based approach when reviewing administrative penalties involving horizontal monopoly agreements, emphasizing the anti-competitive impact over formalistic elements.

17. In the "Concrete Alliance" Antitrust Administrative Penalty Case [(2023) Zui Gao Fa Zhi Xing Zhong No. 29], the SPC clarified that "fixing or altering the price of products" under horizontal monopoly agreements can take various forms. These may include fixing price adjustment ranges, using agreed formulas, or prohibiting unilateral changes without mutual consent.

18. This principle above is consistent with SPC's illustration in the Maoming Concrete Enterprises Horizontal Monopoly Agreement Antitrust Administrative Penalty Case [(2022) Zui Gao Fa Zhi Xing Zhong No. 29], where the SPC upheld the finding that 19 concrete producers had engaged in a horizontal monopoly agreement. Although these enterprises charged slightly different prices due to differences in customer demand, relationships, and settlement terms, the Court found that their coordinated and simultaneous price increases restricted market competition and harmed consumer and public interests.

3. Determination of "concerted practices" as a type of monopoly agreement

19. "Concerted practices" are recognized as a form of monopoly agreement. It refers to situations where competing undertakings, without entering into a written or oral agreement or decision, communicate with each other and tacitly engage in coordinated conduct that excludes or restricts competition. Article 18 of the 2024 Antitrust Judicial Interpretation specifies four factors for identifying concerted practices: (1) uniformity of market behavior; (2) communication or information exchange among operators; (3) market structure and competitive dynamics; and (4) whether a legitimate explanation for the uniform conduct exists. These factors align with those set out in SAMR's Provisions on the Prohibition of Monopoly Agreements, and are consistent with the SPC's judicial practice.

20. Given the inherently concealed nature of "concerted practices," Paragraph 2 of Article 18 allocates the burden of proof based on judicial practice. Where the plaintiff provides preliminary evidence of either (1) and (2), or (1) and (3), suggesting a high probability of concerted conduct, the burden shifts to the defendant to reasonably explain the consistency. If the defendant fails to do so, the court may determine that concerted conduct has occurred. A reasonable explanation may include conduct independently adopted in response to market and competitive changes, such as following or imitating the market behavior of competitors.

21. In the Maoming Concrete Enterprises Horizontal Monopoly Agreement Antitrust Administrative Penalty Case [(2022) Zui Gao Fa Zhi Xing Zhong No. 29], the SPC's second-instance ruling followed the same substantive analysis and burden-shifting approach as set out in Article 18. The Court held that "concerted practice" is a form of horizontal monopoly agreement, and its concealed nature creates challenges for administrative and judicial determination. In this case, consistency of market conduct and information exchange were sufficient to establish the likelihood of concerted conduct, shifting the burden to the undertakings to offer a reasonable explanation.

B. Vertical monopoly agreements

22. While the 2024 Antitrust Judicial Interpretation formally revises only civil-litigation procedure, its effects-based, burden-of-proof approach towards vertical price restrictions or resale price maintenance ("RPM") brings judicial review into closer harmony with SAMR's enforcement practice – and is therefore poised to influence administrative-penalty proceedings as well, since administrative lawsuits may analogously invoke civil-litigation provisions when no specific administrative-procedure rule exists.

1. Allocation of the burden of proof

23. Under Article 21 of the 2024 Antitrust Judicial Interpretation, RPM agreements carry a rebuttable presumption of illegality – once the plaintiff shows the agreement exists, the defendant must prove it does *not* exclude or restrict competition. This change mirrors the 2022 amendment to Article 18(2) of the Anti-Monopoly Law ("AML"), which similarly shifted RPM from a per se illegal category to one subject to rebuttal, and it also serves as a useful reference for allocating the burden of proof in antitrust administrative litigation.

24. It should be noted that, unlike the earlier consultation draft, the finalized 2024 Antitrust Judicial Interpretation omits any special burden-shifting rule for non-price vertical restraints. To date, neither SAMR nor the courts have treated non-price vertical restrictions, on their own, as per se unlawful, and their legal status remains unsettled. By removing a presumption against these agreements, the 2024 Antitrust Judicial Interpretation avoids over-burdening plaintiffs and leaves room for future implementing rules.

2. Standards for assessing anticompetitive effects

25. In contrast to horizontal monopoly agreements – which involve concerted actions among actual or potential rivals – vertical monopoly agreements present more nuanced economic considerations, as they may enhance efficiency even while restricting competition. Different antitrust jurisdictions vary significantly in their legislative and practical approaches to determining whether vertical monopoly agreements should be subject to per se illegality.

26. Under Article 18(2) of the AML, RPM and non-price vertical restrictions are no longer irrebuttably illegal. If a defendant can prove that its vertical agreement does not have the effect of excluding or restricting competition, the agreement is not prohibited under China's AML.

27. Further, Article 22 of the 2024 Antitrust Judicial Interpretation details the factors courts should consider when assessing the anticompetitive effects of vertical agreements. These factors include the agreement's potential to

raise market entry barriers, hinder more efficient operators or business models, and restrict inter-brand or intra-brand competition. Conversely, courts also weigh pro-competitive effects such as preventing free-riding, promoting inter-brand competition, maintaining brand image, enhancing pre- or post-sale services, and fostering innovation. The defendant's significant market power serves as an initial consideration, followed by a comprehensive evaluation of the agreement's competitive benefits and harms.

28. It's noteworthy that although the Interpretation establishes the burden of proof for RPM disputes, courts have not abandoned the fundamental approach of balancing pro- and anti-competitive effects when determining the legality of vertical agreements, including price restrictions. This approach aligns with the object and purpose of the AML and allows for thorough debates between plaintiffs and defendants regarding the competitive impact of vertical agreements in future litigation. The judicial review attitude toward resale price maintenance may thus complement the stringent enforcement landscape.

C. Determination of fines

29. While the 2024 Antitrust Judicial Interpretation does not explicitly address the calculation of fines in antitrust administrative litigation, the SPC has provided guidance through typical cases, emphasizing the principles of proportionality and factual relevance in determining penalties.

1. "Prior-Year" Sales as the base for penalty calculation

30. In the Maoming Concrete Enterprises horizontal monopoly agreement case [(2022) Zui Gao Fa Zhi Xing Zhong No. 29], the SPC held that the "prior year" for calculating antitrust fines should be the year most temporally proximate and factually connected to the unlawful conduct. Because the coordinated price-fixing occurred in 2016 and the investigation only began in 2017, the Court determined that using the 2016 sales figures best reflects the companies' actual operations at the time of the offense. This methodology (1) respects the agency's discretion; (2) preserves enforcement effectiveness and deterrence; and (3) adheres to the principle of proportionality by tying the fine base to the year most relevant to the wrongdoing. The SPC's final judgment upheld the enforcement agency's penalty decision, dismissed the appeal, and affirmed the original ruling.

2. Scope of "prior-year" sales

31. In the "Fire Inspection Services" Horizontal Monopoly Agreement Administrative Penalty Case [(2021) Zui Gao Fa Zhi Xing Zhong No. 880], the Supreme People's Court provided a principled interpretation of the

"prior-year sales" base for calculating antitrust fines and clarified the main factors to consider under the proportionality principle. Specifically:
- The AML does not further limit what constitutes "prior-year sales" when defining the fine base.
- In light of the law's objectives and general rules of statutory interpretation, it is reasonable to construe "prior-year sales" as encompassing an undertaking's total annual sales.
- When determining the fine amount, courts must also weigh factors such as the duration, nature, and severity of the monopoly agreement at issue.
- Applying these principles, the Court held that the penalty imposed in this case conformed to the proportionality requirement.

32. This judgment plays an important role in both supporting and supervising antitrust administrative enforcement and in promoting consistency between judicial review standards and administrative-practice norms.

D. Standardizing enforcement procedures

33. When challenging antitrust penalties, plaintiffs frequently allege procedural defects in the antitrust enforcement agency's decision-making. These challenges, in turn, incentivize enforcement agencies to refine their procedures through judicial review. Commonly contested issues include:
    - **Hearing Rights:** Before issuing a penalty decision, the agency must clearly inform the party of the facts, grounds, and legal basis for the proposed sanction, as well as its rights to submit statements, present defenses, and request a hearing. If the party seeks administrative review, the agency must reiterate the right to a hearing. When a hearing is held, the agency must create and preserve a complete record – including all arguments, questions, and rebuttals. Failure to satisfy any of these obligations is a common ground for judicial challenge.
    - **Validity of Service:** Agencies must serve key documents (e.g., Statement of Objections, Penalty Decision) in strict compliance with the Antimonopoly Law's prescribed methods, addresses, and timelines. Parties often dispute that notices were improperly delivered or untimely, arguing that defective service invalidates the entire proceeding.
    - **Completeness of the Administrative Record:** Agencies are obligated to compile and file a fully complete case file – including the investigation closure report, internal review opinions, evidence logs, and all other procedural documents; undertakings frequently allege that missing materials create a procedural defect and justify invalidating the penalty decision.

III. Judicial Review of Chinese Merger Control Review Decision

34. Historically, civil antitrust litigations between private parties have been relatively common, while administrative litigations against the enforcement authorities have been rare. The Beijing Intellectual Property Court (the "Court") recently issued the judgment on a litigation brought by a pharmaceutical company called T Pharma against the conditional clearance decision of the SAMR on the acquisition of T Pharma's shares by another pharmaceutical company called S Pharma. Notably, this judgment represents the very first judicial review of a merger control decision in China, thus is a landmark ruling in China. It not only resolves many complex and precedent-setting legal issues, but also clarifies both enforcement and judicial perspectives on China's merger control regime.

A. A precedent on plaintiff standing in merger control litigation

35. Determining the plaintiff's standing was a threshold issue in a merger control litigation.

36. In this case, the Court held that, pursuant to Article 25(1) of the Administrative Litigation Law of the People's Republic of China ("ALL"), the addressee of an administrative action, as well as any other citizen, legal person, or organization with a direct interest in the action, has the right to initiate a litigation. Furthermore, according to Article 69(1)(8) of the Interpretation of the Supreme People's Court on the Application of the Administrative Litigation Law (the "Judicial Interpretation of ALL"), if the administrative action does not have a significant practical impact on the legal rights and interests of the party, the court should dismiss the case upon review. Based on these provisions, the court established the criteria for determining whether a plaintiff has standing to sue.

37. The Court first found that the administrative action taken by SAMR in relation to merger control constituted an administrative licensing act. On this basis, the court further clarified the standards for establishing standing in different scenarios.

38. Specifically, the Court ruled as follows:
    - Where SAMR issues a decision not to prohibit the merger, the administrative action does not alter or expand the rights and obligations of the parties to the concentration agreement. As such, it does not affect the parties' legitimate rights and interests, and they therefore lack standing to bring an administrative lawsuit.

- Conversely, if SAMR decides to prohibit the merger or impose restrictive conditions, the administrative action either nullifies the rights and obligations established under the concentration agreement or imposes new legal obligations on the parties post-concentration. In such cases, the administrative action affects the legitimate rights and interests of the parties, and they thus have standing to sue.

39. As the first judicial review case concerning merger control, the standard for determining standing established in this judgment provides important guidance for future cases. It informs how courts should delineate the scope of judicial review and determine admissibility criteria in administrative litigation involving merger control. This case not only enriches the practical application of the ALL, but also constitutes a landmark in the judicial practice of the AML. Moreover, it represents a meaningful judicial exploration into the procedural provisions of administrative litigation.

B. General principle of encouraging operators to implement concentrations in accordance with the AML

40. In this case, the plaintiff, B Pharma, argued during the merger review and litigation process that the AML mandates prohibition as the primary and legally prescribed remedy for concentrations that exclude or restrict competition, while conditional approval should be granted only under exceptional circumstances.

41. However, SAMR contended that Article 6 of the General Principles of the AML explicitly states: "Operators may, through fair competition and voluntary cooperation, implement concentrations in accordance with the law to expand business scale and enhance market competitiveness." This provision establishes the fundamental principle of "exceptional intervention" in merger control regime. Furthermore, Articles 34 and 35 of the AML do not designate prohibition as the sole or primary instrument. It is essential to interpret the specific provisions in Chapter 4 of the AML (including Articles 34 and 35) in conjunction with Article 6, rather than applying them in isolation. Given the general and principled nature of the AML, Chapter 4 does not set forth detailed procedural rules or review standards; rather, it grants enforcement agencies the discretion to refine relevant rules and render different types of review decisions on a case-by-case basis, including the approval of concentrations subject to conditions.

42. In this regard, the Merger Control Review Regulations (Article 39 (1) and (2), and Article 42 (1)) provide that, in order to mitigate or eliminate the exclusionary or anti-competitive effects of a concentration, the parties involved may submit commitment proposals to SAMR, including additional restrictive conditions. SAMR is required to assess the effectiveness, feasibility, and timeliness of such proposals and promptly notify

the applicants of the evaluation results. If a concentration is found to have, or potentially have, impacts of the exclusion or restriction on competition, but the commitments proposed by the operators effectively mitigate these adverse effects, SAMR may approve the concentration subject to additional conditions.

43. The Court ultimately upheld SAMR's position, affirming that the AML should be interpreted in a systematic manner. The judgment further emphasized that, for concentrations with anti-competitive effects, SAMR does not impose an automatic prohibition. A prohibition decision should only be made when SAMR determines that the commitments proposed by the involved parties fail to effectively mitigate the adverse impact on competition.

44. The enforcement and judicial review in this case reaffirm the overarching principle of the AML, which encourages market participants to pursue concentrations in compliance with the law. This approach to merger control enforcement reflects the principle of "exceptional intervention" in China's antitrust framework and underscores the regulatory authorities' commitment to reducing institutional transaction costs for businesses, fostering economic vitality, and continuously optimizing the business environment.

C. Core concern of China's merger review system is addressing competition issues arising from the concentration, in line with international practice

45. In its judgment, the Court explicitly stated that "a concentration that has or may have the effect of excluding or restricting competition" refers to "competition concerns arising directly from the concentration itself." The primary objective of merger control regime is to address competition issues stemming from the concentration, rather than to remedy competition problems that existed *ex ante* the transaction.

46. The principles of merger review affirmed by the Court align closely with the enforcement practices of SAMR. According to the *Guidelines for Horizontal Merger Review* issued by SAMR on December 10, 2024, Article 3 emphasizes that antitrust enforcement agencies support operators in lawfully pursuing concentrations. Where a concentration does not have the effect of excluding or restricting competition, the enforcement agency will approve it in accordance with the law. However, if a concentration has or may have such effects, the agency may either prohibit the transaction or approve it subject to restrictive conditions. Notably, the competition concerns referenced in this provision are those arising from the concentration itself.

47. In the context of this case, the competitive conditions in the Batroxobin injection market prior to the concentration were not within the scope

of the merger control regime. Instead, the key issue under review was whether the concentration itself – specifically, the merger of an existing competitor and a potential market entrant – would give rise to competition concerns. If the commitments proposed by the merging parties could effectively mitigate these concerns and alleviate potential adverse effects on competition, SAMR could approve the concentration with restrictive conditions.

48. The judicial review in this case further confirms that China's merger control system is fundamentally focused on addressing competition concerns arising from concentrations, a principle that is consistent with prevailing practices in other major antitrust jurisdictions worldwide.

49. For instance, under the European Commission's *Commission Notice on Remedies Acceptable Under Council Regulation (EC) No 139/2004 and Commission Regulation (EC) No 802/2004*, the basic principle is that if a concentration raises competition concerns and could significantly impede effective competition, the parties may propose remedies to resolve these issues and secure approval. In practice, the European Commission adheres to this principle. A notable example is the merger review of Novozymes A/S and Christian Hansen A/S, where the Commission assessed the competition concerns posed by the transaction – specifically, the risk that the merger would reduce competition in the market for genetically engineered lactose enzymes, given that Hansen was a potential entrant in this market. The transaction would have eliminated this potential competitive constraint. However, since sufficient potential competitors remained to exert competitive pressure on the merged entity, the Commission imposed restrictive conditions, including requiring the divestiture of Hansen's lactose enzyme production and distribution business as well as Novozymes' related production facilities. The competition concerns identified by the European Commission and its commitment-based approach closely resemble SAMR's review framework in this case.

50. Thus, both the enforcement and judicial review in this case reinforce that China's merger review system remains firmly rooted in competition policy, with a primary focus on addressing competition concerns arising from concentrations. The review process and analytical methods are in line with international best practices, contributing to a more predictable and transparent regulatory environment while reducing institutional transaction costs for multinational companies investing in China.

D. Legal independence of merger control decisions from concentration agreements

51. The transaction between undertakings serves as the basis for review by the market regulatory authority. However, neither the relevant laws and regulations nor the normative documents issued by SAMR provide a clear

interpretation of the relationship between the merger review decision and the transaction itself.

52. However, this relationship is directly relevant and pivotal to determining whether the parties concerned have a substantial interest in the merger review decision under Article 47 of the Administrative Licensing Law of the People's Republic of China and whether they are entitled to procedural rights, such as the right to be informed or to request a hearing in the context of administrative licensing.

53. In this case, the Court explicitly addressed this issue and provided a clear judicial opinion. It maintained that the concentration agreement entered into by the transacting parties and the merger review decision are independent of each other. The legal validity of the concentration agreement arises from the civil legal framework to which it is subject and bears no direct relationship to the outcome of the administrative review. Accordingly, a conditional approval decision does not affect the validity of the concentration agreement, and the parties to that agreement are not considered stakeholders in the review decision.

54. The court's reasoning can be summarized as follows:

55. On one hand, the Share Transfer Agreement (the "Concentration Agreement") signed in 2017 between the parent company of B Pharma and A Pharma is a civil legal instrument, the effectiveness and enforceability of which are governed by civil law and subject to arbitration or court adjudication. The review decision did not modify the contractual rights or obligations of the parties. In essence, the case involves an administrative legal relationship rather than a civil one. Therefore, the administrative license (i.e., the conditional approval decision) does not directly involve the interest relationship between the parent company of B Pharma and A Pharma, nor does it create a substantial interest relationship between them.

56. On the other hand, the obligations imposed by the merger review decision apply only to the entity formed after the concentration, namely, the post-merger entity of A Pharma and B Pharma, and do not directly alter the mutual rights or obligations between the two original parties. The requirement for the parent company of B Pharma to transfer its shares to A Pharma is not an obligation imposed by the merger review decision; rather, it arises from the parties' mutual consent as set forth in the concentration agreement.

57. The resolution of this issue provides important guidance on the procedural legality of administrative licensing in the context of merger control. It clarifies how procedural safeguards under administrative licensing law should be applied in merger review cases and offers practical direction for the future enforcement practices of market regulatory authorities.

IV. The Future of Antitrust Litigation in China

A. Antitrust litigation as a strategic business tool

58. Chinese companies are increasingly leveraging antitrust litigation as a strategic tool in their competitive arsenal. Recent legal developments, notably the Supreme People's Court's judicial interpretation of AML, have lowered evidentiary barriers for plaintiffs and are expected to spur a rise in both civil and administrative lawsuits. This interpretation clarified that plaintiffs can rely on findings from regulatory decisions (such as those by SAMR) in "follow-on" civil suits, shifting certain burdens of proof to defendants and reducing the need for costly market analysis or expert testimony. By easing the plaintiff's burden (for example, dispensing with strict market definition requirements in some cases and presuming certain conduct like resale price maintenance to be illegal), the courts have democratized access to antitrust remedies and lowered the threshold for businesses to initiate litigation.

59. These changes mean that a company harmed by an alleged monopoly behavior – or even a company seeking to challenge a rival's market practices – has a better chance of success in court, making antitrust suits a viable competitive strategy. Businesses are paying closer attention to antitrust enforcement trends and outcomes, knowing that an adverse finding by SAMR can effectively set the stage for private litigation. In parallel, novel forms of administrative antitrust litigation are emerging. Traditionally, administrative challenges in antitrust were rare, but now companies are more willing to take regulators to court over their decisions. For example, in 2025 the Beijing Intellectual Property Court issued a landmark ruling on the first-ever judicial challenge to a SAMR merger control decision. Such cases suggest that administrative litigation – where firms seek judicial review of agency actions like merger approvals or penalties – will play a more prominent role going forward. Both the volume of private civil suits and the willingness to pursue administrative lawsuits are expected to increase as companies recognize the tactical value of antitrust litigation under the more plaintiff-friendly regime.

B. Early developments on public interest litigation and representative actions

60. Public interest antitrust litigation in China remains nascent and underdeveloped. The amended AML opened the door for public-interest lawsuits by empowering the People's Procuratorate to file civil antitrust actions on behalf of the public interest. In theory, this allows prosecutors to sue companies engaged in monopolistic conduct that harms societal welfare, even if no individual plaintiff comes forward. In practice, however, this mechanism is only just beginning to take shape. Chinese procuratorates have

started to explore antitrust public interest cases – reportedly initiating 16 new public-interest antitrust lawsuits in 2024 alone – but these cases are still few, and no established body of case law has formed. To date, there have been no significant precedents of successful public-interest antitrust suits or large-scale collective recovery for consumers, indicating that this tool remains largely theoretical or at least unused in high-profile cases.

61. One potential way public-interest litigation may develop is through representative *actions*. China's civil procedure allows a form of representative litigation (somewhat akin to a class action, but on an "opt-in" basis) where multiple plaintiffs with the same claim designate representatives to sue on the group's behalf. Such mechanisms have seen very limited use in antitrust matters so far. Nevertheless, as awareness grows, there is speculation that representative actions could be employed, for example, by groups of consumers or SMEs affected by cartel overcharges.

62. Going forward, we anticipate cautious growth in this area. The Supreme People's Procuratorate (SPP) has issued guidance signaling that it will prioritize antitrust public interest cases in sectors affecting consumers (such as the internet, public utilities, and pharmaceuticals) and target behaviors like platform exclusivity that harm consumer choice. Representative actions in China may also get a boost from the general trend of heightened antitrust enforcement – if a major antitrust violation captures public attention, we might see either a group action or a procuratorial action to address it. Still, significant questions remain about how these lawsuits will be executed. It is unclear, for instance, how a procuratorate-driven case would interact with any private lawsuits on the same matter, and whether courts will permit parallel public and private claims. As of now, public interest antitrust litigation is an intriguing but underutilized tool. Its evolution may draw on comparisons to the U.S. class action mechanism, but it will likely develop along uniquely Chinese lines, driven by government actors (procuratorates) rather than private class attorneys. Legal professionals should watch for test cases in this area as they will shed light on the feasibility and impact of collective antitrust redress in China.

C. Coordinating administrative enforcement and private lawsuits

63. The interface between administrative enforcement and civil antitrust litigation in China is becoming increasingly important. The new judicial interpretation of AML explicitly addresses the linkage between government enforcement actions and private suits, laying groundwork for a more coordinated approach. In cases of *follow-on litigation*, where a plaintiff files a civil lawsuit after a competition authority has taken action, Chinese courts can now give significant weight to the factual findings of the enforcement decision. The judicial interpretation also permits courts to

stay (suspend) a civil antitrust trial if a related government investigation is ongoing, resuming only after the agency's determination is made. This mechanism prevents inconsistent outcomes and encourages an efficient sequence: regulatory action first, private litigation second.

64. Looking ahead, we expect to see more parallel proceedings in the broad sense – a combination of administrative and civil processes tackling the same alleged monopoly conduct. A likely scenario is how will courts handle situations where a regulatory decision is under appeal (administrative reconsideration or judicial review) at the same time a private follow-on suit is filed? The current interpretation requires that the agency decision be final or court-confirmed before its facts are given weight, which might encourage plaintiffs to wait until enforcement is resolved. We might also see more instances of companies preemptively challenging SAMR's enforcement or merger decisions (as noted above) while simultaneously facing private claims – effectively a multi-front legal battle. Chinese law is beginning to grapple with these complexities: the 2024 interpretation is a start in outlining coordination, but further practical experience will be needed. If parallel civil and administrative suits become common after an administrative action, courts will develop principles on admissibility of evidence, estoppel effects of agency findings, and perhaps even guidelines on damages in follow-on cases.

PART III
Focuses on Data and Digital Era

Re-examination of the Relationship between Anti-Monopoly Regulation and Industry Regulation of Digital Platforms[*]

MENG YANBEI[**]
Professor, Renmin University of China Law School

Abstract

The cross-region, cross-industry and cross-scenario ecological expansion capabilities of digital platforms make it necessary to re-examine the relationship between anti-monopoly regulation and industry regulation. In the pre-digital economy era, there has been a relationship pattern between anti-monopoly regulation and government industry regulation featuring co-existence of each performing its own functions, mutual restraints, checks and balances, overlapping law enforcement, and interactive coordination. The emergence of digital platforms brings about many challenges to anti-monopoly regulation and industry regulation. Since different jurisdictions have different approaches and are exploring whether to and how to make legislation for digital platforms, the relationship between anti-monopoly regulation and industry regulation of digital platforms is dynamic and has regional differences. Due to the current selection of implementing legislation in a more targeted and precise manner for digital platforms in China, the relationship between anti-monopoly regulation and industry regulation of digital platforms in China will still exhibit industry-based differences.

---

[*] The phased outcome of the general project of the National Social Science Fund of China, titled "Research on Anti-monopoly Theory Issues of Platforms" (21BFX115).

[**] Meng Yanbei, Professor of Law School, Renmin University of China.

Re-examination of the Relationship between Anti-Monopoly Regulation and Industry Regulation of Digital Platforms

I. Introduction

1. The new generation of information technologies (e.g., Internet, big data, and artificial intelligence (AI)) and the industries have achieved a deep integration, which is transforming the organization model, service model, and business model of social and economic activities. The new forms of digital economy are based on digital platforms, driven by data elements, and supported by algorithmic technologies. They penetrate and integrate with traditional industries, reconfigured the main bodies, objects, elements and tools of the market, and fundamentally changed the competitive structure, presenting the characteristics of diversified integration and dynamic competition.[1] Digital platform itself is regarded as a standard interface or general-purpose module, and its functions can be expanded through application programs. Based on the extensible code library of the software system, it provides core functions shared by modules that are interoperable with the system, as well as interoperable interfaces. It also serves as a group of subsystems and interfaces that constitute a common structure to develop and distribute derived applications.[2] Compared with traditional economic organizations, digital platforms rely on advanced computing power and algorithmic technology, and adopt free models, user experience, and community content production, etc. as their marketing strategies. They carry out economic activities centered around matching supply and demand and facilitating trades, and have become a new form of economic organization. By reducing information asymmetry, trade cost, and search cost, and by providing new services or establishing large-scale compromise nets, they bring about improved efficiency.[3] They possess basic economic attributes such as economy of scale, economy of scope, network externality, two-sided (multi-sided) market, and driven by algorithms and big data, etc.[4] The cross-region, cross-industry and cross-scenario ecological expansion capabilities of digital platforms pose a risk of disintegration to the regulatory boundaries, functional boundaries and power operation logic of digital platforms, and also bring about challenges to the governance of digital platforms. However, when preventing and curbing the potential market risks that the digital platforms may bring about

---

1   Refer to Chen Yu: The Challenge of Internet Economy to Anti-monopoly Law and System Reconstruction. Journal of Shanxi University of Finance & Economics, Issue S2, 2024.

2   See Venkatesh.V, Tam.K, Y. Hong: "Model of Migration and Use of Platforms: Role of Hierarchy, Current Generation, and Complementarities in Consumer Settings", Management Science, Vol. 56, No. 8(2010), p.1304.

3   See Murati, Erion: "What are digital platforms? An overview of definitions, typologies, economics, and legal challenges arising from the platform economy in Eu." Eur. J. Privacy L. & Tech. (2021): 19.

4   Zhou Hanhua: On the Dual Governance of Antitrust and Regulation of the Platform Economy. China Legal Science, Issue 1, 2023.

due to their strong market force, it is necessary to re-examine the relationship between anti-monopoly regulation and industry regulation in restricting digital platforms.

II. Discussion on the Relationship between Anti-Monopoly Regulation and Industry Regulation in the Pre-Digital Economy Era

2. The basis for exploring the relationship between anti-monopoly regulation and industry regulation is to clear up the relationship between competition policy and industrial policy, as well as the relationship between anti-monopoly law and industry regulation legal system.

(I) Relationship between competition policy and industrial policy

3. Competition policy generally refers to a fundamental economic policy implemented by market economy countries to protect and promote market competition. Its core objective is to ensure that the competitive mechanism functions effectively in the market by protecting and promoting market competition, thereby improving resource allocation efficiency, and enhancing consumer welfare.[5] As a measure taken by the country for promoting industrial development, industrial policy plays the main function of intervening in the market regulation process under the premise of the market mechanism's full regulation of the market supply and demand structure, in order to promote the coordinated development among industries and achieve the rationalization and modernization of the industrial structure, being an important means of national macro-control. Market economy countries will simultaneously employ both competition policy and industrial policy as their policy tools. Even in the United States, where the term "industrial policy" has never appeared in official documents and there is resistance to industrial policy, there also exists a "de facto industrial policy" that emphasizes industrial technology policy.[6]

4. As two important components of a country's economic policy system, competition policy and industrial policy have consistent objectives in most cases, but there is also the possibility of conflicting objectives. Firstly, the pathway through which competition policy and industrial policy achieve their ultimate objectives is different. Generally,

---

5 Wang Xianlin: On Relation between Competition Policy and Trade Policy. Hebei Law Science, Issue 1, 2006.
6 Bin Xuehua, He Qiang: Legislative Evolution of U.S. Industrial Policy and Its Enlightenment to China. Law Science Magazine, Issue 8, 2013.

competition policy promotes the functioning of the market mechanism by regulating monopolistic behaviors and unfair competition behaviors, and it is essentially creating conditions to allow the market mechanism to play its role of resource allocation; however, industrial policy, on the other hand, uses direct or indirect government intervention to replace or influence the role of the market mechanism in resource allocation. Secondly, the scope of application of competition policy and industrial policy is different. Competition policy, as a universal policy, does not have a clear industrial orientation; while industrial policy has direct industries as their object of concern, which are those industries to be promoted, protected, and restricted as determined by the government based on the economic and industrial development situation of the country. Thirdly, the implementation tools of competition policy and industrial policy are different. Competition policy is implemented by prohibiting and punishing monopolistic and unfair competition behaviors; while industrial policy is implemented by fiscal, taxation, financial, pricing, and foreign exchange means, etc. In addition, the implementation node of competition policy and industrial policy is different. The implementation of competition policy is more of a post-event regulation, with only a few cases of pre-event regulation; while the implementation of industrial policy is more of a pre-event regulation, with only a few cases of post-event regulation.[7]

5. Accurately speaking, the debate over the effectiveness and necessity of industrial policy has never ceased in various countries. The effectiveness of industrial policy depends on many factors such as a country's economic system, development level, and historical culture, etc., as well as the definition of the connotation and extension of industrial policy. Therefore, as scholars like Aghion have emphasized, the policy makers shall no longer continue to focus on the dualism debate on whether industrial policy is "needed" or "not needed" by developing economies, but shall shift their focus of work to how to scientifically design and effectively implement a reasonable industrial policy (2012).[8] With the reforms of government functions and economic system in China, the role of the market in resource allocation has become increasingly important, and the conflict between competition policy and industrial policy will be increasingly decreased. The development direction in China in the future is to build a "competition-friendly industrial policy", thereby achieving integration between competition policy and industrial policy.

---

[7] Meng Yanbei: On the Relationship between the Antimonopoly Law Enforcement Agencies and the Government Industry Regulation Organs. Journal of Renmin University of China, Issue 2, 20215.

[8] Refer to Aghion P, Dewatripont M, Du L, Harrison A, Legros P, Industrial Policy and Competition [R], NBER Working Paper, 2012. Quoted from Wang Wen, Sun Zao, Niu Zedong: Industrial Policy, Market Competition and Mismatch of Resources. Economist, Issue 9, 2014.

(II) Relationship between anti-monopoly law and industry regulation legal system

6. Anti-monopoly law is legalization of core competition policy, while the industry regulation legal system embodies the industrial policy, therefore, the relationship between competition policy and industrial policy will have an important impact on the relationship between anti-monopoly law and industry regulation legal system. The differences between anti-monopoly law and industry regulation legal system in terms of legislative objective, adjustment scope and adjustment method have determined the distinctiveness of their impacts and the independence of their effects on national economic development. Therefore, in most cases, both anti-monopoly law and industry regulation legal system will, in accordance with their respective legislative objectives, employ the same or different adjustment methods to independently adjust the industrial and business activities in the economic field. Confronted with industrial competition, both anti-monopoly law and industry regulation legal system are undergoing adjustment. However, as long as there is no conflict, overlapping regulations will not affect the implementation of anti-monopoly law and industry regulation legal system. Furthermore, whether the anti-monopoly law and industry regulation legal system exert their respective functions independently or jointly will not have an impact on the interaction, coordination, restraint, check and balance between them.

7. Anti-monopoly law is dedicated to creating or maintaining a dynamic competitive environment, rather than simply replicating the consequences of competition, or making up for the deficiencies of market competition.[9] Its operation mechanism is passive in nature, mainly relying on a series of clear prohibitive clauses, which set the specific no-go areas for certain business activities. It does not actively guide the specific business strategies of enterprises. Instead, it conveys behavioral restrictions to enterprises in the form of a negative list. Only in extremely rare cases will the anti-monopoly law enforcement agencies meticulously establish legal obligations of initiative. However, the industry regulation laws are just to the contrary, usually setting out the obligations for the operators' initiative. These obligations of initiative are mostly a kind of prior, long-term, and comprehensive intervention, achieving the objective of promoting economic efficiency and industry development by directly intervening in the operation of the agencies to replace the market competition mechanism.

---

9 [US] Stephen Breyer: Regulation and Its Reform. Translated by Li Honglei, et al. Peking University Press, 2022 Edition, Page 194.

(III) Relationship between anti-monopoly regulation and industry regulation

8. Anti-monopoly regulation mainly aims to ensure that the market competition mechanism functions properly, while industry regulation aims to realize system contents that have nothing to do with competition (e.g., industrial safety regulations, and technical standard regulations, etc.). Anti-monopoly law enforcement agencies and government industry regulation organs perform their respective functions in accordance with the law in most of the time. As pointed out by the Judge Breyer, the United States Securities and Exchange Commission (SEC) was dedicated to improving market information. It was an agency for investor protection and information disclosure, rather than an agency for investigating and prohibiting cartels or other anti-competition behaviors.[10] Even though the Congress adopted the *Securities Act*, instructing the SEC to take competition into account in all of its regulatory activities, it still would not take pro-competition as the top consideration factor.[11] Even for such agencies focusing on specific market competition conditions as the United States Federal Communications Commission (FCC), they will not pay more attention to market competition when focusing on the market.

9. Of course, there is not necessarily a conflict between anti-monopoly regulation and government industry regulation, with the possibility of overlapping law enforcement still. The so-called overlapping law enforcement refers to the situation where both anti-monopoly law and industry regulation legal system have overlapping provisions in terms of maintaining competition, and while the anti-monopoly law enforcement agencies are conducting law enforcement against behaviors that harm or restrict competition, the government industry regulation organs can also simultaneously conduct law enforcement against such behaviors in the industry, and as a result, there is an overlap in the jurisdiction of law enforcement. Daniel F. Spulber has noticed the mixed trend of regulation and antitrust quite early. Although he did not further explore the root causes and consequences of such trend, he still analyzed the convergence trend and manifestations of regulation and antitrust.[12] In short, the anti-monopoly enforcement agencies and the government industry regulation organs will form a relationship pattern featuring co-existence of each performing its own functions, mutual restraints, checks and balances, overlapping law enforcement, and interactive coordination.

---

10 Credit Suisse Sec. (USA) LLC v. Billing, 127 S. Ct. 2383, 2396 (2007).

11 Memorandum Amicus Curiae of the Securities and Exchange Commission, Submitted at the Request of the Court, In re Initial Pub. Offering Antitrust Litig., No. 01 CIV 2014 (S.D.N.Y. Dec. 20, 2002.

12 [US] Daniel F. Spulber: Regulation and Markets, Translated by Yu Hui, He Fan, Qian Jiachun, and Zhou Weifu, Shanghai Joint Publishing, Shanghai People's Publishing House, 1999 Edition, Page 595.

III. The Relationship between Anti-Monopoly Regulation and Industry Regulation has gained Attention again in Digital Economy Era

10. Digital platform has demonstrated multiple roles in market operation as an enterprise entity, an intermediary bridge, a provider of capabilities, an infrastructure supporter, an emerging governance force, and even a "new authority", etc.[13] Its core function lies in integrating various interdependent groups in the multi-sided market into a unified whole, shouldering the responsibility for organizing and coordinating resource allocation. In the meantime, it is also responsible for collecting data and managing algorithms, and for establishing and implementing trading rules.[14] Due to the characteristics such as network effect, data self-reinforcement, and increasing returns to scale, etc., digital market always becomes the "Winner-Take-All Markets", but also brings about many challenges to anti-monopoly regulation and industry regulation.

(I) Challenges brought about by digital platforms to anti-monopoly regulation

11. The competitive nature of digital market has shifted from "competition in the market" to "competition for the market". In digital market, products or services possess very strong direct or indirect network effect, which creates barriers to entry and increases market concentration, enabling market forces to sustain. Confronted with challenges brought about by digital economy, the core legislative objective of anti-monopoly law to "maintain market competition" remains unchanged, however, "encouraging innovation" shall become one of the independent legislative objectives of the anti-monopoly law in the digital economy era. In the digital economy era, the anti-monopoly law will regulate behaviors such as algorithm collusion, block-chain collusion, and platform most-favored-nation treatment clauses (MFN), etc. through the Prohibition of Monopoly Agreement System. It will regulate behaviors such as platform self-preferencing and personalized pricing through the Prohibition of Abuse of Market Dominant Position Behavior System, and fulfill the obligation of data portability and interoperability. It will regulate behaviors such as killer merger & acquisition and data-driven merger & acquisition in the digital market through concentration review.

---

[13] Shao Zhanpeng: The Tripartite Attributes and Role Conflicts of Digital Platforms. Zhejiang Academic Journal, Issue 5, 2024.

[14] Refer to Liu Jiejiao: Anti-monopoly Regulation of Digital Platforms: Frontier Issues, Theoretical Difficulties and Strategies. Research on Financial and Economic Issues, Issue 7, 2022.

12. In the digital economy era, after the product supply presents a "multi-product portfolio supply" scenario, the market exhibits a "two-sided or even multi-sided market" pattern, the market competition shows "cross-market competition", and the product or service pricing adopts "free model and cross-subsidy" and other new characteristics, the definition of relevant market, determination of platform market force, assessment of competition harm, and relief measures in the regulatory analysis framework of anti-monopoly law are all confronted with new challenges. For example, when assessing the "competition harm" of digital platform's market behaviors, in quantitative analysis of assessing competition harm, both the standard for maximizing social total welfare and the standard for maximizing consumer welfare are based on the theory of price for their analysis. However, the business models in the digital economy era have changed. Due to the importance of flow and data, as well as the integration of two-sided or multi-sided markets in platform operation, a "zero-price" business model has emerged with free basic products or services. When a multi-sided platform enterprise sets the price of a certain product or service at zero, it will result in the absence of an accurately measurable market price between the user and the product or service, posing challenges to price-based analysis tools and to the analysis paradigm of determining competition harm based on the standard for maximizing social total welfare or the standard for maximizing consumer welfare. For another example, in assessment of competition harm, the anti-competition effect before digital economy era usually refers to the collusive effect and the exclusive effect. The collusive effect means that the competition among competitors is directly restricted, manifested as the consistency of the competitors' behaviors or joint actions; the exclusive effect refers to the situation where one party improperly weakens the competitiveness of the competitors, such as causing a blockade effect of customers and raw materials on the competitors or significantly increasing the competitors' costs. If a behavior results in such an effect, it can generally be determined that there is a "competition harm".[15] In the meantime, the new characteristics in the digital economy, such as two-sided market and cross-border competition of platforms, etc., make it necessary to pay attention to the analysis of transmission effect when assessing competition harm, focus on the leveraged behavior of super platforms and whether the super platforms can conduct leveraged transmission of market force, thereby having a long-term exclusive effect on relevant product markets.[16]

13. In addition, anti-monopoly regulation of digital platforms is also confronted with the challenge of insufficient regulatory measures. Therefore, in the

---

15 Jiao Haitao: Competitive Harm in Anti-monopoly Law and Its Relationship with Consumer Interests. Nanjing University Law Journal, Issue 2, 2022.

16 Meng Yanbei: What is the Anti-Monopoly Law "Against" in the Digital Economy – From the Perspective of "Legislative Objectives". Exploration and Free Views, Issue 7, 2022.

digital economy era, it is also necessary to innovate the regulatory tools. At present, each jurisdiction attaches great importance to innovating regulatory tools, strengthens real-time monitoring and early warning mechanisms, attempts to use technologies such as big data and the Internet of Things (IoT) to comprehensively and dynamically monitor the platform behaviors, identifies monopoly risks and provides early warnings in time, and identities and analyzes the monopoly behaviors making use of the data analysis and pattern recognition capabilities of artificial intelligence (AI), so as to improve the regulatory efficiency and accuracy.

(II) Challenges brought about by digital platforms to industry regulation

14. In the context of digital transformation, some scholars think that there is an institutional tension between the bureaucratic administrative structure and the platform-based ecosystem evolution of digital economy. Taking platform as the hub, this new economic form has established a global operation system with multi-dimensional integration characteristics. The dynamic integration trend of industry boundaries in this form has generated significant institutional friction compared to the traditional departmentalized regulation and territorial jurisdiction models.[17] Some scholars also point out that, the vertical regulatory system and the cross-industry integration trend of the platform economy have revealed a significant institutional tension. Such structural conflict is mainly manifested as follows: Internal conflict between the fragmented allocation of regulatory functions and the integrated development characteristics of digital economy; spatial mismatch between the central-local division of power governance model and the cross-regional operation characteristics of platform enterprises; and in the meantime, the compliance issues of regulatory procedures and the standardization issues of administrative actions have not been systematically resolved yet.[18]

15. The technological innovation of platform economy as well as rapid iteration and dynamic development of business models require that, the regulation must be prompt and agile, and iteration must be made in a timely manner, i.e., it is necessary to carry out agile governance with dynamic, flexible and adaptive characteristics.[19] However, when super platforms

---

17 Tang Yaojia: Research on Digital Economy Regulation. China Financial & Economic Publishing House, 2023 Edition, Page 55.

18 Wang Junhao: A Theoretical System for Regulation with Chinese Characteristics and Its Application. China Social Sciences Press, 2022 Edition, Page 140.

19 Agile governance, as a new public governance model and policy-making tool, was proposed by the World Economic Forum in 2018 to address the challenges posed by the complex and ever-changing Fourth Industrial Revolution to public governance. Refer to Jiang Xiaojuan, Huang Yingxuan: Market Order, Market Supervision and Platform Governance in the Digital Age. Economic Research Journal, Issue 12, 2021.

such as Amazon, Apple, Facebook and Google have transformed from "challenging start-ups" to "super monopolists like the oil tycoons and railway magnates that we have witnessed in history",[20] these super platforms are more like a powerful and invisible complex system that integrates data, capital and technology. This complex system combines the triple advantages of high centralization of power, intelligent management of ruling (dominant) technologies, and distributed extraction of resources (data), forming a power system that not only has a unified will but also has the extraction characteristics of being loose, coupled, and open.[21] Under the traditional approach to industry regulation, what industries require regulation and to what extent they need regulation depend on the characteristics of the industries. However, for digital platforms, different platforms are involved in different industries, and it is difficult to establish a unified regulatory framework for all platforms based on the specific characteristics of each industry.[22] The digital industry regulation is confronted with challenges such as whether obligation of initiative can be imposed on digital platforms, whether and how to adhere to the principle of consistency between online and offline operations, and how to regulate the industrial integration under the framework of two-sided market theory, etc.

(III) The relationship between anti-monopoly regulation and industry regulation of digital platforms shall be dynamically reconfigured

16. Judge Scalia also held the opinion in the Trinko case that, when regulatory agencies "perform antitrust functions", the demand for antitrust law enforcement would decrease.[23] If there is a regulatory structure designed to prevent and remedy anti-competition harm, the additional benefits that anti-monopoly law enforcement provides to competition are often very small, and it is unlikely for anti-monopoly law to take such additional review into account. In contrast, if there is no content in the regulation that performs the anti-monopoly function, then the benefits of anti-monopoly law enforcement would far outweigh its drawbacks.[24] In response to the changes in the business model, technological route and

---

20 Subcommittee on Antitrust, "Commercial and Administrative Law of the Committee on the Judiciary," *Investigation of Competition in the Digital Markets*, https://judiciary.house.gov/uploadedfiles/competition_in_digital_markets.pdf.

21 Fanpeng, Li Yan: Tame Technology Giants: The National Logic of Anti-Monopoly Actions. Beijing Cultural Review, Issue 1, 2021.

22 Editor-in-chief: Huang Yiping: Platform Economy – Innovation, Governance and Prosperity. CITIC Press Group. 2022 Edition, Page 458.

23 See Verizon Commc'ns Inc. v. Law Offices of Curtis V. Trinko, LLP, 540 US 398,412 (2004).

24 See Robert A. Jablon, Anjali G. Patel & Latif M. Nurani, Trinko and Credit Suisse Revisited: The Need for Effective Administrative Agency Review and Shared Antitrust Responsibility, 34 Energy Law Journal 627, 641(2013).

product, and profit model, etc. of digital platforms, the industry regulation organs have also strengthened the real-time regulatory capabilities of the regulation organs over platform enterprises, emphasized that platform enterprises should assume the responsibility for self-regulation, adopted case-specific and differentiated regulatory measures for platform enterprises, granted certain regulatory flexibility to product and service innovations, and established a collaborative regulation among government regulatory agencies, non-government regulatory entities, the regulation objects, and other stakeholders,[25] etc., to cope with the challenges. The industry regulation of digital platforms does not base its control on the occurrence of illegal facts by the operators, nor does it care about how the market force of the operators is acquired. Instead, in order to achieve the regulatory objectives, it requires the specific operators to undertake certain special obligations, thereby prompting the operators to change their market behaviors, and undergoing a structural transformation. At this time, industry regulation of digital platforms is not an anti-monopoly link, and compared with anti-monopoly, the regulation does not require the occurrence of illegal acts as a prerequisite. Industry regulation organs are closer to the market than anti-monopoly law enforcement agencies, and have advantages in technology and information, etc., enabling them to regulate the behavior of the regulation objects in a quicker and more effective manner.[26] For example, some scholars argue that, although there are many challenges in implementing effective regulation of digital platforms, supplementing traditional anti-monopoly law enforcement measures can alleviate specific concerns about digital platforms. They put forward the concept of "Light-Handed Pro-Competitive" (LHPC) regulation innovatively, aiming to enhance market competition intensity, reduce market entry barriers, and in the meantime, better safeguard the benefits that digital platforms provide for consumers. The specific measures for "LHPC" regulation may cover requirements for interconnectivity/interoperability, prohibition of discriminatory behavior, rules for data portability, as well as additional restrictions on certain business practices, etc.[27] During dynamic development of the measures for regulation of digital industry, it is inevitable to make dynamic reconfiguration of the relationship between anti-monopoly regulation and industry regulation of digital platforms.

---

25 Zhou Luyao, Lu Jiaying: From Responsive Regulation to Proactive Regulation: Exploring the Pathway for the Normalized Regulation of Platform Enterprises. Research on China Market Supervision, Issue 9, 2023.
26 Wang Lei: Getting Out of the Myth of Platform Governance: The Benign Interaction Between Regulation and Antitrust. Exploration and Free Views, Issue 3, 2022.
27 See Rogerson, William P., and Howard Shelanski. "Antitrust enforcement, regulation, and digital platforms." U. pa. l. Rev. 168 (2019): 1911.

IV. Direction of legislation for digital platforms during dynamic reconfiguration of the relationship between anti-monopoly regulation and industry regulation

17. The architecture and capabilities of digital platforms enable them to exert control over the ecosystem far beyond the radiation scope of their property rights. In the face of this new market organization form of digital platforms, various jurisdictions are constantly exploring whether and how to regulate digital platforms, and whether separate legislation is necessary for digital platforms.

(I) Jurisdictions in European Union and the United Kingdom, etc. are exploring legislation models for the independent and comprehensive regulation of digital platforms

18. The European Union (EU) has recognized that the EU competition law framework is insufficiently flexible and lagging in dealing with digital platforms. Therefore, it focuses on the powerful market cohesion and transmission effect brought about by the innovative development of digital platforms through their massive user base, vast data, and algorithmic technologies, as well as the negative impacts on users' data privacy and even social democratic fairness. It is committed to exploring the development of new regulatory tools outside the anti-monopoly regulatory framework dominated by the *Treaty on the Functioning of the European Union (TFEU)*. The most important measures taken by EU were the introduction of the *Digital Markets Act* and the *Digital Services Act*. The *Digital Markets Act* adopted by the EU Council in July 2022 has introduced the "gatekeeper" system in legislation for the first time, setting a series of fundamental and discretionary obligations for ultra-large digital platforms that can be recognized as a "gatekeeper", and also establishing a regulatory framework for continuously assessing and monitoring the market behaviors of "gatekeeper" platforms. Unlike the post-event regulation of anti-monopoly law, the EU's *Digital Markets Act* fundamentally emphasizes the importance of pre-regulation. Based on the platform's position in the digital service market and the enterprise scale and other elements, the *Digital Markets Act* predefines the obligations that the platforms should fulfill, and encourages digital platforms to compete fairly in the digital market, thereby enhancing the competitiveness of the digital market and safeguarding the users' diversified options. In the *Digital Services Act*, the EU also attaches great importance to the division of the subjects of duty. It adopts a hierarchical and classified approach to establish a hierarchical responsibility framework, and divides the regulation objects into intermediary service providers of network infrastructure, intermediate platforms providing online services for consumers and sellers,

super-large online search engines, and super-large network platforms. Although the EU's *Digital Services Act* attaches greater importance to the governance of online contents and advertisements, it also emphasizes hierarchical responsibilities and obligations of digital platforms in nature.

19. On May 24, 2024, *Digital Markets, Competition, and Consumers Act (DMCCA)* in the United Kingdom (UK)[28] was approved and took formal effect. *DMCCA* is referred to as the UK version of the *Digital Markets Act*, mainly aiming to control the monopolistic position and ensure that market access is open to smaller participants. For example, large companies are required to enhance their transparency and make their data available to search engines of their competitors; carry out targeted interventions and implement tailor-made behavioral guidelines and so on. It also specifies a series of obligations and prohibited behaviors ought to be followed by large science and technology companies. *EU-UK Trade and Cooperation Agreement* was also signed between UK and EU[29], aiming to supplement *DMCCA* by supporting international cooperation and sharing information with other regulatory agencies.

(II) Jurisdictions in Japan and Australia, etc. are exploring legislation models for the independent but not comprehensive regulation of digital platforms

20. In May 2020, the *Act on Improving Transparency and Fairness of Digital Platforms* was adopted in Japan, mainly aiming to define specific regulation objects, and requiring the Internet platform enterprises that are designated as such objects to be subject to the constraints of this Act.[30] On April 26, 2025, the *Act on Promotion of Competition Related to Specified Smartphone Software* was adopted by the Cabinet of Japan, aiming to create a competitive environment for specific smartphone software, promote innovation by various entities, provide the consumers with more service options, and ensure service security. The Japan Fair Trade Commission (JFTC) will, through a cabinet order, designate software service providers with certain business scales for various specific software subject to the new regulations. Enterprises that meet the standards set by the cabinet order will be referred to as "Designated Providers". This Act will stipulate that the designated providers are prohibited from engaging in certain behaviors and are required to take certain compliance measures, and the details are as follows: (1) The designated providers shall not prevent

---

28 See Digital Markets, Competition and Consumers Act 2024, https://www.legislation.gov.uk/ukpga/2024/13/contents.

29 See The EU-UK Trade and Cooperation Agreement, https://commission.europa.eu/strategy-and-policy/relations-united-kingdom/eu-uk-trade-and-cooperation-agreement_en.

30 Wang Xianlin: International Observations and Domestic Reflections on Anti-Monopoly in Digital Platforms. Journal of University of Chinese Academy of Social Sciences, Issue 5, 2022.

third-party providers from providing their own application stores; (2) The designated providers shall not prevent its users from using third-party billing systems (but this may be applicable to exceptional circumstances); (3) The designated providers shall make the default settings of the smart phone easy to modify, and provide screens for selecting the browser, etc.; (4) The designated providers shall not, without good reasons, offer any form of preferential treatment regarding its services over its competitors in the search results; (5) The designated providers shall not use the data they have obtained about competing applications for their own applications; (6) The designated providers shall not prevent the application developers from using the same level of functionality controlled by the operating system as that provided by them (but this may be applicable to exceptional circumstances).

21. In February 2021, the *News Media and Digital Platforms Mandatory Bargaining Code* was adopted by the Parliament of Australia, aiming to encourage digital platforms and news media to negotiate and bargain with each other, and have the state intervene forcibly for miscellaneous arbitration. Before introduction of this Code, digital platforms often claimed that they provided the news publishers with more than what they could receive in return, and refused to negotiate for fairer terms or compensation. On the basis of referring to Australian Acts, the *Online News Act* was proposed in Canada in April 2022, aiming to address the problems such as insufficient protection for smaller media, and lack of transparency in regulation, and establish a negotiation procedure and regulatory framework, enabling traditional media in Canada to negotiate agreements with digital platforms. And through the intervention of government regulatory agencies, it tries to better protect smaller news media and enhance the transparency of negotiations between media and platforms.[31]

(III) Jurisdictions in Germany, etc. are exploring a non-separate legislation model for regulation of digital platforms

22. Not all jurisdictions would have separate legislation for digital platforms. For example, the 10th Revision of the German *Act against Restraints of Competition* (known as the "digital reform process of anti-monopoly law") took effect on January 19, 2021. This Revision aimed to address the challenges brought about by platforms and big data, and proposed a series of core provisions for improvement of regulation, mainly focusing on the regulation of behaviors abusing market force, including adding "the capability to obtain competition-related data" as a factor in the determination of market dominance, giving priority consideration to

---

31 Chen Hongmei, Zhang Yaoying: Monopoly Regulation, Responsibility Definition, Interest Balance: Extraterritorial Experience and Enlightenment of Digital Platform Governance. Editorial Friend, Issue 8, 2024.

"intermediary power", introducing special regulations for "platforms with cross-market competitive advantages", clearly defining data as the prerequisite for recognizing necessary facility in abusive behaviors, and improving the system for prohibiting the abuse of relative dominant position, etc.[32] On September 26, 2022, the German Federal Ministry of Economic Affairs and Climate Protection has released the ministerial draft for the 11th revision of the German *Act against Restraints of Competition*, and the full title of this ministerial draft is *Ministerial Draft for Optimizing the Competitive Structure and Deriving Benefits from Monopolistic Behaviors in Taxation*. As for the 11th revision of the German *Act against Restraints of Competition*, one of its objectives was to prepare measures for the implementation of the EU *Digital Markets Act*. It was planned to set the legal basis for the implementation of the EU *Digital Markets Act* within Germany in the 11th revision of the German *Act against Restraints of Competition*, thereby establishing a mechanism applicable to integration of the *Act against Restraints of Competition* and the EU *Digital Markets Act*. On November 7, 2023, the 11th revision of the German *Act against Restraints of Competition* took formal effect. Germany mainly achieves the regulation of digital platforms by revising the *Act against Restraints of Competition*, which differs from the EU's separate legislation model for regulation of digital platforms.

(IV) China is also exploring and selecting the legislation model for regulation of digital platforms

23. As for the *Electronic Commerce Law* officially implemented in China on January 1, 2019, it clearly defined the legal responsibilities of e-commerce platform operators, established a series of responsibility norms for e-commerce platform operators, and has for the first time established the normative system related to e-commerce platforms. Among them, the regulations concerning a series of platform responsibilities for audit, cybersecurity maintenance, content management control, trade security guarantee, the publicity of relevant information, as well as the preservation of trade information, intellectual property protection, and consumer rights protection, etc., were highly pertinent and represented the most significant legislative highlight of the *Electronic Commerce Law*. On October 29, 2021, to better promote the standardized and healthy development of platform economy in China, and enhance the pertinence and effectiveness of regulation, the State Administration for Market Regulation (SAMR) organized the drafting of the *Guidelines for Classifying and Grading Internet Platforms (Draft for Comments)* and the *Guidelines for Internet*

---

32 Jia Yuan: The Modernization of Anti-monopoly Regulation for Germany's Abuse of Market Power in the Digital Era – Review of the 10th Revision of the "German Act against Restraints of Competition". Deutschland-studien, Issue 2, 2021.

Platforms to Fulfill Their Primary Responsibilities (Draft for Comments), soliciting comments from the public. However, these two guidelines have not been officially promulgated and implemented. On June 10, 2025, to strengthen the regulation of live-stream e-commerce, protect the legitimate rights and interests of consumers and business operators, and promote the healthy development of live-stream e-commerce, in accordance with laws and regulations such as the *Electronic Commerce Law*, the *Cybersecurity Law*, and the *Law on the Protection of Consumer Rights and Interests*, the SAMR released the draft *Administrative Measures for Supervision of Live-Stream E-commerce (Draft for Comments)* to solicit comments from the public, making specific provisions on the rights and obligations of the subjects such as live-stream platform operators and live-stream room operators, etc. The above legislative actions indicate that the legislation model for digital platforms in China currently opts for legislation in a more targeted and precise manner, which is still under dynamic changes.

V. Conclusions

24. Not only the anti-monopoly law enforcement agencies but also the government industry regulation organs have the legal authority to maintain market competition. Starting from the objective of maximizing the overall social interests, there is no ultimate conflict of interest between anti-monopoly law enforcement agencies and government industry regulation organs. The anti-monopoly enforcement agencies and the government industry regulation organs will form the relationship patterns featuring each performing its own functions, mutual restraints, checks and balances, overlapping law enforcement, and interactive coordination. These relationship patterns will coexist simultaneously and are always changing. The emergence of digital platforms has brought about many challenges to anti-monopoly regulation and industry regulation, and the selection of the legislation model for digital platforms will have an impact on the relationship between anti-monopoly regulation and industry regulation. Since different jurisdictions have different approaches and are exploring whether to and how to make legislation for digital platforms, the relationship between anti-monopoly regulation and industry regulation of digital platforms is dynamic and has regional differences. Due to the current selection of implementing legislation in a more targeted and precise manner for digital platforms in China, the relationship between anti-monopoly regulation and industry regulation of digital platforms in China will still exhibit industry-based differences, and is still in dynamic development.

Anti-monopoly Regulation of Internet Platform from the Perspective of the Public Character

ZHANG CHENYING

Professor & Director, Center for Competition Law,
Tsinghua University, Beijing

Abstract

Internet platforms have undergone a threefold evolution, emerging as new economic hubs that integrate information aggregation, factor production, resource allocation, and rule-making, while functioning as organizational forms through which stakeholders co-create value. Characterized by multi-industry integration, platforms perform ecological functions that reshape production processes and organizational structures, transform modes of resource allocation, and operate as a "third force" between political authority and market power. Unlike the traditional economy, the platform economy exhibits distinct competitive characteristics, posing profound technical, regulatory, and jurisprudential challenges to global antitrust regimes. At its core lies the increasing penetration of platforms into the social and economic order, with their public character becoming ever more salient. However, in the absence of effective regulation, this public character has been alienated, leading to competitive distortions and monopolistic outcomes, particularly manifesting in the non-openness and non-neutrality of data and platform elements. To rectify such distortions and restore competitive order, it is essential to reform the antitrust framework by introducing rules grounded in the logic of abuse of public character. This entails imposing competitive obligations on qualified platform operators, thereby fostering innovation while safeguarding the legitimate rights and interests of all participants in the platform ecosystem.

Anti-monopoly Regulation of Internet Platform from the Perspective of the Public Character

1. The rise of Internet platforms – hereinafter referred to as "platforms" – is one of the three hallmark events of the digital revolution. As a form of market organization, platforms have long existed throughout history. However, with the development of information technology, today's platforms have undergone a qualitative transformation, evolving into new economic hubs that integrate information aggregation, factor production, resource allocation, and rule-making. In doing so, they have reshaped the structure of economic production and become an inseparable part of the economic, political, and cultural spheres.

2. Along with the expansion of platform power, Internet platforms that were originally expected to embody the values of openness, sharing, and circulation have gradually moved toward a form of "feudalization", establishing barriers to entry that result in market failures and exert negative impacts on consumer welfare and innovation, while also posing risks to political security, data security, and individual privacy. In response, scholars have proposed various regulatory approaches from the perspectives of anti-monopoly principles, regulatory techniques, and enforcement paths. The reason the Internet platform challenges tradition on many issues is that it is different starting point and even the bottom logic from the existing anti-monopoly rules which follow the "market" as the analysis basis. The platform has the property of public goods depending on the scale, and the large platform which gradually has the powerful infiltration, social influence, and dominance finally embody the public character. But this public character is alienated by the platform's selfishness, which presents an anti-public character of the data and platform elements, namely abuse of its public character. To correct this kind of monopolistic acts, we need to set up competitive obligation for the appropriate platform and formulate new anti-monopoly rule on the competitive obligation.

I. Analysis of Internet Platforms and the Challenges of Antitrust Regulation

I) Deconstruction of platform and its dual value

3. As a form of business organization, Internet platforms connect multiple participants under a set of defined rules through network technology, thereby enabling the co-creation of value. The connotation of "platform" encompasses three interrelated levels: first, Internet technology serves as the foundational infrastructure for resource integration; second, the platform functions as a carrier for bilateral or multilateral interactions; and third, it represents an organizational form through which relevant actors jointly generate value.

4. The platform ecosystem is primarily composed of three groups: platform operators, in-platform business operators, and consumers. These three categories

of participants are interlinked through five key relationships, which simultaneously constitute legal relationships and embody the logical framework for the realization and transmission of platform value. Modern platforms integrate both a "data base" and "connectivity," which are mutually reinforcing and causally intertwined. "Platformization" is the most fundamental property of the Internet platform – it aggregates individuals with different needs onto a single networked space, enabling each party to fulfill their interests through interactive engagement. The value-creation logic of platform economies lies in reducing transaction costs through "connection" and "aggregation," thereby achieving integrative efficiency. Unlike traditional trading venues, platforms are not only aggregators of data but also producers of data. On the platform, each consumer's preferences and behavioral patterns can be encoded into data, which the platform uses to push personalized content and services, thereby enhancing user stickiness and generating a "lock-in effect." Moreover, platforms exhibit pronounced network externalities and scale effects: the greater the number of users, the more likely it is that diverse and heterogeneous needs will be met, the higher the efficiency of resource allocation, and the stronger the user dependence on the platform.

II) Platform development and subversion of economic pattern

5. Today, by virtue of their extensive resources and market power, Internet platforms have evolved into a new form of economic organization that integrates the industrial chain, fuses value chains, and enhances the efficiency of market resource allocation. Their functions have expanded from virtual domains to encompass the physical economy. At present, ecosystem structures centered on super platforms have already taken shape, and the initial decentralized, peer-to-peer interaction model of the Internet has gradually transformed into a model of "limited decentralization" grounded in platform power.

6. Platforms have fundamentally reshaped the economic landscape in three key dimensions. First, they have altered the processes and organizational forms of economic production. Second, they have transformed the mechanisms of resource allocation. Third, data has emerged as a production factor on par with land, labor, capital, and technology. Through these three structural transformations, platforms have come to serve as both managers of their ecosystems and producers of data elements. Compared to traditional operators along the industrial value chain, they enjoy a competitive edge and have become central actors in the emerging digital economy.

III) Reshaping of competition order and platform economy from the global perspective: anti-monopoly dilemma

7. The rapid rise of the platform economy has introduced a new set of competitive characteristics. No longer constrained by physical space, and amplified by powerful network effects, platforms can theoretically expand

without limit. As a result, the platform economy has given rise to a "single oligopoly competitive monopoly" structure, demonstrating a level of aggressiveness surpassing that of the traditional economy. Antitrust issues under the platform economy are more acute and wide-ranging than those of the industrial era. They extend far beyond competition within defined relevant markets, encompassing structural tensions between traditional and emerging domestic industries, intra-industry competition within the new economy, the configuration of the national economic framework, and even international economic and trade relations. Moreover, the influence of platforms reaches into domains beyond economics, implicating systemic concerns in politics, democratic governance, and consumer privacy.

8. In response, enforcement agencies across jurisdictions have repeatedly initiated antitrust actions in an effort to rein in monopolistic behavior by large platform companies. However, the outcomes have largely fallen short of expectations. The continued reliance on the traditional concept of the "relevant market" reflects a fragmented understanding of platforms, failing to capture their essence as integrated ecosystems. As a result, existing antitrust rules have struggled to effectively address the challenges posed by platform-based economies.

9. Against this backdrop, there is an urgent need to reshape the legal order governing competition. The European Union's introduction of gatekeeper rules outside the conventional antitrust framework, along with the emergence of the New Brandeis School in the United States – which emphasizes the multi-dimensional values of antitrust and the preservation of the competitive process – demonstrates that the regulatory order of antitrust law is undergoing a profound transformation in the era of platform capitalism.

II. Public Character and Its Alienation: The Internal Logic of Platform Monopoly

10. In the era of the digital economy, large-scale Internet platforms exhibit pronounced social and public attributes. The traditional rights-and-obligations framework under private law is no longer sufficient to address the imbalance of legal relationships that has emerged – nor can it rectify the resultant disorder in competitive dynamics.

I) From private interest to public character: the transformation of platform roles

11. The relationship between platforms and users is reflected in two dimensions: the nature of the products and services offered by the platform, and the scope of the platform's managerial power. Specifically, platforms embody the characteristics of public goods and serve as carriers of public

character. At the same time, they perform "quasi-governmental functions," which represent the power dimension of their public character. Platforms are no longer merely private entities; instead, they increasingly assume the nature of public goods. Accordingly, their role has shifted from private operators to public service providers.

12. In economics, goods and services are classified as either private or public. Public goods are defined by non-exclusivity and non-rivalry – traits that often correlate with market failures and necessitate government intervention. In real-world economies, purely public goods are rare, while "quasi-public goods" that lie between public and private categories are widely observed. Platforms already exhibit several attributes of public goods. First, Internet platforms do not exclude new users; on the contrary, more user participation significantly increases the platform's value, demonstrating their non-exclusivity. Second, the utility one user derives from a platform does not diminish that of others, highlighting the platform's non-rivalrous nature.

13. According to the new governance theory, the standard for judging whether an organization has a public character has already "changed from the identity of public character to the behavior of public character". Today, platforms have emerged as a "third power" beyond the traditional dichotomy of the market and the state. Formally, platforms exercise "quasi-legislative," "quasi-judicial," and "quasi-administrative" powers (with "law" here understood as a form of social ordering). Substantively, the platform's management authority carries implications of public governance. Platform operators, in effect, perform the function of maintaining internal competitive order. The essence of platform power lies in its de facto dominance and influence, which stems from the platform's deep penetration into all aspects of daily life, economic production, and even public administration. It is through this expansive influence that platforms have acquired the status of a de facto "third power." As their public character expands, internal platform management becomes not only a matter of private right, but also an economic authority arising from market forces or technological capabilities. Once endowed with public character, platforms undergo a subtle transformation in their competitive role: on one hand, they shift from mere participants in competition to de facto managers of competition; on the other hand, they expand from being market competitors to becoming infrastructures that permeate competition across industries, thereby constituting a new foundation for competition in the digital economy era.

II) From Public character to private interest: role alienation and platform monopoly

14. The tension between the private interest and the public character of platforms constitutes an inherently irreconcilable contradiction. The pursuit of self-interest by platforms leads to a distortion of their original role,

manifesting in an "anti-public" nature. This alienation undermines both platform governance and market governance, ultimately harming the public interest of society.

15. First, the alienation of data elements. Driven by profit-seeking instincts, platforms tend to exercise exclusive control over data resources, thereby transforming data from a public element into a private asset. However, as a non-exhaustible resource, data should not be subject to exclusive possession by any one entity. The monopolization and arbitrary use of sensitive personal data by platforms can infringe upon individual privacy rights. Moreover, since a significant portion of raw data is contributed by users themselves, such data should not be treated as proprietary assets of platforms. Furthermore, platforms often refuse to grant access to key databases, creating data silos that serve to exclude or restrict competition.

16. Second, the alienation of platform elements. The public character of platforms requires them to remain accessible to all qualified users to the greatest extent possible. However, as platforms evolve into super platforms, their intrinsic openness becomes increasingly incompatible with the goal of maximizing private interest. Consequently, platforms may adopt exclusionary or non-interoperable policies. The alienation of platform public character lies at the heart of platform monopolies and serves as a key distinction from monopoly problems in traditional industries. This shift results in an asymmetry between platform "rights and obligations" and between "power and oversight," posing a substantial barrier to fair market competition. Given that platforms exercise quasi-governmental authority in economic management, they should be held to standards of neutrality and subject to external supervision. In response to competitive distortions caused by the alienation of public character, antitrust law must intervene in transactional processes to correct abuses of public power and restore competitive order.

III. Returning to Public Character: The Competitive Obligations of Internet Platforms

17. The disorder in platform competition fundamentally stems from the divergence between private interest and public character. The key to effective platform governance lies in restoring platforms to their normative position as carriers of public character. To this end, the imposition of competitive obligations on platforms – requiring them to foster an open and free competitive environment – serves as a novel regulatory tool that aligns closely with the public nature of platforms. At the same time, it also delineates the boundaries of platform responsibilities.

I) The contours of competitive obligations

18. To shift platforms once again from private interest back toward public character, it is essential that they assume "competitive obligations" aimed at preserving a fair and orderly market environment. These obligations comprise three core dimensions:

19. First, the imposition of competitive obligations must be premised on the platform's public character. The determination of whether a platform possesses such public character serves as a precondition – much like the identification of "market dominance" functions as a prerequisite in cases of abuse of dominance. Second, the purpose of competitive obligations is to restore the "competitiveness" of the platform ecosystem. In practice, this is primarily achieved through ex post enforcement by competition authorities, and the scope of such obligations should be strictly limited to promoting free and fair competition in the market. Third, competitive obligations are predominantly negative in nature – prohibiting certain conduct – while being supplemented by structural obligations. Negative obligations are generally clear and limited in scope, imposing specific prohibitions on platform operators. Structural obligations, by contrast, have a far more significant impact on the business entity and should not be the preferred remedy. Rather, they serve as a fallback mechanism where behavioral obligations fail to achieve the intended competitive outcomes.

II) Fundamental principles of competitive obligations

20. The imposition of competitive obligations on qualified platforms aims to foster competition in the platform economy through institutional design. At the same time, government intervention in platform governance must be appropriately constrained, respecting the platform's business autonomy and safeguarding its legitimate rights, thereby achieving a balance between effective competition and the incentive to innovate. The design of competitive obligations should adhere to the following principles:

21. First, the external boundary of competitive obligations lies in the pursuit of the public interest. From a static perspective, public interest requires the balancing of legal relationships within the platform ecosystem to achieve the most just allocation of rights and responsibilities. From a dynamic perspective, public interest prioritizes economic development and Pareto improvements, which may override static distributional concerns. The principle of public interest thus provides both the regulatory objective and guiding rationale for competitive obligations.

22. Second, the internal boundary of competitive obligations lies in achieving substantive fairness in the market. Regulatory intervention in platform conduct must conform to the principles of legitimacy, proportionality, and minimal impairment, ensuring that interference with commercial activity is reduced to the lowest feasible level. The principle of substantive

fairness focuses on curbing inappropriate platform conduct and serves as the normative foundation for imposing negative competitive obligations.

23. Third, competitive obligation rules should be based on the principle of "openness, neutrality, and reasonable discrimination." Openness requires allowing access to both the platform and its data elements – any party willing to comply with the platform's service agreement and to use its resources in good faith should not be excluded. Neutrality entails that platform managers treat all operators equally and provide a fair competitive environment. The combined principles of openness, neutrality, and reasonable discrimination offer a methodological framework for resolving the competitive concerns posed by dominant platforms.

III) Dynamic perspective of competitive obligations: taking promotion of innovation as the boundary

24. The "Schumpeter–Arrow debate" remains a classical point of reference for understanding the relationship between innovation and competition. However, in the digital economy, platforms exhibit cross-sectoral integration and positive enabling effects, rendering platform-based innovation only partially compatible with the traditional Schumpeter–Arrow framework. In platform markets, this debate traditionally corresponds to the question of how inter-platform competition promotes innovation. Yet, in the platform economy, innovation has evolved into a systemic phenomenon – what is at stake is no longer individual innovation but innovation at the level of the entire platform ecosystem. In this regard, platforms function not merely as participants in innovation but as organizers and managers of an innovation ecosystem. Innovation is carried out by various actors within the platform, characterized by co-creation of value. Mathematically speaking, the promotion of innovation should be understood as a weighted average of platform-led innovation and ecosystem-wide innovation – an integrated process that transcends the scope of the original Schumpeter–Arrow debate.

25. Competitive obligations should thus focus on the impact of platform conduct on internal innovation dynamics, with the goal of preventing a negative innovation cycle caused by abuse of managerial authority. The vitality of a platform's internal innovation ecosystem is closely tied to its competitive environment, and the key lies in preventing inappropriate interference by platform operators with the innovative activities of in-platform business users. Specific forms of such interference include: Firstly, self-preferencing – when platform operators use their dominant position to extend market power into adjacent markets, favoring their own products or services, they undermine the innovation incentives of other operators. Secondly, discriminatory treatment: Unequal access to fundamental platform resources such as search visibility, traffic flow, or data availability may significantly exclude or restrict innovation by disfavored participants. Thirdly, exploitative pricing: Excessive platform usage fees imposed by operators increase the cost of

innovation for smaller entities and startups, thereby dampening their ability to invest in R&D. Finally, killer acquisitions: Refers to large platform companies acquiring startups – not to integrate innovation, but to eliminate emerging competitors with rapid user growth or high potential. Such conduct raises entry barriers and erodes innovation incentives across the market.

IV) Static perspective of competitive obligations: two pairs of relationships with platform operators as the core

26. Platforms, in the course of managing and interacting with merchants and consumers, should also bear corresponding competitive obligations. The State Administration for Market Regulation has explicitly required that platform enterprises uphold principles of "fairness, reasonableness, and non-discrimination" and maintain "objectivity and neutrality" in their dealings with merchants and consumers.

27. The relationship between platforms and merchants involves not only a managerial dimension but also a potential competitive one. Platforms must refrain from leveraging their dual role to gain unfair advantages in internal competition – particularly through practices such as cross-subsidization or self-preferencing. Moreover, platforms should avoid engaging in unreasonable discriminatory treatment among merchants within the platform and should also be closely scrutinized for engaging in predatory pricing practices that lead to the "creative destruction" of traditional industries.

28. Competitive obligations should also address two aspects of platform conduct toward consumers: improper interference with users' freedom of choice, and unjustified encroachments on consumer privacy. Firstly, platforms must respect consumers' freedom of choice, which is a fundamental precondition for the operation of a competitive market and the mechanism of survival of the fittest. Secondly, there exists an inherent tension between consumer privacy and the openness of data. Although the ownership of data remains an unsettled legal issue, data can be classified based on the degree of sensitivity it contains. With technological advancement, data anonymization presents a possible solution. Once the correlation between consumer data and personal identity is severed – either by platform operators or by independent data intermediary agencies using algorithms – certain data can be legitimately opened for use.

IV. Constructing an Antitrust Framework for Internet Platforms: Realizing Competitive Obligations

29. The reform of antitrust rules for Internet platforms should center on regulating platforms' performance of their competitive obligations. At the level of regulatory logic, it is essential to revise the existing antitrust

framework by rethinking the concept of market dominance and establishing a coherent theory and set of rules for the abuse of public character. In terms of the substantive content of platform obligations, the guiding principle should be one of "openness, neutrality, and reasonable discrimination." On this basis, two regulatory rules should be established: first, subject-based prequalification rules, which determine whether a platform qualifies as a public character entity; and second, behavioral remedies as a priority, emphasizing conduct-based interventions over structural remedies. Given that Internet platforms have already evolved into complex ecosystems, it is necessary to rely on governmental oversight to enforce competitive obligations and overcome inefficiencies in resource allocation. In terms of regulatory pathway, antitrust enforcement remains preferable to sectoral regulation, as it better aligns with the overarching goal of restoring competitive order in platform-based markets.

I) Abuse of public character and market Dominance

30. Monopolistic conduct by Internet platforms fundamentally stems from an abuse of public character. Within the current framework of antitrust law, there are two possible approaches to establishing the platform's public character as a necessary precondition. The first approach is to integrate the notion of public character into existing rules under Article 18 of the Anti-Monopoly Law by adopting a more flexible standard of interpretation – such as Paragraph 4, which concerns "the degree of dependence of other operators on the undertaking in transactions," or Paragraph 5, regarding "the difficulty for other undertakings to enter the relevant market." The second approach is to develop an independent standard specifically tailored to the public character of Internet platforms, as exemplified by the "gatekeeper obligations" under the European Union's Digital Markets Act (Draft).

31. Public character constitutes a unique form of market power that is closely related to – but conceptually distinct from – market dominance. In the context of the platform economy, the traditional logic and conclusions associated with the identification of market dominance often lead to paradoxes. Moreover, existing standards for determining market dominance fail to accurately capture the true nature of platform power. Market dominance reflects an undertaking's ability to control the competitive landscape and trading conditions within a specific relevant market. The primary concern of abuse of dominance lies in the firm's conduct that harms upstream or downstream market competition. In contrast, the public character of platforms emphasizes their emergent role as foundational infrastructure in the digital era. Abuse of public character, therefore, is more concerned with the platform's structural impact across broader sectors and industries. Accordingly, public character more accurately reflects the operational logic of platform economies and the sources of

their market power. It follows that, in the context of antitrust regulation of Internet platforms, public character should be treated as an independent analytical category, with its own criteria for assessment.

II) Rule construction for correcting the abuse of public character

32. Antitrust regulation of Internet platforms takes public character as its logical point of departure and aims to correct the alienation of data and platform structures by constructing a system of competitive obligations. At the institutional level, the regulatory framework unfolds across three dimensions: the qualification of obligated entities, the scope of openness, and the modalities of obligation performance.

33. First, the construction of prequalification rules centered on public character. These prequalification rules differ from traditional ex ante regulatory approvals concerning market access or specific conduct. In contrast, antitrust law is grounded in the creation of an open and free competitive environment, and it supervises the legality of platform conduct in a primarily ex post manner, in contrast to sector-specific regulation. The identification of public character may refer to standards in the EU and U.S., and should focus on four key indicators: business scope, platform scale and technical capacity, transaction volume, and user base. In practice, industry regulators should conduct empirical analysis based on the realities of China's platform economy and establish a clear, concise, and quantifiable set of objective standards using economic modeling, with periodic updates.

34. Second, the behavioral rules should follow the principles of openness, neutrality, and reasonable discrimination. Openness and neutrality should be the general rule for platforms with public character, while denial of access to certain operators should be treated as an exception, subject to compelling justification – such as failure to pay reasonable compensation, objective technical barriers, transaction security concerns, or risks to national security. Regarding the content of openness, several distinctions must be made: First, there should be a clear separation between intermediary platform services and data, as the nature and method of opening differ substantially. Second, a distinction should be drawn between public character services and non-public services: the former should remain open and neutral, while the latter may be subject to the platform operator's commercial discretion. Third, in terms of data openness, raw data should be open, whereas processed data and non-anonymized data should not fall within the scope of mandatory openness. Since competitive obligations are primarily negative in nature, a dual-list mechanism should be adopted to guide platform operators – comprising a positive list that recommends categories of platform services and data to be opened under the principles

of openness and neutrality, and a negative list that explicitly prohibits certain conduct. Actions falling outside the negative list should remain within the domain of contractual autonomy.

35. Third, the correction of abuse should prioritize behavioral remedies, along with a re-evaluation of the preventive function of regulation. Since platform ecosystem governance is analogous to corporate governance and constitutes part of a platform's regular operations, behavioral remedies should generally be the primary regulatory response to the abuse of public character. However, behavioral remedies are not always sufficient, and in exceptional cases, structural remedies may be warranted.

II) Regulatory pathways for competitive obligations: antitrust enforcement and sectoral regulation

36. To ensure that Internet platforms fulfill their competitive obligations – that is, to guide them from private interest back toward public character – there are two principal regulatory pathways: antitrust enforcement and sectoral regulation. These two mechanisms are not mutually exclusive, but rather complementary. In the context of regulating platform obligations, the core issue lies in the alienation of data and platform elements, which harms public character. The appropriate response is to open platforms and promote data flows. From this perspective, antitrust enforcement is indispensable, while sectoral regulation plays a vital supplementary role.

37. On the one hand, traditional models of sectoral regulation are not well-suited to the platform economy. First, Internet platforms do not exhibit the defining characteristics of naturally regulated industries. The platform economy is an open, data-driven commercial structure with highly cross-sectoral and fluid boundaries, making it difficult to establish a coherent sectoral regime or dedicated legislation. Additionally, the data on which platforms operate is inherently intangible, duplicable, and multi-possessory, which transcends physical constraints and undermines the conventional justification for natural monopoly regulation. In fact, the very objective of regulating platforms is not to protect a monopoly but to dismantle the capture of public character by private interests – i.e., to combat monopoly itself. Thus, the logic of full-chain sectoral regulation does not apply. Second, conventional tools such as price controls are inapplicable to platforms. Finally, the fragmented nature of sectoral regulation is inadequate for addressing the platform economy's complex ecological structure and legal challenges. In the absence of a unified regulatory authority, overlapping mandates often result in regulatory vacuums.

38. On the other hand, antitrust enforcement and sectoral regulation are fundamentally complementary. First, they provide different but mutually reinforcing perspectives. Antitrust law is based on the principle of free and fair competition; its focus is on dismantling monopolies and restoring

competitive market order through economic means. Sectoral regulators, by contrast, operate from an industry-specific perspective, offering greater expertise in areas such as technical standards, operational norms, and public safety. Second, sectoral oversight remains essential in certain areas of platform operation. From the standpoint of regulatory timing, two scenarios can be distinguished: During regular platform operations, public authorities should supervise the platform's quasi-governmental functions to prevent potential abuses before they occur. Once harm has occurred, government authorities must investigate and impose legal responsibility, including corrective orders – thus serving a remedial function. Finally, sectoral regulation provides crucial support for antitrust enforcement. Restoring the public character of platforms and maintaining a competitive, open market is a foundational value of antitrust law. The reformed antitrust framework – through updated legal standards, institutional mechanisms, and technical tools – can effectively constrain monopolistic behavior. However, sectoral regulators hold technical and informational advantages. Their views are especially important in determining key issues such as the qualification of public character entities and the standards for identifying equivalent competitors. In sum, antitrust enforcement and sectoral regulation should operate in parallel, each performing its respective role to the fullest extent.

Competition Law Regulations on Abuse of Data Advantages

JIA YUAN[*]

Law School of Sichuan University, Chengdu, Sichuan

Abstract

Abuse of Data Advantages in the digital economy era not only induces competition damages such as direct exclusion effect, supply squeeze effect and market blocking effect, but also hinders the flow and use of innovative elements, which is not conducive to the full release of the value of data elements. China's Anti-Monopoly Law and Anti-Unfair Competition Law have both been digitally transformed or in transformation, but how to coordinate the relationship between the two in order to shape the systematic rules of data competition is still inconclusive. In China, it is appropriate to regulate the abuse of data advantages with a hierarchical structure of market dominance and relative trading advantage, while the Anti-Monopoly Law adjusts the exclusive abuse and focuses on guaranteeing the accessibility of specific data, and the Anti-Unfair Competition Law adjusts the exploitative abuse and focuses on safeguarding the right to fair trade.

---

[*] Dr. Jia Yuan, Associate Professor and doctoral supervisor in Law School of Sichuan University, Director of Innovation and Competition Law Research Center.

1. With the rapid advancement of the fourth industrial revolution, marked by big data, artificial intelligence, and the Internet of Things (IoT), human society is gradually entering the digital economy era. China's digital economy is experiencing rapid growth, with digital companies like Huawei, Alibaba, and Tencent emerging as leaders. Government departments and various enterprises have also accumulated significant data volumes during the development of digital cities and digital governance, laying a solid foundation for the next phase of high-quality digital economic development.

2. Data is a core element in the development of the digital economy. Establishing fair and orderly data competition rules is crucial for achieving digital economic development goals. The main obstacle to the development of the digital economy is the lack of free and orderly data flow. Some enterprises and platforms with early-mover advantages have accumulated large amounts of data, hoping to gain more market advantages through continuous data accumulation. However, emerging small and medium-sized enterprises (SMEs) need more data during the digitalization process to participate in fair competition. This has led to increasingly intense conflicts between these two groups. In recent years, frequent data-related anti-monopoly and unfair competition disputes in the practice of digital economic development serve as evidence of this.[1] Additionally, the misuse of data advantages can harm consumer rights and innovation. Therefore, while establishing the data property rights system, it is also necessary to reasonably design and refine the rules for data utilization (i.e., data competition rules). In the process of building data competition rules, it is essential to first study the characteristics of data and their competitive implications. Based on this, summarize and refine the mechanisms of data advantage formation and the characteristics of behaviors that may constitute the abuse of data advantages. Ultimately, improve the existing competition law system by integrating data characteristics and the goal of digital economic development, making it an important part of the data foundation system that highlights innovation leadership. This will ultimately achieve the goal of realizing the value of data elements and promoting the sharing of digital economic development benefits among all citizens.

1. The Necessity of Regulating the Abuse of Data Advantage is Proved

1.1 Data advantage becomes a new source of market power

3. Data serves as a critical input and production factor, in the processes of product development, service provision, and value chain realization. Consequently, the accumulation of data can provide significant competitive

---

[1] Sun Jin: The Inheritance and Innovation of Anti-Unfair Competition Rules in the Era of Digital Economy: Centering on the Third Revision of Anti-Unfair Competition Law [J]. China Law Review, 2023,3.

advantages, primarily in two areas: First, in the Internet economy where data is a key production factor, the more data a company accumulates, the more popular and frequently used its Internet products (such as social media, shopping, games, and videos) become among users. This, in turn, attracts more users and data, which amplifies the company's data advantage through positive network effects. Second, as data becomes a key production factor in more industries, having a substantial amount of data provides companies with a solid foundation for entering new industries and fields. In this context, companies with a significant data advantage are more likely to gain competitive advantages in new industries and markets, thereby achieving indirect network effects. Furthermore, on the basis of both direct and indirect network effects, some large enterprises can build and refine digital ecosystems, becoming super market forces.[2]

4. In the digital economy era, innovation activities are often driven by the utilization of data, particularly in the development of new algorithms like generative AI. This enables operators who possess vast amounts of data to more easily develop new products and services through various algorithms. From a business perspective, moderate data concentration indeed facilitates operators in swiftly developing more innovative and competitive products and services. The OECD's research report indicates that the more data operators have, the higher the marginal utility of data utilization.[3] For instance, in the development of generative AI, companies like Google's Deep Mind and Microsoft's OpenAI have accumulated more data through early and sustained investment, allowing their trained AI to iterate faster than other new entrants. From a market competition standpoint, even if all developers are provided with new data of equal scale and quality, it would not create a fair competitive environment, as operators with a data advantage from the start would have an easier time dominating the market.

1.2 Damage to competition caused by abuse of data advantage

5. As previously mentioned, the data advantage can amplify the scale effect in the digital economy. When an operator gains a data scale advantage, it can continuously attract more users and collect more data, creating a positive cycle that strengthens its data advantage and market power.

---

2   Network effects can be divided into two types: "direct network effects" and "indirect network effects". Direct network effect refers to the interdependence between consumers within the same market, where consumers using the same product can directly increase the utility of other consumers. The indirect network effect mainly arises from the technological complementarity between the basic product and the auxiliary product, which leads to the interdependence of product demand. That is, the value of a product used by users depends on the quantity and quality of the complementary products. The more complementary products a product has, the greater the market demand for that product.

3   See OECD, Big Data: Bringing Competition Policy to the Digital Era, Background Paper, 2016, p.11.

However, if operators abuse their market power to restrict fair access to data by other competitors, such as through forced exclusivity or predatory subsidies, it could undermine the overall market competition order.

6. Moreover, operators with data advantages may exploit the scope effect to monopolize more unrelated markets, thereby building or enhancing digital ecosystems. Data is characterized by non-exclusivity and multi-potentiality, meaning that data collected from one product or service can also be applied to many other products and services, even if these products and services are unrelated. In the traditional economy, operators with competitive advantages could only extend their advantages to adjacent markets such as upstream and downstream markets, with limited market power transmission. However, in the digital economy era, the advantages derived from data can easily be extended to entirely unrelated markets. For instance, the data advantage accumulated through social platforms can enable the platform to more easily enter industries such as gaming, payment, video, and music. The data advantage accumulated through online shopping platforms can also enable the platform to enter industries such as finance, food delivery, and entertainment.[4] Data provides a crucial foundation for the emergence of tech giants in the new era. These tech giants are all building their own large digital ecosystems, which may cover almost every industry. Especially when digitalization has become the primary direction of social and economic development, companies with data advantages can more easily assist traditional industries in their digital transformation, further leveraging the scope economy effect and consolidating their competitive advantages. If this expansion is conducted in a normal and fair manner, it is beyond reproach. However, if an enterprise with data advantage abuses its dominant position and achieves the purpose of expansion by excluding competitors in other markets through unfair and unreasonable ways, it will be regarded as disorderly expansion, which will cause more obvious damage to the effect of competition.

1.3 Damage to innovation caused by abuse of data advantage

7. Data is a source of innovation, but it can also hinder it. As data plays an increasingly significant role in product and service innovation, monopolistic control and misuse of data can significantly impede innovation. Operators with data advantages can limit competitors' innovation by refusing to open data access or by engaging in discriminatory transactions to support their affiliated enterprises while suppressing more

---

4 Jia Yuan and Lan Qian: The Theory of Transmission Effect Theory and the Regulation of Obstructive Abuse of Monopoly in the Digital Economy Era [J]. Journal of Northeast Normal University (Philosophy and Social Sciences Edition), 2023,2.

innovative and competitive rivals.[5] In recent years, frequent acquisitions of innovative startups by companies with data advantages have clearly harmed innovation, especially when these startups develop products or services that surpass the original dominant enterprises. Such acquisitions can directly stifle innovation and competition. Therefore, countries and regions like the United States, Germany, and the European Union have improved their antitrust laws to strengthen the review of such acquisitions. Additionally, the emergence of ChatGPT and Deepseek is seen as a milestone event. The new opportunities brought by the digital revolution, particularly in artificial intelligence, depend on large-scale data and high computing power. Small businesses, which should be the main force in applying and innovating new technologies, may struggle to compete with large enterprises due to the difficulty in obtaining sufficient and high-quality data, leading to reverse selection in the innovation field. Only by promptly regulating the abuse of data advantages that harm innovation can we ensure the healthy development of new fields and business models.

1.4 Harm to consumers caused by abuse of data advantages

8. It is generally believed that consumers can directly benefit and see improved welfare from the development of the digital economy. However, if data advantages are misused by operators, it may lead to exploitation based on information asymmetry. In the era of the data economy, the information gap between operators and consumers has widened. Operators collect data to create user profiles and continuously gather user behavior data, enabling them to more accurately predict user behavior and trends. This gives operators the ability and opportunity to manipulate and control consumers. To further increase marginal profits, operators who gain a data advantage often exploit consumers, even misusing this data. The frequent discussions about big data price discrimination in recent years serve as clear examples.[6] While data advantages can bring more benefits to operators, they should not come at the expense of reducing consumer welfare. Although consumer protection is a primary focus of market regulation and consumer protection laws and regulations, competition law also indirectly protects consumer interests by safeguarding the value of competition. Therefore, the information asymmetry effect amplified in the digital economy era and the resulting loss of consumer welfare should be given due attention and importance.

---

5 Chen Bing: The Competitive Legal Attributes and Regulatory Significance of Big Data [J], Law Science, 2018,8.
6 Zhou Wei: Antitrust Regulations on Personalized Pricing Algorithm [J], Wuhan University Journal (Philosophy & Social Science), 2021,1.

2. The Feasibility of Regulating the Abuse of Data Advantages

2.1 Existing practices of regulating the abuse of data advantages

9. At present, the regulation of abuse of data advantage behavior in the world is mainly divided into the general ex-ante supervision and special legislation model represented by the EU model, and the special ex-ante supervision and endogenous improvement model within the anti-monopoly law represented by the German model.

10. In 2022, the EU introduced the Digital Markets Act, which identifies digital platforms with data advantages as gatekeeper platforms and imposes more prohibitive obligations on these gatekeeper platforms. For example, it prohibits gatekeeper platforms from merging personal data from core platform services with personal data from other services provided by the gatekeeper platform or from third-party services to consolidate personal data. It also requires gatekeeper platforms to respect the differential pricing rights of merchants and allow them to acquire users and conduct marketing activities through the gatekeeper platform.[7] The EU model does not add antitrust provisions to the existing EU competition law system but instead introduces specific legislation to impose more data openness and fair use obligations on large gatekeeper platforms, aiming to prevent and mitigate the abuse of data advantages that could harm market competition and the interests of trading counterparts.

11. In 2021, Germany introduced Article 19a during the tenth amendment to the Anti-Restrictive Competition Act, specifically targeting the monopolistic behavior of ultra-large platforms with a dominant position in cross-market competition. This article prohibits operators with significant cross-market influence from engaging in self-preferencing without justifiable reasons, improperly combining or merging competitive data, hindering the interoperability of products or services, and affecting the portability of data.[8] Additionally, the tenth amendment to the Anti-Restrictive Competition Act revised the original provisions on market dominance,

---

7 Wang Xiaoye: Some Thoughts on Anti-monopoly Supervision of Digital Economy [J], Science of Law(Journal of Northwest University of Political Science and Law), 2021,4.

8 Article 19a, Paragraph 2 of the German Anti-Restraints of Competition Act: The Federal Cartel Office may prohibit the aforementioned operators with significant cross-market competition impacts from: a) Without legitimate reasons, discriminating between their own products or services and those provided by other competitors when providing intermediary services; b) Without legitimate reasons, obstructing other competitors in a market where the operator has not yet achieved a dominant market position but has begun rapid expansion, and such obstruction seriously harms the competitive process; c) Without legitimate reasons, using competition-related data collected in a market where the operator holds a dominant market position, in combination with data collected in other markets, to establish or raise market entry barriers in another market, or to obstruct other operators or require other operators to allow the use of competition-related data; d) Without legitimate reasons, impeding the interoperability of products or services, or affecting data

adding a factor that must be considered: the ability to obtain competitive data.⁹ Furthermore, it specifically added provisions in the section on abuse of market dominance, prohibiting operators with a dominant position from refusing to open data interfaces that are essential for competition.

2.2 Institutional supply in China's Anti-Monopoly Law

12. The 2022 revision of the Anti-Monopoly Law added in Article 9 that 'business operators shall not use data, algorithms, technology, capital advantages, or platform rules to engage in monopolistic practices prohibited by this law.' Article 22, paragraph 2, further clarifies that 'business operators with market dominance shall not use data, algorithms, technology, or platform rules to engage in the abuse of market dominance as described in the preceding paragraph.' However, the supporting systems and rules for these provisions remain unclear. In the rapidly evolving digital economy, improving the anti-monopoly and anti-unfair competition rules related to data is crucial for the high-quality development of China's economy and provides important guidance for competition compliance efforts.

13. The newly revised Anti-Monopoly Law, in Article 9, clearly states that operators may have advantages such as data and algorithms, which can be exploited for monopolistic activities prohibited by this law, including monopoly agreements, abuse of market dominance, and exclusionary or restrictive business concentrations. Therefore, Article 9 is more comprehensive than Article 22, Paragraph 2, and covers a wider range of monopolistic behaviors. In contrast, Article 22, Paragraph 2 does not specify that entities using data and algorithms to abuse market dominance must be data-advantaged companies. This means that even companies that achieve market dominance through other advantages, rather than data, can also be considered as subjects of monopolistic behaviors under Article 22, Paragraph 2. Generally, it is believed that data advantage plays a more significant role in determining market dominance. Therefore, in the design and improvement of future data-related anti-monopoly rules, several key issues should be clarified: first, how to determine market dominance based on data advantage; second, under what circumstances the use of data by operators with market dominance will be deemed as

---

portability, thereby hindering competition; e) Without legitimate reasons, not fully disclosing the scope, quality, and effectiveness of the products or services provided, or otherwise making it difficult for other operators to judge the value of the products or services provided. The burden of proof for such legitimate reasons shall be borne by the operator under investigation.

9 Article 19a (1) of the German Anti Restrictive Competition Act: When an operator conducts business on a large scale in multiple markets, the Federal Cartel Office may determine that it has a significant cross market competitive impact. When determining significant cross market competition impacts, it is important to consider: a) The operator has a dominant position in one or more markets; b) The financial strength or ability to control special resource channels of the operator; c) The operator's vertical integration capability and their business operations in other interconnected markets; d) The operator's ability to control competition related data; e) The significance of the operator's business for third-party entry into the procurement or sales market, as well as the impact of the operator on third-party business operations.

abuse; third, the special characteristics of operators with data advantage in the determination of monopoly agreements; and fourth, the special characteristics of operators with data advantage in the anti-monopoly review of exclusionary or restrictive business concentrations.

2.3 Institutional supply in China's Anti-Unfair Competition Law

14. Following the amendments to the Anti-Unfair Competition Law in 2017 and 2019, the State Administration for Market Regulation (SAMR) released the 'Draft for Public Comments on the Anti-Unfair Competition Law (Amendment Draft)' in November 2022. The primary aim of this revision is to enhance the rules against unfair competition in the digital economy and to regulate behaviors that disrupt market competition order in the development of new economic sectors, business models, and innovative practices. Article 4 of the 'Draft for Public Comments' states, 'The state will improve the fair competition rules for the digital economy. Operators must not use data, algorithms, technology, capital advantages, or platform rules to engage in unfair competitive practices.'

15. First of all, the expression of paragraph 2 of this article is highly similar to Article 9 of the newly revised Anti-monopoly Law, which clearly prohibits operators from engaging in unfair competition by using data and algorithm advantages. In other words, operators may use data and algorithm advantages to engage in monopoly behavior or unfair competition.

16. Secondly, the first paragraph of this article highlights the role of the Anti-Unfair Competition Law in establishing fair competition rules for the digital economy. Through this revision, the state aims to clearly define the boundaries of behavior for digital economy operators, promote fair competition, and set competitive rules. In line with this, the 'Draft for Public Comments' further refines Article 15 of the original Internet Special Provisions, explicitly stating that 'operators shall not use data, algorithms, technology, or platform rules to influence user choices or other means to disrupt the fair competition order of the market.' However, this article does not cover 'unfair competition behaviors conducted by leveraging data and algorithm advantages,' but rather focuses on 'disrupting the fair competition order of the market through the use of data and algorithms to influence user choices.' On one hand, the rules set forth in this article do not assume the possession or abuse of data advantages; on the other hand, the focus of regulation remains on behaviors that may obstruct user choices and does not address other data-related abuses.

17. Meanwhile, Article 17 of the 'Draft for Public Comments' also includes provisions that may be related to data competition rules, stating that 'business operators shall not use technical means or platform rules to violate industry practices or technical standards, improperly exclude or

obstruct other operators from legally providing products or services, disrupting market fair competition.' In the context of the data economy, the provision of products or services, including access and transactions, may involve issues of data access, which aligns with existing practices where platforms restrict other Internet operators from providing product sharing links or data interfaces through their rules. However, this provision also overlooks the prerequisite that operators must have a data advantage. If an operator lacks significant market power, their actions to exclude or obstruct data access are unlikely to disrupt market competition.

3. Hierarchical Construction of Regulation to Abuse Data Advantage

3.1 Gain market dominance based on data advantages

18. To determine whether an operator has gained a dominant market position due to data advantages, it should be analyzed from two perspectives: individual conditions and overall linkage. According to China's Anti-Monopoly Law, a dominant market position is defined as 'an operator's position in the relevant market that allows them to control the price, quantity, or other trading conditions of goods, or to hinder or influence other operators' ability to enter the relevant market.' The law also lists factors such as the market share of the relevant market and the ability to control the sales or raw material procurement markets.[10]

19. To determine whether an operator has a dominant market position due to data advantages, it is essential to first define the relevant market involving data. The commercial use of data typically involves three main stages: data acquisition, analysis, and circulation and trading. Data can also be categorized into personal, corporate, and public data, or classified by industry into transportation, healthcare, retail, and chemical data. Additionally, data can be graded as general, important, and core data. Based on these classification and grading standards, the relevant market involving data can be defined, especially during the circulation and trading of data, where it is easier to identify the supply and demand sides of data transactions. This allows for the use of demand substitution analysis and supply substitution analysis to define the relevant market. A special case in defining the data-related market is the authorized open use of public data. Public

---

10 Anti-monopoly Law of China Article 23 The following factors shall be taken into account in determining whether an undertaking has a dominant market position: (I) the undertaking's market share in the relevant market and the competition situation of the relevant market; (II) the ability of the undertaking to control the sales market or the raw material procurement market; (III) the financial and technical conditions of the undertaking; (IV) the degree of dependence of other undertakings on the undertaking in their trading; (V) the degree of difficulty for other undertakings to enter the relevant market; and (VI) other factors relevant to the determination of the dominant market position of the undertaking.

data collected by government departments is mostly licensed and authorized through an exclusive franchise model. For this part of the publicly accessible and exclusively used data, it essentially forms a single relevant market. Operators who have been granted exclusive rights to use this public data can be more easily identified as having an exclusive monopoly in the relevant market for this part of the public data.

20. For other data-related markets, further analysis using indicators such as market share is necessary to determine whether the operator has a dominant market position. When assessing an operator's ability to control the upstream and downstream markets due to data advantages, the actual availability of data should be considered. If an operator possesses a significant amount of critical data essential for the operations of upstream and downstream players, it is more likely to gain control over these markets. This is evident in the operator's strong bargaining position in data acquisition and licensing, as well as its ability to set prices and terms of transactions.[11]

21. Another key factor in determining a market dominance due to data advantages is the data barrier. If an operator controls market entry by possessing a large amount of critical data, the key consideration is whether this data can or is easily accessible to other operators. For instance, in the early stages of platform economies, the differences in the quantity and quality of data accumulated by different platform operators were not significant. Additionally, the non-exclusivity and multi-user nature of data led to low market entry barriers. However, as competition among platforms intensified, some operators were forced out of the market due to their inability to continue high marketing costs or incorrect development strategies. The remaining platforms accumulated far more data in both quality and quantity than their competitors. As a result, even potential competitors who wanted to enter the market now faced a high market share, creating a blocking effect.

22. Finally, when determining a market dominance based on data advantages, it is crucial to consider the impact of scale and scope effects. When data reaches a certain scale, it can create a positive feedback loop of 'data-user-data', leading to a data lock-in effect. This effect is particularly pronounced in platform economies with strong social and communication features. The scope effect of data enables the establishment or expansion of digital ecosystems by leveraging data. By owning data, companies can more quickly enter various related markets, thereby building their digital ecosystems. This strategy is commonly used by companies with existing data advantages, providing them with cross-market competitive advantages. These advantages, in turn, strengthen their market power in certain related markets.

---

11 Yin Jiguo: Legal Regulation of Big Data Operators Abusing Their Dominant Market Position [J], Studies in Law and Business, 2020, 4.

3.2 Obtain a relatively trading advantage based on data advantages

23. The determination of a relative trading advantage position is generally based on the analysis of the degree of advantage in trading relationships using dependency theory. Article 20 of Germany's Anti-Restrictive Competition Act states, 'If a small or medium-sized enterprise (SME) that supplies or demands certain goods or industrial and commercial services is so dependent on a specific enterprise or enterprise consortium that there is insufficient and foreseeable possibility to switch to other enterprises, then that enterprise has a relative trading advantage position compared to SMEs.' This indicates that the determination of a relative trading advantage position should focus on the lack of sufficient and foreseeable switching possibilities.[12] 'Lack of switching possibilities' means that as a trading counterpart, it is impossible to switch to other operators for transactions, which includes both procurement and sales. The challenge in determining this lies in assessing what constitutes 'sufficient and foreseeable' switching possibilities. The assessment of 'sufficiency' can consider factors such as the number of enterprises in the market that can provide similar goods or services, product and industry characteristics, consumer preferences, and business reputation. For example, well-established chain supermarkets with over a decade of history have accumulated more business reputation compared to newly established supermarket brands. In industries with high entry barriers, it is easier to determine 'sufficiency' than in industries with low entry barriers. The determination of 'foreseeability' typically requires subjective judgment, considering from the perspective of the trading counterpart whether switching to other operators would entail significant sunk costs and transaction risks.[13]

24. In the digital economy era, data has become a crucial input for optimizing numerous products and services, and data itself has become a subject of transactions. The relative trading advantages derived from data require greater attention. In 2021, the tenth revision of Germany's Anti-Restrictive Competition Act introduced Article 20, Paragraph 1a, which states: 'If an operator controls data essential for other operators to conduct their business, other operators will be dependent on this operator. If this operator refuses to share such essential data at a reasonable price, it constitutes an improper obstruction. Additionally, if such data cannot be obtained through public market transactions, refusing to open this data access also constitutes an improper obstruction.'[14] This provision highlights two key

---

[12] Jia Yuan: Research on the Regulation of Abuse of Relative Advantage Position in Germany – The Distinction between Relative Transactional Advantage Position and Relative Market Advantage Position [J]. Legal Studies, 2016,5.

[13] Wang Xiaoye: Legal Regulation for the Abuse of Superior Bargaining Position[J]. Modern Law Science 2016,5.

[14] Jia Yuan: Die Modernisierung der kartellrechtlichen Regulation des Missbrauchs der Marktmacht im Rahmen der Digitalisierung. EinKommentar zur10. GWB-Novelle [J]. Deutschland-Studien, 2021,2.

points: first, having the necessary data for a business may lead to the other party's dependence on the operator; second, the judgment of dependency related to data does not necessarily require the original lack of sufficient and foreseeable alternative options in the transaction. This will significantly impact the determination of relative trading advantages related to data. To clarify the specific obligations of operators who possess essential data, German legislators have introduced a system prohibiting the abuse of a dominant position to refuse to open data. This means that even if an operator does not hold a dominant market position, they must still open their data at a reasonable price if they possess essential data; otherwise, it constitutes an improper obstruction of the market.

25. In practice, it is not uncommon for entities to possess essential data that makes their trading counterparts dependent on them, especially in the platform economy. Whether it is large comprehensive platforms or vertical platforms, they can often win by engaging in a 'winner-takes-all' competition over a long period. The surviving platforms typically have a vast user base and significant user data. The use of big data should be based on its volume; the training of generative AI and other algorithm models, as well as further product development, require massive amounts of data. Operators with vast amounts of data are often concentrated in a few large platforms, making the development and application of new technologies easily turn into a game where only a few major platforms can participate. The American company OpenAI developed the world-renowned ChatGPT AI model due to its deep collaboration with Microsoft, which possesses a large amount of data. The Gemini AI model, capable of challenging ChatGPT, is the result of Google's long-term development and use of its vast data for training. It is widely recognized that large AI models will bring revolutionary changes to various industries, but few companies can participate in big data training and development. This is merely a new opportunity for major platforms to further consolidate their monopoly advantages and status.[15]

4. Developing the Path of Regulating the Abuse of Data Advantage

26. When regulating the abuse of data advantages under competition law, it is essential to clarify the alignment of objectives and the distinct functional roles of anti-monopoly law and anti-unfair competition law. Firstly, both anti-monopoly law and anti-unfair competition law aim to maintain a fair and effective competitive order and promote the healthy development of

---

[15] Chen Yongwei: Beyond Chat-GPT: Opportunities, Risks, and challenges from Generative AI [J]. Journal of Shandong University (Philosophy and Social Sciences), 2023, 3.

the market economy. Secondly, anti-monopoly law focuses on macro-level market competition order, while anti-unfair competition law emphasizes micro-level legitimate competition interests and consumer rights.[16] Lastly, there is a certain division of labor and cooperation between anti-monopoly law and anti-unfair competition law in regulating market power. Anti-monopoly law imposes obligations on operators who have achieved a dominant market position, whereas anti-unfair competition law imposes prohibitive obligations on operators with only a relative trading advantage. Therefore, the regulation of the abuse of data advantages should first identify the characteristics and classification of such abuses, differentiate the levels of market power, and then design a framework and specific rules that align with the value goals and functional roles of anti-monopoly law and anti-unfair competition law.

4.1 Classification of abusive data advantage behaviors

27. The theory of the abuse of market power generally categorizes abusive behavior into two types: obstructive abuse and exploitative abuse. Obstructive abuse aims to exclude competitors and directly restrict competition, ultimately leading to a reduction or elimination of competitors, thereby further consolidating the market power of the operator. Furthermore, obstructive abuse can have spillover effects on other related markets, where operators use their competitive advantage in one market to hinder and exclude competitors in upstream and downstream markets. In contrast, exploitative abuse focuses on the exploitation of trading counterparts (including end consumers) by operators with market power, aiming to gain monopoly profits. When operators with market power engage in exploitative abuse, they directly harm the legitimate rights and interests of trading counterparts, such as their right to choose and fair transactions. They also indirectly enhance and solidify their own market power by increasing revenue and capital strength, thereby undermining market competition.

28. In the digital economy era, both obstructive and exploitative abuses need to be further developed and refined based on existing theories. For instance, with data becoming a core production factor in various industries, a data-centric ecosystem business model has emerged. Operators with market power can not only use obstructive abuses to extend their market advantages to upstream and downstream markets but also to unrelated markets, significantly expanding the scope and likelihood of such effects. Similarly, exploitative abuses now include non-price monopolistic behaviors against trading counterparts, moving beyond the traditional model of unfair high or low prices to infringe on the legitimate rights

---

16 Kong Xiangjun: The Orientation of the Anti-Monopoly Law Concerning Internet Platform from a Macro-Perspective: An Analysis Based on Politic, Policy and Legislation [J]. Journal of Comparative Law, 2021, 2.

and interests of trading counterparts through forced data collection and unfair data usage terms, ultimately solidifying their own data advantages.

29. As previously mentioned, in the development of the competition law sector within the dual system of anti-monopoly and unfair competition laws, the goals of these two laws in maintaining market competition order and promoting economic development have become more aligned, and their functional roles have become increasingly similar. However, the specific division of labor and cooperation between them still requires further clarification. Anti-monopoly law focuses on maintaining macro-level market competition order and protecting effective free competition. Its primary role in regulating the abuse of market power should be to prohibit acts that exclude or restrict competition. In other words, the focus should be on preventing the improper consolidation of market dominance and its transmission to other markets. The protection of consumer rights is a secondary concern. Therefore, the regulation of obstructive abuse should primarily fall under anti-monopoly law. On the other hand, Anti-unfair competition law focuses on protecting the legitimate rights and interests of business operators and consumers. Exploitative abuse should primarily be regulated by unfair competition law. The article will distinguish between monopolistic acts of obstructive abuse of data advantages and unfair competition acts of exploitative abuse of data advantages, and explore the regulatory approaches for the abuse of data advantages.

4.2 Regulation abuses of data advantages in Anti-Monopoly Law: focus on ensuring the availability of specific data

30. Operators who have gained a dominant market position through data advantages may abuse these advantages to exclude and suppress competitors, thereby constituting obstructive abuse. Such improper exclusionary and restrictive competitive practices often take the form of preventing others from fairly accessing relevant competitive data or refusing to open data interfaces. Ensuring the availability of specific data is crucial for creating a fair competitive market environment.[17] Therefore, regulating monopolistic behaviors that abuse data advantages should focus on the following aspects.

31. First, it is necessary to regulate the abuse of data advantages in transactional practices. Operators with data advantages often have the power to set transaction rules, many of which are established through platform regulations. To maintain and strengthen their data advantage, some operators attempt to limit trading partners to only transact with them through transaction rules, thereby continuously keeping transaction data

---

17 Zhou Xiping, Enterprise Data Rights Protection in the Era of Big Data [J]. Law Science, 2022,5.

and related derivative data on their platforms. Whether it's merchants in online shopping platforms, food delivery and group buying platforms, drivers on ride-hailing platforms, or users on social media platforms, they are all, to some extent, constrained and restricted by platform regulations. Of course, such practices should only be considered monopolistic behavior if they severely harm market competition and lack reasonable justification. The greater the data advantage an operator has, the more unequal the rule design, and the more targeted the regulation against specific key competitors, the more likely it is to be deemed a monopolistic practice.

32. Secondly, it is necessary to regulate the refusal of transactions due to the abuse of data advantages. The refusal of transactions due to the abuse of data advantages is similar in terms of identification methods to the traditional refusal of transactions due to the abuse of market dominance, with the only difference being the new scenarios where such behavior occurs. Traditional refusal of transactions often involves products or services that require consideration; if a reasonable offer is made by the counterparty and the transaction is still refused, it may constitute an unjustified refusal of transactions.[18] Refusal of transactions due to the abuse of data advantages can occur in two scenarios: one is the refusal of data transactions (or data authorization), and the other is the frequent refusal to open data access (API interfaces) in practice. The challenge in identifying abusive behavior lies in determining the legitimacy of the reasons. In the context of data transactions, operators with data advantages might cite more legitimate reasons for defense, such as privacy protection, data security, and investment incentives. However, refusing to open data interfaces is more likely to contradict the fundamental principle of internet connectivity, and merely opening data interface requests has a relatively minor impact on privacy protection and data security, making it difficult to justify such behavior as a legitimate reason.[19]

33. Again, it is necessary to regulate the abuse of data advantages in tie-in sales or by imposing unreasonable trading conditions. As previously mentioned, operators with data advantages often attempt to enter more markets by leveraging their data to build or enhance their digital ecosystems. If this is done through normal efficiency improvements and innovations, there is no issue. However, if operators abuse their data advantages to exclude competitors in new markets or exploit trading counterparts by imposing unreasonable trading conditions, it may constitute monopolistic behavior.[20] Common data-related tie-in sales can involve bundling data

---

18 Ning Du: Regulation of Anti-Monopoly Law on Refusal of Transactions: A Review of the Refusal of Transactions Clause in the Anti-Monopoly Guidelines for Platform Economy [J]. Research on Rule of Law, 2021,4.

19 Hou Liyang and He Simai: Legal characterization and Solution of Platform Ban [J]. Law and Economy, 2022,3.

20 Zhan Fu-jing: Antitrust Regulation on the Abuse of Dominant Market Position in the Big Data Field – Logical Development Based on Path Examination [J]. Journal of Shanghai University of Finance and Economics, 2020,4.

transactions or data licensing with other unrelated products or services, forcing trading counterparts to purchase them. Imposing unreasonable trading conditions may involve requiring trading counterparts to return the newly acquired data to the operator after obtaining data authorization, thereby strengthening and consolidating their data advantages.

34. Furthermore, it is also necessary to regulate the abuse of data advantages for self-preferential treatment. Both the EU Market Law and Germany's newly revised Anti-Restrictive Competition Act prohibit self-preferential treatment as a special obligation for super platforms with cross-market competitive advantages. In other words, self-preferential treatment by ordinary operators or platforms is not subject to competition law. However, the abuse of data advantages for self-preferential treatment must meet the following conditions: first, the operator has a strong data advantage, giving them a competitive edge in the cross-market; second, the operator becomes a new competitor in other markets; third, the operator abuses their data advantage to transfer market power to new markets through self-preferential treatment, thereby damaging the competition in these new markets;[21] fourth, the operator's self-preferential treatment significantly enhances their control over the entire digital ecosystem.

4.3 Regulation abuses of data advantages in Anti-Unfair competition Law: focus on the protection of fair trading rights

35. In the identification of unfair competition behaviors that abuse data advantages, we should focus on the core rights and interests of trading counterparts and consumers, namely the right to fair trade. The unfair trading behaviors that abuse data advantages can be refined into exploitative abuse behaviors for regulation.

36. Article 1 of China's Anti-Unfair Competition Law clearly states that the legislative purpose of this law is to protect the legitimate rights and interests of operators and consumers. Article 2, paragraph 2 further specifies that unfair competition behavior refers to acts by operators in their production and business activities that violate the law, disrupt market competition order, and harm the legitimate rights and interests of other operators or consumers. The targets of exploitative abuse are operators and consumers as counterparties in transactions. Since the operators with data advantages regulated by the Anti-Unfair Competition Law are not necessarily those with market dominance, but rather those with a relative trading advantage based on the theory of dependency, exploitative abuse

---

21 Meng Yanbei and Zhao Zeyu: Reasonable regulation of self-preferencing on mega platforms under antitrust law [J]. Journal of Central South University (Social Sciences), 2022, 1.

generally arises from the improper use of such dependency. In practice, common forms of exploitative abuse based on dependency may include big data price discrimination, forcing counterparties to accept unreasonable platform rules and user agreements, etc.

37. First, it is necessary to regulate the misuse of data advantages for big data price discrimination. The phenomenon of big data price discrimination has a long history, particularly on online shopping platforms (such as hotel booking and air ticket sales). Platform operators collect and analyze consumer shopping behavior data to create precise profiles of consumer habits and characteristics. They then use this information to present different prices and transaction terms to consumers, aiming to achieve targeted marketing. While precise marketing is generally encouraged as it can improve resource allocation efficiency and better meet consumer needs, if data advantages are maliciously used to impose unfair high prices or unreasonable transaction terms on some consumers, it may constitute big data price discrimination. Some consumers, upon discovering they have been subjected to big data price discrimination, find it difficult to seek legal redress or switch platforms, as they have become dependent on the platform. The academic community once suggested that anti-monopoly law should regulate big data price discrimination, but since such behavior has a less significant impact on overall market competition and a greater impact on certain consumer groups, the newly revised Anti-Monopoly Law did not include big data price discrimination in its regulatory scope. Therefore, it is necessary to regulate big data price discrimination based on dependency through the Anti-Unfair Competition Law to better protect consumers' legitimate rights and interests.[22]

38. Secondly, it is necessary to regulate the misuse of data advantages and the imposition of unreasonable trading conditions by platform rules. In the platform economy, it is common for platforms to impose unreasonable trading conditions on merchants, riders, and users through setting platform rules and user agreements. Scholars have conducted undercover investigations to reveal the unfair rule-setting issues between a food delivery platform and its riders, but there are few legal cases addressing this issue in practice. The inclusion of clauses in user agreements that allow for the excessive use of data and relax privacy protection obligations has also attracted public and media attention. However, due to the lack of clear legal provisions, there are few enforcement cases. Merchants, riders, or users, as the counterparties in transactions, often lack the willingness and means to sue to protect their rights. Especially when these counterparties have an irrevocable dependence on the platform, few are willing to risk losing the opportunity

---

[22] Liu Wei and Chen Pengyu: A New Perspective of Consumer Interests under the Anti-Unfair Competition Law in the Digital Age [J]. Intellectual Property, 2023, 7.

to continue cooperation or transactions for the sake of so-called rights protection.[23] At this point, the Anti-Unfair Competition Law should intervene to provide clear regulation and protect the legitimate rights and interests of the counterparties in transactions.

Conclusion

39. Our society has entered the fast lane of digital economy development, where from the central to local governments, from enterprises to individuals, all are closely linked to the development of the digital economy based on data utilization. Currently, the commercialization of data still faces numerous bottlenecks, such as insufficient data circulation and restricted openness. The 'data silo' phenomenon has led to a trend of diminishing marginal efficiency in the digital economy. To better leverage large market and vast data resources, it is essential to address the bottlenecks in data utilization and circulation. A key focus should be on regulating the abuse of data advantages through competition laws. Specifically, a 'Guideline for Anti-monopoly Regulation of Data Commercialization' should be formulated based on the newly revised Anti-monopoly Law, to strengthen the regulation of improper exclusionary and restrictive competitive behaviors under the Anti-monopoly Law. This can be achieved also by adding provisions in the proposed revision of the Anti-Unfair Competition Law that prohibit the abuse of a dominant trading position for big data price discrimination or imposing unreasonable trading conditions, thereby protecting consumer rights and other operators' legitimate interests and maintaining fair competition. By doing so, we can inspire market entities to use data fairly and reasonably, create an environment for innovation and creation using data, and foster more new products and services based on data elements, ultimately achieving the goal of empowering the real economy with data and developing new productive forces, thus promoting the high-quality development of digital economy!

---

23 Liu Quan: Public Nature of Internet Platform and its Realization [J]. Chinese Journal of Law, 2020, 2.

Problems of Application of the Essential Facilities Doctrine in China and its Solution

DING MAOZHONG

Ding Maozhong, Professor, Shanghai University of Political Science and Law

Abstract

Although the Anti-Monopoly Law has not adopted the theoretical proposition of directly making provisions for the essential facility doctrine, the supporting regulations prohibiting the abuse of market dominance have always been responsive to this. However, due to the added effect and potential illegal risks of the refusal of transactions provisions in the Anti-Monopoly Law, these supporting regulations about essential facility doctrine have not been applied in practice. Whether it is the conservative or radical approach advocated by the theoretical community for the introduction of essential facility doctrine in the Anti-Monopoly Law, they also have significant shortcomings. The conservative approach contradicts the intention of advocating for the introduction of essential facility doctrine in the Anti-Monopoly Law, while the radical approach will put the uncertainty risk of the Anti-Monopoly Law on the brink of losing control. In fact, China does not need to directly make provisions on the essential facility doctrine in the Anti-Monopoly Law. As long as the "essential" in the provisions of the provisions on Prohibition of Abuse of Market Dominance on the essential facility doctrine is deleted. This not only expresses the basic essence of the essential facility doctrine, but also fully aligns with the refusal of transactions provisions of the Anti-Monopoly Law, and is more convenient and efficient in legislation, and more robust in risk control.

Problems of Application of the Essential Facilities Doctrine
in China and its Solution

I. Presentation of the Issues

1. Essential facility doctrine, also known as essential facility principle, core facility doctrine, etc.,[1] Its basic meaning is that operators with relevant facilities must open them to competitors under specific circumstances to maintain effective competition in the market. The theory originated in the United States, the earliest can be traced back to *the United States Government v. Terminal Railroad Association* case in 1912. The United States Federal Supreme Court held in this case that: the Terminal Railroad Association mastered crossing facilities across the Mississippi River in and out of the St. Louis River, when other similar transportation companies objectively cannot build such facilities. To enable these companies to participate in competition of the relevant market, the Terminal Railroad Association should be in a non-discriminatory manner to enable them to use such facilities.[2] The term essential facility doctrine was first tentatively clarified in 1977 in *Heckert v. Pro Football*, and the District of Columbia Court of Appeals first used this term.[3] Then until 1983 it was further crystallized in *Microwave Communications, Inc. v. American Telephone and Telegraph Company*, in which the U.S. Court of Appeals set forth the following four conditions that should be met for the essential facility doctrine to apply, i.e., that the relevant facilities are controlled by a monopolist; competitors are objectively unable to duplicate the relevant facilities; the owner of the relevant facilities refuses to open up the facilities to competitors, and it is feasible to allow competitors to use of the relevant facilities.[4] During this period, the doctrine began to emerge in the European Union,[5] and was then formally recognized by the European Union in the early 1990s,[6] and has been continuously refined since then.[7] Since the beginning of this century, the doctrine has been applied to varying degrees in other major antitrust jurisdictions around the world, such as Japan.[8]

1　See Jian Wang and Zongze Wu: "On Data as a Necessary Facility in Antitrust Law", in Rule of Law Research, No. 2, 2021; Sulun Zhang: "The Application of the Principle of Necessary Facility of the Competition Law in the Internet Industry", in Journal of Henan Normal University (Philosophy and Social Sciences Edition), No. 1, 2017; and Jian Li, Theoretical Study of Core Facility of Antitrust Law, Shanghai Jiao Tong University Press, 2015 edition, p. 64.

2　See United States v. Terminal Railroad Association, 224 U.S. 383, 406 (1912).

3　See Hecht v. Pro-Football, Inc. 570 F.2d 982, 992 (D.C. Cir. 1977).

4　See MCI Communications Corp. v. American Tel. and Tel.Co., 708 F.2d 1081 (7th Cir. 1983).

5　In the 1974 Commercial Solvents case, the European Court of Justice decided along the lines of the essential facilities doctrine, See Joined Cases 6-7/73, [1974] ECR 223.

6　The term essential facilities was first formally used by the European Court of Justice in 1992 in the Port case, See B & I Line Plc v. Sealink Harbors Ltd (IV/34.174).

7　In the 1996 TV Guide case, the European Court of Justice set out the basic criteria for the application of the essential facilities doctrine. See RTE and ITP v Commission, [1995] ECR 743.

8　See Duan Honglei and Shen Bin, "Study on the Theory of Necessary Facilities in Antitrust in the Field of Internet Economy", in China Applied Law, No. 4, 2020.

2. Long before the Antimonopoly Law was introduced in China,[9] there were voices in the theoretical community calling for the introduction of the essential facility doctrine as well. "Introducing the essential facility doctrine in China is something we must consider in our antitrust law legislation. [...] China should incorporate the must-equipment refusal behavior into the types of abuse of dominant market position behavior, make it explicit in the law, and clearly stipulate that the must-equipment refusal is of proximity illegal behavior."[10] Although the *Anti-Monopoly Law* introduced in 2007 ultimately did not adopt this type of recommendation,[11] the former State Administration for Industry and Commerce responded by promulgating *Rules of the Industry and Commerce Administration Authorities on the Prohibition of the Abuse of Market Dominating Position Behaviors* in 2010. Article 4 of the Rules prohibits operators with market dominance from refusing to trade with their trading counterparts through the following methods without justification: (a) reducing the existing number of transactions with their counterparts; (b) delaying or interrupting an existing transaction with its trade counterparty; (c) refusal to engage in new transactions with their trading counterparts; (d) imposing restrictive conditions that make it difficult for their trading counterparts to engage in transactions with it; (e) refusal to allow their trading counterparts to use its essential facilities with reasonable conditions in their production and business activities. In determining the applicability of paragraph (e) above, the following factors shall be considered: the feasibility of separately investing in and constructing the facility, the extent to which the counterparty to the transaction relies on the facility for its production and business operations, the ability of the operator to provide the facility, and the impact on the operator's own production and business operations.

3. After the State Council's antitrust enforcement agency completed its "three-in-one" reform in 2018, the State Administration for Market Regulation ("SAMR") promulgated the *Interim Provisions on Prohibition of the Abuse of Market Dominance* in 2019, which also made provisions on the essential facility doctrine that were basically the same as those

---

9 In addition to quoting others' original texts, this article will uniformly refer to the Anti-Monopoly Law of the People's Republic of China as simply the Anti-Monopoly Law.

10 Xu Shiying: "The Application of the 'Necessary Equipment Theory' in Regulating the Abuse of Market Advantage", in Yang Zixuan, ed., Studies on Economic Law, vol. 5, Peking University Press, 2007 edition, p. 55.

11 In the course of the formulation of the Anti-Monopoly Law, the essential facilities doctrine has been incorporated into specific provisions of some drafts. For example, in the former Ministry of Commerce's 2004 review draft, it was proposed to stipulate that if it is impossible for an operator to compete with an operator with a dominant market position without accessing the network or other infrastructure owned by the operator with a dominant market position, the operator with a dominant market position shall not deny access to the network or other infrastructure owned by the operator with a dominant market position on reasonable price terms. However, this shall not be the case where the operator in a dominant position in the market is able to demonstrate that access to the network or other infrastructure is impossible or unreasonable for technical, security or other legitimate reasons.

above.[12] During the revision of the *Anti-Monopoly Law*, there have been calls from the academic community to incorporate the essential facility doctrine into the law. "The revision of Chinese *Anti-Monopoly Law* not only requires the introduction of the essential facility doctrine into legislation but also the expansion of its scope of application to include both vertical relationships (without competitive relationships) and horizontal relationships with competitive relationships; simultaneously, in accordance with the aforementioned dual regulatory framework of market dominance and relative advantage, the essential facility doctrine can break away from the existing approach that requires market definition and the determination of market dominance as prerequisites. Instead, it can be applied based on the logic and regulatory framework of relative advantage, thereby restructuring, and redefining the regulatory framework in the context of the tripartite competitive landscape involving platforms, data, and algorithms."[13] Although the revised *Anti-Monopoly Law* of 2022 added several provisions, it still did not adopt such suggestions. However, similar to the *Interim Provisions on Prohibition of the Abuse of Market Dominance*, the SAMR also maintained provisions on the essential facility doctrine in the provisions on *Prohibition of Abuse of Market Dominance* issued in 2023, which are basically the identical as the previous.[14]

4. Therefore, although the *Anti-Monopoly Law* has not yet explicitly addressed the essential facility doctrine, this theory has objectively entered the institutional application phase in China,[15] and has been in practice for over a

---

12 Article 16(1) and (2) of the Interim Provisions on Prohibition of Abuse of Market Dominance stipulate that an operator in a dominant market position is prohibited from refusing to enter into a transaction with the counterparty by the following means without justifiable reasons: (1) materially reducing the number of existing transactions with the counterparty; (2) delaying or interrupting existing transactions with the counterparty; (3) refusing to enter into a new (iii) refusing to enter into new transactions with the counterparty; (iv) setting restrictive conditions that make it difficult for the counterparty to enter into transactions with the counterparty; (v) refusing to allow the counterparty to use its necessary facilities under reasonable conditions in the course of its production and business activities. In determining that an operator has abused its dominant market position in accordance with Paragraph 5 of the preceding paragraph, the feasibility of investing in the construction or development of such facilities with reasonable inputs, the degree of dependence of the counterparty on such facilities for the effective conduct of its production and business activities, the possibility of the operator providing such facilities, and the impact on its own production and business activities, etc., shall be taken into consideration. Like the Provisions of the Administration for Industry and Commerce on Prohibition of Abuse of Market Dominance, the Interim Provisions on Prohibition of Abuse of Market Dominance have also been repealed.

13 Yang Dong: "On the Reconstruction of Antimonopoly Law: Responding to the Challenges of the Digital Economy", in China Law Journal, No. 3, 2020, p. 218.

14 As far as the provisions of the essential facilities doctrine are concerned, the Provisions on the Prohibition of Abuse of a Market Dominance and the Interim provisions on the Prohibition of Abuse of a Market Dominance are identical, i.e., article 16 (1) (e) and (2) of both articles are formulated in the same way.

15 In addition to the above three regulations, China has also made some similar provisions on the essential facilities doctrine in the regulations on the prohibition of the abuse of intellectual property rights to exclude or restrict competition. Article 7(1) of the Provisions on the Prohibition of the Abuse of Intellectual Property Rights to Exclude or Restrict Competition, which was promulgated by the former General Administration for Industry and Commerce (SAIC) in 2015, stipulates that without justifiable reasons, an operator in a dominant position of market dominance shall not exclude and restrict competition when his or her intellectual property rights constitutes a necessary facility for production and business activities, refuse to license other operators to use such intellectual property rights on reasonable terms to exclude or restrict competition. However, considering that: firstly, this regulation has been repealed; secondly, the Provisions on Prohibition of Abuse of Intellectual Property Rights to Exclude or Restrict Competition issued by the State Administration of Market Supervision

decade. However, upon closer examination, it is evident that, apart from the passive and piecemeal application of this theory by courts in a few antitrust civil litigation cases,[16] we have rarely seen antitrust enforcement agencies investigate or prosecute cases based on the provisions regarding this theory in the regulations promulgated at the time. From the perspective of social development over the past decade or so, the first factor that can be ruled out is the lack of specific application scenarios. For example, "given the unique nature of antitrust regulation in the internet sector and the challenges it faces, in situations where competitors must access a platform to effectively compete with the platform owner in another product market, the platform owner's refusal to transact may be difficult to prove step by step through the analysis of the abuse of market dominance. Moreover, for competitors, the primary claim is equal access to the platform, and in such cases, this theory is increasingly being invoked as a basis for antitrust enforcement."[17] This implies that there are issues with the application of this theory in China at present,[18] either at the institutional level or at the enforcement level.[19]

---

in 2023 have made significant modifications to this regulation, the color of the application of the theory of essential facilities has basically "faded", and there is no longer any previous problem. Therefore, this paper in the later discussion of related issues will no longer on the "on the abuse of intellectual property rights to exclude, restrict the competition of the provisions of the provisions of the relevant problems with the above three regulations have the same rationality. In addition, there are some other non-binding normative documents in China that also make similar provisions on the essential facilities doctrine, such as the Antimonopoly Committee of the State Council's Antimonopoly Guidelines on Antimonopoly in the Field of the Platform Economy, issued in 2021 by the Antimonopoly Committee of the State Council. Since these documents are non-binding, they will not be repeated in the discussion of related issues later in this paper.

16 See, for example, the civil judgment of the Intermediate People's Court of Ningbo City, Zhejiang Province (2013) 浙甬知初字第86号), the civil judgment of the Intermediate People's Court of Ningbo City, Zhejiang Province (2014) 浙甬知初字第579号), and the civil judgment of the Intermediate People's Court of Ningbo City, Zhejiang Province (2020) 浙02知民初第182号). It is also worth pointing out that the second instance judgment issued by the Supreme People's Court in late 2023 on the dispute between a Japanese company and a Ningbo company over the abuse of dominant market position also overturned the previous practice of the local courts in applying the doctrine of requisite facilities in the case, see in particular the civil judgment of the Supreme People's Court of the People's Republic of China (2021) Supreme Court of the People's Republic of China, Zhi Civil Final No. 1398.

17 Wang Zhongmei, "Exploring the Applicability of the Principle of Necessary Facilities in Internet Antitrust", in Journal of International Economic Law, No. 1, 2020, p. 120. On the one hand, there are many others who hold such a view, such as Yin Jiguo, "Antitrust Law Regulation of Blocking Behavior of Internet Platforms", in Modern Law Journal, No. 4, 2021, etc. On the other hand, in addition to platforms, specific application scenarios hotly debated in the theoretical community include the fields of intellectual property and data. The former, for example, Ning Lizhi and Yang Nina: "Antitrust Regulation of Patent Refusal License", in Journal of Zhengzhou University (Philosophy and Social Science Edition), Issue 3, 2019; the latter, for example, Yuan Bo: "The Justification and Approach to Compulsory Openness of Necessary Data Antitrust Laws", in Oriental Jurisprudence, Issue 3, 2023.

18 China's current research results on the essential facilities doctrine are relatively abundant, and they can be divided into two categories: one focuses on the institutional introduction of the essential facilities doctrine, especially in the legislation of the Antimonopoly Law; the other focuses on the specific application of the essential facilities doctrine, with a focus on access to platforms, the opening up of data, and intellectual property licensing. However, the theoretical community has paid little attention to the root cause of the problem of why the essential facilities doctrine has been rarely applied in China despite the fact that it has already been provided for in the regulations issued by the antitrust enforcement agencies.

19 One possibility is that the current system is unscientific in its design, which affects enforcement by the antitrust enforcement agencies. Another possibility is that the current system is scientifically designed, but it is just that the antimonopoly enforcement agencies are not acting. It should be noted in particular that if the current system is not scientifically designed, even if there is a suspicion or reality of inaction on the part of the anti-monopoly enforcement agency, then it is appropriate to summarize the problem by saying that the current system is not scientifically designed, and that it is not appropriate to criticize the anti-monopoly enforcement agency harshly in such a case.

II. Review of the Provisions of the Essential Facility Doctrine in China

5. Whether it is the current, the previous or the earliest provisions of abusing market dominance, compared to the refusal to make transaction under the *Anti-Monopoly Law*,[20] those provisions on the essential facility doctrine ("provisions on EFD") all have the same issues, which objectively lead anti-monopoly enforcement agencies to avoid applying the provisions on it as much as possible.

A. Provisions on EFD has additive effect compared to the refusal to conduct transaction under the *Anti-Monopoly Law*

6. Whether before or after the amendment, according to the provisions of Chapter III of the *Anti-Monopoly Law*, there must be three elements constituting a refusal to transact: first, the subject identity, namely, an operator with market dominance; second, the behavior pattern, refusal to transact with the counterparty; and third, the defense, i.e., without justified reasons. However, some scholars argue that all abuses of market dominance, including refusal to transact, should also have an additional constituent element, namely impact on competition, which refers to the exclusion or restriction on market competition. "Although it is difficult to infer the existence of the exclusion or restriction of competition consequence from specific legal provisions, if we consider the historical development of antitrust law in China, particularly its legislative objectives, we may conclude that the exclusion or restriction on market competition is indispensable."[21] It cannot be denied that the constitutive elements of certain abuses of market dominance have been explicitly defined as the aforementioned four factors. Article 21 of the former *Interim Provisions on Prohibition of the Abuse of Market Dominance* and Article 20 of the current *Prohibition of Abuse of Market Dominance* both explicitly stipulate that the SAMR shall determine other abuses of market dominance only if the following conditions are simultaneously met: (1) the operator possesses market dominance; (2) the operator has implemented conduct that excludes or restrict competition; (3) the relevant conduct of the operator lacks justified reasons; and (4) the relevant conduct of the operator has an exclusionary or restrictive effect on market competition. Additionally, both the pre-revised and revised *Anti-Monopoly* Law explicitly provide in their general provisions that operators with market dominance shall not abuse such dominance to exclude or restrict competition.

---

20 The provisions on refusal to deal in Chapter III of the Anti-monopoly Act, "Abuse of Market Dominance", remain unchanged between the pre-and post-amendment periods.

21 Meng Yanbei: "On the Analytical Framework for Prohibiting Abuse of Market Dominance Behavior--Taking the Tetra Pak Antitrust Case as an Example", in Competition Policy Research, Vol. 3, No. 3, 2017, p. 11.

7. Therefore, the constitutive elements of refusal to transact can indeed be four in number, namely, the subject identity requirement, the behavior pattern, the defenses, and the impact on competition. According to this structure the legal basis is not limited to the provisions of Chapter III of the *Anti-Monopoly Law*, but also includes the provisions in the general provisions of the *Anti-Monopoly Law*. There is no doubt that there are significant differences between refusal to transact with three elements and with four. In terms of nature, this directly relates to the positioning of the refusal to transact under the *Anti-Monopoly Law*. When determining the applicability of the anti-monopoly law based on three elements, this means that the *Anti-Monopoly Law* classifies the refusal to transact provision as imposing a general obligation on operators with market dominance not to engage in such conduct. When determining the applicability based on four elements, this means that the *Anti-Monopoly Law* classifies the refusal to transact provision as imposing an obligation on operators with market dominance to undergo special potential competition review. Although determining the provision based on the four elements is more scientific than on the three elements,[22] antitrust enforcement agencies may still rely on the three-element test. Whether before or after the amendment of the *Anti-Monopoly Law*, Chapter III of the *Anti-Monopoly Law* objectively provides sufficient legal basis for antitrust enforcement agencies to determine whether an act constitutes an antitrust violation based on the three-element test.

8. From the provisions on essential facility doctrine in regulations such as the *Prohibition of Abuse of Market Dominance*, it appears that the formal elements required for such provisions should at least include four components. First, there are the subject identity requirement and the defense grounds. The former refers to operators with market dominant position, while the latter refers to the absence of justified reasons. Both are specifically reflected in the first half of the main clause of the first paragraph of the relevant provisions. Second, there is the behavioral pattern requirement, which refers to refusing to transact with transaction counterparts. This is specifically reflected in the fifth item of the first paragraph of the relevant provisions, which states, "refusing to make transaction counterparts use" In addition, the fifth item of the first paragraph of the relevant provisions also includes four restrictive elements in form: first, "in production and business operations"; second, "under reasonable conditions"; third, "its"; and fourth, "essential facilities." Substantively, "under reasonable conditions" and "its" can both be classified as elements of a defense ground. Whether the specific conditions set by the transaction counterparty are reasonable and whether

---

22 For a detailed argument on the relationship between the positioning of the three constituent elements and the four constituent elements and the Antimonopoly Law's provisions on refusal to deal, as well as the choice of which approach is the more scientific, this article will not repeat here, see Ding Maozhong, "The Positioning of the System of Prohibiting Abuse of Market Dominance", in Legal System and Social Development, No. 4, 2021.

the operator has the right to dispose of the relevant facilities fall within the scope of justified reasons for an operator with market dominance to decide whether to engage in a transaction. However, "in production and business operations" and "essential facilities" are difficult to classify under any of the three preceding elements.

9. Although "in production and business operations" is somewhat related to the relevant market definition of the *Anti-Monopoly Law*, i.e., the scope of goods and geographical scope in which operators compete within a certain period of time are basically inseparable from production and business operations, it still differs significantly from the relevant market as part of the constitutive element of the subject identity, including the methods of determination, balancing factors, and specific scope.[23] Although "essential facilities" are related to the dominant position and defense grounds as components of the subject identity, in that "essential facilities" may enable an operator to hold a dominant position and reduce the justified reasons for refusing transactions, there are fundamental differences between them. The most basic manifestation of this is that "essential facilities" do not necessarily enable an operator to hold a dominant position, and the operator is not necessarily required to engage in transactions with the counterpart. Furthermore, "essential facilities" should be considered specific objects in nature. As the name suggests, "essential facilities" refer only to certain specific facilities belonging to operators, not all facilities. According to the provisions on the essential facility doctrine under the *Prohibition of Abuse of Market Dominance*, such facilities should primarily be those that are difficult to construct or develop through alternative investments or development efforts at reasonable costs. This is specifically reflected in the primary considerations listed in the second paragraph of the relevant provisions. This gives "essential facilities" a characteristic like one of the four application conditions for the essential facilities theory proposed by the U.S. Court of Appeals in the *Microwave Communications Company v. AT&T* case, i.e., that "competitors are objectively unable to replicate the relevant facilities." As a result, this becomes a constitutive element parallel to the subject identity, the defenses, and the conduct pattern.

10. Although the elements required to constitute a refusal to transact can indeed be four, approximately five years after the implementation of the *Anti-Monopoly Law*, the anti-monopoly enforcement agencies of State Council and their authorized provincial-level enforcement agencies began to conduct competitive impact analyses in most cases involving the abuse

---

23 "In the course of production and business activities" is a generalized concept, which can be excluded on the basis of whether or not it enters the consumption chain. Relevant market, on the other hand, is a precise concept, the definition of which is often more complicated, and the methodology, rationale and trade-offs involved can be found in the Guidelines of the Antimonopoly Committee of the State Council on the Definition of Relevant Market, and the results of defining the relevant market are usually different from case to case.

of market dominance,[24] including refusals to deal, such as in the cases of Chongqing Qingyang Pharmaceutical Co., Ltd.[25] and Hunan Erkang Pharmaceutical Management Co. Ltd.,[26] Henan Jiuzi Pharmaceutical Co., Ltd.[27] However, there is still a clear difference in the constitutive elements of essential facility doctrine between the *Prohibition of Abuse of Market Dominance* and the theory enforcement agencies applied. Even if we set aside formal issues such as the potential number or specific names of the constitutive elements, the "essential facilities" that serve as the content of the specific object component and the "exclusion or restriction of competition" that serve as the content of the competitive impact requirement are objectively very different. This is at least evident in the following three aspects: First, the former refers to specific facilities, while the latter refers to a certain state that the market may be in. Second, the former is primarily determined based on the possibility of making reasonable investments to construct or develop such facilities separately, while the latter requires consideration of various factors such as market structure, stage of industrial development, and entry barriers. Third, while the former may enable operators to achieve market dominance, thereby increasing the risk of competition being excluded or restricted, the former itself and the operator's market dominance are not inherently unlawful; the latter is illegal in principle and will be prohibited unless with justified reasons.

11. Compared with the refusal to transact as stipulated in Chapter III of the *Anti-Monopoly Law*, the provisions on the essential facility doctrine in the *Prohibition of Abuse of Market Dominance* have one more element in their constituent requirements, namely, the so-called specific object requirement. Even though some provisions in the other four items have been added through revisions, they still only refer to behavioral patterns and do not impose similar restrictions on the subject matter of transactions, such as "essential facilities." In such circumstances, antitrust enforcement agencies prefer to enforce the provisions on refusal to transact under Chapter 3 of the *Anti-Monopoly Law* and the other four items on refusal

---

24 According to rough statistics, about one-fifth of such cases have not been analyzed for competitive impact, such as the case of Inner Mongolia Radio and Television Network Group Co., Ltd. attaching unreasonable trading conditions (Administrative Penalty Decision of Inner Mongolia Autonomous Region Administration for Industry and Commerce, No. 002, Inner Industry and Commerce Punishment Zi [2016]), the case of Suqian Zhengyuan Water Supply Co. Su City Supervision Case [2019] No. 00027 Administrative Penalty Decision), Huaneng Rizhao Thermal Power Co. Limited Limited Transaction and Differential Treatment Case (Shandong Province Market Supervision Administration Lu City Supervision Line Division [2023] No. 5 Administrative Penalty Decision), and so on.

25 See Chongqing Municipal Administration for Industry and Commerce Yu Gongshi Jing Chu Zi [2015] No. 15 Administrative Penalty Decision.

26 See State Market Supervision and Administration of the State Market Supervision and Administration of the State Council [2018] No. 21 Administrative Penalty Decision.

27 See Administrative Penalty Decision of State Market Supervision and Administration of the State Market Supervision and Administration of the State Council [2018] No. 22.

to transact under the *Prohibition of Abuse of Market Dominance*,[28] rendering the provisions on essential facility doctrine in the provisions on the *Prohibition of Abuse of Market Dominance* objectively redundant. Even if antitrust enforcement agencies begin to gradually apply the four elements in cases involving the abuse of market dominance to pursue more scientific enforcement, this does not alter the fact that the provisions of the *Prohibition of Abuse of Market Dominance* regarding essential facility doctrine have become a mere formality. On the one hand, as mentioned earlier, "essential facilities" and "exclusion or restriction of competition" are fundamentally different concepts. On the other hand, according to the provisions of the *Anti-Monopoly Law*, the only additional element that can be added to the elements of abuse of market dominance, including refusal to transact, is the competitive impact element. Undoubtedly, these factors would make antitrust enforcement agencies reluctant to apply the provisions of the *Prohibition of Abuse of Market Dominance* regarding the theory of essential facilities.

B. Compared to the refusal to transact of the Anti-Monopoly Law, the application of essential facility doctrine creates potential legal risks for antitrust enforcement agencies

12. Although the *Prohibition of Abuse of Market Dominance* set forth provisions on the theory of essential facilities, listing factors that antitrust enforcement agencies should consider when determining whether an operator abuses market dominance based on the fifth item, none of them listed directly define what constitutes essential facilities. In response to this, some argue that: "The second paragraph of this provision primarily addresses the criteria for defining essential facilities. Based on the discussion of EU practices in the second and third sections of this article, it can be concluded that for a facility to qualify as an essential facility, the following conditions must be met: (1) the requested product is indispensable to the requesting company; (2) failure to provide the requested product would eliminate all competition in the downstream market; (3) if the matter involves intellectual property rights, failure to provide the requested product would hinder the creation of new products with demand; (4) there is no justified reason for refusing to provide the requested product."[29] Although this view may be open to some debate, it sufficiently reflects the fact that determining what constitutes essential facilities is often no easy task. For this very reason, the *Prohibition of Abuse of Market Dominance* do not directly

---

28 In particular, it should be emphasized that this is only in relation to the provisions on the essential facilities doctrine, such as the Provisions on the Prohibition of Abuse of a Market Dominance, and does not include a comparison with the attitudes of the antitrust enforcement agencies towards the four constituent elements.

29 Hou Liyang and Wang Jirong: "An Examination of the EU Essential Facilities Principle: and the Implications for China", in Wang Xianlin, Editor-in-Chief, Review of Competition Law and Policy, Vol. 1, Shanghai Jiao Tong University Press, 2015 edition, p. 64.

define what constitutes essential facilities. To be precise, the antitrust enforcement agencies of State Council has merely provided a relatively specific list of core factors for determining essential facilities, namely, the feasibility of constructing or developing such facilities through reasonable investment or alternative means.[30] It is evident that determining whether it is feasible to make additional investments or undertake new development and construction of a facility with reasonable inputs is also a challenging task in many cases. At a minimum, this involves issues such as the basic design plan for the relevant facility project, the required resources and their market prices and availability, and a reasonable comparison of the scale of investment and the ability to bear such costs.

13. Although the provisions of the *Prohibition of Abuse of Market Dominance* regarding the theory of essential facilities are clearly more stringent than those of Chapter III of the *Anti-Monopoly Law* regarding refusal to transact, if the anti-monopoly enforcement agency is willing to go to great lengths and overcome difficulties to investigate and handle cases based on the provisions of the *Prohibition of Abuse of Market Dominance* regarding the theory of essential facilities, anti-monopoly enforcement agency should not constitute a violation of the *Anti-Monopoly Law*. As mentioned earlier, whether before or after revision, Chapter III of the *Anti-Monopoly Law* objectively provides sufficient support for anti-monopoly enforcement agencies to make determinations based on the three constitutive elements. The provisions on *Prohibition of Abuse of Market Dominance*, in its provisions on the theory of essential facilities, incorporates the aforementioned three constitutive elements. In terms of nature, the so-called specific object element in this context is, in essence, merely a sufficient condition rather than a necessary condition. Even if the parties concerned file an administrative lawsuit against the antitrust enforcement agency's decision under the *Anti-Monopoly Law*, claiming that the decision of the essential facilities is invalid, as long as the antitrust enforcement agency has not made any errors in determining the subject matter, the conduct pattern, or the

---

30 The possibility for the operator to provide the facility and the impact on its own production and business activities, as enumerated in the Provisions on Prohibition of Abuse of Market Dominance and other provisions on the doctrine of essential facilities, should be in the nature of the elements of the defense. The enumerated degree of dependence of the counterparty on the facility for the effective conduct of its production and business activities can barely be considered as an element for the determination of essential facilities. It is undeniable that essential facilities must have a certain degree of relativity, that is, it must always be relative to what is essential facilities. But this kind of relativity should be more objective and uniform, and can not be changed with the change of the reference object. Because the counterparty in the business, the mode of adoption, have the technology and so on there are often differences, which makes the counterparty directly generalized to the effective implementation of production and business activities on the degree of dependence on the facility as the reference object in the evaluation of the results of the inevitably have a strong subjectivity and differentiation. From a contingent perspective, the degree of reliance on the facility by the counterparty to effectively carry out its production and business activities should be precisely broken down, including the scope of business involving the facility, whether the counterparty is involved in the relevant business, and whether the counterparty owns the facility. The scope of business involving the facility is an important factor in determining the necessary facility, while whether the counterparty is involved in the relevant business and whether the counterparty owns the facility should be categorized as elements of defense. Although the scope of business involving facilities is also relative, it is objective and uniform, so the results of evaluation using it as a reference will be more objective and uniform.

grounds for defense, and provided that the court, in its review of legality or reasonableness, fully respects the discretionary authority of the antitrust enforcement agency within the framework of the *Anti-Monopoly Law*,[31] then even if the court also finds that the decision of the essential facilities in the case is problematic, the decision made by the antitrust enforcement agency is finally unlikely to be deemed by the court as violating the *Anti-Monopoly Law* solely on the basis of the determination regarding the essential facilities. After all, the antitrust enforcement agencies have determined the three constitutive elements in this type of case, thereby meeting the basic requirements for refusal of transactions as stipulated in Chapter III of the *Anti-monopoly Law*.

14. However, if the antitrust enforcement agency determines that the relevant facilities of the parties do not constitute essential facilities and therefore their conduct does not constitute a refusal to transact, then even if the relevant facilities of the parties do not constitute essential facilities, the antitrust enforcement agency may still be in violation of the *Anti-monopoly Law*. Whether before or after revision, from the provisions on refusal to transact under the *Anti-Monopoly Law*, whether the subject matter of the refusal to transact with the transaction counterpart is an essential facility is not a constitutive element of refusal to transact. As mentioned, according to Chapter III of the *Anti-Monopoly Law*, the elements required for a refusal to transact include the subject identity, the conduct pattern, and the grounds for defense. However, the elements required for a refusal to transact can indeed be four, with the additional element being the competitive impact element. Under such circumstance, the legal basis also includes the relevant provisions in the General Provisions of the *Anti-Monopoly Law*. This means that the provisions of the provisions on the *Prohibition of Abuse of Market Dominance* regarding the theory of essential facilities, which emphasize the so-called specific object requirement, can only serve as a sufficient condition under the current circumstances and absolutely cannot be regarded as a necessary condition. Unless the *Anti-Monopoly Law* is amended in the future, any attempt to treat this so-called "specific object requirement" as a necessary condition rather than a sufficient condition, regardless of the method used, would be inconsistent with the refusal to transact provisions of the *Anti-Monopoly Law*. If a complainant or other interested party files an administrative lawsuit against the

---

31 In the case of refusal to deal can be determined in accordance with both the three elements and the four elements, even if it is more scientific to determine in accordance with the four elements, it is not appropriate for the court to negate the antimonopoly law enforcement agency's practice of determining in accordance with the three elements just because it prefers to determine in accordance with the four elements, otherwise it will not only seriously affect the administration of the antimonopoly law enforcement agency in accordance with the law, but will also easily lead to a situation of "judicial substitution of administration", resulting in insufficient motivation for administrative enforcement and inefficient use of judicial resources. Otherwise, it will not only seriously affect the administration of antimonopoly enforcement agencies in accordance with the law, but also easily create a situation of "judicial substitution of administration", which will lead to insufficient motivation for administrative enforcement and inefficient use of judicial resources.

antitrust enforcement agency under the *Anti-monopoly Law* regarding such a decision, and all the elements of the case – including the subject identity, the conduct pattern, the grounds for defense, and the competitive impact requirement – are established, then the decision made by the antitrust enforcement agency shall be deemed unlawful under the *Anti-monopoly Law* by the court.

15. In this situation, antitrust enforcement agencies would naturally be reluctant to investigate cases based on the provisions of the provisions on the *Prohibition of Abuse of Market Dominance* regarding the theory of essential facilities. Otherwise, there would be a flood of complaints against such decisions. On the one hand, such commercial disputes have become increasingly prominent in recent years. For example, on February 29, 2020, ByteDance's office suite Feishu issued an official announcement stating that Feishu-related domains had been completely blocked by WeChat without cause, and that the WeChat sharing API interface had been unilaterally closed. This is not the first time WeChat has taken such measures against ByteDance products. Previously, ByteDance's mobile video social media app Duoshan and its messaging app Feiliao were also unable to share content normally on WeChat. In the view of industry insiders, Feishu's situation is essentially an extension of the ongoing "Tencent-ByteDance" rivalry. From news and information, short videos, social media, and gaming to remote office solutions, the battle between new and established tech giants for user traffic and screen time is intensifying."[32] On the other hand, the stance of antitrust enforcement agencies exerts a strong guiding influence on corporate behavior. For cases where antitrust enforcement agencies have no prior enforcement precedents, companies are generally reluctant to report others to antitrust enforcement agencies for suspected monopolistic practices. Conversely, especially when antitrust enforcement agencies frequently take decisive action or explicitly designate certain issues as priorities for future enforcement, companies are more likely to report others to antitrust enforcement agencies for suspected monopolistic practices.[33]

16. If antitrust enforcement agencies do not continue to choose to investigate cases based on the provisions of the provisions on the *Prohibition of Abuse of Market Dominance* regarding the theory of essential facilities, then there will at least be issues of inconsistent antitrust enforcement or even selective enforcement.[34] However, if antitrust enforcement agencies continue to choose to investigate cases based on the provisions regarding

---

32 Li Xiaoguang and Shi Dan: "Flying Book Battles Weixin, 'Online Office' is Totem", in Business School, No. 4, 2020, p. 77.

33 In addition to the real defense of rights, there is also the possibility of using it to pressure others, especially competitors, to obtain the corresponding commercial benefits.

34 See Huang Berkelium: "Why Selective Law Enforcement? Institutional Motivations and Their Regulation", in Zhongguo xiaoyue juexue (Chinese and Foreign Law), No. 3, 2021.

the theory of essential facilities under the provisions on the *Prohibition of Abusing Market Dominance*, this is highly likely to trigger a significant increase in reports of such cases. Not only would investigating cases based on the provisions regarding the theory of essential facilities under the *Prohibition of Abuse of Market Dominance* significantly increase the workload and complexity of enforcement, but if antitrust enforcement agencies were to conclude that a party's relevant facilities do not qualify as essential facilities and therefore deem their conduct as not constituting a refusal to transact, they would risk violating the *Anti-monopoly Law*. Therefore, even under external pressure, such as when a company lawfully reports to the antitrust enforcement agency that a competitor with market dominance has no justified reason to directly refuse to grant access to its essential facilities, the antitrust enforcement agency would not readily choose to investigate cases based on the provisions regarding the theory of essential facilities under the provisions on the *Prohibition of Abuse of Market Dominance*. This is even more so when there is no external pressure.

III. Considerations on the Integration of the Essential Facilities Doctrine into the Anti-monopoly Law

17. From the review of the provisions on the essential facilities doctrine in the previous section, it seems that the fundamental reason for the current problems in the application of the essential facilities doctrine in China is that the *Anti-Monopoly Law* does not directly stipulate this theory. As mentioned above, not only did the academic community propose early on that the *Anti-Monopoly Law* should introduce the theory of essential facilities, but it also put forward two relatively specific proposals. However, both the conservative and radical proposals have major flaws.

A. Conservative approach is inconsistent with the intent of the Anti-Monopoly Law to introduce the essential facilities doctrine

18. In summary, the conservative approach advocates that, within the traditional framework of prohibiting the abuse of market dominance, the *Anti-Monopoly Law* should directly stipulate that operators with market dominance shall not, without justifiable reasons, refuse to grant access to their essential facilities to transaction counterparts. This approach not only represents the earliest theoretical proposal for incorporating the theory of essential facilities into the *Anti-Monopoly Law*, but also constitutes the mainstream view among those advocating for its adoption. Both before and after the enactment and revision of the *Anti-Monopoly Law*, this approach has garnered significant support.

19. Although, as previously demonstrated, the *Anti-Monopoly Law* did not explicitly address the theory of essential facilities during its formulation or revision, objectively speaking, there are no substantial technical obstacles to adopting a conservative approach in legislation. This is because such an approach still requires the existence of market dominance as a prerequisite, thereby avoiding any subversion or challenge to the traditional prohibition of the abuse of market dominance. Regardless of whether the *Anti-Monopoly Law* adopts a centralized or decentralized approach to legislating against the abuse of market dominance,[35] the only difference in how the conservative approach should be operationalized in the *Anti-Monopoly Law* is that it would be simpler to implement under a decentralized approach than under a centralized approach. It is very clear that the current legislative framework for regulating the abuse of market dominance under the *Anti-Monopoly Law* adopts a concentration-based approach. Even if the enforcement of this approach under a conservative scheme appears somewhat abrupt, this is "of no great consequence." In fact, whether before or after the revision, the provisions of the *Anti-Monopoly Law* prohibiting the abuse of market dominance have followed a similar "precedent." For example, Article 7 of the *Anti-Monopoly Law* prior to revision stipulated provisions for industries where the state-owned economy holds a controlling position, industries vital to the national economy and national security, and industries subject to state-mandated monopolies or exclusive operations. Article 22, Paragraph 2 of the revised *Anti-Monopoly Law* stipulates provisions for platform enterprises abusing their dominant market position. In this context, if the *Anti-Monopoly Law* were to adopt a conservative approach and directly address the theory of essential facilities through a dedicated provision in Chapter III, such an approach would also appear formally acceptable.

20. However, the conservative approach is actually at odds with the intent of the *Anti-Monopoly Law* to introduce the essential facilities doctrine, and this issue appears to have been overlooked by the academic community. "Under the essential facilities doctrine, once a facility is designated as 'core', its owner is obligated to provide access under reasonable terms and conditions and may not refuse to transact. This has significant implications in antitrust law theory. Under the essential facilities doctrine, facility owners no longer enjoy contractual freedom, and the situation of a completely closed market is thereby significantly improved."[36] As can be seen, the theoretical community advocates the introduction of the essential facilities

---

[35] The centralized approach is to provide for all the different abuses of market dominance in one article, while the decentralized approach is to provide for different abuses of market dominance in different articles. The decentralized approach was proposed both when the Antimonopoly Act was enacted and when the Antimonopoly Act was revised.

[36] Li Jian: "The Criteria for Defining Core Facilities in Antitrust Law - The Perspective of Relevant Markets", in Modern Law, No. 3, 2009, p. 60.

doctrine into the *Anti-Monopoly Law* with the aim of imposing stricter legal obligations on entities that possess essential facilities. Even the most conservative approach follows this logic, albeit by limiting the scope of such entities to those that hold a dominant position in the relevant market. "Holders of essential facilities who are in a dominant market position must allow competitors to use them; otherwise, this constitutes an abuse of their market dominance. Any company that owns market-essential facilities or strategic bottlenecks has an obligation to share the essential facilities it controls with competitors, and the conditions for licensing the use of essential facilities must be reasonable and non-discriminatory."[37]

21. This is even more true for radical proposals, which not only seek to expand the scope of entities subject to stricter legal obligations but also aim to broaden the scope of intervention methods. "The introduction of the essential facilities doctrine is closely linked to the emergence of data as a core production factor in the digital economy. The value of data lies in its flow. Incorporating the essential facilities doctrine into the digital economy chapter of the *Anti-Monopoly Law* will facilitate the widespread circulation of data across society. ...The essential facilities doctrine can break through the constraints and limitations of relevant market definition and market dominance assessment, aligning with the relative advantage theory framework, thereby optimizing the prerequisites for competition rules in the digital economy."[38] To distinguish the principle of essential facilities applicable to the industrial era, eliminate semantic misunderstandings of the term "essential," and emphasize the concept of an open core, the principle of essential facilities should be restructured as the principle of open platforms. The open platform principle centers on an open meta-platform, optimizes its constituent elements and implementation pathways, and improves supporting measures. The open platform principle should not be limited to traditional direct competitive markets characterized by refusal to transact. In the digital economy, competition and cooperation often evolve dynamically, with competitors and collaborators changing rapidly. Therefore, the application of the open platform principle should broadly consider both vertical and horizontal relationships, not be confined to competitors or non-competitors, and regulate both current and future competition."[39]

22. In terms of the elements required for a conservative approach, there should be four: the operator holds a dominant position in the relevant

---

[37] Xu Shiying: "Evaluation of the Application of the Principle of Necessary Equipment in Antitrust Law", in Li Mingfa, ed., Anhui University Law Review, vol. 14, Anhui University Press, 2008 edition, p. 5.

[38] Yang Dong and Huang Yinxu: "Study on Setting a Special Chapter on Digital Economy in the Antimonopoly Law", in Competition Policy Research, No. 2, 2021, p. 46.

[39] Yang Dong and Huang Yinxu: "Meta-Platform: A New Theory of Antitrust Law for the Digital Economy," in Journal of the Renmin University of China, Vol. 2, No. 2, 2022, p. 124. It should be noted in particular that the open platform principle and its basic content used later in this article are quoted from this article, and no further annotations will be made to the other generalizations other than quoting the original text.

market, the operator has refused the transaction request of the transaction counterpart, the transaction request of the transaction counterpart involves the use of the operator's essential facilities, and the refusal of the transaction request lacks justifiable reasons. It is clear that these elements are identical to those set forth in the provisions on the *Prohibition of Abuse of Market Dominance* regarding the theory of essential facilities. As demonstrated earlier, whether before or after the revision, pursuant to Chapter III of the *Anti-Monopoly Law*, the elements required for a refusal to transact are, in principle, the subject identity element, the conduct pattern, and the grounds for defense. In fact, this is precisely the set of elements that traditional theory has advocated for regulating refusal to transact. Like the provisions on the theory of essential facilities in the provisions on the *Prohibition of Abuse of Market Dominance*, the conservative approach clearly adds an additional element compared to these provisions. The more elements there are, the more restrictions there are on the imposition of legal obligations. Under the conservative approach, a refusal to transact constitutes an unfair trade practice only if the criteria of subject, conduct, grounds for defense and specific object element are satisfied. However, according to traditional theory or the provisions of Chapter III of the *Anti-Monopoly Law* only the former three elements are necessary. This makes the conservative approach less stringent than the provisions of Chapter III of the *Anti-Monopoly Law* and traditional theory in imposing legal obligations on entities with essential facilities. It is important to note that the elements required for a refusal to transact may indeed four, with the fourth being the competitive impact element; however, in such cases, the legal basis also includes the relevant provisions in the general provisions of the *Anti-Monopoly Law*. Nevertheless, even under such circumstances, the conservative approach achieves the same effect in terms of the legal obligations imposed on entities possessing essential facilities.[40]

B. Radical approach will cause the uncertainty risk of the Anti-Monopoly Law to spiral out of control

23. In summary, the radical approach advocates breaking away from the traditional framework prohibiting the abuse of market dominance, with the *Anti-Monopoly Law* directly stipulating that operator, regardless of whether they hold market dominance, must not refuse to grant access to essential facilities to transaction counterparts without justifiable reasons. This approach primarily represents another specific proposal introduced

---

40 It is quite certain that, even if it were to be incorporated into the law, the Conservative Program would not appear in the General Provisions of the Antimonopoly Act. In this case, if the competitive effect element is to be considered for other refusals to deal under the General Provisions of the Antimonopoly Act, then the conservative program will also need to be considered in addition to this element when applying the conservative program. In other words, the conservative program will still have an additional element.

by academic circles in recent years to incorporate the theory of essential facilities. Since the 13th NPC Standing Committee included the revision of the *Anti-Monopoly Law* in its legislative agenda, the proposal gained momentum following the Central Economic Work Conference in late 2020, which emphasized "strengthening anti-monopoly efforts and preventing the disorderly expansion of capital," reaching a historical peak before the revision of the *Anti-Monopoly Law* was completed. It remains a topic of ongoing discussion to this day.

1. The uncertainty and legal risks of the Anti-Monopoly Law

24. "Antitrust laws in various countries exhibit uncertainty that is not present in traditional law due to the ambiguity of legislative language, the uncertainty of regulatory targets, and the diversification of legal objectives."[41] Whether before or after revision, the *Anti-Monopoly Law* has a high degree of uncertainty, particularly with regard to provisions prohibiting the abuse of market dominance.[42] First, uncertainty is most prominently manifested in the determination of the identity of the operator. Although the *Anti-Monopoly Law* defines relevant markets and market dominance, and the *Anti-Monopoly Law* also stipulates how to determine whether an operator has market dominance, a relatively mature set of methods for defining relevant markets has basically been established in practice; however, both the definition of relevant markets and the determination of market dominance still have significant case-by-case discrepancies and corresponding flexibility in practice. Second, uncertainty is manifested in the determination of behavioral patterns. Regarding the specific acts of abusing market dominance listed in the *Anti-Monopoly Law*, while refusal to transact and restriction of transactions are relatively straightforward, others are typically complex and subject to significant objective disputes. Furthermore, uncertainty is evident in the determination of defenses. Even when addressing the specific circumstances of justifiable reasons listed in the provisions on the *Prohibition of Abuse of Market Dominance*, the parties involved often hold divergent views, let alone the determination of other factors.[43]

25. The *Anti-Monopoly Law* imposes strict legal liabilities for monopolistic conduct, including the abuse of market dominance. Even before the

---

41 Liu Jin: "The Choice of Antitrust Law Enforcement Mechanism under the Perspective of Legal Uncertainty", in Competition Policy Research, Vol. 2, No. 2, 2016, p. 42.

42 On the one hand, when recognized according to the four constituent elements, the element of competitive influence also has such a manifestation. On the other hand, given that the theoretical community has a basic consensus on the strong uncertainty of the Antimonopoly Law, especially on the prohibition of the abuse of dominant position of market behavior, we will not argue in detail on each of the corresponding performance, but only make the necessary elaboration.

43 See Hao Junqi: "On Restorative Remedies for Antitrust in the Platform Economy," in Finance and Economics Law, No. 3, 2023.

revision, the *Anti-Monopoly Law* provided that "Where an undertaking abuses its dominant market position in violation of the present Law, the anti-monopoly law enforcement agency shall order it to cease the illegal act, confiscate its illegal gains and impose on it a fine of not less than 1% but not more than 10% of its sales amount in the previous year." The revised *Anti-Monopoly Law* not only introduced provisions for doubled fines but also added criminal liability. The former is reflected in Article 63 of the revised *Anti-Monopoly Law*, which states that "With regard to any violation of the provisions of the present Law, if the circumstances are especially serious, the effects are especially adverse or the consequences are especially serious, the Anti-monopoly Law Enforcement Agency of the State Council may determine the specific amount of the fine at not less than 2 times but not more than 5 times of the amount of the fine prescribed in Articles 56, 57, 58 or 62 hereof." The latter is reflected in the revised Article 67 of the *Anti-Monopoly Law*. Whoever violates the provisions of the present Law which is serious enough to constitute a criminal offence shall be subject to criminal liability in accordance with the law. The possible criminal liability subjects and behaviors include but are not limited to those specified in the original Articles 52 and 54. Additionally, the provisions of Article 67 are open-ended, meaning that it does not exclude the possibility of criminal liability for severe monopolistic conduct beyond the aforementioned subjects and acts."[44] In this case, the uncertainty of the Anti-Monopoly Law objectively becomes a major risk.

26. However, even with regard to provisions prohibiting the abuse of market dominance, the aforementioned risks are currently largely controllable. "A behavior that would be considered normal competition if carried out by other companies may constitute 'abuse' and be prohibited if by a company with market dominance."[45] It goes without saying that proving the identity of the operator is the basis for antitrust enforcement agencies to investigate and punish abuse of market dominance. On the one hand, it is not easy for antitrust enforcement agencies to define a clear and reasonable relevant market, especially in the digital economy. "The complexity of the digital economy makes the definition of relevant markets an important obstacle to effective antitrust enforcement."[46] On the other hand, unless an operator has a very high market share that can be presumed to constitute market dominance, antitrust enforcement agencies need to make a determination based on various factors such as market share, market competition conditions, and market entry barriers, which is often not an easy task. Even if an operator is presumed by antitrust

---

44 Shi Jianzhong: "The Practical Significance and Content Interpretation of the New Anti-Monopoly Law", in China Law Review, No. 4, 2022, p. 189.

45 Cited in Cao Soldier, Research on Antimonopoly Law, Law Press, 1996 edition, p. 140.

46 See Stigler, G. J. Center Committee for the Study of Digital Platforms Market Structure and Antitrust Subcommittee Center of University of Chicago. 2019.

enforcement agencies to have market dominance due to its very high market share, this presumption can be rebutted.

2. The theory of comparative advantage position is highly uncertain

27. "The comparative advantage position theory emphasizes the relative power of enterprises and argues that when one party to a transaction has market power similar to that of a monopolistic enterprise in certain circumstances, the other party will become 'dependent' on that enterprise, thereby triggering competition law effects."[47] As was the case during the revision of the *Anti-Monopoly Law*, there were calls from the academic community during the drafting of the *Anti-Monopoly Law* to incorporate the theory of comparative advantage position into the *Anti-Monopoly Law*. "The lawmakers of *Anti-monopoly Law* in China should draw on the practical needs of social reality to define the concept, types of conduct, and legal liabilities associated with the abuse of comparative advantage, and incorporate such conduct into the regulatory scope of Law."[48] However, this view has been strongly opposed by the majority and has therefore not yet been adopted in antitrust legislation.[49] "The concept of 'abuse of comparative advantage position' is fraught with uncertainty and may result in significant enforcement costs in practice. Therefore, it should be used with caution."[50]

28. The theory of comparative advantage does indeed have significant uncertainties. Compared with the traditional framework prohibiting the abuse of market dominance, the theory of comparative advantage departs from the prerequisite of a relevant market and instead focuses solely on the relative market power of the relevant operators. First, it is highly unlikely that two operators would be completely equal in strength. On the one hand, assessing an operator's market power involves considering numerous factors, including both internal factors such as organizational structure, number of employees, and capital scale, as well as external factors such as the stage of industrial development, national laws and policies, and the international trade environment. On the other hand, different operators always have certain differences, albeit to varying degrees. Second, different focuses may lead to different comparison results. Take the mutual "accusations" between certain platform companies as an example. If we consider the issue of one platform opening its logistics system to the

---

47 Li Jian: "Questioning the Theory of Relative Advantageous Position", in Modern Law, No. 3, 2005, p. 101.

48 Wang Lijuan and Mei Lin: "Antitrust Law Study on the Abuse of Relative Advantageous Position", in Jurisprudence, No. 7, 2006, p. 67.

49 As a result, this type of debate has turned successively to the revision of the Law of the People's Republic of China Against Unfair Competition, and the situation is now basically the same.

50 Wang Xiaoye: "On the Legal Regulation of Abuse of "Comparative Advantageous Position"", in Modern Law, No. 5, 2016, p. 79.

other's logistics business, Platform A has a dominant position relative to Platform B; however, if one platform opening its payment system to the other's settlement business, Platform B would then have a dominant position relative to Platform A. Furthermore, the stability of comparison results is often poor. Supply and demand relationships can change at any time, and the relative positions of parties involved in transactions may also shift, including transitions from advantageous to disadvantageous positions or vice versa.

29. If the *Anti-Monopoly Law* adopts the theory of comparative advantage position, then operators that may constitute refusal to transact would no longer be limited to with market dominance but would also include with comparative advantage. Unless the *Anti-Monopoly Law* significantly reduces the legal liability for monopolistic conduct or separately establishes lighter legal liability for the abuse of comparative advantage,[51] this would increase the uncertainty risk in the implementation of the *Anti-Monopoly Law* to an uncontrollable extent. First, the determination of comparative advantage does not require the definition of a relevant market, which significantly reduces the investigative burden on antitrust enforcement agencies;[52] second, since different operators inherently possess varying degrees of market power, this provides a basis for broader intervention by antitrust enforcement agencies; furthermore, the criteria for assessing comparative advantage are highly flexible, leaving significant discretion for antitrust enforcement agencies. Moreover, based on practical experience: on the one hand, in pursuit of case handling performance, fiscal revenue, policy effects, or retaliation against enterprises, antitrust enforcement agencies, particularly the over 30 provincial-level enforcement agencies authorized by the State Council's antitrust enforcement agency, may frequently engage in "improper" enforcement; on the other hand, in the current environment where social credibility levels in China are still relatively low, to evade contractual liability or exert pressure on transaction counterparties – particularly competitors – to obtain additional benefits, all operators may occasionally file complaints or reports with antitrust enforcement agencies,[53] or/and continuously exert pressure on such agencies through other means.

---

51 On the one hand, the likelihood of the Antimonopoly Law adopting these approaches for this purpose is minimal; on the other hand, the radical option does not therefore suggest a significant downgrading of legal liability for monopolistic conduct or a separate provision specifically for this purpose.

52 It should be noted that some people believe that the determination of the prohibition of abuse of a position of comparative advantage needs to adhere to the analytical path of "defining the relevant market - determining the position of comparative advantage of the enterprise - determining whether there is an abusive behavior". See Rasen, "The Regulatory Theory and Institutional Composition of the Abuse of Comparative Advantage by Internet Platforms," Global Law Review, No. 1, 2023.

53 This has been amply demonstrated by a number of disputes relating to resale price maintenance that have occurred since the Anti-Monopoly Law came into force and before the completion of the revision of the Anti-Monopoly Law, the most representative of which is the "Moutai Wuliangye Case" behind the refraction of such issues.

3. The principle of an open platform has greater uncertainty

30. In terms of form, the open platform principle not only breaks through the restriction that operators must have market dominance, but also the restriction that operators must have a comparative advantage. Although the platform operators involved may have a comparative advantage or even market dominance, under this principle, antitrust enforcement agencies no longer need to prove whether the platform has a comparative advantage or market dominance. As long as the platform involved falls within the scope of the specified platforms, the operators are included in the basic scope of obligated entities. Additionally, the open platform principle formally breaks through the determination of essential facilities. Although the platforms in question may be classified as essential facilities, antitrust enforcement agencies no longer need to prove whether the platform qualifies as an essential facility. In other words, the open platform principle directly classifies specified platforms as essential facilities.

31. This makes it decisive whether the platform in question falls under the specified platforms, especially when the open platform principle adopts a reversal of the burden of proof in the application of exceptions. The open platform principle is based on openness as the rule and non-openness as the exception. Regarding the burden of proof for whether there are justifiable reasons not to open, one option is for the antitrust enforcement agencies to bear the burden, and the other is for the platform operator in question to bear the burden. If the latter is chosen, then the burden of proof is reversed. In contrast, this approach appears to align more closely with the essence of the open platform principle. If the open platform principle adopts a reversal of the burden of proof in the application of exceptions, then once the platform in question is deemed to fall under the specified platforms, the likelihood of the platform operator being found by antitrust enforcement agencies to have refused to transact by failing to open the platform is very high. Even without a reversal of the burden of proof, the examination of antitrust enforcement agencies of refusal to transact in such cases would at least be more straightforward in form.

32. Although the open platform principle specifies that the platform in question is primarily a meta-platform, this theory is no less robust in terms of uncertainty than the comparative advantage theory, and in some respects even surpasses it. Even if we consider only meta-platforms, first, regardless of whether they are large enterprises, small and medium-sized enterprises, or micro-enterprises, the platforms they operate could potentially become so-called meta-platforms; second, regardless of whether they are e-commerce platforms, lifestyle service platforms, social entertainment platforms, information and news platforms, financial service platforms, or computing application platforms, they could also potentially become so-called meta-platforms; third, regardless of whether they are super-platforms, large

platforms, or small and medium-sized platforms, they could all potentially become so-called meta-platforms. Unless antitrust enforcement agencies explicitly list them in advance, even if a specific list of so-called meta-platforms is compiled beforehand, its scope would remain highly ambiguous, and this is at least currently unlikely to be achieved in China.[54]

33. Therefore, if the *Anti-Monopoly Law* adopts the open platform principle, unless it significantly reduces or adjusts the legal liability for monopolistic conduct, or specifically provides for lighter legal liability for violations of the open platform principle. This will increase the uncertainty risk of the *Anti-Monopoly Law* to an uncontrollable level, especially when the open platform principle adopts a reversal of the burden of proof in the application of exceptions.

IV. Application of the Theory of Essential Facilities in China

34. In terms of how to apply the theory of essential facilities, China should adopt an internalization model at the regulatory level. Specifically, the word "essential" should be deleted from the provisions on the theory of essential facilities in the provisions on *Prohibition of Abuse of Market Dominance*, and there is no need to make explicit provisions on the theory of essential facilities in the *Anti-Monopoly Law*.

A. The internalization model adopted at the regulatory level can still reflect the basic meaning of the essential facilities theory

35. In terms of the directness of expression, the provisions of the provisions on the *Prohibition of Abuse of Market Dominance* regarding the theory of essential facilities are highly direct. Not only do they articulate the fundamental principles of the theory in substance, but they also employ the specific term "essential facilities" in form. This mode of expression for the theory of essential facilities can be referred to as the externalization model. In addition to the externalization model, the theory of essential facilities has another expression method, which involves removing the term "essential" from the provisions of the *Prohibition of Abuse of Market Dominance* that pertain to the theory of essential facilities. This can be referred to as the internalization model. Although it does not use the specific term "essential facilities" in form, it still conveys the basic meaning of the theory of essential facilities in content.

36. As mentioned in the previous section, the basic meaning of the essential facilities doctrine is that operators who own relevant facilities must open

---

54 The fruitless drafting of the Guidelines for the Classification and Rating of Internet Platforms (Draft for Comments) and the Guidelines for the Implementation of the Main Responsibility of Internet Platforms (Draft for Comments) organized by the State Administration for Market Supervision and Administration (SAMSA) is a strong manifestation of this.

them to competitors under certain circumstances in order to maintain effective competition in the market. The specific conditions for this obligation to open facilities are emphasized in formal terms in order to highlight the fundamental reason for requiring external access in principle. In other words, because the relevant facilities are essential facilities, they must in principle be open to external access.[55] This is precisely the starting point of the theory of essential facilities, which directly serves as the argument for why various platforms should be open. "The establishment of a platform antitrust intervention mechanism is based on the attribute of internet platforms as essential facilities. The existence of economies of scale on the demand side gives large internet platforms the status of essential facilities that control network competition, making it feasible and effective to impose active competition obligations on them."[56] Regardless of whether the amendment was made before or after, in the *Anti-Monopoly Law*, such provisions are all concentrated in the defense grounds for refusal to transact.

37. Therefore, the feasibility of making reasonable investments to construct or develop the facility separately, considering factors such as the extent to which the transaction counterparties rely on the facility for their production and business operations, the likelihood of the operator providing the facility, and the impact on its own production and business operations, are also factors that can and should be considered as defenses. Furthermore, the wording of the provisions on the essential facilities theory in the provisions on the *Prohibition of Abuse of Market Dominance* states, "When determining whether an operator has abused its dominant market position in accordance with the fifth item of the preceding paragraph." When an antitrust enforcement agency determines whether an operator with market dominance has a justifiable reason to refuse a transaction where the counterparty seeks to use its facilities under reasonable conditions in its production and business operations, it applies the essential facilities theory. This is substantively consistent with the provisions on the essential facilities theory in the provisions on the *Prohibition of Abuse of Market Dominance*.

B. The internalization model adopted at the regulatory level is fully consistent with the refusal to deal provisions of the Anti-Monopoly Law

38. Although the content of the provisions on the *Prohibition of Abuse of Market Dominance* after the deletion of the term "essential" from the theory of essential facilities is essentially the same as the content before the deletion, compared with the content before the deletion, the method

---

55 See Sun Jin and Cai Qianmeng: "The Rule Remediation of Digital Platform Governance under the Principle of Fair Competition," in Finance and Economics Law, Vol. 1, No. 1, 2023.

56 Rose Zhang: "Paradigm Transformation of Antitrust Legal Regulation of Internet Platforms--Construction of Antitrust Law Prior Intervention Paradigm", in Politics and Law, Vol. 4, No. 4, 2023, p. 162.

39. When the expression of the theory of essential facilities adopts the internalization model, the "facilities" in question should no longer be regarded as specific objective requirements, as is the case with "essential facilities" under the externalization model. On the one hand, they have no specific formal restrictions, which means that all facilities owned by operators with market dominance are first included in the scope of consideration, rather than only certain specific facilities they own. Whether these facilities should be or which facilities should be open to the public is a separate issue. On the other hand, refusing to transact with a transaction counterpart always involves different objects, such as facilities, grain, animals, etc. Whether we exhaustively list or individually list them, unless they are specifically limited as in the externalization mode of the theory of essential facilities, they should not be regarded as specific object requirements in nature merely because they constitute part of the enumerated scenarios. Antitrust enforcement agencies only make basic determinations regarding these objects and do not need to conduct further detailed characterization.

40. It is particularly worth noting that while the phrase "in production and business operations" is difficult to be subsumed under the subject identity, behavioral pattern, or defense grounds of the "essential facilities theory" as stipulated in the provisions on the *Prohibition of Abuse of Market Dominance*, it also cannot be treated as an independent constitutive element like "essential facilities." To be precise, "in production and business operations" is an objective description of the contextual setting in which the essential facilities theory applies, rather than a specific restriction on the scope of application of the theory. The essential facilities theory focuses on the issue of refusal to transact between operators, and primarily between competitors,[57] which objectively concentrates "in production and business operations." As mentioned earlier, even if the term "essential" is removed from the provisions on essential facilities in the provisions on the *Prohibition of Abuse of Market Dominance*, the remaining content can still express the basic meaning of the essential facilities theory. In this case, "in production and business operations" is still an objective description of the context in which the essential facilities theory applies, rather than a specific restriction on the application of the essential facilities theory.

41. The provisions on the *Prohibition of Abuse of Market Dominance* stipulate that the terms "on reasonable terms" and "its" in the theory of essential facilities are both defensible grounds. Whether the specific terms proposed by the transaction counterpart are justifiable and whether the

---

[57] See Liu Xiaochun: "Legal Regulation of Self-Preferential Treatment on Digital Platforms," in Legal Science, 2023, No. 1.

operator with dominant market position has the right to dispose of the relevant facilities are all within the scope of justifiable reasons to decide whether to engage in the transaction. Therefore, after removing the term "essential" from the provisions on the theory of essential facilities in the provisions on the *Prohibition of Abuse of Market Dominance*, the substantive elements of the provisions are reduced to three: the subject identity, the conduct pattern, and the defense grounds. It is very clear that this is now fully consistent with the elements required for refusal to transact as stipulated in Chapter III of the *Anti-Monopoly Law*. Of course, this does not preclude antitrust enforcement agencies from adopting a four-element approach in cases involving the abuse of market dominance to ensure more scientific enforcement.

42. The fact that the refusal to transact is identical in all its elements to the refusal to transact under Chapter III of the *Anti-Monopoly Law* not only makes antitrust enforcement agencies willing to apply the provisions on the *Prohibition of Abuse of Market Dominance* after the removal of the word "essential," but also eliminates any current concerns for them. Even if antitrust enforcement agencies determine that the investigated operator does not constitute refusal to transact solely because they deem it feasible for the transaction counterpart to make reasonable investments to construct or develop alternative facilities or because the transaction counterpart's reliance on the relevant facilities is low, such a determination is made within the framework of the defense grounds. As long as the court fully respects the discretionary authority of the antitrust enforcement agencies within the framework of the *Anti-Monopoly Law* during its review of legality or reasonableness, the agencies should not be directly ruled by the court as violating the *Anti-Monopoly Law* solely on this basis. Although this is essentially no different from the situation previously mentioned, where the antitrust enforcement agencies determined that the relevant facilities of the operators did not constitute essential facilities and thus concluded that their conduct did not constitute refusal to transact.[58]

C. Legislation at the regulatory level is more convenient and efficient when using the internalization model

43. In addition to issues at the regulatory level, such as the conservative approach conflicting with the intent of introducing the essential facilities doctrine into the *Anti-Monopoly Law*, the externalization model is

---

58 It should be noted in particular that, where both the subject matter and behavioral pattern elements are established, it would be quite another matter for the court to "overturn" the findings of the antitrust enforcement agency merely because it does not agree that it is feasible to invest in the construction or development of the relevant facilities with reasonable inputs, or that the counterparty's reliance on the relevant facilities to carry out its production and business activities efficiently is very low. It is another matter for the court to "overturn" the findings of the antitrust enforcement agency simply because it does not agree that it is feasible to construct or develop the facility with reasonable investment or that the counterparty's dependence on the facility for the effective conduct of its business is low.

also problematic when applied to the *Anti-Monopoly Law*. However, the internalization model is the opposite. This expression of the essential facilities doctrine can not only be applied at the regulatory level but also at the *Anti-Monopoly Law* level. As mentioned earlier: on the one hand, the academic community argues that the starting point for introducing the essential facilities theory into the *Anti-Monopoly Law* is to impose stricter legal obligations on operators that possess essential facilities; on the other hand, the provisions on essential facilities in the provisions on the *Prohibition of Abuse of Market Dominance*, after removing the term "essential," are identical in their constitutive elements to the refusal to transact as stipulated in Chapter III of the *Anti-Monopoly Law*. When we adopt the internalization approach to introduce the theory of essential facilities into the *Anti-Monopoly Law*, the legal obligations imposed on operators possessing relevant facilities are as stringent as those imposed by Chapter III of the *Anti-Monopoly Law* and the traditional theory regarding the regulation of refusal to transact.

44. However, unless the *Anti-Monopoly Law* amends its legislative provisions on the abuse of market dominance by adopting a decentralized approach, the formal introduction of the essential facilities doctrine into the *Anti-Monopoly Law* through the internalization model would appear somewhat "incongruous." First, the content of the provisions on the *Prohibition of Abuse of Market Dominance* after removing the word "essential" from the provisions on the theory of essential facilities is quite extensive in terms of volume. In terms of length, it is nearly equivalent to the provisions on the prohibition of abusing market dominance in Chapter III of the *Anti-Monopoly Law*.[59] Second, the provisions of the *Prohibition of Abuse of Market Dominance* regarding the "essential" component of the essential facilities theory, after the term "essential" has been removed, have a relatively broad scope. It not only provides specific examples of potential scenarios involving refusal to transact but also lists specific defenses for one such scenario. Based on previous legislative experience, it would be difficult to incorporate such provisions in a dedicated section under Chapter III of the *Anti-Monopoly Law*, which addresses the prohibition of abuse of market dominance. Additionally, "broad-brush legislation is one of the characteristics of Chinese Anti-Monopoly Law."[60] This is also true of the revised *Anti-Monopoly Law*. It is reasonable to expect that as long as it continues to use the concentration model in its legislation on the abuse of market dominance, this will remain the case. Deleting the word "essential" from the provisions on the *Prohibition of Abuse of Market Dominance* in relation to the theory of essential facilities clearly

---

59 Excluding the provisions on the determination of market dominance, i.e., referring only to the provisions of Article 22 of the revised Anti-Monopoly Law.

60 Shijianzhong: "China's Anti-trust Law's Characteristics, Highlights and Major Shortcomings", in Jurist, No. 1, 2008, p. 14.

conflicts with the concentration model, which is a significant difference from the conservative approach.

45. The legal hierarchy and functions of regulations such as *Prohibition of Abuse of Market Dominance* objectively dictate that such regulations should not only adopt a decentralized structure to prohibit the abuse of market dominance but also effectively specify the prohibited acts of such abuse. This approach is more straightforward in the provisions on the *Prohibition of Abuse of Market Dominance*, where the term "essential" is removed from the provisions on necessary facilities. However, it should be noted that when the provisions on the *Prohibition of Abuse of Market Dominance* eventually adopts an internalization model in expressing the theory of necessary facilities, simply removing the term "essential" will not be sufficient. As mentioned earlier, factors such as the feasibility of making reasonable investments to construct or develop the facility separately are considered under this model in determining whether there are justifiable reasons. Therefore, the content of this provision should at least be placed after the enumerated provisions regarding the elements of the defense grounds for refusal to transact in the provisions on the *Prohibition of Abuse of Market Dominance*.

46. In addition, on the one hand, the *Anti-Monopoly Law* was just revised for the first time in 2022, and it is unlikely that its revision will be initiated again in the short term under normal circumstances. Moreover, the revision of the *Anti-Monopoly Law* is a legislative task at the level of the NPC Standing Committee, and the corresponding procedures are relatively complex. In contrast, the revision of the *Prohibition of Abuse of Market Dominance* is a legislative task at the level of the State Council's anti-monopoly enforcement agency, and not only are the corresponding procedures relatively simple, but it can also be completed in the short term. On the other hand, from the perspective of reasonably controlling legislative costs, matters that can be addressed at the regulatory level should, in principle, not be elevated to the level of the Anti-Monopoly Law. In fact, "although Chinese Anti-Monopoly Law does not explicitly stipulate the essential facilities theory, the provisions on refusal to transact can serve as the normative basis for this principle."[61]

D. The internalization model adopted at the regulatory level is more robust in terms of risk control

47. As shown above, provided that an operator possesses market dominance, the uncertainty risk under the *Anti-Monopoly Law* is currently basically controllable. This is also effectively corroborated by the number of

---

[61] Ning Lizhi and Yu Zhangpeng, "Exploring the Legitimacy of Platform "Banning" Behavior--Analyzing the Application of the Principle of Necessary Facilities", in Journal of Harbin Institute of Technology (Social Science Edition), Vol. 5, No. 5, 2021, p. 39.

monopoly agreements and cases of abuse of market dominance investigated and dealt with by anti-monopoly enforcement agencies since the implementation of the *Anti-Monopoly Law*.[62] From 2008 to 2017, antitrust enforcement agencies investigated 161 cases involving monopolistic agreements and 51 cases involving abuse of market dominance. In 2018, 19 cases involving monopolistic agreements were investigated, with 11 cases concluded; 14 cases involving abuse of market dominance were investigated, with 7 cases concluded. In 2019, 28 monopoly agreement cases were investigated, with 12 concluded; 15 cases of abuse of market dominance were investigated, with 4 concluded; in 2020, 20 monopoly agreement cases were investigated, with 16 concluded; 18 cases of abuse of market dominance were investigated, with 10 concluded; in 2021, 30 monopoly agreement cases were investigated, with 11 administrative penalties imposed, and 11 cases of abuse of market dominance were investigated and handled; in 2022, 18 monopoly agreement cases were investigated, with 16 concluded, and 13 cases of abuse of market dominance were investigated and handled; in 2023, 16 monopoly agreement cases were investigated, with all 16 concluded, and 11 cases of abuse of market dominance were investigated and handled.[63] However, it should be noted that this is still based on the premise that the operator has market dominance, and its significance for risk control goes far beyond this.

48. Although the legislative purpose of the *Anti-Monopoly Law* remains the same before and after revision – "to prevent and prohibit monopolistic conduct and protect fair competition in the market" – both anti-monopoly legislation and enforcement constitute government intervention in nature. While "the market is an effective mechanism for resource allocation, this has been proven by the capitalist economic achievements of most European and North American countries in the 19th century. However, the market is not omnipotent, and the market mechanism has many inherent and insurmountable flaws that lead to its failure and inefficiency in resource allocation."[64] However, "when we say that the government can sometimes improve market outcomes, this does not mean that it always can."[65] "When the means employed by government policy or collective action fail to improve economic efficiency or morally acceptable income

---

62 Since the review of concentration of operators is by nature an administrative licensing act, it is objectively not comparable to the investigation and prosecution of monopoly agreements and abuse of dominant market position by antimonopoly enforcement agencies.

63 See China Antimonopoly Enforcement Annual Report (2019) for data from 2008 to 2017, 2018, and 2019, China Antimonopoly Enforcement Annual Report (2020) for data for 2020, China Antimonopoly Enforcement Annual Report (2021) for data for 2021, China Antimonopoly Enforcement Annual Report (2022), and for data in 2023, see China Antimonopoly Enforcement Annual Report (2023).

64 Wang Quanxing: Topical Studies on Basic Theories of Economic Law, China Procuratorate Press, 2002 edition, p. 80.

65 [US] Mancun: Principles of Economics, translated by Liang Xiaomin, Machinery Industry Press, 2003 edition, p. 10.

distribution, government failure occurs."[66] Moreover, practice has fully demonstrated that the market is often more efficient than the government in allocating resources. Therefore, the Third Plenary Session of the 18th Central Committee of the Communist Party of China, which reviewed and adopted the "Decision on Several Major Issues Concerning Comprehensively Deepening Reforms," specifically emphasized that economic reform is the focus of comprehensively deepening reforms, and that the core issue is to properly handle the relationship between the government and the market, allowing the market to play a decisive role in resource allocation while better leveraging the role of the government.

49. The essential facilities doctrine not only requires operators to open their relevant facilities under specific circumstances but also stipulates that the recipients of such access are primarily their competitors. While our objective is to promote market development, improper implementation could objectively hinder market development. In the preliminary response issued by the US District Court for the District of Columbia in June 2021 to the antitrust civil lawsuit filed by the US Federal Trade Commission and 46 states against Facebook, the judge expressed significant concerns, stating: "If Facebook is treated as an infrastructure provider akin to utilities like water, electricity, or gas, and its ability to refuse services to competitors is restricted accordingly, this would inevitably undermine the incentive for future firms to invest in similar infrastructure, as they would know they would be forced to open such infrastructure to competitors."[67] Once such risks materialize, the impacts are often far-reaching and may even erode the institutional foundations of social innovation. On the one hand, based on current practices, the proportion of cases where it is not feasible to invest in or develop alternative infrastructure due to natural monopolies or other reasons is decreasing, while the proportion of cases where such situations arise due to the application of innovative technologies is increasing. On the other hand, such innovations typically require significant investment and carry high risks of failure. Therefore, unless the expected returns are stable and substantial, businesses will have greater reservations when making such innovation decisions. Compared to the legislative objectives prior to revision, the revised *Anti-Monopoly Law* explicitly includes the objective of "encouraging innovation."

50. On the one hand, assuming that an operator has market dominance as a prerequisite can to a maximal extent limit the scope of government intervention in the application of the essential facilities doctrine. Even if a defense based on justifiable reasons is allowed, the subject of the essential

---

66 [US] Paul A. Samuelson, William D. Nordhaus, Economics, translated by Xiao Chen, China Development Press, 1992 edition, p. 1189.

67 Federal Trade Commission v. Facebook, Inc., MEMORANDUM OPINION, (2020), see https://www.ftc.gov/enforcement/cases-proceedings/191-0134/ facebook-inc-ftc-v.

facilities doctrine is still crucial. At a superficial level, this directly relates to the subject identity requirement; at a deeper level, it directly determines the basic scope of government intervention. The broader the scope of the subject, the broader the basic scope of government intervention.[68] Whether from the perspective of legislation regulating the unilateral conduct of operators in various countries or the application of the essential facilities doctrine, the prerequisite of market dominance of operators results in the narrowest scope of applicable subject identity. On the other hand, operators with market dominance are more likely to engage in conduct that excludes or restricts competition. With regard to unilateral conduct by operators, domestic and international practices have fully demonstrated that conduct such as refusing to transact with transaction counterparts by operators with market dominance is objectively more likely to produce exclusionary or restrictive effects on competition. Even operators with comparative advantage position would not achieve significant or widespread effects through the same conduct, let alone other operators. "How can we better incentivize innovation and foster an environment where innovative outcomes continuously emerge? Theoretical research and practical experience tell us that competition is the foundation of innovation, and the best way to encourage innovation is to strive to create a fair competitive environment."[69]

V. Remainder

51. Although the fundamental meaning of the essential facilities theory determines its practical value for competition governance, it is indeed necessary to introduce this theory into competition governance. However, due to differences in national conditions, the specific legislation of competition governance should not directly copy or replicate foreign practices in the application of the essential facilities theory, but rather should be tailored to local conditions. This is not an isolated case or precedent for the *Anti-Monopoly Law*. Take the regulatory legislation on resale price maintenance (RPM) as an example. Prior to revision, the *Anti-Monopoly Law*, modeled after EU regulations, stipulated in Article 14 that The following monopolistic agreements are prohibited from being reached between operators and their trading counterparties: (1) those fixing the price of commodities for resale to a third party; (2) those restricting the minimum price of commodities for resale to a third party; or (3) other monopolistic agreements as determined by the Anti-monopoly Law Enforcement

---

68 See Zhang Shouwen: "The Theoretical Response of Economic Law to the Development of Digital Economy," in Politics and Law Forum, No. 3, 2023.

69 Feng Zibiao and Wang Jigong: "Competition is the foundation of innovation", in People's Daily, July 29, 2009, p. 7.

Agency of the State Council. In addition to significant theoretical and practical disagreements, the *Anti-Monopoly Law* has also faced issues such as overly stringent legislative standards, widespread violations, and selective enforcement in practice due to RPM. Therefore, the revised *Anti-Monopoly Law* added two provisions to Article 18 regarding RPM: "The agreements prescribed in Items (1) and (2) of the preceding paragraph will not be prohibited if the operators can prove that such agreements do not have effects of eliminating or restricting competition. The agreements between operators will not be prohibited if the operators can prove that their market share in the relevant market is lower than the standard prescribed by the Anti-monopoly Law Enforcement Agency of the State Council and meet other conditions prescribed by the Anti-monopoly Law Enforcement Agency of the State Council."[70]

52. In recent years, the platform economy sector has emerged as a key focus area for the application of essential facilities theory. As the birthplace and major hub for the development of essential facilities theory, as well as the world's two largest antitrust jurisdictions, the United States and the European Union have made significant new developments in this field. The EU published the draft Digital Markets Act (DMA) in December 2020, reached a consensus in March 2022, and approved it in July, with the law set to take effect in November. The core provisions stipulate those platforms with annual turnover of at least 7.5 billion euros or a market capitalization exceeding 75 billion euros over the past three years in the EU, with at least 45 million monthly active users and at least 10,000 business users, control one or more core platform services in at least three member states. These companies must allow third parties to provide services on their platforms, allow users to access data, and allow consumers to connect with other operators outside the platform. The U.S. House Judiciary Committee released four draft bills in June 2021: *the American Choice and Innovation Online Act*, the *Ending Platform Monopolies Act*, the *Augmenting Compatibility and Competition by Enabling Service Switching Act*, and the *Platform Competition and Opportunity Act*. These draft bills aim to introduce a system similar to the "gatekeeper" regime of EU, but subsequent progress has been slow and limited.

53. In response to this, many people in China have suggested that we should adopt the EU's approach. "The *Digital Markets Act* is based on the channel theory to establish a protective framework, providing 'gatekeeper' rules specifically applicable to digital economy companies that control core platform services, and achieving data openness, sharing, and accessibility through a preemptive obligation framework.

---

[70] There is still some divergence of understanding as to the scope of application of the latter paragraph. See Ding Maozhong: "The Normative Determination of the Operator's Contributing to the Monopoly Agreement of Others", in Global Law Review, No. 5, 2023.

Newly issued 'Guidelines on Anti-Monopoly in the Platform Economy Sector' in China continues the analytical framework and approach of traditional anti-monopoly regulations, primarily relying on post-hoc regulatory enforcement for remedial measures, which is insufficient to prevent monopolistic behavior in the platform economy sector. China still needs to draw on the EU's 'gatekeeper' obligations in the platform economy sector to establish an antitrust regulatory framework for the platform economy sector that combines a 'negative list plus exceptions and exemptions' approach, thereby ensuring the healthy and sustainable development of the digital economy market."[71] It can be said that the principle of open platforms advocated in the radical proposal to introduce the theory of essential facilities into the *Anti-Monopoly Law* is identical to this. In fact, there are many similar "versions," such as "anti-monopoly regulation in the digital economy should not be limited to the application of anti-monopoly law; as a shift in anti-monopoly methods and concepts, it can also simultaneously regulate large digital enterprises as a new type of public utility."[72]

54. This is a recommendation that requires careful consideration.[73] On the one hand, there are significant differences between China and the EU in terms of development in the relevant fields. According to the *Internet Trends 2019* report released by Mary Meeker, who is hailed by the industry as the "Queen of the Internet,"[74] in 2019, among the top 30 global internet companies by market capitalization, 18 were from the US, 7 were from China, and only 1 was from the EU. On the other hand, the motives behind the EU's move are highly questionable. Many international scholars have pointed out that the quantitative standards set by the *Digital Markets Act* are at least motivated by two considerations of local protectionism: first, to allow large European platform companies to avoid being designated as "gatekeepers"; and second, to curb the growth of large digital platform companies from China and the United States, thereby aiding less efficient European competitors. The European Commission's preliminary list of 19 'gatekeepers' in March 2023 included only two European companies, while the final list of six 'gatekeepers' in September included only five U.S. companies and one Chinese company. This indicates that the quantitative standards for

---

71 Hu Xiaohong: "The Construction of "Gatekeeper" Obligations in China's Platform Economy under the Perspective of Antitrust Law", in Xuehai, No. 2, 2023, p. 164.

72 Gao Wei: "The New Utility Theory of Platform Regulation," in Legal Studies, Vol. 3, No. 3, 2021, p. 84.

73 See Hong Yingying: "The European Union's Digital Market Law and its Implications for China", in Journal of Shanghai University of Political Science and Law, No. 2, 2023.

74 Apart from the change in the name of the report, Mary Meeker's new releases of this type of report in the last two years have been mainly analyzed and judged in terms of content around the important impact of the new crown epidemic on social development, and have not dealt with the ranking of the market capitalization of companies in the Internet industry. For the original Internet Trends Report 2019, see https://www.sohu.com/a/321315935_818485, last accessed June 16, 2024.

"gatekeepers" under this law are designed to facilitate selective enforcement by the European Commission.[75] This may provide a reasonable explanation for why the United States has made little progress on the gatekeeper regime. It underscores the need for us to proceed with caution to ensure that our country continues to maintain its competitive edge in the global digital economy.

---

[75] Wang Xiaoye: "Whether the EU Model Should Be Introduced for Digital Economy Regulation," in Shanghai Rule of Law News, Nov. 17, 2023, p. B7.

New Development of Anti-Monopoly Regulation on Data in China

CHEN BING[*]
Professor of Law, Nankai University

Abstract

In the context of digital economy, the State Council designated data as a factor of production such as joining land, labor, capital, and technology in China, which not only integrates into all aspects of production and life, but also relates to the creation of a fair competition in the digital economy market with data as the core element. In practice, China has already formulated relevant provisions on data anti-monopoly at the legislative level and regulated data monopoly at the law enforcement level. However, with the development of the digital economy represented by the platform economy, the monopolistic behaviors formed by data elements have become diversified and more hidden, how to effectively regulate data monopolies is still difficult. The main reasons for the inability to effectively regulate data monopolization are that the basic theoretical system related to data is not establish, the legal attributes are not yet clear, and the data infrastructure is not perfect. To effectively regulate data monopolies, it is indispensable to implement precise, agile and interdepartmental comprehensive regulation. At the same time, the construction of the basic theoretical system for data, data circulation and trading system, and data infrastructure should also be further strengthened, to constitute a complete data anti-monopoly regulatory system suitable for China's national conditions.

---

[*] Fund Project: The major project in Judicial Research of the Supreme People's Court (2023) "Research on Judicial Protection of Intellectual Property Rights in Data Interests" (ZGFYZDKT202317-03); The key project of Humanities and Social Science study from the Ministry of Education "Research on the Consideration and Promotion of Human Rights Benchmarks in Global Data Competition" (19JJD820009) Chen Bing, Professor of Law, Vice Dean of School of Law, Director of Center of Competition Law, Nankai University.

1. The Status of Data Monopoly Regulation in China

1.1 The rising status of data elements

1. The 2025 Government Work Report explicitly calls for "developing new productive forces tailored to local conditions and accelerating the construction of a modern industrial system." It also underscores the importance of "speeding up the improvement of foundational data systems, deepening data resource development and utilization, and promoting and regulating cross-border data flows." This reflects the mutually reinforcing relationship between new productive forces and data circulation. Facilitating a reasonable degree of data flow and sharing can significantly boost the growth of the digital economy. China has a wealth of experience in exploring data in the digital economy, the Fourth Plenary Session of the 19th CPC Central Committee made it clear for the first time that data could be distributed as a production factor according to their contributions[1], which means that the State Council formally designated data as a factor of production such as joining land, labor, capital, and technology in China. Data elements have become one of the most important factors of production in digital economy, and the accumulation of data helps market entities to gain competitive advantages and market power[2,3]. New technologies, new industries, and new markets continue to emerge. As a result, the collection, use, trading and sharing of data have become the most common behaviors in the market. At the same time, data-related competitive behavior has gradually attracted great attention from competition enforcement agencies around the world.

2. While the concept of "data monopoly" in the context of the digital economy has not reached a unanimous viewpoint in theory and practice[4], many countries have responded to data-related competition with concrete supervisory actions. As the second largest economy in the world, the Chinese government has also strengthened the regulation of data monopolies and has formulated and issued a series of laws and regulations to supervise data-related monopolies. China introduced the similar concept of "data monopoly" earlier in the wake of the infringement of consumer rights by fintech companies represented by Ant Group. In August 2024, the Shanghai Municipal Administration for Market Regulation investigated Ningbo Senpu Information Technology Co., Ltd. for abusing its dominant market position, ordering it to cease its

---

[1] China Academy of Information and Communications Technology. Report on the Development of China's Digital Economy[R], Beijing: CAICT, 2022.

[2] XU DD: The antitrust governance of advertising supported platforms under the background of digital economy[J]. Southwest Finance, 2020(6): 66-77.

[3] ZHOU HH: On the dichotomy of anti-monopoly and regulation in the platform economy[J]. China Legal Science, 2023(1): 222-240.

[4] CHEN B: Data monopoly: from appearance to truth[J]. Social Science Journal, 2021(2): 129-136.

illegal activities and imposing a hefty fine. This case, the first financial data monopoly case in China, aims to break the monopoly barriers in the financial data sector and set a precedent for fair competition in the data element market.

3. In contemporary society, digitalization is becoming a significant factor in restructuring the allocation of resource, reshaping industrial development, changing competitive landscape, and emerging new industrial forms. However, in practice, certain behaviors that exclude or restrict competition have emerged, hindering the orderly flow of data elements. Data-related monopolies are gradually spreading among various digital industries from fintech industry. Therefore, reasonably dismantling barriers to data circulation and breaking down "data silos" are important concerns in the current governance of the digital economy. As far as the development of the digital industry is concerned, the key lies in the co-enhancement of the sharing level and governance capacity, and the key to realizing fair competition lies in the adoption of effective means to regulate highly data-concentrated markets[5]. In practice, China has responded relatively early to the need for regulating data monopolies at the legislative level. On February 7, 2021, the State Council Anti-Monopoly Commission issued the *Anti-Monopoly Guidelines for the Platform Economy Sector* (hereinafter referred to as the *Anti-Monopoly Guidelines*) and promptly amended the *Anti-Monopoly Law* and related supporting regulations. The newly revised *Anti-Monopoly Law*, effective since August 2022, adds Article 9, which explicitly prohibits monopolistic conduct involving the use of data.

4. However, data monopolization is a complex and systemic issue, with its regulation involving multiple dimensions such as antitrust, anti-unfair competition, data security, cybersecurity, consumer rights protection, and personal information protection.[6] The digital economy is still in a phase of rapid development, and the existing antitrust legal framework faces shortcomings or ineffectiveness when addressing new business models, new technologies, and emerging practices within the digital economy. In practice, due to the special nature of monopolistic behavior using data as a production factor, traditional antitrust supervisory means and evaluation criteria such as relevant market definition methods may not to be applied directly[7]. Additionally, due to a lack of regulatory experience, enforcement agencies may intervene untimely or apply enforcement with inappropriate intensity, resulting in some anti-competitive behaviors not

---

5   Sun H T, Zhou Q Q: The governance dilemma of platform data monopoly and the shared mechanism[J]. Jiangsu Social Sciences, 2023(3): 131-139.

6   Shi Y. T, Zhai W: Anti-Monopoly Regulation Path for "Big Data Killing the Old Customer" Behavior in the Platform Economy[J], Competition Policy Research, 2022(1):56-68.

7   Sun L J, Wei Y H: Legal regulation of data monopoly[J]. Journal of Chongqing University of Posts and Telecommunications (Social Science Edition), 2023(4): 76-87.

being promptly or effectively regulated, or excessive enforcement undermining the incentives of market participants. Therefore, it is urgently necessary to systematically clarify the specific objectives and implementation pathways of anti-data monopolization, and to promote the normalized and systematic regulation of data monopolistic behaviors in a scientific and prudent manner, ensuring the standardized and healthy development of the digital economy.

1.2 Data monopoly has been taken seriously

5. As the most important antitrust law in China, the Anti-Monopoly Law is the basic guideline for regulating and governing data-related monopoly behaviors. In terms of the legal objective, since the multi-objective Anti-Monopoly Law is designed for the economic objectives and non-economic objectives, it is possible to better adapt the existing law to the complex issues brought about by economic development. The issue of whether data constituted an essential facility is extremely controversial[8,9], but in practice, the data-related monopolies have become a significant part by Chinese anti-monopoly enforcement authorities, and there are jurisprudential and legal basis in China's Anti-monopoly Law enforcement system.

6. The addition of data-related monopolization in the Anti-monopoly Law provides clearer guidelines for formulating and improving supporting laws and regulations. Article 9 of China's Anti-Monopoly Law provides that "An undertaking shall not engage in monopolistic conduct prohibited by this Law by data, or an algorithm, technology or capital advantage, or platform rule, among others". This article clarifies the role that data plays in China's antitrust regulation. In addition, Article 22 of the Anti-Monopoly Law states, "An undertaking with a dominant market position shall not engage in the acts of abusing the dominant market position specified in the preceding paragraph by data, or an algorithm, technology or capital advantage, or platform rules, among others."

7. The enactment and revision of supporting laws and regulations also play a complementary role in improving China's Anti-,monopoly Law and regulations, enabling China's Anti-Monopoly Law enforcement authorities to have a complete legal basis for data monopolization and to carry out timely and effective supervision. In fact, prior to the revised Anti-Monopoly Law, the Chinese legislature had imposed restrictions on

---

8   Wang Y C: Data legal person: the governance path of super platform data monopoly[J]. Journal of National Prosecutors College, 2022(6): 145-159.

9   Liu Y, Chen T Y, Chen Y, Zhang B, Pei L: The main manifestations and the path to governance of data monopoly on internet platforms online first[J]. Information Studies: Theory & Application, 2023 (7): 1-10.

an e-commerce business with dominant market position on account of its technological advantage, number of users, control of the relevant industries and other factors, may not abuse the dominant market position to exclude or restrict competition e-commerce data dominance in Articles 22 and 35 of the E-Commerce Law enacted in 2019, businesses are prohibited from abusing their dominant market position in e-commerce data by excluding or restricting competition. This includes factors such as the number of users, control of relevant industries, and other relevant considerations. In the same year, Parts II, IV, and V of the Guiding Opinions on Promoting the Healthy Development of the Platform Economy (2019) and Chapters II, III, and IV of the 'Guidelines' issued in 2021 provide relatively detailed provisions on monopoly agreements, abuse of dominant market position and operator concentration in the new context. These provisions have expanded the field of platform competition regulation for digital governance, and constitute the prototype of China's regulation of data-related monopoly behaviors, but the enforcement framework of the above laws and regulations is still based on the traditional concepts of "monopoly agreement", "dominant position", "concentration of operators" and so on.

8. In March 2022, Opinions of the CPC Central Committee and the State Council on *Accelerating the Construction of a Unified National Market* that "Focusing on increasing anti-monopoly efforts. We will improve legal rules for identifying monopolies and a category-and class-based system for anti-monopoly review of concentrations between undertakings. We will address issues such as platform enterprises' monopoly of data to avoid eliminating and restricting competition by data, algorithms, technology, and other measures". This policy explicitly calls for strengthening the regulation of data monopolization, providing important guidance for further improving the legal framework of the data factor market. It also demonstrates China's increasingly deepened focus on data competition in the field of antitrust regulation.

9. In addition to the counteracting effect on data abuse that can be reflected in economic laws, the rules about data-related monopolistic behaviors provided for in legal provisions on the rights of the Individual and property interest, such as Article 127 of the Civil Code, Article 45 of the Personal Information Protection Law and Article 51 of the Data Security Law. These provisions, from the perspective of personal rights protection, set limitations on the collection, use, and processing of personal information, aiming to prevent the misuse of data that could infringe upon personal rights. Although these regulations need further refinement and clarification in areas such as balancing data circulation with protection and preventing data monopolies by large platform companies, they still hold value in fostering competition.

10. In summary, the Chinese government has earlier recognized that, in the context of the development of the digital economy, undertakings with data advantages, represented by digital platform enterprises, are more likely to engage in such behaviors may have eliminated or restricted competition. Therefore, Chinese market regulatory authorities have focused on platform enterprises, and while the Anti-Monopoly Law and other economic laws and regulations have increased the content of adapted data-related monopoly behaviors, they have also regulated these behaviors in non-economic laws and regulations. With the establishment of many laws and regulations, Chinese market regulatory authorities have gradually begun to strengthen regular and accurate supervision on "data monopoly".

2. China's Data Monopoly Supervision Status and Practice

2.1 The necessity of regulating platform data monopolies

11. The Organization for Economic Co-operation and Development (OECD) maintains that data-driven markets are more concentrated than others, and more susceptible to being monopolized[10]. In September 2020, the inspection team of the National People's Congress Standing Committee carried out by the implementation of the anti-unfair competition law, it was highlighted in the inspection report, pointed out that in recent years, Ali, Tencent and other digital enterprise mergers and acquisition are frequent, suffered from mergers and acquisitions of innovative small and medium-sized enterprises, although they do not reach the current standard of notification prescribed by the State Council and are not subject to the supervision of anti-monopoly law enforcement agencies, but many scholars argue that these concentrations between undertakings have produced a monopoly effect of restricting competition and inhibiting innovation[11]. Internet enterprises, especially digital platforms, have become the key target in China's data-related antitrust supervisory practice[12].

12. In fact, China has a large number of digital platform enterprises, whose industry scale has exceeded 50 trillion dollars as of 2022[13]. Some scholars

---

10 Organization for Economic Co-operation and Development. Data-Driven Innovation: Big Data for Growth and Well-Being[R], Pairs: OECD, 2015.

11 The inspection team of the National People's Congress Standing Committee. Regarding inspection of the Anti-Unfair Competition Law of the People's Republic of China Implementation status report [EB/OL]. (2020-12-26) [2024-04-26]. http://www.npc.gov.cn/npc/c1773/c1849/c6680/fbzdjzfzfjc/fbzdjzfzfjc009/202101/t20210107_309460.html.

12 Zhang W Y: Curbing platform monopoly chaos: How legislation will break the situation[J]. The People's Congress of China, 2021(7): 51-52.

13 China Academy of Information and Communications Technology. Report on the Development of China's Digital Economy[R], Beijing: CAICT, 2022.

assert that most of the major obstacles to the development of data industry have been removed on China, and the cost of data collection has been significantly reduced, especially with the development of Internet technology and the improvement of arithmetic power, all of which have greatly facilitated the excavation of the value of data, whose potential value can be fully utilized with the support of technology. Some scholars argue that a moderate concentration of data can bring significant "dividends," such as economies of scale, which play a prominent role in enriching the types of data and increasing data openness.[14]

13. However, data is often concentrated in the hands of larger platform enterprises, which can lead to serious data abuse issues. The self-regulation of large domestic and international platforms regarding the non-abusive use of concentrated data is concerning. In some cases, these platforms even actively encourage data distribution to become increasingly uneven or polarized, accelerating the development of monopolistic tendencies.[15] Improper use of data not only poses a risk of damage to consumer rights, but also jeopardizes social governance and national security. The risk of data-related monopolization posed by digital platforms has already emerged during the development of the digital economy, and Chinese market regulatory authorities are facing unprecedented pressure to regulate data-related monopoly.

2.2 Enforcement practices for regulating data monopolies

14. Before the addition of data-related aspects to China's Antitrust Law and regulations, there were already mergers and acquisitions in China that were data-related and attracted widespread attention. In the case of the DiDi-Uber merger, Uber (China) sold its China business to Didi Chuxing (DiDi) for US$35 billion. DiDi which has more than 15 million drivers and 300 million registered users, the takeover, which solidified Didi's market dominance, prompted an investigation by the Chinese Ministry of Commerce that ultimately failed to find Didi in violation of any regulations, because the acquisition did not meet the relevant market turnover standards under China's existing antitrust laws. Many scholars think that the mergence may have establish data barriers, abuse data advantages and other behaviors that have the effect of excluding and restricting competition.

15. In terms of the current development of the domestic digital market, it is again true that platform operators use a large amount of concentrated data to gain a dominant position in the market[16], and it is indeed an

---

14 Su Y: Regulatory Limits of Platform Data Monopoly[J]. Journal of the National Prosecutors College, 2022(6):128-144.

15 Cao Y: How to Regulate Data Monopoly? [J], East China Law Journal, 2025(1): 46-59.

16 Li Y J, Xia J C: Potential risks and its preventive strategies of double round monopoly of super platform under the background of digital economy[J]. Reform, 2020(8): 58-67.

observable phenomenon, especially for operators to track users' preferences and daily lives in real time by providing them with free basic services, treating users' personal data as a key input variable, adjusting and optimizing their services in a timely manner, and providing a basis for merchants to place online targeted advertisements based on users' consumption portraits, so as to realize the digital industrialization. This phenomenon has become the main profit model and competitive advantage for many digital platforms,[17] while exacerbating the excessive collection and misuse of data by platform enterprises. This significantly reduces the participation of users and third-party vendors in the digital economy,[18] further leading to the potential risk of "data monopolies" among some leading platforms.

16. These phenomena are particularly evident in the series of cases handled by China's Anti-Monopoly law enforcement institutions, which has investigated and dealt with cases of abuse of dominant market positions such as the Alibaba group required platform-based operators to choose "one out of two" and Meituan required platform-based operators to choose "one out of two", as well as a number of cases of unlawful concentration of business operators. The case is particularly evident in the number of cases in which operators have on illegal concentration of undertakings in the field of platform economy. In response, the Supreme People's Court issued the "Opinions on Ensuring Technological Innovation through High-Quality Judicial Services" in January 2025. By releasing typical cases, it explicitly calls for severe punishment of platform practices such as "choose one of two". It emphasizes strengthening judicial deterrence through punitive damages, preservation measures, and other means, and promotes the coordination between judicial and law enforcement actions.

17. While the crux of the matter for solving data-related monopoly lies in the existence or non-existence of data monopoly. In China's laws and regulations, the word 'data monopoly' is seldom explicitly mentioned, but rather expressed in terms of the use of data monopoly advantage, data advantage, and so on. On the one hand, due to the theoretical system involving data has not been fully established, and there is a great deal of controversy surrounding the data monopoly at the theory level, because some scholars argue that the data itself has a non-competitive, instantaneous and other characteristics are not sufficient to determine the existence of data monopoly; On the other hand, the data is difficult to constitute an essential facility, whether the access restrictions on the

---

17   Su Y: The limits of administrative supervision of platform data monopolies[J]. Journal of National Prosecutors College, 2022(6): 128-144.

18   Liu J. J: Formation Mechanism and Regulatory Analysis of Data Monopoly[J], Journal of Beijing University of Technology (Social Sciences Edition), 2023(1): 71-83.

data constitutes an impenetrable barrier to entry into the market, or the data holding capacity of the market power. Therefore, it is difficult for data to constitute a necessary facility in the sense of monopoly, whether data access restrictions constitute an impenetrable market entry barrier, or whether data holdings can be equated with monopoly power[19].

2.3 Establishing data-specific supervisory measures

18. Data is easily concentrated and exhibits significant economies of scale and scope. Although the initial fixed costs of data are often high, it can generate a positive feedback loop once utilized. In the context of the digital economy, data not only serves as the product itself or the content for providing services, but also plays an important role in business decision-making and strategic implementation. It helps businesses accurately and comprehensively understand and analyze industry and market development trends, effectively assisting in their competitive positioning.[20]

19. Some scholars believe that data monopoly is essentially to seek competitive advantage through the difference in the volume of data calls and the difference in the generation of digital technology[21]. In respect of platform operators involving data monopoly, the root cause of the monopoly lies in the fact that the platform operators have collected a large amount of data far exceeding that of ordinary operators, and restricting other trading conditions by data, platform rules and other methods to eliminate and restrict market competition. However, the main questions are whether the data itself is non-exclusive and cannot be monopolized by other operators, whether the data itself is sufficient to constitute a market controlling force that restricts competition, and whether it is easy to understand data in isolation from the platform's economic structure of the platform and create a bias in understanding. Theoretically, the scale of data does not necessarily constitute dominant market positions, and it is necessary to examine the market power of operators based on their data advantages in the context of multiple dimensions, such as the value, type and validity of data.

20. In addition to Chinese market regulatory authorities regulating and supervising the competitive behavior of platform operators, China's anti-monopoly authorities also focus on industry supervisory to regulate the platform economy, such as the Cyberspace Administration of China, Ministry of Industry

---

19 Li J: The applicability of patent compulsory license and essential facility doctrine:
the connection between the sub-clause 2, article 48 of patent law and anti-monopoly law[J]. Peking University Law Review, 2011, 12(2): 543-560.

20 Ding G. F: Exploring Anti-Monopoly Issues in Data Competition in the Digital Economy Era[J], Economic Law Research, 2023, 24(01): 212-226.

21 Sun H T, Zhou Q Q: The governance dilemma of platform data monopoly and the shared mechanism[J]. Jiangsu Social Sciences, 2023(3): 131-139.

and Information Technology, Ministry of Transport and other departments, which also regulate and supervise the characteristics of the industry, safety risks, and quality of services of the platform operators, for the purposes of promoting standardized, orderly, innovative and sound development of the platform economy, and safeguarding consumers' interests and public interests. During China's anti-monopoly supervisory practice, China's legislature will on the basis of the development status and characteristics of the platform economy, continuously strengthen and improve the regulation, and enhance the pertinence and scientificity of anti-monopoly law enforcement.

3. Practical Challenges in China's Data-Related Anti-Monopoly Supervision

3.1 The relationship between data and competition becomes ambiguous

21. Data plays an increasingly important role in market competition, and with the continuous advancement of technologies like algorithms and powerful computing, data plays different roles in different market competitions. In the current digital economy, competition is no longer confined to traditional market competition; it presents a three-dimensional structure consisting of "platform-data-algorithm."[22] In this structure, the competitive model of data monopoly is not solely caused by data itself but results from the synergistic effects of multiple factors, including platforms, capital, data, computing power, and algorithms. Data monopolies are not limited to a specific industry or sector; they interweave across different domains and levels, making the issue of data monopolies more complex.

22. The relationship between data and competition is showing a dynamic trend. Initially, data was viewed mainly as a static resource, with businesses collecting and storing data to improve their operational efficiency and service quality. As digital technologies evolved, data became one of the core elements of competition for enterprises. However, data monopolies can distort market competition, becoming a tool for a few companies to exclude competitors and raise market barriers. Therefore, it is necessary to correctly examine the relationship between data and competition. In terms of data protection and openness, the two are not opposing forces. Combating data monopolies does not mean restricting data protection, but rather aims to achieve healthy data competition and utilization through scientific, standardized, and effective data flow and sharing.[23]

---

22   Cheng E. F., Yu X. S: Analysis of Data Monopoly and Predatory Pathways in the Digital Economy Era[J], Theoretical Monthly, 2023, (09): 76-83.

23   Chen B: Protection and Competition: The Role of Competition Law in Governing Data Crawling Behavior[J], Political and Legal Forum, 2021, 39(06): 18-28.

23. Given that data plays different roles in various industries and technologies, it is necessary to establish appropriate regulatory measures to address potential anti-competitive effects. Taking generative artificial intelligence as an example, the Chinese government has formulated the "Interim Measures for the Management of Generative AI Services," the world's first regulation targeting generative artificial intelligence, which explicitly states that "monopolistic or unfair competition behavior using algorithms, data, platforms, etc., is prohibited." The training cost of data in generative AI technology is extremely high, making the role of data in such emerging technologies even more critical. Data-related monopolistic behavior directly affects the development of new technologies. Therefore, in the development of the data industry, it is essential to adopt targeted regulatory approaches, taking into account the role of data as a competitive element in the market.

3.2 Difficulty in effectively regulating data-related monopoly behaviors by traditional standards

24. Under the traditional anti-monopoly supervision model, for example, the standard of assessing market shares of operators in the relevant markets based on the proportions of trading amount seems to be not feasible in the digital economy. In the DiDi-Uber merger, it is not difficult to see that China's current Anti-monopoly law is difficult to effectively prevent digital platforms in possession of massive amounts of data to implement the concentration of undertakings and can not effectively regulate the possible existence of monopoly behavior. For example, in terms of analysis methods of internet-related market definition and abuse of dominant market position, Hypothetical Monopolist Testing (HMT) is a generally applicable analytical method that defines the relevant market. In practice, it is assumed that HMT can be conducted through methods such as Small but Significant and Non-transitory Increase in Price (SSNIP) or Small but Significant and Non-transitory Decrease in Quality (SSNDQ). However, in judicial practice, market share in the platform economy is a relatively crude and potentially misleading indicator for evaluating dominant market position[24]. Its position and role in determining dominant market position must be determined based on the circumstances of specific cases.

25. Although the *Guidelines of the Anti-Monopoly Commission of the State Council for Anti-Monopoly in the Field of Platform Economy* and the *Provisions on the Examination of Concentrations of Undertakings* take into account the impact of the standards for declaration standards, proactive investigation, and remedies of concentration of undertakings on the unique characteristics of the platform economy, and affirm the role of

---

24 Cheng X J: The legal regulation research on data monopoly of financial and technical platform [J]. Research on China Market Regulation, 2023(4): 65-68.

data in the market competition, but the data concentration of operators is still lacking in targeted provisions, and the specific evaluation criteria of data monopoly are not clear. Moreover, due to the strict criteria based on the "relevant market → dominance → abuse" paradigm, the post-regulation of many monopoly cases is often time-consuming and difficult, with challenges in determining the relevant elements, and it lacks universality. Additionally, it fails to accurately identify and respond to the distinct behaviors of different types of platforms, often falling into a "one-size-fits-all" approach, which is unlikely to satisfy all parties.[25]

26. In the context of the digital economy, as new technologies such as algorithms and artificial intelligence are widely applied in market operations, supported by factors like platforms, capital, algorithms, and computing power, the manifestations of data monopoly behavior have become more diverse and covert, further complicating the difficulty of determining their illegality.[26] Due to the characteristics of data, the regulatory model for data-related monopolistic behavior must differ from traditional regulatory methods. Although traditional anti-monopoly measures and relevant market definition methods still have some applicability, they are difficult to apply directly and need to be updated and adjusted according to the characteristics of the internet platform's bilateral market structure, network effects, and lock-in effects.[27]

27. In addition, China's Anti-monopoly institutions are still dominated by ex-post supervisions, such as administrative penalties, but some scholars believe that such penalties are not able to give deterrence to platform operators, for example, in the case of China's anti-monopoly authorities imposed a fine of more than 20 billions on Alibaba and Meituan for their 'choose one from two' monopolybehaviors, the market capitalization of two companies has not fallen but risen, and the extent of the increase in their market capitalization is higher than the amount of the fines imposed by the anti-monopoly institutions. Therefore, it is difficult to effectively regulate data-related monopoly behaviors purely by ex-post regulations for antitrust regulation.

28. Traditional antitrust law has strong policy rigidity, making it difficult to adapt to the rapid and innovative development of the platform economy. It lacks the flexibility to respond to new forms of data monopolistic behavior arising from business model innovations on digital platforms. In particular, its post facto prohibitions on specific behaviors may unintentionally harm non-involved companies, leading to significant adjustments

---

25 Same as reference 16 above.

26 Chen B: Responding to the Challenges of Regulating Data Monopolies in China[J], Digital Rule of Law, 2024, (02): 18-30.

27 Li Y., Yuan Z.Z: The Identification of Internet Platform Abuse of Market Dominance Behavior under the Background of Digital Economy[J], Intellectual Property, 2023, (04): 78-107.

in existing business models and increasing uncertainty in innovation and development. Meanwhile, post facto antitrust enforcement is also ineffective in addressing the non-economic harms caused by data monopolies and fails to achieve social value goals effectively. The goal of antitrust law is to maintain market competition; however, post facto enforcement typically only halts specific data monopolistic behaviors and cannot effectively restore market competition or fundamentally resolve the problem of insufficient competition in the market. Under such circumstances, moderate ex ante supervisory should be an important supplement, and eventually regulation should be carried out by a combination of ex ante and ex-post regulation.

3.3 Industry supervision and market regulation should be cooperated

29. China's supervision of data-related competition conduct not only involves the participation of market regulators, but also involves the needs and development of the relevant industry based on the needs of the industry's development of intra-industry competition regulation[28]. For example, since July 2021, the Ministry of Industry and Information Technology initiated the issue of platform inter-connectivity, which later also affected the Chinese market regulatory authorities' attention to the refusing to deal with the other transactional parties without any justifiable cause or self-preferential based on the data. However, industry regulations are influenced by industrial policies and often focus on aspects such as consumer rights protection, personal privacy protection, or trade secret protection. These regulatory measures are often not effectively enforced or implemented, leading to their being sidelined in practical applications. More importantly, existing regulatory measures have not sufficiently considered the commonalities between different regulatory models, which results in a lack of coordination. This causes conflicts or constraints between the regulations, creating an incoherent situation.

30. For example, the phenomenon of overlapping regulation involving industry regulators and market regulators also occurs in the online car-hailing industry and market. In 2021, the Ministry of Transport issued the "Notice on Maintaining Fair Competition in the Market and Accelerating the Compliance of Ride-Hailing Services." In 2022, the National Development and Reform Commission, along with eight other ministries, jointly released the "Opinions on Promoting the Standardized, Healthy, and Sustainable Development of the Platform Economy." Additionally, in 2023, the "Work Plan for Reducing the Excessive Commission Charges by Platform Enterprises on the Transportation Industry" was released.

---

28 Chen B: From tolerance and prudence to normalization: a perfect approach to digital economic regulation[J]. Social Science Journal, 2023(5): 57-67.

These documents explicitly outline anti-monopoly regulations within the regulatory framework, aiming to limit the market dominance of platform companies and prevent the abuse of market power. However, due to the dispersed functions of various departments, regulatory measures often overlap and contradict each other, lacking a unified and coordinated regulatory framework. The aforementioned industry regulations have not fully connected with market regulation, leading to overlaps in supervision and difficulties in enforcement. So it is a challenge to set up the powers and responsibilities between departments so that they can better cooperate with each other[29].

4. Emphasizing and Improving Data Monopoly Supervision.

4.1 Implementing regularized, precise and agile regulatory mechanisms

31. The Chinese government has repeatedly emphasized the regular regulation of the digital economy, raised the level of regulation and supporting platform companies to lead development, create jobs, and better compete internationally. During the annual sessions of the National People's Congress (NPC) and the National Committee of the Chinese People's Political Consultative Conference (CPPCC) of the State Administration of Market Regulation (SAMR), in 2023 Luo Wen, head of the State Administration for Market Regulation, said during an interview on the "Ministers' Passage" said "we need to ensure clarity of rules and process for enforcement and inspections conducive to improve a business environment, and strengthen the regular supervision, especially in key areas such as the digital economy and livelihood protection, and strengthen agile supervision to help strengthen compliance management and provide assistance for enterprise development." The 2025 Government Work Report stated, "Promote the standardized and healthy development of the platform economy, and better leverage its positive role in driving innovation, expanding consumption, and stabilizing employment." Regular and agile supervision has become a regulatory measure adopted by China's anti-monopoly authorities to cope with the context of the digital economy development.

32. In the process of implementing regularized, precise and agile supervisions, firstly, antimonopoly supervision in the field of digital platform economy should be broadened, emphasizing the balance of multiple values and objectives, and paying special attention to innovation in data monopoly

---

29 Chen B: Several online ride-hailing and aggregation platforms were interviewed [EB/OL]. (2023-07-27) [2024-04-26]. https://m.21jingji.com/article/20230727/herald/45521c465aa70b1cb5ee2f0ce360909c.html.

supervision. Secondly, antitrust supervisory measures should be innovated, and scientific and technological supervisory means should be introduced to promote compliance governance and precise regulation of anti-competitive risks of digital economy platform enterprises with scientific supervision, to promote the healthy development of the platform economy. Finally, the rule of platform classification and platform grading should be optimized, and the interconnection regulatory framework can be improved, focusing on perfecting the governmental supervisory system, supplemented by the construction of a diversified regulatory pattern, which will help data monopoly supervision.

4.2 Implementing interdepartmental comprehensive supervision

33. As data has multiple attributes, the interests brought about by data-related monopoly behaviors are not only harmed by a fair competition, but also by the governance of data involving user data, personal information, and even public safety and national security, which requires interdepartmental comprehensive supervision. For example, Data Security Law, Personal Information Protection Law and other laws and regulations also contain provisions on the use of data advantages and platform advantages to implement monopolistic behavior. At the same time, combined with the multiple attributes of data, multi-dimensional and multi-level regulation also helps to clarify the theoretical basis of data, and perfecting the theoretical basis of data is a prerequisite for clarifying how to regulate data monopoly behavior.

34. To this end, the cooperation between internal government industry regulatory departments and market regulatory departments should be strengthened to form a full-chain data regulation system. First, the boundaries between government and market should be clarified. From the perspective of market regulation, the focus is on protecting competition. Improper industry regulations may hinder the cross-industry or cross-domain circulation of data elements, leading to industry data monopolies and restricting market competition. In this case, the coordination between industry regulation and market regulation is crucial. It is important to balance the relationship between competition protection and data value sharing, better protect competition, encourage innovation, and achieve co-creation and sharing of data value.

35. Second, the responsibilities and division of labor among different departments within the government should be clarified. Industry regulatory departments should formulate corresponding data rules based on the characteristics of each industry, while market regulatory departments should be responsible for the formation of a unified national market for data elements. The National Data Bureau should take the lead in coordinating

36. the construction of data infrastructure, managing the construction of local data trading platforms, and establishing unified and reasonable data trading rules, as well as formulating fair data pricing mechanisms.
36. Finally, communication and collaboration between different departments should be further strengthened. Based on the "Guiding Opinions on Deepening the Promotion of Cross-departmental Comprehensive Regulation" issued by the General Office of the State Council, a comprehensive regulatory system for data circulation governance should be improved, enhancing the effectiveness of cross-departmental regulatory coordination.

4.3 Improvement of the basic theoretical system of data

37. According to the characters of data, it really could hardly constitute an element of monopoly, however the various and complicated monopoly behavior related data still requires stronger governance. In 2020, the Chinese government has explicitly stated that link anti-monopoly regulation to the regulation of data collection and use behaviors, especially in relation to innovations in the financial sector. The Chinese government's governance of data monopoly emphasizes more on governance at the source. The Chinese government has carried out exploratory regulation of collection, processing and analysis of data and other aspects, and the increased emphasis on governance at the source involving data-related monopoly behavior can be seen in the intensive introduction of laws such as the Cybersecurity Law, the Data Security Law, and the Personal Information Protection Law.

38. In 2023, the setting up of a National Data Bureau (NDB) it was proposed to advance the development of data-related fundamental institutions and marked a new stage in data protection. In response to data-related monopolization, both source governance and multi-governance have been implemented, and the relationship between data and enterprises has been adjusted at the source to break the data-related monopoly. On January 4, 2024, the National Data Bureau and 17 other departments jointly issued the "Three-Year Action Plan for 'Data Elements X' (2024-2026)," which outlines the goal of forming a relatively complete data industry ecosystem by the end of 2026. It also aims to significantly improve the quality and efficiency of data products and services, with the data industry expected to grow at an annual rate of over 20%. This plan reiterates the importance of improving the foundational data system and sets specific phase targets.

39. Improving the theory of data can mainly focus on three aspects as follow. First, the data property rights system should be clarified to form the interaction between multiple subjects of data, thereby reducing the institutional cost of data transactions and promoting data circulation. Second, the

protection system for data property rights should be improved to enhance the risk control capability of the data factor market. Third, precautionary supervisory measures should be taken to build a multi-law cooperative system with the antitrust law at its core, and fully utilizing the role of market-based governance systems and avoiding excessive supervision.

4.4 Strengthen the construction of data infrastructure

40. Improving and perfecting data infrastructure should be based on a data classification and grading system. Guided by the "Twenty Data Regulations," a classification and grading system for public data, enterprise data, and personal data should be established, along with clear ownership and authorization frameworks. This will provide a clearer regulatory framework for data governance. Public data, as a key resource for national governance, should prioritize the protection of national security and public interests, with strict controls over its commercialization. Enterprise data, on the other hand, should ensure the legitimate rights and interests of market entities while promoting the reasonable allocation and sharing of data property rights. Personal data must be safeguarded to ensure that privacy and security rights are not violated. Establishing this classification and grading system will help form differentiated protection and refined management within data governance, laying the institutional foundation for the development of data infrastructure.

41. Improving and perfecting data infrastructure should focus on data transaction security and compliance. At present, China's data transaction market is still in the exploratory phase, with issues such as unclear data ownership, incomplete transaction rules, and insufficient legal protection remaining prominent. To address these issues, a security and compliance mechanism covering the entire process of data collection, processing, storage, circulation, and use should be built, clarifying the legal boundaries and standards for data transactions. Additionally, there should be enhanced regulation of data transaction platforms to ensure that transactions comply with legal and regulatory requirements, preventing data misuse.

42. Improving and perfecting data infrastructure should aim at improving the data transaction market. Currently, the development of the data transaction market faces many challenges, such as information asymmetry between data supply and demand, incomplete transaction rules, and a single operating model for platforms. In the process of market development, it is important to optimize the mechanism for connecting data supply and demand, promoting the efficient circulation and sharing of data resources between different entities. At the same time, various market participants should be encouraged to actively engage in data transactions, improving data pricing mechanisms and benefit-sharing systems to ensure the reasonable protection of all parties' interests.

4.5 Maintaining fair competition in the data market

43. In response to the frequent occurrence of platform behaviors that hinder the free flow of data elements, such as refusing data interoperability, it is essential to precisely identify and swiftly govern data monopoly and unfair competition practices. First, it is necessary to enrich the factors considered in defining relevant markets and determining market dominance. For example, the market can be defined by testing whether consumers would switch to other platforms if privacy protection measures were significantly reduced but not temporarily, or by assessing whether the platform has the ability to control and process data to determine if it holds market dominance. Secondly, the illegality of platform refusal of data interoperability should be carefully evaluated. Such behavior should only be considered an abuse of market dominance when it has the effect of excluding or restricting competition.

44. Furthermore, it is important to refine the criteria for identifying unfair competition in the data sector by introducing new judgment methods. In AI training, the use of web scraping technology by robots to collect data has become the primary means for data companies to obtain raw materials. The legitimacy and legality of such data acquisition behaviors should not be judged solely based on static data ownership but should be considered in the context of the value brought about by dynamic data innovation. By establishing standards for reasonable use of data, dynamic data rights allocation should be incorporated into judicial decisions, focusing on balancing data security, flow, and value realization. It is crucial to ensure that data companies' necessary costs and reasonable returns during data collection, usage, storage, and trading processes are fully protected, thereby clearly defining, regulating, and encouraging the proper use of data by data companies.

5. Summary

45. With the development of the digital economy, the data-related monopoly behavior have attracted the attention of various countries in the world, and the data-centered digital platform has been subjected to anti-monopoly investigation repeatedly, and the academic community has determined that the data-related monopoly is still have stirred controversy. As data is the most important production factor in the digital economy, the regulation of monopoly behavior derived from it must comply with the basic development law and characteristics of digital industry. At present, China's main regulatory model is to regulate the competitive behavior that may be brought about by the development of the digital economy on the premise of promoting the development of the digital economy and

incentivizing development of the data industry under the premise of safety. Regulatory means in countries around the world are more focused on the impact on the overall market than on the structure of specific behaviors, although there are differences in the regulation of monopoly standards[30]. The same is true for the regulation of data-related monopoly behavior.

46. In general, compared with the data-related anti-monopoly regulatory practices of the European Union and the United States, China is continuously improving its existing antitrust laws and regulations, and continuously incorporating data elements into antitrust regulation. Although there are still controversies over whether and how data can directly form a monopoly, and there is no unanimous opinion on the concept of "data monopoly" either in theory or practice, China's anti-monopoly authorities have formulated a series of laws and regulations on data-related monopoly behavior to regulate potential anti-competitive behavior. It is worth noting that China's existing regulatory tools are not sufficient to fully regulate data-related monopolies, or even accurately identify related monopolies, and it is difficult to match the new monopoly situation spawned by the development of the digital economy. However, China's anti-monopoly authorities have introduced a series of means that are closely aligned with their practices in response to the characteristics of the data elements and competitive behaviors, and have enriched and perfected the anti-monopoly regularization regulatory means by continuously enriching anti-monopoly regulatory tools and implementation methods, strengthening and refining anti-monopoly prior review in the platform economy, helping data enterprises to do a good job of complying with the regulations, and creating a full-cycle, full-chain regulatory mechanism for data competition, so as to achieve the ultimate goal of prospering the data industry market and protecting fair competition in the market.

---

30 Wang X L: Competition Law (2nd edition)[M]. Beijing: China Renmin University Press, 2015: 219.

Monopoly Concerns and Regulatory Approaches in the Artificial Intelligence Industry[*]

ROGER XIN ZHANG
Vice President of Public Affairs, Tencent

DONG YUN
Senior Legal Counsel at Tencen

GUO HANGCHEN
Juris Doctor Candidate, University of Hong Kong

Abstract

While artificial intelligence (AI) has brought substantial benefits to both enterprises and individuals, emerging monopoly concerns associated with its development have become increasingly prominent. In the field of large language model (LLM) foundational services, phenomena such as self-preferencing, refusal to deal, and data-blocking mergers and acquisitions are becoming common. In certain vertical AI applications, issues such as data leakage, algorithmic collusion, algorithmic discrimination, and bundling sales have also surfaced. Faced with these monopoly concerns, current antitrust regulations encounter various difficulties in terms of

---

[*] Funded by: National Social Science Foundation of China, "Research on the Positioning of Competition Policy and Antitrust Issues in the Era of Digital Economy' (23&ZD076); National Social Science Foundation of China, "Research on Difficulties of Competition Law Protection of Personal Information" (23BFX186).
Authors: Roger Xin Zhang (1987-), Vice President of Public Affairs at Tencent, Ph.D., Associate Researcher. His primary research interests are in digital law and competition law. Yun Dong (1990-), Senior Legal Counsel at Tencent. Hangchen Guo (2002-), Candidate for Juris Doctor (JD) at the Faculty of Law, The University of Hong Kong.

Monopoly Concerns and Regulatory Approaches in the Artificial Intelligence Industry

definition of market power, determination of unlawful conducts, and assessment of the legitimacy of defenses. These concerns stem primarily from the covert nature of monopolistic behaviors in the AI industry, lagging of antitrust rules, and lack of capabilities of antitrust regulation to keep pace with technological development. To improve the effectiveness of antitrust regulation in the AI industry, this paper proposes to take a rational view on algorithms; make promotion of data interoperability as a key regulatory objective; set agile regulation and full-cycle resilient regulation as principles of anti-monopoly regulation and expand the relevant rules to improve the regulatory system through establishing internal and external coordinated regulatory mechanisms, promoting smart regulation, and attempting sandbox regulation.

1. With the increasingly widespread application of AI, litigation and administrative enforcement cases involving AI have emerged and gained growing attention. The new business models and competition patterns in the AI industry have raised concerns among antitrust regulators. For instance, many tech giants have chosen to invest in AI startups rather than directly acquire them. This enables tech giants to, without acquiring AI startups, exert control over product innovation, technologies, or key personnel of AI startups through collaborations and investments to circumvent antitrust scrutiny. A typical case is the relationship between Microsoft and OpenAI. Since 2019, Microsoft has invested over $13 billion in OpenAI, which, in turn, is obligated to use Microsoft's Azure cloud platform as its primary cloud service provider and permit its technology to be integrated into various Microsoft products. According to media reports, in June 2024, the U.S. Department of Justice (DOJ) and the Federal Trade Commission (FTC) reached an agreement to initiate antitrust investigations into the dominant positions of Microsoft, OpenAI, and NVIDIA in the AI industry. Under this agreement, the DOJ will lead the investigation into NVIDIA's potential antitrust violations, while the FTC will investigate into OpenAI and review Microsoft's investments in OpenAI, as well as its agreements with other AI companies.[1] In China, although there are no antitrust litigation or administrative enforcement cases involving the AL industry so far, the antitrust cases in other jurisdictions have triggered widespread public debate and in-depth legal discussions on antitrust regulation of AI.[2] This paper aims to outline the existing monopoly risks in the AI

---

[1] See *U.S. Clears Way for Antitrust Inquiries of Nvidia, Microsoft and OpenAI*, on NYTimes.com, https://www.nytimes.com/2024/06/05/technology/nvidia-microsoft-openai-antitrust-doj-ftc.html, accessed on July 3, 2024.

[2] In November 2023, the Beijing Internet Court issued China's first ruling on the copyright of a work generated by AIGC, which has gained widespread public attention. In this case, the Beijing Internet Court found that the defendant had infringed on the plaintiff's rights through an image generated through the plaintiff's input and adjustment of text and parameters in Stable Diffusion. Notably, in this case, the Beijing Internet Court held that AIGC serves as a tool rather than a copyright owner at the output stage; the process by which a user inputs prompt texts into AIGC, which then generates "works," constitutes authorship under copyright

industry, analyze the current challenges in antitrust regulation and the underlying reasons, and put forward some thoughts and recommendations on how to address these monopoly risks in China's AI industry.

I. Monopoly Concerns in the AI Industry

2. Based on current industry status, the AI industry can be broadly divided into two tiers: LLM foundational services and its vertical applications. This paper will examine the primary monopoly risks and concerns associated with each tier.

(A) LLM foundational services

3. Given that the leading AI companies have substantial advantages in terms of computing power, data acquisition, and model training, the segment of LLM foundational services features a high level of market concentration. Several leading companies with robust R&D capabilities and deep resource reserves have successfully developed highly influential LLMs, such as OpenAI's GPT, Google's Gemini, Alibaba Cloud's Qwen, Zhipu AI's GLM, and Baidu's ERNIE Bot. These models not only possess superior computing capabilities and algorithmic advantages but also hold leading market positions, shaping the development trend of their respective sub-sectors. The market position of the leading providers of LLM foundational services is similar to that of the super platforms in the internet sector. Despite the potential efficiency gains from a moderately concentrated market structure, these leading providers of LLM foundational services may leverage their advantageous positions to conduct monopolistic behaviors, such as self-preferencing, refusal to deal, or data-blocking mergers and acquisitions, against other application developers.

1. Self-preferencing

4. Self-preferencing occurs *when a firm sells one or more brands in addition to its own and gives its own brand favorable treatment, or else when it tries to steer customers of some primary product to its own brand of a secondary product or its own repair service.*[3] *Originally understood as a form of differentiated commercial behavior, self-preferencing may give*

---

law. In contrast, while the U.S. Copyright Office similarly concluded in its 2022 "Théâtre D'opéra Spatial" and 2023 "Zarya of the Dawn" registration cases that AIGC also functions as a tool rather than a copyright owner, but the process of inputting prompts followed by AIGC generating output does not qualify as "authorship." See Beijing (2023) No. 0491 Civil First Instance Judgment No. 11279.

3   See Herbert Hovenkamp: "Antitrust and Self-Preferencing", 38(1) Antitrust (Fall 2023), p. 5-8.

rise to leveraging effects[4], and therefore has attracted attention from antitrust scholars. Self-preferencing is not a simple monopolistic strategy, but rather a complex phenomenon encompassing diverse behavioral patterns with manifold manifestations.[5] In the field of LLM foundational services, self-preferencing comes in many varieties, including but not limited to manipulation of search result, display of own products in a prominent position, pre-pre-installation of software, and potential bundling sales.

5. Many AI model providers operate also as digital platforms offering cloud services essential for AI developers. In China, for instance, Baidu operates Baidu AI Cloud, Alibaba operates Alibaba Cloud, and Tencent operates Tencent Cloud. In overseas countries, Microsoft operates Azure, and Amazon and Meta also operate their own cloud platforms. These platforms not only provide cloud services but also leverage their roles as data operators to access third-party data, thus obtaining substantial information or data advantages. Such advantages place platform operators in a superior position when competing with third-party developers who rely on their services. Under these conditions, self-preferencing may come in the form of restricting data interoperability or prioritizing platform operators' own services, thereby distorting market competition. For example, cloud service providers operating their own LLMs might offer cloud services with higher prices or lower quality to competing third-party LLMs and provide preferential treatment (such as better access to computing resources or data training) for their own models. This could constitute self-preferencing under antitrust laws.[6] Self-preferencing may hinder competitors' access to critical datasets or raise the cost of acquiring data. These types of self-preferencing not only undermine the fairness of market competition but also have negative impact on innovation and consumers because they may restrict the emergence of new technologies and services and reduce the diversity of products and services available to consumers.

2. Refusal to deal

6. Refusal to deal is one of the instances of abuse of market dominance explicitly prohibited under China's Anti-Monopoly Law. It is also regarded as an unlawful conduct prohibited by the anti-monopoly laws of most jurisdictions around the world.[7] In AI competition, due to lack of

---

4 See Lan Lei: "A Critical Analysis of the Criticism of Digital Platforms' Self-Preferencing", Oriental Law Review, Vol. 2, Issue No. 2, 2024, p. 123.

5 See Michael A. Salinger: "Self-Preferencing", in the Global Antitrust Institute Report on the Digital Economy, 2020, p.229.

6 See Ding Daoqin: Research on Competition Law Regulation of Generative Artificial Intelligence from the Perspective of Industrial Chain", in Journal of Northwestern Polytechnical University (Social Sciences Edition), Issue No. 1, 2024, p. 102.

7 See Zheng Pengcheng: "Improvement of Antitrust Legislation on Refusal to Deal", in Modern Law Science, Issue No. 5, 2021, p. 158.

computing power, numerous small- and medium-sized model developers are forced to turn to cloud service providers, renting external computing power to support the development and training of their models. However, this path is not without its challenges, as some cloud service providers are direct competitors in AI model development. This dual role may lead certain cloud service providers to refuse to provide cloud computing services to potential competitors in order to maintain their own market position. If the mainstream cloud service providers all restrict the services provided to small- and medium-sized AI developers, these AI developers who depend on these services will face a rapid increase in costs or even an inability to obtain the computing power essential for their AI models. This situation is becoming even more critical given that AI technologies have increasingly become a focal point of international competition. The restriction of access to computing power is gradually evolving into a new form of economic sanction. For example, the U.S. government has recently taken concrete action by instructing its domestic cloud service providers to halt supplying computing power to Chinese AI companies.[8] Considering that U.S. companies have significant advantages in the global cloud service and AI computing power sectors, such polity is highly likely to hinder the research and development progress and innovation capabilities of China's small- and medium-sized AI companies. Additionally, in the AI market, some large platforms control crucial data sources. AI developers, when designing or training models, sometimes need to obtain critical data from these platforms. However, the platforms that control these critical data resources may, in an effort to restrict or exclude competitors, block or limit data interoperability with other developers. Such refusal to deal poses significant harm, as it directly deprives potential competitors in the AI sector of the opportunities to enter the relevant markets and engage in competition.

3. Data-blocking mergers and acquisitions

7. Data is a pivotal resource in the AI industry. To enhance control over data in fierce competition, companies have made acquiring and controlling high-quality data an important goal of mergers and acquisitions. In recent years, cases such as Apple's acquisition of Shazam[9], Facebook's acquisition of WhatsApp[10], have highlighted the central role of data in

---

8   See JW Insights, "U.S. Curbs on China's Access to AI Cloud Computing Power: Short-Term Impacts Manageable, Long-Term Boost to Domestic 'Computing Power + Cloud' Services," published on ifeng.com, available at: https://i.ifeng.com/c/8Woxog3u5Oz, accessed on July 3, 2024.

9   See Music Finance, "Why the Acquisition of Shazam might be Apple's most important investment", in 36Krypton.com, https://36kr.com/p/1722872004609, accessed on 3 July 2024.

10 See Xunpan Cloud: "WhatsApp Acquired by Facebook: Background, Impacts, User Reactions, Development, and Insights," in Sohu News, accessed on July 3, 2024, https://www.sohu.com/a/732969012_121687039, accessed on 3 July 2024.

the decision-making of AI-related mergers and acquisitions. Particularly in the field of generative AI, established companies have an increasingly urgent need to acquire and control high-quality data. This demand has driven them to pursue a series of data-related acquisitions, such as Microsoft's Acquisition of GitHub[11] and Kaggle,[12] etc. Once these mergers and acquisitions are completed, these companies may restrict data sharing or interoperability, particularly with competitors, thereby increasing barriers to enter the AI market and hindering emerging rivals from accessing essential data for AI development at reasonable costs. Such data-driven mergers and acquisitions will therefore strengthen the market position of incumbent AI companies while suppressing new entrants.

(B) Vertical applications

8. In the AI industry, while some companies provide LLM foundational services, many others choose to focus on developing specialized products and services for vertical applications. Leveraging the infrastructure provided by leading companies, such other enterprises create specialized, customized AI applications tailored to specific industries or demands. These vertical applications focus on resolving practical challenges in specific contexts, such as auxiliary medical diagnosis, in-depth financial market analysis, and automated customer service workflows. Through close integration with other industries, these AI companies are able to provide more precise, personalized solutions for their clients, meeting the specific needs of different fields, thereby playing an indispensable role in the AI field. However, several monopoly risks persist with respect to these vertical peripheral applications.

1. Data leakage

9. Due to the substantial volume of user data processed by LLMs, data privacy and security have emerged as critical challenges for the AI industry's development. How to ensure that user data is not improperly collected, leaked, or used for improper purposes by AI companies is currently a key issue for major AI companies. Globally, aside from leading AI companies exploiting their market dominance to collect and leak user data, certain companies may acquire and leak user data of vertical applications through the use of shared third-party platforms. Consequently, the security and privacy of user data in the AI industry are currently under significant threat.

---

11 See: "How to Analyze Microsoft's $7.5 Billion Acquisition of GitHub", on Worktile, accessed on July 3, 2024, https://worktile.com/kb/ask/531396.html, accessed on 3 July 2024.

12 See: "600,000 Talent Pool, Analysis of the Benefits Behind Google's Acquisition of Kaggle," in Tencent Cloud Developer Community, https://cloud.tencent.com/developer/article/1075166, accessed on 3 July 2024.

2. Algorithmic Collusion

10. Algorithmic collusion, as a prominent issue in the current AI industry, poses a significant challenge to market competition order. Since the advent of AI, business operators no longer need to manually collect and process periodic business indicators, such as market supply and demand, price levels, and cost inventory, whereas these business indicators were collected and processed manually in traditional economies. This is because algorithms can automatically update market and operational data, optimizing the allocation of various resources autonomously, thereby achieving profit maximization.[13] Business operators may use algorithmic technologies to track and align prices, or employ "trial balloons"[14] to gauge competitors' reactions to pricing adjustments, so as to facilitate price coordination and supervise competitors' pricing behaviors. This is the so-called price algorithmic collusion. AI platforms can design algorithms and mechanisms that make it easier for companies to carry out price collusion. More specifically, they can effectively reduce communication costs among business operators, identify betrayal by companies involved in collusion, and automatically impose penalties through algorithmic mechanisms, thereby ensuring the long-term stability of price collusion.[15] Therefore, algorithms are no longer merely technologies or tools for communication between individuals; they can unconsciously implement coordinated behavior, or make autonomous decisions based on the analysis of market behaviors from all parties. In scenarios where there is an absence of subjective awareness among business operators, algorithms may automatically establish *de facto* monopolistic agreements, which is often hard to detect.[16] Algorithmic collusion is emerging as a "digital hand" in market competition, leading to an increasing number of platform monopolistic behaviors.[17]

3. Algorithmic discrimination

11. In addition to issues of collusion, algorithms in the AI field may also lead to bias and discrimination, such as biases or discrimination in pricing algorithms. If dynamic pricing algorithms are biased, they may

---

13   See Ding Guofeng: "Legal Regulation of Algorithmic Collusion in the Era of Big Data", in Social Science Journal, Issue No. 3, 2021, p. 127-136.

14   Sofia Olive Ra Pais: "Hub-and-Spoke Agreements and Tacit Collusion: Recent National Decisions and the Competition Market Authority Paper on Algorithms, Competition, and Consumer Harm", Market and Competition Law Review, 2021(1):169-196.

15   See Chen Canqi: "Legal Regulation of Platforms' Abuse of Algorithmic Power", Journal of Hunan University of Science and Technology (Social Science Edition), Issue 6, 2023, p. 158.

16   Ariel E., Maurice E. S: "Artificial Intelligence & Collusion: When Computers Inhibit Competition", University of Illinois Law Review, 2017 (5): 1781-1795.

17   Pasquale F: The Black Box Society: The Secret Algorithms that Control Money and Information, Cambridge MA: Harvard University Press,2015:191.

set different prices for specific companies or consumer groups, resulting in unfair competition in the market or infringing upon consumers' right to fair trade. Furthermore, search engines and recommended systems may prioritize displaying certain companies' products or services, thus marginalizing and restricting other competitors. Overall, algorithmic discrimination not only harms economic efficiency but also causes significant harm to consumer welfare. It not only has an exclusionary effect but also an exploitative effect.[18] Therefore, algorithmic discrimination is also one of the monopoly issues in the AI industry that attract wide public attention.

4. Bundling sales

12. In the AI industry, companies holding a dominant or leading market position may engage in bundling or tie-in sales practices. For example, they may bundle generative AI applications, which are not essential to the other party involved in the transaction, with their existing core products, thereby reducing the trading opportunities of generative AI products with similar functions offered by competitors. This, in turn, distorts the market competition in the field of generative AI products. Currently, certain dominant generative AI service providers tend to engage in such abusive practices, such as bundling and tie-in sales, when offering core products.[19] For instance, in 2024, Amazfit launched its first smart ring, Helio, bundling it with its influential product, the Amazfit Cheetah Pro smartwatch, for sale.[20] Such bundling practices allow Amazfit to leverage its market dominance in one market to another, thereby restricting and impairing fair competition.

II. Dilemma of Antitrust Regulation in the AI Industry and the Causes

13. The emerging monopoly risks in the AI industry urgently require timely intervention from antitrust regulators. However, the current antitrust regulation of the AI industry faces several challenges, and solutions need to be developed based on a deeper understanding of these causes.

---

18 See Li Qian and Niels J. Philipsen: "Anti-monopoly Review of Algorithmic Price Discrimination: A Law and Economics Analysis" in Finance & Trade Law Journal, Issue No. 4, 2023, p. 87-92.

19 See Ding Daoqin: "Research on Competition Law and Regulation of Generative Artificial Intelligence from the Perspective of Industrial Chain," in Journal of Northwestern Polytechnical University (Social Sciences) 2024, Issue 1, p. 102.

20 See Focus Media Network: "Amazfit Helio Ring now available in Europe: Save €149 when bundled with a smartwatch.", Focus Media Network, http://jjxmt.cn/digi/20240617/166222.html, accessed on August 29, 2024.

(A) The dilemma of antitrust regulation in the ai industry

14. The rapid development of AI technology poses significant challenges to antitrust regulation in this field. The following are the key dilemmas faced by antitrust regulation in the AI industry:

1. Difficulty in accurately defining market power

15. Firstly, AI development heavily relies on data, and companies with vast data resources hold inherent advantages in this field. But it is difficult to quantify the value and accessibility of data. This brought challenges to the traditional approach to assess market power, which primarily focuses on market share. =. Secondly, although certain AI companies may possess substantial technological advantages in specific AI segments, this does not necessarily mean they possess market dominance. The rapid development and iterative nature of AI technology make it difficult for any company to maintain a leading position over the long-term. Furthermore, the way in which super-platforms achieve dominant positions differs fundamentally from that in traditional industries. Specifically, super-platforms often operate trading places (i.e., platforms) that offer quasi-public goods, and they can leverage network effects, economies of scale, and consumer lock-in effects to control the market.[21] In the AI field, where data, algorithms, and computing power are core competitive parameters, the assessment of market dominance need to give more weight on non-price factors such as data volume, click rates, algorithmic rules, level of computing power, and active user quantity. These parameters affect AI companies' market competitiveness, and significantly complicate the a of market dominance in the AI industry.[22]

2. Uncertainty in determining the illegality of conduct

16. As a competition-oriented legal system, antitrust law inevitably relies on Competitive harm as the ultimate criterion for determining whether a particular conduct is unlawful.[23] When determining the illegality of monopolistic behavior, we need to analyze whether the conduct in question results in substantive harm to competition. However, in the field of AI, there currently exists no established, objective, unified, or quantifiable standard for assessing Competitive harm resulting from certain

---

21 See Liu Quan: "The Dilemma of Platform Interconnection and the Rule of Law Response", in China Applied Law 2023, Issue No. 3, p. 54-64.

22 See Kong Xiangjun: "On the Macro-Positioning of Antitrust on Internet Platforms – An Analysis Based on Politics, Policies and Law", in Comparative Law Studies, Issue No. 2, 2021, p. 85-106.

23 See Ye Ming and Zhang Jie: "The Rationale and Path of Protecting the Rights and Interests of Personal Information in the Antitrust Law", in Journal of Huazhong University of Science and Technology, Issue. 1, 2023, p. 89.

market conducts. Assessment of competitive harm in the AI industry relies on dynamically changing data that is difficult to measure accurately.[24] Many AI algorithms, particularly deep learning models, operate as "black boxes", as their decision-making processes and outcomes remains unclear. Moreover, AI algorithms continuously self-learn and evolve, meaning that their behaviors and market impact may shift over time. For instance, AI algorithms may influence market conditions to foster collusion among firms, thereby diminishing competition and causing efficiency losses. Additionally, the role of AI algorithms in facilitating collusion can be categorized into various scenarios, with the algorithms playing different roles depending on the scenario. In scenarios where algorithms play a weaker role, they merely act as a medium for human collusion. Whereas in scenarios where algorithms exert a stronger influence, the developers may not have initially intended to collude, nor could they have predicted that the algorithm would lead to collusion. In such cases, the algorithms primarily designed to maximize profits, might eventually adopt collusive strategies through self-learning and experimentation. It is precisely this complexity of AI algorithms that makes it extremely challenging to accurately assess the competitive effects resulting from monopolistic behavior via algorithmic decision-making. Consequently, it remains highly uncertain as to how to determine the illegality of such behaviors.

3. Challenges in determining the legitimacy of defenses

17. In response to the increasingly stringent antitrust scrutiny, AI companies often put forward various defenses to demonstrate that their business activities are not only in line with market mechanisms but also contribute to the health development of the broader economic ecosystem. For example, AI companies might argue that their businesses promote market competition. By introducing innovative technologies and solutions, these companies can dismantle or lower traditional market barriers and create opportunities for other companies to compete; in some cases, they may even create entirely new markets and industries, thereby expanding market opportunities. Furthermore, the widespread application of AI technology can drive the digital transformation of other industries, thereby enhancing overall market competition and innovation. This in turn benefits consumers by offering them more choices with lower prices. Additionally, AI companies might emphasize the positive impacts of their business activities on consumer welfare. Through the use of algorithms, AI companies can gain a more nuanced understanding of consumer needs and be able to offer more personalized products and services. This not

---

24 See Zhang Fuli and Li Luting: "Exploring the Path of Super Platform Interconnection from the Perspective of Publicness", in Journal of University of Science and Technology Beijing (Social Science Edition), Issue No. 3, 2024, p. 127.

only enhances consumer satisfaction and loyalty to the company's product but also contributes to the overall improvement of consumer welfare by providing more efficient and personalized services. Additionally, AI companies can optimize production processes and reduce operational costs, thereby offering consumers more cost-effective products and services. Faced with these myriad defenses, currently, antitrust enforcement agencies often find it challenging to accurately assess the legitimacy of these arguments.

(B) Causes of the antitrust regulatory dilemmas in the AI industry

1. The covert nature of monopolistic behaviors in the AI industry

18. Monopolistic behaviors in the AI industry are often data- and algorithm-driven and tend to be covert. This covert nature manifests in several ways: firstly, data collection is conducted covertly. AI platforms often gather user data through concealed methods. For example, search engines permanently retain users' search histories. Once they collect enough keywords entered by users, they are able to accurately paint the "digital portrait" of users without their knowledge. Secondly, the algorithms used by platforms are non-transparent and complex. AI platforms control the algorithmic design and can manipulate the programming content. This means that AI platforms can integrate unfair consumption patterns into the algorithm design, which are then executed by the algorithm. These unfair consumption patterns (such as "big data price discrimination") and design philosophies (such as "dark mode") are difficult to detect. For instance, during the process of "big data price discrimination," even if a platform is found to have implemented algorithmic price discrimination, it can use technical means to hide such practices. It can also argue that the price fluctuations and price differences are still within a reasonable range.[25] With the widespread application of algorithms and AI in product design and marketing, coupled with non-price factors such as data, algorithms, and computing power, monopolistic behavior in the AI industry has become more complex and covert, making it more difficult to effectively identify.

2. The lag in antitrust rules

19. The traditional economic models upon which antitrust regulations are based were developed under assumptions of a relatively static and mature industry. For antitrust regulations to be effective in the rapidly evolving AI industry, it is essential to constantly monitor the industry's status and

---

25 See Guo Xiaodong: "Jurisprudential Analysis and Regulatory Path of the Power of Digital Platforms", in Journal of Dalian University of Technology (Social Science Edition), Issue. 5, 2024, p. 86.

the latest developments. However, the fast-paced development of the AI industry makes it difficult for existing antitrust theories to reflect changes in the industry.

20. Due to lack of sufficient theoretical preparation, there is a lag in the supply of antitrust rules for the AI industry. For instance, there is currently a lack of clear regulatory guidelines for data monopolies, and the compliance boundaries for data-related competition are very ambiguous. The is no clear and effective regulatory framework applicable to data rights and data circulation, which causes many issues. On the one hand, companies of different scales are unable to use data resources for AI development in a fair and reasonable manner, and on the other hand, improper excessive requirements for interoperability may trigger free-riding behaviors. Additionally, there are limitations in determining algorithmic liability, especially in recognizing unfair competition caused by algorithms and establishing responsibility. Existing laws do not have stringent requirements for algorithm transparency and explainability, making it difficult to effectively regulate algorithmic discrimination. Additionally, the traditional antitrust rules, such as turnover-based merger control notification thresholds, are ill-suited for the digital economy. Such rules cannot effectively address the new changes and challenges posed by the mergers and acquisitions in the AI industry,[26] as the turnover and value of AI companies (especially startups) often diverge significantly. Since the value and revenue of AI companies are no longer directly correlated, it becomes challenging to control the mergers and acquisitions in the AI industry through ex-ante notification and review processes. However, if we solely rely on ex-post control, we may not be able to regulate these mergers and acquisitions in a timely and effective manner.[27]

21. Article 22 of the revised *Anti-monopoly Law of the People's Republic of China* in 2022added provisions on the abuse of market dominance through the use of data, algorithms, technologies, and platform rules in response to changes in the digital economy and assesses market dominance based on companies' capabilities to control data, algorithms, and technology. However, such rules are still not specific enough. It is still difficult to effectively link data and algorithms with the definition of relevant markets and market power in the digital economy. The operability of these provisions needs further improvement.[28] While the methods for determining market dominance and other antitrust tools in traditional industries can still apply to some extent, they

---

26 See Ye Ming and Ran Longyu: "Research on Difficult Issues in Antitrust Regulation of Digital Platform Mergers and Acquisitions," in Electronic Government, Issue 8, 2022, p. 59.

27 In the case of Facebook's acquisition of the instant messaging program WhatsApp, Facebook significantly increased its market power by acquiring additional data from WhatsApp, and in May 2017, the European Commission fined Facebook $122 million for providing misleading information in connection with that acquisition.

28 See Liang Weiliang, "Toward the Age of Meta-Universe: Reflections and Reconstructing Regulation on Data Monopoly", in Modern Economic Discussion, Issue No. 8, 2023, p. 118-119.

cannot be directly applied in the digital economy.[29] Although the China's Anti-Monopoly Guidelines on Platform Economy issued in 2021 list over 40 factors to be taken into account when determining market dominance, they omit the logical relationships between these factors and their respective weights in determining market dominance.[30] Therefore, overall, the existing antitrust rules are still lagging behind the development of AI industry.

3. Regulatory capabilities lagging behind technological development

22. The implementation of monopolistic behaviors in the AI industry differs significantly from that in the traditional industries. In traditional industries, companies typically relied on capital-driven market power to carry out monopolistic behaviors. The deciding advantage is the freedom to set prices without being influenced by other market participants. Therefore, monopolistic behaviors in traditional industries are primarily price-related behaviors. By contrast, the monopolistic behaviors in the AI industry are characterized by data dominance, algorithmic manipulation, and price-related violations. Competition is centered on data, with the attempt to influence or damage competitors' data resources and processing capabilities. Products are frequently offered at low or even zero price. Furthermore, Monopolistic behaviors in AI industry often involve algorithm manipulation, with automated decision-making becoming increasingly prevalent. Market decisions and competitive actions are becoming increasingly automated. Given the non-transparency of algorithms, user and third-party behaviors are often predicted and directed by algorithms in ways that benefit digital platforms.[31]

23. Given that monopolistic behaviors in the AI industry are data-driven and involve algorithmic manipulation, it can be argued that access to sufficient, comprehensive, and accurate data constitutes the fundamental prerequisite for effective antitrust regulation. The integrity of data is crucial to the effectiveness of supervision, as well as the reasonable and precise nature of judgments. From this perspective, data resembles a jigsaw puzzle – every single piece is indispensable for revealing the complete picture.[32] However, in the current AI industry, the majority of data related to market transaction is controlled and used by platform companies. Issues such as data

---

29 See Li Yang and Yuan Zhenzong: "Determination of Abuse of Dominant Position of Internet Platform under the Background of Digital Economy", in Intellectual Property, Issue No. 1, 2023, p. 78.

30 See Yang Liping and Wang Yunbo: "Practical Dilemma and Optimization Path of Monopoly Governance of Exclusive Copyright Agreements of Digital Platforms-Perspective of Public-Private Partnership Governance", in Journal of Beijing University of Posts and Telecommunications (Social Science Edition), Issue No. 5, 2024.https://doi.org/10.19722/j.cnki.1008-7729.2024.0034.

31 See Yang Dong and Li Zishuo: "Regulating Technological Giants: A Re-Examination of Technical Power as a Factor in the Determination of Market Dominant Position", in Academic Monthly, Issue No. 8, 2021, p. 98.

32 See Zhang Chenying: "Rationale and Framework of Anti-monopoly Intelligent Regulation," in Exploration and Free Views, Issue No. 5, 2024, p. 108.

ownership, use, and openness remain unresolved.[33] Government often lacks adequate capabilities to access data, and regulatory authorities are often limited to use publicly available data. Furthermore, the non-transparency of platform algorithms, which are often perceived as "black boxes," makes it difficult for outsiders to understand the underlying development logic and values behind them.[34] Insufficient access to data, asymmetry of information and non-transparency of algorithm heighten the risks of "false positives" or "false negatives" in ex-ante regulatory reviews.[35] Ex-post antitrust investigations require analysis of vast volumes of non-transparent machine learning algorithms and scrutiny of various platform data.[36] However, current antitrust enforcement agencies lack the necessary technologies and skills for analyzing these data and gathering evidence of illegal activities. Therefore, law enforcement agencies are faced with challenges when dealing with various complex monopoly issues in the AI industry.

III. Path for Antitrust Regulation in the AI Industry

24. In the face of concealed, complex, and highly technical monopoly risks in the AI industry, antitrust enforcement agencies must adopt multiple approaches to and conduct full-cycle regulation on monopolistic behaviors in the AI industry, in order to ensure that the development of AI industry complies with regulation. Specifically, the following aspects should be addressed:

(A) Proper cognition for antitrust regulation: a rational view of algorithms

25. Most monopoly risks in the AI industry stem from algorithmic abuse and manipulation. To regulate such risks in an effective and reasonable manner, it is essential to develop a correct understanding of algorithms.

26. Currently, academic community generally agrees that "algorithms are essentially a technology". While technology itself is neutral, it will have value orientation when regulated or governed by institutions, rules, or organizations.[37] In the AI era, humans are increasingly drawn into a complex network ecosystem manipulated by algorithms, which now broadly participate in decision-making processes across various human

---

33 See Mei Xiaying: "The Original Theory of Corporate Data Rights and Interests: From Property to Control", in Peking University Law Journal, Issue No. 5, 2021, p. 35.

34 See Yi Junlin: "Law and Accountability in the Era of Digital Twins – A Perspective on Algorithmic Black Boxes Through Technical Standards", in Oriental Law, Issue No. 4, 2021, p. 77-92.

35 See Sun Jin: "Antitrust Regulation of Digital Platforms," in China Social Science 2021, Issue No. 5, p. 101-127.

36 See Zeng Xiong: "Research on Transition of Antitrust Regulation of Platform Economy in China: Some Thoughts Based on Responsive Regulation Theory," in the Management Journal, Issue 1, 2022, p. 1-12.

37 See Lu Jiangbing: "Neutral Technology and Its Value Bias within Institutional System", in Science, Technology and Dialectics, Issue No. 5, 2000, p. 53-57.

activities. Yet, subject to input data quantity, quality, and algorithmic models, algorithms are inherently embedded with the values – positive or negative – of certain human groups (e.g., algorithm model designers).[38] Algorithms are no longer purely technical tools but have become means for human decision-making or profit-pursuing. As a means, algorithmic technology cannot autonomously seek to infringe upon others' interests; these goals ultimately depend on the individuals or organizations who design or utilize these algorithms, serving the interests of the businesses that design or employ them.[39] In today's increasingly powerful technological landscape, algorithms have emerged as a superpower with decisive influence over the AI industry's development.[40] The influence, dominance, and controlling power inherent in algorithms plays a "decisive" role in the digital economy and society, subtly or overtly reshaping the relationships between different entities in various industries.[41]

27. Based on this, the governance of the monopoly risks caused by algorithms in the AI industry extends beyond the regulation on the algorithmic technology itself, but rather involves addressing new challenges arising from the integration of algorithms into human society.[42] Algorithm operators encode their subjective decision-making and value judgments into various codes, using highly complex algorithmic models and algorithmic decision-making to influence and impact Internet users, third parties, and other stakeholders and society, thereby influencing and controlling the behavior of users, third parties, or the general public. Algorithm operators utilize the "black box" technology to hide intricate ethical issues and various interests. The public and regulators who lack knowledge of algorithms find it difficult to understand the technical principles and interactive mechanisms behind algorithms. If regulators cannot comprehend the underlying interests and recognize the potential monopoly risks of abusing technological power, external regulation will fail.[43] Thus, the effective way to address the algorithmic black box is to curb the abuse of algorithmic power by certain companies through legal means, rather than simply regulating the technical application of algorithms. We should move beyond the technical features of algorithms and focus on their functional role in economic and

---

38 Kirsten M: "Ethical Implications and Accountability of Algorithms", Journal of Business Ethics, 2018(03): 1-16.

39 See Liu Baofu and Liu Hangyu: "Challenges and Responses: How to Promote the Modernization of Social Governance in the Context of Artificial Intelligence," in Journal of Sichuan Administrative Institute, Issue 3, 2023, p. 66.

40 See Zhang Wenxian: "Constructing the Legal Order of An Intelligent Society", in Oriental Law, Issue No. 5, 2020, p. 8.

41 See Chen Canqi: "Legal Regulation of the Abuse of Algorithmic Power by Platforms", Journal of Hunan University of Science and Technology (Social Science Edition), Issue 6, 2023, p. 155.

42 See Jia Kai: "Technical Connotation, Evolutionary Process and Governance Innovation of the Algorithmic Society," in Explorations, Issue No. 2, 2022, p. 164-178.

43 See Tang Linyao: "Algorithm Regulation in the AI Era: Liability and Compliance", in Modern Law, Issue No. 1, 2020, p. 44.

social development.⁴⁴ Governance of monopoly risks caused by algorithmic manipulation must be conducted from multiple dimensions, including technology (algorithms), economics, organization, and law.

(B) Key antitrust regulatory objective: promoting data interoperability

28. The R&D and application of generative AI require substantial data feeding and training, which entails a significant demand for data.⁴⁵ Should leading enterprises in the AI industry engage in arbitrary data blocking practices, the development of generative AI in the industry will be hindered due to the limited access to necessary data for feeding and training.⁴⁶ Consequently, the rapid development of the AI industry is intrinsically dependent on large-scale data availability.⁴⁷ In this context, fostering data openness, sharing, and interoperability, as well as encouraging multi-stakeholder participation in data exchange, becomes particularly crucial. Given the prominent non-competitiveness feature of data resources, i.e., data can be shared and concurrently utilized by multiple entities without diminishing or depleting its intrinsic informational value, regulators can mitigate the resulting asymmetry by compelling dominant firms to open their datasets, thus enabling potential competitors to access and utilize the data. This approach would effectively reduce barriers to entry in the data market, break down the phenomenon of "data silos", and facilitate data interoperability, thereby maximizing the overall value derived from data resources.⁴⁸

29. Requirements for data interoperability can vary in different layers. More specifically, strong interoperability is required at the application layer and weak interoperability is required at the data layer.

30. On the one hand, strong interoperability should be achieved at application layer. When a platform opens an application interface, it means that the platform allows its data to be accessed by other applications. Depending on the level of interoperability, it can be classified as data interoperability (i.e., platforms can access relevant data through interfaces), protocol interoperability (i.e., complementary platforms agree through protocols to interconnect services and data), and full protocol interoperability (i.e., competing platforms can directly access data through

---

44   See Chen Canqi: "Legal Regulation of the Abuse of Algorithmic Power by Platforms", Journal of Hunan University of Science and Technology (Social Science Edition), Issue 6, 2023, p. -160.

45   See Zhao Jingwu, Wang Xin, Li Dawei, etc.: "ChatGPT: Challenges, Development and Governance", in Journal of Beijing University of Aeronautics and Astronautics (Social Science Edition), Issue No. 2, 2023, p. 190.

46   See Huang Yinxu: "Reconstructing an Open and Unified Competition Rule of Law under Web 3.0 Era, in Oriental Law Journal 2023, Issue. 3, p. 104.

47   See Huang Yinxu: "Legal Relationship between the State and Public Data", in Journal of Beijing University of Aeronautics and Astronautics (Social Science Edition), Issue No. 3, 2021, p. 28.

48   See Guo Xiaodong: "Jurisprudential Analysis and Regulatory Path of Digital Platform Power", in Journal of Dalian University of Technology (Social Science Edition), Issue. 5, 2024, p. 89.

interfaces). At application layer, it is essential to impose strong obligations on large platforms that control critical data. These platforms should be required to implement strong interoperability. They should allow all application developers to access the platform and use critical infrastructural data. From an economic perspective, unilateral interoperability exhibits lower efficiency than bilateral interoperability, yielding lower total social welfare and reduced contribution to data utilization efficiency. Consequently, bilateral interoperability should be promoted currently. In practice, even vertically related operators tend to establish biliteral interoperability through agreements. Thus, interoperability should be recognized as an obligation of openness among platforms, requiring important interfaces to be open to other operators without discrimination. In the future, competition regulators should establish clear interoperability standards categorized by platform business types and levels, requiring platform operators to adhere to principles of fairness, transparency, and non-discrimination when sharing data.[49]

31. On the other hand, weak interoperability may be implemented at the data layer, which means the data access should be restricted to what is strictly necessary for the interoperability requester to enter a relevant market. Data access should be limited to raw data held by platforms, with no obligation to open all data. This prevents "free-riding" behavior in the utilization of data.[50] Specifically, it is important to make it clear that the raw data held by platforms are non-exclusive, and recognize that some data possesses both proprietary and competitive characteristics. Certain data may also carry portability rights. Data that is openly shared by platforms for free should exclude processed derivative data. However, platforms should be allowed to charge for the interoperability of derivative data. Furthermore, because platforms source raw data from diverse origins, the raw data are not exclusively owned by platform operators. Given that platforms incur considerable costs in processing and refining data through manual sorting and computational algorithms, derivative data thus assumes added value, qualifying it as a quasi-commodity. Consequently, platforms should be permitted to trade derivative data with other enterprises based on mutual consent. However, data involving personal user privacy, national security, and other sensitive matters, whether raw or derivative, should be strictly protected. Such data should not be collected, transferred, used, or disclosed without proper authorization. Lastly, a pricing framework for data usage should be established. Regulators should encourage data platforms to adopt reasonable pricing

---

49 See Zhang Fuli and Li Luting: "Exploring the Path of Super Platform Interconnection from the Perspective of Publicness," in Journal of Beijing University of Science and Technology (Social Sciences Edition) issue 3, 2024, p.130.

50 See Gao Zhihong: "Public Interest: Legislative Orientation and Institutional Optimization Based on Conceptual Clarification," in Jiangxi Social Sciences, issue 10, 2021, p.183-193.

structures for data interoperability, enabling data providers to offer data to a wider group of users for a fee. This approach should balance the reasonable interests of both data providers and users, motivating platforms to proactively open their data interfaces.[51]

(C) Principles of antitrust regulation: agile and resilient supervision

32. Given the rapid evolution, high-tech nature, and extreme complexity of monopoly risks in the AI industry, the regulation of such risks should adhere to the following principles.

1. Agile regulation

33. Originally conceived for software development, agile regulation emphasizes interaction in the process of software development, collaboration with client, and utilizing tool innovation and iterative approaches to shorten development cycles in response to rapidly changing software environments and demands. Over the years, agile regulation has expanded from software development to other applications, with its core concept being the ability to respond to fast-changing environments with agility. As a principle of competition regulation, agile regulation aims to address the contradiction between the outdated nature of legal frameworks and the rapid iteration of technologies. It involves classifying technological risks to different levels and establishing targeted regulatory framework accordingly.[52] Agile regulation requires the adoption of equally fast, flexible, and adaptive approaches to govern emerging technologies in response to their continuous evolution.[53] Agile regulation not only emphasizes rapid response mechanisms, which is the original meaning of "agile", but also extends further to flexibility, including dynamic regulation, diverse governance tools, classification of risk types, exploration of institutional environments conducive to the development of new technologies and implementation of inclusive and prudent regulation.[54] Considering the high-tech nature and rapid iterative changes of monopoly risks in the field of AI, agile regulation should be applied in this field.

---

51 See *Opinions of the General Office of the State Council on Promoting the Development of "Internet+ Medical Care and Health"*, in Bulletin of the Ministry of Education of the People's Republic of China, issue 22, 2015, p.6-19.

52 See Guo Li: "Smart Regulation Theory and Its Application in Data Element Governance", in Administrative Law Research, Issue No. 5, 2023, p. 28.

53 See Shi Linna: "Risks and Governance Analysis of Artificial Intelligence Development", in Journal of Zhengzhou University of Light Industry (Social Science Edition), Issue No. 2, 2023, p. 60-61.

54 See Zhang Chenying: "The Rationale and Vision of Smart Antitrust Regulation," in Exploration and Free Views, Issue No. 5, 2024, p. 105.

34. Agile regulation has the following characteristics: (1) time sensitivity. Agile regulation requires equally swift regulatory responses to technological and business model innovations. It requires ongoing preparation to address unforeseen risks while innovating regulatory methods amidst the continuous changes in technology and business practices. (2) broad participation. Agile regulation emphasizes collaborative cooperation among multiple stakeholders, encouraging wider involvement in the formulation and regulation of relevant policies and frameworks. This enhances the negotiations and cooperation among stakeholders, fostering a balance of interests that improves the effectiveness and sustainability of policies and systems.[55] and (3) innovation of policy tools. The development of new technologies has placed higher demands on government regulatory methods and tools. Traditional regulatory tools are characterized by delays and inefficiency, while agile regulation requires constant innovation of regulatory tools to enhance the effectiveness of regulation.

2. Full-cycle resilient regulation

35. Resilient regulation refers to the use of more inclusive, redundant, perceptive, and responsive regulatory measures based on a systematic and comprehensive analysis of monopoly risks. It involves a systematic process of *ex-ante* warning, intra-event response and adjustment, and *ex-post* rapid recovery and optimization to improve antitrust regulation.[56] Full-cycle resilient regulation of monopoly risks in AI industry entails two requirements: first, AI serves both as a regulatory tool and a target of regulation. During the process of regulation, emerging technologies like AI, big data, and cloud computing can, on the one hand, be used as a regulatory tool to empower resilient regulation, prevent and resolve the various monopoly risks and contradictions gradually exposed in the AI industry, and enhance the efficiency and effectiveness of regulation. On the other hand, emerging technologies are also subjects of regulation, where regulators identify and predict monopoly risks in the AI industry and develop intervention plans. Only by applying AI appropriately in accordance with the law can AI function as both regulatory tool and target in the process of resilient regulation.[57] Second, regulation should cover the full life cycle of AI products, from constructing language model, establishing and annotating datasets,

---

55 See Shi Lina: "Risks and Governance of Artificial Intelligence Development", in Journal of Zhengzhou University of Light Industry (Social Science Edition), Issue No. 2, 2023, p. 60-61.

56 See Zhai Shaoguo and Zhang Xing: "From Fragile Governance to Toughness Governance: The Issue Transition, Paradigm Shift and Policy Transformation in China's Poverty Governance", in Shandong Social Sciences, Issue No. 1, 2021, p. 76.

57 See Shi Linna: "Risks and Governance Analysis of Artificial Intelligence Development", in Journal of Zhengzhou University of Light Industry (Social Science Edition), Issue No. 2, 2023, p. 61.

training models, to the post-market updates and iterations of AI products. According to *Article 3 of Data Security Law of the People's Republic of China*, "data processing includes the collection, storage, use, processing, transmission, provision and public disclosure of data." The article has already clearly reflected the cycle of data processing. Given that monopoly risk in the AI industry is data-oriented, it may exist throughout the entire lifecycle of AI products. Consequently, antitrust regulation should also adopt a full-cycle perspective in overseeing the entire AI product lifecycle.

(D) Antitrust rules: expanding and supplementing relevant regulations

36. In order to improve the operability of antitrust regulation in the AI industry, it is necessary to refine and amend certain existing antitrust rules that do not align with the characteristics of the AI industry.

1. Determination of market position

37. At present, data, as a basic production factor, not only serves as the foundation of the development of AI companies and an essential part of the products or services produced by the AI companies, but also plays an important role in the market decision-making and strategy implementation of the AI companies. Data can assist AI companies to accurately and comprehensively understand and analyze the development trend, consumer preference, and the characteristics of the AI industry, thus staying in an important position in the AI competition.[58] It can be said that data has become a key element in ensuring the technological innovation and practical application of AI models. In the process of the evolution of AI technology from "humanoid" to "human-like", the demand for, collection and application of massive amounts of data not only opened up new market, but also fostered new type of competitive model.[59] The ability to accumulate data and the volume of data that has been accumulated contribute to a company's competitive advantage and market power. However, data monopoly will arise when the ability to accumulate and control data enables a company to act independently of competitors and, eventually, of consumers, thereby obstructing effective competition or harming consumer welfare.[60] Therefore, when analyzing the market position of companies involved in antitrust cases within AI industry, it should no longer be focused on market

---

[58] See Ding Guofeng: "Research on Antitrust Issues of Data Competition in the Digital Economy Era", in Economic Law Research, Issue. 1, 2023, p. 212-226.

[59] See Chen Bing: "Responding to the Challenges Faced by China's Regulation of Data Monopoly", in Digital Rule of Law, Issue. 2, 2024, p. 24.

[60] See Li Zhaoyang: "From Data Monopoly to Data Access: Competitive Analysis of Data Essential Facility", in Journal of Chongqing University (Social Science Edition), Issue. 6, 2023, p. 190-204.

share alone. Assessment framework centered on data and algorithm should be established, taking into account the characteristics of market competition and monopolistic behavior specific to AI industry. The ability of the involved company to control data can be assessed through factors such as the volume of data under its control, the scarcity of the data, and the difficulty of acquiring the data. Additionally, by examining the computational power it possesses and the maturity of the algorithms it is equipped with, the business's data processing capability can be analyzed through metrics such as computational precision, latency, and throughout. By establishing a correlation between data control and processing capabilities on the one hand, and market position on the other hand, standards for determining the market power of platform enterprises can gradually be developed.[61] Therefore, in the antitrust cases in the AI industry, in addition to considering the price and market share, regulator should also take into account the elements of data, algorithms and technical rules to determine market dominance. A comprehensive approach is needed to assess market dominance, taking into account whether the market barriers are artificially high, legal, or economic, so as to optimize the relevant rules,[62] and correctly determine the market position of the companies involved.

2. Determination of the competitive effects of antitrust behavior

38. When determining the competitive effects or illegality of antitrust behavior in the field of AI, an analysis based on its impact on both business operators and consumers can be conducted.

39. First, from the perspective of business operators, regulators should focus on the exclusionary effect of monopolistic practices on other business operators. In the U.S. antitrust law, the theory of "Raising Rivals' Costs" (RRC) has long been recognized, which suggests that companies may seek or maintain their monopoly position by raising the relative costs of their competitors.[63] Competitive harm caused by monopolistic behavior in the AI industry does not necessarily need to reach a level that would cause other companies to be unable to operate normally in order to be considered illegal. In situations where data are not interoperable, the affected business operators may not exist the market directly, but they will need to seek alternative ways to access users, which can significantly raise the costs of participating in market competition. If the involved company refuses data interoperability without a legitimate reason, it is

---

61 See Ding Qingsong: "Legal Regulation of Monopolistic Practices in the Platform Economy", in China Price Regulation and Anti-Monopoly, Issue. 5, 2024, p. 41.

62 See Huang Yinxu: "Reconstructing an Open and Unified Competition Rule of Law under Web 3.0 Era", in Oriental Law Journal 2023, Issue. 3, p. 105.

63 See Herbert Hovenkamp [US], translated by Xu Guangyao, Jiang Shan and Wang Chen, Federal Antitrust Policy: the Law of Competition and Its Practice, Law Press, 2009 edition, p. 353.

unfairly raising the costs for its competitors. This weakens the competitors' ability to compete and enhances its own market advantage.⁶⁴ This type of harm is something that should be focused on when analyzing the competitive harm or illegality of monopolistic practices in the field of AI.

40. Secondly, for the perspective of consumers, the freedom of choice should be focused. The ultimate goal of the antitrust law is to protect the interests of users, and the reason why some monopolistic practices are deemed illegal is that they can seriously harm the interests of users. Whether tracing the legislative history of antitrust laws or examining the current market landscape of non-price competition, it is clear that antitrust law seeks to protect consumers' interests, which includes ensuring their freedom of choice.⁶⁵ The focus of competition in the AI industry is no longer on "price", but primarily on "data" and "algorithms". Thus, the harm to consumer interests caused by monopolistic behavior in the field of AI differs from the traditional industries. Specifically, the monopolistic practices in the field of AI can harm consumer's information right and right of choice. Whether competition in AI markets is sufficient largely hinges on whether consumers truly possess freedom of choice. Business operators cannot mislead consumers into making choices, nor can they limit the range of choices available to consumers, nor can they force consumers to make choices. Consumers' freedom of choice is embodied in consumers' "active behavior". In order to maintain effective market competition, antitrust laws should protect consumers' "active behavior."⁶⁶ Therefore, when AI platforms, by utilizing their dominance achieved through data advantage and algorithmic power and their abilities to establish and enforce rules and engage in behaviors that infringe on consumers' freedom of choice, such behaviors can be recognized as abuse of market dominance.⁶⁷

3. Accountability

41. Since monopolistic behavior in the AI industry is often the result of business operators abusing their technological advantages and private power, traditional competition law, which focuses on *ex-post* enforcement, struggles to address and remedy the non-economic social harm caused by the distortion of platform power. These non-economic harms, such as data

---

64 See Jiao Haitao: "Platform Interconnection under the Antitrust Law: An Analytical Framework for Abuse of Market Dominance", in Journal of Anhui Normal University (Social Science Edition), 2024, Issue. 4, p. 117.

65 See Ye Ming and Zhang Jie: "The Rationale and Path of Protecting the Interests of Personal Information Through Antitrust Law", Journal of Huazhong University of Science and Technology, Issue. 1, 2023, p. 88.

66 See Jiao Haitao: "Interoperability of Platforms under Antitrust Law: An Analytical Framework for Abuse of Market Dominance", in Journal of Anhui Normal University (Social Science Edition) Issue 4 2024, p. 118.

67 See Chen Canqi: "Legal Regulation of the Abuse of Algorithmic Power by Platforms", Journal of Hunan University of Science and Technology (Social Science Edition), Issue 6, 2023, p. 161.

breaches, damage to transaction fairness, and social inequalities caused by data monopolies, can cause more serious harms to the society.. For example, the infamous Cambridge Analytica incident caused great panic in Western countries and posed a great threat to political ethics and social public interest. However, traditional competition law has had limited capacity to deal with such incidents.[68] Therefore, when refining the liability system for monopolistic practices in the field of AI, it is essential not only to retain traditional antitrust remedies – such as compensation, fines, and orders to cease illegal behavior, but also to strengthen the establishment of the corporate compliance system and the platform gatekeeper system during the *ex-ante* preventive phase based on the unique characteristics of the monopolistic practices in the field of AI. In addition, in addressing the abuse of private power by AI companies, it is imperative to implement measures that prevent AI platforms from acting as managers and operators concurrently on their platforms. The optimal option is structural remedies, which may involve requiring platforms to divest their competing businesses or adopt other effective business separation mechanisms. The second-best option is to require that rules formulated by platforms adhere to principles of fairness, reasonableness, and non-discrimination. The latter is considered as secondary choice because the platform's managerial functions cannot be fully separated, and it is difficult to guarantee or assess whether the platform's rules are truly fair.[69] Indeed, considering that AI platforms compete on an ecosystem basis, both options (i.e., requiring platforms to divest their competing businesses and formulate platform rules on a fair, reasonable and non-discriminatory basis) presents significant challenges.

(E) Antitrust regulatory systems and mechanisms: multidimensional improvement

42. In order to carry out reasonable and effective regulation of monopoly risks in the field of AI, a robust regulatory system is essential. At present, the antitrust regulatory system and mechanism can be improved from the following dimensions.

1. Establishing an internal and external coordinated regulatory system

43. The establishment of a diversified regulatory system is an institutional prerequisite for effectively addressing monopolistic risks in the AI industry. This system encompasses both external regulation and self-regulation.

---

[68] See Guo Xiaodong: "Jurisprudential Analysis and Regulatory Path of Digital Platform Power", in Journal of Dalian University of Technology (Social Science Edition), Issue. 5, 2024, p. 89.

[69] See Jiao Haitao: "Interoperability of Platforms under Antitrust Law: An Analytical Framework for Abuse of Market Dominance", in Journal of Anhui Normal University (Social Science Edition) Issue 4 2024, p. 116.

External antitrust regulation primarily refers to administrative regulation conducted by government agencies. For instance, the regulatory activities conducted by regulatory authorities to preserve competitive market order are typical external regulation. In addition, supervision, feedback and complaint initiated by users of AI products also constitute external regulation. Self- regulation includes both internal and external dimensions. Internally, activities such as data compliance, technology iteration and update, and algorithm optimization may all lead to potential monopoly risks. AI service providers need to establish a comprehensive internal control systems designed to prevent monopoly risk, including measures such as security operation and maintenance, compliance training and learning, risk contingency plans, post-incident reviews, and internal accountability. Externally, AI service providers are required to implement a public-facing early warning mechanism for AI product usage. In instances where users employ AI technologies to engage in illegal or criminal activities (including monopolistic behaviors), the service providers are obligated to intervene by deleting or halting such illegal actions. Only through coordinated external and self-regulation and through multilateral collaboration between government agencies, industry associations, users, and AI operators, can a long-term, sustainable and effective mechanism for mitigating monopolistic risks in the AI industry be established.[70]

2. Promoting smart regulation

44. Given the high-tech nature of the monopoly risks in the AI industry it is necessary to strengthen the monitoring of data ownership, algorithmic collusion and algorithmic black box, and make more efforts on the research and development of regulatory technology in respect of identifying algorithmic collusion so as to improve the fairness and transparency of algorithms through technological innovation.[71] Third-party developers should be encouraged to create data and algorithms governance tools that can monitor personal information protection, data security, data bias, algorithmic fairness, and algorithmic interpretability, such as the "Conceptual Activation Vector Test", This will increase transparency and explainability of the algorithmic "black box", allowing for the detection of discriminatory practices or abusive behaviors.[72] In keeping with the latest technological and industrial trends, it is imperative to leverage emerging technologies to establish big data platforms for monitoring AI market competition. It is

---

[70] See Wei Shunguang: "Legal Dilemma of the Explosive Growth of AIGC and Ways to Address Them: A Reflection Centered on ChatGPT," in Artificial Intelligence Forum, Issue No. 5, 2023, p. 98.

[71] See Hong Zhisheng and Wen Yating: "The Formation and Effect Transmission Mechanism of Negative Externalities in Platform Algorithms in China," in E-Government, Issue No. 11, 2022 p. 48.

[72] See Liu Chao: "Manifestations, Causes and Governance Strategies of Algorithmic Discrimination", in People's Forum, Issue No. 2, 2022, p. 64-68.

also important to actively promote innovative smart regulatory approaches such as "Internet + Competition Regulation", "Big Data + Competition Regulation", and "AI + Competition Regulation", so as to promote smart, agile, and precise antitrust regulation, and enhance reasonable and timely antitrust regulation in the AI industry.[73] As one of the pioneering regions in China's Internet economy development, Zhejiang Province has made some attempt in smart regulation. For instance, "Zhejiang Platform Online" – China's first digital regulatory system for the platform economy – implements targeted regulation on five categories of suspected monopolistic behaviors, including exclusive dealing, big data price discrimination, predatory pricing, vertical monopolistic agreements, and illegal concentrations of business operators. It also employs sophisticated data capture rules and identification models tailored to each specific conduct.[74] Other regional competition regulators can learn from Zhejiang's experience and explore the application of AI technologies to regulate the AI industry in a manner that ensures the ethical development of AI industry.

3. Attempting sandbox regulation

45. Sandbox, a specialized term in the field of computer science, refers to a security mechanism in the field of computer security that provides an isolated environment for running programs. The implementation of sandbox regulation begins with a defined scope (i.e., the "sandbox"). Companies within the sandbox are subject to a prudent and inclusive regulatory approach. At the same time, efforts are made to prevent any issues within the "sandbox" from spreading to the outside world. This approach establishes a fault-tolerant and error-correcting mechanism within the box, with regulatory authorities conducting full-process regulation over the sandbox operations to ensure overall system security. Sandbox regulation is recognized as an optimal solution to avoid the regulatory dilemma where excessive regulation stifles innovation while lack of regulation causes disorder. This approach represents the optimal balance between protection and oversight. Given the highly technical and covert nature of monopoly risks in the AI industry, the determination of monopolistic practices often involves significant uncertainty. However, the sandbox regulatory model can effectively mitigate such uncertainty to a certain extent. From the perspective of the companies subject to regulation, certain commercial practices or AI products using certain algorithms may generate substantial benefits while simultaneously triggering concerns among antitrust regulatory authorities. From the

---

73 See Wang Shucui, Li Jia and Peng Ting: "Research on the Influence Factors of Market Monopoly of Platform Enterprises Based on Grounded Theory", in Science and Technology Management, Issue No. 6, 2024, https://link.cnki.net/urlid/12.1117.G3.20240617.1317.002.

74 See Zhang Chenying: "Rationale and Framework of Anti-Monopoly Intelligent Regulation," in Exploration and Free Views, Issue No. 5, 2024, p. 103.

perspective of regulators, it remains challenging to ascertain or accurately predict the competitive harm arising from such commercial practices or AI products. At this stage, if such commercial practices or AI products are prematurely introduced to market, there will be significant risks for both the companies and the competitive order of the market. If a regulatory sandbox model can be established, both parties can fully communicate with each other on the mechanism behind a new business model or AI product and adopt an *ex-ante* regulatory model with limited authorization to conduct test within the sandbox. During the testing phase, real-time monitoring and dynamic assessments can help control risks, effectively preventing the spread of potential threats. Both parties can communicate and coordinate effectively, reducing the cost of post-launch regulatory of innovative products and, more importantly, accumulating experience for regulators to formulate policies. The *Anti-Monopoly Law*, as the cornerstone of the market economy, is entrusted with the mission of safeguarding competitive market order. For the sake of prudence, it is advisable to implement differentiated regulatory measures within the regulatory sandbox, such as establishing a virtual sandbox where risks can be tested and controlled under simulated conditions before transferring into the actual sandbox. At present, regulatory sandbox is still an emerging concept, particularly in the context of antitrust regulation where no precedent exists. Consequently, a comprehensive set of effective and specific mechanisms is required, including project screening, assessment periods, risk assessment, risk control measures, compensation mechanisms, exit mechanisms, and principal responsibilities.[75]

Conclusion

46. At present, the development of AI technology is rapidly changing, steadily infiltrating every aspect of social economy and daily life. While AI brings many conveniences to enterprises and individuals, the monopoly risks related to it are gradually becoming more prominent. How to regulate AI effectively is an urgent issue both domestically and internationally. In balancing the regulation of AI and the promotion of its development, China can draw on the economic development principles and experiences gained over decades of China's reform and opening-up, prioritizing development as the primary direction while adopting necessary antitrust regulatory measures to ensure a fair and competitive environment for growth. At present, China should accelerate and improve the competition-related legislation in the field of AI, progressively promote AI regulation model tailored to China's specific situation, and actively engage in international coordination on AI regulation. These efforts will constitute the

---

[75] See Zhang Chenying: "Rationale and Framework of Anti-Monopoly Smart Regulation," in Exploration and Free Views, Issue No. 5, 2024, p. 110.

primary direction of China's future AI regulation. At the macro-level of regulation of monopoly risks in the field of AI, the focus should be on industrial policies aimed at promoting AI development, complemented by regulatory policies across multiple fields such as competition, security, and personal data protection, so as to achieve the objective of rapid, healthy, orderly, and secure development of the AI industry. At the same time, when coordinating regulatory policies across different fields, China should maintain the foundational role of competition policies, and timely adjust and update competition regulatory policies and systems to better meet the demands of AI industry development. It is also important to impose necessary regulation on emerging technological sectors to maintain a healthy environment for industrial development and competition. At the micro-level of competition regulation, efforts should be made to bring forward the regulatory work as far as possible. This can be primarily achieved through regulatory talk and administrative guidance between regulators and enterprises, enhancing the companies' understanding of the risks associated with AI technology and the related polices. This proactive approach will enable enterprises make proper compliance arrangements in advance and foster the healthy and rapid development of the AI industry.

China's Antitrust Practice in SEPs: Excessive Pricing and Refusal to Deal

HUANG WEI[*]
Managing Partner, Tian Yuan Law Firm

1. Standard Essential Patents (SEPs) have long been among the most contentious and complex issues in antitrust field. From the "patent wars" in the wireless telecommunications sector to the increasing licensing disputes in emerging fields such as electric vehicles (EVs) and Internet of Things (IoT), SEPs disputes have always been the core battleground.

2. China, as one of the major jurisdictions in global SEP governance, has been shaping its regulatory framework through landmark enforcement actions, judicial rulings, and evolving legislations. In this process, Professor Huang Yong has been at the forefront of SEP governance in China, leading the formulation of many judicial and regulatory rules, and notably, he also possesses a very in-depth industry perspective across various sectors (from telecommunications to EVs, the IoT, etc.). I have gained a lot of fresh perspective from my interactions with Professor Huang Yong.

3. This article focuses on two core antitrust issues in China's SEP landscape: excessive pricing and refusal to deal. Drawing on viewpoints exchanged with Professor Huang Yong and my experience in handling some landmark cases in China, including the *InterDigital case (2013)*, the *Qualcomm case (2015)*, *Yangtze River Pharmaceutical v. HIPI Pharma Tech (2023)*, I aim to elucidate China's antitrust approach to balancing innovation and fair competition.

---

[*] Managing Partner, Tian Yuan Law Firm Secretary General &Deputy Director, Antitrust & Anti-Unfair Competition Committee, ACLA.

I. Excessive Pricing in SEP Licensing: Developments and Insights

1. Antitrust enforcement against excessive pricing

4. China's SEP-related antitrust enforcement traces back to the *InterDigital case (2013)*, where the Chinese antitrust authority scrutinized InterDigital's licensing practices, including alleged setting unfairly high royalties. However, this case ended with Interdigital's voluntary commitments, thus provided limited insights on the authorities' grounds in determining excessive pricing.

5. The landmark *Qualcomm case (2015)*, China's only antitrust penalty case in the SEP field, provided further clarity regarding China's stance. While the antitrust authority did not directly assess royalty rates, it determined the "excessiveness" nature from two perspectives: "charging fees for expired SEPs" and "coercing free cross-licensing". This determination provided important guidance and reference for relevant SEP holders in China's licensing practices at that time.

6. In subsequent years, Chinese antitrust authorities reportedly opened investigations into several major SEP holders. Among these cases, excessive pricing was also a major concern. During the assessment, the authorities paid great attention to, among others, good-faith negotiations, analysis of comparable royalties, issues of double dipping, and abuse of injunctions. However, up to now, no new penalty decisions have been issued, indicating increased regulatory prudence in intervening in the SEP pricing in China.

7. This prudent approach can be further evident by the 2024 *Antitrust Guidelines for SEPs* (the *"SEP Guidelines"*), where the authorities have provided a systematic summary of their approach to regulating the SEP field. For instance:

    - the guidelines explicitly recognize *"balancing the interests of SEP holders and implementers"* as one of the fundamental principles;
    - the guidelines make it clear that *"reasonable royalties can safeguard returns on SEP holders' R&D and innovation"*;
    - the guidelines clarify that violations of good-faith negotiation do not necessarily constitute violations of the antitrust law;
    - the guidelines require royalties to be *"significantly higher"* than comparable rates to merit intervention.

8. These all indicate a more cautious approach taken by the authorities toward regulating excessive pricing in the SEP field.

2. Antitrust judicial cases concerning excessive pricing

9. On the judicial front, Chinese SEP-related cases mainly revolve around royalty-setting. In some cases, such as *TCL v. Access Advance LLC (2024)* and *TCL v. Ericsson (2020)*, implementers also brought antitrust lawsuits against SEP holders for abuse of market dominance, which typically involve alleged excessive pricing. However, all these antitrust lawsuits have ended in settlements, thus there have been no substantive rulings.

10. Nonetheless, recent court rulings regarding excessive pricing disputes related to IPR demonstrate that Chinese courts, particularly the Supreme People's Court (SPC), are very cautious when it comes to antitrust intervention in pricing within innovation-driven sectors.

11. For example, the SPC in its recent judgment on *Yangtze River Pharmaceutical v. HIPI Pharma Tech (2023)*, held that high-price behavior alone does not constitute abuse unless it explicitly restricts competition or harms consumer welfare, and further stressed that industries with high innovation risks require cautious antitrust scrutiny to avoid *"chilling effect"* – *"In the analysis of market competition and innovation risk, the more intense the market competition and the more active the market entry, or the greater the required investment and higher the innovation risk for market entry, the more cautious the analysis and determination of the alleged monopolistic conducts should be"*.

12. The balanced approach is also reflected in the 2024 *Interpretation of the SPC on Several Issues Concerning the Application of Law in the Hearing of Monopoly Civil Disputes* (the *"2024 Judicial Interpretation"*). The *2024 Judicial Interpretation* stipulated that the analysis of excessive pricing shall comprehensively consider factors such as profit, return rate, cost, comparable prices, duration of the pricing, etc., rather than focusing only on certain single indicators. Furthermore, the analysis requires a finding of a *"significant deviation"* from reasonable return rates, profits, or comparable prices, underscoring the SPC's balanced focus on competition protection and innovation incentives.

3. Key Implications: A Balancing Act with Chinese Characteristics

(1) Non-FRAND ≠ antitrust liability

13. The relationship between FRAND-compliance and antitrust violations is a frequently discussed topic in SEP-related disputes. The approach in Chinese antitrust practice has become clearer: whether the SEP holder violates its FRAND commitment is an important consideration in determining excessive pricing, but it does not necessarily equate to antitrust

violations. Antitrust liability hinges on whether the pricing behavior results in demonstrable harms to competition or consumer welfare.

(2) Encouraging innovation while protecting competition

14. China's 2024 amendments to the Anti-monopoly Law (the "*AML*") explicitly incorporate "encouraging innovation" into its legislative purposes, signaling a policymaking balance between market regulation and technological advancement. The *SEP Guidelines*, the *2024 Judicial Interpretation* and judicial precedents all reflect heightened caution in labeling high pricing as monopolistic abuse within innovation-driven sectors. SEP-intensive industries like telecommunications are typical ones, where R&D investments are colossal.

15. This trend echoes with Chinese company's evolving role in global technology competition. Historically mainly positioned as SEP implementers, Chinese firms now have increasingly transitioned to SEP holders. This shift aligns with China's industrial policies prioritizing "indigenous innovation" and "IP monetization".

16. In this regard, Professor Huang Yong has voiced out on multiple occasions that it is necessary to recognize the significant changes in China's industrial stance. He believes that patent value should be fully emphasized, avoiding harm to long-term innovation due to inadequate protection. I share the same view with Professor Huang Yong and anticipate that in future SEP-related cases in China, an effective balance between incentivizing innovation and protecting competition would continue to be maintained.

(3) Multi-faceted assessment of royalty reasonableness

17. Comparable license agreements are a common-used tool for Chinese antitrust authorities to analyze whether SEP royalties are excessive. Key issue remains how to reasonably unpack royalties across diverse agreements - accounting for variables such as licensing context, licensing scope, patent portfolios, fee structure, cross-licensing arrangements, etc.

18. While the *SEP Guidelines* recognize comparable agreements as a benchmark, they offer no definitive threshold for determining when royalties become "*significantly higher*". In practice, this assessment should hinge on whether the alleged overpricing materially distorts downstream competition or harms consumer welfare. Factors such as licensees' ability to effectively compete, consumer choices, etc. should be considered.

19. Meanwhile, the *SEP Guidelines* emphasize that "*reasonable royalties can safeguard returns on SEP holders' R&D and innovation*". This aligns with the 2024 *Judicial Interpretation*, which requires evaluating whether pricing significantly deviates from "*reasonable returns in a competitive market*"

or *"reasonable profits under competitive conditions"*. When conducting the assessment, judicial precedence indicates that multiple economic valuation models shall be applied for cross-verification.

20. In my conversations with Professor Huang Yong, he also repeatedly emphasized that market-based solutions should be encouraged when it comes to pricing innovative products, avoiding excessive administrative or judicial intervention. This aligns with the judicial and regulatory practices I've observed.

(4) Special attention in China's antitrust enforcement focus

21. It is worth noting that the *SEP Guidelines* summarize several aspects of excessive pricing that Chinese authorities pay special attention to, such as: whether royalties are being charged for expired or invalid SEPs or for non-SEPs; whether royalties are reasonably adjusted according to changes in the SEP number, quality, or value; whether royalties are collected repeatedly via non-practicing entities (NPEs).

22. Therefore, SEP holders should pay special attention to issues relating to the license scope, reciprocal cross-license arrangements, regular updates to benchmark royalty rates, and mechanisms to avoid double-dipping during patent transfers.

II. Refusal to Deal in SEP Licensing: Developments and Insights

1. Antitrust enforcement against refusal to deal

23. The core debate over refusal to deal in SEP area revolves around licensing level -specifically, the distinction between "license to all" (LTA) and "access to all" (ATA) licensing approaches:
    - LTA requires SEP holders to license directly to any entity that is willing to take a license in the supply chain, including end-product manufacturers (e.g., smartphone OEMs) and component suppliers (e.g., chipmakers).
    - ATA requires SEP holders to ensure standard accessibility for all implementers, either via a direct licensing or other means (e.g., have-made rights), without offering universal direct licensing.

24. In practice, different SEP holders tend to adopt different licensing models based on their own position and interests, understanding of FRAND commitments, the application fields involved in the license, and the characteristics of the industry. When ATA is applied, implementers excluded from direct licensing (e.g., chipmakers) may challenge the practice as refusal to deal under antitrust law.

25. In China, the issue of SEP refusal to license was widely discussed as early as the *Qualcomm case (2015)*, focusing on whether Qualcomm has an obligation to license at the chip level. Regarding this issue, the penalty decision made by the antitrust authority did not directly negate Qualcomm's licensing model at the end-device level, asserting it constituted a refusal to deal. Instead, it only regarded this licensing model as one of the factors considered in analyzing excessive pricing.

26. Following the *Qualcomm case*, there were no publicly disclosed enforcement cases against refusal to deal in the SEP area. In the *SEP Guidelines*, Chinese authorities seem to adopt a neutral stance toward the dispute around LTA and ATA. Specifically:

    - the guidelines explicitly state that *"in specific cases, whether SEP holder violates the FRAND commitment is an important consideration in determining whether a refusal to license constitutes an antitrust violation"*. That is, regardless of how the FRAND commitment is understood (LTA or ATA), it is only a consideration in determining whether a monopolistic behavior is established, and a violation of the FRAND commitment does not necessarily lead to antitrust illegality.

    - In the section specifically assessing "refusing to license SEPs", the guidelines consider it necessary to assess whether the implementer has factors that affect transaction security (such as poor credit records or deteriorating business conditions) and whether the licensor has objective reasons for being unable to license (such as force majeure).

    - In particular, the guidelines emphasize that the impact of "refusal to license SEPs" on market competition and innovation, consumer interests, and social public interests shall be considered in determining antitrust illegality.

27. This analysis framework provides valuable guidance for SEP holders who take the ATA approach when responding to antitrust challenges from relevant implementers.

2. Antitrust judicial cases concerning refusal to deal

28. On the judicial front, no juridical rulings in China have directly addressed refusal to deal in the SEP context. However, from the recent judgment in *Ningbo Magnetic Materials Co., Ltd. v. Hitachi Metals (2023)*, the SPC overturned the first instance court's determination that Hitachi Metals' non-SEPs constituted "essential facilities", reflecting the Chinese judicial system's cautious attitude towards labelling a refusal to deal as antitrust violation.

29. This cautious attitude can also be seen in the approach to identifying refusal to deal as anticompetitive in the *2024 Judicial Interpretation*, where the court requires that the following conditions be met "simultaneously":

- **Conduct**: whether the operator directly refuses to deal, proposes unreasonable trading conditions, or unreasonably delays negotiations to frustrate a deal;
- **Feasibility**: whether the deal is economically, technically, legally, and operationally viable for both parties;
- **Competition Harm**: whether the refusal to deal excludes or restricts competition in the upstream or downstream markets.

30. In addition, the court needs to further examine whether there are legitimate reasons for the refusal to deal, including whether the counterparty refuses to accept appropriate trading conditions or reasonable requirements, whether the transaction would diminish the operator's legitimate interests, etc.

31. The aforementioned cautious attitude adopted by the court also explains to some extent the rarity of judicial cases involving SEP refusal to deal. Courts prioritize preserving contractual freedom and innovation incentives over intervening in complex licensing negotiations, absent clear market distortions.

3. Key implications: cautious intervention in free market dynamics

(1) FRAND commitment does not create licensing obligations under China's *AML*

32. Back to the "patent war" era in the wireless telecommunications sector, whether FRAND commitment obligates SEP holders to license at the chip level, and whether failing to do so constitutes antitrust violations have been widely discussed.

33. In the *FTC v. Qualcomm (2020)*, the Ninth Circuit Court of Appeals concluded that Qualcomm's OEM-level licensing policy does not constitute an anticompetitive violation of the *Sherman Act*. The court emphasized that even if there were a breach of FRAND commitment, it should be addressed under contract or tort law, not antitrust law.

34. Currently, this dispute persists in SEP licensing in emerging fields such as EVs. For example, the 2022 *Guidelines for SEP Licensing in the Automotive Industry* issued by relevant industrial stakeholders in China advocate that "*SEP holders have an obligation to grant licenses to implementers who intend to obtain a license, regardless of their level in the industrial chain*". This reflects the automotive industry's preference towards this issue.

35. However, the *SEP Guidelines* have presented a relatively clear attitude of the Chinese antitrust authorities, which is that a violation of FRAND commitment does not necessarily lead to a violation of China's *AML*, but is merely a consideration when assessing refusal to deal. In other words, FRAND commitment does not create a licensing obligation under China's *AML*.

(2) The feasibility, efficiency and impacts should be fully considered

36. Regarding SEP holders licensing only at a certain level, multiple factors shall be considered to determine if this constitutes an illegal refusal to deal under China's *AML*:

    - **The economical, technical, legal, and operational feasibility of licensing.** For instance, in terms of patent pool, the operating mechanism of the pool and the authorization scope of the pool licensors shall be considered.
    - **The efficiency of licensing.** For instance, for sectors with complex supply chain, licensing at the end-device level could generate considerable efficiency.
    - **The impacts on the licensor's business model.** For instance, if the licensor's established practice has long been to license at a certain level, requiring the licensor to license to all willing implementers may have an adverse impact on its business model, such as causing great cost to identify and solve double dipping.

(3) Antitrust liability requires demonstrable harm to competition and consumer welfare

37. The *2024 Judicial Interpretation* requires that refusal to deal must "exclude or restrict competition in the upstream market or downstream market" to be considered illegal. The *SEP Guidelines* further emphasize evaluating impacts on market competition and innovation, consumer interests, and public interests. This underscores a restrained approach toward intervening in market practices, focusing on evidence-based harm rather than theoretical risks.

38. In other words, if refusing to license at a specific level does not impede market competition, consumer access to technological improvements, or consumer choice, antitrust intervention should be cautious.

39. I have also discussed this with Professor Huang Yong on many occasions. Professor Huang Yong has explicitly pointed out that "*Antitrust law protects competition, while property rights are the prerequisite for the existence of the market and competition. If the antitrust intervention shakes the foundation of the market and competition, it is very likely to be an excessive intervention and deviate from relevant international consensus*". Professor Huang Yong's insightful understanding fully reflects his international perspective. I believe this will also benefit China's in-depth participation in international competition governance and promotion of high-quality development.

III. Conclusions

40. China's antitrust supervision in the SEP area aims to balance innovation and market competition. Regulators and courts tend to take a cautious stance on contentious issues such as excessive pricing and refusal to deal (licensing levels), intervening only when clear competitive harm is demonstrated. Especially in innovation-driven industries, the focus remains on safeguarding market competition, innovation and consumer welfare, rather than favoring the competitive position of individual firms.

Thank You

As this book approaches publication, I am filled with gratitude. Looking back on four decades of academic pursuit, this Liber Amicorum is both a dialogue with the cutting-edge issues of antitrust around the world and a collective snapshot of colleagues, friends, and students who have contributed to the flourishing of global competition law.

First and foremost, I am deeply indebted to the leaders and colleagues who have guided and supported me at the front lines of legislation and enforcement. From the drafting of the Anti-Monopoly Law to the establishment of competition policy as a fundamental national policy and the fair competition review system; from early explorations in traditional industries to breakthroughs in the governance of the digital economy, it has been their trust and encouragement – both professional and personal – that have sustained my efforts to bridge theory and practice.

I am deeply grateful to friends in academia and practice, at home and abroad. I will always remember the intellectual sparks of every conference, the perseverance required in each research project, and the late nights devoted to solving difficult cases. These exchanges and collaborations have brought us closer in thought and united us in action. I am especially grateful to my international friends. Professor Eleanor Fox, now nearly ninety, has remained steadfastly devoted to the development of Chinese antitrust law for decades. In preparing this volume, she exchanged nearly ten emails with me, carefully verifying every detail. I am equally grateful to Chair Maureen Ohlhausen, Chair Frédéric Jenny, Chair Rasul Butt, Professor William E. Kovacic, and Professor Christopher S. Yoo, whose dedication and passion have illuminated for me the global reach and profound sense of mission embodied in competition law.

I must also express my deep appreciation to the friends and students who have walked alongside me at the Competition Law Center over the decades. In particular, I wish to acknowledge Mr. Tan Ji, Professors Dong Ling, Liu Yannan, Jiang Shan, Xue Yuan, Xiang Jing, Yao Qi, Jin Shanming, Jia Yuan, Ding Maozhong, Lan Lei, Zhang Zhanjiang, Yang Lihua, and Zhou Lixia; Postdoctoral Fellows Zhong Zhenzhen, Jiang Yuhong, and Gu Haixiao; Drs. Dai Bin, Li Zhiyan, Li Zhiqiang, Jiang Tao, Liu Jiaxu, Zhang Yong, Qi Xuedong, Chen Si, Feng Shouzun, Cen Zhaoqi, Dai Shipeng, Huang Yunhua, Li Huiying, Lin Hang, Lian Shichang, Xing Yin, Zheng Duoqing, Wang Xuan, Liu Tan, Deng

Thank You

Zhisong, Zhou Haitao, Liu Dongping, Cui Shufeng, Wang Xiuling, Gao Lei, Wang Lile, Zhang Zhe, Ding Bei, Fan Yunxuan, Jiang Xiaojun, He Rongze, Li Xin, Lu Zaiying, Zhao Zhe, Wang Yuanting, Ye Wei, Zhang Lina, Zhao Dong, Zhu Zhiqi, Liu Qing, Liu Xueming, Zhang Xin, Duan Meimei, Mei Lipeng, Shen Yunyü, Xu Huizhi, Yang Xi, Ran Yiyi, Tian Chen, Wu Jie, Ning Du, Wang Jian, Xiong Yan, Wu Baiting, Ren Wanqiao, Kim Youngjun, Qian Xiaoqiang, Zhang Yu, Liu Kejiang, Zhao Bingling, Gao Huandong, Wang Ankang, Zhao Lili, Yan Wenbin, Tang Jinglun, Wang Zhe, Wang Zichao, Dong Qichao, Xie Jue, Su Runsheng, Ren Chengfu, and Jiao Jie. Their energy, passion, and perseverance have been a wellspring of inspiration, giving me confidence in the next generation of competition law professionals.

I would also like to thank the Concurrences publishing team for their tireless efforts in bringing this book to fruition, as well as Lawyer Bai Yong and Mr. Wang Ziwen for their generous support. Their contributions have added a distinguished finishing touch to this work.

The publication of this Collection embodies collective wisdom and the fruits of long-term dedication to antitrust. I dedicate it to all those who care for and contribute to competition policy and antitrust practice. May these efforts, however modest, advance the rule of competition law in China and across the world.

Professor Huang Yong

Concurrences
Antitrust Publications & Events

The Institute of Competition Law

The Institute of Competition Law is a publishing company, founded in 2004 by Dr. Nicolas Charbit, based in Paris, London and NewYork. The Institute cultivates scholarship and discussion about antitrust issues though publications and conferences. Each publication and event is supervised by editorial boards and scientific or steering committees to ensure independence, objectivity, and academic rigor. Thanks to this management, the Institute has become one of the few think tanks in Europe to have significant influence on antitrust policies.

AIM

The Institute focuses government, business and academic attention on a broad range of subjects which concern competition laws, regulations and related economics.

BOARDS

To maintain its unique focus, the Institute relies upon highly distinguished editors, all leading experts in national or international antitrust: Bill Kovacic, Mario Monti, Eleanor Fox, Laurence Idot, Frédéric Jenny, Ioannis Lianos, Richard Whish, etc.

AUTHORS

8,000 authors, from 85 jurisdictions.

PARTNERS

- Universities: University College London, King's College London, Queen Mary University, Paris Sorbonne Panthéon-Assas, etc.

- Law firms: Baker Botts, Cleary Gottlieb Steen & Hamilton, Baker McKenzie, Jones Day, Norton Rose Fulbright, Skadden Arps, White & Case, etc.

EVENTS

Beijing, Brussels, Dusseldorf, Hong Kong, London, Milan, New York, Oslo, Palo Alto, Paris, San Francisco, Singapore, Warsaw and Washington DC.

ONLINE VERSION

Concurrences website provides all articles published since its inception.

PUBLICATIONS

The Institute publishes Concurrences Review, a print and online quarterly peer-reviewed journal dedicated to EU and national competitions laws. e-Competitions is a bi-monthly antitrust news bulletin covering 85 countries. The e-Competitions database contains over 30,000 case summaries from 8,000 authors.

Concurrences
Competition Laws Review

Concurrences Review

Concurrences is a print and online quarterly peer reviewed journal dedicated to EU and national competitions laws. It has been launched in 2004 as the flagship of the Institute of Competition Law in order to provide a forum for academics, practitioners and enforcers. Concurrences' influence and expertise has garnered contributions or interviews with such figures as Christine Lagarde, Bill Kovacic, Emmanuel Macron, Antonin Scalia and Magrethe Vestager.

CONTENTS

More than 15,000 articles, print and/or online. Quarterly issues provide current coverage with contributions from the EU or national or foreign countries thanks to more than 2,500 authors in Europe and abroad.

FORMAT

In order to balance academic contributions with opinions or legal practice notes, Concurrences provides its insight and analysis in a number of formats:

- Forewords: Opinions by leading academics or enforcers
- Interviews: Interviews of antitrust experts
- On-Topics: 4 to 6 short papers on hot issues
- Law & Economics: Short papers written by economists for a legal audience
- Articles: Long academic papers
- Case Summaries: Case commentary on EU and French case law
- Legal Practice: Short papers for in-house counsels
- International: Medium size papers on international policies
- Books Review: Summaries of recent antitrust books
- Articles Review: Summaries of leading articles published in 45 antitrust journals

BOARDS

The Scientific Committee is headed by Laurence Idot, Professor at Panthéon Assas University. The International Committee is headed by Frederic Jenny, OECD Competition Comitteee Chairman. Boards members include Douglas Ginsburg, Benoît Cœuré, Howard Shelanski, Richard Whish, Wouter Wils, etc.

ONLINE VERSION

Concurrences website provides all articles published since its inception, in addition to selected articles published online only in the electronic supplement.

WRITE FOR CONCURRENCES

Concurrences welcome spontaneous contributions. Except in rare circumstances, the journal accepts only unpublished articles, whatever the form and nature of the contribution. The Editorial Board checks the form of the proposals, and then submits these to the Scientific Committee. Selection of the papers is conditional to a peer review by at least two members of the Committee. Within a month, the Committee assesses whether the draft article can be published and notifies the author.

e-Competitions
Antitrust Case Laws e-Bulletin

e-Competitions Bulletin

CASE LAW DATABASE

e-Competitions is the only online resource that provides consistent coverage of antitrust cases from 85 jurisdictions, organized into a searchable database structure. e-Competitions concentrates on cases summaries taking into account that in the context of a continuing growing number of sources there is a need for factual information, i.e., case law.

- 30,000 case summaries
- 4,000 authors
- 85 countries covered
- 60,000 subscribers

SOPHISTICATED EDITORIAL AND IT ENRICHMENT

e-Competitions is structured as a database. The editors make a sophisticated technical and legal work on all articles by tagging these with key words, drafting abstracts and writing html code to increase Google ranking. There is a team of antitrust lawyers – PhD and judges clerks – and a team of IT experts. e-Competitions makes comparative law possible. Thanks to this expert editorial work, it is possible to search and compare cases by jurisdiction, legal topics or business sectors.

PRESTIGIOUS BOARDS

e-Competitions draws upon highly distinguished editors, all leading experts in national or international antitrust. Advisory Board Members include: Sir Christopher Bellamy, Ioanis Lianos (UCL), Eleanor Fox (NYU), Frédéric Jenny (OECD), Jacqueline Riffault-Silk (Cour de cassation), Wouter Wils (King's College London), etc.

LEADING PARTNERS

- Association of European Competition Law Judges: The AECLJ is a forum for judges of national Courts specializing in antitrust case law. Members timely feed e-Competitions with just released cases.

- Academics partners: Antitrust research centres from leading universities write regularly in e-Competitions: University College London, King's College London, Queen Mary University, etc.

- Law firms: Global law firms and antitrust niche firms write detailed cases summaries specifically for e-Competitions: Clifford Chance, Baker Botts, Baker McKenzie, Cleary Gottlieb Steen & Hamilton, Jones Day, Norton Rose Fulbright, Skadden, White & Case, etc.

Concurrences +
THE COMPETITION LAW PORTAL

21 years of archives
50,000 articles

4 DATABASES

Concurrences
Access to latest issue and archives

- 16,000 articles from 2004 to the present
- European and national doctrine and case law

e-Competitions
Access to latest issue and archives

- 30,000 case summaries from 1911 to the present
- Case law of 85 jurisdictions

Books
Access to all Concurrences books

- 85 e-Books available
- PDF version

Conferences
Access to the documentation of all Concurrences events

- 650 conferences (Brussels, Hong Kong, London, New York, Paris, Singapore and Washington, DC)
- 350 PowerPoint presentations, proceedings and syntheses
- 550 videos
- Verbatim reports

NEW

New search engine
Optimized results to save time

- Search results sorted by date, jurisdiction, keyword, economic sector, author, etc.

New modes of access
IP address recognition

- No need to enter codes: immediate access
- No need to change codes when your team changes: offers increased security and saves time

Mobility

- Responsive design: site optimized for tablets and smartphones

www.ingramcontent.com/pod-product-compliance
Ingram Content Group UK Ltd.
Pitfield, Milton Keynes, MK11 3LW, UK
UKHW021038221225
466318UK00015B/265/J